Transforming Consciousness

Transforming Consciousness

Yogācāra Thought in Modern China

Edited by

JOHN MAKEHAM

OXFORD
UNIVERSITY PRESS

OXFORD
UNIVERSITY PRESS

Oxford University Press is a department of the University of Oxford.
It furthers the University's objective of excellence in research, scholarship,
and education by publishing worldwide.

Oxford New York
Auckland Cape Town Dar es Salaam Hong Kong Karachi
Kuala Lumpur Madrid Melbourne Mexico City Nairobi
New Delhi Shanghai Taipei Toronto

With offices in
Argentina Austria Brazil Chile Czech Republic France Greece
Guatemala Hungary Italy Japan Poland Portugal Singapore
South Korea Switzerland Thailand Turkey Ukraine Vietnam

Published in the United States of America by
Oxford University Press
198 Madison Avenue, New York, NY 10016

Library of Congress Cataloging-in-Publication Data
Transforming consciousness : yogacara thought in modern
China / edited by John Makeham.
p. cm.
Includes index.
ISBN 978-0-19-935813-7 (pbk. : alk. paper) — ISBN 978-0-19-935812-0
(cloth : alk. paper) 1. Yogacara (Buddhism)—China. 2. Philosophy, Chinese.
3. China—Civilization. I. Makeham, John, 1955- editor of compilation.
BQ7500.C6T73 2014
294.3'920951—dc23
2013031769

1 3 5 7 9 8 6 4 2

Printed in the United States of America
on acid-free paper

Contents

Acknowledgments

ON BEHALF OF the contributors, I wish to thank the Chiang Ching-kuo Foundation for International Scholarly Exchange, the Nederlandse Organisatie voor Wetenschappelijk Onderzoek (arranged through the good offices of Axel Schneider), and the Australian Research Council for providing grants that made it possible to carry out the research and conduct the workshops that underpin this volume.

JM, July 2013.

Common Abbreviations

CBETA	Chinese Buddhist Electronic Text Association (CBETA) edition of *Taishō Tripiṭaka* (Taishō Revised Tripiṭaka).
EOB	Tan Sitong, *Renxue.*
FB	Mou Zongsan, *Foxing yu bore.*
HCY	*Haichao yin*, reprinted in MFQ.
MFQ	Huang Xianian (ed.), *Minguo Fojiao qikan wenxian jicheng.*
MFQB	Huang Xianian (ed.), *Minguo fojiao qikan wenxian jicheng bubian.*
T	*Taishō Tripiṭaka* (Taishō Revised Tripiṭaka).
TDQS	Yinshun (ed.), *Taixu dashi quanshu.*
To	Yensho Kanakura et al. (comps.), Tohoku Catalog.
TSTQJ	*Tan Sitong quanji.*
XSLQJ	*Xiong Shili quanji.*

Contributors

Eyal Aviv—teaches in the Department of Religion and the Honors Program at the George Washington University. His research interests are Buddhist philosophy and Chinese intellectual history. His PhD dissertation (Harvard University, 2008) was on Ouyang Jingwu (1871–1943) and the revival of scholastic Buddhism. Recent publications include "Turning a Deaf Ear to Dharma? The Theory of *Śrutavāsanā (聞熏) and the Debate about the Nature of the Hearing and Mind in 20th Century China" (in Chinese; 2009); and "Ambitions and Negotiations: The Growing Role of Laity in 20th Century Chinese Buddhism" (2011). His current research focuses on Yogācāra philosophy in early twentieth-century China through the intellectual biography of Ouyang Jingwu.

Jason Clower—is a buddhologist whose work to date has focused on Mou Zongsan and the life of Buddhist philosophy in the New Confucian movement more generally. Recent publications include *The Unlikely Buddhologist: Tiantai Buddhism in Mou Zongsan's New Confucianism* (2010). His next project is a new English translation of the *Awakening of Faith*. He teaches at California State University, Chico.

Erik J. Hammerstrom—teaches at Pacific Lutheran University in his native Cascadia. He received a PhD in Religious Studies with departmental honors from Indiana University, Bloomington. In 2011 he was awarded Yale University's biennial Stanley Weinstein Dissertation Prize for Best Dissertation on East Asian Buddhism in North America for his dissertation, "Buddhists Discuss Science in Modern China (1895–1949)." He has published articles in *Theology and Science*, the *Chung-Hwa Buddhist Journal*, and the *Journal of Chinese Religion*. As an extension of his work on Chinese Buddhism, together with Gregory Scott he established the *Database of Modern Chinese Buddhism*.

John Jorgensen—is adjunct associate professor in the College of Asia and the Pacific, The Australian National University, and his doctoral dissertation (Australian

National University, 1990) was on Chan and poetics. Chief publications include *Inventing Hui-neng, the Sixth Patriarch: Hagiography and Biography in Early Ch'an* (2005); three volumes of translation in the Collected Works of Korean Buddhism [vol. 3, *Hyujeong: Selected Works*; vol. 7-2, *Gongan Collections II*; vol. 8, *Seon Dialogues*] (2012); and a translation with Eun-su Cho, *The Essential Passages Directly Pointing at the Essence of the Mind: Reverend Baegun (1299–1375)* (2005). He has published many articles on East Asian Buddhism and Korean new religions.

Chen-Kuo Lin—is Distinguished Professor, Department of Philosophy, National Chengchi University, Taiwan and holds a PhD (1991) in Buddhist philosophy from Temple University. His research interests include Buddhist philosophy (Madhyamaka, Yogācāra), Chinese philosophy (Neo-Confucianism, Taoism), and comparative philosophy. In addition to many book chapters and journal papers, he has also published three books (in Chinese): *Emptiness and Modernity: From the Kyoto School, Modern Neo-Confucianism to Multivocal Hermeneutics* (1999); *A Passage of Dialectics* (2002); and *Emptiness and Method: Explorations in Cross-Cultural Buddhist Philosophy* (2012). He has held several visiting positions: International Institute of Asian Studies and Leiden University (European Chair of Chinese Studies, 1999–2001), Chinese University of Hong Kong (Philosophy, 2005), and Harvard University (Pusey Fellow, 2012). He is a past president of the Taiwan Philosophical Association (2008–2009) and received a Distinguished Research Award from the National Science Council in 2011. Currently he also serves as the Convener of Philosophy (Religious Studies) Section, National Science Council, Taiwan.

Dan Lusthaus—a leading scholar of Yogācāra Buddhism, has published extensively on Indian, Chinese, and Japanese philosophy. His publications include *Buddhist Phenomenology: A Philosophical Investigation of Yogācāra Buddhism and the* Ch'eng wei-shih lun (2002); *A Comprehensive Commentary on the Heart Sutra (Prajñāpāramitā-hṛdaya-sūtra) by K'uei-chi* (translated in collaboration with Heng-Ching Shih; 2001); and numerous articles on Buddhist, Hindu, and Daoist thought. He has taught at UCLA, University of Illinois Champaign-Urbana, and Boston University, and has been a Research Associate at Harvard University since 2005.

John Makeham—is Professor of Chinese Studies in the College of Asia and the Pacific, The Australian National University (ANU), and a Fellow of the Australian Academy of the Humanities. His research interests are in Chinese philosophy and intellectual history, with a special interest in Confucian thought and the influence of Sinitic Buddhist philosophy on Confucian philosophy. Educated at ANU, has held academic positions at Victoria University of Wellington, University of Adelaide, National Taiwan University, Chinese University of Hong Kong, and ANU. He has recently completed an annotated translation of Xiong Shili's *New Treatise on the Uniqueness of Consciousness*. He is editor of the monograph series, *Modern Chinese Philosophy*.

Thierry Meynard S.J.—is Professor of Philosophy at Sun Yat-Sen University, Guangzhou. Since August 2012, he has also been director of The Beijing Center for Chinese Studies, a study program established in 1998. In 2003, he obtained his PhD in philosophy from Peking University, presenting a dissertation on Liang Shuming. From 2003 to 2006, he taught philosophy at Fordham University, New York. He has authored *The Religious Philosophy of Liang Shuming: The Hidden Buddhist* (2011) and *Confucius Sinarum Philosophus (1687): The First Translation of the Confucian Classics* (2011).

Viren Murthy—teaches Transnational Asian History at the University of Wisconsin-Madison and specializes in modern Chinese and Japanese intellectual history. His book, *The Political Philosophy of Zhang Taiyan: The Resistance of Consciousness*, was published in 2012. He is currently working on a project on pan-Asian thought in Japan, China, and India.

Scott Pacey—completed his doctorate at the Australian National University in 2011. His dissertation was on the Chinese monastic Taixu (1890–1947) and the major Chinese and Taiwanese monastics that he influenced. After graduating, he was a Golda Meir Postdoctoral Fellow in the Department of East Asian Studies at the Hebrew University of Jerusalem. He is presently Lecturer in Buddhist Thought and Practice at the University of Manchester. His current research focuses on debates between Buddhists and Christians in the 1950s and 1960s in Taiwan, and contemporary Buddhism in the PRC.

John Powers—is Professor of Asian Studies in the College of Asia and the Pacific, The Australian National University. He specializes in Buddhist philosophy and Tibetan history and has published twelve books and more than sixty articles on a wide range of subjects. Among these are five books and several articles on Yogācāra topics, including a translation of the *Saṃdhinirmocana-sūtra* (*Wisdom of Buddha*; 1995) and a study of Yogācāra hermeneutics (*Hermeneutics and Tradition in the Saṃdhinirmocana-sūtra*; 1993). He is also co-chair of the Yogācāra Section of the American Academy of Religion.

Transforming Consciousness

Introduction

John Makeham

HISTORICALLY, CHINESE THOUGHT has been most profoundly influenced by two external intellectual traditions: disciplinary-based Western thought and Indian Buddhist thought. Western thought began to be introduced into China by Jesuit missionaries in the late-sixteenth century; disciplinary-based Western thought began to be introduced from Japan in the late-nineteenth century. In contrast, Indian Buddhist thought was first introduced into China two thousand years ago. Precisely because Buddhist thought was an integral part of the Chinese cultural landscape for so long, it shaped styles of reasoning, constructs of the world, and ways of comporting oneself in society. This legacy has profoundly influenced how Chinese people view themselves collectively and individually, and also how they deal with other people. Buddhism also shaped the development of indigenous Chinese traditions of religion, philosophy, art, and literature.

The Western roots of many aspects of modern Chinese thought have been well documented. Far less well understood, and still largely overlooked, is the influence and significance of the main exemplar of Indian thought in modern China: Yogācāra Buddhist philosophy. This situation is all the more anomalous given that the revival of Yogācāra thought among leading Chinese intellectuals in the first three decades of the twentieth century played a decisive role in shaping how they engaged with major currents in modern Chinese thought: empirical science; "mind science," or psychology; evolutionary theory; Hegelian and Kantian philosophy; logic; and Confucian thought in a modernizing China. The influence and legacy of Indian thought have been ignored in conventional accounts of China's modern intellectual history. This history urgently requires rewriting so that the role played by a major non-Western system of thought in the formation of Chinese responses to modernity is duly acknowledged and its historical and contemporary implications are no longer ignored. This volume seeks to redress this imbalance and in doing so change the way we understand China's modern intellectual history.

Within the context of a broader renewal of interest in traditional philosophical writings (including selected indigenous Chinese Mahāyāna texts) in the late-Qing period (1644–1911), the corpus of Yogācāra writings attracted unparalleled attention. China's Yogācāra revival—specifically the Weishi 唯識 (Nothing but Consciousness) School—from the late 1890s to the 1930s was spearheaded by two generations of prominent intellectuals: monastics, lay believers, and secular figures alike. Why was Yogācāra so attractive to Chinese intellectuals of that period?

Yogācāra (*Yuqie xingpai* 瑜伽行派; yogic practice) is one of the two most influential philosophical systems of Indian Mahāyāna Buddhism, along with Madhyamaka. Other names for the Yogācāra School include the Way of Consciousness (Vijñānavāda), and Nothing but Consciousness (Vijñapti-mātra). Historically, both Weishi 唯識 (Nothing but Consciousness) and Faxiang 法相 (*dharma-lakṣaṇa*; dharma[1] characteristics) were synonymous with the Yogācāra School in China. After the Tang Dynasty, the term was used to denote the famous pilgrim and monk Xuanzang's 玄奘 (602–664) Yogācāra School, but it soon became a mildly derogatory expression used by its opponents, who mocked the Yogācāras for pursuing the "characteristics of dharmas" rather than the real nature of dharmas (*faxing* 法性). Despite this, the Yogācāras later adopted the term, and in Japan it continues to be the official name of this school (Hossō in Japanese).

As the name implies, Yogācāra focuses on meditative practice, as well as epistemology and logic. Competing traditions of Yogācāra thought were first introduced into China during the sixth century, with the Weishi School rising to preeminence in the seventh century. By the Yuan Dynasty (1271–1368), however, key commentaries of this school had ceased being transmitted in China, and it was not until the end of the nineteenth century that a number of them were re-introduced into China from Japan, where their transmission had been uninterrupted. Crucial to the late-Qing revival of interest in Yogācāra thought was the friendship between the Japanese lay Buddhist scholar Nanjō Bun'yū 南條文雄 (1894–1927) and the Chinese lay Buddhist scholar Yang Wenhui 楊文會 (1837–1911). Between 1891 and 1896, Nanjō sent a total of 235 Buddhist texts to Yang, including thirty Yogācāra works that had long ceased being transmitted in China.[2] Within a few short years, Yogācāra was being touted as a rival to the New Learning from the West, boasting not only

1. Physical and mental phenomena.

2. Chen Jidong 陳繼東, "Shinmatsu ni okeru Yuishiki Hōsō tenseki no kankō ni tsuite 清末における唯識法相典籍の刊行について" (On the Publication of Yogācāra Texts at the End of the Qing Dynasty), *Indogaku Bukkyōgaku kenkyū* 44, no. 2 (1996): 811.

organized, systematized thought and concepts, but also a superior means to establish epistemological verification based on its accounts of the processes of cognition and the nature of reality.

Aims of this volume

A number of informative studies have been undertaken on aspects of Yogācāra thought in the writings of individual figures from the early decades of the twentieth century. The sheer complexity of historical, linguistic, hermeneutic, and doctrinal issues, however, has meant that to date, no study has been undertaken to demonstrate (1) the nature and significance of the revival of Yogācāra thought as a response to the challenges of modernity in the first four decades of the twentieth century and (2) its broader impact on the development of modern Chinese philosophical thought. By coordinating and drawing on the combined resources of a unique body of expertise in a highly innovative collaborative undertaking, we believe this volume has made it possible to address these two important areas of study. The project from which this volume has drawn its findings involved the collaboration of a network of specialists around the globe—Australia, China, Canada, Germany, Israel, Taiwan, and the United States—to pool the strengths of scholars of Buddhism (covering Indian, Tibetan, Chinese, Korean, and Japanese traditions of Buddhism) and scholars of Chinese intellectual history. Over a three-year period (2009–2011), project members met regularly to present and discuss chapter drafts at focused, themed workshops.

This volume sets out to achieve three goals. The first is to explain why this Indian philosophical system proved to be so attractive to influential Chinese intellectuals at the very moment in Chinese history (1890–1930) when traditional knowledge systems and schemes of knowledge compartmentalization were being confronted by radically new knowledge systems introduced from the West. The next goal is to demonstrate how the revival of Yogācāra thought informed Chinese responses to the challenges of modernity, in particular modern science and logic. The third goal is to highlight how Yogācāra thought shaped a major current in modern Chinese philosophy: New Confucianism. A further aim, related to this last one, is to show why an adequate understanding of New Confucian philosophy must include a proper grasp of Yogācāra thought because only then can we understand why New Confucianism's most influential theorists all sided with Sinitic Buddhism—that is, traditions such as Huayan, Tiantai, and Chan, which first developed in China—in constructing their philosophical systems. Their implicit or explicit affirmations of the inherent enlightenment (*benjue* 本覺) doctrine associated with Sinitic traditions of Buddhism highlight a feature of New Confucian philosophy that is generally muted or absent in contemporary accounts that emphasize the movement's connections with Confucian traditions of the Song and Ming periods.[3]

Before turning to introduce in some detail several themes that run across multiple chapters in this volume, the following section will provide an overview of Yogācāra in China before its revival in the early decades of the twentieth century, focusing on the most salient landmarks and facts in that history.[4] (John Powers' opening chapter to this volume in part I introduces the Indian origins of Yogācāra.[5])

1. *Yogācāra in China: Pre-twentieth century overview*

1.1 Fifth to eighth centuries in China

Yogācāra ostensibly begins with the fourth-century Indian thinkers Asaṅga (Wuzhao 無著) and Vasubandhu (Shiqin 世親); their ideas began to appear in China almost immediately. The precise details of the earliest introductions of Yogācāra materials to China are unclear, but among the first were two texts translated by *Dharmakṣema (Tan Wuchen 曇無讖; 385–433) near the beginning of the fifth century: **Bodhisattvabhūmi-sūtra* (*Pusa di chi jing* 菩薩地持經; Stages of the Bodhisattva Path),[6] and **Bodhisattva Prātimokṣa* (*Pusa jie ben* 菩薩戒本; On Conferring Bodhisattva Vinaya). This second text contains excerpts from the *Yogācārabhūmi-śāstra* (*Yuqie shidi lun* 瑜伽師地論; Discourse on the Stages of Concentration Practice; alt. Treatise on Grounds for Disciplined Practice),[7] which was intended as a ritual text for practicing Mahāyāna clerics, thus suggesting

3. In English, the term "New Confucian" is to be distinguished from "Neo-Confucian." New Confucianism is a modern neoconservative philosophical movement, with religious overtones. Proponents claim it to be the legitimate transmitter and representative of orthodox *ru* 儒 ("Confucian") values. The movement is promoted and/or researched by prominent Chinese intellectuals based in China, Taiwan, Hong Kong, and the United States.

4. This section is based substantially on notes generously provided by Dan Lusthaus, John Jorgensen, and John Powers. I am also grateful to Michael Radich for constructive critical feedback on this section.

5. When referring to the chapters of individual contributors to this volume, the convention adopted is simply to cite the author by name with no reference to chapter title or page number. Where reference is made to other works authored by the volume's contributors, full citation details are provided.

6. This text describes the practices and outcomes of those practices for the bodhisattva in the Mahāyāna tradition.

7. Composed in India between 300 and 350, it was translated into Chinese by Xuanzang between 646 and 648. In East Asia its authorship is traditionally attributed to one Maitreya, but in Tibet its authorship is attributed to Asaṅga.

that at this point Yogācāra was treated not only as a doctrinal entity, but was also being used as a core part of monastic practice.

The *Bodhisattvabhūmi*, however, does not discuss some of what came to be considered the signature doctrines of Yogācāra, such as the eighth consciousness (*ālayavijñāna; alaiye shi* 阿賴耶識);[8] the three natures (*trisvabhāva; san xing* 三性);[9] and "nothing but consciousness" (*vijñapti-mātra; weishi* 唯識). The text credited with introducing those ideas is the *Saṃdhinirmocana-sūtra* (*Jie shenmi jing* 解深密經; Discourse Explaining the Thought) (all but its introduction and chapter colophons are included in full in later sections of the *Yogācārabhūmi*). This text also appears in China in the first half of the fifth century.

Another sutra that appeared early in China containing Yogācāra ideas, though mixed with *tathāgatagarbha* (matrix of buddhas; *rulaizang* 如來藏)[10] ideas (for which see the chapters by John Powers and Eyal Aviv in this volume), is the *Laṅkāvatāra-sūtra* (*Lengqie jing* 楞伽經; Sutra on [the Buddha's] Entering [the Country of] Lanka), first translated into Chinese by *Dharmakṣema between 412 and 433. So we see that *Dharmakṣema was perhaps the first recognized importer

8. The term *ālayavijñāna* is translated as "base consciousness" in this volume. In the Chinese tradition it is also rendered as "store consciousness" (*zangshi* 藏識). As John Powers explains in his chapter in this volume, the base consciousness

> provides a mechanism for rebirth because it is the primary factor that moves from one life to the next and retains the seeds of volitional actions, carrying them toward the future. It also explains continuity of personality and memory within a particular life and the resumption of attitudes and past impressions after periods of meditative trance in which the continuum of consciousness is suspended.

By retaining the impressions of past experiences, the base consciousness "perfumes" new experiences on the basis of that previous conditioning. These habituated tendencies "condition the seeds that constitute the mental stream, similar to the way in which perfume pervades a cloth. The general disposition of any given mental continuum is a reflection and function of these accumulated tendencies."

9. The first nature is the nature of existence produced from attachment to imaginatively constructed discrimination (*bian ji suozhi xing* 遍計所執性; *parikalpita-svabhāva*). The second nature is the nature of existence arising from causes and conditions (*yi ta qi xing* 依他起性; *paratantra-svabhāva*), and hence ultimately is a false construct. The third nature is the nature of existence being perfectly accomplished (*yuancheng shixing* 圓成實性; *pariniṣpanna-svabhāva*). As Dan Lusthaus observes, however, since the notion of self-nature "presumes self-hood, it too must be eliminated. Thus the three self-natures are actually three non-self-natures." See his entry, "Yogācāra School" in *Encyclopedia of Buddhism*, ed. Robert E. Buswell, Jr., vol. 2 (New York: Thomson Gale, 2004), p. 918. See also John Powers's chapter in this volume.

10. The *tathāgatagarbha* doctrine is the idea that the potentiality for buddhahood exists embryonically in all sentient beings.

of Yogācāra texts to China, having introduced the *Bodhisattvabhūmi* as well as a monastic disciplinary rules (*prātimokṣa*)[11] text based on it and the *Laṅkāvatāra.*

1.1.1 *First major wave*

Among learned scholastics interested in systematics and textual exegesis, sixth-century Chinese Buddhism was primarily a battleground between competing versions of Yogācāra, starting with the disputes that broke out between translators Bodhiruci (Putiliuzhi 菩提流支; d. 527) and Ratnamati (Lenamoti 勒那摩提; d.u.) when, in 508, they attempted jointly to translate Vasubandhu's **Daśabhūmi-vyākhyāna* (*Shidi jing lun* 十地經論; Commentary on the Discourse on the Ten Stages [of the Bodhisattva Path])[12] or *Dilun* (Stages Treatise) for short. Bodhiruci and Ratnamati fought bitterly over how to interpret the text, and their conflicting interpretations carried over even after the project was finished, leading their disciples to found two competing schools that doxographers later labeled as the Southern Dilun and Northern Dilun, respectively.

There were numerous issues of contention between the two schools that increased over the course of the sixth century, such as whether the base consciousness (*ālayavijñāna*) was the problem that needed to be overcome (the northern position) or something akin to the *tathāgatagarbha*, which is realized and reaches its pure form with full enlightenment (the southern position); whether "buddha nature" (*foxing* 佛性) meant "buddhahood" that was acquired rather than inborn (the northern position) or an inherent nature associated with *tathāgatagarbha*, the universal nature of all sentient beings (southern position); and so on. The two Dilun schools, which were basically competing versions of Yogācāra, were dominant for the first half of the sixth century until Paramārtha (see below) arrived in China.

1.1.2 *Second major wave*

Paramārtha (Zhendi 真諦; 499–569) was from Ujjain in western India. He translated numerous foundational Yogācāra texts, including a partial translation of the *Yogācārabhūmi-śāstra* called **Viniścayasaṃgrahaṇī* (*Juedingzang lun* 決定藏論; Compendium of Ascertainments), which introduced the idea of an **amalavijñāna* 阿摩羅識: a "pure consciousness" that his followers considered to be a ninth consciousness beyond the *ālayavijñāna*; *Madhyānta-vibhāga* (*Zhong bian fenbie lun* 中邊分別論;[13] Differentiation of the Middle and Extremes); Vasubandhu's

11. A type of monthly group "confessional" ritual that is also part of the initiation into the monastic community (*saṃgha*). It involves a communal recitation of the rules of monastic discipline.

12. The ten stages through which a bodhisattva proceeded on the way to *nirvāṇa*.

Viṃśatikā (alt. *Viṃśikā*) (*Weishi ershi lun* 唯識二十論; Twenty Verses); Dignāga's (sixth-century) *Ālambana-parīkṣā* (*Wu xiang si chen lun* 無相思塵論; Treatise on Considerations [of The Fact That] Objects of Thought Have No Characteristics);[14] and, most importantly for the school that built itself on his translations, Asaṅga's *Mahāyāna-saṃgraha* (*She dasheng lun* 攝大乘論; Compendium of the Great Vehicle; *Shelun* for short) as well as Vasubandhu's commentary on it (*She dasheng lun shi* 攝大乘論釋). Paramārtha's style of Yogācāra was called Shelun 攝論, and it largely eclipsed the Dilun schools by the end of the Sui and beginning of the Tang dynasties (early seventh century).

An apocryphal text written in China but purporting to be the work of a well-known second-century Indian scholar-monk named Aśvaghoṣa (whose attested works give no evidence of Mahāyāna affiliation), with the title *Dasheng qixin lun* 大乘起信論 (Awakening of Mahāyāna Faith), was also claimed to have been translated by Paramārtha. While modern scholarship has shown that in language, style, vocabulary, and underlying models it has more in common with writers and translators *other than* Paramārtha, traditionally it was accepted as his text or as having been written by a member of his school. *Dasheng qixin lun* quickly struck a chord among East Asian Buddhists, who assigned it a central role in their thinking. Today it remains one of the foundational texts in Korea and still strongly influences the thinking of East Asian Buddhists. *Dasheng qixin lun* proposed a version of Yogācāra blended with "matrix of buddhas" thought that its interpreters took to mean a grounding of all reality in One Mind that is inherently enlightened.

1.1.3 *Third major wave*

Another translator, who is frequently overlooked, is Prabhākaramitra (Boluojiapomiduoluo 波羅迦頗蜜多羅; 564–633). He arrived in the Chinese capital, Chang'an, in 627 from Magadhā in central India and promoted both Madhyamaka and Yogācāra texts. One of Prabhākaramitra's notable translation assistants was Wŏnch'ŭk/Woncheuk 圓測 (613–696), who arrived from Korea around

13. This is the title given in Paramārtha's translation; Xuanzang translated the title as *Bian zhongbian lun* 辯中邊論.

14. Historically this text has different Chinese titles, just as it has different Chinese translations. See the discussion in Dan Lusthaus's chapter. Lusthaus suggests *Treatise on Considerations about Sense-objects as Lacking Materiality* as a possible rendering for *Wu xiang si chen lun* 無相思塵論. Xuanzang's rendering, *Guan suoyuan yuan lun* 觀所緣緣論, can be translated as *Treatise on Discerning the Conditions for the Causal Support of Consciousness*. In this volume, Dan Lusthaus opts for *Investigation of What Lies behind Perceptual Objects*. The Sanskrit can be rendered more simply as *Investigation of Ālambana*, *Investigation of the Object* or *Investigation of the Percept*. It was Xuanzang's rendering that was followed in the early decades of twentieth-century China.

the same time. Wŏnch'ŭk later joined Xuanzang's translation committees, becoming a prominent disciple of Xuanzang who vied with Kuiji 窺基 (632–682) for succession when Xuanzang died (Kuiji prevailed).

At the same time that Prabhākaramitra was working in the Chinese capital, Xuanzang arrived in India. Against a background of doctrinal disputes in China involving the two Dilun schools and Paramārtha's school, Xuanzang was motivated to travel to India in 629, believing that these disputes could finally be resolved if a complete translation of *Yogācārabhūmi-śāstra* was made available in China.

He returned to China in 645, with over 600 texts, 74 of which he translated, including new versions of translations by his predecessors. Xuanzang attempted to recreate as much of the Indian context for Buddhist thought and practice as he could through his translations in order to help Chinese students reach a proper understanding of doctrine and practice.

Aside from the travelogue of his journey through Central Asia and India (*[Da Tang] Xiyu ji* ([大唐]西域記; Record of Western Lands), all his works were faithful translations of Indic originals, with the exception of the *Cheng weishi lun* 成唯識論 (Demonstration of Nothing but Consciousness), which was a composite of commentaries on Vasubandhu's *Triṃśikā* (*Weishi sanshi lun song* 唯識三十論頌; Thirty Verses). In order to buttress his own claim as rightful successor to a "lineage" through Xuanzang, Kuiji claimed that *Cheng weishi lun* was strictly based on ten Indian commentaries, with the opinion of sixth-century Indian Yogācāra exponent Dharmapāla (Hufa 護法) invariably prevailing. More recently, it has been argued that often it is the interpretations of the seventh-century Yogācāra master Sthiramati (Anhui 安慧) that is the authoritative position (demonstrable by comparing Sthiramati's commentary, the only one of the supposed ten that is extant today, with *Cheng weishi lun*).[15] Additionally, *Cheng weishi lun* draws on a variety of sources other than *Triṃśikā* commentaries. Be that as it may, it is important to bear in mind that Kuiji's *Cheng weishi lun shuji* 成唯識論述記 (Commentary on *Demonstration of Nothing but Consciousness*) is important for providing crucial glosses on *Cheng weishi lun*, the foundational text of the East Asian Yogācāra tradition. As one of the texts preserved in Japan and only reintroduced into China between 1891 and 1896, it had a seminal impact on the revival of Yogācāra in the twentieth century.[16]

15. Hidenori Sakuma, "On Doctrinal Similarities between Sthiramati and Xuanzang," *Journal of the International Association of Buddhist Studies* 29, no. 2 (2006[2009]): 357–382; Dan Lusthaus, *Buddhist Phenomenology: A Philosophical Investigation of Yogacara Buddhism and the Ch'eng Wei-shih Lun*, Curzon Critical Studies in Buddhism Series (London: Routledge, 2002), chapter 15.

16. In his chapter, John Jorgensen reveals that this text also played an important role in the revival of interest in Buddhist logic in Meiji Japan.

As Eyal Aviv notes in his chapter in this volume, for the influential Buddhist layman Ouyang Jingwu 歐陽竟無 (1871–1943) and his generation, "it was the only way to unlock the meaning of *Demonstration of Nothing but Consciousness.*"

Due to Kuiji's successful efforts to lay exclusive claim to the authoritative interpretation of *Cheng weishi lun*, his claim that it is Dharmapāla's text and that it would serve as the basic catechism of his school, with Dharmapāla becoming the first patriarch of the Weishi tradition, has been accepted in East Asia to this day. In a certain sense that battle—often framed as the *Awakening of Mahāyāna Faith* approach versus the Dharmapāla-Xuanzang-Kuiji approach—continues up to the present, and certainly sparked lively debate among twentieth-century Chinese intellectuals (see the chapters by Dan Lusthaus, Eyal Aviv, Lin Chen-kuo, and John Makeham in this volume).

Finally, Yijing 義淨 (635–713), seeking to follow in Xuanzang's footsteps, traveled to India in 671 and returned to China in 695. His interest was primarily in monastic discipline (*vinaya*), and so he began translating *vinaya* texts while still abroad and continued to do so after returning to China. In addition, he translated works important to Yogācāra, including commentaries by Dharmapāla on Dignāga's *Ālambana-parīkṣā* and on Vasubandhu's *Viṃśikā* (*Cheng weishi baosheng lun* 成唯識寶生論).

Kuiji was succeeded by Huizhao 慧沼 (650–714), the second patriarch of the Weishi School, who in turn was succeeded by Zhizhou 智周 (668–723). Without new translations to nourish it, however, the Weishi School was reduced to writing subcommentaries on subcommentaries, thus losing its vitality after a few centuries.

Among learned scholastics, Chinese Buddhism during the sixth and seventh centuries was dominated by various competing strands of Yogācāra (Northern and Southern Dilun, Shelun, Weishi, etc.). Even the so-called Sinitic Mahāyāna schools—Chan, Huayan, Pure Land, and to some extent Tiantai—were strongly influenced by Yogācāra models. Over time, however, Chinese Buddhists distanced themselves from their Yogācāra roots by (1) embracing supplemental doctrines, some already mixed with Yogācāra in India, such as matrix of buddhas thought, and some purely Chinese inventions, such as the theory of inherent enlightenment (*benjue* 本覺), which espouses the view that all sentient beings are already enlightened; and (2) leveling harsh polemical attacks against Yogācāra doctrine, especially against the type of Yogācāra introduced by Xuanzang in the seventh century. Since these polemical arguments continued to be repeated by the surviving Sinitic Buddhist schools over the centuries, and were reiterated in Korea and Japan, a revival of Yogācāra would entail responding to 1400 years of denigration and hostile interpretations that had become deeply ingrained in Chinese Buddhist sensibilities.

1.1.4 *Post-Tang decline*

Studies of Yogācāra texts continued into the tenth century in Chang'an and on Mt. Wutai, but after the death of the doctrinal synthesizer Yongming Yanshou 永明延壽 (904–975), many key Yogācāra texts were lost. We know from Japanese and Korean catalogues that in the tenth and eleventh centuries, Yogācāra texts, especially those on logic, were written in China but have not survived.[17] Moreover, the school identified as "Faxiang" continued to exist in Yanjing under the Liao Dynasty and in the capital territory region of Northern Song (Bianjing, i.e., modern Kaifeng) and later in Zhengdingfu (modern Zhengding, south of Beijing) under the Northern Song through the Jin Dynasty and even into the Yuan Dynasty. The Khitan *Tripiṭaka* contained a number of Yogācāra works, and Liao inscriptions provide evidence of the existence of several Liao Yogācāra scholars.[18]

By the 1130s, there were at least three centers of Yogācāra studies in China: Zhendingfu, the Bianjing to Luoyang area, and Hangzhou. Several Yogācāra monasteries, which had been founded by refugees from the north after the Jurchen invasion in 1127, survived as Yogācāra centers well into the Yuan Dynasty, and there is evidence that Yogācāra continued to be studied in Zhendingfu into the Yuan period.[19]

1.2 Late-Ming to early Qing Yogācāra studies

Despite a hiatus in Yogācāra studies lasting around two centuries, a revival occurred in the sixteenth and seventeenth centuries. Between 1511 and 1647 or thereabouts, at least thirty-five works on Yogācāra were written; virtually all were in the form of commentaries. The range of texts commented on was limited. Eight commentaries were written on Xuanzang's *Cheng weishi lun*, two on Vasubandhu's *Triṃśikā*, five on Vasubandhu's *Mahāyāna-śatadharmā-prakāśamukha-śāstra* (*Dasheng baifa mingmen lun* 大乘百法明門論; Lucid Introduction to the One Hundred Dharmas); four on Dignāga's *Ālambana-parīkṣā* (*Guan suoyuan yuan lun* 觀所緣緣論); eight on logic (*yinming* 因明); and seven on Xuanzang's *Bashi guiju song* 八識規矩頌 (Verses on the Structure of the Eight Consciousnesses). Two were written on a debate supposedly conducted in India where

17. Yang Weizhong 楊維中, *Zhongguo Weishizong tongshi* 中國唯識宗通史 (A General History of the Weishi School in China), 2 vols. (Nanjing: Fenghuang chubanshe, 2008), pp. 861–862.

18. Chikusa Masaaki 竺沙雅章, *Sō-Gen Bukkyō bunkashi kenkyū* 宋元佛教文化史研究 (Studies on the History of Buddhist Culture during the Song and Yuan Periods) (Tokyo: Kyūkosha, 2000), pp. 28, 5–7.

19. Chikusa Masaaki, *Sō-Gen Bukkyō bunkashi kenkyū*, p. 21.

Xuanzang established a proposition of true "nothing but consciousness" and defeated all his opponents.[20]

It appears that the major Yogācāra commentaries[21] were lost in the Northern Song period (960–1127), and so all attempts to interpret those Yogācāra texts still in circulation had to rely on quotations and explanations found in *Huayan jing shuchao* 華嚴經疏鈔 (Subcommentary on the Flower Ornament Sutra) by the Huayan patriarch Chengguan 澄觀 (738–839) and *Zongjing lu* 宗鏡錄 (Record of the Lineage Mirror) by the Chan scholar-monk Yanshou 延壽 (904–975).[22] Access to, and the ability to read, Sanskrit texts had of course long ceased. Most of the late-Ming Yogācāra commentators were Chan monks, and so there was also a marked tendency for them to introduce Huayan, Tiantai, and Chan into their interpretations, and to reconcile so-called attributes/characteristics (*xiang* 相; *lakṣana*) and nature (*xing* 性; *(sva)bhāva*, i.e., *tathāgatagarbha*) themes, relying heavily on *Dasheng qixin lun* to do so.[23]

With the importation from Japan in the late-Qing period of the major lost commentaries written by Kuiji and several other Tang-Dynasty Yogācāra scholars, most of the Ming-Dynasty texts became redundant. Two qualified exceptions to this observation are the Ming scholars Mingyu 明昱 (1527–1616) and Zhixu 智旭 (1599–1655), each of whom wrote eight commentaries on Yogācāra texts. Specifically, their respective commentaries on Dignāga's *Ālambana-parīkṣā* were frequently cited in Ouyang Jingwu's 歐陽竟無 (1871–1943) pioneering 1914 commentary on this work, *Guan suoyuan yuan lun shijie* 觀所緣緣論釋解 (Interpretative Exposition on the *Ālambana-parīkṣā*). *Ālambana-parīkṣā* was an influential text in the early twentieth-century revival of Yogācāra (as discussed below).

---

20. Shi Shengyan 釋聖嚴, "Ming mo de Weishi xuezhe ji qi sixiang 明末的唯識學者及其思想" (Late-Ming Yogācāra Scholars and Their Thought), *Zhonghua Foxue xuebao* 1 (1987): 21–23. For the last two titles, see also Ono Genmyō 小野玄妙, *Bussho kaisetsu jiten* 佛書解說大辭典 (Encyclopedia of Buddhist Literature with Explanations), 11 vols. (Tokyo: Daitō shuppansha, 1932–1936), vol. 3, pp. 78a-b, 232b.

21. In particular, three indispensable commentaries on *Cheng weishi lun* written in the Tang period: Kuiji's *Cheng weishi lun zhangzhong shuyao* 成唯識論掌中樞要 (Essentials of *Cheng weishi lun* in the Palm of One's Hand); Huizhao's *Cheng weishi lun liaoyi deng* 成唯識論了義燈 (Lamp of the Discerned Meaning of *Cheng weishi lun*); and Zhizhou's 智周 (668–723) *Cheng weishi lun yanmi* 成唯識論演祕 (Elaboration of the Esoteric in *Cheng weishi lun*). Key commentaries written by these same three authors on Buddhist logic had also ceased being transmitted in China by the late-Ming period.

22. Shi Shengyan, "Ming mo de Weishi xuezhe ji qi sixiang," p. 4.

23. Shi Shengyan, "Ming mo de Weishi xuezhe ji qi sixiang," pp. 26–27; see also William Chu, "The Timing of Yogācāra Resurgence in the Ming Dynasty (1368–1643)," *Journal of the International Association of Buddhist Studies* 33, nos. 1–2 (2010): 5–25.

Commentary writing on Yogācāra texts continued on into the early Qing period, particularly on *Bashi guiju*. There appears, however, to have been a long period between the early and the late-Qing periods when Yogācāra was largely ignored.

The revival of Yogācāra in the late-Ming period prefigures the resurrection of Yogācāra studies in late-Qing and Republican China. Like the late Qing, in the late Ming, Buddhism was greatly weakened by the corruption of the monastic establishment; state restrictions on Buddhism in the name of control over popular sectarian Buddhist movements that threatened the state; and the impact of foreign ideas. The level of monastic education had fallen, and monks often transgressed the precepts.[24] There was also a thirst for new ideas as people tired of Cheng-Zhu (Cheng Yi 程頤 [1033–1107] and Zhu Xi 朱熹 [1130–1200]) Neo-Confucian orthodoxy. Some began to call for a more equal society and others turned to Catholicism, attracted also by the new scientific ideas introduced by the Jesuits.[25] Therefore a demand emerged for a more robustly intellectual Buddhism than that offered by Chan or Pure Land piety. We might also note the revival of interest in Buddhist epistemology and logic, closely associated with Yogācāra, in the late Ming.

The arrival of Christian missionaries in China in the sixteenth century initiated a series of confrontations between the Europeans and adherents of traditional Chinese systems who faced unprecedented attacks on their doctrines and practices. The Jesuit missionary Matteo Ricci (1552–1610) and other Christians brought their message directly to the Chinese populace, and some wrote treatises that attempted to refute Chinese Buddhism.[26] Jiang Wu has shown how Chan master Feiyin Tongrong 費隱通容 (1593–1661) used Buddhist logic to counter Ricci and other Christians.[27] Specifically, Tongrong adapted the Buddhist proof

24. Jiang Canteng 江燦騰, *Zhongguo jindai Fojiao sixiang de zhengbian yu fazhan* 中國近代佛教思想的諍辯與發展 (Debate and Development in Modern Chinese Buddhist Thought) (Taipei: Nantian shuju, 1988), pp. 87–92.

25. Jiang, Canteng, *Zhongguo jindai Fojiao sixiang de zhengbian yu fazhan*, pp. 110–111, 118–121.

26. An example of this polemical literature is Ricci's treatise *Tianzhu shiyi* 天主實義 (The True Meaning of the Lord of Heaven). A collection of Chinese responses was compiled by the lay Buddhist scholar Xu Changzhi 徐昌治 (1582–1672) in his *Shengchao poxie ji* 勝朝破邪集 (Collection that Destroys Heterodoxy), published in 1633. This mainly includes Confucian works, but there are a number of Buddhist responses to Christianity in the last part of the collection.

27. Jiang Wu, "Buddhist Logic and Apologetics in 17th Century China: An Analysis of the Use of Buddhist Syllogisms in an Anti-Christian Polemic," *Dao: A Journal of Comparative Study*, 2.2 (June 2003): 273–289. This summarizes some of the research of his PhD dissertation, "Orthodoxy, Controversy and the Transformation of Chan Buddhism in Seventeenth-Century China," Harvard University, 2002.

sequence (often referred to as a "Buddhist syllogism"[28]) and used it to devise three major arguments against the Christian doctrine of God. According to Jiang,

> Even in the Tang dynasty, when the study of Buddhist logic was promoted by Xuanzang, there is no evidence that Buddhist logic was successfully used in actual debates as an apologetic tool. In this sense, the emergence of Buddhist logic in the context of the seventeenth-century anti-Christian movement signaled a new development in Buddhist apologetics.[29]

Such efforts set a precedent in which Yogācāra was construed as an authentically Buddhist system that provided conceptual resources for defending Buddhism against foreign attackers. Thus, when reformers sought to adapt Buddhism in response to the challenges of modernity in the early twentieth century, some followed the lead of these seventeenth-century thinkers and looked to Dignāga and other logicians for philosophical ammunition.

2. *Yogācāra thought in modern China: An overview*

Section 1 sought to provide a succinct account of the history of Yogācāra in China before the twentieth century. Section 2 now takes us to the main subject of this volume: the reception of Yogācāra in the early decades of twentieth-century China. It does this by introducing three major themes that run throughout the volume: science, logic, and New Confucian thought, and their relation to Yogācāra. An introduction to these three themes anticipates several key questions animating discussions in the individual chapters of the volume: What role did the Yogācāra revival in the early decades of the twentieth century play in Chinese responses to the challenges of modernity? Why did Chinese intellectuals turn to a tradition that was not Chinese? How did the promoters of Yogācāra respond to the intellectual and institutional authority now commanded by science? In what ways

---

28. The full form of the standard *yinming* three-part inference or "syllogism" is as follows:

1. *pakṣa* (*lizong* 立宗; thesis): Sound is impermanent.
2. *hetu* (*yin* 因; reason) or *liṅga* (*xiang* 相; mark): because produced.
3. *dṛṣṭānta* (*yu* 喻; example):

   [a] Whatever is produced, that is known to be impermanent, like a pot, etc.
   [b] Whatever is permanent, that is known to be unproduced, like space (*ākāśa*), etc.

See Dan Lusthaus's entry under *nengli* 能立 in the *Digital Dictionary of Buddhism*, www.buddhism-dict.net.

29. Jiang Wu, "Buddhist Logic and Apologetics in 17th Century China," p. 286.

was logic significant for the reception of Yogācāra in modern China? Why does *Dasheng qixin lun* 大乘起信論 (Awakening of Mahāyāna Faith) loom so large in the history of the modern reception of Yogācāra? What was the relation between Yogācāra and the development of New Confucian thought?

2.1 Yogācāra and science

The decades immediately before and after 1900 witnessed a profound process of intellectual and institutional translation in which Western disciplinary models challenged, superseded, and widely displaced traditional schemes of knowledge classification in China. At the forefront of this process of epistemological upheaval was that flag-bearer of modernity, the juggernaut called science, a category that itself was rapidly expanding in disciplinary and subdisciplinary complexity. With the tide of Western learning ever strengthening, and institutional support for traditional schemes of knowledge compartmentalization disappearing in the wake of the abolition of the civil examinations in 1905,[30] the traditional category of "Natural Studies" (*gezhi* 格知; inquiring into and extending knowledge) was being fundamentally displaced by *kexue* 科學, modern science.

Since the early twentieth century, science had been the criterion used to distinguish "religion" (*zongjiao* 宗教) from "superstition" (*mixin* 迷信). Within this context, demonstrating Buddhism's compatibility with science was necessary if it was to gain intellectual and political acceptance. How did the promoters of Yogācāra respond to the intellectual and institutional authority now commanded by science? The range of responses or positions is surprisingly varied, ranging from efforts to show that Buddhism is scientific, right through to arguments designed to show how science validates Yogācāra. What is consistent is the view that science and soteriology are not incompatible, a view underpinned by the conviction that Yogācāra provided a superior means to establish verification.

2.1.1 *The relevance of Yogācāra to science*

OF ATOMS AND *ĀLAMBANA-PARĪKṢĀ*

Against the backdrop of a renaissance of interest in logic and in Yogācāra philosophy in the late-Qing and early Republican periods, the logician Dignāga's *Ālambana-parīkṣā* (Discerning the Conditions for the Causal Support of Consciousness) commanded considerable fascination in China during the 1910s and 1920s. *Ālambana-parīkṣā* is a debate text in which popular Indian Realist theories about atoms are subjected to sustained analytical critique. Some of these theories

30. The civil service examinations had played a key role in government administration as well as in the fabric of social and intellectual life since 650.

proposed that an *ālambana* (*suoyuan* 所緣)—a cognitive object from which mental impressions are derived—is composed of individual or clustered groups of atoms. In *Ālambana-parīkṣā* Dignāga sets out a deconstructive argument and a constructive argument. The deconstructive argument refutes the thesis that either individual atoms or groups of atoms are capable of functioning as a percept; the constructive thesis is the proposition that what we actually cognize are mental images (*ākāra*; *xiang* 相) of our own making. As Dan Lusthaus notes in his chapter in this volume:

> Although eventually the *Ālambana-parīkṣā* was superseded in India (and later Tibet) by more sophisticated and complex critiques of atomism, none of those later works reached China and East Asia until the twentieth century. Thus, *Ālambana-parīkṣā* represents the high water mark in the East Asian appropriation of Indian Buddhist critiques of atomism, and as such received much attention among twentieth-century Chinese intellectuals for its seeming relevance to modern scientific atomic theories as well as contemporary trends in the psychology and philosophy of perception.

Such alignments of Yogācāra with science could of course also be used to further agendas internal to Buddhist polemics. In the case of the Buddhist scholars Ouyang Jingwu and Lü Cheng 呂澂 (1896–1989), one such aim was to critique "false Buddhism" and promote "genuine Buddhism" (see below and also Lusthaus, Aviv, and Lin).

In one essay dating from the period when he was in Japan (1906–1911), the revolutionary, scholar, and philosopher Zhang Binglin 章炳麟 (Taiyan 太炎) (1869–1936) had argued that Chinese versions of Yogācāra texts on Buddhist logic and reasoning—having only recently become available again after a hiatus of many centuries—made it possible once again to gain a proper understanding of China's earliest writings on logic. On the face of it,[31] in some ways this is curiously similar to the position advocated by Lü Cheng that without a careful consideration of Sanskrit or Tibetan counterparts, a number of Chinese versions of

31. Despite having identified problems with the claim that the *Dasheng qixin lun* was a genuine Indian scripture, Zhang's personal commitment to its teachings seems not to have been affected: "The Buddha's teachings are concerned solely with developing interpretative accounts of Suchness (*zhenru* 真如 [*tathatā*]) and so it is necessary to verify Suchness as it actually is. In order to develop accounts of Suchness it is necessary to verify the 'matrix of buddhas' (*rulaizang* 如來藏 [*tathāgatagarbha*]). Rather than calling this [Buddhism] a religion it would be better to refer to it as 'that which provides philosophical verification based on evidence.' " Zhang Taiyan, "Lun Fofa yu zongjiao, zhexue yi ji xianshi zhi guanxi 論佛法與宗教、哲學以及現實之關係" (The Relationship between Buddhism, Religion, Philosophy and the Real World), *Zhongguo zhexue* 6 (1981): 300.

those texts would be difficult to understand and to reconcile with each other. Lü sought to demonstrate this with the example of *Ālambana-parīkṣā*. For Lü there was far more here at stake than scholarly one-upmanship: he wanted to demonstrate that Sinicized forms of Buddhism are corrupt and incompatible with the project of modernity and at the same time sought to defend the soteriological import of Yogācāra doctrine (see the chapters by Lusthaus and Lin).

As chief exponents and representatives of the movement that sought to "return to the roots" of original Indian Buddhism, with special attention being paid to Yogācāra teachings, Lü and his teacher Ouyang Jingwu were opposed to the doctrine of "inherent enlightenment" that had developed in China, on the grounds that it is founded on the notion of the matrix of buddhas—the idea that the potentiality for buddhahood exists embryonically in all sentient beings—and hence this is only faith-based and not true Indian Buddhism.

One of Ouyang's and Lü's principal targets of criticism was Aśvaghoṣa's *Dasheng qixin lun*, the most influential "matrix of buddhas" text in the tradition of Sinitic Buddhism, but which since the late-nineteenth century had been characterized by leading Japanese scholars as a Chinese forgery. For its critics it was the embodiment of what was wrong with East Asian Buddhism. Despite the attacks on the scripture's authenticity, it continued to be defended and revered as a genuine, if perhaps problematic, Buddhist text. The cultural "pull" of this text is such that even Ouyang himself later in life changed his views about *tathāgatagarbha*, as Eyal Aviv reveals in his chapter. We can perhaps even see the philosopher, Rural Reconstruction Movement leader, and teacher Liang Shuming 梁漱溟 (1893–1988) as revealing traces of a similar "matrix of buddhas"-like disposition. As related by Thierry Meynard in this volume,

> Liang had an ontological faith in the sense that he believed there was a foundational reality of human experience and of the world. As a Buddhist himself, he started with the existential questions of human suffering and impermanence. He adopted the Yogācāra method in order to deconstruct all the elements of experience. In the end, Liang believed that beyond the illusory elements of experience he would find an ontological reality, or Suchness. We can say that Liang had a real faith in Suchness, something that was beyond his words and beyond his intelligence but which could be experienced.

The alignment of Yogācāra with scientific rationality—such as the critique of atomism in *Ālambana-parīkṣā*—served to bolster the authority of the criticisms that Lü Cheng and others directed at "false Buddhism," as exemplified by *Dasheng qixin lun*. Despite this (or perhaps also because of this), Ouyang and Lü—sometimes characterized as the modern defenders of the

Dharmapāla-Xuanzang-Kuiji or Weishi School of Yogācāra—both came under attack from a number of quarters (not least the so-called New Confucians; see Lin, Clower, and Makeham). As Eyal Aviv points out, as a consequence of this,

> much of our view of them [has been] informed by polemical literature created by their opponents who doubted the patriotism of Ouyang and his followers and the 'Chinese-ness' of their Yogācāra teachings. They also saw them as criticizing everything that Chinese Buddhism stood for, one important aspect of which was the *tathāgatagarbha* teachings.

TELESCOPES, MICROSCOPES, AND ETHER

Scott Pacey argues that the influential Buddhist monastic Taixu 太虛 (1890–1947) was more than a Buddhist reformer: he was also an intellectual who contributed to broader, ongoing debates about modernity in Chinese society. Sympathetic to science, Taixu even called for the study of science in order to spread Buddhism. By attempting to show that Yogācāra was compatible with science, he hoped to propagate Buddhism, more generally. On the one hand, he called for Yogācāra to be discussed using scientific terminology, referring to this as the "new Yogācāra"; on the other hand, he also attempted to show that Yogācāra could help improve scientific method. In this latter respect, Yogācāra was particularly useful because it enables one to overcome flawed observation and to observe reality directly, thereby leading to improved scientific observations. According to Pacey, "This led Taixu to suggest that in the future, 'Yogācāra methods could . . . increase the limited powers of telescopes and microscopes.' Yogācāra would improve on the scientific method, augmenting scientists' powers of observation, so that they could use their scientific instruments to full effect."

Taixu's vision of a "modernized Buddhism" was articulated under the rubric of "Buddhism for the human world" (*renjian fojiao* 人間佛教) or "Buddhism for human life" (*rensheng fojiao* 人生佛教). Both notions gained further theoretical refinement in the hands of Taixu's student Yinshun 印順 (1906–2005). Then, due to an influx of monks from the mainland beginning in 1949, the Taiwanese Buddhist world inherited the legacy of Taixu's (and Yinshun's) re-articulated Buddhisms. Subsequently, members of a new generation of Buddhist monks and nuns—most notably represented by Xingyun 星雲 (b. 1927), Shengyan 聖嚴 (1930–2009), and Zhengyan 證嚴 (b. 1937)—devoted themselves to the implementation and realization of many of Taixu's reforms and proposals. Taixu's use of Yogācārā philosophy thus must be placed within the context of his broader aim, which was to demonstrate how Buddhism should be used to develop and benefit human life. Although he did not claim that Yogācārā was preeminent among the Buddhist schools in China, he did believe that it was the one most able to contend with Western scientific thought on its own terms. Alongside

Madhyamaka it thus formed an important component of his refutations of Western scientific materialism, theistic religion, and social theory (such as communism, socialism, and anarchism). It was in this way that Taixu was instrumental in using Yogācāra to inform subsequent developments in twentieth-century Chinese Buddhism.[32]

For other Chinese intellectuals, Yogācāra provided a means by which to interpret and to understand science, and so make it more accessible to Chinese people. An example of this approach is Tan Sitong's 譚嗣同 (1865–1898) pioneering attempt to use Yogācāra to explain contemporary neurophysiology. Tan completed his draft of *Renxue* 仁學 (A Study of Benevolence) in 1897. One of the basic characteristics of Tan's understanding of *ren* (benevolence) is "interconnectedness" (*tong* 通), a notion derived from Huayan Buddhism and applied in his efforts to synthesize Confucius's concept of *ren*, Mozi's notion of ungraded concern, the *ālaya* consciousness of Yogācāra Buddhism, Christian love, and even ether, centripetal force, and gravitational force. In Huayan Buddhist thought, *tong* relates to the idea that the boundary between the absolute (*li*) and phenomena (*shi*) is nonexistent, thus allowing a metaphysical interpenetration of the two realms—an idea that in turn can be seen to be connected to themes in *Dasheng qixin lun* and early hybrid Yogācāra thought.

Tan identified the brain, the nervous system, and electricity as all being composed of the same psychophysical substance: ether (*yitai* 以太). When ether was running free in space, it was electricity.[33] As with benevolence, ether is produced by the mind. As Erik J. Hammerstrom points out, until Einstein's work appeared, the idea that physical and mental phenomena are composed of ether was still very much a live theoretical concept within physics, allowing Tan to unite the world of ethics, morals, and politics with that of physical matter. In his first essay Pacey relates how Tan "provided an answer to the unexplained relationship between electricity and consciousness by combining discoveries about the brain's electrical functions with Yogācāra's cognitive architecture." Not long after this, as John Jorgensen relates, the reformer, philosopher, and scholar Liang Qichao 梁啓超 (1873–1929) maintained that Western enlightenment and scientific

32. The Wuchang Buddhist Seminary (Wuchang Foxue Yuan 武昌佛學院)—strongly associated with Taixu—exerted a lasting influence on the institutions and thought of modern Chinese Buddhism through its network of individuals, seminaries, and periodicals that connected Chinese Buddhists in different parts of China. For members of the "Wuchang School," as Erik J. Hammerstrom shows in his chapter, "Yogācāra served as an indispensable resource for understanding and critiquing the complexities of modern mind science."

33. The distinction echoes one made by Neo-Confucian Zhang Zai 張載 (1020–1077) between his concept of *taixu* 太虛 (Ultimate Void) and *qi* 氣 (vital stuff).

discovery were governed by the cerebrum, or *manas* (the seventh consciousness), and that Chinese rote memorization belonged to the *manovijñāna* (the sixth consciousness or mental consciousness).

MIND SCIENCE

Yogācāra also played an important role in enabling Buddhists and, more generally, Chinese intellectuals to interpret the new discipline of psychology. By the late 1870s in Germany, scientific methods such as experimentation and the development of physiological tools provided the impetus for psychology to be differentiated from philosophy as a science. And although there were attempts after this in the United States to consolidate links between philosophy and psychology (most notably by William James), by the turn of the twentieth century psychology had begun to be established as an independent academic discipline, even if courses were still referred to as moral or mental philosophy. The establishment of independent psychology departments was, however, a gradual process, as departmentalization in American tertiary institutions only began in earnest in the 1890s. China's first association dedicated to the study of psychology was not founded until 1921. At Peking University, psychology courses continued to be taught in the Philosophy Department in the 1910s through to the early 1920s; it was not until 1926 that the Psychology Department was established and the Philosophy Department ceased offering psychology courses.

As Hammerstrom clearly describes in his chapter, a major topic to which Buddhist writers in the 1920s applied Yogācāra was that of modern mind science. (Hammerstrom adopts the term "modern mind science" instead of "psychology" in order to represent the novelty of this field in China at the time.) The theories of mind science that were being translated in China at the time "were not part of a stable discipline, but belonged to one where competing viewpoints on basic methodological assumptions vied for dominance." He shows how concepts drawn from Yogācāra such as "karmic seeds" and the "base consciousness" helped Chinese Buddhists, in particular, to "answer certain questions that were causing problems for modern mind science, such as the processes by which instinct and memory occurred."[34]

---

34. Writing in 1932, Xiong Shili 熊十力 (1885–1968)—who was generally disdainful of psychology—even opined that "Today, psychologists have what they refer to as the sub-conscious. It is even possible that they have some glimpse into the deep source of seeds and so talk about them [in such terms]." See *Xin weishi lun* 新唯識論 (New Treatise on the Uniqueness of Consciousness), literary redaction (1932), *Xiong Shili quanji* 熊十力全集 (The Complete Writings of Xiong Shili) (Wuhan: Hubei jiaoyu chubanshe, 2001), vol. 2, p. 105.

2.1.2 *The scientific validation of Yogācāra*

An appeal was also made to the claim that science could validate the insights of Yogācāra. Sometimes this involved accounts that appealed to unfolding trends in human history, some deep rooted, others less so. Thierry Meynard introduces the intriguing example of Liang Shuming, who

> attempted to understand how Yogācāra teachings could have appeared so early in human history, describing the intellectual precocity (*zaoshu* 早熟) of Yogācāra as being the sublime product of genius such as that of Asaṅga and Vasubandhu. Because of its complexity, their teaching was not understood at that time. Only today, in the modern age, have people begun to understand Yogācāra because modern Western science is showing people the validity of Yogācāra.

Zhang Taiyan similarly appealed to historical trends to argue that science could validate the insights of Yogācāra, making the point that only in recent times had scholarly advances in science in China developed enough to appreciate the insights of Yogācāra:

> There is a good reason for my singular respect for *faxiang* 法相 [an alternative name for the Weishi School]. Modern scholarship [in China] has gradually followed the path of "seeking verification in actual events." Of course the detailed analysis carried out by Han Learning scholars [textual and philological scholars of the Qing Dynasty] was far superior to that which scholars in the Ming were able to achieve. [Analogously,] with the beginnings of [modern] science [introduced in China in the late nineteenth century] scholars applied themselves with even greater precision. It is for this reason that *faxiang* learning was inappropriate to the situation in China during the Ming but is most appropriate in modern times. This was brought about by the trends that have informed the development of scholarship.[35]

Zhang also approvingly cited the words of his friend and *fin de siècle* Buddhist networker, Gui Bohua 桂伯華 (1861–1915), who had also studied under Yang Wenhui:

> Gui Bohua also said, "Over the recent three hundred years the style of scholarship has become vastly different from that of the Song and

35. Zhang Taiyan, "Da Tiezheng 答鐵錚" (Reply to Tiezheng), in *Zhang Taiyan ji* 章太炎集 (Collected Writings of Zhang Taiyan), ed. Huang Xia'nian 黃夏年 (Beijing: Zhongguo shehuikexue chubanshe, 1995), p. 19.

Ming periods. The evidential scholarship of Han Learning was the forerunner of science, and science is the forerunner of *faxiang*. This is because that which *faxiang* discusses must be verified in reality, and its doctrines must thoroughly adhere to principle. In character it is the same as science." These words can be said to understand the trend in scholarship.[36]

2.1.3 Using Yogācāra to critique science

The relationship between Yogācāra and science was not restricted to how Yogācāra might contribute to interpreting or even enhancing science. Nor were attempts to secure the authority of Yogācāra made by appealing only to the claim that science could validate Yogācāra—Yogācāra was also used to critique science and scientists. Scott Pacey demonstrates how Taixu emphasized the similarities between Einstein's theory of relativity and Yogācāra, yet concluded that the theory of relativity lacked Yogācāra's level of comprehensiveness. "He could therefore invoke Einstein—whom he called 'the greatest contemporary scientist'—in support of Yogācāra, while showing his ideas to be inadequate when compared with Buddhism."

The philosopher Xiong Shili invoked Bertrand Russell for a similar purpose. Bertrand Russell and Dora Black arrived in China in October 1920 and stayed nine months, based in Beijing and giving lectures across the country. Xiong began to teach at Peking University in 1922. In one of his lectures titled "Zhexue wenti 哲學問題" (Philosophical Problems), Russell remarked that "nothing in the world is more real than momentary things."[37] In expounding on the fundamental Buddhist doctrine that "dharmas do not abide even momentarily"[38] Xiong singled Russell out for maintaining "what is temporary is real"; just as on another occasion when critiquing some arguments on atomism proposed by traditional Indian Realist philosophers, he criticized Russell for purportedly asserting that "cameras are able to see things."[39]

Hammerstrom, in turn, cites the fascinating example of Wang Xiaoxu 王小徐 (1875–1948), one of China's first great modern scientists and a founding member

---

36. Zhang Taiyan, *Zi shu xueshu cidi* 自述學術次第 (My Sequence in Learning), in *Zhuo Han san yan* 葑漢三言 (Three Books by Zhang Taiyan) (Shenyang: Liaoning jiaoyu chubanshe, 2000), p. 166.

37. Song Xijun 宋錫鈞 and Li Xiaofeng 李小峰 (comps.), *Luosu ji Bolake jiangyan ji* 羅素及勃拉克講演集 (Collected Essays of Russell and Black) (Beijing: Weiyiri baoshe, 1922), p. 11.

38. Xiong Shili, *Xin weishi lun*, vol. 2, p. 43.

39. Xiong Shili, *Weishi xue gailun* 唯識學概論 (A General Account of Yogācāra Learning), *Xiong Shili quanji*, vol. 1, p. 107.

of Academia Sinica. Following the lead of Liang Shuming, Wang argued that empiricism—the basis of science—was merely the operation of inferential cognition/logical inference (*biliang* 比量; *anumāna pramāṇa*), concluding that "because of this, science was thus not capable of proving the truths that were described in Buddhism, which had been apprehended by the direct perception (*xianliang* 現量; *pratyakṣa pramāṇa*) utilized by advanced practitioners of the Buddhist path."

The issue Wang touches upon also highlights an important yet curiously overlooked reason that many intellectuals in the 1910s and 1920s regarded Yogācāra as representing a legitimate epistemological position. This issue concerns positivist epistemology, which, in some of its formulations, seems close to being a variation of epistemological idealism. Epistemological idealism, of course, is one of the main ways in which Yogācāra (nothing but consciousness [*vijñapti-mātra*]) has been, and continues to be, represented. John Powers provides a clear account of Yogācāra epistemological idealism based on the *Saṃdhinirmocana-sūtra*:

> All perceptions are mediated and interpreted by the mind; no aspect of the outside world appears directly to awareness. Sense impressions of phenomena relay information to the mind and are then interpreted, and the cognitions of a particular agent reflect the physical realities of his or her species and perceptual faculties, background, language, and life experience. There are no pure experiences outside of meditation, and all cognitions have an interpretive overlay.

Taking a different focus, Lambert Schmithausen chooses instead to describe the basic epistemological stance of Yogācāra as the view "that there are no entities, especially no material entities, apart from consciousness, or, more precisely, apart from the various kinds of mind [*citta*] and mental factors or mind-associates [*caitta*]." Dan Lusthaus, however, cautions that

> the key Yogācāric phrase *vijñapti-mātra* does not mean (as is often touted in the scholarly literature) that "consciousness alone exists," but rather that "all our efforts to get beyond ourselves are nothing but projections of our consciousness." Yogācārins treat the term *vijñapti-mātra* as an epistemic caution, not an ontological pronouncement.[40]

---

40. Lambert Schmithausen, *On the Problem of the External World in the Ch'eng weishi lun* (Tokyo: The International Institute for Buddhist Studies, 2005), p. 9; Dan Lusthaus, *Buddhism and Phenomenology: A Philosophical Investigation of Yogācāra Buddhism and the Ch'eng Wei-shih Lun* (London: RoutledgeCurzon, 2003), p. 5.

And even though discussion of the particular distinction highlighted in Schmithausen's and Lusthaus's respective accounts was not in vogue in 1920s China, it would not have affected the point raised in Wang's critique. The so-called science and philosophy of life debates (or science and metaphysics debates) of 1923[41] in China reveal that even some of the harshest critics of metaphysics promoted an epistemological stance that (unexpectedly) shares key similarities with the doctrine of nothing but consciousness.

The chief protagonists in the debates were the philosopher (later a politician, and even later a retrospectively-identified New Confucian) Zhang Junmai 張君勱 (Carsun Chang; 1886–1969), critic of scientism and materialism, and the geologist Ding Wenjiang 丁文江 (1888–1936), critic of metaphysics. The intellectual historian Charlotte Furth sees the debate between Zhang and Ding as a direct outcome of an agenda pursued in Liang Shuming's *Dongxi wenhua ji qi zhexue* 東西文化及其哲學 (Eastern and Western Cultures and Their Philosophies), according to which Eastern and Western civilizations each possessed its own inherent form of philosophical and ethical principles and that at the heart of the contention was an attempt "to expose the underlying forces responsible for the two world systems and to reveal the primary axioms upon which a future Chinese society would have to be based."[42] Hammerstrom similarly relates:

> These debates were over competing visions of modernity in China, and even competing visions of science. One of the main battle lines was between those who supported a view of science founded upon values from the Enlightenment, and those, like Carsun Chang, who favored a worldview strongly inspired by Romanticism and Romantic science.

In his essay "Xuanxue yu kexue 玄學與科學" (Metaphysics and Science), Ding advocates an epistemological stance he calls "skeptical idealism," which he associates with the theories of perception subscribed to by Huxley, Darwin, Spencer, William James, Karl Pearson, and Ernst Mach:

> Because they hold that sense perception is the only method by which we can know objects (*wuti*), our concepts of objects are psychological phenomena and hence we say it is idealism. As to whether there are things in

41. Brought together in Zhang Junmai 張君勱 et al. (eds.), *Kexue yu renshengguan* 科學與人生觀 (Science and Philosophy of Life) (Shanghai: Yadong tushuguan, 1923). See also Erik Hammerstrom's discussion of these debates in his chapter in this volume.

42. Charlotte Furth, *Ting Wen-chiang: Science and China's New Culture* (Cambridge, MA: Harvard University Press, 1970), p. 99. Liang himself would certainly have insisted that it was three, not two, civilizations that were relevant, although at that time India was less so.

> the realm beyond sense perception or behind self-consciousness, or what kind of things objects are, they all maintain that this is not known (*bu zhi* 不知)[43] and should not be discussed, hence we say "skeptical."[44]

He contrasts the position of the skeptical idealist with that of the metaphysician, who claims that independent of the mind[45] there exist noumena (*benti* 本體), such as Berkeley's notion of God and Zhang's notion of self. In charting the demise of metaphysics and the rise of science, Ding parodies the metaphysician's position as follows:

> By the second half of the nineteenth century even psychology, the guard dog of metaphysics, had become independent. Thereupon metaphysics retreated from fundamental philosophy into ontology. Without any sign of repentance they [the metaphysicians] continued to put on airs in the face of philosophy saying, "You are unable to study self-awareness or the noumena that lie beyond sense perception. You deal with the physical not the metaphysical. You are dead and I am living."[46]

Even though most of the proscience participants in the debates would probably have rejected skeptical idealism as a concession to metaphysics, it remains a curious fact that skeptical idealism was well entrenched among the promoters of positivism in China. This concern about noumena (*benti* 本體) being inherently unknowable was placed prominently on the intellectual agenda in China through the pioneering translator Yan Fu's 嚴復 (1853–1921) introduction of positivist philosophy. Contemporary Tsinghua University philosopher Hu Weixi 胡偉希, argues that like Huxley, Spencer, and Mill, Yan Fu was committed to the epistemological premise that human knowledge is bound by the limits of sensory experience:[47]

> He concurred with Spencer's division of the world into the phenomenal and the unknowable, maintaining that all [genuine] knowledge is knowledge which relates only to the phenomenal world. Hence, [Yan said] "there

43. It may be that Ding actually means "unknowable."

44. Zhang Junmai, *Kexue yu renshengguan*, pp. 12, 13.

45. Literally "patterns of the mind" (*xinli* 心理).

46. Zhang Junmai, *Kexue yu renshengguan*, p. 16.

47. See also Wang Hui, "The Fate of 'Mr. Science' in China: The Concept of Science and its Application in Modern Chinese Thought," in *Formations of Colonial Modernity in East Asia*, ed. Tani E. Barlow (Durham, NC: Duke University Press, 1997), p. 40.

is no way we can learn about what is not of this world and even if one should attempt to do so it would have no bearing on human affairs." Denying that "*benti*" can be known was not some occasional, casual remark on his part but was the core of his entire philosophical thinking.[48]

There is thus perhaps more than irony in the fact that Yan Fu should have cited Buddhist views in his support of Mill's claim that human knowledge is bound by the limits of sensory experience.[49] Yan began his translation of Mill's *A System of Logic* in 1900 and the work was published in 1905. Intriguingly, this is exactly the period when the revival of interest in Yogācāra began in China.

2.2 Yogācāra and logic

The third volume of Joseph Levenson's trilogy *Confucian China and its Modern Fate*, titled *The Problem of Historical Significance*, attempts to show how a particular "system of ideas passed out of contemporary reality into history, how what was once living tradition was handed over to traditionalists."[50] The late-Qing Confucian, like the modern diasporic Jew, was confronted by what Vera Schwartz refers to as the separation of history and value, in which intellectuals were compelled to find "value" in places other than in their own tradition.[51] The case of Yogācāra differs from that of Confucianism: Yogācāra was privileged precisely for what it represented in terms of "value" rather than what it represented in terms of emotional attachment to "tradition," even if individual thinkers varied in their attitudes to the question of the significance of the relationship that Yogācāra had with the Chinese past and indeed with the recovery of the Chinese past.

---

48. Hu Weixi, *Zhuan shi cheng zhi: Qinghua xuepai yu ershi shiji Zhongguo zhexue* 轉識成智—清華學派與 20 世紀中國哲學 (Transforming Consciousness into Wisdom: The Tsinghua School and Twentieth-Century Chinese Philosophy) (Shanghai: Huadong shifan daxue chubanshe, 2005), pp. 124–125.

49. Yan Fu, *Mule Mingxue* 穆勒名學 (Mill's *A System of Logic*), in his *Yan yi mingzhu congkan* 嚴譯名著叢刊 (Collection of Famous Writings Translated by Yan Fu), vol. 8 (Shanghai: Shangwu yinshuguan 商務印書館, 1931), p. 58.

50. Henry F. May, H. Franz Schurmann, and Frederic Wakeman, "University of California: In Memoriam, December 1970," http://content.cdlib.org/xtf/view?docId=hb629006wb&doc.view=content&chunk.id=div00025&toc.depth=1&brand=oac&anchor.id=0, accessed May 6, 2007.

51. Vera Schwartz, review of *The Mozartian Historian: Essays on the Works of Joseph R. Levenson*, eds. Maurice Meisner and Rhoads Murphey, *History and Theory* 17, no. 3(1978): 358. See also Joseph R. Levenson, *Confucian China and Its Modern Fate: A Trilogy* (Berkeley and Los Angeles: University of California Press, 1968), p. x.

What role did the Yogācāra revival in the early decades of the twentieth century play in Chinese responses to the challenges of modernity? A particularly common view is that intellectuals of the time regarded Yogācāra as a sophisticated knowledge system that could serve as an authoritative alternative to the knowledge systems being introduced from the West; that it was an "indigenized" intellectual resource that could be co-opted to counter the challenges posed by the logic, philosophy, psychology, and science of the West. Whatever the merits of this explanation (one that is supported by statements made by protagonists of the day), it still does not account for why Chinese intellectuals should have turned to a tradition that might well be regarded as inherently non-Chinese.

The conventional explanation is that even though Yogācāra had its roots in Indian thought, it was still considered a "Chinese" system because for early twentieth-century Chinese intellectuals its most influential historical interpreters were Chinese commentators, extending back to early Tang times. (And as noted above, even in the late-Ming period, it was employed as an aid in critiquing the foreign religion of Christianity.) The conventional explanation fails, however, to account for modern scholars such as Ouyang Jingwu and Lü Cheng, who were part of a movement that sought to "return to the roots" of original Indian Buddhism (see Aviv, Lusthaus, and Lin) with special attention being paid to Yogācāra teachings and texts. Lü, in particular, emphasized the importance of fluency in Sanskrit and Tibetan, reflecting a trend that had already begun in Japan in the mid-Meiji period (see Jorgensen).[52]

The conventional account also fails to give due recognition to how new knowledge systems—and despite its long history, Yogācāra *did* constitute a new knowledge system in late-Qing, early-Republican China—were used by some as tools in the recovery of tradition. European and Asian confrontations with modernity often differ in significant ways. European modernities commonly involve a radical repudiation of the past and of tradition in favor of innovation and individual creativity with a vision of a new social order and a new regime of knowledge. While some Asian modernities, such as the May Fourth Movement in China, follow a similar route and propose the adoption of Western science, philosophy, and political thought, others (particularly movements led by people with a strong commitment to a traditional system like Buddhism or Confucianism) valorize and reappropriate classical (or imagined classical) traditions, texts, beliefs, and practices and mobilize them in the service of nationalistic agendas in response to an encounter with Western modernity.

52. Nanjō Bun'yū went to London to study Sanskrit with F. Max Müller in 1876 and this is when he met Yang Wenhui. Nanjō began lecturing on Sanskrit at Tokyo University in 1885.

Zhang Taiyan is a prominent exemplar of this second approach. Against the backdrop of an intellectual climate in Japan and China during the decades on either side of 1900, in which a premium had come to be placed on logic as a precondition for the development of philosophy, Zhang was one of the first Chinese intellectuals to follow the lead of Japanese scholars such as Kuwaki Genyoku 桑木嚴翼 (1874–1946) and Murakami Senshō (alt. Senjō) 村上専精 (1851–1929) in maintaining that classical Chinese philosophers had developed indigenous forms of logic. Significantly, he further argued that Chinese versions of Yogācāra texts on Buddhist epistemology and logic (*yinming* 因明; *hetuvidyā*)[53]—having only recently become available again after a hiatus of many centuries—made it possible once again to develop a proper understanding of China's earliest writings on logic.

In Japan, the study of Western logic began in earnest in 1874 when the philosopher Nishi Amane 西周 (1829–1897) published *Chichi keimō* 致知啓蒙 (Primer on the Extension of Knowledge), a work based on J. S. Mill's *A System of Logic*, and the first exposition of formal logic and inductive logic in Japan.[54] Parallel to this was a renewed interest in Buddhist logic. As Jorgensen notes in his chapter in this volume, Murakami Senshō, the most famous Meiji scholar of Buddhist logic, had already published his *Inmyōgaku zensho* 因明學全書 (Complete Works on Logic Studies) in 1884, and the texts that Nanjō Bun'yū sent to Yang Wenhui between 1892 and 1896 included copies of Kuiji's commentaries and writings on logic and epistemology—including Kuiji's key commentary *Yinming ru zhengli lun shu* 因明入正理論疏 (Commentary on *Entryway into Logic*), a discussion of the Sanskrit text *Nyāyapraveśa* [Entryway into Logic][55]), which had not been transmitted in China—as well as Japanese commentaries on texts dealing with Indian systems of logic developed in the Yogācāra tradition.

In the 1890s, however, the attitude of many Japanese scholars to Chinese philosophy and to the history of Chinese philosophy was highly critical. Identifying logic as the hallmark of order (*soshiki* 組織) and system (*keitō* 系統; *taikei* 體系),

---

53. *Yinming* (knowledge of reasons) is the Chinese interpretation of Buddhist reasoning and logic: *hetuvidyā*. See Christoph Harbsmeier, *Language and Logic in Traditional China*, in *Science and Civilisation in China*, vol. 7, pt. 1 (Cambridge: Cambridge University Press, 1998), pp. 358–408. On the introduction of logic into China and the development of Chinese logic, see Joachim Kurtz, *The Discovery of Chinese Logic* (Leiden: Brill, 2011).

54. See Barry Steben, "Nishi Amane and the Birth of 'Philosophy' and 'Chinese Philosophy' in Early Meiji Japan," in *Learning to Emulate the Wise: The Genesis of Chinese Philosophy as an Academic Discipline in Twentieth-Century China*, ed. John Makeham (Hong Kong: Chinese University Press, 2012), p. 60.

55. An introductory text on Dignāga's logic, compiled by Śaṃkarasvāmin (sixth century) and translated by Xuanzang.

and the prerequisite for genuine philosophical discourse, there was widespread consensus that Chinese philosophy lacked systemization; that in method and organization it was simple and naïve; and that it fell far short of the standards set by Western philosophy. In 1898, the Buddhist scholar Matsumoto Bunzaburō 松本文三郎 (1869–1944) bluntly asserted: "There is no study of logic in Chinese philosophy. Not only do the Chinese lack logic in their speculative thinking, we are not even able to find logical organization in Chinese philosophy."[56]

The criticisms of Japanese scholars subsequently influenced the high regard that Chinese intellectuals such as Wang Guowei 王國維 (1877–1927), Liang Qichao 梁啟超 (1873–1929), Liu Shipei 劉師培 (1884–1919), and Zhang Taiyan came to place on logic as a precondition for the development of philosophy, as indeed did the views of a minority of Japanese scholars who found evidence of the development of logic in early China. These developments in turn stimulated Chinese scholars to make significant efforts to identify logic in the writings of the pre-Qin masters, in particular in *Xunzi* and in *Mozi*.

As I have argued elsewhere,[57] Zhang, in particular, applied the benchmark of Yogācāra Buddhist philosophy to assess the philosophical merit of individual pre-Qin texts such as *Xunzi*, *Mozi*, and *Zhuangzi*, seeking to show how early Chinese texts "bear witness" to insights into realities that transcend individual cultures but are most fully and systematically articulated in Yogācāra systems of learning; and that classical Chinese philosopher-sages had attained an awareness of the highest truths, evidence of which can be found in their writings. He was also a pioneer in attempting to show how Indian logic and epistemology could be used to recover the meaning of ancient Chinese philosophical texts—such as his analysis of a key passage in *Mozi* in his 1909 essay, "Yuan ming 原名" (Tracing the Origins of [Philosophers of] Names)[58]—in ways that Western logic could not.

This was no mere exercise in philosophical archaeology—there was a pronounced political dimension articulated in Zhang's philosophical reconstructions. In his celebrated commentary, *Qi wu lun shi* 齊物論釋 (An Interpretation of "Discourse on Making All Things Equal"; 1910), he develops an extended, complex Yogācāra reading of the "Qi wu lun" (Discourse on Making All Things Equal) chapter in *Zhuangzi*. Zhang interpreted the title of the chapter to mean

56. Matsumoto Bunzaburō, "Shina tetsugaku ni tsuite 支那哲學について" (On Chinese Philosophy), 5.4 (1898): 172.

57. John Makeham, "Zhang Taiyan, Yogācāra Buddhism, and Chinese Philosophy," in Makeham, *Learning to Emulate the Wise*, pp. 115–123.

58. Zhang Taiyan, "Yuan ming" (1909), in his *Guogu lunheng* 國故論衡 (Discourses on the National Heritage Weighed in the Balance) (Shanghai: Shanghai guji chubanshe, 2004), p. 121.

"Discourse on Making All Things Equal" (rather than "Equalizing Discourse on Things" or "Equalizing Human Discourse"). By "equal," Zhang is not advocating some form of relativism or treating all things as having equal value; rather, he is proposing that when characteristics/attributes (*xiang* 相) and names/concepts (*ming* 名) are abandoned all that remains is the undifferentiated state of Suchness (*zhenru* 真如; *tathatā*). It is from this perspective that he understood the title to mean "making all things equal": "To equalize that which is not equal is but the base attachment of lowly persons; [to realize] the equality of inequality is the profound discourse of the most exalted wisdom. Unless one abandons names and attributes, how can this wisdom become realized?"[59]

As Viren Murthy explains in his chapter, in *Qi wu lun shi* Zhang connects the term "equalization; making equal" (*qi* 齊) with "equality" (*pingdeng* 平等) in order to shift a "subjective stance from seeing things as equal, that is without high and low, to an epistemological position in which one is detached from the words and concepts that make our world possible." Murthy shows how "equalization" was targeted at the concept of universal principle (*gongli* 公理) promoted by prominent late-Qing intellectuals such as Yan Fu and Liang Qichao, who used it to legitimize the state; and by the reformer and scholar Kang Youwei 康有為 (1858–1927), who advanced the idea that the universal principle is realized when the world evolves to a perfectly egalitarian society without national divisions. In the case of the universal principle's being linked to state-and society-building, Zhang objected that this would entail sacrifice to a collective; and in the case of achieving an egalitarian society, he argued it would eradicate difference through some type of evolutionary paradigm. According to Murthy, Yogācāra Buddhism and Zhuangzi allowed Zhang to deal with such problems at the level of epistemology. He did this by "criticizing value judgments in order to delve into the epistemological conditions for the possibility of these judgments, so that one could eventually go beyond them. . . . Zhang claims that the universal principle and evolution, which echo Hegel's philosophy, are both variations on a basic structure of confusion, alienation, and domination; in short, such phenomena emerge from consciousness. His goal is to overcome the confusion at the source of such phenomena."[60] As John Jorgensen describes in his chapter,

59. Zhang Taiyan, "Qi wu lun shi ding ben 齊物論釋定本" (Definitive Edition of An Interpretation of "Discourse on Making All Things Equal") in *Zhang Taiyan quanji* 章太炎全集 (Complete Works of Zhang Taiyan), vol. 6 (Shanghai: Shanghai renmin chubanshe, 1986), p. 61.

60. Capitalism can be seen to exhibit early globalizing impetuses retrospectively identified in modernity. In this same chapter, Viren Murthy further proposes an epistemological shift related to capitalism to explain the equation of Yogācāra with science and modern philosophy. Murthy's chapter also features a discussion of another key aspect of modernity: subjectivity.

> Zhang linked Yogācāra with revolution, justifying violence to eliminate caste or class discrimination, and with anarchism, which likewise sees rulers as nothing more than bandits. . . . Yogācāra could provide a philosophy of equality through its "wisdom of equality" (*pingdengxing zhi* or *samatā-jñāna*) that was achieved by converting the self-centered seventh *vijñāna* (consciousness) into a wisdom that removed attachment to ego and so achieved true equality.

For Zhang, this self-transformation provided the basis not only for soteriology but also for political revolution. Indeed, already in his 1906 essay, "Jianli zongjiao lun 建立宗教論" (On Founding a Religion), Zhang had appealed to the Buddhist concept of equality (*pingdeng* 平等) as a justification for overthrowing the Manchu government of China.

2.3 Yogācāra and Confucianism

The modern Buddhist scholars Ouyang Jingwu and Lü Cheng were part of a movement that sought to "return to the roots" of original Indian Buddhism, with special attention being paid to Yogācāra teachings, and so they were opposed to the doctrine of "inherent enlightenment" that had developed in China. Therefore, New Confucianism—as represented principally by Xiong Shili and Mou Zongsan 牟宗三 (1909–1995)—can be seen as the product of a sustained and conscious attempt to distance itself from the views of Yogācāra's modern defenders, despite New Confucianism's having grown in philosophical sophistication through sustained critical engagement with Yogācāra's conceptual frameworks and problematics. It is this ideological double-identity—ignored in conventional accounts—that this volume brings into sharp relief for the first time.

2.3.1 Yogācāra and Liang Shuming

Retrospectively identified as one of the founding fathers of New Confucianism, Liang Shuming's relationship with Yogācāra is complex, not least because it changed over time. Thierry Meynard shows that in his earlier writings, Liang followed Dignāga (and post-Dignāga Yogācāra epistemology) in maintaining that there are only two valid sources of knowledge: inferential cognition/logical inference (*biliang* 比量) and direct cognition/perception (*xianliang* 現量). When he wrote *Dongxi wenhua ji qi zhexue*, however, Liang expressed dissatisfaction with Yogācāra epistemology. As Meynard explains, even though Yogācāra epistemology was able to explain the functioning of the mind, ultimately it saw

> the mind as an obstacle to overcome: by deconstructing the mental operations we may succeed in neutralizing them, not letting them operate, and be liberated from them. Although Liang continued to uphold this overall project of liberation, he wanted to accommodate, within the mental operations, some room for judgments that could bear positive meanings.

These positive meanings included moral judgments, and Liang introduced a new mode of knowledge: moral intuition (*zhijue* 直覺). Meynard continues:

> From this revised epistemology, Liang could link the three modes of knowledge to three moral options presented to individuals and to cultures. The three cultures of the West, China, and India, respectively, represented three moral options: the development of the self and of the nation (in the West and based on *biliang*), the deepening of harmonious relations with others (in Confucianism and based on *zhijue*) and the radical quest for transcendence (in Buddhism and based on *xianliang*).

Believing that Chinese culture was not yet developed to a stage that would enable it to enter a Buddhist cultural period (unlike India), Liang promoted Confucian moral values as a necessary preparatory stage on the path to Buddhism—a sort of convenient/skillful means (*upāya*).[61] (As with Taixu's account of Yogācāra as the mature expression of the purest philosophy and purest science [see Scott Pacey's chapter on Taixu], strong traces of social Darwinism are also evident in Liang's philosophy of culture.)

This did not, however, mean that Liang abandoned his personal engagement with Yogācāra philosophy. As Meynard relates,

> With Yogācāra, Liang completely embraces the discourse of reason of his age, and yet, with Yogācāra, he is able also to subvert reason from within, showing that the discourse of reason is altogether limited. In this sense, Yogācāra has truly enabled a modern discourse of reason, in which reason is able to criticize itself.

The subversion of reason referred to here is Liang's creative transformation of Yogācāra, whereby he developed a special mode of valid cognition he first referred to as intuition (*zhijue*) and later as moral reason (*lixing* 理性). According to Meynard,

61. John Hanafin, "The Last Buddhist," in *New Confucianism: A Critical Examination*, ed. John Makeham (New York: Palgrave, 2003), pp. 187–218.

> This change of terminology, from intuition to moral reason, manifests Liang's shift from epistemological problems to ethical issues, applying Buddhist epistemology to Confucian ethics. . . . Here again, Liang's focus on morality is truly modern. Because he considered morality important as such, he made it an independent mode of reason, distinct from the transcendental reason of religion and distinct from the instrumental reason of worldly affairs.

2.3.2 *Yogācāra and Xiong Shili*

Together with Liang Shuming, Xiong Shili is conventionally regarded as a founding figure of the modern New Confucian school of philosophy and is widely recognized as one of the most original and creative Chinese philosophers of the twentieth century. And as Jason Clower points out, for Liang and Xiong alike, "Yogācāra was both a resource and a foil, a philosophy from which they borrowed ideas and also against which they defined themselves by contrast."

Over the past three decades, there has been a widespread tendency to portray Xiong narrowly as a Confucian philosopher, who also happened to criticize Buddhist philosophy, but whose philosophical achievements lie in his accounts of the relationship between ontological reality (*ti* 體) and manifest functioning (*yong* 用); the principle of Change (易); and the two concepts "contraction" (*xi* 翕) and "expansion" (*pi* 闢) derived from *Yijing* 易經 (Book of Change). Scholars who share this view claim to find evidence of Xiong's Confucian persuasion in his sustained critiques of Yogācāra thought.

Xiong's main critique of Yogācāra philosophy (as principally represented by *Cheng weishi lun* or the so-called Weishi tradition associated with Dharmapāla and Xuanzang) is that it had hypostasized the doctrine of conditioned arising (*yuanqi* 緣起)[62] into a doctrine of seeds, effectively creating a structural realism. It also entails various forms of ontological dualisms and even ontological pluralism, with seeds posited as the ontological basis of all things. One of Xiong's key objections to Yogācāra is that by positing seeds as causes of cognitive objects, the mind becomes bifurcated into a subject part and an object part, and its inherent oneness thus becomes artificially and mistakenly severed. To address this, Xiong appealed to the inseparability of ontological reality (*ti*) and its phenomenal functioning (*yong*), criticizing the Yogācāra position as advocating the manifestation of reality through function (*ji yong xian ti* 即用顯體) where function is understood actually to exist, which for Xiong amounted to bifurcating ontological reality and the phenomenal world. Xiong's position can be seen to be implicitly consistent with the views expressed in the *Awakening of Mahāyāna*

---

62. That is, everything arises from causes and conditions and has no inherent self-nature.

Faith, in that the latter does not present the phenomenal world as ontologically distinct from the all-pervading, undifferentiated absolute reality (*dharmakāya;* the "truth body" associated with buddhahood). Rather, it posits ignorance as hindering us from realizing that the phenomenal world lacks independent existence, self-nature, reality (see Makeham, chapter 8).

It is a curious fact that, too often, Xiong's uncompromising critiques of Yogācāra philosophy seem to have provided a convenient pretext for scholars to ignore other key elements of Buddhist thought in his constructive philosophy. As I argue in my chapter, Xiong's critiques are grounded in the Mahāyāna doctrine of conditioned arising and the doctrine that the phenomenal world is not ontologically distinct from undifferentiated absolute reality (*dharmakāya*), a thesis he develops using the noumenal reality/manifest functioning (*ti-yong*) conceptual polarity. Critically appropriating important terms, concepts, and problems from Yogācāra philosophy (strongly mediated through its Chinese interpretation), Xiong Shili went on to develop these elements into his own ontology: a metaphysics in which the primary ontological realm of "Fundamental Reality" (*benti* 本體) transforms and permeates all things such that Fundamental Reality and phenomena are seen to cohere as a single whole.

Xiong is not the only "New Confucian" to suffer this fate. Recently, in a similar vein, Thierry Meynard has argued that

> in the last twenty years, many studies in Mainland China have analyzed Liang's thought from the standpoint of Confucianism, considering him to be the forerunner of today's Contemporary New Confucianism. . . . [The] labeling of Liang as a Confucian or as a New Confucian prevents a comprehensive understanding of his thought and life that would articulate, in a meaningful way, both Confucianism and Buddhism.[63]

Similarly, as Jason Clower and Wing-cheuk Chan have each recently shown, Mou Zongsan's philosophical system cannot be grasped without also understanding the role of Sinitic Buddhist philosophy within his thought.[64]

---

63. Thierry Meynard, *The Religious Philosophy of Liang Shuming: The Hidden Buddhist* (Brill: Leiden, 2010), pp. xi, xii, xiii.

64. Jason Clower, *The Unlikely Buddhologist: Tiantai Buddhism in Mou Zongsan's New Confucianism* (Brill: Leiden, 2010). Wing-cheuk Chan, "On Mou Zongsan's Hermeneutic Application of Buddhism," *Journal of Chinese Philosophy* 38, no. 2 (June 2011): 174–175. For a discussion of the role of Huayan Buddhism in New Confucian Tang Junyi's thought, see Yau-Nang William Ng, "Tang Chün-i's Idea of Transcendence: with Special Reference to his Life, Existence, and the Horizon of Mind-Heart" (PhD diss., University of Toronto, 1996), pp. 194–202.

Xiong also drew substantial (albeit largely unacknowledged) philosophical inspiration from the *Dasheng qixin lun* and the doctrine of nature origination (*xingqi* 性起), as resources to affirm the phenomenal world, the life-world, and not simply to repudiate it. The *Dasheng qixin lun* also has a more contemporary connection with Xiong Shili. After Xiong published the literary redaction of his *Xin weishi lun* 新唯識論 (New Treatise on the Uniqueness of Consciousness) in 1932, two of his more trenchant critics were Ouyang Jingwu—the founder of the China Inner Learning Institute (Zhina Neixue Yuan 支那內學院)—and the Buddhist scholar Lü Cheng. (Xiong had, in fact, first studied Yogācāra together with Lü Cheng under the tutelage of Ouyang.) As already noted above, seeking to "return to the roots" of Indian Buddhism, Ouyang, Lü, and their colleagues promoted "true" Buddhism over "false" Buddhism, criticizing such core Sinitic Buddhist doctrines as "inherent enlightenment" and "returning to the source."

In 1943, the year Ouyang died, an extended series of polemical exchanges took place between Lü Cheng and Xiong Shili on the question of whether human nature is innately quiescent (*xing ji* 性寂) or innately enlightened (*xing jue* 性覺), the details of which are set out in Lin Chen-kuo's chapter in this volume. At the most general level, this question touched upon the very legitimacy of the philosophical foundations of East Asian Buddhism. More specifically, this point of contention bears directly on a range of issues, including the interpretation of the doctrine that "the nature of the mind is inherently pure" (*xinxing ben jing* 心性本淨) and methods of cultivation. In regard to these two matters, Xiong upheld the view that the inherently awakened (and hence dynamic) nature of the mind can be personally realized through the "inner realization" of our own minds and is associated in particular with the teachings of the *Dasheng qixin lun*. (Later, Mou Zongsan accorded "inherent enlightenment" a central role in his philosophical system by attributing to it the capacity for "intellectual intuition.") Lü Cheng, on the other hand, upheld the Yogācāra view (represented by Xuanzang and Kuiji) that although "the nature of the mind is inherently pure," realization of that purity requires a transformation of consciousness.[65]

In more recent times, the standoff between the views upheld by Xiong, on the one hand, and by Ouyang and Lü, on the other, has resurfaced in the context of controversies surrounding so-called Critical Buddhism. Critical Buddhism is an intellectual movement initiated in the mid-1980s Japan by the Buddhist scholars Hakamaya Noriaki 袴谷憲昭 and Matsumoto Shirō 松本史郎.[66] Critical

65. The notion of innate clarity of mind has a long pedigree in India and is attested in Pāli texts.

66. Jamie Hubbard and Paul L. Swanson, (eds.), *Pruning the Bodhi Tree: The Storm over Critical Buddhism* (Honolulu: University of Hawai'i Press, 1997).

Buddhism takes aim at any doctrine that posits an eternal, metaphysical substratum, underlying ground, or "locus" on which everything else is ontologically grounded, as it is contrary to the Buddha's teachings on impermanence. In particular, Critical Buddhism regards Sinicized forms of Buddhism as false Buddhism and as incompatible with the project of modernity because they are not founded on rational critique. As Lin Chen-kuo points out, "Like Habermas, the Critical Buddhists choose to carry out the project of modernity because they see that both the West and Buddhism share the same idea of enlightenment, namely as a quest for liberation from ignorance and domination."[67]

In setting out his understanding of the concept of "transformation" —a metaphor for ontological reality—in the *New Treatise*, for example, Xiong describes one of its characteristics in the following terms: "Wondrously transforming, unfathomable; the myriad things are unequal. Equal by virtue of being unequal, and so each is as what it is as." This is exactly the sort of notion of equality (which, as we have seen, was shared by Zhang Taiyan) that Critical Buddhists object to because, as Paul Swanson explains, "if one assumes a single basis and underlying reality for all things—that good and evil, strong and weak, rich and poor, right and wrong, are fundamentally 'the same'—there is no need or incentive to correct any injustice or right any wrong or challenge the status quo."[68] In Xiong's case, "a single basis and underlying reality for all things" is just what "transformation" is, in the same way that the pure buddha-nature intrinsic in all things (the matrix of buddhas concept)—the all-pervading, undifferentiated absolute reality (*dharmakāya*)—functions in *Dasheng qixin lun*.

Critical Buddhists regard *Dasheng qixin lun* to be emblematic of so-called topical Buddhism or topical philosophy—"notions of a universal, ineffable, preconceptual ground or 'topos' from which all things are produced and to which they return at death"[69]—because of such constructions as "truth body" (*dharmakāya*) and "matrix of buddhas" that seemingly contradict the doctrine of no-self. These constructions, in turn, are foundational for such doctrines as inherent enlightenment (*benjue* 本覺), a doctrine that appears to be inconsistent with the doctrine of dependent arising.

As it happens, in modern China it has been topical philosophy (in the form of New Confucian metaphysics, especially Mou Zongsan's New Confucianism) that has emerged victorious over scholastic forms of Critical Buddhism (Ouyang

---

67. Lin Chen-kuo, "Metaphysics, Suffering, and Liberation: The Debate between Two Buddhisms," in Hubbard and Swanson, *Pruning the Bodhi Tree*, p. 305.

68. Paul L. Swanson, "Why They Say Zen is Not Buddhism," in *Pruning the Bodhi Tree*, p. 7.

69. Jacqueline Stone, "Some Reflections on Critical Buddhism," *Japanese Journal of Religious Studies* 26, no. 1(1999): 161.

Jingwu and Lü Cheng).[70] Clearly, topical philosophy continues to have strong support in Chinese intellectual communities. Xiong's *New Treatise* provides us with the first substantive attempt to respond to the modernist challenge of providing Chinese philosophy with "system";[71] and he did this in the form of an ontology. Thus understood, Xiong's *New Treatise* is also a response to modernity and, in its own Buddhist way, very much part of "a quest for liberation from ignorance and domination,"[72] even if the path he followed was metaphysics and not scientific rationality.

2.3.3 Yogācāra and Mou Zongsan

Clower presents a stark account of the fate of Yogācāra among New Confucian philosophers after World War II:

> Mou Zongsan and Tang Junyi 唐君毅 (1909–1978) removed Yogācāra from the New Confucian agenda. They no longer found Yogācāra important. And indeed since then, Yogācāra has lingered far from the center of the Chinese intellectual scene. . . . Mou demoted Yogācāra to the second poorest kind of Mahāyāna philosophy, and Tang ranked it dead last.

Mou instead directed most of his creative energy to Immanuel Kant while Tang turned his to Hegel. Not only did Mou and Tang consider Yogācāra a spent force, they passed that belief on to later Confucians such that today in mainstream New Confucian philosophy it is barely even of historical interest. Clower further argues:

> The New Confucian project is based partly on national *ressentiment* directed toward the West, and to the considerable extent that New Confucians are also cultural nationalists, they wish to match Chinese cultural

70. In his chapter on Ouyang, Eyal Aviv insists that Ouyang should not be too readily associated with the Japanese Critical Buddhist movement because where the Critical Buddhists completely reject the *tathāgatagarbha* doctrine, later in his life Ouyang revealed a more sympathetic attitude to it.

71. Ever since the early 1900s, Chinese intellectuals have sought to respond to claims initially made by Japanese scholars that Chinese philosophy lacks systemization; that in method and organization it is simple and naïve; and that it falls far short of the standards set by Western philosophy. I discuss this in detail in "The Role of Masters Studies in the Early Formation of Chinese Philosophy as an Academic Discipline," in Makeham, *Learning to Emulate the Wise*, pp. 73–101.

72. Lin Chen-kuo, "Metaphysics, Suffering, and Liberation," p. 305.

> products against those specifically from the West, rather than from one of its former colonies. . . . Yogācāra is Indian and hence it is irrelevant to their nationalist purposes.

Mou did not, however, entirely wash his hands of Yogācāra. On the one hand, writes Clower,

> Mou used Yogācāra as a stand-in for two of his rivals, Ouyang Jingwu and Lü Cheng of the Inner Learning Institute, whom he loathed as traitors to Chinese culture, and for Immanuel Kant, whom he regarded with "admiration and competitiveness," as both the epitome of the Western philosophical tradition and also a Western analog to Yogācāra's emphasis on the empirical mind at the expense of the transcendental mind.

On the other hand, Mou continued to draw inspiration from Yogācāra. Despite his ultimate and unambiguous privileging of Confucian philosophy over Buddhist philosophy, as Clower has elsewhere pertinently remarked,

> What makes Mou noticeable . . . is his catholicity of interest and breadth of reading in Buddhist writings and willingness to proclaim the philosophical superiority of Buddhists to Confucians and the necessity for Confucians to submit themselves to Buddhist tutelage, and then to openly re-organize and re-evaluate the whole Confucian philosophical tradition in an explicitly Buddhist way.[73]

The principal doxographical methodology to be applied to this reevaluation is Mou's appropriation of the Sinitic Buddhist method of "doctrinal classification" (*panjiao* 判教) and his application of it to the whole of Chinese philosophy. Within this scheme, Mou identified the Tiantai paradigm of the Perfect Teaching (*yuanjiao* 圓教) as providing a theoretical model to demonstrate how Kant's ideal of due correspondence between virtue and happiness can be achieved without appeal to God. He further insisted that certain Song and Ming Neo-Confucians had articulated the most perfect "Perfect Teaching."

Mou identifies Yogācāra thought as a dialectical stage in a process of philosophical development, which for him culminates in the Tiantai Perfect Teaching. Yogācāra's dialectical value lies in having produced an "ontology with attachment," a key component of his dual ontology: a "phenomenal ontology" (*xianxiangjie*

---

73. Jason Clower, *The Unlikely Buddhologist*, p. 3; see also Serina N. Chan, *The Thought of Mou Zongsan* (Leiden and Boston: Brill, 2011).

de cunyoulun 現象界的存有論) or "attached ontology" (*zhi de cunyoulun* 執的存有論) and a "noumenal ontology" (*bentijie de cunyoulun* 本體界的存有論) or "non-attached ontology" (*wuzhi de cunyoulun* 無執的存有論). Whereas the former enables humans to realize their noumenal nature, the latter enables humans to function in the phenomenal world. Xiong Shili's analysis of phenomenon in the context of his "ontological reality"/"manifest functioning" ontology (see Makeham, chapter 8) can also be regarded as having found further development in Mou's "phenomenal ontology."

This volume shows that just like Xiong Shili's and Liang Shuming's philosophical systems, so too Mou Zongsan's philosophical system cannot be grasped without also understanding the role of Sinitic Buddhist philosophy within that system, a salient feature of which is the creative tension between Yogācāra and "matrix of buddhas" (*tathāgatagarbha*) approaches to salvation. This reinforces the importance of recognizing the vital role Buddhist philosophy has played in the construction of New Confucian philosophy and the ongoing presence it still retains in the historical constitution of New Confucian philosophy. Despite this, the Indian roots of Chinese philosophy—traditional or modern—continue largely to be ignored. It is hoped this volume will show why this is no longer a tenable position.

PART I

The Indian and Japanese Roots of Yogācāra

I

Yogācāra: Indian Buddhist Origins

John Powers

INDIAN BUDDHIST PHILOSOPHY is a rich mosaic of commentary on canonical sources, scholastic codification of doctrines, and innovative, original perspectives developed in debate with rival Buddhists as well as non-Buddhists. The situation in India was fluid, and some thinkers adopted differing perspectives in different works. Attribution is often difficult, because famous figures were sometimes associated with texts of dubious authenticity. Others, like Vasubandhu (*ca.* fourth century), shifted their philosophical alliances, and some later thinkers, like Kamalaśīla (fl. 713–763) and Śāntarakṣita (725–788), developed syncretic philosophies that mingled elements of different traditions. The major Indian philosophers have been retrospectively assigned to "schools" by Buddhist doxographers, and these divisions have been accepted with some qualifications as useful heuristic devices by many contemporary scholars, but it is doubtful that most Indian thinkers would have acknowledged (or even considered) these attributions.[1]

Indian Buddhist doxography

Broadly speaking, there were two main divisions among Indian Buddhists: (1) Mahāyāna (Great Vehicle), which accepted as canonical discourses (*sūtra*) attributed to the Buddha that began to appear in India centuries after his death;

1. The doxographical system developed in Tibet divides Buddhist philosophy into four schools. There are two "Hīnayāna" schools (Vaibhāṣika and Sautrāntika) and two "Māhayāna" schools (Cittamātra—or Yogācāra—and Madhyamaka). Tibetans further posited various subschools and syncretic schools that incorporated tenets from more than one tradition. The seeds of this doxography were present in India, as attested by the characterization of Buddhist tenets in Vinītadeva's (*ca.* seventh century) *Ālambana-parīkṣā-ṭīkā (dMigs pa brtag pa'i 'grel bshad)*, Tibetan Tripiṭaka, sDe dge edition (Tibetan Buddhist Resource Center, n.d.), vol. 3452, W22704, p. 370), in which he attributes distinctive views to Buddhists belonging to Vaibhāṣika (Bye brag tu smra ba), Yogācāra (rNal 'byor spyod pa), and Madhyamaka (dBu ma pa). (W: is "work"; it is the designation used by the Tibetan Buddhist Resource Center.)

and (2) the Mainstream schools (traditionally eighteen in number, but Indian Buddhist literature records more), which are pejoratively labeled "Hīnayāna" (Inferior Vehicle) by their Mahāyāna rivals. Both groupings contain a diverse range of perspectives, philosophical ideas, and polemics. Some philosophers apparently identified themselves with a particular tradition, whereas others were probably less exclusive in their affiliations.

Even within these broad divisions, there was considerable overlap. Chinese pilgrims who traveled to India expressed surprise when they found Mahāyānists and Hīnayānists living in the same monasteries and participating in communal events.[2] Nāgārjuna (*ca.* second century), regarded by tradition as the founder of the Madhyamaka ("Middle Way") school and one of the most influential Mahāyāna philosophers, apparently spent part of his working life in a Hīnayāna monastery and composed works that argue Mahāyāna ideas using Hīnayāna sources.[3]

Within the Mahāyāna camp, later Buddhist doxographers designated two main schools: (1) Madhyamaka, which accepted the Perfection of Wisdom discourses (*Prajñā-pāramitā-sūtra*) as canonical and emphasized dialectical debate and the use of *reductio ad absurdum* (*prasaṅga*) arguments to refute rivals' theses without advancing countertheses of their own; and (2) Yogācāra (Yogic Practice School), which valorized meditation and focused on issues of psychology and epistemology. The most influential figures of the first group are Nāgārjuna and Candrakīrti (*ca.* seventh century), and the brothers Asaṅga and Vasubandhu (*ca.* fourth century) are regarded by tradition as the founding figures of Yogācāra. Their work was explicated and their philosophical visions developed by a number of outstanding commentators, including Sthiramati (*ca.* sixth century) and Vinītadeva, and the epistemological turn of this group was expanded by Dignāga (*ca.* fifth-sixth centuries), Dharmakīrti (*ca.* seventh century), and their successors, including Devendrabuddhi (*ca.* seventh century), Śākyabuddhi (*ca.* eighth century), and Ratnakīrti (*ca.* eleventh century). In China, Dharmapāla (*ca.* sixth century; Hufa 護法) and Paramārtha (499–569; Zhendi 眞諦) are influential figures for early Yogācāra, along with Xuanzang 玄奘 (602–664), who studied in India and returned with a number of core works (see the Introduction to this volume.)

In the Tibetan Buddhist canon, Asaṅga, Vasubandhu, and their commentators are designated as belonging to the "Mind Only" (Sems tsam) School,

---

2. For example, the Chinese pilgrim Xuanzang traveled in areas included in modern-day Bangladesh, where he observed that in some monasteries monks of these rival traditions lived in harmony. He described the situation in Vāśibhā Monastery, a Hīnayāna institution where 700 Mahāyāna monks resided. See Thomas Watters, *On Yuan Chwang's Travels in India*, vol. 2 (London: Hesperides Press, 1996), pp. 164–165.

3. Joseph Walser, *Nāgārjuna in Context: Mahāyāna Buddhism and Early Indian Culture* (New York: Columbia University Press, 2005).

implying that they propounded an idealist philosophy,[4] and the works of Dignāga, Dharmakīrti, and their successors are collected in a section labeled "Epistemology" (*Tshad ma*) and assigned to the Mainstream Sautrāntika school (mDo sde),[5] despite their close historical and doctrinal association with Yogācāra and their overt Mahāyāna commitments. Contemporary scholars increasingly treat both groups as a single—though highly diverse—philosophical tradition.

This is also true in East Asia. The twentieth-century Chinese reformer Lü Cheng 呂澂 (1896–1989), for example, adopted Yogācāra as the system best suited to his agenda of creating a modern Buddhism, and he chose Dignāga's *Ālambana-parīkṣā* (Investigation of the Percept[6]) as a paradigmatic text for commentary.[7] Other modern Chinese Buddhists also took an expansive view of Yogācāra, and many regarded the indigenous pseudepigraphic work *Dasheng qixin lun* 大乘起信論 (Awakening of Mahāyāna Faith) as a normative Buddhist text that accorded with Yogācāra thought.[8]

Yogācāra philosophy

The most important scriptural source for Indian Yogācāra is the *Saṃdhinirmocana-sūtra* (Discourse Explaining the Thought), attributed to the Buddha but probably composed around the third century C.E. This is a mature Mahāyāna work that negatively characterizes the emphasis on logic and debate now associated with Madhyamaka. It valorizes meditative practice and focuses on epistemological issues.[9] Written as a *sūtra* (discourse delivered by the Buddha), it is a polemical

---

4. This tradition is also known by other names, including Consciousness School (Vijñānavāda), and Nothing but Consciousness (Vijñapti-mātratā).

5. They are generally placed in the somewhat odd category of "Sautrāntikas Who Follow Reasoning" (Rigs pa rjes 'byung gi mdo sde pa). The other branch of this school, according to Tibetan doxographers, is "Sautrāntikas Who Follow Scripture" (Lung gi rjes 'byung gi mdo sde pa). Sautrāntika literally means "follower of the sūtras," so it is strange to have one group designated as followers of scripture and another as followers of reasoning.

6. The meaning of this title is variously interpreted in the Chinese and Tibetan commentarial traditions, as is reflected in the different renderings adopted in this volume; see glossary.

7. This is discussed in detail by Dan Lusthaus in this volume.

8. For example, see Jason Clower, *The Unlikely Buddhologist: Tiantai Buddhism in Mou Zongsan's New Confucianism* (Leiden: E. J. Brill, 2010), pp. 115–116, which discusses Mou Zongsan's 牟宗三 (1909–1995) attribution of the text to Paramārtha.

9. Despite negative characterizations of people who waste their energies on logic and debate at the expense of meditative practice, the text contains discussions of logic, and this was later a core focus of Yogācāra thinkers, including Vasubandhu, and of the Epistemologists, including Dignāga, Dharmakīrti, and their successors.

text that is the locus classicus for a number of seminal Yogācāra doctrines, including the three wheels of doctrine (*dharma-cakra*); the three natures (*trisvabhāva*); and the base consciousness (*ālayavijñāna*).[10] It also contains an important statement to the effect that objects of perception are "nothing but consciousness" (*vijñapti-mātratā*), but stops short of a blanket denial of the existence of external objects. Rather, the text's position appears to be that all perceptions are mediated and interpreted by the mind; no aspect of the outside world appears directly to awareness. Sense impressions of phenomena relay information to the mind and are then interpreted, and the cognitions of a particular agent reflect the physical realities of his or her species and perceptual faculties, background, language, and life experience. There are no pure experiences outside of meditation, and all cognitions have an interpretive overlay. In this sense, the Yogācāra position is one of epistemological idealism, but the *Saṃdhinirmocana* is agnostic regarding the ontological status of external objects.

The text also denies the ultimate existence of mind, which is a collection of cognitions that arise and pass away from moment to moment. There is no substantial entity underlying these transitory cognitive events, and so mind, like its contents, is empty of inherent existence. In the developed Yogācāra system, a list of fifty-one mental factors (*caitta*) that accompany minds was developed. "Minds" refers to the operations of the six primary consciousnesses, which are aware of their respective referent natures (for example, an eye consciousness is aware of a sensation as a visual phenomenon). Mental factors are related to minds and arise in tandem with each moment of cognition in varying combinations.[11] These are divided into six groupings: (1) five omnipresent mental factors (*sarvatraga*): contact, mental engagement, sensation, discrimination, and volition; (2) five determining mental factors (*viniyata*): aspiration, belief, mindfulness, stabilization, and knowledge; (3) eleven positive mental factors (*kuśala*): faith, conscience, shame, noncraving, nonhatred, nondelusion, enthusiasm, serenity, vigilance, indifference, and nonharming; (4) six primary afflictions (*mūlakleśa*): desire, anger, ignorance, pride, doubt, and false views; (5) twenty secondary afflictions (*upakleśa*): lethargy, excitement, belligerence, resentment, concealment, jealousy, spite, miserliness, deceit, deception, haughtiness, harmfulness, nonshame, nonembarrassment, nonfaith, laziness, nonconscientiousness, forgetfulness,

10. For a discussion of its philosophy that highlights its polemical tropes, see John Powers, *Hermeneutics and Tradition in the Saṃdhinirmocana-sūtra* (Leiden: E. J. Brill, 1993).

11. This schema only relates to the five sensory consciousnesses and mental consciousness, and not afflicted mentality (*kliṣṭa-manas*) or base consciousness (*ālaya-vijñāna*). Only the first six consciousnesses have intentional objects, and so they also have accompanying mental factors.

nonintrospection, and distraction; and (6) four indeterminate mental factors (*aniyata*): sleep, remorse, investigation, and analysis.

The *Saṃdhinirmocana* comprises ten chapters of uneven length. Each begins with an introduction to a tenth-level (*bhūmi*) bodhisattva, who then poses questions to the Buddha. Many concern ambiguous or contested notions that were the basis of debate between rival factions, and the Buddha declares the intention behind his utterances. In some places, he also provides hermeneutical guidelines for determining what he really meant, and this is the apparent basis for the title "*Discourse Explaining the Thought*."[12] The tensions in the text are based on the presupposition of the canonicity of a large corpus of discourses, all attributed to the Buddha but written over the course of centuries, many long after he had passed away. Some Mainstream traditions like the Sthaviravādins took a conservative approach (as does the modern Theravāda school, which claims descent from them), while Mahāyānists accepted the Perfection of Wisdom discourses and a range of other texts that in some cases only appeared centuries later. Some of this literature was apparently in a state of flux, and dated Chinese versions show considerable interpolation, emendation, and editing.[13] In this situation, it is hardly surprising that groups that accepted as canonical later texts that only began to circulate long after the death of their purported author and that changed over time would have difficulty resolving apparent contradictions within their textual corpus.

The *Saṃdhinirmocana* attempts to provide hermeneutical guidelines, while also denouncing the positions of rivals—particularly those identified as Mādhyamikas in later tradition—along with adherents of Mainstream factions. In addition, it has the Buddha propound new doctrines that became part of the developed Yogācāra tradition.

In the first four chapters, the Buddha discusses the relation between phenomena and the ultimate truth (*paramārtha*). The ultimate truth is declared to be the final nature of phenomena and cannot ontologically be separated from them. He gives the analogies of a conch and its white color and a *vīnā* (Indian lute) and its melodious sound and declares that just as the two factors (a thing and its qualities) may be differentiated by thought but are one entity, so also ultimate truth—which is equated with emptiness (*śūnyatā*), Suchness (*tathatā*), and reality-limit (*bhūta-koṭi*)—is inherent in phenomena and can only be differentiated from them by thought. These chapters contain several anecdotes about

---

12. For a discussion of how the title is interpreted in India, China, and Tibet, see Powers, *Hermeneutics and Tradition in the Saṃdhinirmocana-sūtra*, pp. 28–40.

13. Lewis Lancaster provides an interesting discussion of how dated Chinese sūtras exhibit significant differences in "The Oldest Mahāyāna Sūtra: Its Significance for the Study of Buddhist Development," *The Eastern Buddhist* 8, no. 1 (1975): 30–41.

misguided people who attempt to discover the truth through argumentation and logic, and the Buddha (or his interlocutors) declares that this is doomed to fail. Only those who engage in introspective meditation can grasp the ultimate truth, and they are true followers of the Buddha. This is an obvious broadside aimed at Mādhyamikas, but they are not named, and it may be that at the time the text was composed neither Madhyamaka nor Yogācāra had settled into "schools." Rather, there were probably rival factions within the broad spectrum of Mahāyāna that were influenced by the scholastic *abhidharma* traditions but rejected some of their conclusions and that viewed the Perfection of Wisdom discourses and other Mahāyāna works as normative.[14] Some emphasized dialectics and logic, while others valorized meditative practice as the core element of the Buddhist path and as the best way to attain advanced levels of realization.

Psychology and meditation theory

In chapter five of the *Saṃdhinirmocana*, the Buddha describes the base consciousness, which is a subtle substratum underlying all aspects of mind. It is composed of "seeds" (*bīja*), which are the latent residua of a person's actions. Every volitional action deposits a predisposition within one's mental continuum, which represents a propensity to perpetuate that sort of action and also guarantees the karmic repercussions of one's moral choices. As the metaphor of seeds implies, they lie dormant until the proper conditions for their manifestation are present and then give rise to mental states that resemble the original impulses that led to their creation. A popular metaphor associated with this process is often referred to as "perfuming" in contemporary discussions of Yogācāra. This translates the Sanskrit term *vāsanā*, which designates predispositions or habituations. In this context, perfuming refers to the idea that these tendencies condition the seeds that constitute the mental stream, similar to the way in which perfume pervades a cloth. The general disposition of any given mental continuum is a reflection and function of these accumulated tendencies.

The base consciousness is said to be like a river, with each moment of the continuum characterized by the seeds it contains. When the appropriate conditions are present, a seed will produce its effects, and the individual reaps the karmic consequences of previous actions. Moreover, the fruition of the seeds produces a tendency to continue in the same general cognitive direction. Beings tend to repeat patterns of behavior during their lives; the base consciousness model accounts for this.

---

14. *Abhidharma* is a general term referring to scholastic presentations of Buddhist doctrine. The early *abhidharma* (lit. "higher doctrine") was based on discourses attributed to the Buddha and attempted to synthesize their doctrinal statements into consistent dogmatic systems.

It is, however, also possible to make changes and reorient one's mind, and the base consciousness doctrine indicates how this might occur. If one engages in lying, for example, this sort of behavior will become easier and more spontaneous, and the habit becomes progressively more difficult to break. If, however, a person confronts this negative tendency and decides to become more truthful, the latencies created by past falsehoods can gradually be lessened, and one can make a conscious move toward truth telling. As this is cultivated, truthful propensities become stronger and one's virtue becomes ingrained. A core tenet underlying this is the notion of the luminous nature of mind (*prabhāsvara-citta*), which has a long pedigree in Indian Buddhism. It is found in the Pāli canon and is also propounded in a number of Mahāyāna discourses.[15] The mind is of the nature of clear light, and defilements are adventitious (*āgantuka-kleśa*). They are developed by immoral behavior, but once eliminated they have no basis for reoccurrence. When the mind has been purified of all stains, one undergoes a fundamental existential experience, "transformation of the basis" (*āśraya-parāvṛtti*), following which one's mind becomes "stainless consciousness" (*amala-vijñāna*), and all the seeds in the mental continuum reflect one's perfected virtue. This is the decisive moment in the progression toward buddhahood.

In some Yogācāra texts, however, some beings are declared to be incorrigible. Either as a result of a defect in their psychophysical continuums or due to negative actions that have eliminated their "roots of virtue" (*kuśala-mūla*), they are utterly disinclined toward religious pursuits and cannot cultivate the qualities that contribute to progress on the Buddhist path. These beings are referred to as "*icchantika*," a term of uncertain derivation. It appears to imply that they have extreme desires that prevent them from looking beyond selfish short-term interests.[16] This notion created considerable controversy in East Asia and was one of the main debating points with respect to Yogācāra texts. The Tiantai and Huayan schools—which asserted that all beings have the potential for

15. For example, in the "Paṇhita-vagga" of the *Aṅguttara-nikāya*, edited by Richard Morris (London: Pāli Text Society, 1961), I.10.6, p. 10 vol. 2, the Buddha declares: "Monks, the mind is luminous, but it is afflicted by adventitious defilements that come from outside of it." See also Ian Charles Harris, *The Continuity of Madhyamaka and Yogācāra in Indian Mahāyāna Buddhism* (Leiden: E. J. Brill, 1991) and Konstantin Regamey, *Three Chapters from the Samādhirājasūtra* (Warszawa, Poland: Towarzystwo naukowe Warszawskie, 1938), p. 25.

16. Karashima Seishi, "Who Were the Icchantikas?" *Annual Report of the International Research Institute for Advanced Buddhology* (March 2007): 67–80, associates *icchantika* with the Pāli term *icchati*, where it has the sense of "imagines," "maintains," or "claims." This is cited by Charles Muller under the entry *chanti* 闡提 in the Digital Dictionary of Buddhism (http://www.buddhism-dict.net). He adds that it might refer to dogmatic monks who were opposed to ideas they regarded as deviations from true doctrine. The Sanskrit *icchā* means "desirous" or "willful."

buddhahood—rejected it.[17] Some East Asian Buddhists interpreted the concept as indicating that some beings had degenerated to a point of depravity that would lead to suffering in future lives, but held that they might be redeemed in the future provided that they met with virtuous teachers and changed their ways. A minority view asserted that there are some beings who cannot be saved, and in the end nothing can be done for them.

Buddha nature

These concepts are related to discussions of the doctrine of "matrix of buddhas," according to which all beings have the potential for buddhahood because their most fundamental minds share the luminous nature described above. When all cognitive defilements have been eliminated and the good qualities of a buddha (generosity, ethics, patience, compassion, wisdom, etc.) have been perfected, one becomes a buddha. According to Mahāyāna, buddhas were once ordinary beings who made the right decisions in past lives, renounced negative behaviors, cultivated virtue, successfully attained advanced meditative states, and performed prodigious acts of compassion. Any being can make the same choices, and all have the cognitive potential for the highest level of awareness.

These notions are conceptually related to East Asian developments that propound the existence of a fundamental, universal "buddha nature" (*buddhatva*) that is inherent in all beings (and, in some formulations, all phenomena) and that makes buddhahood possible.[18] In early Indian sources, buddha nature and

---

17. This idea did not generate significant controversy in India, but became a major source of debate in East Asia. When the short version of the *Mahāparinirvāṇa-sūtra* (Discourse of the Great Final Release), translated by Faxian (法顯; 337–*ca.* 422), appeared in China in 418, it indicated that an *icchantika* can never attain nirvana. The later translation by Dharmakṣema (385–433) of a longer text of the same title in 421 stated that they are able to do so. The latter position subsequently was generally viewed as definitive in East Asia, and the "controversy" was regarded as settled by most commentators. There are precedents in India for the idea that some beings are fundamentally incorrigible, particularly in Asaṅga's work *Treatise on the Stages of Concentration Practice*, which declared that some beings have a "determinate lineage" (*gotrastha*) and that others "lack determinate lineage" (*agotrastha*). The latter lack the capacity to attain nirvana. The Chinese debates occurred in the context of questions about the doctrine of "matrix of buddhas" (*tathāgatagarbha*; *rulai zang* 如來藏). Asaṅga's *Treatise* does not address this notion and so his comments on lineage (*gotra*) are not really pertinent to the concerns that were debated in East Asia. See Ming-Wood Liu, "The Problem of the Icchantika in the Mahayana *Mahāparinirvāṇa-sūtra*," *Journal of the International Association of Buddhist Studies* 7, no. 1(1984): 57–82.

18. This notion became fundamental to East Asian Buddhism, but is not derived from Indian Yogācāra texts. It appears to be an East Asian development with uncertain Indic precedents.

the matrix of buddhas were equated with emptiness: all phenomena lack any inherent nature or essence and are collections of parts that come into being and change due to causes and conditions external to themselves. Thus, the psychophysical continua of all beings are in a constant state of flux, and the future trajectory of a particular individual depends on morally significant choices made at the present time and the influences of past karma. Because they are empty of inherent existence, beings have the capacity to change, and a sustained program of positive actions, outstanding acts of virtue, and successful meditative cultivation can serve to move a practitioner toward the final apotheosis of buddhahood.

In East Asia, however, buddha nature is generally interpreted as a numinous reality that pervades all things. Buddhahood is not something brought about by a program of training in which qualities one did not previously possess are sequentially developed, but rather is the result of the actualization of an innate essence, one that is coextensive with the universe itself. It pervades all reality and is the most fundamental nature of all beings, and when they follow the Buddhist path the qualities they develop are resonances of this potential. When adventitious obscurations are eliminated, it can shine forth in its primordial purity, but nothing new has been added. Negative traits have been completely removed, and the buddha nature—which has been exactly what it is since beginningless time—is fully manifest. At this point one becomes what one has always potentially been: a buddha.

The base consciousness

The doctrine of base consciousness entails an implicit rejection of solipsism because each mental continuum is specific to an individual.[19] As the term implies, the base consciousness is foundational according to Yogācāra epistemology. The system posits eight consciousnesses; the other seven emerge from the base consciousness and are affected by its constitution at the moment of their arising. The other consciousnesses are: the five sense consciousnesses; mental consciousness (*manovijñāna*); and afflicted mentality (*kliṣṭa-manas*). The last of these generates negative mental states and is the primary factor involved in perpetuating the misguided apprehension of subject-object duality.

The base consciousness serves a number of important functions in Yogācāra psychology. It provides a mechanism for rebirth because it is the primary factor

19. An example of a detailed refutation of solipsism is Dharmakīrti's *Saṃtānāntara-siddhi* (Establishment of the Existence of Others' Continuums), To. #4219; Kitagawa Hidenori 北川秀則, "A Refutation of Solipsism: Annotated translation of Saṃtānāntarasiddhi," *Indo koten ronrigaku no kenkyū: Jinna (Dignāga) no taikei* インド古典論理学の研究: 陳那 (Dignāga) の体系 (Studies in Ancient Indian Logic: Dignāga's System) (Kyoto: Suzuki gakujutsu zaidan, 1965): pp. 407–429 (originally published 1955).

that moves from one life to the next and retains the seeds of volitional actions, carrying them toward the future. It also explains continuity of personality and memory within a particular life and the resumption of attitudes and past impressions after periods of meditative trance in which the continuum of consciousness is suspended.

According to Yogācāra soteriology, in the state of buddhahood the eight ordinary consciousnesses cease and one develops nonconceptual wisdom (*jñāna*). Buddhas perceive the world through direct perception unmediated by conceptual categories, and the five sense consciousnesses evolve into wisdom consciousnesses that spontaneously accomplish the aims of oneself and others (*kṛtyānuṣṭhāna-jñāna*). Mental consciousness becomes a faculty that directly penetrates the reality of things (*pratyavekṣaṇa-jñāna*), which perceives the general and specific characteristics of phenomena as they really are, without the mediation of conceptuality. The base consciousness no longer functions because all the seeds of ordinary cognition have been replaced by the purified qualities of buddhahood. At this point, the mind operates on the level of the "great mirror-like wisdom" (*mahādarśa-jñāna*), which views phenomena from a completely neutral perspective, with no conceptual overlay, free from any attachment or bias. One no longer apprehends the false dichotomy between subject and object. One's perceptions are unmediated by any cognitive overlay, one views reality just as it is (*yathā-bhūta*), and one acts spontaneously to aid others in overcoming their mental afflictions and developing awareness.

Yogācāra and Buddhist Hermeneutics

The *Saṃdhinirmocana-sūtra* (Discourse Explaining the Thought) proposed a schema for interpreting contested doctrines attributed to the Buddha; this schema appropriated the traditional notion that he taught differently for different individuals and audiences depending on their respective capacities and predilections. This explains how the Buddha could apparently contradict himself and still be an omniscient sage who was free from error: the contradictions in discourses attributed to him are only apparent. Like a skillful physician, the Buddha dispensed the appropriate spiritual medicine to each patient, and he was not concerned with formulating a doctrinally consistent system.

There was, however, an underlying thought behind all his utterances, which he declares fall into two categories: (1) interpretable (*neyārtha*) statements; and (2) definitive (*nītārtha*) statements. The first includes expedient teachings delivered to trainees of inferior capacity, such as Hīnayāna doctrines, while the latter were intended for more advanced audiences, that is, Mahāyānists.

The Buddha proposes a schema for sorting out his contested teachings: they can be divided into three "wheels of doctrine." The first wheel comprised

Hīnayāna doctrines such as the four noble truths (*ārya-satya*) and dependent arising (*pratītya-samutpāda*). These were expounded for Hīnayāna audiences and served the pragmatic purpose of setting them on the Buddhist path and refuting non-Buddhist systems, but were only intended as an introductory instruction for beings of limited understanding.

In the first wheel, the Buddha focused on phenomena (*dharma*) and their functions, while "hiding" emptiness. The second wheel is associated with the Perfection of Wisdom discourses; in these sermons the Buddha undermined the implicit message of his earlier dispensation and declared that all phenomena—including his own previous statements—are empty of inherent existence and are dependent on causes and conditions. This problematized the excessive adherence of his Hīnayāna audiences to his words and their literal meaning and served to move them toward a more sophisticated level of understanding. It also helped them to overcome the tendency to develop a substantialist view.

For some, however, this blanket deconstruction led to an extreme view of nihilism, and to correct this he subsequently taught a third wheel, in which he went into greater detail regarding what was and was not being negated.

The Tibetan scholar Tsong kha pa (1357–1419) refers to the third turning as the "wheel of good differentiations" (*legs par phye ba'i chos 'khor*) because in this cycle of teachings the Buddha elucidated exactly how his followers should understand his pronouncements regarding emptiness.[20] His clarification included a new model for interpreting cognitions, according to which they can be divided among three natures (*trisvabhāva*): (1) attachment to imaginatively constructed discrimination (*parikalpita*); (2) the other-dependent (*paratantra*); and (3) the thoroughly real (*parinispanna*).[21] The first is the mistaken conceptual

20. Tsong kha pa bLo bzang grags pa, *Drang nges rnam 'byed legs bshad snying po* (Sarnath: Pleasure of Elegant Sayings Printing Press, 1973), pp. 29.4–29.18.

21. This is often misleadingly translated as "perfected" or consummated." These terms imply that it is changed, altered, and perfected by the actions of meditators, but Buddhist literature makes it clear that this is ultimate reality. It is equated with emptiness (*śūnyatā*), ultimate truth (*paramārtha*), and reality limit (*bhūtakoṭi*), all of which refer to the ultimate reality, something that never changes. This is reflected in the standard Tibetan translation, *yongs su grub pa*, "thoroughly established," "thoroughly real." It is important as a meditative object: meditators focus attention on it, and this serves to eliminate afflictions and produce wisdom consciousnesses. It is referred to in some meditation texts as an "object of observation for purification" (*viśuddhālambana*). If it were the end result of a process of perfection through religious training, it could not serve this function. Monier Monier-Williams notes that it can mean "developed" but he also indicates that it means "perfect," "real," "reality," "existing," etc. See *A Sanskrit-English Dictionary* (Delhi: Motilal Banarsidass, 1979), p. 596, col. 3.

overlay ordinary beings attribute to the phenomena of experience: imaginatively constructed discrimination. It includes such notions as an enduring self or essence and subject-object duality. These ideas are false and can be weakened by grasping the conceptual ramifications of Buddhist doctrines, empirical observation, and reasoning. They can only be comprehensively extirpated by meditative training.

The other-dependent is connected with the concept of dependent arising, according to which all phenomena come into being in dependence upon causes and conditions, change from moment to moment, and eventually disintegrate and pass away. This is conventionally valid but is not the ultimate truth. The ultimate truth is that all phenomena are empty of inherent existence, but those who correctly understand dependent arising have a more accurate apprehension of the nature of reality than those who operate on the level of imaginatively constructed discrimination.

The thoroughly real character is equated with emptiness and suchness and is declared to be the way things really exist. The Buddha states that when the conceptual overlay of imaginatively constructed discrimination is no longer superimposed on the other-dependent one grasps the thoroughly real. This is what advanced meditators realize, but its ramifications are only fully apprehended by buddhas. Those who take the ultimate truth as their object of meditation progressively eliminate cognitive afflictions and purify their mental continua, and for this reason it is characterized as an "object of observation for purification" (*viśuddhālambana*). It is described as an antidote (*pratipakṣa*) to mistaken ideas and afflicted cognitions.

Imaginatively constructed discrimination is related with "entitylessness in terms of character" in the sense that it is not produced and does not cease, and so it is devoid of the characteristics mistakenly attributed to imaginatively constructed phenomena by deluded beings. Imaginatively constructed phenomena do not exist by way of their own character (contrary to false impressions), and so they cannot be said to be produced.

Other-dependent phenomena are associated with "entitylessness in terms of production" in the sense that they depend on causes and conditions for their arising, changes, and cessation. Thus they too lack inherent existence because they require factors external to themselves. The thoroughly real is also linked to entitylessness and is characterized as "entitylessness in terms of the ultimate" because, like all phenomena, it lacks inherent existence. It is merely the absence of the false conceptual overlay of the imaginatively constructed superimposed on the other-dependent, and so it has no separate or real essence.

The three wheels schema was used by Yogācāra exegetes to valorize their own doctrines and relegate those of their rivals to inferior status. Tsong kha pa is probably correct in his opinion that it is not meant to include all Buddhist teachings. He points out that many statements attributed to the Buddha—including norms relating to monastic conduct such as the proper dimensions and wearing of robes—cannot coherently be assigned to any of the three wheels of doctrine.[22] They are associated with Hīnayāna discourses, but Tsong kha pa believes that monks should understand them literally whatever their doctrinal affiliation. The three wheels schema includes core Buddhist tenets such as the four noble truths and dependent arising, the discourses on emptiness in the second wheel, and the differentiations of the third wheel, which he contends mainly comprise the teachings of the *Saṃdhinirmocana-sūtra* and related works.

Yogācāra in India

Yogācāra philosophers cited the *Saṃdhinirmocana* and considered it their main scriptural source, but they were also strongly influenced by the Perfection of Wisdom texts and by Mainstream philosophical systems. Many of the ideas presented in the *Saṃdhinirmocana* are not well developed, which is also true of the Perfection of Wisdom literature. Indian Buddhist philosophers who wrote philosophical treatises and commentaries on canonical texts developed new exegetical models to explain apparent contradictions in the Buddha's teachings and also borrowed from other traditions, creating new systems of thought.

Vasubandhu and Asaṅga began their monastic careers in Hīnayāna *abhidharma* lineages and attempted to synthesize a range of Buddhist teachings into their philosophies. According to traditional accounts, early in his monastic career Asaṅga belonged to the Hīnayāna Mahīśasika lineage and later converted to Mahāyāna. Following a period of intense study of the Buddhist canon, he meditated in a cave hoping to receive a vision of the future buddha, Maitreya. After three years of unsuccessful practice, he decided to abandon his

22. Tsong kha pa, *Drang nges rnam 'byed legs bshad snying po*, pp. 27.14–28.16. In his *Legs bshad snying po'i dka' 'grel bstan pa'i sgron me* (Lamp for the Teaching: Commentary on the Difficult Points in the Essence of Good Explanations), Dpal 'byor lhun grub comments: "All sūtras spoken in the first, middle, or final time are not differentiated individually into the interpretable and the definitive by this sūtra. For example, the statement [by the Buddha at the time of first turning the wheel of doctrine] to the five ascetics, 'A roundish lower robe should be worn,' and also sūtras of the middle cycle that explicitly teach impermanence and so forth, and those sūtras of concordant suitability spoken during the definitive cycle are not differentiated individually as the interpretable and the definitive." Dpal 'byor lhun grub, *Legs bshad snying po'i dka' 'grel bstan pa'i sgron me* (Buxaduar: Sera Monastery, 1968), p. 34.

quest, but as he left the cave he noticed that running water had worn rivulets in the rock near the entrance, which he took as a sign that he should persevere. Three more years passed, and again he decided to give up, but he saw birds flying by the entrance, and their wings brushing across the stone left marks in it: another sign.

After a total of nine years of solitary practice, Asaṅga believed that he was no closer to his goal than when he began, but as he walked away from the cave along a road he saw a man selling needles he claimed had been sharpened by rubbing cotton wool on steel. This encounter convinced Asaṅga to return to his meditation, but after a further three years he had still failed to encounter Maitreya. Leaving the cave, he walked along the road toward a town and along the way he saw a dog lying on its side and suffering horribly from running sores. These had become infected with maggots, and Asaṅga felt profound compassion for the suffering animal. He decided to help relieve its suffering, but as a Buddhist he could not kill the maggots. He decided to cut off pieces of his own flesh to feed them, but as he raised a knife to do this, the dog transformed into the radiant form of Maitreya.

This was what he had been training for during his twelve years in the cave, but Asaṅga was somewhat annoyed that it had taken the bodhisattva so long to respond to his efforts. Maitreya informed Asaṅga that he had been in the cave standing in front of him all along but that Asaṅga's cognitive obscurations had prevented him from realizing this. Maitreya showed him the stains on his robes left by Asaṅga's discarded food and told him that the impulse of pure compassion he had generated when seeing the dog had cleared away his defilements and allowed him to experience the bodhisattva face to face.

Following this encounter, Maitreya became Asaṅga's teacher and he transported him to Tuṣita Heaven, where he revealed five texts that became core sources for the Yogācāra tradition.[23] Some modern scholars attribute them to a human figure they term "Maitreyanātha," but there is no extant Indic source that treats the author of these texts as a human sage, nor is there any mention in extant Indic literature of a person who corresponds to this description. Buddhist

23. According to Tibetan tradition, the "Five Treatises of Maitreya" are: (1) *Abhisamayālaṃkāra* (Tib. *mNgon par rtogs pa'i rgyan*: Ornament for Clear Realizations); (2) *Mahāyāna-sūtrālaṃkāra* (Tib. *Theg pa chen po'i mdo sde'i rgyan;* Ornament for the Great Vehicle Discourses); (3) *Mahāyānottara-tantra* (Tib. *Theg pa chen po'i rgyud bla ma'i bstan*: Sublime Continuum of the Great Vehicle); (4) *Dharma-dharmatā-vibhāga* (Tib. *Chos dang chos nyid rnam par 'byed pa*; Differentiation of Phenomena and Pure Being); and (5) *Madhyānta-vibhāga* (Tib. *dBus dang mtha' rnam par 'byed pa*; Differentiation of the Middle Way from Extremes). In East Asian traditions, the *Abhisamayālaṃkāra* is not attributed to Maitreya, and he is credited with the *Yogācārabhūmi-śāstra*.

tradition in India, Tibet, and East Asia accepts the notion that these texts were revealed by the future buddha.

In Indian and Tibetan sources, Asaṅga is credited with the massive *Yogācārabhūmi-śāstra* (Treatise on the Stages of Concentration Practice), which develops a comprehensive vision of Buddhist thought. It assigns Hīnayāna teachings to lower rungs of a hierarchy and describes the path to buddhahood from a Yogācāra perspective. Asaṅga's *Abhidharma-samuccaya* (Compendium of Higher Doctrine) was conceived as a Mahāyāna *abhidharma* that incorporates aspects of non-Mahāyāna schools within an overarching Yogācāra framework. His *Mahāyāna-saṃgraha* (Compendium of the Great Vehicle) reads like a Yogācāra textbook that outlines the main features of the system in relation to various aspects of Buddhist thought.

Whereas Asaṅga's contributions were mainly of a scholastic nature, Vasubandhu was an original and innovative thinker. According to traditional biographies, both brothers had Hīnayāna affiliations in their early lives, but Asaṅga converted to Mahāyāna and subsequently convinced Vasubandhu to follow his lead. Vasubandhu's biography reports that after his change of heart he was so distraught by his former calumnies against Mahāyāna that he decided to cut out his tongue, but his brother persuaded him to use it to defend the tradition.

In his early life Vasubandhu studied with masters of the Vaibhāṣika tradition, and their system was the basis for his scholastic masterpiece *Abhidharma-kośa* (Storehouse of Higher Doctrine). After writing the root text, he sent a copy to his former teachers, who declared it to be an excellent distillation of their system and asked him to compose an autocommentary to further elucidate its details. During the process of composition, however, he had debated its philosophical ramifications with Buddhist and non-Buddhist rivals and had become dissatisfied with Vaibhāṣika. Vasubandhu was an independent thinker, and when he wrote his commentary he sometimes adopted the perspective of the rival Sautrāntika School and refuted the positions of his former teachers. When they saw the finished product, they denounced him as an apostate and severed relations with him, but Vasubandhu was apparently more concerned with philosophical consistency than with rigidly adhering to any sectarian position.

After converting to Mahāyāna he composed a number of influential works that are stylistically elegant and philosophically astute. These include *Madhyānta-vibhāga* (Differentiation of the Middle and Extremes), which focuses on epistemology and meditation theory and practice. He considers the Madhyamaka perspective on emptiness and concludes that it fails adequately to account for the ontological status of subject and object and their interrelation. In the opening chapter he summarizes his position in a verse:

Imagination of the unreal exists
But duality does not exist in it.
But emptiness exists in it, and that [imagination] in it [emptiness].
Thus it is said that everything is neither empty nor nonempty,
Because of [imagination's] existence, [the object's] nonexistence, and [emptiness'] existence;
And this is the middle way.[24]

As Gadjin Nagao notes[25] this passage is similar to a famous verse in Nāgārjuna's *Mūlamadhyamaka-kārikā* (Fundamental Verses on the Middle Way), in which he asserts:

Whatever is dependently arisen
Is explained to be emptiness.
That, being a conventional designation,
Is the middle way.[26]

In Vasubandhu's formulation, imagination of the unreal (*abhūta-parikalpa*) creates mental images, and ordinary beings apprehend them as real and veridical. They subsequently act on their beliefs, and these actions have real effects; thus imagination of the unreal cannot simply be regarded as utterly nonexistent, like a square circle or the son of a barren woman. Phenomena are empty but emptiness depends on an empty thing that is its referent. Emptiness is ultimately real and is associated with the ultimate truth and suchness, but it is also empty, and so in this sense it shares the same ontological status as phenomena.

Vasubandhu's biographies report that he was a master of dialectical debate who defeated many rivals, both Buddhist and non-Buddhist. In classical India, public debates between rival philosophers and factions were often sponsored by rulers and were a form of popular entertainment. The stakes in these contests were high: winners enjoyed royal patronage and gained new followers while the

24. Gadjin Nagao (ed.) *Madhyāntavibhāga-bhāṣya* (Tokyo: Suzuki Research Foundation, 1964), pp. 17–18. The bracketed material is inserted on the basis of Vasubandhu's explanation in the commentary. In the commentary, he explains the middle way as follows: "Everything is neither totally empty nor totally nonempty," and he cites the Perfection of Wisdom as a scriptural source.

25. Gadjin Nagao, *Mādhyamika and Yogācāra: A Study of Mahāyāna Philosophies* (Albany: State University of New York Press, 1991), pp. 189–199.

26. J.W. de Jong (ed.), *Mūlamadhyamakakārikā* (Madras: Adyar Library, 1977), p. 35.

defeated parties were sometimes ordered to convert to their rivals' systems or exiled. Many of these competitions were waged between adherents of different religions who held different scriptures as normative, and so they could not cite their own texts in their arguments. A neutral format for debate was needed and Vasubandhu proposed one in his *Vāda-vidhi* (Procedures for Disputation), which outlined a framework within which rival factions could argue on the basis of shared epistemological premises, along with standard rules of grammar and logic.

Yogācāra and idealism

Vasubandhu's *Viṃśikā* (alt. *Viṃśatikā*; Twenty Verses on Nothing but Consciousness) and *Triṃśikā* (Thirty Verses) explore the ramifications of the doctrine of nothing but consciousness. How this should be interpreted is one of the most hotly debated topics among contemporary Yogācāra scholars. Dan Lusthaus contends that Yogācāra philosophers reject metaphysical idealism. He compares the Yogācāra agnosticism regarding the ontological status of external objects to Husserl's *epoché* and claims that like Husserl, the Yogācāras "bracketed" this question.[27] Lusthaus provides a wealth of Indic and East Asian source material to bolster his arguments, but there is no Yogācāra text of which I am aware that uses terminology similar to the notion of *epoché* in Husserl's phenomenology, nor does any Indian member of the Yogācāra tradition use language that suggests he posited a bracketing of the ontological status of external objects.

Other Western scholars assert that Yogācāra espouses an idealist view that denies the existence of external objects.[28] This is also the position of Tibetan exegetes who follow Tsong kha pa, who assert that in the Yogācāra system the base consciousness holds and maintains the seeds of volitional actions and that their fruition is a resultant object of observation that arises in the same moment as the cognition that perceives it. Because there is no temporal gap, the two must be one entity, produced entirely from one or more seeds.

---

27. Dan Lusthaus, *Buddhist Phenomenology: A Philosophical Investigation of Yogācāra Buddhism and the Ch'eng Wei-shih lun* (London: RoutledgeCurzon, 2002). Lusthaus presents his case for rejecting the notion that Yogācāra espouses metaphysical idealism in his article, "What Is and Isn't Yogācāra," http://www.acmuller.net/yogacara/articles/intro-uni.htm. This also provides an erudite overview of Yogācāra in India and East Asia.

28. See, for example, Ashok Kumar Chatterjee, *The Yogācāra Idealism* (Delhi: Motilal Banarsidass, 1987), and Jay L. Garfield, *Empty Words: Buddhist Philosophy and Cross-Cultural Interpretation* (New York: Oxford University Press, 2002).

In the *Triṃśikā*, Vasubandhu explains how the doctrine of nothing but consciousness should be understood:

> *When no object is apprehended*
> *By consciousness,*
> *Then, established in appearance-only,*
> *With no object there is no grasping subject.*[29]

According to Vinītadeva, this means that

> when one completely eliminates [the false notion of] an object, then consciousness does not appear as an object external to the mind. Such a mind is established in nothing but mind.[30]

Sthiramati, commenting on the same passage, asserts:

> When consciousness does not perceive things as external to mind, does not see them, does not apprehend them, and does not posit them, then it perfectly apprehends the pure meaning. Then one is no longer like a blind person and, having eradicated the grasping of consciousness, one is established in the nature of mind itself. . . . Thus, one does perceive neither the constructed object nor the constructor of the object, and one attains equanimous transcendental wisdom. One eradicates the last traces of subject and object, and the mind is established in its own nature.[31]

The locus classicus of the doctrine of nothing but consciousness is a passage in the eighth chapter of the *Saṃdhinirmocana*, in which the bodhisattva Maitreya asks the Buddha whether or not objects of observation viewed in meditation are the same as the mind or different. The Buddha informs him that they are not different. Alex Wayman contends that this passage should be understood as referring only to experiences in introspective meditation and denies that it constitutes a denial of the ontological status of external objects.[32] His comments,

---

29. Ashok Kumar Chatterjee (ed.), *Vasubandhu's Vijñapti-mātratā-siddhi with Sthiramati's Commentary* (Varanasi: Kishor Vidya Niketan, 1980), p. 129.

30. Vinītadeva, *Triṃśikā-ṭīkā* (*Sum cu pa'i 'grel bshad*), To. #4070, sDe dge edition vol. *hi* (New York: Tibetan Buddhist Resource Center, n.d.), W23703–1454, p. 119.

31. Sthiramati, *Triṃśikā-bhāṣya* (*Sum cu pa'i bshad pa*), To. #4064, sDe dge edition vol. *shi* (New York: Tibetan Buddhist Resource Center, n.d.), W23703–1454, p. 119.

32. Alex Wayman, "Yogācāra and the Buddhist Logicians," *Journal of the International Association of Buddhist Studies* 2, no. 1 (1979): 67.

however, ignore a following passage in which Maitreya extends his question to objects perceived in ordinary experience. Maitreya asks: "Are the appearances of the forms of sentient beings and so forth, which abide in the nature of images of mind, 'not different' from the mind?" The Buddha replies: "Maitreya, they are 'not different.' However, because childish beings with distorted understanding do not recognize these images as cognition-only, just as they are in reality, they misconstrue them."[33]

Lambert Schmithausen comments that this may be "the oldest, or at least the oldest extant, Yogācāra text that clearly expresses universal idealism,"[34] a view that echoes the consensus of Buddhist commentators in India and Tibet. In his commentary on this chapter, Jñānagarbha (eighth century) states that the Buddha's response indicates that "those objects that are images are also not different from this mind."[35] He expands on this idea: "An object of observation is an appearance of mind in the aspect of an object and, moreover, it is not different from cognition because it is observed simultaneously."

The passage from the *Saṃdhinirmocana* is also quoted by Asaṅga in the *Mahāyāna-saṃgraha* in support of his contention that the doctrine of nothing but consciousness is proven by both scripture and reasoning. He asserts:

> The reasoning is also indicated by this scripture. When the mind is in meditative equipoise, in terms of whatever images that are objects of knowledge—blue and so forth—that are seen, mind is seen. Blue and so forth are not objects that are different from mind. By this reasoning, bodhisattvas should infer that all cognitions are nothing but consciousness.[36]

Similarly, the Korean monk and disciple of Xuanzang, Wŏnch'ŭk 圓測 (613–696), asserts that the passage confirms that "those objects that are images

---

33. John Powers, *Wisdom of Buddha: The Saṃdhinirmocana Mahāyāna Sūtra* (Berkeley, CA: Dharma Publishing, 1995), pp. 153–155.

34. Lambert Schmithausen, "On the Problem of Spiritual Practice and Philosophical Theory in Buddhism," in *German Scholars on India*, ed. Cultural Department of the Embassy of the Federal Republic of Germany, New Delhi (Varanasi: Chowkhamba Sanskrit Series Office, 1973), p. 240. See also Lambert Schmithausen, "On the Vijñaptimātra Passage in *Saṃdhinir-mocanasūtra* VIII.7," *Acta Indologica* 6 (1984): 433ff.

35. Jñānagarbha, *Ārya-saṃdhinirmocana-sūtre-ārya-maitreyakevala-parivarta-bhāṣya* (*'Phags pa dgongs pa nges par 'grel pa'i mdo las 'phags pa byams pa'i le'u nyi tshe'i bshad pa*), To. #4033 (Tokyo: Ōtani University Press, 1980), *Sems tsam* vol. 2 (*bi*), p. 321b.

36. Translated from Étienne Lamotte, *La Somme de Grand Véhicule d'Asaṅga (Mahāyānasaṃgraha)* (Louvain-le-Neuve: Institut Orientaliste, 1973), Tome II, p. 27.

are also not different from this mind."[37] He adds that even objects of observation of distracted minds are not separate from consciousness but the minds of childish beings are mistaken, and so these beings think of the things they perceive as external objects. He adds: "When they abandon external objects then they pacify incorrect minds; when they pacify incorrect minds then they realize the middle way."[38]

The seminal passage in *Saṃdhinirmocana* is philosophically connected with another idealist statement in chapter five that states: "An eye consciousness arises depending on an eye and a form in association with consciousness. Functioning together with that eye consciousness, a conceptual mental consciousness arises at the same time, having the same objective referent."[39] Tsong kha pa comments that if there were an ontological distinction between an object and the cognition of it then there must be a temporal sequence.[40] This also appears to be Dignāga's conclusion in his autocommentary to *Ālambana-parīkṣā*:

> Depending on the power of an "eye" and an internal form, a perception that appears as an object that cannot be distinguished from sense objects arises. Moreover, these two are mutually causal, and this has always been so. Sometimes from the maturation of the potency the cognition is produced in the aspect of a referent, and sometimes from its aspect a potency [is produced]. . . . Thus because an internal sense object is endowed with two factors it is posited as a referent.[41]

In an extended discussion of the idealist implications of the *Saṃdhinirmocana*, Wŏnch'ŭk develops his contention that the text denies the existence of external

---

37. Wŏnch'ŭk 圓測, *Ārya-gambhīra-saṃdhinirmocana-sūtra-ṭīkā* (Ch. *Jie shenmi jing shu* 解深密經疏; Tib. *'Phags pa dgongs pa zab mo nges par 'grel pa'i mdo'i rgya cher 'grel pa*) (Delhi: Delhi Karmapae Choedhey, Gyalwae Sungrab Partun Khang, 1985), *mDo 'grel*, vol. *thi* (119), p. 217.5.

38. Ibid., p. 218.1. He adds that the mind's perception of objects is not like the rays of the sun illuminating external objects; rather, like an image in a mirror, something appears to be an external object but is only of the entity of mind: "Objects of direct perception arise from the entity of [the consciousness itself], and so the sūtras say that although it is not the case that any phenomenon apprehends another phenomenon, at the time when a consciousness is produced it appears as similar in character to those [things], due to which it is said that those things are apprehended."

39. John Powers, *Wisdom of Buddha*, p. 71.

40. Tsong kha pa, *Drang nges rnam 'byed legs bshad snying po*, pp. 70.17–71.10.

41. Dignāga, *Ālambana-parīkṣā-vṛtti* (*dMigs pa brtag pa'i 'grel pa*) (New York: Tibetan Buddhist Resource Center, n.d.), *bsTan 'gyur*, W23703–1490, p. 173, v. 8a. (*bsTan 'gyur* means "translations of treatises." It is one of the two divisions of the Tibetan canon; it contains commentaries, philosophical treatises, etc.)

objects. He points out that there are numerous cases of perception in the absence of external referents, such as dreams, in which one perceives things and responds to them as real but later recognizes them to be nonexistent. Similarly, when one fully apprehends the nature of consciousness and enters into meditative states in which one directly perceives nothing but consciousness, one realizes that the phenomena of ordinary experience are like dreams. They appear as real, and deluded beings respond to them as such, but buddhas know that they are merely mental creations.

Wŏnch'ŭk also asserts that different types of beings perceive the same thing in different ways. When humans view a body of water, their innate predispositions cause them to identify it as a substance they can drink or a place to bathe, while fish relate to it as their habitat; gods see ambrosia, and hungry ghosts (*preta*) see pus and blood. There is no one "true" version of any cognition; each species has its own cognitive apparatus and predispositions, and the perceptions of individuals are also colored by their life experiences, gender, age, and the relative soundness of their minds and senses.

The consensus of the Yogācāra tradition is that all objects are objects of consciousness. The mind is unable to contact objects directly and only perceives things by way of the senses. Sense data is then interpreted by the mind in accordance with one's predispositions, and so there is no possibility of an unmediated apprehension of the world for ordinary beings. One important conclusion of this line of reasoning is that the objects of experience are empty of inherent existence. They depend on subjective cognition, but because the referents of cognition are empty, subjects similarly lack any enduring essence. Those who fully grasp this insight overcome the false subject-object duality, and they become indifferent to the things of the world. If everything is merely a mental image like a dream, there is no reason to grasp some illusions and reject others.

Concluding remarks

The Yogācāra philosophers—Asaṅga, Vasubandhu, Sthiramati, Vinītadeva, Dignāga, Dharmakīrti, etc.—shared a number of philosophical commitments and similar epistemological emphases and concerns. Whether their collected works constitute a "school" is open to debate. There is considerable divergence among thinkers assigned to this group by Buddhist doxographers, and it is unlikely that its members regarded themselves as members of a school. Asaṅga and Vasubandhu accepted the *Saṃdhinirmocana-sūtra* and the Perfection of Wisdom texts as authentic statements by the Buddha and developed philosophies that explored the ramifications of these works, but they also incorporated elements of *abhidharma* and other aspects of Buddhist thought in their philosophies. Dignāga, Dharmakīrti, and their successors mainly relied on reasoning that was based on Buddhist principles, but was less dependent on reference to scripture to make points and develop conclusions. Their audience included non-Buddhists who rejected the authority of Buddhist scriptures, and so the Epistemologists relied on independent reasoning, shared epistemological assumptions, and rules of logic and grammar in developing their views.

Although most contemporary scholars agree that the similarities within this group of thinkers warrants a general acceptance of them as constituting a coherent (if in some cases loosely affiliated) tradition, some of the doxological categories developed by traditional Buddhists are problematic. For example, according to the dGe lugs pa system of commentary on Yogācāra,[42] Asaṅga was the "opener of the chariot way" (*shing rta*) of Mind-Only, which implies that he consciously knew himself to be the person prophesied by the Buddha to explicate his statements in the third wheel of doctrine. But Tibetan tradition also holds that he was a third-level bodhisattva, and the dGe lugs pa believe that in order to attain this status one must hold the Madhyamaka view of emptiness. Tibetan doxographers regard the Mind-Only view as inferior to that of Madhyamaka, and so Asaṅga could not have reached the third level by following Mind-Only. Thus the dGe lugs pa posit a tortured explanation according to which Asaṅga was really a closet Mādhyamika but spent most of his working life explaining and developing a system he ultimately rejected because he knew that the Buddha wanted him to do so and had predicted that he would.

Traditional attributions may be flawed or questionable, but there is no doubt that the Yogācāra philosophers developed highly sophisticated philosophies and had a significant impact on Indian thought, both within and outside Buddhist circles. For centuries Yogācāra was the dominant tradition in several of the north Indian monastic universities that were the main institutional bases for the transportation of Buddhism from India through Central Asia to East Asia, and later into Tibet and Mongolia.

In India, following its efflorescence during the fourth–seventh centuries, Yogācāra became incorporated with Madhyamaka in the systems of syncretic philosophers like Śāntarakṣita and Kamalaśīla, but the Epistemologists remained a separate tradition until the demise of Buddhism on the subcontinent in the thirteenth century. After the seventh century, there were few influential or original thinkers, and most Yogācāras were mainly devoted to commentary on existing works, rather than developing original insights.

When Xuanzang visited India in the seventh century, he studied at Nālandā Monastery, the greatest center of Buddhist learning in the world at that time. His studies focused on Yogācāra, and when he returned to China he brought

42. The dGe lugs pa is the Tibetan school founded by Tsong kha pa (1357–1419).

copies of the *Saṃdhinirmocana* and other Yogācāra works, which he subsequently translated. He also wrote commentaries, including *Cheng weishi lun* 成唯識論 (Demonstration of Nothing but Consciousness), which is a composite of commentaries on Vasubandhu's *Triṃśikā*. Traditionally he is purported generally to follow Dharmapāla's interpretation, but also notes divergent opinions. His disciple Kuiji 窺基 (632–682) is regarded by Chinese Buddhist tradition as the first patriarch of the Weishi or Faxiang School (*Faxiang zong* 法相宗), which is based on Xuanzang's work. Despite its demise after the Tang Dynasty (618–907), Yogācāra remained an influential current of thought throughout Chinese Buddhist history. During the Tang Dynasty it was one of the most important Indian Buddhist systems in China and was widely studied. In the late Ming Dynasty (1388–1644) there was a resurgence of interest in Yogācāra during which a number of new independent Yogācāra treatises were composed (see the Introduction to this volume), and again in the twentieth century Yogācāra emerged as the system of choice for prominent intellectuals—both secular and monastic—who wanted to develop a Buddhist response to modernity.

Despite the disappearance of Buddhism from India, Yogācāra thought traveled throughout the Mahāyāna Buddhist world and was highly influential in Tibet and East Asia. Commentary on Yogācāra texts and topics, as well as ongoing dialectical debate, is a feature of contemporary Tibetan monastic education, and there has been a significant resurgence of interest in Yogācāra on the part of modern Non-Sectarian (Ris med) scholars. The dGe lugs pa monastic educational system includes lengthy periods of study of Yogācāra texts and topics, and Tsong kha pa, the founder of the tradition, composed several major works that discussed the philosophical ramifications of Yogācāra. And even though for centuries Yogācāra was no longer a separate school in China, it continued to influence Buddhist philosophers, and its twentieth-century modern revival (and subsequent decline) constitutes a new chapter in a long story that began millennia ago in India.

2

Indra's Network: Zhang Taiyan's Sino-Japanese Personal Networks and the Rise of Yogācāra in Modern China

John Jorgensen

Far away in the heavenly abode of the great god Indra, there is a wonderful net which has been hung by some cunning artificer in such a manner that it stretches out infinitely in all directions. . . . The artificer has hung a single glittering jewel in each "eye" of the net, and since the net itself is infinite in dimension, the jewels are infinite in number. . . . Each of the jewels reflected in this one jewel is also reflecting all the other jewels, so that there is an infinite reflecting process occurring.

FRANCIS H. COOK, Hua-yen Buddhism: The Jewel Net of Indra[1]

ALTHOUGH YOGĀCĀRA FAILED to gain a permanent foundation in Chinese thought, it contributed to debates at critical times in Chinese history when need has been felt for a more systematic, logical, and critical form of thought than the more intuitive and essence/nature-oriented outlook that usually dominated Chinese thought. Thinkers drew upon it as a resource in the late Ming period, and in modern China it has been used by some of China's most influential philosophers and even by a number of revolutionaries. It has been especially employed as an aid in the resistance to incursions of foreign thought and religion such as Christianity. Because many of the resources of Yogācāra had been lost in China, some of these philosophers, Buddhists, and revolutionaries had to look to Japan, where

1. Francis H. Cook, *Hua-yen Buddhism: The Jewel Net of Indra* (New York: Pennsylvania State University Press, 1977), p. 2.

Yogācāra had survived largely intact. Indeed, without the books printed by the Chinese lay Buddhist scholar Yang Wenhui 楊文會 (1837–1911) and provided by the Japanese lay Buddhist scholar Nanjō Bun'yū 南條文雄 (1849–1927), this Faxiang 法相 or Dharma Characteristics (Yogācāra School founded by Xuanzang's 玄奘 [602–664] disciple Kuiji 窺基 [632–682][2]) revival in modern China may have not even got off the launching pad. The influences of Japan on Faxiang and its proponents were varied and complex, as can be seen in the case of the Chinese intellectual and revolutionary Zhang Taiyan 章太炎 (1869–1936). Zhang had personal connections with people influenced in many ways by Yogācāra or Hossō (the Japanese pronunciation of Faxiang) thought, and in turn Zhang was indirectly influenced through reading Japanese works on Yogācāra and allied or rival systems of thought.

In Indra's net, many individuals and ideas reflect each other, so that in the same network there were Chinese and Japanese, autocratic oppressors and anarchist revolutionaries, preservers of Buddhism and developers of Buddhism, Japanese who used Buddhism to justify imperial expansion and keeping the workers in their place, and Chinese who desired to overthrow their oppressors and change the social system, some even allying themselves with Japanese totalitarians to do so. Buddhism was only one jewel in the net, for in the late nineteenth to early twentieth century, China and Japan were confronted with a wide spectrum of ideas and philosophies, ranging from attempted modernizations of Confucianism and Buddhism, to Christianity, science and pseudoscience, socialism and anarchism, democracy and nationalism, or desperate attempts to preserve the old order. The ideological crosscurrents are intricate, just like Yogācāra doctrine itself, which is so multifaceted that it could be interpreted to suit many a position, just like a wish-fulfilling gem.

It is this multifaceted network surrounding Zhang Taiyan that will be examined here. Although a number of Chinese intellectuals in the Qing Dynasty were interested in Yogācāra, often for practical solutions to political and religious problems, by the late Qing, the Chinese who wished to revive Faxiang had to look to Japan for lost Yogācāra texts and to the Japanese experience for models of Buddhist modernization. The reasons for the Japanese preservation of Yogācāra/Hossō were institutional and historical. The Hossō School and its centers survived from around the seventh century to the present due to the support of eminent families and an abundance of resources. Secondly, Hossō entered into a Japanese environment that had yet to develop fixed ideas about Buddhism. A predominant set of Japanese Buddhist values had yet to be formed, and so Hossō

2. As noted in the Introduction, historically, both Weishi 唯識 (nothing but consciousness) and Faxiang 法相 (*dharma-lakṣaṇa*; dharma characteristics) were used as translations for the Yogācāra School in China.

in its early period did not encounter any strong opposition, unlike Xuanzang's Faxiang in Tang-Dynasty China. Therefore, this chapter examines Yogācāra in Japan as background before turning the focus onto Zhang Taiyan and his network.

1. Yogācāra in Tokugawa and Meiji Japan

1.1 Hossō in Japan

In Japan many regarded Yogācāra, or Hossō, as the basis for Buddhist scholarship. This is illustrated by the saying, "*Kusha, kusha* 俱舍 (*Abhidharma-kośa*; Storehouse of Higher Doctrine) three years, Yuishiki 唯識 (*vijñānavāda*; nothing but consciousness) eight years."[3] *Abhidharma-kośa* was a text written by Vasubandhu (fourth century) that outlines the classifications of the components of existence and experience and then critiques them. In Japan it was used as preparation for the study of Yogācāra. The term *yuishiki* 唯識, usually considered a translation of *vijñānavāda*, or "nothing but consciousness," was widely used in East Asia to describe the core doctrine of Yogācāra. Faxiang/Hossō, used as a translation of *dharma-lakṣana*, "characteristics/marks of the dharmas," had a more sectarian nuance, and so most East Asians separated *weishi/yuishiki* from other Faxiang/Hossō tenets.[4]

Faxiang (Hossō) was first introduced into Japan by Dōshō 道昭 (629–700) who went to China in 653 and studied with Xuanzang, who introduced Yogācāra in its full Indian form to China. Later, Hossō as an institution was generally neglected and only revived in the Tokugawa era (1603–1868) due to individuals who did not belong to the Hossō sect. Tokugawa Buddhist scholars clearly regarded the *Abhidharma-kośa* and *vijñānavāda* as an essential basis for the study of many Buddhist doctrines, as is evidenced by the considerable literature produced on these topics. Such research continued well into the Meiji period, and even a cursory tally of works on *vijñānavāda* shows that over a hundred were written in the Tokugawa and about fifty in the Meiji.[5] Thus Hossō scholarship remained vital until the early 1900s.

---

3. Quoted in Hattori Masaaki 服部正明 and Ueyama Shunpei 上山春平 (eds.), *Bukkyō no shisō 4: Ninshiki to Chōetsu Yuishiki* 仏教の思想4：認識と超越、唯識 (Buddhist Thought 4: *Vorstellung*, Transcendence and Nothing but Consciousness) (Tokyo: Kadokawa shoten, 1970), p. 170.

4. This understanding is also that of Taixu 太虛 (1871–1943) in his argument with Ouyang Jingwu 歐陽境無 (1890–1947), for which see the chapter in this volume by Eyal Aviv.

5. Ono Genmyō 小野玄妙 (comp.), *Bussho kaisetsu daijiten* 佛書解説大辞典 (Bibliographical Encyclopedia of Buddhist Texts), 11 vols. (Tokyo: Daitōshuppansha, 1932–1936).

1.2 Non-Buddhist Indian studies in the Tokugawa

Two non-Buddhist Indian philosophical texts that came to Japan were a commentary on Iśvarakṛṣṇa's *Sāṁkhya-kārikā* (Verses on Sāṁkhya) translated by Paramārtha (499–569) between 548 and 569 as *Jinqishi lun* 金七十論 (**Suvarṇasaptati;* On the Golden Seventy Verses) and Maticandra's (sixth or seventh century) *Daśapadārtha śāstra* (Treatise on the Ten Metaphysical Categories) translated in 649 by Xuanzang as *Shiju yi lun* 十句義論. Sāṁkhya was a significant philosophical rival for Yogācāra in India, and elements in it could easily be confused with the *tathāgatagarbha* and *ālayavijñāna*[6] notions in the Yogācāra that Paramārtha[7] supported. This brought those who supported his legacy into conflict with "orthodox" Faxiang. According to Yuki Reimon, this conflict was at the heart of many disputes over *vijñānavāda.*[8] *Daśapadārtha śāstra* (Treatise on the Ten Metaphysical Categories) is a Vaiśeṣika[9] text. It was possibly translated because it dealt with universals in a realist fashion, something Buddhist logicians like Dignāga (*ca.* 480–540) and Dharmakīrti (*ca.* 600–670)[10] (or their precursors), whose ideas were crucial to Xuanzang's Faxiang, were opposed to.[11]

---

6. The terms *tathāgatagarbha* and *ālayavijñāna* are difficult to translate into English. *Tathāgatagarbha* is variously translated as "womb of the thus gone ones" or "matrix of the buddhas," while the Chinese *rulaizang* 如來藏 suggests "store of the thus come." It is sometimes seen as the potential to become a buddha, a potential that is hidden by contaminants, and is awaiting an opportunity to appear. *Ālayavijñāna*, or "base consciousness" is the eighth consciousness that stores seeds that can produce results, good and bad. It is also translated as *zangshi* 藏識, the "store consciousness."

7. Paramārtha was an early translator of Yogācāra texts into Chinese, but because his version of Yogācāra allowed for the existence of the *tathāgatagarbha*, his works became controversial, some even alleging that he introduced an alien doctrine into Yogācāra, although his translations may have reflected a version of Yogācāra found in India.

8. Yūki Reimon 結城令聞, "Kinsei yuishiki kenkyū no aru keifu ni tsuite no hyōron 近世唯識研究の或る系譜についての評論" (An Evaluation of Certain Lineages of Research on *Vijñānavāda* in Modern Times) in *Bukkyōshigakkai 30 nen kinen ronshū: Bukkyō no rekishi to bunka* 仏教史学会 30 年記念論集: 仏教の歴史と文化 (Collected Essays Commemorating the Thirtieth Anniversary of the Buddhist History Association: Buddhist History and Culture), compiled by Bukkyōshi gakkai (Kyoto: Dōhōsha, 1980), pp. 894–907.

9. Vaiśeṣika held that everything is composed of atoms, and also that souls (*ātman*) exist. Both atoms and souls are imperceptible. However, perception and inference show that all existing things are *padārtha* (named and experienced categories). This school was associated with the practice of logic. See Erich Frauwallner, *History of Indian Philosophy*, trans. V. M. Bedekar (Delhi: Motilal Banarsidass, 1973), 2: 3–180.

10. Dignāga pioneered Buddhist logic and wrote on epistemology and perception. Dharmakīrti built on the work of Dignāga, striving for greater certainty in logic. His works did not reach China until modern times.

11. Promed Kumar, "The *Nyāya-vaiśeṣika* and the Buddhist Controversy over the Problem of Universals," *East and West* 47, nos. 1–14 (December 1997): 95–104.

The first East Asian commentaries on the *Jinqishi lun* (On the Seventy Golden Verses) and *Shiju yi lun* (Treatise on the Ten Metaphysical Categories) were written in Tokugawa Japan, and many scholars interested in Hossō wrote about them.

1.3 Reform and reason

Buddhist logic as preserved in Japan attracted the attention of a number of Chinese reformers from the late Qing period onward. A core part of *vijñānavāda* was *hetuvidyā* or a Buddhist logic that clarified the relationships of the proposition or thesis, the reason, and their connection illustrated via an example. This logic was first described in the *Yogācārabhūmi-śāstra* (Discourse on the Stages of Concentration Practice) and was systematized by Dignāga. The Chinese only translated the simplest of the textbooks on the most formal type of Buddhist logic and not those that introduced epistemological issues. In the Tang Dynasty, there were many commentaries on the *Nyāyapraveśa* (*Yinming ru zhengli lun* 因明入正理論; Entryway into Logic), a "brief introductory manual on Dignāga's logic"[12] as translated by Xuanzang in 647, but most were soon lost since the Chinese were not concerned with logic, and the Faxiang School disappeared after being replaced with the more intuitive Chan and Huayan. The only commentary to the *Nyāyapraveśa* to survive was Kuiji's *Yinming ru zhengli lun shu* (Commentary on *Entryway into Logic*), commonly known as the "Great Commentary" (*Dashu* 大疏).

This Chinese understanding of Buddhist logic was introduced into Japan by the monk Genbō 玄昉 (d. 746).[13] By the Meiji era, the most important studies were made by Jōdo shinshū (True Pure Land School, traced back to Shinran 親鸞 [1173–1262]) scholars. In Japan, logic was introduced as an accompaniment to *vijñānavāda*, and the Hossō scholars largely reproduced the major errors found in the Chinese works. According to Watanabe Shoko, although Hossō monks produced many commentaries, they lacked understanding of even some basic items.[14]

The scholar-monk Hōtan 鳳潭 (1654–1738) listed eighty-four works on logic extant in his day, and more were written later,[15] yet Nakamura Hajime

12. Christoph Harbsmeier, *Science and Civilisation in China*, vol. 7, pt. 1: *Language and Logic* (Cambridge: Cambridge University Press, 1998), p. 361.

13. After studying *vijñānavāda*, Genbō went to China, where he stayed for twenty years, returning to Japan in 735, bringing many texts to Kōfukuji. This was the so-called fourth transmission of Faxiang to Japan.

14. Watanabe Shoko 渡辺照宏, *Nihon no Bukkyō* 日本の仏教 (Japanese Buddhism) (Tokyo: Iwanami shinsho, 1958), p. 14.

15. Nakamura Hajime 中村元 (trans.), *Inmyō nisshōri ronsho* 因明入正理論疏 (Commentary on *Entryway into Logic*) in *Kokuyaku issaikyō: WaKan senjutsubu: Ronshobu 23* 国訳一切経: 和漢撰述部、論疏部 (Japanese Translation of the Tripitaka: Sino-Japanese Texts: Commentaries) compiled by Iwano Masao 岩野真雄, rev. ed. (Tokyo: Daitō shuppansha, 1982), p. 14.

(1912–1999) and others have appropriately dismissed much of these works as full of errors, starting from Xuanzang's translations and Kuiji's "Great Commentary" on logic. Xuanzang and Kuiji added scriptural proof to the perceptive and inferential bases of proof that the Indian Buddhist logicians had recognized as valid. Moreover, because Kuiji misunderstood some of the basics of the logical system, this largely blighted the entire tradition because his was the most authoritative and widely read commentary. Part of Nakamura's argument is that Buddhists defended their religion and tried to refute Sāṁkhya principles of the law of contradiction and the law of the excluded middle,[16] but part is an indictment of Kuiji's slavish adherence to the Chinese exegetical methods of *xungu* 訓詁 (glossing) without respect for the Sanskrit meaning.[17] Nakamura even accuses Xuanzang of not understanding the definitions or rules of Indian logic, charging that he failed to discriminate between two forms of inference—*parārtha-anumāna* and *svārtha-anumāna*—the former being used to persuade others and the latter being used for proof to oneself.[18] Harbsmeier, however, has attempted to defend Xuanzang and the later logicians.[19]

The Japanese writers on logic concentrated on the issues of contradiction and thirty-three errors in debate, or rather, of inference. These were made up of nine errors in the propositions, four mistaken causes that cannot be established, six causes that are uncertain as to their truth and falsity, the four contradictions, and ten erroneous illustrations. Nakamura Hajime dismisses much of this scholarship as not so much a development of logic as a specific discipline but rather as an art of dialogue for highly ritualized Dharma assemblies. One had to know this art before being admitted to the debates in these assemblies. Moreover, this Buddhist logic in Japan involved a spirit of protection of the doctrine and gave highest authority to Kuiji's interpretations. Much of the commentarial literature was directed to maintaining that Kuiji was correct, and so was part of Hossō orthodoxy, and less about logic itself. Yet it was considered indispensable in interpreting *vijñānavāda* texts. Another limitation was a tendency from the late Heian period onward for Buddhist logic to be treated as a secret in-house transmission, so this Buddhist logic was restricted to scholarly monks who wanted to interpret the "true import" of the philosophical passages in Buddhist scriptures.

These Japanese commentaries were not theoretical in orientation, tending to be philological and not a development of the logic itself. Nakamura notes that in the several hundred texts produced over a millennium, there is no real

16. Nakamura, "Inmyō," p. 4.

17. Nakamura, "Inmyō," p. 5.

18. Nakamura, "Inmyō," p. 7.

19. Harbsmeier, *Language and Logic*, pp. 368–369.

contribution to the development of reasoning or logic, unlike the work done by Dharmakīrti and others in India. Written in classical Chinese, they did not spread beyond the walls of a few scholastic monasteries and did not influence mathematics or science in Japan. It was only from the Meiji period, with the introduction of Western formal logic, that Japanese intellectuals realized they needed logic for modern development.[20] This began in earnest in 1874 when Nishi Amane 西周 (1829–1897) published *Chichi keimō* 致知啓蒙 (Primer on the Extension of Knowledge), a work based on Mill's *A System of Logic* and the first exposition of formal logic and inductive logic in Japan.[21]

This interest in reason and logic was all part of the response to the early Meiji persecution of Buddhism and the search for modernization. As Buddhism was to be remolded as an Eastern philosophy, the idea arose that logic was an integral part of this new Buddhism. However, even before the end of the Tokugawa period, Echō Chikū 慧澄癡空 (1780–1862),[22] began the process of modernizing Buddhist logic by writing his *Inmyō sanjūsanka honsahō kensanshi* 因明三十三過本作法犬三支 (On the Three Pseudo Members in the Basic Operations of the Thirty-Three Errors of Logic) in Japanese.

Perhaps the greatest contributor was the Jōdo shinshū (True Pure Land) scholar monk Kirara Kōyō 雲英晃耀 (1824–1910), who published an annotated edition of the *Yinming ru zhengli lun shu* (Commentary on *Entryway into Logic*) in 1881. In the postface, Ogurusu Kōchō 小栗栖香頂 (1831–1905) (later to debate Yang Wenhui in China) wrote about how logic had originally been the domain of the Nara schools (six schools of doctrinal studies introduced into Japan in the seventh and eighth centuries), then of Shingon (True Word or Mantra School founded by Kūkai, 774–835), and now of Jōdo shinshū.[23] Kirara, who wrote a series of volumes on logic, ranging from detailed commentaries to introductions and lectures, adopted Echō's practice of writing in Japanese. However, he introduced comparisons with Western logic from 1884, plus an advocacy of the use of this logic in practical situations. Kirara suggested that Buddhist logic should be applied beyond the bounds of Buddhist debates and used in everyday life, believing it could contribute to a modern society.

20. Nakamura, "Inmyō," pp. 20–24.

21. See Barry Steben, "Nishi Amane and the Birth of 'Philosophy' and 'Chinese Philosophy' in Early Meiji Japan," in *Learning to Emulate the Wise: The Genesis of Chinese Philosophy as an Academic Discipline in Twentieth-Century China*, ed. John Makeham (Hong Kong: Chinese University Press, 2011), p. 60.

22. Washio Junkei 鷲尾順敬 (comp.), *Zōtei Nippon Bukke jinmei jisho* 増訂日本佛家人名辞書 (Revised and Expanded Dictionary of A Dictionary of Names of Japanese Buddhists) (Tokyo: Tokyo bijutsu, 1911), p. 807.

23. Nakamura, "Inmyō," p. 14.

The most famous Meiji scholar of logic, Murakami Senshō 村上専精 (1851–1929), another Jōdo shinshū believer, continued Kirara's work.[24] In 1871, Murakami began studying the *Cheng weishi lun shuji* 成唯識論述記 (Commentary on *Demonstration of Nothing but Consciousness*) written by Kuiji. Around 1875, he took the lectures of Kirara on the "Great Commentary" (*Yinming dashu*) of Kuiji, and he later published his notes and studies as the *Inmyōgaku zensho* 因明學全書 (Complete Works on Logic Studies) in 1884, and by 1885 he was lecturing on *vijñānavāda* and logic at the Sōtō Zen sect university in Tokyo, and then in the Tetsugakukan (Philosophy Hall). He also lectured on the Sāṁkhya text, *Sāṁkhyakārikā* (On the Golden Seventy Verses), suggesting that there is a relation between the *Sāṁkhyakārikā* and *vijñānavāda* texts.[25] Murakami later became the third person to be a lecturer in Indian philosophy at Tokyo University, from 1884 to 1890. He followed in the footsteps of Hara Tanzan 原坦山 (1819–1892), and likewise promoted Buddhism as a philosophy and tried to demonstrate its unity.[26] Between them, Murakami and Kirara published about fifteen books on logic during the Meiji period; most were by Kirara.

Besides the Jōdo shinshū monks, other scholars of the *vijñānavāda* and *Dasheng qixin lun* 大乗起信論 (Awakening of Mahāyāna Faith) also wrote on logic, such as Saeki Gyokuga 佐伯旭雅 (1828–1911) and Fujii Genju 藤井玄珠 (1813–1895).[27] There were many others. It is clear that the modernizing Buddhist scholars were most interested in logic and reason.

1.4 Vijñānavāda, Sanskrit, and reason in the Middle Meiji

All of these threads were brought together by modernizing scholars who were heirs to the above pioneering studies. They included Nanjō Bun'yū 南條文雄 (1849–1927), Kasawara Kenju 笠原研壽 (1852–1883), Takakusu Junjirō 高楠順次郎 (1866–1945), and many of those connected with Inoue Enryō's 井上 円了(1858–1919) Tetsugakukan and Tokyo University.

Some of the founders of the New Buddhism 新仏教 (*shin Bukkyō*),[28] such as Hara Tanzan, tried to link Buddhism to Indian philosophy and to the latest

---

24. Nakamura, "Inmyō," pp. 20–27.

25. Tamura Kōyū 田村晃祐, *Kindai Nihon no Bukkyōshatachi* 近代日本の仏教者たち (Modern Japanese Buddhists) (Tokyo: NHK Raiburari, 2005), pp. 100–106; Miyamoto Shōson 宮本正尊, *Meiji Bukkyō no shichō: Inoue Enryō no jiseki* 明治仏教の思潮: 井上円了の事績 (The Intellectual Tide of Meiji Buddhism: Inoue Enryō) (Tokyo: Kōsei shuppansha, 1975), pp. 54–59.

26. Miyamoto, *Meiji Bukkyō no shichō*, pp. 60–63.

27. Ono, *Bussho kaisetsu daijiten*, 1:185a, 191a, 205b; for Fujii, 185c, 201a.

28. New Buddhism was a modernized Buddhism that was meant to be logical, scientific and not religious, possessing a psychology and philosophy capable of supporting Japan against the incursions of Christianity and colonialism.

advances in Western medicine and possibly psychology. Others, such as Murakami Senshō and possibly Kasawara Kenju, began to link their Buddhism with Western systems of logic, or at least reform it into a rival to Western logic. A key to this was *vijñānavāda*, Indian studies, *Dasheng qixin lun*, and logic. Most of the leading Buddhist scholars and educators in the Meiji were involved with these four concerns. This is evident from an examination of two overlapping groups, those who promoted Buddhism in Japan and those who studied overseas, especially with F. Max Müller (1823–1900) at Oxford and his associates in Europe. A major role was played by the leader of the Nishi Honganji faction of Jōdo shinshū, Ōtani Kōson 大谷光尊 (1850–1903), who sponsored many of the young Jōdo shinshū scholars to study overseas. It was he who sent missionaries to Okinawa, Taiwan, Amoy (Xiamen), Singapore, Vladivostok, Hawaii, the United States, Korea, and China.[29]

Two of the Honganji students sent to Europe were Nanjō Bun'yū and Kasawara Kenju, both of whom went to England to study Sanskrit with F. Max Müller in 1876. They studied Sanskrit Buddhist sutras and the Sanskrit text of *Jinqishi lun* 金七十論 (On the Golden Seventy Verses).[30] Nanjō wrote a *Catalogue of the Chinese Translation of the Buddhist Tripitaka*, published in 1883, and also worked with Müller, H. Kern, and Izumi Hōkei (1923) on editions and translations of Mahāyāna sutras.[31] Nanjō returned to Japan in 1884, and the next year he commenced lecturing on Sanskrit at Tokyo University. This was the start of modern Sanskrit studies in Japan.[32] It was Nanjō's study of Sanskrit and the Tripitaka catalogue in London that brought him to the attention of Yang Wenhui in 1876.[33] At their first meeting in London, Yang presented Nanjō with his *Dasheng qixin lun xu* 大乘起信論序 (Prolegomenon to the *Awakening of Mahāyāna Faith*), and they began to exchange Buddhist texts from 1891.[34] Many of these books were on *vijñānavāda*, logic, *Dasheng qixin lun*, and even *Hasshū kōyō* 八宗綱要 (Essential Tenets of the Eight Schools) and *Sangoku Buppō dentsū engi* 三國佛法傳通緣起 (Circumstances of the Transmission of the Buddha-dharma Through the Three

29. Miyamoto, *Meiji Bukkyō no shichō*, pp. 24–26.

30. Tamura, *Kindai Nihon no Bukkyōshatachi*, pp. 166–168; Miyamoto, *Meiji Bukkyō no shichō*, pp. 105–106.

31. Miyamoto, *Meiji Bukkyō no shichō*, p. 106.

32. Miyamoto, *Meiji Bukkyō no shichō*, pp. 109–110; Tamura, *Kindai Nihon no Bukkyōshatachi*, p. 171.

33. Chen Jidong 陳継東, *Shinmatsu Bukkyō no kenkyū: Yō Bun'e o chūshin toshite* 清末仏教の研究：楊文会を中心として (Late-Qing Buddhist Research: Centered on Yang Wenhui) (Tokyo: Sankibō Busshorin, 2003), p. 125.

34. Chen, *Shinmatsu Bukkyō no kenkyū*, pp. 137, 143.

Countries [India, China, Japan]) by Gyōnen 凝然 (d. 1321). These books were important in forming the New Buddhism.

1.5 Consequences

Research on Buddhist logic continued well into the Meiji period, and even a cursory tally of works on Yogācāra in Ono Genmyō's *Bussho kaisetsu daijiten* (Bibliographical Encyclopedia of Buddhist Texts) gives over one hundred Tokugawa texts and about fifty Meiji texts. The main Meiji group seems to have been the one centered on Saeki Gyokuga 佐伯旭雅 (1828–1891) in Kansai. The group produced many books and lectures and wrote much on Buddhist logic.

Therefore, when Nanjō Bun'yū began to send Buddhist texts to Yang Wenhui, it was natural that he included among them not just Yogācāra texts by Chinese scholars that had been lost in China since the Yuan Dynasty, but also some of the texts by Japanese scholars. Among them were the *Ryakujutsu Hossōgi* 略述法相義 (A Brief Description of the Meanings of Dharma Characteristics) by Ryōkō Monsho 良光聞證 (1634–1688), the *Inmyō daiso zuigenki* 因明大疏瑞源記 (Notes on the Fortunate Source, the *Great Commentary on the Entry into Logic*) by Hōtan, the 1884 *Inmyō sanjūsanka honsahō kahon* 因明三十三過本作法科本 (Table of the Basic Operations of the Thirty-three Errors in Logic) by Kirara Kōyō, and the 1765 *Hossō Daijō genron* 法相大乘玄論 (i.e., *Daijō issai Hossō genron*; On the Profundities of All Dharma Characteristics in Mahāyāna) by Kiben 基辨 (1718–1791), a Hossō monk. In addition, *Kanjin kakumushō* 觀心覺夢抄 (Abstracts on Contemplation of the Mind to Waken One from the Dream State) by Ryōben 良遍 (1194–1252), a Hossō popularizer, and the *Inmyō shisōi shaku* 因明四相違釋 (Explanations of the Four Contradictions in Logic) by Genshin 源信 (942–1017), a prolific Tendai scholar, were sent, as well as editions of the *Jinqishi lun* (On the Golden Seventy Verses) and *Dasheng qixin lun* collated by Fujii Genju (1813–1895).[35] All were sent between 1892 and 1896. Later, Hōtan's work on logic was reprinted in 1928 by the Commercial Press of Shanghai.[36]

These works probably influenced the Chinese Buddhists in their interpretation of and enthusiasm for Yogācāra, and so Wen Tingshi 文廷式 (1856–1904) and Song Shu 宋恕 (1862–1910) went to study Yogācāra in Japan[37] where they would have imbibed some Japanese approaches to forming a new Buddhism. Their Japanese teachers had lived through a persecution of Buddhism as a religion, and it is likely that they tried to counter the critique that Buddhism was illogical or lacked

35. For lists of the texts sent to China, see Chen, *Shinmatsu Bukkyō no kenkyū*, pp. 156, 158, 520, 528, 542–543, 566.

36. Harbsmeier, *Language and Logic*, p. 363.

37. Chen, *Shinmatsu Bukkyō no kenkyū*, pp. 185–185.

logic by emphasizing logic and the scientific study of religion in the style of Max Müller.[38] Thus, Sugiura Sadajirō 杉浦貞二郎 (1870–1947) collaborated with Edgar Arthur Singer in 1900 to publish *Hindu Logic as Preserved in China and Japan* in Philadelphia.[39] Likewise, *Dasheng qixin lun*, which had been attacked by a number of leading Japanese Buddhist scholars as a Chinese forgery, an idea reported by the reformer, philosopher, and scholar Liang Qichao 梁啓超 (1873–1929) in 1922 in great detail,[40] was attacked via Yogācāra thought by Yang Wenhui's pupil, Ouyang Jingwu 歐陽竟無 (1871–1943), on the grounds that it was *tathāgatagarbha*-influenced (that is, as positing an essence or substrate, the womb/matrix for becoming Buddha) and hence merely faith-based and not true Indian Buddhism.[41]

This suggests that the Chinese Buddhists, who experienced their own setbacks from 1898 when monasteries began to be confiscated for schools and Buddhism was condemned as superstition, an oppression lasting to 1930,[42] may have adopted some of the Japanese strategies. Hence Ouyang Jingwu and Liang Qichao thought religion to be superstition,[43] and Ouyang attacked *Dasheng qixin lun*. Following this, other Buddhists took up Yogācāra, such as the reformer Han Qingjing 韓清淨 (1884–1949) and his Sanshi Xuehui 三時學會 from 1924.[44] It is this hypothesis of Japanese experience and influence as reflected in the Chinese fascination with Yogācāra that needs to be tested. In this chapter I will concentrate mainly on the networks linking Yang Wenhui, Nanjō Bun'yū, and Zhang Taiyan, with most emphasis on the latter, and exclude Confucianism from consideration.

---

38. James Edward Ketelaar, *Of Heretics and Martyrs in Meiji Japan: Buddhism and its Persecution* (Princeton, NJ: Princeton University Press, 1990), pp. 41, 137, 144, 162, 186–187.

39. Harbsmeier, *Language and Logic*, p. 358.

40. Liang Qichao, *Dasheng qixin lun kaozheng* 大乘起信論考證 (Evidential Study of the *Awakening of Mahāyāna Faith*) (Taipei: Taiwan shangwu yinshuguan reprint of 1922 text), preface.

41. Li Xiangping 李向平, *Jiushi yu jiuxin: Zhongguo jindai Fojiao fuxing sichao yanjiu* 救世與救心：中國近代佛教復興思潮研究 (Salvation of the World and Salvation of the Mind: Studies on the Tide of Modern Chinese Buddhist Revivalist Thought) (Shanghai: Shanghai renmin chubanshe, 1993).

42. Holmes Welch, *The Buddhist Revival in China* (Cambridge, MA: Harvard University Press, 1968), pp. 11–14, 142–143, 147–148; Jiang Canteng 江燦騰, *Zhongguo jindai Fojiao sixiang de zhengbian yu fazhan* 中國近代佛教思潮的諍辯與發展 (Debates and Developments in Modern Chinese Buddhist Thought) (Taipei: Nantian shuzhu, 1998), pp. 406–408, 433.

43. Welch, *The Buddhist Revival in China*, pp. 204–205, 208.

44. Cheng Gongrang 程恭讓, "Sanshi Xuehui Qingjing jushi de wannian zhushu yu sixiang 三時學會清淨居士的晚年著書與思想" (The Late Works and Thought of Layman Qingjing of the Society of the Three Ages), *Shijie zongjiao yanjiu* 71, no. 1(January 1998): 44–51.

2. *Zhang Taiyan and Indra's network*

Late-Qing intellectuals were able to observe the collapse of monastic Buddhism in China and to witness the survival and role of Buddhism in a rapidly modernizing Japan. They had a thirst for ideas that could rescue China from its weakness and suffering under an increasingly inept Manchu regime. Lay Buddhists and many intellectuals of the Gongyang 公洋 branch of Confucian studies who also researched Buddhism[45] realized they needed ideas to reform politics and values to transform society in order to strengthen China and create social justice. They also required a philosophy to counter Christianity and the West if China was to preserve its identity. They found in Buddhism a neglected resource that suited China and that could be used to criticize the social inequality and self-serving interests in Chinese society. They thought that Buddhism could be used to champion equality, people's rights, the salvation of all beings from suffering, and even evolution.[46]

Zhang Taiyan was a revolutionary and master of traditional scholarship, an anti-Manchu activist, and an independent thinker with anarchist tendencies (see the chapter by Viren Murthy in this volume for some of these aspects of Zhang's thought), whose ideas influenced those of the monk reformer Taixu 太虛 (1890–1947)[47] and who had a very extensive circle of friends and students, including the influential publisher and Yogācāra researcher Fan Gunong 範古農 (1881–1951).[48] Zhang saw Yogācāra as the most applicable form of Buddhism to address the above-listed needs. It could provide a philosophy of equality through its "wisdom

---

45. Ma Tianxiang 麻天祥, *Wan Qing Foxue yu jindai shehui sichao* 晚清佛學與近代社會思潮 (Late Qing Buddhist Studies and Modern Social Thought) (Taibei: Wenjin chubanshe, 1992), 1: 65. The Gongyang branch of studies refers to a group of commentators on the *Spring and Autumn Annals* who sought knowledge useful for government and society in such texts, and did not restrict themselves to philology. Also called the New Text School. Liang Qichao said that it "was fashionable for scholars of the New Text School to read the Buddhist literature." Sin-Wai Chan, *Buddhism in Late Ch'ing Political Thought* (Hong Kong: Chinese University Press, 1985), p. 29. See also note 60 for another contemporary observation on the connections of Gongyang scholars and Buddhism.

46. Ma Tianxiang, *Wan Qing Foxue*, vol. 1, pp. 13–15, 18, 69–72.

47. Li Guangliang 李廣良, "Fofa yu geming: Taixu Dashi de geming sixiang 佛法與革命:太虛大師的革命思想" (The Buddha-dharma and Revolution: Master Taixu's Revolutionary Thought) *Shijie zongjiaoyanjiu* 世界宗教研究 (Studies in World Religions) (2002.3): 61.

48. Fan met Zhang Taiyan in Japan in 1908 and studied Yogācāra while in Japan. In 1929 he became the editor of Shanghai Buddhist Books (Shanghai Foxue shuju 上海佛學書局). Late in life he published at least three books on Yogācāra. See "Fan Gunong" entry, http://buddhistinformatics.ddbc.edu.tw/dmcb/Fan_Gunong (accessed 29/01/2012) and Meng Lingbing 孟令兵, "Lüeshu Shanghai Foxue shuju chuangshi yinyuan (xia) 略述上海佛學書局創始因緣（下）" (A Brief Description of the Foundation of the Shanghai Buddhist Book Store), http://www.hkbuddhist.org/magazine/534/534_04.html (accessed 29/01/2012).

of equality" (*pingdengxing zhi* 平等性智; *samatā-jñāna*) that was achieved by converting the self-centered seventh *vijñāna* (consciousness) into a wisdom that removed attachment to ego and so achieved true equality.[49] Although Wang Fuzhi 王夫之 (1619–1692), Gong Zizhen 龔自珍 (1793–1842), and Tan Sitong 譚嗣同 (1865–1898) had foreshadowed such approaches,[50] theirs had been isolated voices, and their ideas had not been further developed. Therefore, Chinese Buddhist laypeople and reformers such as Yang Wenhui and Zhang Taiyan looked to Japan for resources and inspiration.

Recalling earlier experiences, Zhang Taiyan wrote in his *Zhuo Han weiyan* 菿漢微言 (Subtle Words of Zhang Taiyan; post-face 1917)[51] that after 1906 he wanted to study Vaiśeṣika and Sāṁkhya (see earlier for these Indian schools of philosophy), and that soon after he began to lecture on *Zhuangzi* using the Guo Xiang 郭象 (d. 312)[52] commentary. Zhang, however, often found Guo's comments unsatisfactory, and so "To explain the 'Qi wu' chapter I matched it with Yogācāra and Huayan. As soon as the so-called *maṇi* (jewel) light appears, it gives off different colors according to your view, and this unhindered, complete interpenetration of Indra's net alone clarified *Zhuangzi*."[53] This field of intersecting viewpoints, plus Zhang's activities as a revolutionary interested in anarchism, Western philosophy, and Confucian evidential studies (*kaozheng* 考證) and his many personal contacts, illustrates the complex web surrounding Yogācāra studies and reevaluations of Confucianism in China and Japan from the 1880s into the 1910s.

2.1 Zhang Taiyan's personal networks

Zhang Taiyan's varied interests involved him with many people over his career as a scholar and revolutionary. His main teacher, Yu Yue 俞樾 (1822–1906), was a specialist in evidential (*kaozheng*) scholarship. Yu was also influenced by Sun

49. Ma Tianxiang, *Wan Qing Foxue*, vol. 1, pp. 13, 69–70. Sin-Wai Chan, *Buddhism in Late Ch'ing Political Thought*, pp. 27, 39, indicates that Yang Wenhui and Kang Youwei stressed the Buddhist ideal of equality, with Kang using this equality in discussions of society.

50. Ma Tianxiang, *Wan Qing Foxue*, vol. 1, pp. 15, 69–70. This was first mentioned by Liang Qichao, who read Tan Sitong's *Renxue* 仁學 (A Study of Benevolence) as it was being written. Scott Pacey's chapter on Tan Sitong mentions Tan's interest in Wang Fuzhi.

51. Zhuo Han was one of the styles Zhang used. 菿 is a loan graph for *zhuo* 倬. Li Yu 李昱, "'Zhuo Han' jie '菿汉'解" (On 'Zhuo Han'), *Jinyang xuekan* (2008.1): 119–122.

52. Guo Xiang was a theorist of Profound Learning (*Xuanxue* 玄學), a synthesis of Classical Daoism and the philosophy of the *Yijing*.

53. Approximate translation based on Japanese translation by Takata Jun 高田淳, *Shinkai kakumei to Shō Heirin no Seibutsuron tetsugaku* 辛亥革命と章炳麟の斉物論哲学 (The 1911 Revolution and Zhang Binglin's Philosophy of the Equalization of Things) (Tokyo: Kenbun shuppan, 1984), p. 24.

Yirang 孫詒讓 (1848–1908),[54] especially his writings on *Mozi*, and by Wang Xianqian 王先謙 (1842–1918), who studied *Xunzi* and *Zhuangzi*. Additionally, Yu was informed by the scholarship of Gu Yanwu 顧炎武 (1613–1682).[55] Many of these threads of thought are reflected in Zhang's own work, and it is one of the reasons Zhang befriended Tatemori Kō 館森鴻 (1863–1942) in Taiwan in 1898 and visited Japan together with this reformist scholar of Confucianism who introduced Western ideas into the Japanese version of evidential scholarship (*kōshōgaku*).[56] It was Tatemori who showed Zhang the works of Terui Takakuni 照井全都 (Ittaku 一宅 [1818–1881]). Terui admired *Xunzi* and wrote on *Zhuangzi*. Zhang appreciated both studies, despite Terui's anti-Buddhist feelings.[57] In this way, Yu Yue's influence brought Zhang into contact with Japanese scholars while he was fleeing the Qing authorities by going to Taiwan.

Although Zhang had little concern with Buddhism early in his life, his teacher Yu Yue had a side interest in Buddhism, and Zhang's father was also interested in Chan Buddhism.[58] This probably made it easier for Zhang to study Buddhism seriously—as philosophy—when his friends recommended Buddhist texts, rather than as simply grist to the mill of his evidential studies. These friends included Xia Zengyou 夏曾佑 (1863–1923), Song Shu 宋恕 (1862–1910), Huang Zongyang 黄宗仰 (1864–1921), and Su Manshu 蘇曼殊 (1884–1918). Moreover, when Zhang Taiyan was employed as a journalist for the *Shiwu bao* 時務報 (China Progress), an organ sponsored by Zhang Zhidong 張之洞 (1837–1909), a cautious reforming official and military modernizer,[59] he came into contact with a circle that studied

---

54. Sun Yirang was a philologist who created an edition of *Mozi*, commented on the *Zhouli* 周禮 (Zhou Rites), and pioneered studies of oracle bone script.

55. Fukushima Shun'ō 福嶋俊翁, "Shin Ju Yu Kyokuen to sono *Kongōkyōchū* 清儒兪曲園とその金剛経注" (Yu Yue of the Qing and his Commentary on the *Diamond Sutra*) in *Fukushima Shun'ō chosakushū* 福嶋俊翁著作集 (The Collected Works of Fukushima Shun'ō) (Tokyo: Mokujisha, 1973), vol. 3, p. 233 (reprint of an article from *Zengaku kenkyū* 7, no. 9 (1928). Gu Yanwu was a philologist and geographer who criticized Neo-Confucian philosophy, advocating a return to the study of the Classics by ignoring any commentaries written after the Han dynasty. He sought practical knowledge and was opposed to Manchu rule.

56. Tang Zhijun 湯志鈞, *Kindai Chūgoku no kakumei shisō to Nihon* 近代中国の革命思想と日本 (Japan and the Revolutionary Thought of Modern China), trans. Chigono Michiko 児野道子 (Tokyo: Nihonkeizai hyōronsha, 1986), pp. 197–203.

57. Tang Zhijun, *Kindai Chūgoku no kakumei shisō to Nihon*, pp. 207, 209–212.

58. Takata Zhijun, *Shinkai kakumei to Shō Heirin*, pp. 31–32, 15; Jer-shiarn Lee, *Chang Ping-lin (1869–1936): A Political Radical and Cultural Conservative* (Taipei: The Liberal Arts Press/Wenshizhe chubanshe, 1993), p. 56.

59. Seungjoo Yoon, "Literati-Journalists of the *Chinese Progress (Shiwu bao)* in Discord, 1896–1898)," in *Rethinking the 1898 Reform Period: Politics and Cultural Change in late Qing China*, ed. Rebecca E. Karl and Peter Zarrow (Cambridge, MA: Harvard University Asia Center, Harvard East Asian monograph, 2002), pp. 48–75.

Buddhism, the so-called "seven sages of Shanghai" (*haishang qi zi* 海上七子). Although not all members of this circle were closely connected with Zhang Taiyan, they did have an impact on him, and this illustrates the importance of Buddhism, especially Yogācāra, in Chinese intellectual life of the 1890s onward. Contemporary observers, such as Inaba Kunzan 稲葉君山 (1876–1940), writing in 1914, and participants such as Liang Qichao, recognized that many Gongyang school scholars were interested in Yogācāra.[60]

This group of seven were Sun Baoxuan 孫寶瑄 (1874–1924), Wu Jiarui 吳嘉瑞, Wang Kangnian 汪康年 (1860–1911), Hu Weizhi 胡惟志 (d.u.), Liang Qichao, Tan Sitong, and Song Shu. They attempted to match Buddhist doctrines with science.[61] Wu Jiarui, who was praised by Tan Sitong as "the first instructor in Buddhism," was also the lecturer on Buddhism to the "seven sages,"[62] but there are few clues to the content of the lectures. Xia Zengyou introduced Buddhism to Sun Baoxuan, a former official and relative of Li Hongzhang 李鴻章 (1823–1901). Sun, a bibliophile, befriended Zhang Taiyan. Sun read Western scholarship (in translation) voraciously. An advocate of people power and a parliamentary system, he read Adam Smith, Kant, and all kinds of philosophy and politics. In this he was influenced by Song Shu. Around 1901 he discussed the expulsion of the Manchu rulers.[63] Sun was initially more partial to Pure Land and Chan, but under Xia's guidance from 1901 he studied *Abhidharma-kośa* (Storehouse of Higher Doctrine), Kuiji's *Cheng weishi lun shuji* (Commentary on *Demonstration Nothing but Consciousness*) and *Yogācārabhūmi-śāstra* (*Yuqie shidi lun* 瑜伽師地論; Discourse on the Stages of Concentration Practice). Moreover, of the more than

60. Mori Noriko 森紀子, "Ryō Keichō no Butsugaku to Nihon 梁啓超の佛学と日本 (Liang Qichao's Buddhist Studies and Japan)," in *Kyōdō kenkyū: Seiyō kindaishisō juyō to Meiji Nihon* 共同研究：西洋近代思想受容と明治日本 (Joint Research: The Acceptance of Modern Western Thought and Meiji Japan) comp. Hazama Naoki 狭間直樹 (Tokyo: Misuzu shobō, 1999), pp. 194–197.

61. For this group, see the chapter in this volume by Thierry Meynard; Ge Zhaoguang 葛兆光, "Zijia baozang de shi er fude 自家寶藏的失而復得" (The Loss and Recovery of Our Own Treasure), *Shixue jikan* (2010.1): 67–78; and Murao Susumu 村尾進, " 'Banki sensen': *Jimu hō* jiki no Ryō Keichō 万木森々：時務報時期と梁啓超" (The Luxuriant Forest: Liang Qichao and the *China Progress* Period), in *Kyōdō kenkyū: Seiyō kindaishisō juyō to Meiji Nihon*, comp. Hazama Naoki, p. 41; and Mori, "Ryō Keichō no Butsugaku to Nihon," pp. 194–228.

62. Hanshan si 寒山寺, "Liang Qichao zaonian de shiyou xuefo yuan 梁啓超早年的師友学佛緣 (The Buddhist Connections of the Teachers and Friends of Liang Qichao in his Early Years)," http://www.hanshansi.org/bianjibu/xzzq/2001/03/2011/992.html, accessed 22/01/2012.

63. Liu Yajun 劉雅軍, "Cong *Wangshanlu riji* kan Sun Baoxuan shijie lishi renshi yu biangeguan de zhuanbian 從《忘山廬日記》看孫寶瑄世界歷史認識與變革觀的轉變" (Changes in Sun Baoxuan's Understanding of World History and in His Views on Reform as Seen from his Wangshan lu Diary), *Shixue yuekan* (2011.2): 134–136.

200 volumes on Buddhism in Sun's collection, virtually all had been printed by Yang Wenhui (many of which Yang had obtained from Japan), and so were likely a resource for the "seven sages" and Zhang.[64]

In 1896 Wang Kangnian was selected by Zhang Zhidong to lead the *China Progress*,[65] and Liang Qichao was made editor-in-chief.[66] This journal advocated reform and self-strengthening, but under pressure from Zhang Zhidong and his observation of the failure of reforms, Wang became increasingly conservative from 1898. Despite their differences in outlook, it was Wang who invited Zhang Taiyan to write for the paper, and these connections gave Zhang an introduction to the Japanese journalist Yamamoto Baigan 山本梅岸 (1852–1928).[67]

The famous Liang Qichao had been introduced to Buddhism from 1891, but it was Xia Zengyou who truly influenced Liang. Liang joined the "seven sages" in 1896, mixing with Song Shu, Zhang Taiyan, and Tan Sitong.[68] Elements of Yogācāra can be found in aspects of Liang's thought. For example, in writing about education, he theorized that Western enlightenment and scientific discovery was governed by the cerebrum or *manas* (the seventh consciousness) and Chinese rote memorization belonged to the *manovijñāna* (the sixth consciousness).[69] In 1899, Liang, in exile in Japan, while lecturing on the reform of Chinese religion, used *Indo shūkyōshi* 印度宗教史 (History of Indian Religion) and similar texts by Anesaki Masaharu 姉崎正治 (1873–1949). From 1902 he came under the influence of Inoue Enryō's philosophy.[70] By the 1920s, however, under Anesaki's influence, Liang began to investigate early Buddhism.[71] As we shall

64. Ge, "Zijia baozang de shi er fude," p. 68; Mori, "Ryō Keichō no Butsugaku to Nihon," p. 199.

65. Yoon, "Literati-Journalists of the *Chinese Progress*," p. 54.

66. Ibid., p. 56.

67. Murao, "'Banki sen-sen,'" p. 40; Lü Shunzhang 呂順長, "Yamamoto Baigan to Ō Kōnen no kōyū 山本梅岸と汪康年の交遊 (The Friendship between Yamamoto Baigan and Wang Kangnian)," *Shittenōji Kokusai Bukkyō Daigaku kiyō* 四天王寺国際仏教大学紀要 45(2008.3): 30–31. For Wang's politics, see Liao Mei 寥梅, *Wang Kangnian: Cong minquanlun dao wenhuabaoshuzhuyi* 汪康年: 從民權論到文化保守主義 (Wang Kangnian: From Peoples' Rights to Cultural Conservatism) (Shanghai: Shanghai guji chubanshe, 2001).

68. Mori, "Ryō Keichō no Butsugaku to Nihon," pp. 197–198; Murao, "'Banki sen-sen,'" p. 40.

69. Murao, "'Banki sen-sen,'" pp. 44, 54, 58. The *manas* appropriates the perceptions as "mine" and the *manovijñāna* or mental consciousness takes as its objects past perceptions (memory) and the future (hopes, calculations). That Liang used these terms does not guarantee he was using Yogācāra concepts in the strict sense, for other Buddhist schools also used these terms.

70. Mori, "Ryō Keichō no Butsugaku to Nihon," pp. 201–202.

71. Mori, "Ryō Keichō no Butsugaku to Nihon," p. 214 ff.

see, Zhang Taiyan was also deeply influenced by Anesaki and Inoue Enryō, but it is not clear whether Liang encouraged Zhang to consult the views of these two Japanese authors.

Xia Zengyou was a key figure in these networks, introducing many of the individuals involved to Yogācāra, while acting as a loyal disciple of Yang Wenhui. Xia was informed by Gongyang scholarship, especially the scholarship of Gong Zizhen 龔自珍 (1793–1842), and by the latest Chinese translations of Western and Japanese works on science, philosophy, and politics. Deeply involved in discussions of reformist politics, Xia was considered the most versed in Buddhism of these circles.

Xia was the first friend to introduce Zhang Taiyan to Buddhism. They met in 1894 and Xia recommended that Zhang read the **Saddharma-puṇḍarīka-sūtra* (*Fahua jing* 法華經; Lotus Sutra), the *Avataṃsaka-sūtra* (*Huayan jing* 華嚴經; Flower Ornament Sutra), and the *Mahāparinirvāṇa-sūtra* (*Niepan jing* 涅槃經; Nirvana Sutra), and although Zhang did so, initially they had little effect on him. Xia was an adherent of Faxiang as the only true Buddhism, studied *Cheng weishi lun* and disagreed with the *Laṅkāvatāra-sūtra*, no doubt because of its introduction of *tathāgatagarbha* (matrix of the buddhas) doctrine into an otherwise Yogācārin text. Xia, however, was prepared to apply the teachings of Buddhism to the issues of race and equality, asserting in 1897 that the theory of equality was initiated by the Buddha, and referred to the idea that even animals have the Buddha-nature. In turn, this may have influenced Zhang's theory of equality that appears in Zhang's *Qi wu lun shi* 齊物論釋 (An Interpretation of "Discourse on Making All Things Equal"), a commentary on a chapter of *Zhuangzi* (see Viren Murthy's chapter in this volume).[72]

Xia, a disciple of Yang Wenhui, was delighted when Nanjō sent a copy of Kuiji's *Cheng weishi lun shuji* to Yang.[73] Yang told Xia that the weakness of Buddhism in China was due to Chan, and in Japan its weakness was due to Jōdo shinshū.[74] This probably confirmed Xia in his devotion to the Faxiang version of Yogācāra. Xia was thus the first link between Zhang and the Yang-Nanjō relationship. Yang Wenhui was the godfather of the Yogācāra revival in China. As part of a Chinese embassy to London, Yang encountered Nanjō Bun'yū in 1878,[75] having already heard about Nanjō while in China in 1876. This meeting initiated a long-term

72. Takata, *Shinkai kakumei to Shō Heirin*, pp. 32–33. As Viren Murthy shows, however, Zhang himself saw no contradiction in mixing ideas from *Dasheng qixin lun*—a *tathāgatagarbha*-influenced text—with ideas derived from Yogācāra.

73. Chen Jidong, *Shinmatsu Bukkyō no kenkyū*, pp. 188–189.

74. Chen Jidong, *Shinmatsu Bukkyō no kenkyū*, p. 241.

75. Chen Jidong, *Shinmatsu Bukkyō no kenkyū*, pp. 121–125.

exchange of Buddhist texts, letters, and views. Yang in turn published many Yogācāra texts and encouraged his disciples and associates to study those texts in order to revive Chinese Buddhism, counter Christianity, and correct misunderstandings about Buddhism.

The second link to Zhang Taiyan was Song Shu. Song had studied in Japan from about the age of twenty-five, buying books on the Meiji Restoration. Song's thought was complex, at times contradictory, but mainly directed at reform of politics and abolition of practices such as foot-binding. He studied all the branches of Neo-Confucian idealism, but also advocated materialism, science, and modernization.[76] In 1889 he studied the *Dafang guangfo Huayan jing helun* 大方廣佛華嚴經合論 (Combined Discussions of the *Flower Ornament Sutra* of the Buddha of Vast Expanse) and the *Mahāratnakūṭa-sūtra* (*Dabaoji jing* 大寶積經; Accumulation of Sutras of Great Treasures) in the monastic residence of Qibao Monastery in Hangzhou. Song compared Buddhist texts with what he knew of Western theory,[77] as did Zhang in the early 1900s. Song was involved in reformist politics: he met Kang Youwei four times in 1895 and corresponded with Liang Qichao.[78]

In 1897, Song resumed his studies of Buddhism, this time with the Japanese priests of the Jōdo shinshū 浄土真宗 branch in Shanghai. Studying under Matsubayashi Kōjun 松林孝純 (1856–?)[79] he read Japanese works such as the *Hasshū kōyō* (Essential Tenets of the Eight Schools) and *Kyōgyō shinshō* 教行信證 (Passages Revealing the True Teachings, Practice, Faith, and Realization of the Pure Land).[80] The latter is a key Jōdo shinshū text written by Shinran 親鸞 in 1224. The former was no doubt more useful to Song, as it is a summation of the main schools of Japanese Buddhism, including Sanron 三論 (Madhyamaka or Middle Way), Hossō, and Kegon. It was a textbook for beginners in serious study of Buddhist doctrine and was widely used in Meiji Japan. In 1897, when Zhang was

76. Hu Zhusheng 胡珠生 (comp.), *Song Shu ji: Zhongguo jindai renwu wenji congshu* 宋恕集: 中國近代人物文集叢書 (Song Shu's Collected Works: Collected Books of Modern Chinese People) (Beijing: Zhonghua shuju, 1993), 2 vols. (continuous pagination), pp. 3–4.

77. Hu Zhusheng, *Song Shu ji*, pp. 1093, 1095.

78. Hu Zhusheng, *Song Shu ji*, p. 1102.

79. Matsubayashi was a Jōdo shinshū missionary. After studying Nanjing dialect in Osaka, he was sent in 1881 to Suzhou to learn the local dialect. He later taught in the Japanese school of the Jōdo shinshū branch temple in Shanghai, and in 1883 was connected with the compilation by Yu Yue of a large collection of poems by Japanese written in Chinese, the *Dongying shixuan* 東瀛詩選 (Selected Japanese Poems). Later he was a translator for the Japanese army during the Sino-Japanese War and he published translations from Japanese texts in Shanghai. Kawabe Yutai 川邊雄太, "*Tōei shisen* hensan ni kansuru ichi kōsatsu, 東瀛詩選編纂に関する一考察" (An Examination of the Compilation of the *Dongying shixuan*), http://nippon-chugoku-gakkai.org/utf8/wakate/4th/408.pdf; accessed 10 June 2010.

80. Hu Zhusheng, *Song Shu ji*, p. 1107.

thirty, Song had Zhang read the *Sanlun* (Madhyamaka) treatises, but Zhang did not like them. When Zhang encountered *Dasheng qixin lun*, however, he was impressed and continued to read it. Song then introduced Zhang to other Buddhist texts, in particular the *Dabaoji jing* (Accumulated Sutras of Great Treasures).

Song had also studied with Yu Yue. In 1898 Song wrote to Yu describing the activities of Matsubayashi and the survival of Buddhism in Japan, and the introduction of philosophy into Japanese universities. He noted the division of philosophy into Eastern and Western philosophy, with Eastern philosophy divided into Indian and Chinese philosophy, the former being Buddhism and the latter represented by Confucianism, Daoism, and the pre-Qin philosophers. He mentioned in passing the studies by Nanjō Bun'yū.[81]

In 1898, Zhang fled to Taiwan, and Song wrote to him with material on Chan that Zhang increasingly came to appreciate. The following year Zhang left Taiwan for Japan. As soon as he arrived in Japan, he paid his respects at the tomb of the monk Gesshō 月性 (1813–1858) (see below)[82] in the grounds of Kiyomizudera in Kyoto, and after that he met Sun Yat-sen in Yokahama through the offices of Liang Qichao.[83] After Zhang returned to China, the Boxer Rebellion erupted, and the Qing government's failure to respond adequately led Zhang on the path to revolution.[84] He openly criticized the Manchu government, fleeing again to Japan in 1902 to avoid arrest.

On his return to China in 1903, Zhang continued his anti-Manchu propaganda, and this time was arrested and imprisoned from 1903 to 1906 in Shanghai. It was during this term of imprisonment that Song Shu encouraged Zhang to study the Yogācāra texts, including the *Yogācārabhūmi-śāstra*, *Cheng weishi lun*, and *Yinming lun* in depth.[85] Zhang mentions the *Yogācārabhūmi-śāstra* in particular.[86]

After he was released from prison, at Sun Yat-sen's invitation, Zhang again left for Japan, and joined the Tongmenghui or Chinese Revolutionary Alliance,

81. Hu Zhusheng, *Song Shu ji*, p. 588.

82. For an account of the last years of this monk, see Mark Ravina, *The Last Samurai: The Life and Times of Saigō Takamori* (Hoboken NJ: John Wiley and Sons, 2004), pp. 70–76.

83. Takata, *Shinkai kakumei to Shō Heirin*, pp. 34–35; see Gao Jingcheng 高景成, "Zhang Taiyan nianpu 章太炎年譜" (Chronological Biography of Zhang Taiyan), in *Zhang Binglin zhuanji huibian* 章炳麟傳記彙編 (Collected Biographical Materials on Zhang Binglin), comp. Cuncui xueshe 存萃學社 (Hong Kong: Datong tushu gongsi, 1978), p. 236.

84. Jer-shiarn Lee, *Chang Ping-lin*, pp. 110–112.

85. Jer-shiarn Lee, *Chang Ping-lin*, pp. 57, 114–121; Takata, *Shinkai kakumei to Shō Heirin*, p. 15.

86. Xu Shoushang 許壽裳, "Zhang Binglin 章炳麟," in *Zhang Binglin zhuanji huibian*, comp. Cuncui xueshe, p. 49, and quotation at p. 146.

founded in Japan in 1905 with the aim of overthrowing Manchu rule and establishing a republic. Zhang edited their journal, *Minbao* 民報, and stayed in Japan until 1911. Meanwhile, Song visited Japan in 1903 and had a "brush talk" with Nanjō and other Japanese scholars. Song had been consulting with Japanese monks and scholars from as far back as 1898, studying the Meiji Restoration, Zen, philosophy and Kuiji's commentary on the *Yinming lun*.[87] Therefore, when Song arrived in Japan in 1903, he went to see Zhang Taiyan just before the latter's departure, and he talked to Japanese philosophers and to Nanjō before returning to China late in the year with many books.[88]

Song's main interest in Buddhism was Buddhist logic,[89] so as he continued to hold brush conversations with Japanese scholars, including Inoue Tetsujirō, he inquired about who were the best scholars in each of the fields of Buddhism. In 1903 he first met Nanjō who introduced him to the current state of scholarship on Buddhist logic in Japan. Song actively promoted *yinming* logic to his own students, as is evident in a series of poems written in 1901 while he was in Hangzhou.[90] In 1898 he had studied Kuiji's key commentary *Yinming ru zhengli lun shu* 因明入正理論疏 (Commentary on *Entryway into Logic*)—a discussion of the Sanskrit text *Nyāyapraveśa*—with Matsubayashi, and he even drafted a book on logic that was never published.[91] In 1905, Song returned to China to take up a post as an education advisor in Shandong, where he seems to have advocated that *yinming* logic be introduced into the curriculum.[92] Finally, in 1908, he returned to his home district but fell ill and died in 1910.

Huang Zongyang, the next figure in this circle, was active in Shanghai, where he was well known. Huang was a considerable scholar, for he supposedly knew Japanese and English, and had studied Sanskrit.[93] In 1902, Huang organized the Aiguo xueshe 愛國學社 (Patriotic Society), which Zhang Taiyan also joined

87. Hu Zhusheng, *Song Shu ji*, pp. 1108–1112.

88. Hu Zhusheng, *Song Shu ji*, pp. 1118–1120.

89. Chen Jidong, *Shinmatsu Bukkyō no kenkyū*, p. 184.

90. Song Shu, *Liuzhai beiyi* 六齋卑議 (Humble Deliberations of Liuzhai), collated and printed by Huang Qun 黃群 (1883–1945) of Yongjia, in *Jingxiang lou congshu* 敬鄉樓叢書 (Collected Books from the Jingxiang Pavilion), 1928, appendix 2a. It suggests that the popularity of Chan had caused the demise of *yinming* studies, and mentions Kuiji's *Yinming ru zhengli lun shu*.

91. Hu Zhusheng, *Song Shu ji*, p. 941.

92. See Shen Haibo 沈海波, "Song Shu yu yinming xue 宋恕與因明學" (Song Shu and Buddhist Logic Studies)," *Haichaoyin* 77, no. 4 (1996): 10–14.

93. Welch, *The Buddhist Revival in China*, pp. 16–18. There is a question as to whether Huang studied Sanskrit or just the Siddham script.

in 1903. They had probably met in 1902. Zongyang believed that human rights were a natural given, that the Way was based on self-respect, and that Buddhism was necessary to moral education. Because morality was the basis for society, so Buddhism too was necessary for society. He also thought that Buddhism and a politicolegal system were crucial for national salvation. "The reason Japan has prospered is that it has Buddhism and a politico-legal system; the reason India collapsed was because it had Buddhism but no politico-legal system."[94]

Another figure in this network was the poet and romantic Su Manshu (1884–1918). Su had a serious interest in the study of Buddhism, Sanskrit, anarchism, and revolution. Born of a Chinese father and Japanese mother in Yokahama, he had been sent to study in Kang Youwei's Datong School in Shanghai, returning to Japan in 1903.[95] Su became a monk in 1904, but politically he opposed Kang Youwei, and associated rather with Chen Duxiu 陳獨秀 (1879–1942) and the anarchist couple Liu Shipei 劉師培 (1884–1919) and He Zhen 何震 (fl. 1903–1919). Su again returned to Japan in 1907 where he stayed with Liu Shipei and He Zhen and met Zhang Taiyan.[96] In the journal run by Liu and He, the *Tianyibao* 天義報 (Natural Justice), Zhang penned a preface to Su's proposed five-volume Sanskrit grammar, or *Fanwendian* 梵文典,[97] which shows Su and Zhang had similar interests.[98] The project was eventually abandoned, with only the first volume completed. Zhang wrote the preface, Liu Shipei wrote another, and there were dedicatory poems by He Zhen and Chen Duxiu.[99]

Around 1908, Su and Zhang wrote "An Admonishment of All Buddhist Disciples" and "A Manifesto to Both Officials and Commoners," in which they defended Buddhism against those who were campaigning in China to convert Buddhist monasteries into Western-style schools. They claimed that ambitious and vulgar monks were ruining Buddhism, and that the remedy was Buddhist scholarship, the study of Sanskrit, and the translation of sutras into modern Chinese. They also wrote that India was the source of Buddhism and so should be studied.

94. Cited in Li Xiangping 李向平, "Ershi shiji Zhongguo Fojiao de 'geming zouxiang' 二十世紀中國佛教的'革命走向' " (The Revolutionary Tendencies of Twentieth-Century Chinese Buddhism)," *Shijie zongjiao yanjiu* (2002.3): 44.

95. Liu Wu-chi, *Su Man-shu* (Boston, MA: Twayne, 1972), pp. 24–32.

96. Liu Wu-chi, *Su Man-shu*, pp. 39–40, 44–45.

97. Probably based on the 1886 text, *Sanskrit Grammar*, written by Max Müller and others.

98. Takata, *Shinkai kakumei to Shō Heirin*, pp. 50, 55, note 11; Liu Wu-chi, *Su Man-shu*, pp. 46–47.

99. Liu Wu-chi, *Su Man-shu*, pp. 48–49; Liu Yazi 柳亞子 (comp.), *Su Manshu quanji* 蘇曼殊全集 (Complete Works of Su Manshu), 5 vols. (Beijing: Xinhua shudian, 1985), 1: 104.

In October 1908, Yang Wenhui invited Su Manshu to Nanjing, where he was to teach English and translate two letters in "Sanskrit" sent by the Ceylonese Buddhist revivalist and writer Anagārika Dharmapāla, the secretary of the Mahabodhi Society in India, which he had founded in 1893. Su told Yang that the letters requested that monks be sent to India and Japan to study the scriptures, especially of Yogācāra and *dhyāna* (meditation). Su's work with Yang lasted only three months.[100] During this period, Xia Zengyou arrived and discussed Buddhism with Su and Yang, and as a letter by Yang indicates, Xia was using Buddhism for political purposes.[101] Su likewise thought of Buddhism as having a revolutionary use. He wrote that if you do not truly recognize the nonexistence of the marks of self, person, sentient being, and life you cannot talk of revolution. Only when you are "without attachment to the mind, and the mind subsequently has nothing to change can you talk of having reached revolution."[102] After the brief interlude in China, Su returned to Tokyo in 1909, but by this stage he had largely dropped out of the network.

Zhang continued to promote Buddhism but he was also concerned with revolution and anti-imperialism, befriending a number of Indian exiles in Japan, hoping that the Indians would throw off the British yoke just as he was working to remove the Manchu hold over the Chinese. In 1911 he wrote:

> In the past when I was in Edo [Tokyo] I had many comrades from India. I made a promise to travel west (to India) and at that time to devote myself to restoration [Indian independence], but this [promise] is yet to be fulfilled. . . . Even though I have written on the profound principles of Laozi and Zhuangzi, in reality I have yet to discuss them in depth with scholars. . . . We must search for a person to explain them, but not so far away as the West, but closer, in India. Together we would investigate Śākya [Buddha] and the extant works of the six [non-Buddhist] masters that would be most beneficial in India. With the body of layman Vimalakīrti, and imitating Dharma Master Kuiji's work, even though I will investigate [Kuiji's] inferences, there should be no doubt.[103]

100. Liu Wu-chi, *Su Man-shu*, pp. 58–61; Liu Yazi, *Su Manshu chuanji*, 1: 108.

101. Li Hongyan 李洪岩, "Xia Zengyou zhi shengping yu xueshu 夏曾佑之生平與學術 (The Life and Scholarship of Xia Zengyou)," 2002, http://www.acriticism.com/article.asp?newsid=3056, accessed 13/11/2011. Brought to my attention by Axel Schneider.

102. Cited in Li Guangliang, "Fofa yu geming," p. 60.

103. Takata, *Shinkai kakumei to Shō Heirin*, p. 87.

This was written shortly after Zhang introduced Yogācāra into his commentary on *Zhuangzi* to promote the morals he felt necessary for a new society. During this period, Zhang tried to learn Sanskrit in a group, this time with an Indian scholar, but this lasted only two meetings.[104] Zhang's interest in Indian philosophy and *Zhuangzi* was deepening. Besides Yogācāra, he was most interested in Sāṁkhya and Vaiśeṣika, noting that both were represented by texts in Chinese in the Buddhist canon.

Soon after, in 1911, Zhang returned to China, giving a farewell lecture to some thirty Japanese monks on Buddhism, recommending Hossō, but Tendai (Ch. Tiantai), Kegon (Ch. Huayan), and Jōdo (Pure Land) monks criticized this.[105] At this point, Zhang's life and networks changed. Song Shu was dead, Su Manshu was estranged, and Yang Wenhui died in 1911. The connections with Japan were also being loosened, for in 1911 another of Zhang's associates, Takeda Hanshi 武田範之 (1863–1911), also died.

2.1.1 *Zhang Taiyan, the Hossō network, and political activism*

"The view of society as being impermanent and the bodhisattva's view of human life led me to follow the path of revolution."
QU QIUBAI 瞿秋白 (1899–1935)[106]

As the above quotation illustrates, Buddhism in the late nineteenth and early twentieth centuries was often associated with political activism. This was truer in China, but Japan also provided some examples, even for Zhang Taiyan, who debated with some of those whom we would normally consider to have been his political enemies.

Martyr to the Restoration, revolutionary, and erstwhile Hossō monk Gesshō (1813–1858) was idolized by Chinese revolutionaries and monks. The first time Zhang Taiyan visited Japan, he went to Kiyomizudera in May 1899 to pay his respects at Gesshō's tomb, "for dying in the service of the king," noting also that many monks and Buddhists flocked there. After the failure of the Hundred-Days Reform advocated by Kang Youwei, Zhang was attracted to Gesshō's deeds as those of a bodhisattva because they were selfless actions for the people or state.[107]

104. Takata, *Shinkai kakumei to Shō Heirin*, p. 66.

105. Gao Jingcheng, "Zhang Taiyan nianpu," p. 240 for 1911 entry.

106. Qu Qiubai was a pioneering Marxist literary critic and leader of the Chinese Communist Party from 1927. Cited by Li Guangliang, "Fofa yu geming," p. 57.

107. Takata, *Shinkai kakumei to Shō Heirin*, pp. 35–36.

He remained a hero for Zhang, as he is mentioned in his 1906 "Jianli zongjiao lun 建立宗教論" (On Founding a Religion) along with Mozi, Zongmi 宗密 (780–841) and other anti-dictatorship heroes.[108]

While the link between Hossō or Yogācāra and revolution—as seen in the cases of Gesshō and Zhang—may seem coincidental, a product of the times and personal networks, the evidence from Zhang suggests there is a connection with elements of Yogācāra thought. Other Buddhists involved in revolutionary action or political change, ranging from Chinese monk revolutionaries such as Huang Zongyang, who was involved in insurrections and plots from 1905 and read anarchist tracts,[109] as well as Japanese Buddhist military adventurers and imperialists such as the monks Takeda Hanshi (1863–1911) and Kitabatake Dōryū 北畠道龍 (1820–1907), had connections with either Zhang or Yogācāra. The element in Yogācāra that appealed to revolutionaries and military adventurers may have been the passage in the *Yogācārabhūmi-śāstra*, translated by Xuanzang as *Yuqie shidi lun* (Discourse on the Stages of Concentration Practice), that was summarized in the maxim "to kill one to benefit the many," which saw such altruistic killing as the actions of a bodhisattva and the overthrow of tyrannies as justified:

> So if this bodhisattva has seen a robber bandit who is about to kill many beings out of a thirst for their valuables . . . he will have already produced the thought, "If I eliminate the life of these evil sentient beings I will fall into the *nāraka* [hell]. If I do not eliminate them, they will undergo the great suffering of uninterrupted karma. I would rather kill them and fall into the *nāraka* [hell] so that in the end they will not undergo uninterrupted suffering." . . .
>
> Again, if the bodhisattva sees the supreme ruler and officials of the highest rank who violently hate sentient beings and have no kind concerns, and act only oppressively, and the bodhisattva, having seen this, will give rise to a mind of kind concern, and produce a delight in benefiting and comforting those beings, and if he in accord with his powers, removes or expels those of highest rank, he will due to this causation not violate the bodhisattva precepts and will produce much merit.[110]

---

108. Nishi Junzō 西順蔵 and Kondō Kuniyasu 近藤邦康, *Shō Heirin shū* 章炳麟集 (Collected Writings of Zhang Binglin) (Tokyo: Iwanami shoten, 1990), p. 185.

109. Welch, *The Buddhist Revival in China*, p. 16.

110. Maitreya, *Yuqie shidi lun*, CBETA (Chinese Buddhist Electronic Text Association [CBETA] edition), T30n1579_p0517b06-21.

Zhang Taiyan drew upon this text and the Chinese Buddhist "militant" attitude in his call to revolution and to overthrow the Manchu rulers. In an address on July 15, 1907, in Kanda to an estimated seven thousand Chinese students, who saw Zhang as a revolutionary leader,[111] he used this idea as part of the drive for the expulsion of the Manchu government:

> Confucianism and Christianity [as religions] definitely are useless, so ultimately what teaching (*jiao*) can be used? Our China was originally called a Buddhist country, and the reason of Buddhism causes those of highest intelligence to believe in it, and the precepts of Buddhism cause the most stupid people to believe, so it is most useful from top to bottom. But the Buddhism circulating today also has many impurities and is not the same as the original teaching, so we must devise means to reform it so it will be useful. . . . We today need to use the two schools of Huayan and Faxiang to reform the old Dharma. What the Huayan School says is that we must universally liberate sentient beings and donate our heads, eyes, and brains to people, which is most beneficial for morality. What the Faxiang School says is that all dharmas are nothing but mind, that all formed matter has no formed mental objects, all being illusory vision, illusory imagination. . . .
>
> There is a theory that Buddhism looks on all sentient beings as equal and so there is no need to produce volkist (*minzu*) thought and no need to speak of expelling the Manchu and restoring the Chinese. These people in particular do not understand that Buddhism values equality above all, and therefore we must remove such obstacles to equality. The Manchurian government treats our Chinese race unequally, so why shouldn't we expel them? . . .
>
> According to Buddhist preaching, the expulsion of the Manchu and restoration of the Chinese is properly our duty. Moreover, Buddhism hates the power of the ruler. The Mahāyāna monastic regulations all say, "If the king of the country is violent and oppressive, and the bodhisattva has the power, he should remove and expel him." It is also said, "To kill one person and save many people is the action of a bodhisattva." Other sutras and shastras on the two items of king and bandits all show this. Therefore the Buddha was the son of a king, and left home to be a monk. This [action] is in agreement with the stories of restoring the people's rights.[112]

111. Xu Shoushang, "Zhang Binglin," p. 52. Xu was present and recorded the speech.

112. That is, the Buddha rejected the monarchy for which he was destined and adopted a kind of democracy. The Manchu ruler was a monarch, so the implication is clear.

> Therefore the promotion of Buddhism is to raise the moral views of society, which is most important, and also for raising the moral views of our revolutionary army, which is also most important.[113]

Some of the vocabulary Zhang used and quoted is similar to that in the *Yuqie shidi lun* and not like that of the other Buddhist texts that justify violence in the protection of the Dharma or innocents such as one of Zhang's favorite sutras, the rambling *Mahāratnakūṭa-sūtra* (Accumulation of Sutras of Great Treasures).[114] In this way, Zhang linked Yogācāra with revolution, justifying violence to eliminate caste or class discrimination, and with anarchism, which likewise sees rulers as nothing more than bandits. Yet many revolutionaries and Buddhists could not agree with this, even those who used violence. One who disagreed was the Sōtō Zen monk Takeda Hanshi (1863–1911).

In 1893 Takeda was involved with the Genyōsha 玄洋社 (Black Ocean Society), a society of Japanese adventurers in Korea that promoted the cause of a war between China and Japan. Takeda participated in Japanese military actions during the Tonghak Rebellion of 1894. In 1895 he allegedly participated in the bloody assassination of Queen Min, who headed the pro-Chinese party in Korea. Takeda was imprisoned in Hiroshima, and after an amnesty in 1896 he became an abbot, and sometime after 1900 it is said he drafted a declaration of revolution for Sun Yat-sen. In 1901, Takeda joined the nationalist Kokuryūkai 黒龍會 (Black Dragon/Amur River Society) of Uchida Ryōhei 内田良平 (1874–1937), and in 1904 he was appointed the missionary in charge of the propagation of Sōtō Zen in Korea. In 1906, when Itō Hirobumi 伊藤博文 (1840–1909) became the governor-general of Korea, Uchida, a member of Itō's staff, invited Takeda to Korea. There, Takeda met the leader of the pro-Japanese Ilchinhoe 一進會, Yi Yonggu 李容九 (1868–1912), widely regarded in Korea as a traitor. Takeda became Yi Yonggu's advisor.

In 1910 he secretly planned with the head of the main Buddhist organization in Korea, the Korean Buddhist Research Association, and abbot of Haein

---

113. Xu Shoushang, "Zhang Binglin," pp. 49–50.

114. *Upāyakauśalyajñānōttarabodhisattvaparipṛcchā* (*Dasheng fangbian hui* 大乘方便會; Sutra on the Skillful Means of Mahāyāna), translated by Zhu Nanti 竺難提 in 420 (and part of the Ratnakūṭa-sūtra [*Dabaoji jing* 大寶積經; Treasury Sutra], CBETA T11n0310_p0604c07-27), justifies killing one evil person to save 500 bodhisattvas. All these texts are related to the *Nirvana Sutra*. See Kim Hosŏng 金浩星, "*Bagavatdogītā* to *Daijōnehankyō* ni okeru bōryoku, sensō no shōtōka mondai 「バガヴァッド·ギーター」と「大涅槃経」における暴力、戦争の正当化問題," (The Justification of Violence and War in the *Bhagavad-Gītā* and the *Mahāyāna-Nirvāṇa-Sūtra*), *Kankoku Bukkyōgaku Seminar* 韓国仏教学 SEMINAR (Journal of Korean Buddhist Seminar: Korean Students' Association of Indian and Buddhist Studies, Tokyo) 9 (2003): 149–166, esp. p. 151, note 9, citing Fernando Tola and Carmen Dragonetti, "Buddhism and Justification of Violence," *Hokke bunka kenkyū* 27 (2001): 63–100, which lists all the texts.

Monastery, Yi Hoegwang 李晦光 (1862–1933), to make Korean Buddhism, then called Wŏnjong 圓宗, subordinate to Sōtō Zen. A nationalist backlash led by the pro-Imje 臨濟 (J. Rinzai) Sŏn 禪 Buddhists quickly put an end to these nefarious schemes. In 1911, Takeda died in Tokyo.[115]

Takeda Hanshi was one of Zhang Taiyan's drinking companions, and in 1908 he initiated a debate in the press with Zhang. Takeda said that the *Minbao* should be used as a voice of the people and not as a mouthpiece for Buddhism. Zhang replied that Buddhism would raise the morality of the people, but Takeda regarded this as unrealistic, writing that despite Zhang's Buddhist erudition, he was still not enlightened and only used doctrinal explanations, which in Zen terms was totally inadequate. For Zhang, "public equality is all that is needed for government," and this made Buddhism the basis for revolution.[116]

Opening his reply, Zhang wrote that Laozi and Zhuangzi, then Buddhism, tried to correct avariciousness in society, whereas Confucianism was of little benefit to the morality of the people.[117] Buddhism was the only force for real morality, and this is why he used Buddhism in the *Minbao*. Takeda argued that India had been conquered because too many people had become monks and so there was no one to defend the country.[118] Zhang retorted that when China's power was at its height, during the Tang Dynasty, Buddhism also was at its most popular, but when Confucianism was at its height, China was weak. Zhang criticized Japan as a feudal society, and asserted that China was less feudal, with a greater equality of classes, and that should be restored.[119] The argument then shifted to discussion of Buddhism proper, bringing in ideas from the *Dasheng qixin lun* and Yogācāra.

---

115. Summarized from Nagao Ryōshin 中尾良信, "Uchiyama Gudō to Takeda Hanshi 内山愚童と武田範之" (Uchiyama Gudō to Takeda Hanshi), *Hanazono Daigaku Jinken ronshū* 15: *Ko no jiritsu to tasha e no mezashi* 花園大学人権論集 15: 個の自立と他者への目差し (Hanazono University Theses on Human Rights: Individual Independence and Regard for the Other) (Tokyo: Hihyōsha, 2008), pp. 100–108; Sōtōshū jinmei jiten kai 曹洞宗人名辞典会 (comp.), *Sōtōshū jinmei jiten* 曹洞宗人名辞典 (Dictionary of Sōtō Sect People) (Tokyo: Kokusho kankōkai, 1977), p. 235. For a description of the plot to kill Queen Min, see Peter Duus, *The Abacus and the Sword: The Japanese Penetration of Korea, 1895–1910* (Berkeley: University of California Press, 1995), pp. 110–112. Takeda may have been one of the Japanese civilian toughs. On Uchida and the Ilchinhoe, see pp. 202, 217, 232–235. See also Hwansoo Kim, "'The Future of Korean Buddhism Lies in My Hands': Takeda Hanshi as a Sōtō Missionary," *Japanese Journal of Religious Studies* 37, no. 1 (2010): 99–135, who has some doubts as to whether Takeda took part in the assassination of Queen Min.

116. Takata, *Shinkai kakumei to Shō Heirin*, pp. 47–49.

117. Nishi and Kondō, *Shō Heirin shū*, pp. 356–357, "Reply to Bōan."

118. Nishi and Kondō, *Shō Heirin shū*, p. 358.

119. Nishi and Kondō, *Shō Heirin shū*, pp. 362–363.

In the exchange, both refer to Vasubandhu's **Mahāyāna-śatadharmā-prakāśamukha-śāstra* (*Baifamingmen lun* 大乘百法明門論; Lucid Introduction to the One Hundred Dharmas), which lists one hundred dharmas as expanded from the seventy-five dharmas of the *Abhidharma-kośa* (Storehouse of Higher Doctrine).[120] Notably, they introduce Aśvaghoṣa (putative author of *Dasheng qixin lun*) and *ālayavijñāna* (base consciousness), no doubt having in mind *Dasheng qixin lun*, and Zhang referred to Paramārtha's theory of *amalavijñāna* or ninth pure consciousness. This put Zhang squarely in the camp of the mainstream of Japanese (and Chinese) thought concerning *vijñānavāda* that reconciled *tathāgatagarbha* (matrix of the buddhas) thought with *vijñānavāda*, using Paramārtha's work and *Dasheng qixin lun*.

According to Jacqueline Stone, *Dasheng qixin lun* "subsumes the *ālayavijñāna* concept within that of the *tathāgatagarbha* by redefining the former as none other than the pure mind as perceived through unenlightened consciousness."[121] This enabled a relationship to be opened up between the polluted mind and the enlightened mind. In other words, the *Dasheng qixin lun* tries to establish a bridge or avenue for the unenlightened to reach enlightenment. For many Chinese and Japanese Buddhists, the Faxiang/Hossō version of Yogācāra failed to provide such an avenue (for it gives no connection between the *tathāgatagarbha* and the *ālayavijñāna*),[122] and this is why arguments ensued between Taixu and Xiong Shili 熊十力 (1885–1968)—who were clearly sympathetic to a type of *Dasheng qixin lun*-influenced Yogācāra—and Ouyang Jingwu and Lü Cheng 呂澂 (1896–1989), who largely maintained the Xuanzang/Kuiji version of Yogācāra.[123] *Dasheng qixin lun* also explains why the apparently pure can appear to be defiled: it is

---

120. Hirakawa Akira 平川彰, "Jo 序," in *Shin Butten kaidai jiten* 新仏典解題事典 (New Bibliographical Dictionary of Buddhism), ed. Mizuno Kōgen 水野弘元 (Tokyo: Shunjūsha, 1966), p. 19.

121. Jacqueline I. Stone, *Original Enlightenment and the Transformation of Medieval Japanese Buddhism* (Honolulu: University of Hawai'i Press, 1999), p. 6. *Dasheng qixin lun*, CBETA T32.576b7-11:

> Mind as arising and ceasing: In dependence upon the matrix of the buddhas there is mind that arises and ceases. That is to say, the non-arising and non-ceasing are harmoniously integrated with the arising and ceasing; they are neither the same nor different. It is called the base consciousness. This consciousness has two senses . . . What are the two? First, the sense of awakening, and second, the sense of non-awakening. (Translation by John Makeham, John Powers, and Mark Strange.)

122. See Peter N. Gregory, *Tsung-mi and the Sinification of Buddhism* (Honolulu: University of Hawai'i Press, 2002), p. 232, for a more detailed explanation.

123. See the chapters by Eyal Aviv and Chen-kuo Lin in this volume, discussing whether the process of the purification of the defiled mind comes from within or without, especially the March 23, 1943, letter sent by Xiong to Liang Shuming and Lü Cheng, and the subsequent debate translated in Lin's chapter.

merely due to the differences of perspective of the observer, whether enlightened or not. By identifying the *ālayavijñāna* with the *tathāgatagarbha*, an explanation, albeit slightly unsatisfactory, was provided for the origin of evil or ignorance within pristine thusness.[124] Moreover, the *Dasheng qixin lun* account rejected the tendency to predestination found in the Faxiang/Weishi version of Yogācāra with its ideas of inherent natures or seeds which would deny salvation to some beings,[125] something anathema to Zhang Taiyan and most East Asian Buddhists.

It is unclear if Zhang had read any particular Hossō authors or scholars of Yogācāra in Japan, for he had studied on his own in China. There are some clues, such as the reference to Paramārtha's *amalavijñāna* (pure consciousness) and to the *tathāgatagarbha* as understood by Faxiang. Also, Zhang referred to Japanese scholars who compared Aśvaghoṣa's philosophy (probably referring to *Dasheng qixin lun*) to that of Hegel.

Zhang thus preferred the mixture of *tathāgatagarbha* and Yogācāra with Huayan that most Japanese favored, for unlike the Faxiang of Xuanzang and Kuiji, it championed universal enlightenment. Zhang modified this mixture to promote equality and altruistic courage. He used it to encourage morality and to advocate revolution to overthrow a corrupt government. According to Zhang, morality, courage, and revolution depend on self-reliance, which although found in Chan had long been lost in China. What were needed, he asserted, was universal salvation and a philosophy, which Yogācāra promised. This revolution had to begin with self-transformation, which was to be achieved via the *ālayavijñāna* (base consciousness).[126] Orthodox Hossō claimed that there was no universal salvation.

It was this need for philosophy and its application to politics that would have made Zhang ignore the Yogācāra of Japanese monks like Fujaku 普寂 (1707–1781), for Fujaku had rejected *hetuvidyā* logic as a non-Buddhist intrusion into Buddhism that had only been introduced as a temporary expedient to argue against non-Buddhists. According to Fujaku, the Buddha had not used it. Vasubandhu and Dignāga had introduced a complex, alien element into the meditative world of the buddhas and bodhisattvas, an element only applicable in conventional truth.[127] Given that traditional Buddhist scholarship in Japan appeared to Zhang to have no relevance to his mission, he turned to Japanese academics who applied

124. Gregory, *Tsung-mi*, pp. 181–182.

125. Stone, *Original Enlightenment*, p. 15.

126. Analysis by Chen Jidong 陳継東, "Yuishiki no kanōsei (1): Shō Heirin no ba'ai 唯識の可能性(I): 章炳麟の場合 (The Possibilities of *Vijñānavāda* (1): The Case of Zhang Binglin)," *Gendai Mikkyō* 現代密教 14 (2001): 155–164.

127. Nishimura Ryō 西村玲, "Kachi to fukachi no airo: Kinsei Fujaku no Hossō-hihan 可知と不可知の隘路: 近世普寂の法相批判" (The Impasse of Knowable and Unknowable: The Critique of Hossō by Fujaku of the Tokugawa Period), *Nanto Bukkyō* 南都仏教 82 (2002): 141–144.

Western philosophy to the Buddhism of the Paramārtha version of Yogācāra that accommodated *tathāgatagarbha* and the promise of an equal, universal salvation.

2.2 Impersonal Networks

2.2.1 *Yogācāra, Science, and Philosophy*

Modern Chinese and Japanese scholars of Yogācāra may be differentiated on the basis of their aims and methods. One group sought to preserve traditional Buddhism against the state and Christianity, with the aid of modern publication and scholarship. This group chiefly adhered to the Xuanzang line. In China this includes figures such as Yang Wenhui, Ouyang Jingwu, Lü Cheng, Han Shanqing, and Zhou Shujia 周叔迦 (1899–1970); and in Japan it includes Saeki Gyokuga, Saeki Jōin, Kirara Kōyō, and others, with the less orthodox coming out of the Jōdo shinshū camp, including Nanjō. On the other hand, there were groups that wanted to make Buddhism scientific and relevant to political concerns and to the issues of modern philosophy. In China this group included Tan Sitong, Zhang Taiyan, Xiong Shili, Taixu, and possibly Su Manshu and Liang Shuming; and in Japan, Hara Tanzan, Nishida Kitarō 西田幾多郎 (1870–1945), and Senō Giro 妹尾義郎 (1889–1961).[128]

As Zhang wrote in 1907 to the "anarchist" Lei Shaoxing in *Minbao*:

> If you ask why I esteem only Faxiang [and not Chan, which had unfortunately stopped studying the *Laṅkāvatāra-sūtra* (*Lengqie jing* 楞伽經; Sutra on [the Buddha's] Entering [the Country of] Lanka)], I have another theory. That is, modern scholarship has gradually taken the road of seeking truth through facts, and evidential (*kaozheng*) scholars have analyzed the principles of things. This (analysis) is far beyond what the Ming Confucians could do. The (evidential scholars) almost understood the bases of science, and their use of the mind was further refined. It is for this reason that the study of Faxiang was not suited to the Ming period, but is most suited to the modern age.[129]

---

128. An attempt at such a classification of Buddhists has been made by Ko Yŏngsŏp 고영섭, "Han, Chung, Il samguk ŭi kŭndae Pulgyohak yŏn'gu pangbŏpnon 한.중.일 삼국의 근대불교학 연구방법론 " (Examination of the Methodology of Modern Buddhist Studies in Korea, China and Japan), *Pulgyo hakbo* 51 (February 2009): 170–173. I have modified his list, and of course, not all of these scholars specialized in Yogācāra.

129. Nishi and Kondō, *Shō Heirin shū*, p. 254; cited also in Kim Cheran 김제란, "Tong Sŏhak ŭi maegaerosŏ ŭi yusikhak ŭi yuhaeng 동.서학의 매개로서 唯識學의 유행" (The Prevalence of the Nothing but Consciousness School as the Intermediation of Eastern and Western Cultures: On the Relationship of the Nothing but Consciousness School and the Philosophy of Bergson), *Pulgyo hakbo* 47 (August 2007): 231. Square brackets indicate Zhang's auto-commentary. For similar passages by Zhang and Gui Bohua, see John Makeham, "Zhang Taiyan, Yogācāra Buddhism and Chinese Philosophy" in *Learning to Emulate the Wise: The Genesis of Chinese Philosophy as an Academic Discipline in Twentieth-Century China*, ed. John Makeham (Hong Kong: Chinese University Press, 2012), p. 105.

Zhang then proceeds to criticize Chan and Tiantai Buddhism for their shortcomings. Similarly, Zhang said to Gui Bohua 桂伯華 (1861–1915), a loyal pupil of Yang Wenhui: "In the present age scientific reason grows clearer by the day. I fear Huayan and Tiantai will have nobody paying attention to them, so if it is not Faxiang then nobody [in the Buddhist world] will lead them." He also said, "Han Studies are a precursor to science. Science in turn is a precursor to Faxiang."[130]

Zhang and others saw Yogācāra as akin to science because it seemed logical, systematic, and analytic. It possessed a methodology in *hetuvidyā* (Buddhist logic) that enabled the testing and refutation of rival theories such as those of Sāṁkhya and Vaiśeṣika, as well as an epistemology and "psychology."[131] This led them back to Indian philosophy, on the one hand, and to the application of modern Western philosophy to Yogācāra, on the other. This interest in Indian philosophy and the application of Western philosophy was greatly stimulated by developments in Japan.

Possibly the first person to use the term "Indo tetsugaku 印度哲學" (Indian philosophy) and to equate that with Buddhism was Hara Tanzan (1919–1892), presumably in 1879 when he gave lectures at Tokyo University on *Dasheng qixin lun* following the commentary of the Huayan scholar-monk Fazang 法藏 (643–712). He also brought his interest in Western medicine, in particular studies of the nervous system, into play. Hara quoted with approval the opinion of Henry Steel Olcott (1832–1907) that the word "religion" was not applicable to Buddhism, which was rather a moral philosophy. Hara said it is appropriate to call it a philosophy of mind nature, and best to call it an Indian philosophy.[132] This statement by Hara is dated 1887 in a published document.[133] But in a lecture on March 22, 1884, Hara had already stated: "Indian philosophy (that is, Buddhism) is roughly divided into teaching, principle, practice and result."[134]

130. Zhang Taiyan, "Taiyan xiansheng zishu xueshu cidi 太炎先生自述學術次第" (The Scholarship of Mr. Taiyan as Described by Him in Sequence), in *Zhang Binglin quanji huibian*, comp. Cuncui xueshe (Hong Kong: Datong tushu gongsi, 1978), p. 256.

131. Kim Cheran, "Tong Sŏhak ŭi maegaerosŏ ŭi yusikhak ŭi yuhaeng," pp. 231–232.

132. Miyamoto, *Meiji Bukkyō no shichō*, pp. 150–153. For Olcott's views and this theme, see David L. McMahan, "Modernity and the Early Discourse of Scientific Buddhism," *Journal of the American Academy of Religion* 72, no. 4 (December 2004): 909–911, dating Olcott's statement to 1881. Olcott had trained in mesmerism.

133. Quoting Nakamura Hajime in Satō Tetsurō 左藤哲朗, *Dai-Ajia shisō katsugeki: Bukkyō ga musunda mō hitotsu no kindaishi* 大アジア思想活劇：仏教が結んだもうひとつの近代史 (The Tumultuous Thought of a Greater Asia: Another Modern History Formed by Buddhism) (Tokyo: Sanga, 2008), p. 36.

134. Hara Tanzan, *Tanzan Ōsho zenshū* 坦山和尚全集 (Collected Works of Reverend Tanzan) (Tokyo: Kōyūkan, 1909), p. 29.

In the same article in which Hara quoted Olcott, he wrote:

> There are various names for mind (意), but in Japan there is only the word *kokoro* 心. However, in India there are the preceding five *vijñānas* (eye . . .), the sixth *manovijñāna* (mental consciousness), the seventh *manas* (mind), and the eighth *ālayavijñāna* (base consciousness) . . . and in Western psychology there are the three abilities of intellect, feeling, and intention.[135]

In 1870 he wrote about a linkage between a Yogācāran, or rather *Dasheng qixin lun*, analysis of the *vijñānas* (consciousnesses) and Western theories of anatomy and the nervous system, claiming that Buddhism had made a great discovery. According to him, of the three kinds of mind-consciousness:

> One is the true mind of numinous awareness and pure wisdom; second is the mental substance of collection and grasping [in Sanskrit it is called *ādāna* (appropriating consciousness) . . . what Western medicine calls vitality/life force]; and third is the emotional consciousness of thought and cogitation [this is the mind's volitional consciousness, entirely the false mind of the *kleśa-vijñāna* (afflicted consciousness)]. . . . In looking at the books of doctors . . . [the old Chinese medicinal theories are often grossly wrong; here I am referring to Westerners' investigations of mind and body] there is one great error, which is that they take the brain to be the source of the conscious spirit.

Hara then identifies the brain as the source of the true mind, and the spine marrow as the substance of the mind of collection and grasping that has no conscious knowledge. He suggests that the spine marrow flows into the brain and is compounded (和合), which in Buddhism is called the compounded consciousness, in other words, the *ālayavijñāna* (base consciousness) of *Dasheng qixin lun*.[136] Hara attempted to prove his theories by way of what he termed practical evidence, and although his theories were never adopted, they did have the effect of linking the *Dasheng qixin lun* version of Yogācāra, medical science, and Indian philosophy.

2.2.2 Indian Studies: Sāṁkhya, Vaiśeṣika, and hetuvidyā

Sāṁkhya, Vaiśeṣika, and Buddhist logic were significant in Yogācāra because doctrinally, Sāṁkhya and Vaiśeṣika were philosophical rivals to Yogācāra, and Buddhist

135. Hara, *Tanzan Ōsho zenshū*, pp. 55–56.

136. Hara, *Tanzan Ōsho zenshū*, p. 99, "Nōseki itairon 腦脊異體論" (On the Differences between Brain and Spine)," translation tentative.

logic was an indispensable element in the logical refutation of these and other doctrines. Therefore, in the Meiji period, a number of studies were published on the Sāṁkhya text **Suvarṇasaptati* (On the Golden Seventy Verses), such as Ōuchi Seiran's 大内青巒 (1845–1918) *Kinshichijūron bikō ebon* 金七十論備考會本 (Text Assembling Detailed Investigations of the Golden Seventy Verses). Commentaries on the Vaiśeṣika *Daśapadārtha-śāstra* (Treatise on the Ten Metaphysical Categories) were published in 1890 and 1896, as well as lectures given on it at the Tetsugakukan. Inoue Enryō also compiled much material on Sāṁkhya and Vaiśeṣika, especially from Yogācāra sources and from the Tokugawa period commentaries on **Suvarṇasaptati* and *Daśapadārtha-śāstra*.[137]

Zhang Taiyan was also aware that these two texts existed in the Buddhist canon, and having obtained Sanskrit copies of these texts he compared them with the Chinese translations. Interestingly, at this time he turned his attention to *Zhuangzi*.[138] Zhang's interest probably resided in countering materialism and the notion of an eternal soul and its connection with ignorance, as well as learning more about India. Perhaps Zhang foresaw the problem of the *tathāgatagarbha* (matrix of buddhas) or *ālayavijñāna* (base consciousness) and its possible confusion with the *ātman* of Sāṁkhya, an accusation leveled against the *tathāgatagarbha* of *Dasheng qixin lun* by Ouyang Jingwu and Lü Cheng, the champions of Faxiang in China.[139]

Moreover, there was a belief at the time that Buddhism was based on Sāṁkhya, a view proposed by Richard Garbe in 1892 and Hermann Jacobi in 1896 and 1898, especially in connection with causation, with the movement from ignorance through the twelve-fold chain of causation, often called in Chinese *liuzhuan* 流轉, the word Zhang mentioned in connection with the Lokāyata (an Indian system of materialism that allowed no soul).[140] Paramārtha probably translated the *Sāṁkhya-kārikā* (Verses on Sāṁkhya) into Chinese as a means to counter such allegations that he was asserting the existence of an underlying soul because of his linkage of *tathāgatagarbha* and *ālayavijñāna*. Zhang and others also had to take Sāṁkhya and Vaiśeṣika into account because the Yogācāra and Faxiang texts argued against these rival Indian philosophies so strongly.

137. Inoue Enryō 井上円了, *Gedō tetsugaku* 外道哲學 (Philosophies of the Non-Buddhists of India) (Tokyo: Tetsugakukan, 1897), pp. 205, 491–550.

138. Takata, *Shinkai kakumei to Shō Heirin*, pp. 23–24.

139. Jiang Canteng, *Zhongguo jindai Fojiao sixiang de zhengbian yu fazhan*, chapters 13–15, pp. 543–618. In this volume, see Eyal Aviv's chapter on Ouyang Jingwu for Ouyang's changing views on *tathāgatagarbha* and Dan Lusthaus's chapter on Lü Cheng for his claims that *tathāgatagarbha* was not genuine Buddhism.

140. Cf. Murakami Shinkan 村上真完, "Sānkuyaha no sekaikan to Bukkyō サーンクヤ派の世界観と仏教 (The World View of Sāmkhya and Buddhism)," *Risō* 642 (Spring 1989): 14–15.

The issue of logic or *hetuvidyā* likewise became important in Buddhism for internal debates and for use in countering the rivals of Yogācāra, although Madhyamaka (School of the Middle Way) also used it to refute Vaiśeṣika and Sāṁkhya. Yet in China interest in Buddhist logic largely died out, whereas in Japan it was pursued by Hossō scholars, albeit with many errors. Buddhist logic was of great concern to Meiji-period Japanese. As we have noted, Kirara Kōyō (1824–1910) in particular introduced comparisons with Western logic in 1884. His work was followed up by Murakami Senshō (1851–1929), who lectured on Kuiji's *Yinming ru zhengli lun shu* (Commentary on the *Entryway into Logic*) and on **Suvarṇasaptati*. Many others also wrote on *hetuvidyā*. In turn, this scholarship on logic became an object of interest for Chinese Yogācāra scholars such as Song Shu and Zhang Taiyan.

Elements of logic are found among the early Indian systems of philosophy, not just the Vaiśeṣika but also Mīmāṃsā and Lokāyata.[141] Because refutation of these non-Buddhist theories was so important, we find many works on logic by conservative Hossō scholars and by Jōdo shinshū scholars[142] who had made the first moves to modernization. Because *shōsō* 性相 studies (that is, the combination of Yogācāra, *Dasheng qixin lun*, Huayan texts, and *Abhidharma-kośa* texts) were considered the basics for the study of Buddhist doctrine in Tokugawa Japan, many monks turned their hand to Buddhist logic.[143]

It was only when Kirara and Murakami began to compare this tradition of *hetuvidyā* (Buddhist logic) with Western formal logic that any major changes in themes or methodology took place.[144] Perhaps the first clues to this were introduced by Nanjō Bun'yū, who in an 1887 lecture gave a brief and vague account of the origins of Buddhist logic, but then claimed there were two systems of logic[145]: one derived from Gautama (Buddha) and one derived from Kaṇāda, author of the *Vaiśeṣika-sūtra*. He compared the metaphysical logic of the former with Aristotelian logic, noting that the latter was the basis of Western science.[146] In 1891, Murakami stressed that logic was an operation of thought that sought to find the truth and to determine which of a number of propositions was true by the proper

141. Takemura Shōhō 武邑尚邦, *Inmyōgaku: Kigen to hensen* 因明學: 起源と變遷 (Buddhist Logic Studies: Origins and Vicissitudes) (Kyoto: Hōzōkan, 1986), p. 7ff.

142. List in Takemura, *Inmyōgaku*, p. 346.

143. Takemura, *Inmyōgaku*, p. 165.

144. Takemura, *Inmyōgaku*, p. 213.

145. Nanjō based himself on *The History of India* by Mountstuart Elphinstone (1779–1859).

146. Takashi Dairyō 高志大了 and Nanjō Bun'yū 南條文雄, *Inmyō dai'i* 因明大意 (Essentials of Buddhist Logic) (Kyoto: Hōzōkan, 1887), pp. 11–14; the entire text is only 16 pp.

use of language.[147] He discussed the relationship of language and thought, introduced Western logic, and compared Western logic with the *hetuvidyā* of Vasubandhu and Dignāga at some length. Murakami also addressed the issue of whether *hetuvidyā* is Buddhist or non-Buddhist,[148] concluding that just as Western sciences are related to logic, so too Buddhism is related to *hetuvidyā*.[149]

In countering the notion that people must have a nation or government, in his anarchist mode Zhang Taiyan referred to Buddhist logic in relation to self-contradiction and improper reasoning. In his notes to this he mentions the three elements of inference or syllogism; proposition, reason, and example. He used this to demonstrate why certain propositions about nationalism and nation were problematic.[150] Zhang was probably also told about Buddhist logic by Song Shu, who had purchased Murakami's *Inmyōgaku zensho* (Complete Works on Logic Studies).[151] We thus see Zhang applying Buddhist logic to his interpretation of *Zhuangzi*,[152] for he had read the *Yinming ru zhengli lun* (*Entryway into Logic*; the *Nyāyapraveśa* by Śaṅkarasvāmin) while he was in prison, which had been brought by a friend (Song Shu?).[153]

Conclusion

Zhang Taiyan and many members of his network were influenced by developments in Japan. This influence went beyond politics and technology, and extended into the complex realms of Yogācāra thought. Initially, Yang Wenhui's publication enterprise provided vital resources for Yogācāra studies by printing long-lost Yogācāra texts that had been preserved in Japan and sent to Yang by Nanjō Bun'yū and his colleagues. Many of these books were purchased by Sun Baoxuan, who lent them to members of the "seven sages of Shanghai" circle and to others. Xia Zengyou, a disciple of Yang, had introduced Sun and Song Shu to Yogācāra. He also encouraged Zhang to study Buddhism, and Song followed this up by offering Zhang Yogācāra texts to study while he was imprisoned in Shanghai between 1903 and 1906.

---

147. Murakami Senshō 村上専精, *Inmyōgaku zensho* 因明學全書 (Complete Works of Buddhist Logic Studies) (Tokyo: Tetsugaku shoin, 1891), p. 3.

148. Murakami Senshō, *Inmyōgaku zensho*, p. 41ff.

149. Murakami Senshō, *Inmyōgaku zensho*, pp. 44–45.

150. Zhang Taiyan,"Wu wu lun," in Nishi and Kondō, *Shō Heirin shū*, pp. 269–270.

151. Hu Zhusheng, *Song Shu ji*, p. 359.

152. Kobayashi, *Shō Heirin to Meiji shichō*, p. 126.

153. Takata, *Shinkai kakumei to Shō Heirin*, p. 43.

Song and Zhang, like Liang Qichao before them, went to Japan, where they learned more about Yogācāra from leading champions of Japan's New Buddhism, who introduced Western scholarly methodology in an attempt to transform Buddhism from a religion of faith into a logical philosophy compatible with science. Therefore, much attention was directed at Buddhist logic. The Chinese fascination with Yogācāra was driven in part by this Japanese experience of the modernization of Buddhism and the role Hossō or Yogācāra had to play in it. Some Chinese further saw Buddhism, especially Yogācāra, as an aid to revolution. Zhang Taiyan was in the vortex of these complex developments, reflecting the many philosophies, ideas, and political theories that appeared around him like a jewel in Indra's net.

PART 2

Early Appropriations

3

Tan Sitong's "Great Unity": Mental Processes and Yogācāra in An Exposition of Benevolence

Scott Pacey

TAN SITONG 譚嗣同 (1865–1898) wrote his magnum opus—*Renxue* 仁學 (An Exposition of Benevolence; hereafter, EOB)—in 1896 and 1897.[1] It was published posthumously both in Yokohama in *Qing yi bao* 清議報 (China Discussion) between 1898 and 1901, as well as in Shanghai in the *Yadong shibao* 亞東時報 (East Asia Times).[2] The work represents Tan's attempt to bring together the prominent ideas on the late-Qing intellectual landscape under the rubric of Confucian *ren* 仁 (benevolence). Although the plurality of influences at work in EOB has been widely acknowledged, the presence of Yogācāra concepts in the book has been less extensively researched.[3] This chapter will examine two ways in which Yogācāra contributed to the scheme Tan advanced in EOB. First, it will demonstrate that Yogācāra's cognitive architecture played an important role in his philosophical

I gratefully acknowledge the support I received from the Australian Friends of the Hebrew University and the Louis Frieberg Center for East Asian Studies, when I was a Golda Meir Postdoctoral Fellow at the Hebrew University of Jerusalem in 2011–2013.

1. Tan Sitong, "Renxue," in *Tan Sitong quanji* 譚嗣同全集 (The Complete Works of Tan Sitong) [TSQ], ed. Cai Shangsi 蔡尚思 (Beijing: Zhonghua shuju, 1981), vol. 2, pp. 289–374. The English translations in this chapter are taken from T'an Ssu-t'ung [Tan Sitong], *An Exposition of Benevolence: The Jen-hsuëh of T'an Ssu-t'ung*, translated by Chan Sin-wai (Hong Kong: The Chinese University Press, 1984). In the following references, Chan's translation will be indicated by "EOB," and Tan's original (in his collected works) by "TSQ."

2. These two versions are different; the latter was included in his collected works. See Chan Sin-wai, "Introduction to 'An Exposition of Benevolence,'" in *An Exposition of Benevolence*, pp. 13–14.

3. Erik Hammerstrom provides a focused assessment of Tan's discussion of Yogācāra, science, and New Thought in his "Buddhists Discuss Science in Modern China (1895–1949)," PhD diss., Indiana University, 2010, pp. 107–121.

system alongside other theories of mind drawn from Neo-Confucianism, science, and the Christian-based New Thought movement. Second, it will show that along with these other views, Yogācāra was central to Tan's utopian social project. As such, Yogācāra helped enable Tan to achieve two aims of late-Qing modernizers: delineating the relationship between Chinese and Western ideas, and showing how they could be applied in ways that contributed to Chinese reform efforts.

The eclectic nature of the text is reflected in the brief reading list Tan provided at the beginning of EOB. In addition to Neo-Confucian scholars and Buddhist texts, he includes such diverse entries as the writer Tao Yuanming 陶淵明 (365–427)—who penned China's quintessential literary depiction of the ideal society, "Taohua yuanji 桃花源記" (Peach Blossom Spring)—and the New Testament. He also recommends reading scientific works.[4] Although his engagement with such a complex array of influences may appear unwieldy, he was conversant with many of the cutting-edge ideas of his time. Liang Qichao 梁啟超 (1873–1929) said of EOB that "while it is undeniable that it contains many inconsistent, disorderly, and childish arguments, still it broke so entirely free and independent of the fetters of the traditional thinking that it had no equal throughout the Ch'ing period."[5] It is this novel incorporation of diverse modern and traditional ideas that has established the book's importance in Chinese intellectual history.

It is also because of Tan's pioneering use of Yogācāra in this intellectual synthesis that EOB is significant. Moreover, although later thinkers such as Taixu 太虛 (1890–1947) and members of the Wuchang School[6] sought to demonstrate Yogācāra's superiority over science rather than focusing on their similarities, as Tan tended to do, by dealing with science and Yogācāra in the same context, Tan helped lay the foundations for Taixu's and the Wuchang School's general intellectual projects.

Tan's reading list also provides an indication of his Buddhist orientation. He mentions the foundational text of the Huayan School (Huayan zong 華嚴宗)—the *Avataṃsaka-sūtra* (*Huayan jing* 華嚴經; Flower Ornament Sutra),[7] the Chan School (School of Mind; Xin zong 心宗), and the Faxiang School (Dharma Characteristics School; Faxiang zong 法相宗) as bearing upon the topic of

4. T'an, EOB, p. 65; Tan, TSQ, p. 293.

5. Liang Ch'i-ch'ao, *Intellectual Trends in the Ch'ing Period*, trans. Immanuel C. Y. Hsü (Cambridge, MA: Harvard University Press, 1959), p. 108.

6. On the Wuchang School, see Hammerstrom's chapter in this volume.

7. The Huayan School, which traditionally considers Dushun 杜順 (557–640) its founding patriarch, emphasizes the interconnectivity of the phenomenal world. *Huayan jing* illustrates this using the image of a net with jewels (representing phenomena) in each knot. Each jewel is linked with the others through the strands of the net; each individual jewel also reflects all of the other stones. (For the Indra's net metaphor, see John Jorgensen's chapter.) The text, and the school, describes how phenomena are characterized by both unity and individuality.

benevolence.[8] It is only later in EOB that he specifically mentions *Cheng weishi lun* 成唯識論 (Demonstration of Nothing but Consciousness) and the *Dasheng qixin lun* 大乘起信論 (Awakening of Mahāyāna Faith)—works of central importance in this volume.[9] Tan's advocation of the *Huayan jing*, however, and his later reference to *Cheng weishi lun* (both of which form part of the Faxiang textual corpus as established by Kuiji 窺基 [632–682]), indicate his partiality to Yogācāra. For many intellectuals, *Dasheng qixin lun* was a Yogācāra text as well. As we shall see, for Tan, the basic ideas he found in Yogācāra resonated with the other accounts of mental functioning that he encountered in the late Qing intellectual context.

Intellectual background: utopia and the primacy of the mind

EOB is a complex work, and before examining it in detail, it is prudent first to consider the diverse intellectual influences on Tan and how they come together in the book. Tan wrote EOB soon after a time in which the notion of benevolence itself had undergone analysis and scrutiny. After the classical scholar Yan Ruoqu 閻若璩 (1636–1704) challenged the traditional attribution of the *Shang shu* 尚書 (Classic of History) and the *Daxue* 大學 (Great Learning), other evidential scholars such as Dai Zhen 戴震 (1724–1777), Jiao Xun 焦循 (1763–1820), and Ruan Yuan 阮元 (1764–1849) began to reexamine classical texts. Dai saw in Neo-Confucian Zhu Xi's 朱熹 (1130–1200) reading of benevolence—which he characterized as amounting to the overcoming of desire—the creation of an incorrect dualism between principle and desire.[10] Ruan built on earlier philological analyses of the character for benevolence ("person," or *ren* 人 and "two," or *er* 二)

8. T'an, EOB, p. 64; Tan, TSQ, p. 293. Practitioners of Chan—or in Japanese, Zen—engage in meditation as a path to insight. The term *faxiang*—or "dharma characteristics"—was originally used by Huayan exegetes to denote what they saw as Yogācāra exponents' excessive attention to the external features of phenomena rather than their more fundamental, internal qualities. Despite this, it eventually became an accepted name for Yogācāra. See A. Charles Muller, "Translator's Introduction," in Shun'ei Tagawa, *Living Yogācāra: An Introduction to Consciousness-Only Buddhism*, trans. A. Charles Muller (Boston, MA: Wisdom Publications, 2009), p. xxi.

9. *Cheng weishi lun* is Xuanzang's 玄奘 (602–664) account of Yogācāra teachings. Tradition accepts that the work is mostly based on Dharmapāla's 護法 (sixth century) commentary on Vasubandhu's 世親 (fourth century) *Triṃśikā* (*Weishi sanshi lun song* 唯識三十論頌; Thirty Verses). The *tathāgatagarbha*, or matrix of buddhas, doctrine propounded in *Dasheng qixin lun* exerted a profound influence on East Asian Buddhism.

10. Benjamin A. Elman, "The Revaluation of Benevolence (*Jen*) in Ch'ing Dynasty Evidential Research," in *Cosmology, Ontology and Human Efficacy: Essays in Chinese Thought*, ed. Richard J. Smith and D. W. Y. Kwok (Honolulu: University of Hawaii Press, 1993), p. 63; Justin Tiwald, "Dai Zhen on Human Nature and Moral Cultivation," in *Dao Companion to Neo-Confucian Philosophy*, ed. John Makeham (New York: Springer, 2010), pp. 399–422.

to claim that it "was the fulfilment of human desires, not their denial."[11] Jiao, in turn, had emphasized the social importance of benevolence and desire, and explained that the sages had devised rituals on this basis.[12]

Tan followed on from these reassessments to regard benevolence through a multifaceted lens, although he deviated from Neo-Confucian understandings of the term. This can partly be ascribed to the intellectual climate in which his career unfolded, when the inherited Confucian tradition was seen as incapable of providing an impetus for progress like science and Christianity. Some, however, sought to locate a progressive dynamic within the Neo-Confucian corpus of texts. The historian of late imperial China, Joseph Levenson, shows these efforts to be epitomized in the writings of the reformer and scholar Kang Youwei 康有為 (1858–1927), who in *Xinxue weijing kao* 新學偽經考 (On the False Classics of Xin-Period Learning; 1891), *Kongzi gaizhi kao* 孔子改制考 (On Confucius as a Reformer; 1897), and the *Datong shu* 大同書 (Book on the Great Unity),[13] presented Confucianism as aligned with the modern ideal of progress.[14] Kang explained that society would move through the stages of "disorder" and "approaching peace" to the Great Unity.[15] In *Datong shu* he wrote: "Confucius's Era of Complete Peace and Equality, the Buddha's Lotus World, Lieh Tzu's Mount Tan P'ing, [and] Darwin's Utopia, are realities [of the future], and not empty imaginings."[16] The Great Unity was within reach; moreover, it was sufficiently similar to the utopian ideals of other systems to be mentioned alongside them. Tan also exemplified this eclectic approach.

Datong shu was published after EOB,[17] but Tan did not meet Kang until 1898, although he had earlier read his *Xinxue weijing kao*.[18] Nevertheless, both Kang

---

11. Elman, "The Revaluation of Benevolence," p. 67.

12. Elman, "The Revaluation of Benevolence," pp. 73–74.

13. This was a work in progress when Tan was writing EOB; the first two parts were published in 1913, and it was published in its entirety in 1935, after Kang's death. Although Tan learned of Kang's ideas from his students, it is apparent that he arrived at the ideas in EOB independently. See Luke S. K. Kwong, *T'an Ssu-T'ung, 1865–1898: Life and Thought of a Reformer* (Leiden: E. J. Brill, 1996), pp. 166–168.

14. Joseph Levenson, *Confucian China and Its Modern Fate: A Trilogy* (Berkeley and Los Angeles: University of California Press, 1968), vol. 1, p. 81.

15. Wolfgang Bauer, *China and the Search for Happiness: Recurring Themes in Four Thousand Years of Chinese Cultural History*, trans. Michael Shaw (New York: The Seabury Press, 1976), p. 302.

16. K'ang Yu-wei, *Ta T'ung Shu: The One World Philosophy of K'ang Yu-wei*, trans. Laurence G. Thompson (London: George Allen & Unwin, 1958), p. 84.

17. Liang Qichao initially stated that Tan intended his book to be an elaboration of Kang's ideas, but later dropped this claim. See Kwong, *T'an Ssu-T'ung*, pp. 165–168.

18. Ibid., pp. 125–126.

and Tan operated within a common intellectual milieu—one in which Confucianism's compatibility with modernity was being articulated. In EOB, Tan therefore claimed that in the Age of Universal Peace, "with repentance, everybody can acquire the moral character of the religious founder, and can then do without the religious founder, and everybody can acquire the power of the ruler, and can then do without the ruler. At such a time, everyone can enjoy democracy everywhere."[19]

His belief in Confucianism's progressive nature can also be attributed to his educational background. Tan was taught by three of Hunan's top Neo-Confucian scholars: Ouyang Zhonggu 歐陽中鵠 (1849–1911), Liu Renxi 劉人熙 (1844–1919), and Tu Qixian 涂啟先 (1834–1900).[20] All were exponents of the Neo-Confucian thought of Wang Fuzhi 王夫之 (1619–1692), and in 1889, Tan proclaimed himself Wang's disciple.[21] His own understanding of benevolence in turn bears the intellectual imprint of Wang through his teachers Ouyang, Liu, and Tu. According to Stephen Platt, Tan was particularly interested in Wang's *Siwen lu* 思問錄 (Record of Thoughts and Questions), in which Wang stressed that the "Way" needed a vessel in the world to take shape.[22] Tan learned from Wang that to understand the Way, one must study the phenomenal world—a belief that found a natural corollary when he encountered science in the 1890s.[23]

Tan also developed Wang's views on the Way and vital stuff—or *qi* 氣— into "a hypothesis covering all of human society, namely, that society itself could be considered an instrument. . . . According to Tan's reading of Wang Fuzhi, then, to possess the latent Way, and thereby enjoy peace and prosperity, society must first be changed."[24] China's defeat in the Sino-Japanese War (1894–95) convinced him that China was in need of reform;[25] in an 1895 letter to his friend Bei Yunxin 貝允昕 (1865–1927), he advocated broad-scale Westernization, and supported his view with the thought of Wang Fuzhi, stating that since there was a unity between the Way and *qi*, "when *ch'i* changed, the Way should change accordingly. . . . To adopt Westernization in China was in fact to practise universal truth."[26] Tan's

19. T'an, EOB, p. 220; Tan, TSQ, p. 370.

20. Stephen R. Platt, *Provincial Patriots: The Hunanese and Modern China* (Cambridge, MA: Harvard University Press, 2007), pp. 68–69.

21. Chan Sin-wai, *Buddhism in Late Ch'ing Political Thought* (Hong Kong: The Chinese University Press, 1985), p. 59.

22. Platt, *Provincial Patriots*, p. 73.

23. Ibid., pp. 73–74.

24. Ibid., p. 73.

25. Chan, "Introduction to 'An Exposition of Benevolence,' " p. 7.

26. Chan, *Buddhism in Late Ch'ing Political Thought*, p. 64.

progressive and reformist views thus had a Neo-Confucian foundation through Wang. As we shall see below, these were bolstered with ideas from Yogācāra, lending his utopian vision a Buddhist aspect as well.

Tan would have found in Neo-Confucianism certain correlations with the Yogācāra he would encounter in the mid-1890s. In EOB, although Tan listed Wang as one of the thinkers students of benevolence should read, he did so alongside a number of other Neo-Confucians who delineated relationships between the mind, the phenomenal world, and morality. Zhou Dunyi 周敦頤 (1017–1073) attributed a moral aspect to Heaven and to the Supreme Ultimate (*taiji* 太極)—"the source of all things in the universe"[27]—including benevolence and righteousness (*yi* 義).[28] Zhang Zai 張載 (1020–1077) developed a form of monism in which *qi*, as the basic substance of the universe, had inherent moral qualities.[29] For Lu Jiuyuan 陸九淵 (1139–1193) "the universe and the mind are one."[30] Wang Yangming 王陽明 (1472–1529) held that "the mind or *xin* [心] and the Principle or *li* [理] are identical."[31] Finally, for Huang Zongxi 黃宗羲 (1610–1695), mind was "fundamentally indeterminate substance," or *qi*, "and derivatively reason."[32] The Neo-Confucian figures Tan listed thus held that the basic constituent of the universe had a moral aspect, and that this was intimately linked with mind. There are parallels between this view and Tan's later equation of benevolence with the scientific concept of ether, the origin of which he traced back to Yogācāra's cognitive architecture.

Chan Sin-wai has noted that when intellectuals looked for ways to bolster Confucianism in response to Christianity and science, they "did not simply lament the fact that Confucianism was no longer practicable, but sought alternatives for the bolstering of the Chinese tradition."[33] As John Makeham notes in the Introduction, while some intellectuals (Ouyang Jingwu and Lü Cheng) searched for an "original Indian Buddhism," others understood Buddhism in its received, Sinitic form. For them, Buddhism was a Chinese system of thought that was

---

27. Siu-chi Huang, *Essentials of Neo-Confucianism: Eight Major Philosophers of the Song and Ming Periods* (Westport, CT: Greenwood Press, 1999), p. 32.

28. Ibid., p. 26.

29. Hao Chang, *Chinese Intellectuals in Crisis* (Berkeley: University of California Press, 1987), p. 81. In the early 1890s, Tan studied Zhang's works. See Chan, *Buddhism in Late Ch'ing Political Thought*, pp. 60–61.

30. Huang, *Essentials of Neo-Confucianism*, p. 173.

31. Ibid., p. 194.

32. Chung-Ying Cheng, "Reason, Substance, and Human Desires in Seventeenth-Century Neo-Confucianism," in *The Unfolding of Neo-Confucianism*, ed. William Theodore de Bary (New York: Columbia University Press, 1975), p. 497.

33. Chan, *Buddhism in Late Ch'ing Political Thought*, p. 3.

deemed compatible with science and superior to Western philosophy.[34] Certain members of Tan's generation were thus strongly influenced by Buddhism. Kang esteemed Buddhism highly in his treatment of the Great Unity,[35] and prior to 1911, Liang Qichao argued that Buddhism could "be utilized to cultivate morality for the cause of revolution, to serve as a unifying ideology and as a philosophy which could be paralleled with Western philosophy."[36] And as Viren Murthy has written in this volume, Zhang Taiyan 章太炎 (1868–1936) used Madhyamaka and Yogācāra—and Daoist—concepts to articulate a new, revolutionary social vision in his response to global modernity.

As part of this environment in the mid-1890s, Tan delved into the study of Buddhism and—reflecting his interest in Westernization—science. In 1896 he met Liang Qichao in Beijing,[37] and he subsequently discussed both topics with him and his associates in Shanghai.[38] It was during this time that he also met the layman, Yang Wenhui 楊文會 (1837–1911).[39] Yang had established the Jinling Sutra Press (Jinling Kejingchu 金陵刻經處) in 1866 in Nanjing, and, like Tan, maintained an interest in both Buddhism and science. After working in the Qing embassy in London between 1878 and 1881 (and again between 1886 and 1888), he brought a range of scientific instruments back to China.[40] As John Jorgensen relates in his chapter in this volume, from 1891 Yang also procured a range of Buddhist texts from Japan.[41] It was after Tan's extended discussions with Yang—which included conversations on "Buddhism and Western Learning"—that he wrote EOB.[42]

Tan was also an avid reader of scientific works produced at the Jiangnan Arsenal by the British missionary John Fryer (1839–1928), whom he met in Shanghai

---

34. Ibid., p. 7.

35. Ibid., pp. 39–40.

36. Ibid., p. 42.

37. See ibid., p. 67; Kwong, *T'an Ssu-T'ung*, p. 117.

38. Ibid., pp. 123, 140.

39. Chan, *Buddhism in Late Ch'ing Political Thought*, p. 69.

40. Holmes Welch, *The Buddhist Revival in China* (Cambridge, MA: Harvard University Press, 1968), p. 4.

41. Guo Peng 郭朋, Liao Zili 廖自力 and Zhang Xinying 張新鷹, "Yang Wenhui de Foxue sixiang 楊文會的佛學思想" (The Buddhist Thought of Yang Wenhui), in their *Zhongguo jindai Foxue sixiang shigao* 中國近代佛學思想史稿 (A History of Recent Chinese Buddhist Thought) (Chengdu: Bashu shushe, 1989), pp. 3, 283–284.

42. Zhang Hua 張華, *Yang Wenhui yu Zhongguo jindai Fojiao sixiang zhuanxing* 楊文會與中國近代佛教思想轉型 (Yang Wenhui and the Transformation of Modern Chinese Buddhist Thought) (Beijing: Zongjiao wenhua chubanshe, 2004), p. 318.

in 1893 and 1896.[43] Together, they discussed science,[44] and his comments indicate that they specifically discussed the mind. In a letter to Ouyang Zhonggu, Tan cited Fryer's claim that "there is a new method whereby we can fathom the *qi* 氣 and nerves of a person's brain, picturing the things that are presently in [the subject's] mind, hence knowing what sort of dreams he has. [They can even] use machines to make dreams, that is to [make people] dream according to the machines . . ."[45] It is clear that through Fryer, Tan would have been privy to unique views not only on the explanatory power of science, but also on its capacity to probe the mind—a key concern of the Neo-Confucianism to which he had been introduced in his youth, as well as of Buddhism.

Benevolence and ether

Tan was thus informed by an array of perspectives on the mind—Neo-Confucian, Buddhist, and scientific. In EOB, these diverse influences coalesced in his treatment of benevolence, which he explained using terms drawn from each. At the very beginning of the text, Tan wrote that "the phenomenal world, the world of the void, and the world of sentient beings are permeated with something extremely vast and minute"—the ether (*yitai* 以太). Ether featured prominently in nineteenth-century physics;[46] by the latter part of the century it was thought to permeate the universe and serve as the vehicle for transmitting light. According to Tan, however, ether (like benevolence) was produced by the mind,[47] and it was therefore to be equated with the eight consciousnesses of Yogācāra.[48]

Tan would have found support for the importance of ether and its relationship to the mind in a book by Henry Wood entitled *Ideal Suggestion through Mental Photography*, which John Fryer translated as *Zhixin mianbingfa* 治心免病法 in 1896. Wood stated that ether conveyed thought, and Fryer added, in his translation, that

43. In 1868, Fryer had begun translating scientific works for the Chinese government at the translation department in the Jiangnan Arsenal in Shanghai. In the 1890s, he also edited *Gezhi huibian* 格致匯編 (Chinese Scientific Magazine).

44. David Wright, *Translating Science: The Transmission of Western Chemistry into Late Imperial China, 1840–1900* (Leiden: Brill, 2000), p. 124.

45. Tan's quotation of Fryer, cited in Wright, *Translating Science*, p. 124; Tan, TSQ, pp. 458–459.

46. For an analysis of Tan's usage of this concept, see Wright, "Tan Sitong and the Ether Reconsidered," *Bulletin of the School of Oriental and African Studies* 57.3 (1994): 558–563. On ether theories more generally, see Wang Xiwei 王錫偉, "Lun 'yitai' shuo de xiandai renshilun yiyi 論'以太'說的現代認識論意義" (The Modern Epistemological Significance of Ether Theory), *Jiangsu shehui kexue* 2(2007): 36–38.

47. Chan, "Introduction to 'An Exposition of Benevolence,'" p. 18.

48. Ibid., 23–24.

> recently, Western countries have discovered that the myriad things have in them a circulating quality called "ether." Even inside the farthest star there cannot be a vacuum; it must be filled with this "ether." This "ether" is even in the particles of the terrestrial atmosphere. . . . No matter where or what it is, it cannot be avoided. Without ether, light from the sun and planets would not reach the Earth's surface. . . . Thoughts are transmitted according to the same principle. Regardless of the distance, or whether the five senses can perceive it, when one is moved to emit a thought, ether will channel it to the minds of others.[49]

The ether-benevolence construct was not only produced by the mind,[50] it was "a manifestation of the consciousness of the entire universe, connecting the physical, mental, and spiritual realms."[51] It also served a metaphysical function, holding together matter and astral bodies, familial and social relationships, and the Buddhist conception of the cosmos.[52] Using Yogācāra terminology, Tan explained that while all things in the universe came from benevolence, "benevolence is the source of heaven, earth, and the myriad things: thus there is nothing but mind [*weixin* 唯心]; thus there is nothing but consciousness [*weishi* 唯識]."[53] As "an object projected by nothing but consciousness,"[54] ether was thus an aspect of

49. Fryer, cited in Zou Zhenhuan 鄒振環, *Yingxiang Zhongguo jindai shehui de yibai zhong yizuo* 影響中國近代社會的一百種譯作 (One Hundred Translations that Influenced Modern Chinese Society) (Beijing: Zhongguo duiwai fanyi chuban gongsi, 1996), p. 108. Wood mentions ether on page 52:

> We find that the great force called thought has scientific relations, correlations, and transmutations; that its vibrations project themselves in waves through the ether, regardless of distance and other sensuous limitations; that they strike unisons in other minds and make them vibrant; that they relate themselves to like and are repelled by the unlike; that their silent though forceful impact makes a distinct impression; in fact, that they are substantial entities, in comparison with which gold, silver, and iron are as evanescent as the morning dew.

See Henry Wood, *Ideal Suggestion through Mental Photography: A Restorative System for Home and Private Use; Preceded by a Study of the Laws of Mental Healing*, 6th ed., (Boston, MA: Lee and Shepard Publishers, 1893), p. 52. Zou suggests that Wood's book is a possible source for his particular conception of ether, along with *Guangxue tushuo* 光學圖說 (Pictorial Explanations of Optics)—another of Fryer's translations, published in 1890. See Zou, *Yingxiang Zhongguo*, pp. 109–112.

50. Chan, "Introduction to 'An Exposition of Benevolence,'" p. 24.

51. Wright, "Tan Sitong and the Ether Reconsidered," p. 556.

52. T'an, EOB, 68; Tan, TSQ, p. 294.

53. T'an, EOB, 62; Tan, TSQ, p. 292.

54. Chan, *Buddhism in Late Ch'ing Political Thought*, p. 93; T'an, EOB, p. 136; Tan, TSQ, p. 331.

cognition.[55] Benevolence therefore united nineteenth-century physics, the Neo-Confucian understanding of *qi* as having a moral aspect, and Yogācāra's emphasis on cognitive experience.

Neurophysiology

In EOB, Tan also sought to show how Yogācāra's eight consciousnesses cohered with scientific knowledge of the brain.[56] The period of Tan's career had seen remarkable advances in the fields of biology and brain science.[57] In his chapter in this volume, Hammerstrom notes Gustav Fritsch's (1837–1927) and Eduard Hitzig's (1839–1907) discoveries linking brain function, movement, and electricity. Early in the nineteenth century, Charles Bell (1774–1842) and François Magendie (1783–1855) determined that electrical signals were sent from peripheral nerves to muscles, and from sense organs to the central nervous system. The Nobel Prize winner Ramón y Cajal (1852–1934) made discoveries about the structure of nerve cells, and that signals were conveyed between them.[58] Meanwhile, in 1875, Richard Caton measured the first EEG signals.[59] The work of nineteenth-century researchers led to the view that

> brain function is electrically mediated. Each nerve cell is a sophisticated electrical element capable of generating a resting potential and of rapidly changing that potential through a reversal of its intrinsic membrane charges. These action potentials constitute a continuous stream of signals flowing through the vast system of neurons that is our brain. Somehow the stream of electrical signals is related to the stream of what we call consciousness.[60]

Reflecting this state of knowledge, Tan equated the brain itself with electricity.[61] He explained that the nervous system was like a series of wires,[62] and that

---

55. See also Chan, *Buddhism in Late Ch'ing Political Thought*, p. 87.

56. As John Jorgensen notes, Hara Tanzan had already linked the brain and spine to the consciousnesses of Yogācāra in Japan in 1870.

57. See J. Allan Hobson, *The Dreaming Brain* (New York: Basic Books, 1988), chapter 4.

58. Ibid., p. 95.

59. Ibid., p. 100.

60. Ibid., p. 108.

61. T'an, EOB, 69: Tan, TSQ, p. 295.

62. T'an, EOB, 73; TSQ, p. 295.

thoughts produced movement in brain nerves and had unique electrical outputs. But he also identified Yogācāra's eight consciousnesses with the cerebrum and the cerebellum.[63] Accordingly, the cerebrum had both a "substance" (*ti* 體), which was the eighth, or base consciousness, and a "function" (*yong* 用), which was Yogācāra's sixth, thinking consciousness.[64] The cerebellum, too, had both a substance (the seventh, evaluating consciousness, or *manas*), and a function (the sense consciousnesses).[65] Tan thus provided an answer to the unexplained relationship between electricity and consciousness by combining discoveries about the brain's electrical functions with Yogācāra's cognitive architecture.

A likely source for some of Tan's information about the brain may have been a series of school textbooks translated and published by John Fryer at the Jiangnan Arsenal. These were written from the perspective of Scientific Temperance Instruction, which held that alcohol was a form of poison and the cause of illness. The books, however, also contain much information on human biology.[66] Tan referred to the brain's physical structure when he subsumed a physical explanation of the visual system within the broader context of Yogācāra, explaining that "the circular cavity in front of the cerebrum is a mirror in which is reflected all the images of heaven, earth, and the myriad things."[67] He thus connected the operation of the visual consciousness to a specific point in the skull.

Tan also relied on Yogācāra's cognitive model when explaining topics that fell within the purview of the then-new discipline of psychology, including how we dream, the cause of insanity, and how we could achieve benevolent interconnections with others. He wrote that dreams and insanity arose when the thinking consciousness (the sixth) was connected, but the ego-centered consciousness (the seventh) was only partially connected. Tan apparently meant that the seventh

---

63. Tan thus ascribed spiritual functions to anatomical structures of the brain, as Descartes had done when asserting that the pineal gland was the repository for the soul. I am grateful to Dan Lusthaus for this observation. For Descartes's theory compared to those of his predecessors and contemporaries see Gert-Jan C. Lokhorst and Timo T. Kaitaro, "The Originality of Descartes Theory about the Pineal Gland," *Journal of the History of the Neurosciences* 10, no. 1 (2001): 6–18.

64. Digital Dictionary of Buddhism, s.v. "*yishi* 意識," by C. Muller, accessed February 29, 2012, http://buddhism-dict.net/ddb.

65. T'an, EOB, p. 209; Tan, TSQ, 364. See Digital Dictionary of Buddhism, s.v. "*siliangshi* 思量識," by C. Muller, accessed June 3, 2012, <http://buddhism-dict.net/ddb.

66. These are: *Haitong weisheng bian* 孩童衛生編 (Health for Little Folks; 1894), *Youtong weisheng bian* 幼童衛生編 (Lessons in Hygiene; 1895) and *Chuxue weisheng bian* 初學衛生編 (First Book in Physiology and Hygiene; 1896). See Ruth Rogaski, *Hygienic Modernity: Meanings of Health and Disease in Treaty-Port China* (Berkeley and Los Angeles: University of California Press, 2004), pp. 118–120.

67. T'an, EOB, 135; Tan, TSQ, p. 331.

consciousness was partially—although not completely severed from the base consciousness, thus depriving it of data used in cognition. This resulted in the continued belief in the existence of the self, but a disbelief in the existence of dharmas. Tan wrote of such individuals: "Their cerebrum is still conscious, while their cerebellum is semi-conscious."[68]

To understand why Tan felt this was important, we may consider that dreams and insanity were interlinked in late nineteenth-century psychology, when "dreaming was seen as capable of inducing both hysterical paralysis and paranoia; and vice versa, psychosis was seen as a breakthrough of the dream process. Thus many pre-Freudian authors regarded the dream as nocturnal insanity."[69] Tan dealt with this dual concern of nineteenth-century psychology with reference to Yogācāra's cognitive processes. He explained that data received by the five sense consciousnesses was channeled to the cerebrum (which housed the base consciousness), while the cerebellum (which embodied the function of the five sensory consciousnesses and the evaluating consciousness) created dreams on the basis of this information. He added that the evaluating consciousness of children was not fully formed, and therefore they did not dream. Meanwhile, the Daoist "perfect man" (*zhiren* 至人) also did not dream, but for a different reason: data from the sense consciousnesses did not "ferment," meaning that dreams would not arise.[70]

The idea that fools and sages did not dream is frequently referenced in Chinese literature and philosophy.[71] Zhuangzi states that "True Men [*zhenren* 真人] of old slept without dreaming and woke without cares."[72] Tan's views on dreams and insanity, however, also reflect contemporary physiological understandings of the brain. For scientists of this period, "insanity was a disease of the brain,"[73] and dreams had physical causes. Johannes Müller (1801–1858) suggested that dreams resulted from bodily movements; Wilhelm Wundt (1832–1920) and Alfred Maury (1817–1892) proposed they arose from internal and external bodily sensations. George Trumbull

68. T'an, EOB, 210; Tan, TSQ, p. 364.

69. Hobson, *The Dreaming Brain*, p. 51.

70. T'an, EOB, 210; Tan, TSQ, p. 365.

71. See, for example, two articles that appeared in *Shenbao* 申報 in the years preceding Tan's composition of EOB: author unknown, "Meng yuan xiao ji 夢緣小記" (Notes on the Reasons for Dreams), *Shenbao* 5989 (December 19, 1889); author unknown, "Shuo meng 說夢" (On Dreams), *Shenbao* 6018 (January 17, 1890).

72. A. C. Graham, trans., *Chuang-tzŭ: The Seven Inner Chapters and Other Writings* (London: Unwin Paperbacks, 1986), p. 84.

73. William Wingfield, "The Asylum: Its Construction and Deconstruction," in *Psychotropic Drugs and Popular Culture: Essays on Medicine, Mental Health and the Media*, edited by Lawrence C. Rubin (Jefferson, NC: McFarland, 2006), p. 26.

Ladd (1842–1921), Joseph Delboeuf (1831–1896), Karl Scherner (1825–1889) and Karl Binz (1832–1913) also put forward physiological theories of dreams.[74]

It is difficult to determine precisely where, and if, Tan had been exposed to such theories. As mentioned above, he reported that he had discussed dreams and the mind with John Fryer. However, these physiological accounts were also part of a general discourse concerning these subjects. An article appearing in an 1888 issue of *The Century*, for example, provided an overview of dream research, and stated that "there is no proof that babies dream at all. . . . The condition of the babe in sleep is precisely such as might be expected from its destitution of recorded sensations."[75] An 1897 piece appearing in the magazine *Zhi xin bao* 知新報 (The Reformer China) reported on an article appearing in the *Scientific American Supplement*, which concluded that dreams are constructed from sensations and memories. The Chinese article added that "thus children have few dreams, and elderly people have many dreams."[76]

Tan was concerned not only with showing the concordance between Yogācāra and science. He also equated concepts in the *Great Learning*—a key text in Neo-Confucianism—with Yogācāra's cognitive system:

> [w]hen the first five kinds of consciousness are transmuted into the Wisdom of Perfect Achievement [cognition with unrestricted activity;[77] *cheng suozuo zhi* 成所作智], this is what the *Great Learning* means when it says, "Cultivate the person and the person is cultivated." The so-called eyes, ears, nose, tongue and body in Buddhism are collectively called the 'person' in Confucianism. When Confucius told Yan Hui of the "four dont's," he spoke with due reference to the rites that Yan Hui should observe when he looked, listened, spoke, or moved. Such straight-forward remarks show that the store consciousness [or base consciousness; *zangshi* 藏識] of Yan had already been transformed into wisdom. Only when the transformation of one's store consciousness has been achieved can one be benevolent.[78]

74. See Hobson, *The Dreaming Brain*, pp. 23–51.

75. J. M. Buckley, "Dreams, Nightmare, and Somnambulism," *The Century* 36, no. 3 (July 1888): 448.

76. Author unknown, "Mengli jingshuo 夢理精說" (A Discussion of Dream Principles), *Zhi xin bao* 28 (1897): 25. The article refers to a piece appearing in a June 19 issue of *Scientific American Supplement*. See, author unknown, "The Theory of Dreams," *Scientific American Supplement* 1120 (June 19, 1897): pp. 17909–17910. This article, in turn, takes its information from "The Theory of Dreams," *Literary Digest* 14, no.10 (January 9, 1897): 303, which is the translation of a piece that appeared the previous year in the French journal *Cosmos*. See L. Ménard, "La Théorie des Rêves," *Cosmos* 619 (December 5 1896): 585–586.

77. *Digital Dictionary of Buddhism*, s.v. "*cheng suozuo zhi* 成所作智," by C. Muller, http://buddhism-dict.net/ddb (accessed February 21, 2012).

78. T'an, EOB, 138; Tan, TSQ, p. 332.

For Tan, clearly there were no impediments to identifying correlations between the major features of his intellectual world. Regardless of the exact sources of his knowledge, he thus combined nineteenth-century physiology with Confucian, Daoist, and Buddhist elements to present a novel understanding of how the mind worked.

New Thought

Alongside Neo-Confucianism and Yogācāra, New Thought provided another theory of mental processes that informed Tan's conception of mind in EOB. Reflecting his concern for China's future after its 1895 defeat in the Sino-Japanese War, Tan felt that China was suffering the results of negative karma accrued by generations of tyrannical rulers,[79] and that this would result in the devolution of the Chinese people.[80] Changing this course was again a question of mental reformation; he remarked that since a "kalpa destiny is created by the mind, it certainly can be resolved by it too."[81] This could be achieved by turning to Buddhism, or the ideas of the aforementioned Henry Wood[82]— a central figure in the New Thought movement then popular in the United States. As noted above, Tan had read John Fryer's translation of Wood's *Ideal Suggestion through Mental Photography* after it was published in 1896.

Alongside Neo-Confucianism and Yogācāra, New Thought provided another theory of mental processes that informed Tan's conception of mind in EOB. Like Scientific Temperance Instruction, New Thought was concerned with the root cause of illness; however, New Thought attributed this cause to incorrect modes of thinking rather than to alcohol. The movement emerged from an environment in which various forms of mental healing—the early progenitor of which was Phineas Pankhurst Quimby, a practitioner of "mental therapeutics"[83]—were being popularized. Quimby held that disease arose in the mind, and that physical cures could be enacted through psychological therapy.[84] Wood's book was one

79. T'an, EOB, 193; Tan, TSQ, p. 356. Citing this section of Tan's text, Geremie Barmé situates him in a lineage of pessimistic thinkers leading up to 1980s PRC intellectuals. See Geremie R. Barmé, "To Screw Foreigners is Patriotic: China's Avant Garde Nationalists," *The China Journal* 34 (July 1995): 209–234.

80. T'an, EOB, 167; Tan, TSQ, p. 344.

81. T'an, EOB, 194; Tan, TSQ, p. 356. A kalpa is the length of time between universes in the cosmic cycle of creation and destruction.

82. T'an, EOB, 195–96; Tan, TSQ, p. 357.

83. Eva S. Moskowitz, *In Therapy We Trust: America's Obsession with Self-Fulfillment* (Baltimore: The Johns Hopkins University Press), p. 11.

84. Ibid., pp. 10–18.

of a number of publications in the 1890s that helped mental healing techniques attain widespread popularity.[85]

According to Dell deChant, "New Thought's primary beliefs are idealistic in character";[86] it holds that the "universe is mental," and "all material-physical phenomena result from one's mental states."[87] Wood himself wrote:

> God made man a "living soul," and therefore he *is* a soul, not *has* a soul. His body is a temporary material correspondence; a set of instruments for his convenience on the plane of sense. . . . Just behind the seen and material human organism there is a sensuous mind, the most outer and fleshly of the immaterial part, which pertains especially to the body and acts directly upon it. Next within is the intellectual zone, and still deeper, in the innermost, is the spiritual ego, the divine image. This is the Christ-plane, where dwells the perfect humanity.[88]

Wood outlined a method of spiritual practice, explaining that ultimately "the physical organism is only the soul made manifest,"[89] and that "the practical universe to each one is that which is built of thoughts, mental states, and delineations."[90] He advocated a process of moving one's ego up the planes of consciousness to the highest level—that of the "Christ-plane," to realize that reality was an emanation of God. In this transcendental scheme, the "soul must rise superior to environment, dominate body, and free itself from degrading and long-continued servitude."[91]

A key part of the required cultivational practice involved meditating on certain statements that were printed on separate pages in the second part of the book. Examples include: "I am soul," "spirit is the only substance" and "I am not

85. Moskowitz, *In Therapy We Trust*, p. 18. On this aspect of New Thought, see Eva Moskowitz, "The Therapeutic Gospel: Religious Medicine and the Birth of Pop Psychology, 1850–1910," *Prospects* 20 (1995): 57–86.

86. Dell deChant, "The American New Thought Movement," in *Introduction to New and Alternative Religions in America*, vol. 3, ed. Eugene V. Gallagher and W. Michael Ashcraft (Westport, CT: Greenwood Press, 2006), p. 81.

87. deChant, "The American New Thought Movement," p. 82.

88. Henry Wood, *Ideal Suggestion through Mental Photography*, p. 33. For the Chinese translation, see Wute Hengli 烏特亨利 [Henry Wood], *Zhixin mianbingfa: erjuan* 治心免病法：二卷, translated by Fu Lanya 傅蘭雅 [John Fryer] (Shanghai: Gezhi shushi kanben, 1896).

89. Wood, *Mental Photography*, p. 72.

90. Ibid., p. 84.

91. Ibid., p. 86.

body." It is not difficult to see how intellectuals with an interest in Buddhism in the late Qing would have been receptive to Wood's ideas. According to Kay Alexander, New Thought arose "within self-consciously Christian circles," but it "developed nationwide against a background of wider interest in comparative religions,"[92] including Buddhism.[93] New Thought certainly resonates with possible idealistic trends in Yogācāra texts. As John Powers explains in this volume, this is exemplified by the third-century text *Saṃdhinirmocana-sūtra* (*Jie shenmi jing* 解深密經; Discourse Explaining the Thought), in which the Buddha states that objects of perception and cognition are the same. Wood's ideas on mental purification also correspond, superficially, with the practical aims of Yogācāra.

There are also parallels between New Thought's assertion that there is an essential, pure nature internal to the self, and the Buddhist *tathāgatagarbha* (*rulaizang* 如來藏; matrix of buddhas) as discussed in popular Buddhist texts such as *Dasheng qixin lun* (Awakening of Mahāyāna Faith) and the *Laṅkāvatāra-sūtra* (*Lengqie jing* 楞伽經; Discourse on [the Buddha's] Entering [the Country of] Lanka), according to which a pure, undefiled inner nature exists in sentient beings and will be revealed when delusion is cast aside. Of course, New Thought and Yogācāra are fundamentally different, and juxtaposing them in the scholarly arena is rightly questionable (at best). In the context of the late Qing, however, finding correlations between Chinese and Western thought was a key concern of reform-oriented intellectuals. The identification of a common truth underlying both lent legitimacy to Sinitic ideas and served to reify their value. There was clearly much in these two philosophies for them to work with.

Chang Hao considers "Mahayana Buddhism and Confucianism" to have been more important "in articulating [Tan's] belief in the spiritual power of the human mind" than New Thought.[94] Wood's influence, however, might be detected in Tan's views on how science and technology could enable us to decrease our dependency on the physical body. According to Tan, human physiology could be altered so the body could sustain itself solely from the atmosphere—like the Daoist practice of "swallowing air."[95] A method might be invented that would reduce the heavy, physical particles of the body,[96] so that humans became only "wisdom and

---

92. Kay Alexander, "Roots of the New Age," in *Perspectives on the New Age*, ed. James R. Lewis and Gordon Melton (Albany: State University of New York Press, 1992), p. 35.

93. Ibid., 36.

94. Chang, *Chinese Intellectuals in Crisis*, p. 84.

95. The prominent Taiwanese monastic, Xingyun expressed similar views in 2001. See Xingyun 星雲, "Renjian Fojiao de lantu (er) 人間佛教的藍圖 (二)" (A Blueprint for Buddhism in the Human World (II), *Pumen xuebao* 普門學報 6 (November 2001): 24.

96. T'an, EOB, 213; Tan, TSQ, p. 366.

soul," which could possibly be achieved through eugenics.[97] Whereas "soul is an attribute of wisdom; body is an attribute of karma consciousness"; however, "with equality, body can become soul."[98] Tan's emphasis on the primacy of mind, as reflected in Neo-Confucianism, Sinitic understandings of Yogācāra influenced by *Dasheng qixin lun*, and New Thought, led to him considering that the body may well be transcended altogether.[99]

Yogācāra and utopia in EOB

Kwong notes that in EOB, "a perfect society was possible because of the supposed, transformative efficacy of mental power (a là Henry Wood via Fryer)."[100] This human transcendence of the physical brings us to the final part of EOB, in which Yogācāra, along with the various influences mentioned above, played a role: the work's utopian social project.

In an influential study, Krishan Kumar argues that three factors distinguish utopianism from other conceptions of the ideal life: its emphasis on science, the notion that utopias could exist in time, and the idea of progress—that utopia could be actualized in the future.[101] Utopianism was secular and humanistic, and it embodied a belief that "there is nothing in man, nature, or society that cannot be so ordered as to bring about a more or less permanent state of material plenty, social harmony and material fulfillment."[102] This meant that non-Western conceptions of the ideal society were not true utopias; Chinese ideal states such as the Confucian Great Unity were "backward-looking ideological slogans" that were "based on their vision of the good life."[103] As a result, only through an

---

97. T'an, EOB, 213; Tan, TSQ, p. 366.

98. T'an, EOB, 62. Tan, TSQ, p. 291. Tan was, however, critical of "the Western concept of soul," and what he claimed was the ascription of souls only to human beings. See T'an, EOB, p. 95; Tan, TSQ, p. 310. On Jewish, Christian, and Islamic perspectives on animals, see G. H. Bousquet, "Des Animaux et de leur traitement selon le Judaïsme, le Christianisme et l'Islam (Animals and Their Treatment According to Judaism, Christianity, and Islam)," *Studia Islamica* 9 (1958): 31–48. Bousquet finds evidence in the OT and Talmud suggesting that animals are similar to humans and thus have souls. The NT, on the other hand, has much less to say about animals. I thank Dan Lusthaus for drawing my attention to this issue.

99. However, the question as to whether Tan was ultimately a materialist or idealist is difficult to resolve conclusively, and was taken up with vigor by Marxist writers in China after TSQ's publication in 1954. For an account of this debate, see Chan, "Introduction to 'An Exposition of Benevolence,' " pp. 25–34.

100. Kwong, *T'an Ssu-T'ung*, p. 159.

101. Krishan Kumar, *Utopianism* (Milton Keynes, UK: Open University Press, 1991).

102. Ibid., p. 29

103. Ibid., p. 34.

exposure to the West in the nineteenth century did China develop true utopian schemes, such as Kang Youwei's *Datong shu* and the social ideals of the Taiping Rebellion.[104] In a similar vein, in his study of Tan's thought, Chang Hao asserts that the "transcendental and ahistorical" nature of EOB "militate against the view of history as a temporal process directed toward the future."[105] Thus, EOB "does not issue (as K'ang Yu-wei's philosophy did) in any futuristic utopianism."[106]

However, EOB can be considered utopian in some important ways. Tan clearly advocated the use of science and technology, particularly to augment human development. He also had a conception of progress, both in terms of human evolution and in terms of the ideal future society. Both of these visions were ultimately Buddhist in nature and depended on human action for their realization. Tan described this society as it would be when Amitābha was present on earth:

> People will then be well provided for and happy, mountains and rivers will look like mirrors, thusness [Suchness] will prevail in the dharma realm, and the people will have attained Buddhahood, while those who have not will surely attain it when the earth is about to be destroyed, if not at the time when the world enjoys great prosperity."[107]

Although these social conditions recall the Pure Lands of Buddhist cosmology, Tan advocated their re-creation on earth through science, and a form of individual cultivation he found support for in Neo-Confucianism, New Thought, and Yogācāra. This would create a world in which "the people will have universally attained Buddhahood."[108] Reflecting further influences from the West, Tan noted that this future society would be akin to the one described in Edward Bellamy's best-selling 1888 novel *Looking Backward: 2000–1887*,[109] which told the story of

104. Ibid., pp. 34–35.

105. Chang, *Chinese Intellectuals in Crisis*, p. 103.

106. Ibid.

107. T'an, EOB, 214; Tan, TSQ, p. 367.

108. T'an, EOB, 220–221; Tan, TSQ, p. 370.

109. Hammerstrom notes the importance of this book as an example of futuristic science-fiction in the late Qing. See "Buddhists Discuss Science," pp. 96–97. A translation by the Welsh missionary Timothy Richard was published in *Wanguo gongbao* 萬國公報 (The Globe Magazine) in 1891 and 1892. See Martin Bernal, *Chinese Socialism to 1907* (Ithaca, NY: Cornell University Press, 1976), p. 22. In his translation of EOB, Chan suggests that in the relevant passage, Tan was referring to the story of Rip van Winkle (p. 217, n. 392). According to Guo Yanli, the editors of the earlier 1981 edition of *Tan Sitong quanji* likewise did not identify the phrase "*bainian yi jue* 百年一覺" (waking after a hundred years) as the title of a book, and understood Tan as referring to Rip van Winkle, the story of which was

a Boston man who fell into a trance and awoke in 2000 amid a socialist utopia. However, Tan established mental processes as the most important driver of the historical process; he advocated mental reformation as the way to avoid the terrible consequences of China's karmic burden and move toward a brighter future.

Conclusion

Both Tan and EOB continued to exert an influence long after his death. Zhang Kundi 張昆弟 (1894–1932) recalled that in 1917, in a meeting with Mao Zedong 毛澤東 (1893–1976) and Cai Hesen 蔡和森 (1895–1931), Mao opined that China needed a thinker like Tolstoy to clear away old modes of thinking and proclaimed that "before there was Tan Sitong; now there is Chen Duxiu 陳獨秀 [1879–1942]. Their spirits are great—something that, to be honest, conventional learning (*suxue* 俗學) cannot equal."[110] After the publication of *Tan Sitong quanji* in 1954, EOB also played a role in the materialism versus idealism debate. Tan's attempts to link Yogācāra's cognitive architecture to the brain's physiology, in a sense, was

---

published in the *Shenbao* in 1872 as "*Yi shui qishi nian* 一睡七十年" (A Seventy-Year Slumber). However, the title of Bellamy's novel, *Looking Backward*, was in fact translated by Timothy Richard as *Bainian yi jue* 百年一覺 and published in 1894. See Guo Yanli 郭延禮, *Wenxue jingdian de fanyi yu jiedu: Xifang xianzhe de wenhua zhi lü* 文學經典的翻譯與解讀: 西方先哲的文化之旅 (The Explanation and Translation of Literary Classics: The Cultural Travels of Past Western Thinkers) (Jinan: Shandong jiaoyu chubanshe, 2007), pp. 280–282. In 1891 and 1892, Richard's translation had also been serialized in *Wanguo gongbao* under the title *Huitou kan jilüe* 回頭看紀略 (Looking Backward). In *Huitou kan jilüe*, however, Richard saw the blueprint for a future Chinese society. He imbued the book with a stronger Christian message than that of the original, inserting a passage at the end about Christian forgiveness. In the original, Julian West kneels beside his love (Edith), and "confessed with tears how little was my worth to breathe the air of this golden century, and how infinitely less to wear upon my breast its consummate flower. Fortunate is he who, with a case so desperate as mine, finds a judge so merciful." See Edward Bellamy, *Looking Backward, 2000–1887* (Cambridge, MA: Belknap Press of Harvard University Press, 1967), p. 311. According to Liu Shulin, in Richard's translation, West "then said 'Never before have I harboured a desire to be of aid to the world. Now, I was not at first qualified to live in this world. But I have already promised heaven that having arrived here, I will completely change; I desire to benefit people.' Edith said, 'God is supremely merciful. After repenting for one's past sins, one is forgiven.' With this, West became peaceful" (p. 132). However, Liu expresses doubt that this Christian message was influential on Tan. See Liu Shulin 劉樹林, "Li Timotai yu 'Huitou kan ji lüe' 李提摩太與《回頭看紀略》: 中譯美國小說的起源 (Timothy Richard and 'Looking Backward': The Origin of the Chinese Translation of American Novels)," *Meiguo yanjiu* 1 (1999): 122–138.

110. Mao Zedong 毛澤東, *Mao Zedong zaoqi wengao* 1912.6-1920.11 毛澤東早期文稿 1912.6-1920.11 (Mao Zedong's Early Manuscripts 1912.6-1920.11), edited by Zhonggong zhongyang wenxian yanjiushi 中共中央文獻研究室 and Zhonggong Hunan shengwei Mao Zedong zaoqi wengao bianjizu 中共湖南省委《毛澤東早期文稿》編輯組 (Changsha: Hunan chubanshe, 1990), p. 639.

also a precursor to contemporary neuroscientific studies of Buddhist meditation, in which scientific and Buddhist concepts enter into a mutually supportive relationship.[111] His attempt to find common features between Buddhism and science also prefigured the approach of both Taixu and the Wuchang School, while his hopes for an ideal society were a precursor to Taixu's "Pure Land in the human world" (*renjian jingtu* 人間淨土): the vision of a society guided by Buddhism.

Hammerstrom notes that after EOB's publication, Buddhists did not continue to engage with ether—the concept had become untenable after the theory of relativity's dramatic transformation of the scientific world.[112] Something else, however, had changed as well. Although Yogācāra was not the only pillar for Tan's thought in EOB, along with other theories of mind, it was an important one; while Tan tried to show how Yogācāra and other theories of mental functioning cohered with one another, Taixu (who was a great admirer of EOB[113]) worked from the perspective of Yogācāra to identify deficiencies in scientific theories. By this time, it was not only the scientific environment that had been altered—China's religious landscape had been shaken by the new antireligious trends of the May Fourth generation.

In both historical contexts, however, Yogācāra served an important function in the broader Buddhist engagement with Western science, religion, and philosophy. Therefore, while the specific uses to which Tan put Yogācāra did not endure, his juxtaposition of it alongside both traditional ideas and the products of modernity was a demonstration of its intellectual relevance that lasted well into the twentieth century.

111. See, for example, Antionino Raffone, Angela Tagini, and Narayanan Srinivasan, "Mindfulness and the Cognitive Neuroscience of Attention and Awareness," *Zygon: Journal of Religion and Science* 45, no. 3 (2010): 627–646; Zhou Changle 周昌樂, "Cong dangdai naokexue kan chanding zhuangtai dacheng de kenengxing ji qi yiyi 從當代腦科學看禪定狀態達成的可能性及其意義 (The Possibility and Significance of Attaining the State of Meditative Concentration Viewed from the Perspective of Contemporary Brain Science)," *Hangzhou shifan daxue xuebao [shehui kexue ban]* 3, no. 5 (2010): 17–23.

112. Hammerstrom, "Buddhists Discuss Science," p. 118.

113. Taixu, "Taixu zizhuan 太虛自傳" (An Autobiography of Taixu), in *Taixu dashi quanshu* 太虛大師全書 (The Collected Works of Master Taixu) (CD-ROM), ed. Yinshun 印順 (Xinzhu: Caituan faren Yinshun wenjiao jijinhui, 2005 [1940]), vol. 29, p. 191.

4

Equality as Reification: Zhang Taiyan's Yogācāra Reading of Zhuangzi *in the Context of Global Modernity*

Viren Murthy

ALTHOUGH BEST KNOWN in the late Qing for his nationalism and his scholarship, Zhang Binglin 章炳麟 (Taiyan 太炎) (1869–1936) also promoted a unique vision of equality in his *Qi wu lun shi* 齊物論釋 (An Interpretation of "Discourse on Making All Things Equal"; 1910; hereafter *An Interpretation*). Zhang was extremely proud of this piece, in which he presents a Yogācāra Buddhist interpretation of the second chapter of the *Zhuangzi* 莊子[1]. Zhang believed that he had constructed a unique reading and exclaimed that in his interpretation of this text, "each character is worth one thousand gold pieces."[2] One of the reasons he was so content with this text is that he believed he had analyzed passages in the second Inner Chapter of *Zhuangzi* that had befuddled interpreters ever since the time of Zhuangzi (*ca.* 300 BC). Moreover, he claimed that he was able to do this precisely because he drew on Yogācāra thought.

Although scholars have recently turned their attention to Zhang's interpretation of *Zhuangzi*, they have generally remained focused on the Chinese intellectual context and have hence overlooked the wider significance of Zhang's work. I argue that we can understand the wider significance of *An Interpretation* by placing these ideas in the context of modern European philosophy and in turn

1. The *Zhuangzi* is one of the key texts in the Daoist canon, attributed to the eponymous Daoist thinker, Zhuangzi, who lived during the fourth century BC.

2. Tang Zhijun 湯志鈞, *Zhang Taiyan nianpu changbian* 章太炎年譜長編 (An Extended Chronological Biography of Zhang Taiyan), 2 vols. (Beijing: Zhonghua shuju, 1979), p. 346.

historicizing modern philosophy in relation to global capitalism. My theoretical position goes against a current trend of invoking the notion of "alternative modernities," which we see in the subtitle of Kobayashi Takeshi's well-known book on Zhang Taiyan, *Zhang Taiyan and Meiji Thought: Another Modernity*.[3] I contend that rather than focusing on national or regional particularity, we should see the antinomies of modern philosophy as expressing contradictions involved in a capitalist world imbricated in commodity exchange, bureaucracy, and a world system of nation-states. In particular, in a society where each day people must deal with commodities, money, or bureaucracy, the concept of formal equality, which is indifferent to particularity, becomes increasingly salient. In this environment, people begin to perceive an antinomy between impersonal forces and their particular subjective experience. We should hence not be surprised that modern German philosophy, from Hegel onward, has been constantly attempting to overcome such antinomies, and specifically, the antinomy between subject and object.

In late-Qing China, although his exposure to German idealism was limited, Zhang's interpretation of Yogācāra goes beyond German idealism by affirming a type of particularity that philosophically transcends the above-mentioned opposition between various modern antinomies of philosophy, such as subject and object and universality and particularity. We shall see Zhang explain the significance of his thought by explicitly placing Zhuangzi and Hegel in opposition. The significance of Zhang's reading of *Zhuangzi* in light of Yogācāra is not merely that he brought two distinct traditions together or that he was a comparative philosopher before his time. Rather, we must understand Zhang's work in relation to a larger global problematic of equality and also in relation to a trend toward criticizing modernity. From this perspective, I shall argue that Zhang's approach dovetails with that of recent post-Hegelian philosophers in France, such as Gilles Deleuze.

The various figures discussed in this volume can be divided roughly into those who attempted to mobilize Yogācāra to promote a particular political vision and those who were interested in scholarship. Although Zhang is famous as a scholar, I would place him in the former camp, along Taixu, Tan Sitong, and others. As with Germany and Japan, because China was a late-comer to the global capitalist system, a number of intellectuals attempted at the same time to join and then overcome this system. In *An Interpretation*, Zhang makes this gesture toward overcoming at an abstract level, but does not quite grasp its conditions of possibility in capitalism.

---

3. Kobayashi Takeshi 小林武, *Shō Heirin to Meiji shichō: mō hitotsu no kindai* 章炳麟と明治思潮：もう一つの近代 (Zhang Taiyan and Meiji Thought: Another Modernity) (Tokyo: Kenbun shuppan, 2006).

The Epistemology of Equality in the late Qing: Gongli *and the unification of subject and object*

During the late nineteenth and early twentieth centuries, in response to domestic and international crises along with defeats in numerous wars, late-Qing officials and intellectuals took the Meiji reforms as a model to transform the Chinese empire into a strong nation-state. The domestic side of this transformation involved the emergence of a new category of people inextricably connected to equality: "citizens." Citizens were formally equal, required recognition by the state, and would be schooled to identify with the nation. The concept of equality is made possible and promulgated through two interrelated structures of capitalist society, the modern bureaucratic state and an economy of commodity exchange on the market.

The intellectual historian Wang Hui describes the social and political transformations that gave birth to the new category of the citizen and the aggregate "the people" in a manner that brings out its philosophical significance:

> The formation of the people must legally abstract and separate each individual from various communal, local place, and kinship relations and then construct formally equal national citizens. The latter can participate in the activities of the sovereign nation either as a unit or as a group. This political process simultaneously follows the development of industry, the expansion of the city and increase in the power of money, the formation of professional society, the establishment of a market system, and so on.[4]

The above passage describes what Jacques Bidet calls the dual structures of modernity, namely market and organization, both of which entail abstraction and equality.[5] This abstraction is mediated by relations of domination and subordination in a global capitalist system of nation-states. In late-Qing China, the idea of human equality and equality in general were inextricably linked to the global processes of territorialization, nation-building, and the spread of capitalism. All of these processes involve a degree of formal rationality associated with the development of large bureaucracies, a modern legal system, and a world of commodities created for exchange. The processes associated with formalization and rationalization occurred at both global and national levels, and as a result, late-Qing thinkers, and Zhang Taiyan, in particular, confronted these two interrelated

4. Wang Hui 汪暉, *Zhongguo xiandai sixiang de xingqi* 中國現代思想的興起 (The Rise of Modern Chinese Thought), 4 vols. (Beijing, Sanlian shudian, 2004), vol. 4, p. 1399.

5. Jacques Bidet, *L'état-monde: libéraliseme, socialisme et communisme à l'échelle globale* (Paris: Presses Universitaires de France, 2011), p. 12.

realms as they constructed their political thought. Consequently, late-Qing intellectuals used equality and other related concepts to make sense of their world and to conceive of political ideals at global and local, as well as at collective and individual, levels.

The interconnection between local groups, society, and the state in the theoretical realm corresponded to an institutional process that entailed the expansion of state power through local organizations or groups. The Qing government was initially hostile to the reformers' proposals of 1898, which emphasized giving more power to the localities. During the early 1900s, however, the government implemented the so-called New Government Policies through which the Qing state penetrated various dimensions of society. Prasenjit Duara describes the New Government Policies of the late Qing as a "Chinese pattern of state strengthening—closely interwoven with modernizing and nation-building goals."[6] He notes that "all regimes, whether central or regional, appeared to respect the administrative extensions of state power in local society . . . whatever their goals, they assumed that these new administrative arrangements were the most convenient means of reaching rural communities."[7]

In the context of the abstraction associated with the above state-building process, late Qing intellectuals began to propose the idea of the universal principle (*gongli* 公理), which was in some sense the metaphysical ground that justified many of the social and political transformations associated with this period. This principle mimics the rationalizing tendency of the state, but it represents a logic that transcends the boundaries of the state.

The universal principle was scientific and also had direct implications for moral and political philosophy. It can form numerous compounds, such as "the universal principle of science," and the "the universal principle of evolution," but in general it resembles Georg Lukács's description of modern rationalism as the equation "of formal, mathematical and rational knowledge with knowledge in general and 'our' knowledge."[8] From the perspective of science, all things were equal before the universal principle; it was a type of abstract standard to which all things conform. Hence, reformist proponents of the universal principle faced an aporia between the broad scope of the universal principle and the more limited nature of the nation-state. Zhang would to some extent exploit this aporia using Yogācāra.

6. Prasenjit Duara, *Culture, Power and the State: Rural North China, 1900–1942* (Stanford, CA: Stanford University Press, 1988), p. 2.

7. Ibid., p. 3.

8. Andrew Feenberg, *Lukács, Marx and the Sources of Critical Theory* (Totowa, NJ: Rowman and Littlefield, 1981), p. 102.

Moreover, although the universal principle does include some type of moral imperative, late-Qing intellectuals began to perceive a gap between *gongli* as scientific principle and *gongli* as moral principle, and hence they had to reinscribe moral categories into the scientific side of the universal principle or the seemingly amoral movement of the material world. This gap between the scientific and the moral is once again related to the difference between subject and object, and *gongli* had to unite the two. Among reformers, Kang Youwei 康有為 (1858–1927) perhaps went the farthest to couch scientific concepts in Confucian terminology. As early as 1886, Kang linked the Confucian ideals to a type of scientific principle of the universe: "All things have humanity, righteousness and rituals, not only humans" and spoke of rituals as "the necessity of things" (*wu zhi bi ran* 物之必然).[9] However, this necessity implied a world beyond Confucius. Kang Youwei's follower, Fan Zhui 樊錐 (1872–1905), explicitly linked the universal principle to equality in a way that develops the above paradigm:

> With respect to heaven's producing things, all things are one. That which is one is the universal principle and the universal principle is equality. . . . Since all things come from heaven, all things are heaven. Moreover, the infinite heaven is also equal. If everything is equal, then everything is the same.[10]

The above passage brings all things under one principle and subsumes the myriad things in the world under the umbrella of sameness. We should not think of this sameness merely as spatial but also as temporal. The idea of evolution extends this idea of the repetition of the same in the context of history and temporal difference. As Liang Qichao 梁啓超 (1873–1929) explained at around the same

---

9. Jiang Yihua 姜義華 and Wu Genliang 吳根樑 (comps.), *Kang Youwei quanji* 康有為全集 (The Complete Works of Kang Youwei) (Shanghai: Shanghai guji chubanshe, 1987), vol. 1, pp. 191–192, cited in Wang, *Zhongguo xiandai sixiang de xingqi*, vol. 2, p. 749.

10. Cited in Wang Ermin 王爾敏, *Wan Qing zhengzhi sixiang shilun* 晚清思想史論 (Late-Qing Intellectual History) (Taipei: Taiwan wuying shuguan, 1995), p. 228.

11. Liang Qichao, "Bianfa tongyi xu 變法通義序" (Preface to a General Proposal for Reform; 1896), in *Liang Qichao wenji* 梁啟超文集 (The Collected Essays of Liang Qichao), ed. Chen Shuliang 陳書良 (Beijing: Beijing yanshan chubanshe, 1997), p. 1.

12. Yan Fu, "Tian yan lun, xu yu anyu 天演論, 序與案語" (Preface and Annotations to Huxley's *Evolution and Ethics*)," in *Shehui jubian yu guifan chongjian: Yan Fu wenxuan* 社會巨變與規範重建：嚴復文選 (Great Social Change and Reconstruction of Models: Selected Works of Yan Fu), ed. Lu Yunkun 盧雲昆 (Shanghai: Shanghai yuandong chubanshe, 1996), p. 328. Yan Fu uses a different character, *li* 例, for "principle," which usually means example, but I think that in the context *gongli* signifies something like the universal principle.

time: "In the past one thousand years, there has been no time without change and no event that has not changed. This is the way of the universal principle and is not caused by human action."[11] Here Liang posits a principle of change outside of human action. But change is not random. A number of late-Qing intellectuals conceived of the combination of the universal principle and change as the equivalent of social evolution. For example, Yan Fu 嚴復 (1854–1921) spoke of "the universal principle of evolution."[12]

As I mentioned above, because the universal principle was sufficiently abstract, people drew on it to make different political conclusions. Yan Fu and Liang Qichao used the universal principle and the idea of evolution to legitimize the state; however, Kang went a step further and contended that the universal principle is only realized when the world evolves to a perfectly egalitarian society without national divisions:

> The age of heavenly peace is the great community; human equality and the great community of the human race themselves are definitely the universal principle. However, the inequality of things is their condition. If the conditions are not correct, even if one forces people with national laws, and oppresses people with monarchical power to make people follow the universal principle, one will not be able to put it into practice successfully.[13]

Kang Youwei, of course, combines Confucian and evolutionary theories to develop his political vision, but later reform-oriented intellectuals would more directly invoke theorists such as Hegel to make the above-mentioned link between abstract universal principles, equality, and history. For example, in a 1905 volume of the journal *Qingyi bao* 清議報 (The China Discussion), which Liang Qichao edited in Japan, Guan Yun 觀雲 wrote an essay titled "The Conflict between Equality and China's Old Morality" that repeated some of Kang's points in an explicitly Hegelian framework:

> From Hegel's discussion of ethics and according to the principle that his philosophy establishes, the world is an expression of a great spirit and the individual is just a small part of this great spirit . . . Hence all things such as states, families, societies, and countries do not have the goal of developing the individual, but only that of developing the great spirit of the world. According to Hegel's theory, the myriad things of the world are equal as one. It appears that there are differences, but in actuality there are none . . .

---

13. Kang Youwei, *Da tong shu* 大同書 (Book on the Great Unity), annotated by Chen Deyuan 陳得媛 and Li Chuanyin 李傳印 (Beijing: Huaxia chubanshe, 2002 [1935]), p. 145. See also Wang, *Zhongguo xiandai sixiang de xingqi*, vol. 2, p. 771.

> Socialism and cosmopolitanism both take equality as their moral foundation and thus they both can be deduced from Hegel's theory.[14]

Although part of Guan Yun's purpose in this essay is to extol equality, like Kang and to some extent Hegel, Guan also uses the concept of equality in order to legitimate partial inequality by making distinctions between the civilized and the barbarian and the intelligent and the stupid. He explicitly links equality to civilization. "The more civilized a country is, the more it strives for equality and barbarian countries do the opposite."[15] As we have seen in the above quotation, equality is a result of evolution, and hence to attain equality, one must support evolution, which might involve inequality. "If one wants to attain equality, the situation is such that one must take from the wise and hard-working and give to the stupid and lazy. As a result all will be stupid and lazy and the world will regress. Thus those who speak of equality must separate people into two classes."[16] In other words, according to Guan, to attain the equality that corresponds to the evolution of the world, one must ensure that the wise and hardworking are richer than the stupid and lazy, since in this case, the stupid and lazy have an incentive to change, which will eventually promote overall evolution. Although Guan does not directly use racial categories, he produces a logic that obliterates difference, since ultimately equality can only be reached when all people become the same, that is, "wise and hardworking."

One of Zhang Taiyan's aims in his interpretation of Yogācāra and *Zhuangzi* was precisely to criticize the above two characteristics of the universal principle, which we have seen in the writings of Yan Fu, Liang Qichao, Kang Youwei, and their followers. Zhang had two fundamental problems with the universal principle. The first is the way in which the universal principle is linked to state-and-society building and thus demands sacrifice to a collective. Second, the universal principle legitimates the eradication of difference through some type of evolutionary paradigm. Yogācāra Buddhism and *Zhuangzi* allowed Zhang to deal with such problems at the level of epistemology. Zhang conceives of this eradication of difference as the inevitable outcome of the distinction between civilization and barbarism, which is in turn linked to the scientific worldview associated with the universal principle. This latter point is crucial. If Zhang were merely interested in undermining the distinction between civilized and barbarian, he would perhaps have had little use for Yogācāra. Zhang, however, sought to go beyond criticizing

---

14. Zhang Dan 張枬 and Wang Renzhi 王忍之 (eds.), *Xinhai geming qian shi nian jian shilun xuanji* 辛亥革命前十年間時論選集 (Selected Writings from the Decade before the 1911 Revolution) (Beijing: Sanlian shudian, 1977), vol. 2, part 1, p. 21.

15. Ibid., p. 22.

16. Ibid., p. 23.

value judgments in order to delve into the epistemological conditions for the possibility of these judgments, so that one could eventually go beyond them.

Zhang's critique of the universal principle from the standpoint of equalization

From 1900 Zhang actively propagated anti-Manchu nationalism, and his revolutionary writings eventually led to his incarceration in Shanghai from 1903 to 1906. In jail, Zhang avidly read the Buddhist scriptures, especially the *Yogācārabhūmi-śāstra* (*Yuqie shidi lun* 瑜伽師地論; Discourse on the Stages of Concentration Practice). Reading these scriptures helped him to endure his difficult years in jail, and the experience left an indelible mark on his writings between 1906 and 1910. After his release from jail, he fled to Tokyo, where he edited *Minbao* 民報 (The People's Journal) and often wrote essays that inflected critical politics with Buddhist epistemology. In short, Zhang argued that most religions, including "science," overlooked the role of human activity or karma (*ye* 業) in creating the phenomenal world.

Zhang claims that the universal principle and evolution, which echo Hegel's philosophy, are both variations on a basic structure of confusion, alienation, and domination; in short, such phenomena emerge from consciousness. His goal is to overcome the confusion at the source of such phenomena. Hence Zhang contrasts Zhuangzi with Hegel and notes that according to Zhuangzi's philosophy of the equalization of things:

> There is no correct place, no correct taste, no correct color; it lets each things be what it wants. The understanding cannot grasp the extent to which this surpasses the universal principle. As Zhuangzi says, "All things are so and all things are permissible (*wu wu bu ran, wu wu bu ke* 無物不然，無物不可)." The literal meaning of this phrase is the same as Hegel's "all events are in accord with principle and all things are virtuous and beautiful (*shi shi jie heli, wu wu jie shanmei* 事事皆合理，物物皆善美)."[17] The former, however, takes people's hearts and minds to be different and difficult to even out, while the latter posits a final end, which is the process by which things are realized. This is a fundamental and huge difference.[18]

17. This must be Zhang's rendition of the "real is the rational and the rational is real."

18. In Jiang Bin 姜玢 (ed.), *Ge gu ding xin de zheli: Zhang Taiyan wenxuan* 革故鼎新的哲理：章太炎文選 (The Philosophy of Discarding the Old and Establishing the New: Selected Writings of Zhang Taiyan), (Shanghai: Shanghai yuandong chubanshe, 1996), p. 304.

Zhang notes the formal similarity between his own ideal and Hegel's theory of spirit, some version of which late-Qing thinkers used in discussions of equality. But this formal similarity overlooks a more fundamental difference. This difference concerns Hegel's propensity to subsume the particular under a larger structure in contrast to Zhuangzi's/Zhang Taiyan's attempt to think the unique particular. In Zhang's view, the political implications of such a distinction are clear. The Hegelian model promotes transforming the different or the other into the same, and we have seen examples of this practice in the writings of Kang Youwei and his disciples. According to Zhang one cannot evaluate the particular using some external standard. There a quasi-existential overtone to his work, in that existence merely is. The difference, however, is that, in Zhang's view, existence in its immediacy is always already mediated by confused consciousness, and hence one requires practice and discipline before a deeper realm of singularities reveals itself. Zhang's *An Interpretation* is largely concerned with uncovering this more fundamental experience.

An interpretation of "Discourse on Making All Things Equal"

Scholars have shifted between arguing that "An Interpretation" affirms particularity or individualism and claiming that it extols community and universality.[19] In fact, Zhang's interpretation of the *Zhuangzi* is complex because by combining Zhuangzi's idea of equalization, Yogācāra Buddhism, and elements of German idealism, Zhang aims to criticize both the universality of the universal principle and the particularisms embodied in individualism and nationalism. One way in which he does this is by claiming that both universality and particularity are produced by the processes of karmic consciousness. If we follow Moishe Postone[20] in thinking of the opposition between particularity and universality as being at the center of modern thought conditioned by capitalism, we can interpret Zhang as struggling to think of a way to escape this opposition, even though he does not theorize this opposition in relation to history. We have already seen him negate the universal as principle, and throughout his writings on Buddhism he negates the individual or particular self.

---

19. The two extremes are represented by Wong Young-tsu and Wang Hui, respectively. See Wong Young-tsu, *Search for Modern Nationalism: Zhang Binglin and Revolutionary China, 1869–1936* (Hong Kong: Oxford University Press, 1989); and Wang, *Zhongguo xiandai sixiang de xingqi*.

20. Moishe Postone, *Time, Labor and Social Domination: A Reinterpretation of Marx's Critical Theory* (Cambridge, UK: Cambridge University Press, 1993).

But more specifically, Zhang constantly gropes for a way to express something beyond mundane concepts, such as universality and particularity. Thus Zhang begins his interpretation by showing that we must understand Zhuangzi's idea of "equalizing things" from a perspective that is different from how we usually grasp such terms:

> "Equalizing things" refers to absolute equality. If we look at its meaning carefully, it does not refer only to equality between sentient beings, such that there is no inferior and superior. It is only when [dharmas] "are detached from the characteristics of speech; detached from the characteristics of naming cognition; and detached from of them as objects," that one understands absolute equality. This is compatible with the "equalization of things."[21]

Zhang asks how Zhuangzi's notion of "*qi wu*" in "Qi wu lun 齊物論" (Discourse on Making All Things Equal) should be understood and, in so doing, brings Zhuangzi, modern Western philosophy, and Yogācāra together. *Qi* is an important concept in *Zhuangzi*, which Zhang connects to *pingdeng* 平等 (equal; equality), and this term, *pingdeng* refers to both Western concepts of equality and to that used in *Dasheng qixin lun* 大乘起信論 (Awakening of Mahāyāna Faith).[22] The initial response he considers is that it is similar to the Western concept of equality in that it gets rid of hierarchical distinctions between high and low. This might entail that it represents a transition from feudal hierarchical relations to relations of modern citizenship and capitalism. Zhang does not completely reject this view, but he draws on Yogācāra to point to something more fundamental.[23]

---

21. Zhang Taiyan, "Qi wu lun shi," in *Zhang Taiyan quanji* 章太炎全集 (The Complete Works of Zhang Taiyan), 8 vols. (Shanghai: Shanghai renmin chubanshe, 1982–1986), vol. 6, p. 4.

22. *Dasheng qixin lun*, CBETA T32n1666_p0576a11-13: "Therefore all the dharmas since the very beginning transcend characteristics of discourse, transcend the characteristics of naming, and transcend the characteristics of cognitive objects. They are absolutely undifferentiated, changeless, and indestructible. There is nothing but this One Mind and for this reason it is nominally called Suchness." 是故一切法從本已來，離言說相、離名字相、離心緣相，畢竟平等、無有變異、不可破壞。唯是一心故名真如，以一切言說假名無實。(Translation by John Makeham, John Powers, and Mark Strange.)

23. As both John Jorgensen and Scott Pacey point out in chapters 2 and 3, a number of scholars in the late-Qing and early Republican periods regarded *Dasheng qixin lun* as closely aligned with Yogācāra, if not an actual Yogācāra text. Doctrinally, this is a problematic position, the roots of which can be traced to developments in sixth-century China, and complicated by the fact that traditionally its translation was attributed (again problematically) to Paramārtha (499–569), a scholar-monk closely associated not only with

He invokes the notion of absolute equality drawn from *Dasheng qixin lun*, which shifts one's subjective stance from seeing things as equal—that is, without high and low—to an epistemological position in which one is detached from the words and concepts that make one's world possible.

Zhang attempts to go beyond both the empty universality of abstract equality and the isolating particularity of confused experience by focusing on language. He cites the following sentence of the *Laozi* as he brings Zhuangzi and Yogācāra into dialogue: "'Is it only the human mind that is wild and cannot be fixed?' The human mind only arises because of names, images, and discrimination. Names reflect everything. By appropriating them transformations grow deeper. Hence the most sublime way is to use names to get rid of names."[24] From this perspective, the point of *An Interpretation* is to go beyond names and discrimination, even though one must do this through the use of names. In order to describe this dialectic of detachment from names, images, and the mind, Zhang draws on a passage from the *Yogācārabhūmi-śāstra* to show how to make distinctions that point beyond mundane ideas of sameness and difference:[25]

> What are the four thorough investigations? They are the investigation of the name, the investigation of the given thing, the investigation of designations for essential nature, and the investigation of the designations for particularity. With respect to these, investigation of the name means that the bodhisattva sees with regard to the name that it is just a name. Likewise, with regard to a given thing, seeing that it is just a given thing is the investigation of the given thing. With respect to designations for essential nature, clearly seeing those as just designations for essential nature is investigation of designations for essential nature; and with regard to designations for particularity, seeing those as just designations for particularity.[26]

Yogācāra, but also with *tathāgatagarbha* thought. Zhang himself believed that *Dasheng qixin lun* was a Yogācāra text written by Aśvaghoṣa. See Zhang Taiyan, "*Dasheng qixin lun* bian 大乘起信論辯" (Disputing the *Awakening of Mahāyāna Faith*), *Minbao* 民報 19 (1908), reprinted in *Xiandai fojiao xueshu congkan* 現代佛教學術叢刊 (Collectanea of Modern Buddhist Scholarship) (Taipei: Dasheng wenhua chubanshe, 1978), vol. 35, pp. 9–12. With respect to the text I am discussing, *An Interpretation*, it is also clear that Zhang cites *Dasheng qixin lun* with other texts that are uncontroversially considered to be Yogācāran, such as the *Yogācārabhūmi-śāstra*.

24. Zhang Taiyan, "Qi wu lun shi," p. 4.

25. The fifteenth volume of the *Yogācārabhūmi*.

26. Zhang Taiyan, "Qi wu lun shi," p. 4. Translation follows Janice Dean Willis, *On Knowing Reality* (Delhi: Motilal Banarsidass Publishers, 2002), p. 134.

The chapter from which this passage is drawn describes certain meditative practices that enable one to separate the name, the thing, designations of essential nature, and particularity. By pointing out that names are just names, Zhang (invoking the authority of Asaṅga, the putative author of the text) separates particular names from various attachments that one associates with those names in daily life. By distinguishing between the word and experiences in which words are coupled with other designations of things, one begins to see other possibilities in these words and things. Zhang is already practicing this with words such as *qi* (equalization) and *pingdeng* (equality), since he is causing us to think about equality differently. Similarly, by stressing that designations of essential nature and particularity are just designations (*jiali* 假立), Asaṅga/Zhang underscores the active dimension or positing. In other words, it is the human subject who posits these designations. Zhang goes on to cite a passage that explains how such meditative separation can lead to knowledge:

> What is knowing precisely, in detail, the investigated name? You should know that the bodhisattva, having investigated the name as name only, knows that name precisely; to wit, he determines that "This name is the linguistic unit (*yi* 義; [*artha*]) for a given thing"; likewise "the linguistic unit for conceptualizing, the linguistic unit for viewing, and the linguistic unit for attributing (*jiali* 假立; [*upcāra*])." If, for a given thing originally conceived as form, a name is not decided upon, no one would thus conceive of that given thing as form; and not conceiving it, he would not exaggerate or cling to it. And not clinging to it, there would be no expression in discourse. Thus he knows it precisely, in detail. This is said to be knowing the investigated name precisely in detail.[27]

The point of this passage concerns the idea that names are what enable desire to have an object, and thus the first step in liberating oneself from attachment is to understand what a name is. If the form is not decided upon, there will be no clinging. Here we see the agency of the subject again insofar as the emphasis is placed on positing or designating (*jiali* and *jia jian* 假建). However, this is also a reflex clinging, connected to our grasping, which is in turn is connected to our karmic past. Asaṅga seeks to break this structure by pointing to the indeterminacy of language, which becomes determinate through clinging. At this point, there is a phenomenological moment in which one moves toward the things themselves.

---

27. Zhang Taiyan, "Qi wu lun shi," pp. 4–5. Willis, *On Knowing Reality*, p. 136, translation modified based on the Chinese text.

> What is knowing precisely, in detail, the investigated thing? For any given thing, the bodhisattva, having investigated it as a given thing only sees that given thing, while conceived of as "form," etc., and while associated with all the expressions [for it], is in itself inexpressible. This is the second knowing in detail, namely, knowing precisely, in detail, the investigated given thing.[28]

Here Asaṅga discusses a type of knowing that is separate from discursive thought and names. Because, at this point, one realizes that the thing is inexpressible, it is difficult to grasp what the object of such knowledge would be or even whether we are dealing with objects. After all, without names the bodhisattva would appear to face a nonreified world, which Zhang would call the world of equalization. Part of what Zhang wants to show is how reification emerges, and this is the first step toward overcoming it.

Janice Dean Willis translates *satkāyadrsti* as the "reifying" view, which suggests that Asaṅga's project, and by extension Zhang's, is one of dereification. In a section of the *Yogācārabhūmi* just before the one Zhang cites, Asaṅga connects reification to the perspective of the self:

> The discursive thought concerning "I" and the discursive thought concerning "mine" engender the reifying view (*satkāyadrsti*; *sajiaye jian* 薩迦耶見 or *shen jian* 身見), and the root of all other views, namely the root of pride (*māna*) and egoism (*asmi-māna*), and the root of all other self-centered views.[29]

Reification here refers to when people see their self as real, but this originary reification leads to a number of derivative reifications. These derivative reifications emerge because people bring things together with names as a whole. Therefore, the process of separation—that is, seeing names as only names, and so on—is the beginning of a process of dereification. Zhang mobilized Yogācāra in order to combat and counter the reification that was increasingly pervading China as it entered the global capitalist world and that intellectuals promoted using concepts such as the universal principle. Placing the emphasis on reification would support Dan Lusthaus's reading of Yogācāra as anti-idealism.[30] The reified view

28. Willis, *On Knowing Reality*, p. 136; Zhang Taiyan, "Qi wu lun shi," p. 5.

29. Willis, *On Knowing Reality*, p. 128

30. Dan Lusthaus, *Buddhist Phenomenology: A Philosophical Investigation of Yogācāra Buddhism and the Ch'eng Wei-shih Lun*, Curzon Critical Studies in Buddhism Series (London: Routledge, 2002).

takes as independently existing the view of objects that the subject perceives. The meditative practices outlined by Asaṅga are meant to deconstruct this view to facilitate the appearance of that which lies concealed.[31] Zhang cites another passage from Asaṅga that expresses the complexity of this process:

> What is knowing precisely in detail, the investigated designations for essential nature? It is that knowing whereby the bodhisattva, with regard to a given thing conceived of as "form," etc., after having investigated its designations for essential nature as designations only, knows and well knows in detail that in designations relating to that given thing there is only the mere semblance of essential nature, and that in truth essential nature is lacking there. For him, seeing that "essential nature" as but a magical creation, a reflected image, an echo, a hallucination, the moon's reflection in the waters, a dream and an illusion, he knows that this semblance is not made up of that essential nature. This is the third knowing precisely, in detail, which is the sphere of most profound knowledge.[32]

Asaṅga criticizes the reified or idealized object. One posits essential nature in places where it is lacking just as one immediately takes the reflected image for the real or believes in hallucinations. From this perspective, dereification requires a different type of mediation, the mediation of meditative practice, which will allow one to disaggregate and dissolve the object of immediate unreflective experience. Through the practice of investigating the designations for essential nature, one sees that the essential nature of things is produced by one's own activity and does not exist independently.

Zhang, however, cites one more step in the above meditative practice, which is knowing in detail the investigated designations of particularity:

> That knowing by the bodhisattva, after having investigated the designations for particularity as designations only attached to the given things called "form" etc., sees designations for particularity as having non-dual (*bu er* 不二) meaning. The given thing neither completely has a nature nor lacks a nature (*bhāvo nā-bhāvah; fei youxing fei wuxing*). It is not present, since it is not "perfected," owing to its having an expressible "self." And it is not altogether absent, since in fact it is determined to have an inexpressible essence. Thus from the stance of absolute truth (*paramārthasatya;*

31. From this perspective, one can compare this project with Heidegger's unconcealment (*Unverborgenheit*), which also attempts to go beyond and beneath surface experiences.

32. Willis, *On Knowing Reality*, p. 137; Zhang Taiyan, "Qi wu lun shi," p. 5.

> *shengyidi* 勝義諦), it does not have form (*rūpī*; *youse* 有色), yet from the stance of relative truth (*samvrtisatya*; *shisudi* 世俗諦) it is not formless, since form is attributed to it. As with presence and absence, or formed and formless, just so is whatever is shown or not shown, and so forth. All enumerations of designations for particularity should be understood in just the same manner.[33]

Zhang has still not explained what remains when one removes names, but again opposes the inexpressible to the expressible in order to stress indeterminacy. Things paradoxically have nature and are present when they are inexpressible, and thus his position anticipates contemporary neo-Heideggerians, such as Graham Harman, who speaks of objects as receding from consciousness: "[T]he world is constantly torn between the being of things and the oversimplified surfaces through which they appear to us."[34] From Asaṅga's perspective, the oversimplified surfaces can be seen as such when one separates names from things themselves. Zhang invokes Asaṅga to stress the difference between the reified view of particularity and the essence in a world free from reification. If we associate ordinary visions of equality as sameness with the world of reification, we can say that Zhang uses Yogācāra and Zhuangzi's views of equalization (*qi*) to go against the reified world.

Zhang explains how the above passages from Asaṅga relate to the *Zhuangzi* by claiming that they serve to illuminate a number of key passages. Specifically, he claims that the idea that "words are not the mere chirping of birds, but they have something to say," is the same as Asaṅga's seeing that the name is only a name. "Using a horse to point out that a horse is not a horse" is the same as Asaṅga's "not clinging to it, one cannot express it." He then contends that "If everything is one, then is there language?" is the same as Asaṅga's "with respect to the given thing, one sees that it is only a thing" and "essential nature is separate from language." Zhang then compares "If one follows a completed mind and takes it as a teacher, who is without a teacher," to Asaṅga's "seeing designations for essential nature only as designations for essential nature." He juxtaposes Zhuangzi's "If one affirms and negates before something is complete in the heart-mind, this is like taking nothing for something" to Asaṅga's "there is only a semblance of essential nature and in truth essential nature is lacking."[35]

---

33. Willis, *On Knowing Reality*, pp. 137–138 mod.; Zhang Taiyan, "Qi wu lun shi," p. 5.

34. Graham Harman, *Heidegger Explained: From Phenomenon to Thing* (Chicago: Open Court, 2007), p. 2.

35. Zhang Taiyan, "Qi wu lun shi," p. 5.

These various examples return to a single issue: the relationship between names, reification, and reality. In the first citation, Zhuangzi separates words from the chirping of birds, in that they have meaning, but it is not fixed. Because the meaning of words is not fixed, words can be separated from things, as in Asaṅga's paradigm. The famous passage, "using a horse to show that a horse is not a horse is not as good as using a non-horse to show that a horse is not a horse" has a number of interpretations, but most relate it to the problem of naming. As A. C. Graham explains, this passage is basically saying that one need only name something else "a horse" and then what we used to refer to as horse is no longer a horse.[36] Chad Hansen connects name to perspective and contends that from another perspective a horse could be described as something else, such as a group of bones and skin, or, to use a more modern example, a conglomeration of atoms.[37] Such an interpretation also overlaps with the idea that any interpretation is always incomplete and that names and language are indeterminate.

Zhang himself proposes an interpretation that anticipates that of Hansen when he discusses Zhuangzi's critique of Gongsun Long. Gongsun Long tried to show that a "white horse" was not a horse, because "horse" names form and "white" names color. In Zhang's view, Gongsun Long does not go far enough because he does not go beyond cognitive objects: "Zhuangzi says that to use cognitive objects (*jing* 境) to show that consciousness is not a cognitive object is not as good as to use that which is not a cognitive object to show that consciousness is not a cognitive object."[38] He then provides the following example, when discussing the passage about the horse:

> This living horse is originally an agglomeration of the various elements such as earth, water, fire, and wind. How can one say that it belongs to the living? If one says that earth, water, fire and wind are also living things, then when a number of living things become one living thing, even though one says "horse" this is just a posited name (*jiaming*).[39]

By comparing this to Asaṅga, Zhang reads Zhuangzi's statement about a horse as part of larger practice associated with self-negation and dereification. He explicitly makes the same point immediately before the above citation.

---

36. A. C. Graham, "Chuang Tzu's Essay on Seeing Things as Equal," *History of Religions* 9 (November 1969– February 1970): 241.

37. Chad Hansen, *A Daoist Theory of Chinese Thought* (Hong Kong: Oxford University Press, 1992).

38. Zhang Taiyan, "Qi wu lun shi," p. 18.

39. Zhang Taiyan, "Qi wu lun shi," p. 19.

If one speaks broadly, heaven and earth originally have no substance and the myriad things do not arise. If one thinks of them from the perspective of attachment to (the reality of) dharmas (*fazhi* 法執), then *qian* and *kun* do not perish. Because one thinks from the perspective of attachment to self (*wozhi* 我執), things appear. Both of these are confusions of the cognitive faculty and the understanding. Some use language to refute the idea of signification or meaning, but they do not use argument to refute the idea of a horse, and fall into the cracks of Gongsun Long's words.[40]

In the next two comparisons, Zhang shows how we prereflectively take things as real and compares this point that we have seen Asaṅga make with Zhuangzi's example of those people who do not have a complete mind (*cheng xin* 成心) and then take what is not there as something that is there. Zhuangzi's point that everyone has a teacher in the completed mind, refers to the fact that everyone can break free of the reifying tendencies of consciousness by following practices that begin with the mind, namely the disaggregation meditations mentioned above.[41]

Zhang then continues his exploration of language and reality through Asaṅga and Zhuangzi and moves closer to describing a realm separate from language. Indeed, if it is the case that without language there are no distinctions, then Zhang's knowledge of other things would be what Hegel describes as "naïveté of emptiness," which depicts a "night in which all cows are black."[42] This would lead to a politics of the same, which was exactly the position that Zhang hoped to mobilize Asaṅga and Zhuangzi to attack. In the following passages, however, Zhang inscribes difference and negativity in the realm separate from conventional language and perception. This would be something like writing under erasure, a new use of vocabulary, precisely the type of redescription to which he refers above. He explains:

One only uses traces to guide transformations. Without words nothing can appear and words have the nature of returning. Thus one uses words to signify things. This is what is said in the following passage [from *Zhuangzi*]: "In speaking there are no words. One speaks one's whole life

40. Zhang Taiyan, "Qi wu lun shi," p. 19.

41. Here again, the similarity to Hegel's discussion is intriguing. In particular, Hegel contends that everyone can use their understanding to gain conceptual knowledge. Of course, here Zhang attempts to describe a nonconceptual practice that Hegel would label esoteric. G. W. F. Hegel, *Phänomenologie des Geistes* (Frankfurt am Main: Surkamp, 1986), p. 20.

42. Hegel, *Phänomenologie des Geistes*, p. 22.

> and has never spoken. One does not speak throughout one's life and has never stopped speaking (*wei chang bu yan*)."[43]

Scholars have remarked about the way in which the radical changes taking place during the late Qing required scholars to develop new terms in order to make sense of their world and translate new concepts. Before standardized Japanese translations became hegemonic, late-Qing intellectuals such as Yan Fu borrowed creatively from classical texts in order to create new meanings. Zhang goes beyond this general practice, since he is not just mining the myriad characters in classical Chinese to come up with hypothetical equivalents to Western terms.[44] Rather, he is more reflexive about the incompleteness of the process in which language signifies, but he simultaneously tries to lead language beyond itself. He formulates a radical critique of what he considers to be distinctions and value judgments that have become hegemonic, and so he must not only use arcane terms but also constantly invoke paradoxes that push language and signification to its limits. Perhaps nowhere are these paradoxes more forceful than when he is discussing his use of language in this text:

> To refute a theory with a theory is not a theory of equalization. Why? This is because one establishes the refutation. When we say something is equalization, it already goes against equalization. Why? This is because one excludes the unequalized. That is why the "Yu Yan 寓言" chapter [of *Zhuangzi*] says, "Without words there is equalization. Equalization and words are not equal. Words and equalization are not equal."[45]

Reading the above passages together suggests that Zhang's "equalization" does not refer merely to an ineffable state. To name something as equalization would already fix and reify it, which is why one is not interested in refuting a theory. Rather, one uses language to go beyond language. Zhang is precisely trying to affirm the tension between words and equalization, which points to things from the standpoint of dereification or enlightenment, in which things do not have a clear identity, but at the same time, they do have a certain singularity. He makes this point in a key passage in this text: "To equalize the unequal is

43. Zhang Taiyan, "Qi wu lun shi," p. 6.

44. This is the process Lydia Liu describes as "translingual practice," through which we can say that "new" (neither Chinese nor Western) meanings are produced primarily as an unintended consequence. Zhang, however, is much more reflective about the production of new meaning. See Lydia Liu, *Translingual Practice* (Stanford, CA: Stanford University Press, 1995).

45. Zhang Taiyan, "Qi wu lun shi," p. 6.

the position of the lowly scholar, but to see the equal in the unequal is the theory of the elevated philosopher."[46] The above passages may seem opaque, but given the above discussion, we can infer that the latter position, in which equal and unequal exist together, refers to a deeper level beyond mundane language, which Zhang sees both Asaṅga and Zhuangzi portraying.

Although Zhang draws on premodern thinkers to make his point, it is interesting that his argument overlaps with certain trends in post-Hegelian philosophy in France and Germany. Zhang explicitly opposes his philosophy of equalization to Hegel's teleological vision of history, and so a comparison with Hegel could be instructive. To some extent, Zhang's discussion of going beyond refutation echoes Hegel's criticism of one-sided theories in the *Phenomenology*, when he berates positions that seek either "agreement" (*Beistimmung*) or "contradiction" (*Widerspruch*) and argues that one must comprehend the way in which a given position is connected to its opposite in an overarching unity. Hegel explains his position in an oft-cited beautiful metaphor:

> The bud disappears with the emergence of the flower and one could say that each of these are refuted (*widerlegt*). Likewise the fruit of the flower is explained as a false being of the plant as the truth of the former replaces that of the latter. These forms do not merely separate from one another; rather, they suppress each other as irreconcilable. However, their flowing nature makes them moments of an organic unity, where they not only do not contradict one another, but each is as necessary as the other and this same necessity constitutes first the life of the whole (*das Leben des Ganzen*).[47]

Here as well, we have an attempt to overcome one-sidedness, but Hegel stresses a type of necessity that is greater than any of the particulars. Notice that it is the same necessity (*gleiche Notwendingkeit*) that governs all of the various particulars. Here we see the epistemological function of equality working in Hegel's text. Zhang would contend, like post-Hegelian philosophers, that both the parts and the overarching unity are reifications and one needs to penetrate to a more fundamental phenomenological level to grasp a different type of reality. Indeed, the meditative practices of the detachment found in Asaṅga are supposed to break us free from such types of false necessity. It is possible to interpret Zhang as groping for a concept of difference free from conceptualization, beyond or before reifications of subject and object. Although their respective methods of going

46. Zhang Taiyan, "Qi wu lun shi," p. 4.

47. Hegel, *Phänomenologie des Geistes*, p. 12.

beyond reification differ from Zhang and from each other, ever since Nietzsche and Heidegger, philosophers have searched for a realm before the distinctions and logics that envelop our world.

To some extent, we find this gesture expressed clearly in Henri Bergson and more recently in Gilles Deleuze. In particular, in Deleuze's interpretation of Bergson, he distinguishes "difference" from "determination." According to Deleuze, Hegel's dialectic represents a linear movement because his idea of difference is exterior to the thing itself and hence inevitably involves both determination and contradiction. We see this in a number of the antinomies that pervade his thought, such as the opposition between being and nothing, or between particularity and universality. Deleuze is clearly attempting to draw on Bergson to think his way outside such oppositions and claims that in Bergson's view, "not only will vital difference not be a determination, but it will rather be the opposite—given a choice (*au choix*) it would select indetermination itself."[48] Of course, were it merely indetermination, Hegel could retort that in essence Bergson is simply unable to think difference and thus the phrase "given a choice" is crucial. In other words, it would be best not to choose between the determinate/indeterminate opposition, but from our usual conceptual grid, this type of "vital difference" can only appear as indeterminate. In later works, such as *Qu'est-ce que la philosophie?* Deleuze continues this idea and speaks of philosophy in relation to a lived transcendental (*un vécu transcendental*),[49] which plays with the paradox of being both lived and transcendental, at the same time particular and universal. In these ways, Deleuze attempts to point to a realm beyond hegemony, false necessity, and reification. In other words, although the role of phenomenology is to grasp the lived separate from conceptual confusion, the separation between phenomenon and self is itself problematic and hence the actual thing itself can only be expressed through specific paradoxes. Indeed, in the Buddhist context, the self itself is the root of confusion and reification. To express something like the above paradoxical determinations, Zhang cannot stop at leaving words, concepts, and mind. He affirms some type of mark made in this nonconceptual space.

Similar to Bergson and Deleuze, Zhang attempts to avoid the contradiction between the universal and the particular, or the antinomies between the equal and the unequal, which he sees in Kant and Hegel and the various theorists of the universal principle. Of course, Zhang contends that it is not just because of Hegel that we are stuck in more mundane antinomies related to language and concepts;

---

48. Gilles Deleuze, "La conception de la différence chez Bergson," *Etudes bergsoniennes* 4 (1956): 92; "Bergson's Conception of Difference," translated by Melissa McMahon in *The New Bergson*, ed. John Mullarkey (Manchester: Manchester University Press, 1999), p. 50, translation modified.

49. Gilles Deleuze, *Qu'est-ce que la philosophie?* (Paris: L'éditions de minhuit, 1991), p. 9.

rather our whole conceptual framework, generated by attachments to the self and to objects, confronts us as a type of inescapable logic. Zhang claims that such a Yogācāra analysis of the production of categories actually anticipates Kant's idea of categories as the conditions for the possibility of experience.[50] However, unlike Kant, Zhang repeatedly points out that these categories are not eternal but produced contingently by our desire. Like post-Hegelian philosophers, Zhang decenters the world of subjects and objects and positions a more primordial phenomenological realm. Access to such a realm, however, is premised on various practices leading to self-negation.

Conclusion: Situating Zhang Taiyan's reading of Yogācāra and Zhuangzi *historically*

If the above analysis is correct, we are left with the question of how to explain the convergence between Zhang Taiyan and post-Hegelian philosophy. One approach would be to conclude that Yogācāra Buddhists and Zhuangzi spoke to universal philosophical issues and in some way anticipated issues in modern French and German philosophy. Zhang Taiyan then discovered their hidden meaning. Such an interpretation, however, overlooks the selective nature of Zhang's reading of Yogācāra and indeed the selective nature of philosophical interpretations of Yogācāra. There is no doubt that such epistemological discourses existed, but during the time of Asaṅga, such abstract Buddhist epistemologies coexisted with a number of other theories, such as those about heaven and hell or reincarnation. In other words, Zhang brings Yogācāra Buddhists and Zhuangzi closer to the epistemological space of modern philosophy and modern scholarship, by extracting Yogācāra epistemology from its larger original context. From this perspective, when making the comparison to Western philosophy, we are dealing with Zhang's Yogācāra, rather than with some transhistorical body of doctrines. Given Zhang's active role in interpreting Buddhist texts, we should probably call Zhang a "post-Hegelian" philosopher. Indeed, he is closer to Schopenhauer, Nietzsche, and Bergson in both time and in thought than he was to Hegel. However we cannot explain this confluence of ideas merely on the basis of texts. Although Zhang was somewhat familiar with Nietzsche and Schopenhauer, his knowledge of these texts was limited to what he read in translation. So rather than merely understanding the texts of Zhang and Yogācāra, one needs to understand the social contexts that encouraged doctrines to be read one way rather than another.

One must thus ask how this epistemological space, which entailed concepts of subject, object, abstraction, and equality, and their potential overcoming,

---

50. Zhang Taiyan, "Qi wu lun shi," pp. 13–14.

came to be. Clearly at this point, in the Chinese case we could point to the growing popularity of science and the mingling of science and Yogācāra, which Erik J. Hammerstrom examines in his contribution to this volume. I am in some sense adding a footnote to Hammerstrom's argument, by contending that the conditions for the possibility of the equation of Yogācāra with science and modern philosophy, concerns a larger epistemological shift related to global capitalism and the various structures that it entailed. In the first section of this essay, we have seen the ways in which capitalism entered China during the late Qing, and I suggest that this contributed to changing epistemologies in late-Qing China.

Perhaps the most important presupposition of modern philosophy and epistemology concerns the opposition between the subject and object, and behind this opposition lies the negation of previous categories of hierarchy. One of the essential elements of a scientific worldview is reification, in that objects are supposed to exist independently of subjects. In modern philosophy, subject and object are thought of in the abstract, separated from their various particular relationships. Reification, seeing the world as populated by things, brings with it notions of equality, namely that all objects are the same insofar as they are things.

Politically this change has been both liberating and oppressive. The history of political movements is replete with examples of minorities using the concept of equality to claim rights qua humans, thus negating their particularity. On the flipside, this negation of particularity implies that minorities cease to be minorities. Indeed Marx has been reproached for negating the identity of Jews as Jews in his famous essay "On the Jewish Question," where he argued for an emancipation from religion rather than for religious freedom. Zhang Taiyan himself could be seen as juggling with some of these same contradictions. On the one hand, one can hardly find a stronger proponent of the nation-state, and we have seen how the concept of equality is embedded in modern bureaucracy and concepts of national citizenship. Such concepts of identity and difference pervade Zhang's work as he underscored the difference between Han and Manchu identity, which presupposed the self-same identity of both the Han and the Manchu ethnicities. This has led some scholars to think of Zhang as a multiculturalist.[51]

On the other hand, Zhang's philosophical works pose the question of identity, equality, and sameness at a deeper level. Rather than working with pre-established reified categories of Manchu and Han, in *An Interpretation*, Zhang looks

51. Perhaps "national multiculturalist" would be more precise. For a cogent exposition of this standpoint, see Wong, *Search for Modern Nationalism*. Wong has recently criticized my position in favor of his in a review of my recent book on Zhang Taiyan, *The Political Philosophy of Zhang Taiyan: The Resistance of Consciousness* (Leiden: Brill, 2011). For Wong's review see Wang Rongzu 汪榮祖 (Wong Young-tsu), "Book Review: Viren Murthy, *The Political Philosophy of Zhang Taiyan: The Resistance of Consciousness*," *Zhongyang yanjiuyuan*

at the formation of identity and equality in general. We can locate the emergence of the dominance of identity and equality in a tripartite structure associated with the capitalist world, namely the commodity form or commodity exchange, bureaucratic organization, and global capitalist world system. In other words, with the abolition of particular and naturalized privilege, status, and rank, the concept of equality emerges; however, the price one pays for this concept is the obliteration of particularity—a new type of domination.

Zhang Taiyan spent his early career in late-Qing China and then wrote his famous essays on Buddhism and Daoism in Meiji Japan at a time when both countries were in the midst of being incorporated into this world of capitalist domination. Early twentieth-century China experienced increasing bureaucratization with only limited market exchange, while Meiji Japan, especially the late Meiji, represented a place where the processes of both bureaucratization and commodification were further developed than in China. Once Zhang went to Japan, he came in contact with a number of Japan scholars and activists, many of whom were critical of the modernization processes taking place in Japan at the time.

In this context, Zhang mobilizes *Yogācāra to attack* the origins of the concept of abstraction at the heart of much of modernity, but does not simply posit an unchanging concrete identity as the site of resistance. Rather, Zhang invokes the equalization of things, which goes beyond conventional ideas of identity and difference. The ideal that Zhang proposed appears to us today as a utopia, one that has yet to find institutional form. It is a world in which the concrete is not separated from the abstract universal, where individuals are not alienated from the structures that govern them, and where equality does not imply the denuding of particularity, as it does in abstract models of citizenship. The above analysis suggests that like post-Hegelians, such as Schopenhauer, Zhang uses transhistorical categories to analyze and combat the above reification and alienation. To this extent, his project could not understand its own conditions of possibility in historically specific concepts, such as commodity and capital. However, his critique of reification remains important in light of the modernizing paradigm that came to dominate much of twentieth-century Chinese intellectual history. The task that remains, of course, is how to transform the social conditions that constantly reproduce reification. This would be the social analog to the Buddhist idea of overcoming attachments (*zhi* 執).

---

jindaishi yanjiusuo jikan 77 (2012): 147–158. I have responded to his essay: Mu Weiren 慕唯仁 (Viren Murthy), "Chongxin sikao Zhang Taiyan yu xiandaixing: dui Wang Rongzu jiaoshou de huiying 重新思考章太炎與現代性：對汪榮祖教授的回應" (Reconsidering Zhang Taiyan's Modernity: A Response to Professor Wang Rongzu), *Zhongyang yanjiuyuan jindaishi yanjiusuo jikan* 78 (2012): 179–185.

PART 3

Yogācāra and Modern Science

5

Taixu, Yogācāra, and the Buddhist Approach to Modernity

Scott Pacey

TAIXU 太虚 (1890–1947) is one of the most important Chinese Buddhist monastics of the twentieth century. He is known chiefly for his attempts to demonstrate the relevance of the Dharma (*fa* 法; the Buddha's teachings) to the intellectual landscape of the post–May Fourth era. To underscore the Dharma's resonance with scientific and ideological trends in an intellectual context antagonistic to religion, Taixu presented his views under the rubric of "Buddhism for human life" (*rensheng Fojiao* 人生佛教; a term he introduced in 1928),[1] and later (from 1933),[2] "Buddhism for the human world" (*renjian Fojiao* 人間佛教). Although he ultimately judged his reform efforts to have failed,[3] his ideas became increasingly influential after his death and eventually entered into mainstream Buddhist discourses in China and Taiwan.

Although Taixu typically discussed Buddhism from a variety of different angles, Yogācāra often featured in his efforts to demonstrate to intellectuals that Buddhism could further their modernist projects. In a study of Taixu's views on Yogācāra, Li Guangliang points out that "although Taixu promoted Yogācāra,

I gratefully acknowledge the support I received from the Australian Friends of the Hebrew University and the Louis Frieberg Center for East Asian Studies, when I was a Golda Meir Postdoctoral Fellow at the Hebrew University of Jerusalem in 2011–2013.

1. See Taixu 太虛, "Duiyu Zhongguo Fojiao geming seng de xunci 對於中國佛教革命僧的訓詞" (Instructions to Chinese Buddhism's Revolutionary Clergy), in *Taixu dashi quanshu* 太虛大師全書 [TDQS] (The Complete Works of Master Taixu) (CD-ROM), ed. Yinshun 印順, vol. 17 (Xinzhu: Caituan faren Yinshun wenjiao jijinhui (2005 [1928]), p. 597.

2. See Taixu, "Zenyang lai jianshe renjian Fojiao 怎樣來建設人間佛教" (How to Establish Buddhism for the Human World), in TDQS, vol. 24 (2005 [1933]), p. 431.

3. See Taixu, "Wo de Fojiao geming shibai shi 我的佛教革命失敗史" (The History of the Failure of My Buddhist Revolution), in TDQS, vol. 29 (2005 [1937]), pp. 61–63.

he did not endorse using Yogācāra doctrines to reconstruct Chinese Buddhism. His intention was merely to turn Yogācāra into one resource in the development of Chinese Buddhism."[4] Taixu was not alone in taking this approach—other Buddhists during his career also considered Yogācāra capable of mounting an effective Buddhist response to Western scientific disciplines and thought.[5] According to them, Yogācāra, like science, addressed the nature of the noumenon, discussed epistemology and causality, and had a system of logic.[6] For Taixu, these positive correlations with Western modernity were evidence of Buddhism's veracity. At the same time, he maintained that Buddhism could expose and rectify inadequacies in contemporary Western science, philosophy, and ideology. It therefore warranted serious intellectual attention from intellectuals who were interested in these ideas.

This chapter will show that Yogācāra played an important role in Taixu's presentation of Buddhism as modern, even though he himself maintained an essentially conservative doctrinal position. He understood modernity as referring to ideas that originated in Euro-America. Countries that were "individualistic" or "socialistic," that were "scientifically developed," and that had already passed through a phase of "industrial revolution" were modern in this sense.[7] For Taixu, modernity therefore entailed coherence with current trends of Western origin. On this basis, the following analysis will focus on his use of Yogācāra in discussions of contemporary science and Western philosophy, including social evolution, psychology, the theory of relativity, biology, and the reformation of the individual. The chapter will draw on Taixu's writings and speeches from the time of the May Fourth movement in 1919, with its calls to replace religion with science and democracy, through to the 1930s.

The focus of the chapter, however, will be on Taixu's writings from the 1920s. While this period saw the rise of an antireligious movement associated with Marxism, other aspects of the time made it hostile to religion as well. The Guomindang (GMD), which formed a national government in 1927, assumed that "society was knowable and changeable by science," and "that history was moving toward a new stage in which the harmful legacies of the past (especially ignorance and superstition)

---

4. Li Guangliang 李廣良, *Xinshi de liliang: Taixu weishixue sixiang yanjiu* 心識的力量: 太虛唯識學思想研究 (The Strength of Consciousness: Research on Taixu's Thought Yogācāra) (Shanghai: Huadong shifan daxue chubanshe, 2003), p. 48.

5. Chen Bing 陳兵 and Deng Zimei 鄧子美, *Ershi shiji Zhongguo Fojiao* 二十世紀中國佛教 (Twentieth-Century Chinese Buddhism) (Beijing: Minzu chubanshe, 2000), pp. 227–228.

6. Li, *Xinshi de liliang*, pp. 22–24.

7. Taixu, "Zenyang jianshe xiandai Zhongguo de wenhua 怎樣建設現代中國的文化" (How to Establish a Modern Chinese Culture), in TDQS, vol. 20 (2005 [1935]), p. 125.

could be dealt a fatal and definitive blow."[8] Beginning in the early twentieth century, "'science' often came to be the touchstone in dividing between 'religion' (compatible with science) and 'superstition' (unscientific), so that the three formed a triangle in modernist rhetoric."[9] Within this context, demonstrating Buddhism's coherence with science was necessary if it was to gain intellectual and political acceptance.

Taixu's discussions of the similarities between Buddhism and modern ideas from the West were therefore expedient, but also reflected his firm beliefs.[10] He located a model for Buddhism's modernization in Sun Yat-sen's "Three Principles of the People" (*Sanminzhuyi* 三民主義)—the driving ideology of the GMD—which he considered to have successfully merged traditional Chinese culture with modernity.[11] Like *Sanminzhuyi*, Taixu thought that Buddhism could adapt to new contexts while preserving its unchanging, fundamental tenets.[12] The multidimensional nature of his engagement with the world of non-Buddhist ideas, some of which were antithetical to religion, thus points to the complexity of Taixu's thought, and suggests that he should be considered more than an exclusively Buddhist thinker.

Taixu's views were forged in opposition to the atheistic tendencies of the 1920s. In 1922, the Anti-Christian Student Federation (Feijidujiao xuesheng tongmeng 非基督教學生同盟), and an outgrowth of this organization, the Anti-Religion Federation (Feizongjiao tongmeng 非宗教同盟), had opposed the World Student Christian Federation (Shijie Jidujiao xuesheng tongmeng 世界基督教學生同盟) meeting in Beijing.[13] The years 1923 and 1924 also saw the beginning of a debate between advocates of science and those of metaphysics concerning which was most suited to the formation of a viable "philosophy of life."[14] Zhang

8. Vincent Goossaert and David A. Palmer, *The Religious Question in Modern China* (Chicago and London: University of Chicago Press, 2011), p. 62.

9. Ibid., p. 50.

10. Taixu, "Rensheng Foxue de shuoming 人生佛學的說明" (An Explanation of Buddhism for Human Life)," in TDQS, vol. 3 (2005 [1928]), p. 209.

11. Ibid., p. 208. Taixu identified his own plans for Buddhist reform with those of *Sanminzhuyi*. See Don A. Pittman, *Toward a Modern Chinese Buddhism: Taixu's Reforms* (Honolulu: University of Hawai'i Press, 2001), p. 169. For Taixu's original discussion, see Taixu, "Duiyu Zhongguo Fojiao geming seng de xunci," pp. 598–604.

12. Taixu, "Xin yu rongguan 新與融貫" (The New and the Blended), in TDQS, vol. 1 (2005 [1937]), p. 450.

13. See Tatsuro Yamamoto and Sumiko Yamamoto, "II. The Anti-Christian Movement in China, 1922–1927," *The Far Eastern Quarterly* 12, no. 2 (1953): 133–147; Douglas Lancashire, "Introduction," in *Chinese Essays on Religion and Faith*, trans. Douglas Lancashire (Hong Kong: Chinese Materials Center, 1981), pp. 6–10.

14. Danny Wynn Ye Kwok, *Scientism in Chinese Thought 1900–1950* (New Haven, CT: Yale University Press, 1965), p. 135.

Junmai 張君勱 (1886–1969) led the metaphysicians in this debate, arguing that science did not embody a moral outlook. They were opposed by thinkers such as Ding Wenjiang 丁文江 (1887–1936), Chen Duxiu 陳獨秀 (1879–1942), and Hu Shi 胡適 (1891–1962),[15] who argued that science did embody a worldview—one in which "the outlook on life is reduced to science" and "the evaluation of good and evil is also reduced to scientific cognition."[16]

Perhaps as a response to these intellectual currents, at a 1928 lecture in Paris, Taixu explained that Buddhism shared similarities with science, religion, and philosophy, but also that it was different from them.[17] However, he also stressed throughout his career that Buddhism encompassed much scientific knowledge. Its compatibility with science and its provision of a moral framework thus resolved the dilemma faced by intellectuals in 1923 and 1924, and meant that Buddhism was well placed to serve as the worldview for modern society. His writings on Yogācāra were integral to his demonstration of this, as well as to his broader project aimed at establishing a preeminent place for Buddhism on the intellectual landscape of modern China more generally.

The New Yogācāra

Although Taixu argued that Buddhism was aligned with modernity, his stance on Yogācāra was essentially traditional. Chinese Buddhists had two terms for Yogācāra at their disposal: *Weishi* 唯識 (nothing but consciousness), which emphasized cognitive processes; and *Faxiang* 法相 (dharma characteristics)—a derogatory name used by exegetes of the Huayan School (Huayan zong 華嚴宗) who regarded Yogācāra scholars as focusing narrowly on "the superficial manifestations of things."[18] In contrast to his prominent contemporary Ouyang Jingwu 歐陽竟無 (1871–1943), whom Eyal Aviv discusses in detail this volume, Taixu opposed the division of *Faxiang* and *Weishi*, stating that "their content is

15. Ibid., p. 150.

16. Yang Guorong, "The Debate between Scientists and Metaphysicians in Early Twentieth Century: Its Theme and Significance," *Dao: A Journal of Comparative Philosophy* 2, no. 1 (2002): 4.

17. Taixu, "Foxue yu kexue zhexue ji zongjiao zhi yitong 佛學與科學、哲學及宗教之異同" (The Differences and Similarities between Buddhism, Science, Philosophy and Religion), in TDQS, vol. 20 (2005 [1928]), p. 19.

18. A. Charles Muller, "Translator's Introduction," in Shun'ei Tagawa, *Living Yogācāra: An Introduction to Consciousness-Only Buddhism*, trans. A. Charles Muller (Boston, MA: Wisdom Publications, 2009), p. xxi. The Huayan School, which privileged the teachings of the *Avataṃsaka-sūtra* (*Huayan jing* 華嚴經; Flower Ornament Sutra), stressed the interdependence and relativity of phenomena.

fundamentally the same."[19] He thus frequently combined the two terms. In 1933, he explained that

> the conjoined terms, "*Faxiang*" and "*Weishi*," express the fact that the mind manifests all dharmas: the "five kinds of dharmas" (*wu fa* 五法),[20] the "three aspects" (*san xiang* 三相)[21] and so on. [The term] "*wei* 唯" means "not detached." "*Shi* 識" refers to the fact that of the one hundred dharmas (*bai fa* 百法), in addition to the eight consciousnesses (*ba shi* 八識) and the fifty-one mental associates/factors (*wushiyi xinsuo* 五十一心所),[22] the other forty-one dharmas cannot exist detached from the mind either.[23]

In holding these views, Taixu did not advocate any radically new doctrinal interpretations; in general he upheld a position founded on Xuanzang's 玄奘 (602–664) *Cheng weishi lun* 成唯識論 (Demonstration of Nothing but Consciousness) and Kuiji's 窺基 (632–682) *Cheng weishi lun shuji* 成唯識論述記 (Commentary on the *Cheng weishi lun*).[24]

Taixu also differed with Ouyang over how to interpret *Dasheng qixin lun* 大乘起信論 (Awakening of Mahāyāna Faith). He considered this to be a legitimate Indian text even though serious doubts had been raised concerning its traditionally accepted history—that it was composed by Aśvaghoṣa 馬鳴 (ca. 80–150) and translated into Chinese from Sanskrit by Paramārtha 眞諦 (500–569).[25]

---

19. Ibid., p. 20. Taixu, "Faxiang weishixue gailun 法相唯識學概論" (An Overview of Dharma-Characteristics–Consciousness-Only), in TDQS, vol. 9 (2005 [1932]), p. 1151.

20. Here, Taixu probably means the five skandhas.

21. Arising, abiding, and ceasing.

22. See the detailed description in John Powers's chapter in this volume.

23. Taixu, "Faxiang weshixue gailun," pp. 1165–1166; *Digital Dictionary of Buddhism*, s.v. "*baifa* 百法," by C. Muller, http://buddhism-dict.net/ddb>.(accessed June 23, 2011):

> According to the Yogācāra 唯識 school, all experiential phenomena are divided into the five categories of: mind 心, mental factors 心所, form 色法, factors not directly associated with mind 心不相應行法, and unconditioned dharmas 無爲法. In mind group there are eight; within mental factors there are fifty-one, among which are the five which function pervasively 五遍行, the five that function only in regard to specific objects 五別境, the eleven good factors 十一善, the six primary afflictions 根本煩惱, the twenty secondary afflictions 隨煩惱 and the four indeterminate dharmas 四不定. In the group of form there are ten, in the group that are not directly associated with mind, there are twenty-four, in the unconditioned, there are six 六無爲, totaling one hundred.

24. Li, *Xinshi de liliang*, 163.

25. Francesca Tarocco, "Lost in Translation? The Treatise on the *Mahāyāna Awakening of Faith* (*Dasheng qixin lun*) and Its Modern Readings," *Bulletin of the School of Oriental and African Studies* 71, no. 2 (2008): 323–343.

For example, in his study of the text, Liang Qichao 梁啟超 (1873–1929) concluded that it was of Chinese origin.[26]

In addition, whereas the *Dasheng qixin lun* held that Suchness and reality were entwined and that Suchness could be perfumed, Ouyang maintained that Suchness and reality were separate.[27] In other words, Ouyang's "assumption that there are two separate worlds, the world of higher or 'real' truth versus the world of inferior or 'worldly' truth, or the development of dharma-nature versus the world of dharma-character," could not be reconciled with the *Dasheng qixin lun*'s position: that these two worlds were "merely the two aspects of the same thing."[28] Taixu's acceptance of the *Dasheng qixin lun*'s basic position, however, like his equation of *Faxiang* and *Weishi*, marked him as an upholder of the Chinese Buddhist tradition.

Taixu did, however, believe that a new approach to Yogācāra was necessary in the modern era. In a 1920 speech, he explained that this was because

> recent scientific advances have achieved extraordinary results, and theistic religion has completely lost its basis. Science has gradually occupied the domain of philosophy. The only path remaining for philosophy now is one of metaphysics . . . [however] doubt now exists that metaphysics can offer us anything in the way of knowledge, or that what it can know is useless.[29]

Although Taixu clearly recognized the importance of science, like many Chinese intellectuals of the post–World War I generation, he traced the source of conflict to its misuse. In the absence of philosophy and theism, something else was needed to guide scientific inquiry so that it could be used for peaceful and constructive purposes. He suggested that while Yogācāra could make substantial contributions in this regard,[30] it would need to be presented in ways that accorded with twentieth-century intellectual trends. He therefore called for Yogācāra to be discussed using scientific terminology[31] and referred to this as the "new Yogācāra."[32]

---

26. Ibid., 333.

27. Wing-tsit Chan, *Religious Trends in Modern China* (New York: Columbia University Press, 1953), p. 114.

28. Ibid., pp. 114–115.

29. Taixu, "Xin de weishilun 新的唯識論" (A Treatise on the New Yogācāra), in TDQS, vol. 8 (2005 [1920]), p. 606.

30. Ibid., p. 607.

31. Ibid., p. 610.

32. Ibid.

Aside from advocating a new mode of expression, the content of Yogācāra would remain the same. According to Wing-tsit Chan,

> Taixu calls his theory new because, he says, it is elucidated with modern ideas, makes use of modern science, and agrees with Einstein's Theory of Relativity. . . . Actually, his understanding of Western philosophy is extremely superficial. And he has not offered a new theory of ideation.[33]

Although Taixu's views on Yogācāra may not have been doctrinally innovative, the links he identified between Yogācāra and non-Buddhist ideas caused him to conceive of it in unique ways. When he went into sealed confinement for three years on Putuo Mountain from 1914,[34] he took works on Yogācāra with him, demonstrating the importance he attached to the school during these early phases of his intellectual development.[35] He also took books on "psychology, logic, ethics, and philosophy."[36]

In the years prior to Taixu's confinement, he had also read numerous works that embodied the ideals of science and progress. These included Zhang Taiyan's 章太炎 (1868–1936) "Jianli zongjiao lun 建立宗教論" (On Founding a Religion),[37] Kang Youwei's 康有為 (1858–1927) *Datong shu* 大同書 (Book on the Great Unity), Tan Sitong's 譚嗣同 (1865–1898) *Renxue* 仁學 (An Exposition of Benevolence), and Liang Qichao's *Xinmin shuo* 新民說 (On the New Citizen),[38] as well as works by Tolstoy, Kropotkin, Bakunin, Proudhon, Marx, and Kōtoku Shūsui.[39] He also read Yan Fu's 嚴復 (1854–1921) 1903 translation of Herbert Spencer's *The Study of Sociology* (*Qunxue siyan* 群學肆言).[40] Taixu's subsequent work bore the legacy of these early influences and demonstrated his belief that Buddhism had important links to science and society, while also critiquing them from his Buddhist standpoint.

---

33. Chan, *Religious Trends in Modern China*, pp. 124–125. Romanization modified.

34. Taixu, "Taixu zizhuan 太虛自傳" (Autobiography of Taixu), in TDQS, vol. 29 (2005 [1940]), p. 208.

35. Chan, *Religious Trends in Modern China*, p. 119.

36. Taixu, "Taixu zizhuan," p. 209.

37. Taixu, "Wo de Fojiao gaijin yundong lüeshi 我的佛教改進運動略史" (A Brief History of My Buddhist Reform Movement), in TDQS, vol. 29 (2005 [1940]), p. 74.

38. Taixu, "Taixu zizhuan," p. 191.

39. Ibid., 194.

40. Taixu, "Wo de Fojiao gaijin yundong lüeshi," p. 69.

The scientific method

The links between science and Buddhism can be seen from Taixu's discussions of one of the pillars of Western modernity: the scientific method itself. Although he considered the scientific method to be flawed, he also believed that it could be improved on through the introduction of concepts from Yogācāra. The underlying problem with the scientific method was that it relied on the imperfect observations of deluded beings. For example, in a 1919 piece entitled "Materialist Science and the Study of Yogācāra," he explained that research on optics and electricity had shown all phenomena to consist of impermanent false forms (*jiaxiang* 假相) that were in a continual state of flux.[41] Although science had verified this, Yogācāra would provide a basis for it to be perceived more directly through the five eyes (*wuyan* 五眼).[42] With one of these, the buddha eye (*foyan* 佛眼), one would be able to see that everything is of one mind (*yixin* 一心), and the "two characteristics" (*er xiang* 二相)[43] would disappear.[44]

Furthermore, in 1924, he explained that scientific observations did not take the relationship between the mind and the phenomenal world into account. As a result, the theories scientists developed on the basis of their observations were misguided.[45] Despite this, Taixu also criticized the basis of science in materialism, stating that "the three worlds are nothing but mind (*weixin* 唯心), the ten thousand dharmas are nothing but consciousness (*weishi* 唯識)."[46] In the absence of Yogācāra, scientists were thus faced with two problems: first, their reliance on flawed observation; and second, their false understanding of the phenomenal world and its relation to cognition.

Taixu did accept that science and Buddhism were different; whereas science presented a method he characterized as "narrow,"[47] Buddhism constituted a "broad scientific method."[48] Both approaches, however, were useful and pursued

---

41. Taixu, "Weiwu kexue yu weishi zong xue 唯物科學與唯識宗學" (Materialist Science and the Study of Yogācāra), in TDQS, vol. 22, 2005 [1919], p. 818.

42. Ibid., p. 819. The five eyes is a notion taken from *Yogācārabhūmi-śāstra* (*Yuqie shidi lun* 瑜伽師地論; Discourse on the Stages of Concentration Practice): the physical eye; the heavenly eye; the wisdom eye, the dharma eye; and the buddha-eye.

43. The universal and particular characteristics of Suchness.

44. Taixu, "Weiwu kexue yu weishi zong xue," p. 819.

45. Taixu, "Renshengguan de kexue 人生觀的科學" (The Science of the Philosophy of Life), in TDQS, vol. 23 (2005 [1924]), pp. 4–5.

46. Ibid., p. 813.

47. Taixu, "Renshengguan de kexue," p. 6.

48. Ibid., p. 5.

truth from different levels of depth: "Buddhism's explanations are deep but its level of detail is shallow," whereas "science's explanations are shallow but its level of detail is deep."[49] Taixu therefore saw the future of Yogācāra and science as one in which they could complement one another.[50] In time, scientists would come to appreciate Buddhism's explanatory power. He provided a further example of this by stating that among the "worldly methods of seeking knowledge, science is more excellent," but that Buddhism could "improve" the "six senses and eight consciousnesses," increasing one's capacity to observe reality directly,[51] thus leading to improved scientific observations. This led Taixu to suggest that in the future, "Yogācāra methods could . . . increase the limited powers of telescopes and microscopes."[52] Yogācāra would improve on the scientific method, augmenting scientists' powers of observation so that they could use their scientific instruments to full effect.

Biology

As might be expected from this comment, Taixu also considered Buddhist texts to embody knowledge on microbiology. Erik J. Hammerstrom has shown how the effort to demonstrate the Buddha's awareness of microbiological science led Taixu to search for evidence in lesser-known texts, thus promoting them to new positions of prominence.[53] In 1919 and 1923, he referred to a phrase from the *Pini riyong lü* 毗尼日用綠 (Record of the Vinaya for Daily Use) to show that the Buddha was aware of the existence of microorganisms—before Antonie van Leeuwenhoek's (1632–1723) observation of them in the seventeenth century. Taixu also used a citation from the *Saddharma-smṛty-upasthāna-sūtra* (*Zhengfa nianchu jing* 正法念處經; Sutra on the Bases of Mindfulness of the True Dharma) as evidence that the Buddha had knowledge concerning the existence of gametes and cells. The notion that the Buddha had advanced microbiological knowledge later became a common theme in the 1920s.

While Buddhism embodied existing biological knowledge, Yogācāra could be used to fill gaps in our understanding of processes such as reproduction. In

49. Taixu, "Yue *Weishi xin lun* jianshu 閱'唯識新論'簡述" (A Concise Account of My Reading of "A New Treatise on Yogācāra"), in TDQS, vol. 25 (2005 [1935]), p. 169.

50. Taixu, "Xin de weishi lun," p. 610.

51. Taixu, "Zhen xianshilun zongyilun (shang) 真現實論宗依論（上） (On True Realism: On the School's Basis [Part 1])," in TDQS, vol. 18 (2005 [1927]), p. 159.

52. Taixu, "Renshengguan de kexue," p. 54.

53. Erik J. Hammerstrom, "Early Twentieth-Century Buddhist Microbiology and Shifts in Chinese Buddhism's 'Actual Canon,' " *Theology and Science* 10, no. 1 (2012): 3–18.

1923, drawing from the *Yogācārabhūmi-śāstra* (Discourse on the Stages of Concentration Practice),[54] Taixu explained that it was the base consciousness that in fact enabled male and female gametes to form a zygote, thereby creating the first fetal stage (the first of eight stages of fetal development).[55] Without this, the gametes would disperse.[56] Further proof, according to Taixu, came from those who had developed the "divine eye"—they had confirmed the Buddhist account of reproduction contained in the *Yogācārabhūmi*. In contrast, biologists had as yet been unable to observe directly the process of zygote formation.[57] (In fact, although Taixu may have been unaware, the German zoologist Oskar Hertwig [1849–1922] had observed this process in sea urchins in 1875.[58]) Superior methods of Buddhist observation had therefore enabled important biological information to be obtained centuries before the discoveries of Western scientists.

Psychology

As Hammerstrom shows in this volume, the Wuchang School, with which Taixu was associated, regularly published articles on Buddhism and psychology during the 1920s. As with the scientific method more generally, Taixu saw Yogācāra and psychology as capable of working together, although performing different functions. In a 1924 essay, Taixu suggested that both could be used to "regulate the mind,"[59] while Buddhism's ten good deeds (*shi shanfa* 十善法) could moderate the mind and behavior. Furthermore, psychology would be used to explain "the motivations [behind] ethics," and "scientific rationality [would be used to] moderate direct perception."[60] From the perspective of social ethics, psychology and Yogācāra could clearly work in tandem, with Buddhism taking a lead role in the area of morality, and psychology furnishing research on specific mental functions.

---

54. On this text, see the "Summary of the Yogācārabhūmi-śāstra" by Dan Lusthaus and Charles Muller, which is available at: www.acmuller.net/yogacara/outlines/YBh-summary-utf8.htm (accessed June 14 2010).

55. On the stages of fetal development, see *Digital Dictionary of Buddhism*, s.v. "*bawei taizang* 八位胎藏," by C. Muller, http://buddhism-dict.net/ddb (accessed July 17, 2010).

56. Taixu, "Fo yi jin jie 佛疑今解" (A Contemporary Explanation of Buddhist Uncertainty), in *Faxiang weishixue* 法相唯識學 (Dharma-Characteristics–Consciousness-Only) (Beijing: Shangwu yinshuguan, 2006 [1923]), vol. 2, p. 417.

57. Ibid., p. 419.

58. Ernst Mayr, *The Growth of Biological Thought: Diversity, Evolution, and Inheritance* (Cambridge, MA: The Belknap Press of Harvard University Press, 1982), pp. 665–666.

59. Taixu, "Renshengguan de kexue," p. 43.

60. Ibid.

Besides suggesting that psychology and Yogācāra could perform these different roles, Taixu also felt they shared common knowledge regarding the senses and certain cognitive functions. In the context of the 1920s, this was an important verification of Buddhism's compatibility with modern science. He thus explained that the Buddhist five sensory faculties (*wu gen* 五根)[61] should be equated with the nervous system.[62] The first six consciousnesses were the subjects of psychological investigations, whereas the independently arising thinking consciousness (*dutou yishi* 獨頭意識)—the sixth consciousness—was what psychologists called the "imagination." [63] Meanwhile, the sensory abilities (*shengyi gen* 勝意根) were akin to nerves joined to organs, such as the optic or auditory nerves.[64]

Ultimately, however, Taixu claimed that Yogācāra provided a more expansive account of the mind's mental processes than psychology.[65] Yogācāra's "*shi* 識," or "consciousness," was broader than the psychological definition (which encompassed only knowledge and emotions).[66] Moreover, certain aspects of the mind that were unknown to psychologists were well understood in Yogācāra. For example, although psychologists discussed the subconscious and the unconscious, they were unaware of the seventh consciousness—or *manas*, which erroneously leads us to arrive at the idea of selfhood—and the base consciousness, which is the "storehouse" of our accumulated karma.

In a 1932 piece, Taixu specifically referred to "behavioral psychology" (*xingweipai zhi xinlixue* 行為派之心理學) and "introspective psychology" (*neixing xinlixue* 內省心理學),[67] which were two prominent schools during the period of his career. (A contemporary comparison of the two stated that behaviorism focused on the acquisition of qualitative data on "memory, forgetting, sensation, association, learning, and the like," while introspection focused on "the conscious middle term in the reaction chain and nothing more."[68]) According to Taixu, both schools were hindered by their inability to perceive these deep structures of the

61. The visual, hearing, olfactory, gustatory, and tactile faculties.

62. Taixu, "Faxiang weishixue gailun," pp. 1196–1197.

63. Ibid., pp. 1189–1190.

64. Taixu, "Bashi guiju song jianglü 八識規矩頌講錄" (Records of a Lecture on *Verses on the Structure of the Eight Consciousnesses*), in TDQS, vol. 9 (2005 [1931]), 918.

65. Taixu, "Faxiang weishixue gailun," pp. 1189–1190.

66. Taixu, "Weishi sanshilun jiangyao," p. 691.

67. Taixu, "Faxiang weishixue gailun," p. 1202.

68. Samuel W. Fernberger, "Behavior versus Introspective Psychology," *The Psychological Review* 29, no. 6 (1922): 411.

mind, for which practice in "meditation and wisdom" was required.[69] Furthermore, the psychological conception of cognition (*sixiang* 思想) only covered the mind's investigative (*xun* 尋) and scrutinizing (*si* 伺) functions, or the observation of coarse and fine objects respectively—which was a smaller range of functions than had been identified in Yogācāra.[70]

Taixu held that the root of the problem was psychology's basis in materialistic science, which assumed that life was subject to mechanistic laws.[71] He explained, however, that recent developments in science—such as relativity—had shown that matter existed only in interdependent relationships. As a result, "old nineteenth-century materialism" was now untenable.[72] With its detailed discussion of the relationship between the mind and the phenomenal world, Yogācāra was clearly in a position to advance science into the postmaterialistic age.

This approach to scientific explanations of mental functioning distinguished him from a figure who, in many ways, was his predecessor, Tan Sitong. Taixu had read Tan's *Renxue* (An Exposition of Benevolence) early in his career, and later wrote that he loved it "so much that I could not part with it."[73] Although Tan claimed that all "Western Learning" stemmed from Buddhism,[74] the emphasis of the book is on the essential agreement between different religious perspectives and branches of science. Whereas Tan had sought to locate Yogācāra's cognitive architecture in the brain, Taixu held that the "physical mind" (*routuan* 肉團) was merely a "form dharma" (*sefa* 色法);[75] that is, an object of sensory perception, rather than the mind itself (*xinfa* 心法) or its mental functions (*xinsuo* 心所). And even though psychologists assigned memories a physical location within the brain, the brain was too small to store all of them. According to Taixu, the base consciousness provided a superior explanation for the retention of memory.[76] His approach was thus more closely aligned with that of the more critical Wuchang School.

69. Taixu, "Faxiang weishixue gailun," p. 1202.

70. Taixu, "Bashi guiju song jianglü," p. 914.

71. Taixu, "Fa yu ren zhi yanjiu 法與人之研究" (Research on the Dharma and Human Beings), in TDQS, vol. 9 (2005 [1931]), p. 1321.

72. Taixu, "Fa yu ren zhi yanjiu," p. 1323.

73. Taixu, "Taixu zizhuan," pp. 189–191.

74. Tan Sitong, "Renxue," in *Tan Sitong quanji* 譚嗣同全集 (The Collected Works of Tan Sitong), ed. Cai Shangsi 蔡尚思 (Beijing: Zhonghua shuju chuban, 1981), vol. 2, p. 317; T'an Ssu-t'ung, *An Exposition of Benevolence: The Jen-hsuëh of T'an Ssu-t'ung*, trans. Chan Sin-wai (Hong Kong: The Chinese University Press, 1984), p. 107.

75. Taixu, "*She dasheng lun* chufen jiangyi 攝大乘論初分講義" (Initial Division of Lectures on the *Compendium of the Great Vehicle*), in TDQS, vol. 8 (2005 [1925]), p. 502.

76. Taixu, "Faxiang weishixue gailun," pp. 1195–1196.

Social evolution

While Taixu's early interest in revolutionary social theories had subsided by the 1920s, his concern with Buddhism's social role remained throughout his life. One of the most important contributions to twentieth-century Chinese Buddhism came in the form of his "Pure Land in the human world" (*renjian jingtu* 人間淨土) concept in 1926—the notion that rather than focusing on attaining rebirth in the Pure Lands, this world itself could be "purified" by making Buddhism the basis of individual and social life.[77]

As noted above, Taixu indicated in one of his autobiographical accounts that he had read Yan Fu's translation of Herbert Spencer's *The Study of Sociology*. Yan Fu himself "gravitated to Spencer's side and held that evolution was a law or force that could be generally applied to the domains of nature and social ethics."[78] Displaying the influence of this social Darwinism, Taixu himself proposed an evolutionary scheme that saw Buddhism elevated to become a feature of advanced societies. In doing so, he directly asserted that Buddhism, rather than being the outmoded product of a premodern age, in fact surpassed conventional understandings of modernity. It was during such a time that Yogācāra would be treated as a form of "perfect science."

He explained this in some detail in 1927, when he wrote that social evolution's first stage was one of idolatrous semihuman people who were primarily occupied with survival. In the second stage, society was characterized by theistic religion and a system of government. Eventually, theism was discarded in favor of mathematics, ethics, rationality, and science. The third stage saw the rise of what Taixu called the "supermen" (*chaoren* 超人), who aspired to sagehood and practiced techniques of mental cultivation, such as Chan, Jainism, Yoga, Confucianism, and Daoism. The final stage consisted of the "super-supermen" (*chao chaoren* 超超人), who were Buddhists. At this time, the scientific outlook of earlier stages would give way to the study of the various schools of Buddhism: Chan, Pure Land, Huayan, Tiantai, and Yogācāra. During this final stage:

> Zhenyan Pure Land studies are a pure aesthetics. Huayan and Tiantai studies are a pure literature. The wisdom that comes from knowing that all dharmas are empty is a pure philosophy. Yogācāra is a pure philosophy,

---

77. Taixu coined this term in 1926, although his previous writings display elements of this idea. See Taixu, "Jianshe renjian jingtu lun 建設人間淨土論" (Treatise on Establishing the Pure Land in the Human World), in TDQS, vol. 24 (2005 [1926]), pp. 349–424.

78. Wang Hui, "The Fate of 'Mr. Science' in China: The Concept of Science and Its Application in Modern Chinese Thought," *Positions* 3, no. 1 (1995): 25.

> and a pure science. From this it can be seen that the Dharma spoken of by the Buddha can encompass everything spoken of by humanity.[79]

Taixu thus situated Buddhism at a higher level than the knowledge systems of the second, scientific stage of civilization, which clearly corresponded with the West. And from among the other Buddhist schools, he placed Yogācāra in a privileged position in relation to science, making it the perfect form of modernity's most important feature.

Taixu developed this scheme in opposition to other theories that were attracting attention in the 1920s. One of these belonged to Liang Shuming 梁漱溟 (1893–1988), who, in his influential 1921 book *Dongxi wenhua jiqi zhexue* 東西文化及其哲學 (Eastern and Western Cultures and Their Philosophies), rejected Buddhism as a suitable basis for society. As Thierry Meynard shows in this volume, although Liang himself was a Buddhist, he chose Confucianism as a middle path between what he considered Western scientific and Indian transcendental culture. Taixu's scheme also contrasted with that of Auguste Comte, who suggested that society passed through "theological," "metaphysical," and "positivist" stages.[80] (In 1930, Taixu criticized this Comtean scheme on the grounds that it established firm boundaries between religion, philosophy, and science that did not exist, since each one of these categories contained aspects of the others.[81]) Taixu's presentation of Buddhism established it as sharing the scientific aspects of Western culture, as well as the worldly aspect of Confucianism.[82] Encompassing and surpassing both, Buddhism, according to Taixu, was at the peak of the civilizational typologies. As such, Taixu implied that modernists who were interested in science and social progress should turn away from Comte and Liang, as well as from Marxists touting a postreligion future, to embrace Buddhism.

Physics

Taixu also claimed that Yogācāra could complete scientific theories concerning more fundamental physical processes. One special target for him in this regard was Einstein's theory of relativity, which had been introduced to China in 1917 by

79. Taixu, "Zhen xianshilun zongyilun (shang)," p. 159.

80. See George Perrigo Conger, *New Views of Evolution* (New York: The Macmillan Company, 1929), p. 176.

81. Taixu, "Minguo yu Fojiao 民國與佛教" (The Republic and Buddhism), in TDQS, vol. 22 (2005 [1930]), p. 1243.

82. Taixu, "Foxue yu xin sixiang 佛學與新思想" (Buddhism and New Thought), in TDQS, vol. 20, p. 43.

the scientists Xu Chongqing 許崇清 (1888–1969) and Li Fangbai 李芳柏 (1890–1959) after their studies in Japan.[83] The post–May Fourth intellectual climate provided fertile ground for the theory's popularization. It was praised by Bertrand Russell during his stay in China in 1921, and further popularized by Einstein's own visit in 1922. According to Danian Hu, "Not a single Chinese physicist or mathematician between the 1920s and the 1940s publicly opposed the theory."[84] Relativity was thus a landmark feature of China's intellectual vista in the 1920s, and given its prominence, to show how Yogācāra could identify the theory's inadequacies and render it complete would have been an astonishing demonstration of Buddhism's modernity.

In 1927, Taixu attempted to do this by responding to an explanation of relativity provided in 1922 by the Scottish naturalist and professor at the University of Aberdeen J. Arthur Thomson (Tang Musheng 湯姆生). Thomson's explanation had appeared in a four-volume work entitled *An Outline of Science*, which was published in Chinese in 1923 and 1924 under the title *Hanyi kexue dagang* 漢譯科學大綱.[85]

Thomson explained notions of space, time, and matter with a story about an "intelligence" that, upon arriving in a field, initially lacked these concepts. Eventually, it learned to distinguish between itself and the outside world, creating a dualistic view of reality. When it observed a flower with a wasp on it, the intelligence initially regarded both as part of a unified world external to the self. When the wasp flew into the intelligence's hand, it discovered that there were different points in space, and arrived at concepts such as "here" and "there." After being stung by the wasp, the intelligence also learned about different points in time, and thus gained the ability to distinguish between "before" and "after." Having thus conceptualized space and time, it subsequently went on to develop ideas concerning matter.[86]

Thomson's story was intended to illustrate the principles of relativity. Taixu, however, claimed it was useful for both explaining Yogācāra and simultaneously pointing out the flaws in Einstein's theory:

---

83. Danian Hu, "The Reception of Relativity in China," *Isis* 98, no. 3 (2007): 541.

84. Ibid., 545.

85. For the original passage see J. Arthur Thomson (ed.), *The Outline of Science: A Plain Story Simply Told*, vol. 4 (New York: G. P. Putnam's Sons, 1922), pp. 1032–1033. For the Chinese translation, see Tang Musheng 湯姆生 [J. Arthur Thomson], *Hanyi kexue dagang* 漢譯科學大綱 (An Outline of Science: Chinese Translation), (Shanghai: Shangwu yinshuguan, 1923–1924), vol. 13, p. 50.

86. Taixu, "Ai'ensitan xiangduilun yu Weishilun 愛恩斯坦相對論與唯識論 (Einstein's Theory of Relativity and Yogācāra)," in TDQS, vol. 21 (2005 [1927]), pp. 616–617.

> Although this explanation of the origins of knowledge concerning space, time, and matter has not reached the level of depth of the explanation concerning this origin in the base consciousness, it is near enough! It speaks of a primitive real essence (*zhenti* 真體)[87]—an intelligence completely lacking in experience. We may call this the base consciousness. When it suddenly appears here, it first experiences the environment, and all things within it, as an entirety (*quanti* 全體). The natural world and the body with senses (*genshen* 根身) appear simultaneously to the base consciousness. The body and the environment are then understood to be two things. Next, the *manas* grasps the base consciousness as something internal to the self. The intelligence thus has a body, and assumes this to be its center of thought. It begins to distinguish between "here" and "there." Then, the consciousness, considering the body to be real, gives rise to the distinction between the self and those things attached to the self (*wo wosuo* 我我所). Following on from this, the first six consciousnesses divide and combine different things in the environment: this flower, the wasp, this hand, the wasp which is first at the flower and then is by the hand, then material objects, space, time—all of these "burning lamps" (*chiran* 熾然)[88] appear to oneself. Analysis of these material things from a distance leads to the establishment of different points in time, small particles, and material things such as molecules, atoms and electrons. Although Einstein's theory of relativity is impoverished and incomplete, it is in agreement with Yogācāra.[89]

Taixu's interpretation therefore emphasized the similarities between relativity and Yogācāra, while claiming that the theory of relativity lacked Yogācāra's level of comprehensiveness. He could therefore invoke Einstein—whom he called "the greatest contemporary scientist"[90]—in support of Yogācāra, while showing his ideas to be inadequate when compared with Buddhism.

In 1937, Taixu again referred to contemporary scientific literature in some detail with the intention of showing how Yogācāra accorded with new scientific developments.[91] The basis of his discussion was a speech given by the

87. *Digital Dictionary of Buddhism*, s.v. "*zhenti* 真體," by C. Muller, http://buddhism-dict.net/ddb (accessed March 25, 2012). This is "the true form of something."

88. Ibid., s.v. "*chiran* 熾然," by C. Muller (accessed March 25, 2012).

89. Taixu, "Ai'ensitan xiangduilun yu weishilun," pp. 617–-618.

90. Ibid., p. 616.

91. See Taixu, "Xin wulixue yu Weishixue 新物理學與唯識學 (The New Physics and Yogācāra)," in TDQS, vol. 21, 2005 [1937], pp. 596–618.

British physicist Sir James Jeans (Qinsi Jueshi 秦斯爵士). Entitled "The New World Picture of Modern Physics," this originally appeared in a 1934 issue of the journal *Science*. It appeared in Chinese translation in *Eastern Miscellany* in 1937.[92]

Jeans's speech had focused on what he called "the new physics." He declared that the old physics was akin to a mansion that had been shaken by a series of earthquakes. The principles of physics could "only be made comprehensible in the form of parables," and "no parable can remain true throughout its whole range to the facts it is trying to explain. . . . The fundamental mistake of the old-fashioned physicist was that he failed to distinguish between the half-truths of parables and the literal truth."[93] He added that space and time were "mere mental frameworks of our own construction."[94] Casting doubt on the reliability of sensory perception, Jeans explained:

> Physical science, assuming that each message must have had a starting point, postulated the existence of "matter" to provide such starting points. But the existence of this matter was a pure hypothesis; and matter is in actual fact as unobservable as the ether, Newtonian force, and other unobservables that have vanished from science. Early science not only assumed matter to exist but further pictured it as existing in space and time. Again, this assumption had no adequate justification; for there is clearly no reason why the whole material universe should be restricted to the narrow framework along which messages strike our senses. To illustrate by an analogy, the earthquake waves which damage our houses travel along the surface of the ground, but we have no right to assume that they originate in the surface of the ground; we know, on the contrary, that they originate deep in the earth's interior.[95]

As a result, "the whole picture, and the manifold dimensions of space in which it is drawn, become pure mental constructs—diagrams and frameworks we make for ourselves to help us understand phenomena."[96]

---

92. Qinshi Jue (Sir [James Hopwood] Jeans), "Xiandai wulixue de xin shijieguan 現代物理學的新世界觀" (The New World Picture of Modern Physics), trans. Tang Zhongling 湯鍾靈, *Dongfang zazhi* 34, no. 6 (1937): 65–77; James Hopwood Jeans, "The New World-Picture of Modern Physics," *Science* 80, no. 2071 (September 7, 1934): 213–222.

93. Ibid., p. 214.

94. Ibid., p. 215.

95. Ibid., p. 215.

96. Ibid., p. 217.

Such comments led Taixu to conclude that since nineteenth-century physics was deficient, the only remaining option was to renovate it using the tools provided by Yogācāra. When Jeans stated that scientific truths could be expressed only through the use of metaphors, Taixu claimed this was akin to the difference between the posited reality (*anlidi* 安立諦)—the attempt to express truths about reality using language—and unposited reality (*fei anlidi* 非安立諦), or ultimate truth. Similarly, Jeans's example of our inability to directly sense the origin of an earthquake was akin to perceptions that travelled through our sensory organs, but whose origins—in the base consciousness—we were unaware of.[97] Finally, the notion that reality was a mental construction—and, as Jeans stated in his speech, the inability to distinguish between objective and subjective reality—meant that science had, as Taixu predicted, finally verified the existence of the base consciousness. Scientists were therefore realizing what Yogācāra scholars already knew: that "the world of external objects and the views of the internal mind are of the same nature."[98]

Taixu and Cassirer

In 1929, Taixu gave a speech entitled "The Person of Culture and the Base Consciousness."[99] He recalled encountering the idea of the "person of culture" (*wenhuaren* 文化人) on the German leg of his Euro-American tour in 1928 and 1929. Although he did not provide the source of this idea—he may not have known—it would appear that he was referring to *Philosophy of Symbolic Forms*, the three volumes of which the German philosopher Ernst Cassirer (1874–1945) published in 1923, 1925, and 1929. The speech indicates that Taixu was not only interested in responding to science from the perspective of Yogācāra but that he also saw it as a useful vantage point from which to approach Western thought more generally, including contemporary European philosophy.

Cassirer held that culture manifested in various "symbolic forms" throughout history, including "myth, religion, language, science, [and] art."[100] He emphasized the creative power of the individual to make history, against what he called the "physicalist" determinism of Comte, the "psychological" determinism

97. Taixu, "Xin wulixue yu weishixue," p. 600.

98. Ibid., p. 602.

99. Taixu, "Wenhuaren yu alaiyeshi 文化人與阿賴耶識" (The Person of Culture and the Base Consciousness), in TDQS, vol. 20, pp. 237–242.

100. Enno Rudolph, "Symbol and History: Ernst Cassirer's Critique of the Philosophy of History," in *The Symbolic Construction of Reality: The Legacy of Ernst Cassirer*, ed. Jeffrey Andrew Barash (Chicago: University of Chicago Press, 2008), p. 7. Here, Rudolph is summarizing Hans Blumenberg.

of Spengler, and the "metaphysical" determinism of Hegel.[101] In contrast to Kant, Cassirer held that "there is no 'primary datum' underlying the creative activity of consciousness. Every primary datum is already spiritually imbued, even the simplest spatial perceptions, like left and right, high and low."[102] Therefore, "the question [of] what absolute reality should be outside that totality of spiritual functions, what the 'thing in itself' might be in this sense . . . [is] a falsely put problem, a phantom of thought."[103] Cassirer instead compared human beings to artists; interaction with the environment was creative and imbued it with meaning.[104] It was recognition of one's own creative power, and the manipulation of symbolic formations, that would enable humanity to become liberated from them. Thus, "a healthy consciousness must in every act, shuttle back and forth throughout the aeons of cultural development and knit all of them into the act."[105] In advocating a complex, ever-changing conception of culture, and a human integration with its products that led to ultimate liberation, Cassirer "points toward a future of symbolic forms so rich that man's present culture appears very primitive indeed."[106]

Taixu augmented various aspects of this theory with concepts from Yogācāra. In agreement with Cassirer, he explained that "the person of culture has two aspects: one is historical, and one is social."[107] While people bore the legacy of their cultural past; this could be the foundation on which to build a new, superior culture.[108] However, he diverged from Cassirer when he added that the person of culture—which he also called the "universal person" (*yuzhouren* 宇宙人)—should be subject to a "Buddhist education."[109]

Taixu explained it was the base consciousness that determined interpersonal differences; this was how unique individuals such as Confucius and the Buddha could appear.[110] The influence of environmental factors on Confucius's and the

101. Ibid., p. 12.

102. Robert S. Hartman, "Cassirer's Philosophy of Symbolic Forms," in *The Philosophy of Ernst Cassirer*, ed. Paul Arthur Schilpp (Evanston, IL: Library of Living Philosophers, 1949), p. 293.

103. Ernst Cassirer, *Philosophie der symbolischen Formen*, I, 47 f., cited in Hartman, "Cassirer's Philosophy of Symbolic Forms," pp. 294–295.

104. Ibid., pp. 300–301.

105. Ibid., p. 305.

106. Ibid., p. 332.

107. Taixu, "Wenhuaren yu alaiyeshi," p. 237.

108. Ibid.

109. Ibid., p. 239.

110. Ibid., pp. 241–242.

Buddha's base consciousness led them to become exemplary individuals. Taixu saw the cultural person as one who could "absorb the common qualities of the world" and yet also develop the "uncommon qualities" that made them unique and stand above others (like Confucius and the Buddha).[111] By supplying the right influences, the base consciousness could therefore be deliberately molded.

Taixu delivered another speech the next year—one that provided readers with a summary of what a Buddhist education might entail. He explained that the concepts of "nonself" and "nothing but mind" should form the basis of a universal worldview.[112] As was the case with science, Taixu saw much that was of value in the person of culture, but the fact that the concept was so compatible with Yogācāra was evidence of its veracity. He did, however, continue to present Buddhism as a superior overarching framework in which Cassirer's theory would need to be situated in order to render it complete. Taixu's person of culture can also be read alongside his critique of Liang Shuming's promotion of Confucian culture (which Thierry Meynard discusses in this volume), because Buddhism could encompass the best of Liang's cultural typologies while remaining true to itself as a superior worldview and the pinnacle of modernity.

Conclusion

Taixu features prominently in histories of Chinese Buddhism, but less so in intellectual histories of modern China. He was, of course, a monastic, and throughout his life he was committed to the promotion of a Chinese Buddhist worldview. Yet he also maintained a broad engagement with China's republican intellectual scene, to which he contributed from his Buddhist perspective. Perhaps he has been difficult to place as a historical figure because he was such a divisive figure in the Buddhist world (his ideas were far from universally accepted) and was not a secular intellectual. Although he did not fit in either camp, as the chapters in this volume show, the boundary between the secular and the religious was permeable for other late-Qing and republican intellectuals as well.[113] When we consider Yogācāra's role in bridging these two spheres during the period, Taixu's

111. Ibid, p. 242.

112. Taixu, "Cong wuwo weixin de yuzhouguan dao pingdeng ziyou de renshengguan 從無我唯心的宇宙觀到平等自由的人生觀" (From a Nonself–Mind-Only Worldview to an Egalitarian and Free Outlook on Life), in TDQS, vol. 22 (2005 [1930]), p. 986.

113. Furthermore, later in Taiwan and the PRC, the nuances of his ideas were rejected by Buddhists in favor of his broad approach to an engaged Buddhism. This is because "Buddhism for the human world," as a general concept, had great currency whereas many of his specific ideas did not accord with ideological or scientific developments in the ensuing decades, or were too divisive for broad acceptance.

importance as an active agent at the heart of this confluence of trends becomes clear.

Taixu can therefore be considered a republican-era intellectual (rather than just a Buddhist reformer) who contributed to ongoing discussions of modernity from his unique stance in traditional Chinese Buddhism. He was concerned with showing that rather than being superstitious and outmoded, Buddhism was capable of furthering modernist projects more effectively than Western scientific, philosophical, and ideological instruments themselves. In his wide-ranging essays and speeches on diverse subjects that included scientific knowledge and its foundations, as well as society and the individual, Yogācāra played an important part in this critical assessment of modernity. While on the one hand, it was evident through Yogācāra that Buddhism shared important similarities with his conception of Western modernity, on the other, he saw Yogācāra as capable of correcting the deficiencies of modernity. Yogācāra was therefore a crucial aspect of his overall intellectual project in that it helped him articulate a modern Buddhist approach to engaging with Western science, philosophy, and ideology—which he felt was the only viable path for China's future.

6

Yogācāra and Science in the 1920s: The Wuchang School's Approach to Modern Mind Science

Erik J. Hammerstrom

AS SEVERAL OF the chapters in this volume make abundantly clear, one of the primary reasons for the popularity of Yogācāra thought among Chinese intellectuals in the early twentieth century was the potential it was perceived to hold for connecting China's philosophical past to modern science. For example, in the late 1890s Tan Sitong 譚嗣同 (1865–1898) used Yogācāra to link contemporary neurophysiology with a Confucian ethical metaphysics. Two decades later Liang Shuming 梁漱溟 (1895–1988) made a similar claim by arguing that modern science had actually made it much easier to understand the complexities of Yogācāra doctrine. And, before eventually turning to Kant, Mou Zongsan 牟宗三 (1909–1995) saw in Yogācāra an example of a premodern theory of empirical knowledge present in China. In the main, thinkers of the period pointed to Yogācāra's systematic nature as being its most scientific aspect. Zhang Taiyan 章太炎 (1868–1936) displayed this attitude early on, but this was still a common perception in 1929, when Jiang Weiqiao 蔣維喬 (1873–1958) declared that lay people were studying Yogācāra because it was "rigorous, systematic and clear, and close to science."[1]

During the 1920s, a number of other writers used Yogācāra thought in their discussions of science in general, and of dogmatic scientism[2] in particular. By drawing on Yogācāra thought, Buddhists were able to make substantial

1. Jiang Weiqiao 蔣維喬, *Zhongguo Fojiao shi* 中國佛教史 (History of Chinese Buddhism) (Shanghai: Guji chubanshe, 2004/1929), p. 325.

2. Scientism is the idea that all aspects of knowledge and life can only be answered through recourse to materialist science. The best study of the history of this mode of thinking in modern China remains David W. Y. Kwok, *Scientism in Chinese Thought* (New Haven, CT: Yale University Press, 1965).

criticisms of the materialism upon which scientism was based. They also used Yogācāra to examine and critique the epistemological underpinnings of the scientific method, which was being held up during the 1920s as a foolproof method for reaching truth. For example, Tang Dayuan 唐大圓 (1890–1941) and Wang Xiaoxu 王小徐 (1875–1948) both argued against strict materialism by citing the Yogācāra doctrine that "the myriad dharmas are nothing but consciousness." And while Wang used Buddhist logic to place limits on the authority of the scientific method, Tang held Yogācāra up as the "scientific method of Buddhism."

Beyond these uses of Yogācāra thought, a major topic to which Buddhist writers in the 1920s applied Yogācāra was modern psychology (which I refer to in this paper as "modern mind science" in order to highlight for the reader its novelty in China during the time under consideration). The fact that some Buddhists would draw from the complex theories of the mind and cognition found in Yogācāra thought as they sought to understand and delimit the developing field of modern mind science is not surprising. The goal of this chapter is to explain how an early concern with understanding mind science through early Buddhist doctrine gave way to an emphasis on Yogācāra among one group of Buddhist intellectuals. The turn to the Yogācāra concepts of karmic seeds and the storehouse consciousness allowed Buddhists affiliated with the Wuchang Buddhist Seminary (Wuchang Foxue Yuan 武昌佛學院) to answer certain intractable questions then facing mind science, such as the processes by which instinct and memory occurr.

In this chapter I focus on the circle of students and teachers at the first modern Buddhist seminary, a seminary closely associated with Taixu 太虛 (1890–1947).[3] This "Wuchang School" can be viewed as another major inheritor of the great lay Buddhist Yang Wenhui's 楊文會 (1837–1911) legacy in modern Chinese Buddhism. Indeed, the Wuchang School was arguably more successful in the long term than Ouyang Jingwu's 歐陽竟無 (1871–1943) China Inner Learning Institute (Zhina Neixue Yuan 支那內學院), which is discussed in other chapters of this volume. Whereas Ouyang's students Lü Cheng 呂澂 (1896–1989) and Xiong Shili 熊十力 (1885–1968) are rightly famous for their contributions to modern discourses about Yogācāra, the Wuchang School exerted a lasting influence on the institutions and thought of modern Chinese Buddhism that should not be overlooked. For members of this school, Yogācāra served as an indispensable resource for understanding and critiquing the complexities of modern mind science.

3. Taixu's own discussions of the scientific nature of Yogācāra are studied in chapter 5 by Scott Pacey.

Yogācāra and A Place for Buddhism in Modern China

The use of Yogācāra in Buddhist discussions of science cannot be understood independently of changes that occurred in Chinese society in the early twentieth century. The 1920s saw the intensification of debates that had begun two decades earlier regarding the definitions and relative values of science, religion, and superstition. Arguments over this complex of terms reflected the larger social and political shifts taking place in China, as various voices and agents within society sought to determine what was beneficial to the modern nation (science and possibly religion), and what was harmful (superstition).[4] As part of these shifts, the attitude of local elites and local- and national-level governmental agencies toward temple practice and clergy changed. As voices of power, their ideas mattered. So too did the voices of intellectuals, whose writings disseminated new ideas. One result of this was that traditional elements of society, such as Buddhist institutions, found their roles redefined, sometimes for the worse, such as when government agencies seized temple lands in order to build schools and post offices.[5] Such seizures, however, were carried out in a piecemeal fashion, and although they were threatening to Buddhist institutions, systematic discourses on the rejection of religion in China did not really take hold until the 1920s.[6] When that occurred it became imperative for Buddhists to argue for their relevance within the modern nation then being envisioned by Chinese thinkers. Among other things, such as locating Buddhism with respect to the state, this was done by arguing for the scientific nature of Buddhism.[7] Writers such as Tang Dayuan and Wang Xiaoxu turned to Yogācāra and the cognate field of Buddhist logic as they argued for the overlap of Buddhism and science. Both of these men, and the members of the Wuchang School, were influenced in their discussions by the so-called science and philosophy-of-life debates of 1923, which had a major impact on the Chinese intellectual world.[8]

The science and philosophy-of-life debates were sparked by a lecture given by Carsun Chang (Zhang Junmai 張君勱, 1886–1969) in Beijing in late 1923 in which he called into question the growing tide of scientism that claimed that all

4. Rebecca Nedostup, *Superstitious Regimes: Religion and the Politics of Chinese Modernity* (Cambridge, MA: Harvard University Press, 2009).

5. Vincent Goossaert, "1898: The Beginning of the End for Chinese Religion?" *Journal of Asian Studies* 65, no. 2 (May 2006): 307–336.

6. Vincent Goossaert and David Palmer, *The Religious Question in Modern China* (Chicago: University of Chicago Press, 2011), p. 51.

7. Erik Hammerstrom, "Buddhists Discuss Science in Modern China, 1895–1949," Ph.D. thesis, Indiana University, 2010, pp. 10–16, and *passim*.

8. See also the Introduction to this volume for a discussion of these debates.

problems of society, including issues related to ethics, would one day be solved by materialist science. This lecture touched off a debate between nearly two-dozen thinkers who published articles attacking one another's positions. The status of these exchanges as a unified debate was established when many of the essays were collected by Hu Shi 胡適 (1891–1962) and Chen Duxiu 陳獨秀 (1879–1942), and published in late 1923 as the volume *Kexue yu rensheng guan* 科學與人生觀 (Science and Philosophy of Life). Although the participants did not focus on an explicit set of topics, there are a number of themes that appear in their works.[9] Despite the characterization of the debates put forward by those in support of scientistic worldviews, the debates were not waged between the supporters of science and its detractors, nor between supporters of progress and conservative elements. These debates were over competing visions of modernity in China, and even competing visions of science. One of the main battle lines was between those who supported a view of science founded upon values from the Enlightenment, and those, like Carsun Chang, who favored a worldview strongly inspired by Romanticism and Romantic science. Most relevant for the discussion here is that the former group tended to support mechanistic materialism, whereas the latter tended to support vitalism and idealism; and these positions had major impacts on the participants' views of modern mind science. In particular, various writers sparred over the extent to which human psychological processes were determined by strict rules of cause and effect, analogous to, and inspired by, the laws of classical physics. As we shall see below, the debate over these very issues formed a major part of the impetus for members of the Wuchang School to turn to Yogācāra.

Mind science occupied an important position for moderns of all types in the 1920s: on the one hand, materialists supported it because they believed it would allow them to do away with fuzzy subjectivity, while on the other hand, idealists thought the study of the mind held the key to even higher levels of understanding. By the 1920s, the biological and physical sciences had already demonstrated their efficacy to the general Chinese population by means of the medicine and technologies they made possible. If science was going to become the totalizing system that some groups felt it should be, it had to extend its reach into the complex world of human actions and emotions through sociology and modern mind science. Behaviorist psychology held the hope for the materialists that the sum total of human conduct could be explained by making a specific inventory of the stimulus-response potentials of human beings. Once complete, they believed that

9. Summarized in Chow Tse-tung, *The May Fourth Movement: Intellectual Revolution in Modern China* (Cambridge, MA: Harvard University Press, 1960), pp. 333–337; and much more extensively treated in David W. Y. Kwok, *Scientism in Chinese Thought*, pp. 135–200.

this inventory of the rules by which specific responses follow automatically from specific stimuli would give scientists the ability to quantify, explain, and predict human thoughts and behavior the same way that classical physics could predict the reactions of matter to physical forces. This understanding of the mind, favored by debate participants such as Tang Yue 唐鉞 (b. 1891),[10] removed the need for subjectivity, and treated humans as predictable machines.

Modern mind science held promise for those on the other side of the debates as well. For those with idealist leanings, the study of the mind was still essential to the project of understanding the individual, central to modernity. The difference was that writers like Carsun Chang and others favored philosophies that were less materialistically reductive[11] and placed more emphasis on subjective experiences (such as could be found in the work of Henri Bergson).

Thus, even though they did not agree on the basic methodological assumptions under which modern mind science should operate, by the late 1920s, it was generally agreed by most Chinese thinkers that it was important. Even the Buddhist writings examined here stressed the importance of studying mind science, and its centrality to a variety of fields of inquiry, and its importance fueled the turn to Yogācāra.

Yogācāra and Science: A Few Examples

In seeking resources for talking about modern mind science among the many riches of the Buddhist intellectual tradition, a tradition in which reflection upon and description of the mind holds a central place, Republican thinkers turned repeatedly to Yogācāra thought.[12] Ideas from Yogācāra, including its logic, were used in different ways during the Republican period as Buddhists participated in the "community of scientific discourse"[13] developing in China. As John Jorgensen points out in his chapter, the idea that Yogācāra could be placed alongside science had its roots in Japan, and was promoted in China in the writings of Zhang Taiyan. Zhang's writings set an important tone, and several of the points Zhang mentioned briefly would become major themes for later writers. Like others of his time, he emphasized the systematic nature of Yogācāra thought, the fact that

10. Kwok, *Scientism in Chinese Thought*, p. 128.

11. Chow, *The May Fourth Movement*, p. 334.

12. Some thinkers did draw from other Buddhist concepts, notably Liang Qichao, whose lecture-cum-article was one of the first to relate Buddhism systematically to the modern mind sciences. This is discussed below.

13. This concept, which comes from the work of Wang Hui, is discussed in greater detail below.

it has a developed system of epistemology and logic (*yinming* 因明) for analyzing truth claims, and, most importantly in the context of the present chapter, constitutes a science of the mind on par with the modern mind science then being developed in the West.

Yogācāra provided an important rhetorical tool for a wide variety of Buddhists (even those who did not otherwise write about Yogācāra) for locating their tradition in relation to modern science and Western thought in general. By the 1920s, many Buddhists had adopted the understanding that the concept "the myriad dharmas[14] are nothing but consciousness" (*wanfa weishi* 萬法唯識) was *the* onto-epistemological position of Mahāyāna vis-à-vis Western philosophy (which was generally described as tending toward the extremes of materialism or idealism).[15] When Buddhists invoked this concept to reject strict materialism they also rejected the scientism that embraced it. Such critiques were, however, not usually part of detailed comparisons of Yogācāra thought and Western thought in general or science in particular. Instead, as mentioned above, many writers simply made vague comments about the "systematicity" of Yogācāra thought.

One notable exception to this tendency was *Weishi de kexue fangfa* 唯識的科學方法 (The Scientific Method of Yogācāra) by the lay Buddhist scholar Tang Dayuan, a member of the Wuchang School. A prolific lecturer, writer, and magazine editor, Tang and his writings have not yet attracted much scholarly attention, but his role as a popularizer of Yogācāra in Republican-era China certainly merits further study.[16] *The Scientific Method of Yogācāra* was perhaps his largest work. It was an edited version of lectures he delivered at Zhonghua 中華 University in Wuchang and Dongnan 東南 University in Shanghai

---

14. Here best understood as referring to all phenomena generally.

15. Erik Hammerstrom, "The Expression 'The Myriad Dharmas are Only Consciousness' in Early 20th Century Chinese Buddhism," *Chung-Hwa Buddhist Journal* 23 (2010): 71–92.

16. Although originally a practitioner of Pure Land Buddhism and a refuge disciple of Yinguang 印光, Tang became a close associate of Taixu during the 1920s and an important lay lecturer on Yogācāra in the Hunan and Jiangnan regions. He was instrumental in establishing the Wuchang Buddhist Seminary and was its chief lecturer on Yogācāra during its run in the 1920s. In addition to writing dozens of articles for a number of Buddhist periodicals, he also edited the *Haichao yin* 海潮音 (Sound of the Sea Tide) [hereafter *HCY*] for a time, and established his own journal *Dongfang wenhua* 東方文化 (Eastern Culture) in 1926. Yu Lingbo 于凌波, *Zhongguo jindai Fomen renwuzhi* 中國近代佛門人物志 (Biographies of Early Modern Chinese Buddhists), (Taipei: Huiju, 1999), vol. 5, pp. 254–269. Most of his writings were on Yogācāra, and although he may not have left the same lasting impression as thinkers like Xiong Shili or Lü Cheng, he certainly seems to have done a great deal to popularize Yogācāra among the Buddhist laity in the 1920s and 1930s.

in the mid-1920s.[17] Despite its title, this work was not a systematic comparison of science and Yogācāra; instead, it was primarily an explanation of basic Yogācāra doctrine that took the form of a commentary on the *Cheng weishi lun* 成唯識論 (Demonstration of Nothing but Consciousness), and between one half and one third of the work is made up of charts outlining various aspects of Yogācāra thought. Nevertheless, given the work's size, there is much that could be said about it; here I will just briefly mention what Tang actually did say about science, and how he viewed the relationship between it and Yogācāra.

When he did mention science, much of Tang's work is defensive in tone, and often he took aim at scientists as a group, chiding them for their wrongheaded views on several issues. By scientists, it is fairly clear that Tang actually meant proponents of materialist scientism. He was particularly critical of them for their misleading talk about matter. Tang stated that science today emphasizes aspects of material culture (*wuzhi wenming* 物質文明), such as securing clothing and shelter, but that people do not understand that this "matter" (*wuzhi* 物質) is "merely the characteristics (*xiang* 相; *lakṣaṇa*) of self and of dharmas that are produced through the transformation of nothing but consciousness."[18] In addition to criticizing the materialism of the scientistic worldview on philosophical grounds, Tang also cautioned that such an utilitarian view of the world, when combined with the social evolutionist doctrine of the survival of the fittest, would lead to much violence and suffering.[19] This was a widespread sentiment among Buddhists at the time.[20]

Tang was also highly critical of scientists' narrow view of cause and effect. For the 1929 edition of *The Scientific Method of Yogācāra*, Tang added a third section dedicated entirely to a discussion of causality.[21] His decision to include this new section was likely due in no small part to the central role that discussions of rules of psychological cause and effect played in the science and

17. *The Scientific Method of Yogācāra* first appeared as a monograph in 1926 published by the Shanghai Lay Buddhist Association. In 1929, Tang added a third section (the section on causality, which I discuss below) and had the entire work reprinted in two parts in *HCY*. (*HCY* 10.5 [1929], in *Minguo Fojiao qikan wenxian jicheng* 民國佛教期刊文獻集成 [Collection of Republican-Era Buddhist Periodical Literature], ed. Huang Xianian 黃夏年, 209 vols. [Beijing: Beijing Tushuguan, 2006] [hereafter MFQ] 172:493–517; and *HCY* 10, no. 6 [1929]; MFQ 173:29–57.) The entire revised work was also reprinted as a monograph later that same year. As I have not been able to locate any copies of either version of the monograph, I have drawn here from the version found in *HCY*.

18. MFQ 172:505.

19. MFQ 172:506.

20. Erik Hammerstrom, "Buddhists Discuss Science in Modern China," pp. 233–241.

21. MFQ 173:53–57.

philosophy-of-life debates. In this section, Tang sought to make clear that there was a difference between cause and effect as talked about in science, and how it was talked about in Yogācāra. The idea that both Buddhism and science studied cause and effect was a fairly popular notion during the period among those who wanted to show the scientificity of Buddhism. Tang argued that scientists only believe in the operation of cause and effect in the present time period, by which he meant one's present lifetime. They do not take account the action of cause and effect across the "three times" (*san shi* 三世), which for him meant the operation of karma from lifetime to lifetime.[22] To support this view he cited at length a summary of Sarvāstivādin arguments for the reality of the three worlds as found in the *Abhidharma-mahāvibhāṣā-śāstra*.[23] (This idea was actually part of a larger Sarvāstivādin argument that was refuted by Yogācāras, but Tang was not concerned with this issue.) He then cited the *Cheng weishi lun* to support his claim that karma operates across the three times, and to show that an effect appears in the same location and immediately after the demise of its cause.[24] Tang's aim was to undermine both materialist scientism's attachment to presently-manifesting dharmas, and their denial of the operation of karma between lifetimes, and he turned to Yogācāra and closely related Sarvāstivādan ideas to support his point.

Although Tang had a negative attitude toward certain principles of dogmatic scientism, he did appreciate the scientific method (a fact that is clear from the title of this work), and he sought to borrow some of the cultural cachet it had built up in China by the mid-1920s. At the very beginning of *The Scientific Method of Yogācāra*, Tang offered a brief explanation of the scientific method. Science, he said, is composed of classified fields of learning, like physics, chemistry, and psychology. What they have in common is a method for seeking the truth of things by carrying out experiments, and systematizing the results of those experiments. Tang then said that in Buddhism, there is Yogācāra, which also offers a detailed verification of the truths of reality. Yogācāra uses the same method, and can be viewed as the scientific method of Buddhism. His goal in writing this work was to provide a detailed, systematic explanation of Yogācāra thought, which he saw as akin to the scientific method. Later in the work, Tang wrote:

---

22. MFQ 173:53.

23. *Apidamo da piposha lun* 阿毘達磨大毘婆沙論 (Great Commentary on the Abidharma). Tang cited a passage found at CBETA, T27n1545_p0396a13. An English translation of this passage appears in K. L. Dhammajoti, *Sarvāstivāda Abhidharma* (Hong Kong: Centre of Buddhist Studies, The University of Hong Kong, 2007), pp. 147–149. The Sarvāstivādins (*yiqie you bu* 一切有部) represented a major later school of *abhidharma* thought in Indian Buddhism, and many of their views were incorporated into Yogācāra. The *Mahāvibhāṣā* is one of the central philosophical texts of that school.

24. MFQ 173:55–56. *Cheng weishi lun*, CBETA, T31n1585_p0012c1528.

> Today's scientists all emphasize experimentation and arrogantly think they understand everything, but they do not know that practitioners of Yogācāra emphasize experimentation. These practitioners use their whole bodies as the experimental apparatus, so there is no time when they are not carrying out experiments, and there is nowhere that is not a laboratory.[25]

This was clearly a response to scientists who failed to appreciate what Tang believed to be the overarching empirical nature of Yogācāra. Such a viewpoint is fairly ironic given the fact that at the time he was writing those words there were people within the Buddhist community itself who felt that Yogācāra was all talk, and lacked a strong foundation in practice.[26]

More thorough analyses of the scientific method were carried out using the discipline of Buddhist logic, which is closely associated with Yogācāra in China. The most famous example of this appeared in the works of Wang Xiaoxu, one of China's first great modern scientists, a founding member of the Academia Sinica, and a friend of Joseph Needham.[27] Wang was also a devout Buddhist, and in several much-reprinted writings from the late 1920s, he followed the example set forth by Liang Shuming (as discussed in Thierry Meynard's chapter in this volume) by arguing that the very empiricism upon which the scientific method—and thus science—is based could be described as simply the operation of *inferential cognition* (*biliang* 比量; *anumāna pramāṇa*). Wang expanded on Liang's analysis by using this to conclude that science was thus not capable of proving the truths described in Buddhism, which had been apprehended by the *direct perception* (*xianliang* 現量; *pratyakṣa pramāṇa*) utilized by advanced practitioners of the Buddhist path. In making this argument, Wang relied on the categorical distinctions made in Buddhist logic between different types of cognition (*pramāṇas*). Wang's work was popular among Buddhists and remains in print today, but some non-Buddhists, notably Hu Shi, the influential public intellectual and disciple of John Dewey, were highly scornful of Wang's views. That scorn,

25. MFQ 172:507.

26. Yinguang, Tang Dayuan's own refuge master, wrote several highly critical letters to Tang in this vein. In one such letter, Yinguang reminded Tang that Buddhism is for liberation and not just for turning into philosophy. He also chided Tang for teaching about "medicine that he had not himself taken." Yinguang 印光, *Yinguang dashi quanji* 印光大師全集 (Collected Writings of Master Yinguang), 7 vols. (Taipei: Taiwan Fojiao chubanshe, 1991), vol. 1, pp. 202–203.

27. Joseph Needham, *Science and Civilization in China* (Cambridge: Cambridge University Press, 1956), vol. 2, p. 418.

however, only stimulated the support of the wider Buddhist community, especially in the early 1930s.[28]

Outside of these discussions of the scientific method, the primary systematic use of Yogācāra thought to discuss modern science among Buddhists in the 1920s appeared not in any general assessment of science *qua* science, but in Buddhists' attempts to relate their tradition to the nascent field of Chinese psychology, which they did for several historical reasons. One such reason was the aforementioned science and philosophy-of-life debates. Another more proximate reason for Buddhist interest in modern mind science in the 1920s was its recent appearance in China. Just as Western logic began to be taken seriously as individual disciplines in China in the 1920s,[29] the modern field of psychology did not gain wide attention in China until that same decade. Finally, the appearance of China's first association dedicated to the study of psychology in 1921 roughly coincided with the founding of the Wuchang Buddhist Seminary the following year. That latter institution had a significant impact on the development of Buddhist modernisms[30] in China, and because of the prominent inclusion of Yogācāra studies in its curriculum, its members made extensive use of Yogācāra in the articulation of those modernisms.

The Wuchang School

The history of the Wuchang Buddhist Seminary and its importance in modern Chinese Buddhism has long been recognized by scholars.[31] Although it only

---

28. For a summary of both Wang's thought and the events of his life, see Erik Hammerstrom, "Science and Buddhist Modernism in Early 20th Century China: the Life and Works of Wang Xiaoxu," *Journal of Chinese Religion* 39 (2011[2012]): 1–32. For an English translation of one of his main works, as well as of his exchange with Hu Shi about that work, see Douglas Lancashire (ed. and trans.), *Chinese Essays on Religion and Faith* (San Francisco: Chinese Materials Center, 1981).

29. Joachim Kurtz, "Coming to Terms with Logic: The Naturalization of an Accidental Notion in China," in *New Terms for New Ideas: Western Knowledge & Lexical Change in Late Imperial China*, ed. Michael Lackner et al. (Brill: Leiden, 2001), pp. 147–175.

30. The term "Buddhist modernism" has been widely used by Buddhist scholars in the past few decades to refer to the many types of world Buddhism that have developed under the influence of the key forces of modernity, including especially post-Enlightenment rationalism and notions about religion derived from Protestant Christianity. For more on this term, and a study of the development of Buddhist modernism using Anglophone sources, see David L. McMahan, *The Making of Buddhist Modernism* (New York: Oxford University Press, 2008).

31. Shi Dongchu 釋東初, *Zhongguo Fojiao jindai shi* 中國佛教近代史 (The Early Modern History of Chinese Buddhism), 2 vols. (Taipei: Dongchu chubanshe, 1974), vol. 1, pp. 206–207.

operated from 1922 to 1926 in its original incarnation, the Wuchang Buddhist Seminary was important for a number of reasons. Inspired by Yang Wenhui's Jetavana Hermitage (Qihuan Jingshe 祇洹精舍), this school became the prototype of the modern Buddhist seminary. There, Taixu and his colleagues formulated a curriculum based on lay academies and Japanese seminaries, and the ideas they pioneered eventually spread as dozens of other new seminaries appeared in China, many of which adopted parts or all of the Wuchang system. Of note here is the fact that Yogācāra and the related field of Āgama literature were central to their studies, and when members of this school responded to the popularity of mind science in the Chinese intellectual world, they eventually turned to Yogācāra for the resources it contained.

The Wuchang Buddhist Seminary began as the idea of several laymen from the Wuchang area who were inspired by lectures given by Taixu. In 1922, they took up a collection for the purpose of establishing a modern Buddhist Seminary in Wuchang, which they invited Taixu to oversee. The seminary opened in the fall of 1922 with a class of more than eighty students. After the first year, due to the reportedly poor quality of the students, the first- and second-year classes were combined, and they ultimately graduated together in 1924. During the summer of 1924, Taixu expressed his desire to accept only monks as students and to begin running the seminary according to rules for Chan monasteries. The board of directors rejected this suggestion, and the incoming class of 1924 included a number of lay people as students.[32] That fall, Taixu left his position at the seminary citing health reasons, though this was probably a face-saving *upāya* carried out when Taixu realized that the Wuchang Buddhist Seminary was not entirely his to run as he saw fit. At this point the monk Shanyin 善因 (n.d.) took responsibility for overseeing the school. Two years later, fewer than four years after it first opened its doors, the board was forced to suspend the activities of the seminary after Northern Expedition forces appropriated the school's buildings for use as a barracks. The seminary returned to operation as a research center in 1932, but closed again in 1934 due to unrest caused by the first stirrings of the Second Sino-Japanese War.

Although it operated for only a short time as a physical school with a distinctive curriculum, the Wuchang Seminary also housed a school in another sense of the word, and it was in this sense that it ultimately had its greatest impact. The Wuchang Buddhist Seminary served as a starting point for a network of individuals, seminaries, and periodicals that connected Buddhists in different

---

32. Gao Zhennong 高振農, *Fojiao wenhua yu jindai Zhongguo* 佛教文化與近代中國 (Buddhist Culture and Early Modern China) (Shanghai: Shehui kexue chubanshe, 1992), p. 68.

parts of China. The Wuchang School was not unique in this: these kinds of networks were a common feature of Chinese Buddhism at the time, as evidenced by both the networks developed among Shanghai's lay Buddhists in the 1920s,[33] and the networks of Japanese and Chinese intellectuals formed during the late Qing that are discussed in John Jorgensen's chapter of this volume. Many of the teachers and students present during the first run of the Wuchang Seminary from 1922 to 1926 went on to serve in important positions as abbots of temples, heads of other major Buddhist seminaries, and founders and editors of major Buddhist periodicals.[34] More than simply a network of affiliation, members in the Wuchang School also shared a common project: the development of a Buddhist modernism. The exact dimensions of this modernism were somewhat fluid, as the individuals articulating it responded to the many historical changes that took place during the Republican period. Nevertheless, it is possible to define certain elements of this project, and the discursive tools that students and teachers at the seminary developed to carry it out grew organically from the curriculum of the school and the texts around which that curriculum was centered.

Students at the Wuchang Buddhist Seminary studied from a wide range of Buddhist scriptures, as well as Buddhist logic and Yogācāra. According to the charter for the school drawn up by its board of laymen, during the first year students were to begin their studies with texts including the *Dasheng qixin lun* 大乘起信論 (Awakening of Mahāyāna Faith), *Nyayāpraveśa* (Entryway Into Logic), and the **Śūraṃgama-sūtra* (Sutra of the Sam of Heroic Progress), *Vajracchedikā-prajñāpāramitā-sūtra* (Diamond Sutra), and various translations of the **Mahā-prajñāpāramitā-hṛdaya-sūtra* (Heart Sutra), as well as Madhyamaka thought and Indian Buddhist history. According to the plan, their study of important Yogācāra texts was to begin at the start of the second year (in the third semester), with the *Cheng weishi lun*, *Mahāyānasaṃgraha* (Compendium of the Great Vehicle), and

33. These networks have been studied in Brooks Jessup, "The Householder Elite: Buddhist Activism in Shanghai, 1920–1956," Ph.D. thesis, University of California-Berkeley, 2010.

34. A full accounting of the impact of the Wuchang School is beyond the scope of this paper, but as examples of the nature of its members' contributions one can note that students from the graduating class of 1924 went on to establish (often with Taixu's assistance, and often at his request) two of the most influential and longstanding of the Republican Period's Buddhist seminaries, the Minnan Buddhist Seminary (Minnan Foxue Yuan 閩南佛學院) in Fuzhou, and the Sino-Tibetan Institute (Han Zang jiaoli Yuan 漢藏教理院) in Sichuan; as well as half a dozen other, shorter lived seminaries. They also launched and edited a number of periodicals beyond the *Haichao yin*, including *Ren haideng* 人海燈 (Altar-lamp of Humanity), *Xiandai sengqie* 現代僧伽 (Modern Saṃgha), and *Zhengxin* 正信 (True Faith).

Saṃdhinirmocana-sūtra (Discourse Explaining the Thought).[35] It was also during the second year that the students were to study Western ethics and (most relevant for this chapter) mind science.[36] Along the way, the students also studied *abhidharma* literature, though the prominent monk Fafang 法舫 (1904–1951) reported that during his time as a student in the first class at the seminary the *abhidharma* classes were not nearly as popular with his fellow students as classes on the *Cheng weishi lun*.[37]

The emphasis that teachers and students placed on the texts in this curriculum had an influence on the topics they wrote about over the next decade. For example, Taixu, Tang Dayuan, and other members of the Wuchang School participated in the debate over the authorship of the *Dasheng qixin lun*, which is discussed in several other chapters in this volume.[38] This chapter explores another aspect of the project of the Wuchang School: the use of Indian Yogācāra thought to integrate Buddhism into the discourse of modern mind science. The primary source materials used here to reconstruct that position are the articles published by members of this school in various Buddhist periodicals, principally the *Haichao yin* 海潮音 (Sound of the Sea Tide, hereafter HCY), which was in many ways the voice of the Wuchang School.[39] Some of the individuals whose works are cited here were teachers at the seminary, such as the laymen Tang Dayuan and Zhang Huasheng 張化聲 (b. 1880), the monk Shanyin, and two of the seminary's students, the monks Fafang and Manzhi 滿智 (n.d.).

35. These last two titles are the two central texts of Yogācāra thought, and there are multiple translations of each in the Taishō.

36. "Foxue Yuan zhangcheng 佛學院章程" (Rules for the Buddhist Seminary), *Foxue xunkan* 佛學旬刊 (Buddhist Studies Weekly), no. 26 (1922), MFQ 8:156–157. The term *abhidharma* (*apidamo* 阿毗達磨) refers collectively to the various schools of doctrinal commentary and interpretation that arose in Indian Buddhism during the millennium centered on the year zero of the Common Era.

37. Fafang, *Weishi shiguan ji qi zhexue* 唯識史觀及其哲學 (The History of Yogācāra and its Philosophy) rpt. (Taipei: Tianhua chubanshe, 1998/1950), pp. 2–3.

38. For a thorough treatment of the roots of this debate in Japanese scholarship and the form it took in Republican China, see also Eyal Aviv, "Differentiating the Pearl From the Fish Eye: Ouyang Jingwu (1871–1943) and the Revival of Scholastic Buddhism," Ph.D. thesis, Harvard University, 2008, pp. 119–165.

39. All periodicals used in this chapter are cited according to their appearance in Huang Xianian 黃夏年 (ed.), *Minguo Fojiao qikan wenxian jicheng* 民國佛教期刊文獻集成 (Collection of Republican-Era Buddhist Periodical Literature), 209 vols. (Beijing: Beijing Tushuguan, 2006); and Huang Xianian 黃夏年 (ed.), *Minguo Fojiao qikan wenxian jicheng bubian* 民國佛教期刊文獻集成. 補編 (Supplement to the Collection of Republican-Era Buddhist Periodical Literature), 86 vols. (Beijing: Beijing Tushuguan, 2007). Following scholarly convention, these two works are referred to as MFQ and MFQB, respectively.

In treating all of these figures as part of a common "school," it is important to consider the roles Taixu did and did not play in its formation. In chapter 6, Scott Pacey outlines the many ways in which Taixu felt that the study of Yogācāra could supplement what he saw as the deficiencies of modern science. Although Taixu clearly served as an inspiration and leader for the direction that the school initially took, others in this group contributed their own ideas. As such, their writings should not simply be viewed as extensions of Taixu, or even of his reformist project more generally, but rather the result of a collaborative environment in which masters and disciples, teachers and students, worked together to draw from Indian thought in the context of modern China. This is important for two reasons: first, because Taixu had already resigned from the seminary by the time much of the work cited here was penned; and second, because the majority of the individual works Pacey cites in his chapter were written during this period, a period when Taixu was probably learning as much from those around him as they were from him. I will show that this was especially the case with Zhang Huasheng, who was responsible for bringing a detailed knowledge of modern mind science to the Wuchang School. After Taixu's departure, Zhang seems to have been important in setting the direction that members of the Wuchang School took in studying Yogācāra for what it could say to and about modern mind science. But why did the members of this school feel compelled to use Yogācāra to address modern mind science in the ways that they did? And what "mind science" were they and other Chinese thinkers familiar with in the 1920s?

Modern Mind Science in China

As the members of the Wuchang School reached to Yogācāra to argue for a place for Buddhism in modern China, they also responded to the general newfound popularity of modern mind science in China and to the specific problems related to that discipline that were most commonly discussed at the time. Although the first translated book on modern mind science appeared in China in 1889,[40] it was among members of the May Fourth Movement that mind science first became popular. As noted earlier, in this chapter I am intentionally using the term "mind science" instead of "psychology"[41] in order to emphasize the unsettled, contested

40. Zhang Jingyuan, *Psychoanalysis in China: Literary Transformations, 1919–1949* (Ithaca, NY: Cornell East Asia Program, 1997), pp. 37–38.

41. The modern Chinese word for psychology–*xinlixue* 心理學–was originally a Japanese neologism and was first introduced into Chinese in 1896 by Liang Qichao. Federico Masini, *The Formation of Modern Chinese Lexicon and Its Evolution Toward a National Language: The Period from 1840 to 1898*, Journal of Chinese Linguistics Monograph Series, no. 6. (1993), p. 209.

nature of the discipline as it existed both in China and in the West during that period. Although chemistry and biology were well established, and physics had become the "queen of the sciences" in the West by the end of the nineteenth century, psychology was still a young discipline, and there were many competing theories in the field during the early decades of the twentieth century. By the early 1920s, the reductive school of behaviorism was beginning to hold sway, but it had not yet reached the dominance it would hold in later decades. Thus, the theories of mind science that were being translated in China during the time in which they were being studied by the Wuchang School were not part of a stable discipline, but belonged to one in which competing viewpoints on basic methodological assumptions vied for supremacy.

Two factors influencing the rise of modern mind science in China were a series of lectures given by Bertrand Russell in Beijing in 1920, later published as *The Analysis of Mind*; and the return of Chinese students of psychology from Europe and America that started around the same year.[42] In August 1921, the first organization dedicated to the study of modern mind science, the Chinese Psychological Society (Zhongguo xinli xuehui 中國心理學會), was formed.[43] Beginning the following year, the association began publishing the journal *Xinli* 心理 (Psychology). Although articles on psychology were already appearing in the broader Chinese periodical press,[44] *Xinli* was the only periodical solely dedicated to the subject to appear in Chinese until 1928.[45] An examination of the contents of the first five years of this journal carried out in 1927 by Siegen Chou of Stanford University helps to place the Wuchang School's efforts to use Yogācāra to examine mind science into their proper context. During those five years, one of twenty-one categories of articles that appeared in the journal was "Systematic Psychology." According to Chou, this category included articles on "Buddhist psychology[46]; introspective vs. behaviorist psychology; Wang Yang[ming]'s

42. Zhang, *Psychoanalysis in China*, pp. 10; 40.

43. Louise T. Higgins and Zheng Mo, "An Introduction to Chinese Psychology–Its Historical Roots until the Present Day," *The Journal of Psychology* 136, no. 2 (March 2002): 229.

44. Zhang, *Psychoanalysis in China*, p. 24.

45. In total, *Xinli* ran to fourteen issues from 1922 to 1927. In this run were 150 original articles, 20% of which were by the editor. It also included 330 summaries of articles from other journals. Most of the pieces that appeared were translations of Western articles. Geoffrey Blowers, Boris Tat Cheung, and Han Ru, "Emulation vs. Indigenization in the Reception of Western Psychology in Republican China: An Analysis of the Content of Chinese Psychology Journals (1922–1937)," *Journal of the History of Behavioral Sciences* 45, no. 1 (Winter 2009): 25.

46. I have not been able to examine all of the issues of *Xinli*, but according to a note by the editor in HCY (MFQ 175:420b), it is likely that the article referred to in this list is an article by Liang Qichao that was reprinted in HCY in 1930; see note 73 below.

psychology (1472–1528); life of Freud and progress of his thought; [Zhu Xi]'s (1130–1200) and [Xunzi]'s (about 300 B. C.) thoughts on psychology."[47] From this list, it appears that Zhang Yaoxiang 張耀翔 (1863–1964), the president of the society and chief editor and contributor to the journal, took seriously its stated purpose, which was to create a synthesis of new ideas from Western mind science and ideas from Chinese classical culture. In the 1924 article "Wang Yangming xinlixue 王陽明心理學" (The Psychology of Wang Yangming), Neo-Confucian views on the nature of mind were compared with those of modern psychology.[48]

Xinli was one of the primary vehicles through which ideas about modern mind science were translated in China, and it was also the principal site in which the beginnings of "indigenous" modern mind science were constructed. Because it was blazing new territory, the overall quality of the articles in the journal was not particularly high. Although technical terms like "consciousness" and "disorder" were used, they were not explained in much detail. This was still an important journal, and its orientation lay close to that of the Buddhists whose work is covered here. One can regard the authors whose work appears in *Xinli* as participating in the same general project as our Buddhists: the construction of modern mind science that combined elements of both modern Western theories and traditional ones. In the case of the Buddhists of the Wuchang School, these theories were drawn not from the classical Chinese tradition, but from Indian theories about the mind as contained in Yogācāra thought. I shall return to these below.

During the 1920s at least, the nature of modern mind science was an open question in China. Although mind science, in the form of behaviorist psychology, held great promise for China's ardent materialists, they did not monopolize the discourse. For example, far from being a mouthpiece for supporters of scientism, *Xinli* carried articles on "superstitious" practices, including fortune telling based on the interpretation of dreams.[49] The inclusion of such elements in discussions of mind science continued, but the 1930s saw a narrowing of the discussion as the professionals who were beginning to dominate the field increasingly turned their attention to psychometric techniques, such as I.Q. tests.[50] Based on the decline in articles appearing in the Buddhist press on the topic, it seems that Buddhists also lost interest in theoretical discussions of Buddhist mind science by

---

47. Siegen K. Chou, "Trends in Chinese Psychological Interest since 1922," *The American Journal of Psychology* 38, no. 3 (July 1927): 487–488.

48. Wang Zhen 汪震, "Wang Yangming xinlixue 王陽明心理學" (Wang Yangming's Psychology), *Xinli* 3, no. 3 (September 1924): n.p.

49. Blowers et al., "Emulation vs. Indigenization in the Reception of Western Psychology in Republican China," pp. 28–29.

50. Ibid, p. 30.

the mid-1930s. Concomitant with their general loss of interest in mind science, the number of articles linking it with Yogācāra declined dramatically.

The mid-to-late 1920s was thus the high point for a wide range of philosophical discussions of modern mind science by Buddhists and non-Buddhists in China, but there were a few other notable Buddhists who wrote and lectured about mind science before that period. One of these was Tan Sitong, whose use of Yogācāra thought is covered in more detail in Scott Pacey's chapter 6 in this volume. Tan made several points relevant to the current discussion of mind science in his *Renxue* 仁學 (Study of Benevolence), and those comments reflected current issues in the field in the late nineteenth century. As these issues remained important themes for Buddhist authors in the early twentieth century (including Taixu, who, as Pacey notes, had read *Renxue*), before discussing the writings of the Wuchang School I will mention a few of these points. As is well known, one of Tan's central arguments in *Renxue* is that all physical and mental phenomena are composed of ether (*yitai* 以太). Until Einstein's work on Relativity appeared this was still very much a live theoretical concept within physics. For Tan, it allowed him to unite the world of ethics, morals, and politics with that of physical matter. Nowhere is this unification more apparent than in his explanation of the human nervous system. Tan declared that the brain, the nervous system, and electricity are all composed of the same psycho-physical substance: ether.[51] When ether takes substantial form, it manifests itself as, among other things, brains and nervous systems. When it runs free in space, it is electricity.[52] This idea was not entirely new: as Jorgensen points out, Hara Tanzan made a similar attempt to use Buddhist ideas to identify the common substance of the spine and the mind in Japan in the 1880s.

Tan's ideas are best understood within the context of the development of mind science. In 1870, the Germans Gustav Fritsch (1837–1927) and Eduard Hitzig (1839–1907) discovered that electrical stimulation of the brain caused parts of the body to move. This led many to speculate on the connection between electricity and the mind, and during the course of the 1870s more motor "centers" were identified through observation of direct stimulation.[53] The ether was a way

51. Tan Sitong 譚嗣同, *Renxue* 仁學 (An Exposition of Benevolence), in *Tan Sitong quanji* 譚嗣同全集 (The Complete Works of Tan Sitong), 2 vols. (Beijing: Zhonghua shuju, 1981), vol.1, pp. 302–303. For an English translation of this section, see T'an Ssu-t'ung, *An Exposition of Benevolence: The Jen-hsueh of T'an Ssu-t'ung*, trans. Chan Sin-wai (Hong Kong: Chinese University of Hong Kong, 1984), pp. 83–84.

52. Tan, *Renxue*, 1:295; T'an, *An Exposition of Benevolence*, pp. 69, 72.

53. Raymond E. Fancher, *Pioneers of Psychology*, 3rd ed. (New York: Norton, 1996), pp. 90–91.

to reconcile the two seemingly disparate phenomena of the brain and electricity. And the connection between electricity and thought began to appear in a broad range of Chinese writings. By the end of the first decade of the twentieth century, several stories of science fantasy revolving around the use of electric devices to read and control thoughts had appeared in Chinese fiction journals, popularizing this connection between the two among literate Chinese.[54]

The 1870s witnessed a fairly substantial shift in modern mind science, eventually paving the way for those who sought to use Yogācāra thought to relate the two. Although the discovery of electrical stimulation marked a new era in localizing motor functions within specific parts of the human brain, the period also witnessed a retreat from the view that each region of the brain controlled one specific higher-level faculty, such as greed or shame. This theory, first popularized by Franz Josef Gall (1752–1828), led to the rise of phrenology.[55] From the 1870s, scientists were no longer looking for these control centers, "but sought instead to demonstrate how complex psychological processes in general might be created out of the basic elements of sensation, movement, and their memory traces."[56] It was these sorts of complex processes (especially memory and instinct) that members of the Wuchang School explained using Yogācāra.

Mind science began to see the mind as a complex system of interrelated processes, in which memory was an integral part. By the late 1910s, it was demonstrated that memory was not localizable within one specific region of the brain.[57] This raised a number of questions about the location and functioning of memory that would become very important for scientists, philosophers, and for the Wuchang School. Tan, for his part, was writing at a time when some in the scientific community still thought it possible to localize the functions of memory within the brain, and he followed suit in his writings. Although he did not speak directly of memory, Tan did identify the cerebrum (*da'nao* 大腦) as the location of the *ālayavijñāna*, the container of the karmic "seeds" that follow one from rebirth to rebirth discussed in Yogācāra.[58] A similar identification of the supposedly nonmaterial consciousness with the material object of the brain would draw the strong rejection of Buddhists in the late 1920s, but it must be remembered that in Tan's ether-centered cosmology, mental and

54. David Pollard (ed.), *Translation and Creation: Readings of Western Literature in Early Modern China, 1840–1918* (Philadelphia: John Benjamins Co., 1998), pp. 195, 204–405.

55. Fancher, *Pioneers of Psychology*, p. 75.

56. Ibid, 95.

57. Ibid, 96–97.

58. Tan, *Renxue*, 1:331, 364; T'an, *An Exposition of Benevolence*, pp. 69, 135, 209.

material phenomena were not qualitatively different. Nevertheless, Tan was at the forefront of those breaking with a longstanding belief among Chinese literati who had, until the 1880s, vigorously opposed any attempt by the Western translators of science to locate the mind, memory, or anything remotely resembling a soul in the brain.[59] Tan was not the only one to do this, but the ideas that he put into the *Renxue* were the first attempt by a Chinese Buddhist to deal with a range of concepts being translated into China from the West. These attempts were carried on by the next generation of Buddhist thinkers, and groups such as the Wuchang School.

Wuchang School Writings on Mind Science

The curriculum of the Wuchang Buddhist Seminary was modeled after both modern secular schools and Japanese seminaries, and one of the elements of that curriculum was the study of modern sciences. As with much of the Wuchang School's activity, students' study of science was in part the product of Taixu's interests, but was developed by a group of teachers and students. As Pacey demonstrates in chapter 6 in this volume, Taixu showed an early interest in both the relationship between Yogācāra and science and the critique of modern mind science. Taixu had taken works on modern mind science with him into confinement in 1914, and as early as 1922 he was actively making claims about it (notably, that he felt Yogācāra was much greater in scope than modern mind science). The following year, in an important lecture that he gave at the first meeting of the World Buddhist Federation (Shijie Fojiao lianhehui 世界佛教聯合會), later published in HCY, Taixu called for the study of the sciences in order to help in the propagation of Buddhism. Although he felt that science could support Buddhism, it would never be able to surpass the truths contained therein.[60] In this article, Taixu roughly identified the purviews of the various sciences, but did not call for a specific study of any one of them. It is interesting to note that at this point Taixu (mis)understood mind science to "consist only of various explanations for spiritual phenomena."[61] Apart from the discussion of a number of issues related to mind science in lectures and articles on other topics, it was not until 1925 that one sees members of the Wuchang School emphasizing the study of the relationship between Buddhism and modern mind science. That year, HCY

59. Benjamin A. Elman, *On Their Own Terms: Science in China 1550–1900* (Cambridge, MA: Harvard University Press, 2005), p. 293.

60. Taixu, "Fofa yu kexue 佛法與科學" (The Buddha-dharma and Science), *HCY* 4, no. 8 (1923), MFQ 157:12–17.

61. MFQ 157:13.

published five major articles on mind science, four articles by three members of the Wuchang School, and one by the noted Japanese Buddhologist Kimura Taiken 木村泰賢 (1881–1930). Each of the following three years saw the appearance of at least one more major article on mind science by a member of the Wuchang School. In this section I will assess the Wuchang School's approach to mind science, which began with discussions of Indian Buddhist thought preserved in the Chinese canon as the Āgamas, before focusing on Yogācāra concepts of the storehouse consciousness and its karmic seeds.

The first two articles from the Wuchang School devoted to the study of Buddhist mind science to appear in print were transcripts of lectures given by Zhang Huasheng 張化聲 (b.1880), presumably at the Seminary.[62] Although little is known about his life, it is clear that Zhang was a central figure in the early Wuchang School. He taught Madhyamaka and Chinese studies at the seminary from 1924 to at least 1925, edited HCY for a time, and, most importantly, brought knowledge of Western sciences and philosophy to the seminary.[63] He also shared responsibility for teaching *abhidharma*.[64] His articles can be considered programmatic in that he established several of the features that would characterize the Wuchang School's approach to mind science. He should also be seen as an important leader in the Wuchang School in that his work was generally more technical than the work of Taixu, which could indicate that Zhang was one of the main conduits by which knowledge of modern mind science passed into the school.

Although covering slightly different topics, Zhang's two articles can be viewed as a whole, and after providing a distinct summary of each I will treat them in this manner. In his first article, "Yichu yu yijie duiyu xinlixue shang zhi yaodian 意處與意界對於心理學上之要點" (The Mind-Field and the Mind-Element vs. the Main Points of Psychology) Zhang was primarily concerned with identifying the

---

62. Zhang Huasheng 張化聲, "Yichu yu yijie duiyu xinlixue shang yaodian 意處與意界對於心理學上之要點" (The Mind-Field and the Mind-Element vs. the Main Points of Psychology), *HCY* 6, no. 2 (1925a), MFQ 161:296–300; and Zhang Huasheng, "Fojiao xinlixue yu xiyang xinlixue teyi zhi dian 佛教心理學與西洋心理學特異之點" (A Few Points on the Special Differences between Buddhist Psychology and Western Psychology), *HCY* 6, no. 3 (1925b), MFQ 161:429–433.

63. Yu Lingbo 于凌波 (ed.), *Xiandai Fojiao renwu cidian* 現代佛教人物辭典 (Dictionary of Modern Buddhist Personages), 2 vols. (Taipei: Foguang, 2004), vol.1, p.966a-c. Beyond his writing on Buddhist mind science, Zhang published several other articles on the relationship between Buddhism and various sciences, notably "Se ji shi kong, kong ji shi se zhi lihua tan 色即是空，空即是色之理化談" (A Discussion of Form Is Emptiness, Emptiness Is Form [from the Standpoint of] Physics and Chemistry), HCY 5, no. 12 (1924), MFQ 161:21–28.

64. At the Wuchang seminary, Zhang and Shi Yiru 史一如 (1876–1925) taught the courses in *abhidharma* using a text Shi had translated from Japanese. Fafang, *Weishi shiguan ji qi zhexue*, pp. 2–3.

weak points of Western mind science, and then demonstrating how the interrelated Buddhist concepts of the mind-field (*yichu* 意處; *mana-āyatana*) and the mind-element (*yijie* 意界; *mano-dhātu*) could provide an explanation for phenomena that mind science could not explain. Both concepts were important in Indian *abhidharma* thought, and both were incorporated into Yogācāra as it developed out of *abhidharma*. Although Zhang used them primarily as examples of *abhidharma*, their importance in Yogācāra allowed his students to pivot in their studies from the former to the latter. This is because the two concepts he invoked lie at the core of Yogācāra theory on the process by which human consciousness arises. The former term, mind-field, is used to refer to the central functions of cognition (functions also collectively referred to as the "mind-king" [*xinwang* 心王]). The latter term, mind-element, encompasses the "compositional elements of consciousness," and includes both the *manas* (seventh consciousness) and *âlaya* (base or eighth) consciousnesses.[65]

Zhang began his article by defining the main terms he would be using. He discussed mind science first, saying that although it was a branch of scientific research, properly speaking it was just a kind of metaphysics (*xing er shang de xue* 形而上的學) and, if one was being very strict about it, is a kind of philosophy and not a science.[66] He then outlined the method of mind science, which he said is to study the functions of the mind. In an effort to avoid being labeled a branch of metaphysics, scientists of the mind do experiments, but they only return mechanistic formulations of the mind's function. Here, Zhang is implicitly criticizing behaviorism, and this would remain common among members of the Wuchang School. After defining mind science, Zhang very briefly defined the concepts of the mind-field and the mind-element using short citations from the *Abhidharma-kośa* (Storehouse of Higher Doctrine). For the concept of the mind-field, he focused on its role as the gate by which various activities of the mind, known as mental factors (*xinsuo* 心所), are formed. In defining the mind-element he focused on its role in supporting the continuation of consciousness through the three times of past, present, and future. It will become clear that it was important for Zhang to focus on this aspect of the mind-element in light of the criticisms he made of mind science.[67]

The basic problem with modern mind science, as Zhang saw it, was that mind science focused on the function of the mind but did not address the

65. *Digital Dictionary of Buddhism*, s.v. "Yichu 意處," (article by C. Muller, et al., http://buddhism-dict.net/ddb).

66. MFQ 161:296.

67. MFQ 161:297. The mental factors are the activities of cognition that occur external to the essential nature of the mind, which are collectively referred to as *xinwang*, a term discussed above.

question of its fundamental reality (*benti* 本體). Because of this, modern mind science could not provide adequate explanations for a number of different phenomena, including latency and instinct, reaction, memory, dreams, and abnormal mental states (such as hypnosis). Three-quarters of this article is taken up with Zhang's various explanations of these problems, each of which begins with some reference to mind science, and is followed by a statement on how the concepts of the mind-element and mind-field can provide an answer to the problem. For example, in the section on instinct, Zhang identified some of the problems theorists were having in identifying the factor that could account for unlearned behavior that manifested at certain points in a creature's life. Zhang's solution was to say that the "seeds of instinct" (*benneng zhi zhongzi* 本能之種子) are stored in the mind-field and mind-element, where they later manifest (*xianxing* 現行).[68] Zhang uses these key concepts from Yogācāra, which are discussed at length in the *Cheng weishi lun*, but he does not identify them explicitly as deriving from Yogācāra.

In his second article, Zhang continued with several of the same themes (e.g., that mind science is really metaphysics and that Buddhism can supplement it). He also provided a more thorough history of modern mind science, as well as a justification for viewing Buddhism as a kind of mind science in its own right. Zhang said that many fields of inquiry had evolved within Buddhism over the millennia, and he admitted that an independent school of Buddhist mind science is difficult to identify. Nevertheless, he cited the doctrine of "the three worlds are nothing but mind, the myriad dharmas are nothing but consciousness" (*sanshi wei xin, wan fa wei shi* 三世唯心, 萬法唯識) to argue that in Buddhism all phenomena are mental phenomena.[69] The implication of this claim is that all of Buddhism can be viewed as a type of mind science. Zhang followed this with a brief history of Buddhist mind science, which he divides into three periods: (1) the period of the Vinaya and the Āgamas; (2) the period of the Nikāyas (which contributed, among others, the concepts of *xinsuo* and *xinwang* discussed above);[70] and (3) the period of Yogācāra. Zhang stressed that each of these three stages

68. MFQ 161:298.

69. MFQ 161:429.

70. Zhang's periodization of Buddhism in this manner was not entirely correct. Each of these terms–Vinaya, Āgama, and Nikāya–refers to a collection of texts, composed in an era of early Buddhism. The Vinaya is comprised of the various collections of monastic rules established by Buddhist communities before the start of the Common Era. Āgama and Nikāya are each used to refer to the collections of texts created by the various schools of *abhidharma* thought in Indian Buddhism. Whereas "Āgama" (*Ahan jing* 阿含經) is used to refer to those texts preserved in the Chinese canon, "Nikāya" is used

relied upon what had come before, and this orientation can be seen in Zhang's own use of a wide range of Buddhist ideas about the mind.[71]

Following his brief account of the evolution of Buddhist mind science toward Yogācāra, Zhang laid out an equally brief history of Western mind science, which he divided into two types. The first to appear historically was philosophical mind science, the development of which he described from Plato to Spencer, with specific emphasis on Kant. He did note that in the past ten years scientists had become dissatisfied with the metaphysical nature of this mode of inquiry, and had begun constructing a scientific mind science, which was still very much in its infancy. Continuing his implicit criticism of behaviorism, Zhang stated that this science tends to view the mind as a machine.

An analysis of both of his articles reveals that Zhang's use of Buddhism is primarily focused on Mainstream Buddhist doctrines such as the five *skandhas* (*yun* 蘊), twelve *āyatanas* (*chu* 處), and eighteen *dhātus* (*jie* 界).[72] On this point alone his work bears similarity to that of some other writers during the period, such as Liang Qichao 梁啓超 (1873–1929), whose presentation to the Chinese Psychological Association on Buddhist mind science focused particularly on the five *skandhas*, although he did make some reference to Yogācāra thought.[73] It is also likely that Zhang was influenced by the work of Kimura Taiken, whose article "Early Buddhist Psychology," appeared in Chinese translation in HCY in August

for the divisions of texts used in the Southern Buddhist traditions. Technically speaking, both designations can include the works of a number of different sects (also referred to as "nikāya") of Buddhism. Zhang is historically inaccurate in that the Chinese Āgamas include works by earlier *abhidharma* schools, as well as those of later schools, such as the Sarvāstivāda, mentioned above. Hirakawa Akira, *A History of Indian Buddhism: From Śakyamuni to Early Mahāyāna* (Honolulu: University of Hawai'i Press, 1990), pp. 71–72.

71. MFQ 161:429–430.

72. These Buddhist concepts are collectively referred to as the "three categories" (*san ke* 三科). The five *skandhas*, twelve *āyatanas* 處, and eighteen *dhātus* 界. The five *skandhas*, or aggregates, are used to explain the contingent, compositional nature of human existence, and to highlight its lack of intrinsic essence or selfness. The twelve *āyatanas* and eighteen *dhātus* are concepts that appeared in *abhidharma*, which were incorporated into Yogācāra. They are used to explain how consciousness arises out of the interaction of the six sense organs (eyes, ears, nose, tongue, body, and mind) and their specific sense-objects. The *āyatanas* are the six sense organs and their objects, whereas the *dhātus* includes the six consciousnesses produced from their interaction.

73. This lecture, which first appeared in the journal *Xinli*, was reprinted in HCY in 1930, although not without an editorial comment stating that Liang had incorrectly identified the third *skandha*, *saṃjñā*, as the source of memory. Liang Qichao, "Fojiao xinli qiance 佛教心理學淺測" (A Brief Account of Buddhist Psychology), *HCY* 11, no. 6 (1930), MFQ 175:407–420.

1925.[74] This article focused entirely on doctrines found in the Āgamas, such as the *āyatanas*; and in it, Kimura made no reference to Yogācāra, and almost no reference to modern mind science.

Zhang's work makes much implicit use of Yogācāra thought, an important element in the Wuchang School's discussion of mind science. Zhang used a number of Mainstream Buddhist ideas to discuss mind science, but, as mentioned above, these concepts also hold important places in Yogācāra thought. Given that Zhang several times cited the idea that "the myriad dharmas are nothing but consciousness," it is not too far of a stretch to imagine that Zhang saw his work as relying heavily on Yogācāra. At the end of his first article, Zhang reported that although the *āyatanas* and *dhātus* may be ideas from Hīnayāna, his group was researching what importance the idea that "the myriad dharmas are consciousness-only" held for mind science. Zhang clearly saw the exploration of Yogācāra views as they related to modern mind science as the next step in the school's work. This is indeed what happened, and that research followed along lines already laid out by Zhang. The two themes that marked the work of the Wuchang School after Zhang were efforts to explain memory and instinct using Yogācāra ideas, and the refutation of materialist readings of mind science, particularly as expressed in the increasingly dominant school of behaviorism.

A key point that can be seen in Zhang's work, especially in light of the goals of the present volume, is the importance that fairly Indian modes of Buddhist thought took on for Chinese Buddhists in their responses to modern sciences. As they engaged with modern mind science, East Asian Buddhists turned first to Mainstream Buddhist ideas, which they often encountered through important Yogācāra and pre- Yogācāra sources (like the *Abhidharma-kośa*). The historical and doctrinal affinity of Yogācāra to certain forms of Mainstream Buddhist thought, such as that of the Sarvāstivāda, formed a bridge by which Mahāyāna Buddhists in twentieth-century China could study and take advantage of the riches present in Mainstream Buddhist texts for analyzing the mind without sacrificing their Mahāyāna ideals. Such usage was not limited to Buddhist approaches to mind science, however. As Eyal Aviv shows in this volume, the tendency to use *abhidharmic* literature as an entry point into a deeper study of Buddhist doctrine was clearly part of the intellectual development of Ouyang Jingwu as well. For his part, Zhang provided a simplified explanation of the relationship that made this possible by saying that although the writers of the Âgamas developed complex schemes of the mind, it was left to the Yogācāras

74. Kimura Taiken 木村泰賢, "Yuanshi Fojiao zhi xinlixue 原始佛教之心理學" (Psychology in Original Buddhism), *HCY* 6, no. 6 (1925), MFQ 162:259–270.

to determine the ontological status of phenomena vis-à-vis the categories of matter and mind.[75]

As previously noted, the question of how memory is formed, stored, and functions was of key interest to both scientists and philosophers of the mind in the late nineteenth and early twentieth centuries. The related phenomenon of instinct occupied a position of similar importance. Behaviorism and related materialist positions needed to establish a physical location for memory, but since the existence of a singular "memory center" in the brain had been generally disproven by the late 1910s, mind science had to find other ways to locate and account for memory. Instinct also continued to prove a thorny problem, especially to the behaviorists, who wanted to formulate, through experimentation, a catalog of all the specific responses provoked by specific stimuli; and the variable and complex role that instinct plays in motivating actions was not easily incorporated into behaviorist models. The topics of instinct and memory were also important for philosophers like Henri Bergson, as well as those who supported vitalism and other aspects of what could be termed "Romantic science."

As noted above, Zhang attempted to explain the functioning of both memory and instinct the following year using the concepts of mind-field and mind-element. That same year, one of the monastic students at the Wuchang Seminary published the most detailed treatment of instinct from the viewpoint of Yogācāra Buddhism. Building on Zhang's equation of instinct and the seeds discussed in Yogācāra, the monk Manzhi wrote an article in which he made extensive use of the *Cheng weishi lun* to explain the role of karmic seeds in the Yogācāra system of eight consciousnesses.[76] Manzhi is an interesting figure in that he was both a member of the first graduating class of the Wuchang Buddhist Seminary and a student at the China Inner Learning Institute from 1924 to 1925. Based on the analysis Lin Chen-kuo provides in this volume of Lü Cheng's teaching activities in the mid-1920s, it is likely that Manzhi studied Yogācāra and Buddhist logic while there. After his brief stint at the institute, Manzhi helped with several of Taixu's endeavors, teaching at the newly formed Minnan Buddhist Seminary (Minnan Foxue Yuan 閩南佛學院) in 1926, and taking charge of setting up the Sino-Tibetan Institute (Han Zang Jiaoli Yuan 漢藏教理院) in Chongqing in 1932. Unfortunately, he disappeared from the historical record by the mid-1930s.[77]

75. MFQ 161:430.

76. Manzhi, "Xinlixue zhi benneng yu weishizong zhongzi zhi guanxi 心理學之本能與唯識宗種子之關係" (The Relationship between Instinct in Psychology, and Seeds in the Nothing but Consciousness School), *HCY* 6, no. 5 (1925), MFQ 162:152–157.

77. Yu Lingbo, *Xiandai Fojiao renwu zhi*, 2.1438c–1439c.

Although he claimed that he was not trying to support functionalism in general, Manzhi did say in his article that he wanted to help that school of thought deflect some of the criticisms that it received from the behaviorists, who disliked the functionalists' emphasis on instinct. Manzhi began by explaining some of the basic aspects of the concept of instinct. He claimed that instinct was something discussed primarily by vitalist researchers, and referred to a motive force aimed at specific goals, which is inherited by an ethnic group. The idea that instinct is something that creatures are born with led Manzhi to ask (in a manner pregnant with meaning in the East Asian Buddhist context) how it would be possible to study what comes before birth.[78] Manzhi then rehearsed some of the primary discussions of the day regarding instinct, but found each of them lacking in some way. The central problem for Manzhi was that the functionalists, and anyone who focused on instinct, studied only its manifestations but did not investigate its roots. He said the real substance of instinct, its cause, is the karmic seeds stored within the *ālayavijñāna* and that the manifestations of instinct that the functionalists study is merely the manifestation (*xianxing*) of those seeds. He said that talking about instinct only from the standpoint of its effects (whether objective or subjective) is like looking at the reflection of a flower in a mirror, or of the moon in water.[79] What was needed was an examination of the causes of instinct.

The anti-behaviorist bent of the Wuchang School should be obvious from the works cited thus far, but at least one member of the group was not content to let those criticisms stand as their final word. Although he had left the seminary in 1924, Taixu continued to have a strong influence on its students, especially those who, like Manzhi, graduated in the first class. In 1927 and 1928, Taixu published articles criticizing the mechanistic viewpoint of behaviorism.[80] The first of these articles is the more general of the two, and there Taixu was critical of another extreme he saw in a different stream of modern mind science: the tendency of any school to posit the existence of any kind of soul or vital essence. As a Buddhist, he was suspicious of any doctrine that relied on the existence of a permanent, substantial essence that determined human behavior, and he stated again that what some in the field of biology understand to be the functioning of a kind of hidden power (by which he means the *élan vital* of the vitalists) comes from the seeds of the eighth

78. MFQ 162:153.

79. MFQ 162:157.

80. Taixu, "Xingweixue yu xinlixue 行為學與心理學" (Behaviorism and Psychology), *HCY* 8, no. 1 (1927), MFQ 167:39–49; and Taixu, "Zai lun xinlixue yu xingweixue 再論心理學與行為學" (Discussing Behaviorism and Psychology Again), *HCY* 9, no. 1 (1928), MFQ 169:282–284.

consciousness.[81] Thus, some members of the Wuchang School seemed to have been as concerned with the extreme of vitalism (which they saw espoused in some forms of modern mind science) as they were with the mechanistic determinism of behaviorism.

Conclusion

A wide range of actors took part in the translation of modern science into China in the late nineteenth and early twentieth centuries. Rather than adopt the interpretation offered by certain participants in the science and philosophy-of-life debates, who viewed that translation as the process of truth overcoming an ignorance rooted in stale tradition and wild metaphysical speculation, we should see the translation of science as a lengthy process in which complexes of ideas were taken up, contemplated and commented upon, and incorporated into indigenous modes of thought. This was nowhere more evident than in the indigenization of modern mind science. Buddhists played their part in this process, and as they did so the questions posed by the rapidly changing field of mind science helped them breathe new life into their explorations of Buddhist doctrine, such as that contained within Yogācāra. As this volume makes clear, the members of the Wuchang School were not the only ones writing about Yogācāra at the time, nor were they the only ones discussing the intersection of Yogācāra and science. They did, however, represent an important stream of thought during the period.

In this chapter, it has been shown that more than other forms of Buddhist thought, Yogācāra provided the foundation that enabled Buddhists to relate to modern psychology, a newly-introduced science that played an important symbolic role in Chinese intellectual negotiations around modernity and modern values. In the Wuchang School, the application of Yogācāra thought to this science was first called for by Taixu, but was carried out by others, notably Zhang Huasheng and Manzhi. Although they all agreed that "the myriad dharmas are nothing but consciousness," they did not start with Yogācāra directly; instead, they began their exploration of the connections between modern science and Buddhist thought by means of the doctrines of earlier forms of Indian Buddhism, doctrines that overlap to a considerable degree with Yogācāra ones. In developing their Buddhist mind science, these writers demonstrated their awareness of the state of the field by focusing their discussions on areas of heated debate within it: memory, instinct, and the relative strengths of behaviorism and functionalism.

81. MFQ 167:48.

By examining these writings, I hope it has been shown that "the Wuchang School" is a useful concept with which to approach certain patterns in the intellectual history of modern Chinese Buddhism. Study of this school is one way to bring some of the important contributors to China's Buddhist modernisms out from behind the large shadow cast by Taixu. Further study of the networks it engendered will likely yield important conclusions about the shape and spread of those modernisms. The concept of the Wuchang School is also very important in the context of this book, which focuses primarily on certain lay thinkers, and does not otherwise cover the development of Yogācāra studies among China's monastics. In this regard, one could fruitfully compare the Yogācāra writings of Lü Cheng with those of another of Yang Wenhui's grand-disciples, Fafang. Like Lü, Fafang spent several years studying Sanskrit and Pāli (although unlike Lü, he did this in India and Sri Lanka). Fafang's Yogācāra thought is only touched on briefly here, but he did leave behind at least one major work on the topic at the end of his tragically short life.[82] His writings, and those of other monastic graduates of the Wuchang Buddhist Seminary represent an important branch of modern Chinese Yogācāra studies, one which started from the same roots as those described in this book, but which grew in different directions.

82. This is a collection of lectures he gave at the Tung Lin Kok Yuen 東蓮覺苑 in Hong Kong in May, 1949: *Weishi shiguan ji qi zhexue* 唯識史觀及其哲學 (The History of Yogācāra and its Philosophy), first published in 1950, and still in print today.

PART 4

Yogācāra and Confucian Thought

7

Liang Shuming and his Confucianized Version of Yogācāra

Thierry Meynard

YOGĀCĀRA WAS REVIVED in China by progressive Buddhist circles as an attempt to demarcate Buddhism from other popular forms of religious expression that were considered irrational and superstitious. At the same time, non-Buddhist intellectuals such as Zhang Taiyan 章太炎 (1869–1936) also participated in its revival. In this chapter, I shall examine the case of Liang Shuming's 梁漱溟 (1895–1988) involvement in the revival of Yogācāra in modern China.[1] The chapter consists of four sections. In the first three sections, I shall look at the early phase of Liang's engagement with Yogācāra, from 1909 to 1921. During this period, Liang was both a student and a teacher of Yogācāra, using two complementary methods: historical-critical exegesis, which distances itself from tradition and reorganizes the history of that school (section 1); and philosophical exegesis, which expresses its doctrine with modern concepts, mostly drawn from Western philosophy (section 2). I then present Liang's manual of Yogācāra (section 3). If Liang had stopped there he would have been a pioneer of Yogācāra studies in Chinese academia. Liang, however, was also an original thinker and, from the early-1920s he developed his own version of Yogācāra, as an intellectual foundation for his own social engagement in the world. The fourth and last section will therefore deal with the creative phase of Liang's use of Yogācāra.

1. For a general presentation on Liang Shuming's life, see Guy Alitto, *The Last Confucian* (Berkeley: University of California Press, 1979). For a more recent approach, making the case that Liang was a Buddhist, see Thierry Meynard, *The Religious Philosophy of Liang Shuming, The Hidden Buddhist* (Leiden: Brill, 2011).

1. *The historical-critical exegesis of Yogācāra*

Liang was a self-taught Buddhist. Having no formal training in Buddhism, he admitted to being at a loss when confronted with so many schools and theories.[2] Yet, as his Buddhist writings reveal, his sharp mind enabled him to capture the subtleties of Buddhist thought. In 1909, at the age of sixteen, he started reading Buddhist discourses and treatises, and with more intensity, in 1911, during a period of self-imposed seclusion. He read the *Foxue congbao* 佛學叢報 (The Miscellany of Buddhist Studies), a monthly journal published in Shanghai.[3] Some Yogācāra materials were published there, for example, Ouyang Jingwu's 歐陽竟無 (1871–1943) "*Guan suoyuan yuan lun* shijie 觀所緣緣論釋解" (Interpretation of the *Treatise on Discerning the Conditions for the Causal Support of Consciousness*).[4] Liang, however, was not immediately convinced by Yogācāra. We shall see how early on he expressed some reservations about a teaching he considered too worldly. He was, however, attracted to the school because of his own interest in meditative practice, and from then he started a critical examination of the history of the school and of its teaching.

1.1 From early reservations about Yogācāra to teaching it

Despite the new scholarship on Yogācāra introduced by Ouyang, Liang's initial views on that school remained largely negative. Liang's early prejudice is clearly expressed in his first academic essay, "Jiuyuan jueyi lun 究元決疑論" (On Finding the Foundation and Resolving the Doubt; 1916). In this essay, he adopted the usual doxographical classification of Sinitic Buddhism recognizing two main schools: the Dharma Characteristics School (*xiangzong* 相宗) and the Dharma Nature School (*xingzong* 性宗). Yogācāra was considered as belonging to the Dharma Characteristics School because it limited itself to analyzing only the dharma-attributes, that it is the ever-changing phenomena. The Dharma Nature School was seen to be superior because it allowed the mind to grasp the true nature of things and Buddhahood. Therefore, in Liang's first published essay he

---

2. Liang Shuming, "Wo de zixue xiaoshi 我的自學小史" (A Short History of My Self-Learning), in *Liang Shuming quanji* 梁漱溟全集 (The Complete Works of Liang Shuming) 8 vols. (Ji'nan: Shandong renmin chubanshe, 1989–1993), vol. 2, p. 692.

3. *Foxue congbao* was published by Youzheng shuju Press. There were a total of twelve issues, from October 1912 to June1914.

4. Ouyang Jingwu, "*Guan suoyuan yuan lun* shijie," *Foxue congbao* 11 (1914-05-01): 1–29. The *Ālambana-parīkṣā* (Treatise on Discerning the Conditions for the Causal Support of Consciousness) was written by Dignāga (*ca.* 480–540) and is discussed in more detail in Dan Lusthaus's chapter.

talked about Yogācāra as the Dharma Characteristics School, a term that was not neutral but derogatory.

It seems that at that time Liang had not yet read Xuanzang's (*ca.* 600–664) *Cheng weishi lun* 成唯識論 (Demonstration of Nothing but Consciousness), referring only to the *San wuxing lun* 三無性論 (Treatise on the Three Non-natures) and the *Foxing lun* 佛性論 (Treatise on the Buddha Nature), two treatises translated by Paramārtha and displaying a strong ontology.[5] Although Liang adopted this ontologized interpretation of Yogācāra by Paramārtha, in which an ontological foundation, or Suchness, is posited as the basis of the myriad of dharmas, Liang's preference still lay with the "school of nature," for providing a superior account of fundamental reality (*benti* 本體), according to a well-established tradition in China.

Liang's seminal essay was noticed by the president of Peking University, Cai Yuanpei 蔡元培 (1868–1940), who invited him to teach Indian philosophy at Peking University.[6] At the time, Buddhist philosophy was a branch of Indian philosophy within the academic curriculum of the philosophy department.[7] In the context of the revival of Yogācāra, Liang recanted his early prejudice and became a proponent of the school. Yet Yogācāra's popularity made Liang quite worried. The teachings of that school are complex, and he was horrified to hear popular interpretations of Yogācāra doctrines, such as the belief that the eight consciousnesses really exist. This meant that instead of helping people to get rid of attachments, Yogācāra was in fact being used to create more illusions and attachments. Even worse, some Buddhist monks and laymen, who had not studied the teaching thoroughly, were disseminating incorrect interpretations. Because of his own study of Yogācāra, Liang was able to find errors in the understanding of two famous Buddhist laymen, Zhang Kecheng 張克誠 (1865–1922) and Jiang Weiqiao 蔣維喬 (1873–1958). Zhang Kecheng, also called Jingru 淨如, was invited in 1917 as an adjunct faculty to lecture on Buddhism at Peking University,

---

5. Liang Shuming, "Jiuyuan jueyi lun," in *Liang Shuming quanji*, vol. 1, p. 8. *Cheng weishi lun* presents different interpretations of Yogācāra, including the one that Xuanzang considered orthodox. The *San wuxing lun* and the *Foxing lun* belong to a different interpretative tradition, based on an ontological frame of thought (nature, or nature as nonnature). *San wuxing lun* is usually attributed to either Asaṅga (fourth century) or Vasubandhu (fourth century). *Foxing lun* is questionably attributed to Vasubandhu.

6. Cai Yuanpei became the president of Peking University starting December 1917, just a few months after the publication of Liang's essay.

7. See Thierry Meynard, "Introducing Buddhism as Philosophy: The Cases of Liang Shuming, Xiong Shili and Tang Yongtong," in *The Genesis of Chinese Philosophy as an Academic Discipline in Twentieth-century China*, ed. John Makeham (Hong Kong: Chinese University Press, 2012), pp. 183–212.

presumably the first such appointment.[8] Liang, however, thought that Zhang did not have a good understanding of Yogācāra and made serious mistakes. For example, Zhang wrongly understood the self-authenticating aspect of cognition as bringing a moral judgment about good and evil.[9] Also, in his popular *Guan suoyuan yuan lun qianshuo* 觀所緣緣論淺說 (Explanation of the *Treatise on Discerning the Conditions for the Causal Support of Consciousness*), Zhang wrongly interpreted the notion of "conditions for the causal support of consciousness" (*suoyuan yuan*所緣緣).[10] For Liang, Zhang Kecheng fell into objectivism by holding that the base consciousness leads to the establishment of a "correct principle" (*zhengli* 正理). Zhang's objectivist understanding was opposed to Liang's own understanding of Yogācāra as going beyond reason and concepts. Liang further suggested that Zhang may have made mistakes because he was relying on Ming commentaries.[11]

The same concern for orthodoxy made Liang criticize the educator and Buddhist scholar Jiang Weiqiao. Jiang had published a very popular book about seated meditation in 1914[12] and later studied Yogācāra with Zhang Kecheng. In 1918, one year after his master, Jiang also lectured on Yogācāra at Peking University. It is no wonder that Liang could find the master's mistakes in his disciple.[13]

As we can see, Liang took his Yogācāra studies very seriously. He thought that Yogācāra had not been correctly transmitted in China for more than a thousand years and that the later commentaries were not reliable. He saw Buddhist monks

---

8. Zhang Kecheng was an officer in charge of criminal cases but, feeling too much pressure, he gave up his job in 1911 and went into retreat in Guangji Temple 廣濟寺 in Beijing. For biographical details on Zhang Kecheng, see Yu Lingbo于淩波, "Jindai Weishixue de fuxing yu fazhan 近代唯識學的復興與發展" (The Revival and Development of the Weishi Studies in Modern Times), in *Weishi sanlun jinquan* 唯識三論今詮 (Modern Explanation of Three Treatises of Weishi) (Taipei: Zhongda faxing, 1994).

9. Cf. Liang Shuming, *Weishi shuyi* 唯識述義 (Outline of Yogācāra, 1920), in *Liang Shuming quanji*, vol. 1, p. 289. According to *Cheng weishi lun*, the transformation of consciousness is the result of consciousness' being bifurcated into an object part and a seeing or perceiving part. A third part, the self-authenticating aspect, confirms the perceiving part.

10. Ibid., p. 301.

11. Liang considered that Zhang Kecheng was probably influenced by two late-Ming commentators of the *Cheng weishi lun*, the monk Zhixu 智旭 (1599–1655), who wrote *Guan suoyuan yuan lun zhijie* 觀所緣緣論直解 (Direct Explanation of the *Treatise on Discerning the Conditions for the Causal Support of Consciousness*), and the monk Mingyu 明昱 (1527–1616), who wrote *Guan suoyuan yuan lun huishi* 觀所緣緣論會釋 (Collected Interpretations of the *Treatise on Discerning the Conditions for the Causal Support of Consciousness*).

12. Jiang Weiqiao, *Yinshizi jingzuofa* 因是子靜坐法 (The Method for Seated Meditation of Yinshizi) (Beiping: Shangwu yinshuguan, 1914). There was an expanded edition in 1922.

13. Liang, *Weishi shuyi*, p. 253.

and laymen in high demand to give lectures and to publish on Yogācāra but he considered that many of them did not thoroughly study the teaching. Acknowledging only Ouyang Jingwu's authority, Liang took it upon himself to adopt the modern methods of Buddhist scholarship in order to retrieve the authentic teaching.

1.2 Yogācāra and practices of meditation

In 1918, Liang taught a class on Indian philosophy at Peking University. The manual that came out the following year, *Yindu zhexue gailun* 印度哲學概論 (Introduction to Indian Philosophy) showed Liang's strong interest in meditation. When Liang describes meditation, he refers mainly to the method described in the **Śūraṃgama-sūtra* (*Lengyan jing* 楞嚴經; Sutra of the Samādhi of Heroic Progress).[14] In his manual, Liang quoted this text extensively. Accordingly, from the perspective of the mind at rest, the flow of consciousness in the mind is an illusion, or as expressed in **Śūraṃgama-sūtra*:

> You should know Ānanda that when the Buddhist disciples in the *stabilizing meditation* have their mind stable, clear and correct, they cannot be disturbed by the ten kinds of *deva-māra*. Only then can they fully understand the origin of all the categories of beings. As the origin of the categories becomes apparent, they can contemplate the source of the hidden, fleeting, and pervasive flux.[15]

Next, the **Śūraṃgama-sūtra* explains how to reach this stage though an elaborate process in which external teachings and erroneous ideas arise in the mind to be negated, one by one. Although the Buddhist practitioner knows that the five aggregates or *skandhas* (form, sensation, perception, volition, consciousness) are empty, his mind generates wrong ideas that become like seeds, themselves producing unwanted results. None of the erroneous ideas that come to the mind are presented here as heresies to avoid. On the contrary, they reveal a mental path

14. A Sanskrit counterpart for this sutra is not extant. Despite controversy about its origin, the sutra has become very influential in Chan Buddhism.

15. *Yindu zhexue gailun*, *Liang Shuming quanji*, vol. 1, p. 67; original text in *Da foding rulai miyin xiuzheng liaoyi zhupusa wanxing shoulengyan jing* 大佛頂如來密因修證了義諸菩薩萬行首楞嚴經 (The Sutra on the Mantra Spoken from above the Crown of the Great Buddha's Head, and on the Hidden Basis of the Tathāgatas' Myriad Bodhisattva Practices Leading to Their Verification of the Definitive Meaning), CBETA T19n0945_010, 0151c11. English translation here is from the Chinese: *The Shurangama Sutra: Sutra Text and Supplements*, with commentary by Hsuan Hua (Burlingame, CA: Buddhist Text Translation Society, 2003), p. 269.

that has to be experienced by the individual. The distance traveled by the mind here is most relevant. Through concrete meditation, the mind stays for a while with these ideas, measures and experiences them, and finally rejects them.

Liang sees the meditative practice as the work of reason in eliminating wrong ideas, in destroying them, until nothing but consciousness remains. In other words, Yogācāra logic and meditation are tightly connected. At the end of the process, consciousness itself is destroyed, allowing the mind to enter into the "dark primordial truth" (*mingdi* 冥諦), which is nonconceptual, and in which the mind is "no longer affected by cause and effect and is correctly focused" (*wuwei zhengding* 無為正定), and knows the absolute without knowing that it knows.[16]

Besides the **Śūraṃgama-sūtra*, Liang also refers to a foundational text for meditative practice in Yogācāra, the *Yogācārabhūmi-śāstra* (*Yuqie shidi lun* 瑜伽師地論; Discourse on the Stages of Concentration Practice).[17] Liang probably used the new edition published by Ouyang Jingwu. Liang had a special interest in this text because of its emphasis on concrete techniques of "meditative concentration" (*samādhi*).[18] In the first stage of meditation, the five hindrances have completely disappeared and unwholesome intentions cease. Although one can experience an intense unified bliss, a subtle mental activity remains and therefore this *samādhi* is qualified as "conceptual thought" (*vitarka*; *youxun* 有尋) and "analytical thought" (*vicāra*; *yousi* 有伺). This means that conceptualization and reflection still occur at that level. For Liang, this proves further that philosophical thinking and meditative practice come together: "First, from thinking activity to stabilization of the mind, and then, from stabilization of the mind to thinking activity, and further on, with the depth of thought depending on the stabilization of the mind, and with the degree of stabilization depending on thought."[19] Liang therefore understood Yogācāra as an integrated experience including the rational and the extrarational. Both elements are necessary. Without the meditative practice, ideas appear in the mind, but are not really experienced by it, bringing no

16. *Yindu zhexue gailun*, p. 67. *Mingdi* translates the Sanskrit term *prakṛti*, taken from Sāṃkhya, and introduced in medieval times to China through Buddhist texts.

17. This is the definitive text of Yogācāra. Composed in India between 300 and 350, it was translated into Chinese by Xuanzang 玄奘 from 646 to 648. In East Asia the putative author is thought to be Maitreya 彌勒, but the Tibetan tradition considers it to have been composed by Asaṅga 無著.

18. Quite strangely, Liang mentioned this text only once in his *Weishi shuyi*, stating that Yogācāra's epistemology developed successfully because it recovered the capacity for direct cognition (*xianliang*) through the exercises of "meditation and stabilization of the mind" (*chanding* 禪定). Therefore, Liang sees the Yogācāra theory of direct cognition as "both a by-product of the Yogācāra practice, as well as an explanation of Buddhist Yogācāra" (p. 305).

19. *Yindu zhexue gailun*, p. 70.

result but only a catalogue of different opinions. Without philosophical reason, however, experience is fundamentally blind. For Liang, the Buddhist method uses both religious practice and philosophical inquiry.

We need also to observe that reason works as a tool by which erroneous ideas are discarded.[20] This *via negativa* works as a kind of mental purification, which prepares the Buddhists for leaving the world. Liberation is obtained only through canceling out the ongoing production of consciousness, negating all elements of perception as ultimately false and illusory. The process is therefore purely rational, and Liang called it: "to cancel understanding through understanding" (*yi lijie quxiao lijie* 以理解取消理解).[21] The meditative practice leads to a transcendental wisdom. In this sense, Liang says that Buddhism is religious not only in its method of meditation, but also in its aim, that is, to leave the world and to access a reality that lies beyond.[22]

1.3 Critical study of Yogācāra: Founder, canon, interpreter

Following his class on Indian philosophy, in 1919 Liang offered a class on Yogācāra and so came to study its teachings systematically for the first time. He read two works by Kuiji 窺基 (632–682), *Cheng weishi lun shuji* 成唯識論述記 (Notes on *Demonstration of Nothing but Consciousness*) and *Yinming ru zhengli lun shu* 因明入正理論疏 (Commentary on *Entryway into Logic*).[23] He read also the *Nyāyamukha* (*Yinming zhengli menlun* 因明正理門; Introduction to Logic) by Dignāga 陳那 (sixth century),[24] as well as the *Nyāyapraveśa* (*Yinming ru zhengli lun* 因明入正理論; Entryway into Logic) by Dignāga's disciple, Śaṃkarasvāmin 商羯羅主.[25] In 1920, Liang published the notes of this class as *Weishi shuyi* 唯識述義 (Outline of Yogācāra).[26]

20. Ibid., p. 70.

21. Ibid., p. 158.

22. See *Yindu zhexue gailun*, p. 66.

23. This latter text is referred as the *Dashu* 大疏 (Great Commentary).

24. This text was translated from Sanskrit into Chinese by Xuanzang. The Japanese scholar-monk Kirara Kōyō 雲英晃耀 (1824–1910) published an edition of this text in 1881. Kirara stressed the practical use of Buddhist logic, especially in the public debates of the courts and of the national assembly. See the chapter by John Jorgensen in this volume.

25. This text was also translated by Xuanzang. Many Weishi scholars commented on this text, the most influential being Kuiji.

26. Liang, *Weishi shuyi*, p. 269. Liang was able to write only the first part of *Weishi shuyi* because of insomnia—an illness he suffered throughout his life—and so had to stop the class. At the beginning of 1920, he agreed, quite reluctantly, to publish the existing draft.

During the Republican era, many scholars emphasized the use of new methods of critical scholarship when dating and establishing the authorship of works. Modern approaches to history allowed scholars to establish intellectual influences between writers and between schools. Liang Shuming applied these methods to reassess the origin of Yogācāra. The Chinese tradition held that Yogācāra was established by Maitreya,[27] who purportedly received the teaching of the *Saṃdhinirmocana-sūtra* (*Jie shenmi jing* 解深密經; Discourse Explaining the Thought) from the Buddha.[28] Today, modern scholars are very cautious about the authorship of this text. In the first chapter of this volume, John Powers relates that it was probably composed around the third century C.E. Liang accepted the tradition that the *Saṃdhinirmocana-sūtra* was a discourse of the Buddha, but he stated that Maitreya was the real founder of the Yogācāra School. Because Maitreya himself dictated the five treatises to his student Asaṅga 無著 (fourth century), Liang next considered Asaṅga as the proper founder of the Yogācāra School, taking also into consideration the fact that Asaṅga wrote the *Mahāyānasaṃgraha* (*She dasheng lun* 攝大乘論; Compendium of the Great Vehicle).[29] Finally, he concluded, from the point of view of the development of Yogācāra, it was Vasubandhu, and not his brother Asaṅga, who was the real founder:

> It is better to say that the Yogācāra School goes back to Maitreya rather than to say it goes back to Śākyamuni Buddha; but it is even better to say that it goes back to Asaṅga rather than to say it goes back to Maitreya, and in fact the real founder of the school in India is Vasubandhu.[30]

Through the question of authorship and school lineage, Liang was paying respect to intellectual history. Later on, he continued to value the results of critical historicism. For example, in 1923, he acknowledged the conclusions of Japanese scholars and Ouyang Jingwu that traditional attributions of authorship for the **Śūraṃgama-sūtra* and the *Dasheng qixin lun* 大乘起信論 (Awakening

---

27. A shadowy figure thought to have lived from around 270–350.

28. Liang, *Weishi shuyi, Liang Shuming quanji*, vol. 7, p. 267. For an English translation from the Tibetan, see John Powers, *Wisdom of the Buddha: The Saṃdhinirmocana Mahāyāna Sūtra* (Berkeley, CA: Dharma Publishing, 1995). This discourse in ten chapters contains the earliest presentation of the essentials of Yogācāra. Although no Sanskrit version survives, there are five Chinese translations and three in Tibetan. The most authoritative Chinese translation was by Xuanzang.

29. It is a major text of Yogācāra. Even though the Sanskrit original is not extant, Tibetan and Chinese versions are preserved.

30. Liang, *Weishi shuyi*, pp. 267–268.

of Mahāyāna Faith) were dubious.[31] Since Liang did not have access to Sanskrit texts, however, his research on the question of authorship was limited. Also, he did not grant himself enough time to delve into difficult research, since he left the university a few years after.

Liang also delineated the corpus of Yogācāra by listing the canon established in Kuiji's *Cheng weishi lun shuji*. Interestingly, it seems that Xuanzang himself did not establish a canon, and so Liang considered Kuiji, in agreement with the tradition, as the real founder of Yogācāra in China.[32] Kuiji's canon includes six sutras and eleven treatises (*shijing shiyilun* 六經十一論). The first "sutra" mentioned in Kuiji's canon is the *Avataṃsaka-sūtra* (*Huayan jing* 華嚴經; Flower Ornament Sutra).[33] Although this sutra is mentioned first, in fact, it is not specific to Yogācāra, but was used as the general framework for Mahāyāna teachings, providing a very complete explanation of the buddha's state and the bodhisattva's quest for awakening through ten stages. The second sutra in the canon is the *Saṃdhinirmocana-sūtra*, which includes the seminal teachings of the school. The third sutra is the *Laṅkāvatāra-sūtra* (*Lengqie jing* 楞伽經; Discourse on [the Buddha's] Entering [the Country of] Lanka).[34] This text evidences many ideas from Yogācāra, but, according to modern scholarship, it does not represent mainstream Indian Yogācāra. Although it is quoted seven times in *Cheng weishi lun*, Xuanzang expressed a differing view on several occasions.[35] Indeed, this text is quite late and also drew on the ontological concept of *tathāgatagarbha*, or womb or matrix of the buddhas.[36] Of the remaining three sutras designated by Kuiji, none was translated into Chinese.

Therefore, of the six sutras in Kuiji's canon, we can say that the only one available in Chinese and which could be considered representing authentic Yogācāra is the *Saṃdhinirmocana-sūtra*. Kuiji included in his canon some sutras that his master Xuanzang probably would not have recognized as Yogācāra, especially

31. Preface of the third edition (1923), in *Yindu zhexue gailun*, p. 28. The *Awakening of Mahāyāna Faith*, though of uncertain origin, came to occupy a central place in the development of Buddhism in East Asia.

32. Liang, *Weishi shuyi*, p. 268.

33. It was translated in Chinese by Buddhabhadra 佛陀跋陀羅 (*ca.* 420), and later by Śikṣānanda 難陀 (*ca.* 700).

34. This "sutra" is supposed to record the actual words of the Buddha when he entered Sri Lanka and it sets out the workings of human consciousness.

35. Francis Cook, *Three Texts on Consciousness Only* (Berkeley, CA: Numata Center for Buddhist Translation and Research, 1999), p. 437.

36. See Kogen Mizuno, *Essentials of Buddhism*, translated by Gaynor Sekimori (Tokyo: Kosei Publishing, 1996), p. 45.

those displaying an ontological tendency, such as the *Laṅkāvatāra-sūtra*. Liang inherited from Kuiji a very plastic understanding of Yogācāra. At one point, Liang even included *Dasheng qixin lun* in the Yogācāra corpus.[37] Indeed, the boundaries of Yogācāra were quite blurred at that time. As John Jorgensen points out in chapter 2, Yang Wenhui 楊文會 (1837–1911) held that *Dasheng qixin lun* summarized and unified Yogācāra and Huayan. This made it possible for Liang to go one step further and insert it into the Yogācāra School. As Lin Chen-kuo demonstrates in his chapter, Lü Cheng 呂澂 (1896–1989) later on rejected such an inflated corpus for the school.

As we can see, Liang's dependence on Kuiji for his understanding of Yogācāra was tremendous. At that point, we should have expected his *Weishi shuyi* to draw from Kuiji's canon. However, the canonical writings selected by Kuiji expose theories and explanations that are difficult to reconcile with one another. This led Liang to affirm that the ultimate reference in Yogācāra should be *Cheng weishi lun*, thereby opting for a text that presents the advantage of a systematic exposition of the fundamental Yogācāra teachings. When Liang refers to *Cheng weishi lun*, however, in fact he means the *Cheng weishi lun shuji* by Kuiji, since he conflated the two works. The confusion was already present in *Yindu zhexue gailun*:

> Kuiji, the Great Disciple [of Xuanzang], the Great Master of the Ci'en Temple, collected and revised ten interpretations of the Yogācāra, and he composed the *Cheng weishi lun* [sic], making a complete and uniform explanation. The merit of establishing the school belongs to Kuiji.[38]

In his *Weishi shuyi*, Liang restated this in similar terms:

> All the texts of Yogācāra and *yingming* studies are from the hands of the Great Master of the Ci'en Temple. Because the *Triṃśikā* (Thirty Verses) came to receive ten interpretations that were divergent, Kuiji revised the text and, mostly following the explanation of Dharmapāla, he composed the *Cheng weishi lun*. He successfully unified Yogācāra. Today, when the specialists talk about Yogācāra, in fact, they talk only about the *Cheng weishi lun*.[39]

37. Liang, *Weishi shuyi*, p. 269.

38. *Yindu zhexue gailun*, p. 56.

39. Liang, *Weishi shuyi*, p. 268.

Liang here follows Chinese Buddhist historiography, considering Kuiji as the first patriarch of the Dharma Characteristics School in China. He seems to ignore Xuanzang completely, probably considering him only a transmitter and translator of texts. How is it possible that Xuanzang was eclipsed by Kuiji in the Republican era? The immediate reason that comes to mind is the novelty of *Cheng weishi lun shuji*, which had ceased being transmitted in China for centuries and had been re-introduced into China from Japan. Also, as with many intellectuals, Liang was sensitive to the systematic nature of the *Cheng weishi lun shuji*. The scientific quality of Yogācāra was not only to be displayed in the content of the teaching, but also in the exposition, which had to be systematic and comprehensive.[40] As a result, Liang's understanding of Yogācāra depended almost exclusively on Kuiji's interpretation. In an interview at the end of his life, Liang recalled, that for several decades in his life he was never without a copy of *Cheng weishi lun shuji*, even while eating or sleeping.[41]

1.4 Yogācāra's position within Buddhism

When Liang was writing his Yogācāra manual, he was also maturing his scheme of the three cultures he later described in *Dongxi wenhua ji qi zhexue* 東西文化及其哲學 (Eastern and Western Cultures and their Philosophies). In this arrangement, Buddhism in general, and Yogācāra in particular, were considered as specific to India. Therefore, Liang came to insist more and more on the foreignness of Buddhism and Yogācāra in relation to China. This shift from Chinese Buddhism to Indian Buddhism was partly due to the academic community's new focus on the roots of Buddhism. But it was also due to Liang's own elitist view of Buddhism being the preserve of a few people in China. This shift did not come easily. As mentioned above, in his first essay Liang had criticized Yogācāra for staying at the level of the dharmas and being unable to grasp the true nature of Buddhahood. In *Yindu zhexue gailun* he started showing more sympathy for Yogācāra, devoting one short chapter to discuss Yogācāra and the debate between "emptiness" (*kong* 空) and "existence" (*you* 有), which duplicated

40. According to Dan Lusthaus, the idea of writing a systematic account of Yogācāra was not the original intent of Xuanzang, but he had to yield to Kuiji's request. Later, Kuiji wrote his own commentary on the *Cheng weishi lun* as a way to reinforce the doctrinal dimension of the teaching. Therefore it is Kuiji's commentary that "gives the *Ch'eng wei-shih lun* its catechismic flavor, not the *Ch'eng wei-shih lun* itself." Dan Lusthaus, *Buddhist Phenomenology: A Philosophical Investigation of* Yogācāra *Buddhism and the Ch'eng Wei-shih Lun*, Curzon Critical Studies in Buddhism Series (London: Routledge, 2002), p. 397.

41. See Ma Tianxiang 麻天祥, *Liang Shuming shuofo* 梁漱溟說佛 (Liang Shuming's Buddhism) (Wuhuan: Hubei renmin chubanshe, 2006), p. 192.

the debate between the Dharma Nature School and the Dharma Characteristics School.[42] There, Liang attempted to strike a balance between the two and put them on an equal footing, rebuking the Yogācāra theory of the third turning of the wheel and its claim to represent the final truth without need for further explication (*nītārtha*).[43] In *Weishi shuyi*, Liang came back to the issue:

> Yogācāra originally raised the matter by distinguishing existence and non-existence, affirming that false imagining (*bianji* 遍計 [*parikalpa*]) is unreal, but other-dependence (*yita* 依他 [*paratantra*]) is real. Indeed, false imagining is as unreal as the horn of a rabbit or the feather of a turtle. But other-dependence is as real as the relation between a cow and a horn, or between a sheep and the wool. And so, real or unreal are ways to speak. The Prajñā School, however, directly understands that the unknowable (*wude* 無得) does not fall into the confrontation of opinions, and so, from the standpoint of emptiness, it sweeps away all confrontations of opinions, because its concept of emptiness is not a confrontation of opinions. Therefore, even though the two schools talk about emptiness and nothingness, they do not mean the same thing.[44]

Here Liang attempted to step away from the controversy between the Dharma Characteristics School and the Dharma Nature School, to evaluate fairly their respective limitations and strengths, according to their own perspectives. Liang did, however, have to face the fact that in the history of Chinese Buddhism, as well as in his own personal intellectual history, it was Yogācāra that had been the victim of the Dharma Nature School, the former being utterly misunderstood and rejected by the latter. In order to correct this imbalance, Liang came to take the opposite stance, claiming not only that Yogācāra was necessary to Mahāyāna Buddhism, but also that it constituted the whole of Buddhism:

> If there was no Yogācāra in Mahāyāna Buddhism and there was only the ineffable of the Prajñā School, then we would need the teaching of Hinayāna. Of course, this would not be acceptable. In reality, the theory

42. *Yindu zhexue gailun*, pp. 123–143.

43. According to Yogācāra, the Buddhist teaching has been historically delivered in three steps, or turnings of the wheel, the first turning corresponding to the teaching of Hinayāna, the second turning to the general teaching of Mahāyāna, and the third to Yogācāra's own specific teaching, considered the ultimate teaching. See John Powers's discussion in chapter 1.

44. Liang, *Weishi shuyi*, p. 269.

> of Mahāyāna Buddhism cannot be established without Yogācāra. There is no way to explain Mahāyāna Buddhism without Yogācāra. If we look for philosophy in Buddhism, it is only to be found in Yogācāra . . . I even dare to say that Yogācāra represents the teaching of the whole Buddhism.[45]

This last statement seems to contradict the passage above in which Liang explained that the Dharma Characteristics School and the Dharma Nature School complement each other. But, I think that two reasons can be advanced to understand Liang's exaltation of Yogācāra. First, he promoted Yogācāra because it seemed to him that this school was the most needed in the China's Chan-dominated Buddhist discourse, a discourse that Liang considered as empty talk, completely disengaged from the real world. As Scott Pacey shows in his chapter, Tan Sitong 譚嗣同 (1865–1898) appreciated Buddhism for its Chineseness. On the contrary, Liang came to value Buddhism for its foreignness, as being similar to and even better than what the West could offer to China. Second, Liang came to regard Yogācāra as representing all of Buddhism, because even though he studied Kuiji's interpretation of Indian Yogācāra, he remained committed to the Chinese interpretation of Yogācāra, which he first learned in Paramārtha's texts. In other words, because Liang found the ontology of the Dharma Nature School inside the Dharma Characteristics School, he could claim that the latter represents the whole of Buddhism, including both the explanation of the dharmas and of buddhahood.

As a general evaluation of Liang's brief endeavor with Yogācāra studies, we should recognize that he faced some limitations. Although he tried to keep informed on the most recent research, he had no access to the Yogācāra literature in Sanskrit or Tibetan, and he did not deal directly with the texts of Asaṅga and Vasubandhu that were available in Chinese translations. Yet, Liang's exegesis developed a very modern approach, adopting the method of historical criticism in order to reassess the history and the teachings of the school and, in this sense, he undertook pioneering work.

2. The philosophical exegesis of Yogācāra

As I have shown above, Liang's exegesis of Yogācāra was influenced by the rise of modern Buddhist scholarship. The historical-critical exegesis of Yogācāra encountered another type of exegesis, that is, a philosophical exegesis of Yogācāra. Liang inserted himself into this new intellectual trend. Rejecting the scholastic tradition that had blocked true understanding, Liang attempted

45. Ibid., p. 269.

to understand Yogācāra from the standpoint of important philosophical questions and through the use of Western concepts. Yet unlike other philosophical interpretations of Yogācāra, we shall see that Liang attempted to preserve the orthodoxy of the teaching and refused to allow the school to be used for a political ideology.

2.1 The seven sages of Shanghai

Ge Zhaoguang 葛兆光 of Fudan University in Shanghai has been involved in the vast project of understanding Chinese intellectual history from the perspective of external influences. He recently published an article dealing with the question of the re-introduction of Yogācāra from Japan in the late-Qing and early Republican era, stating: "The re-introduction of the Yogācāra classics from Japan provided the intellectual world and Buddhism in China with resources for a Buddhist answer to Western science and philosophy."[46] Ge shows that, as the texts were being progressively published, their influence went much beyond Buddhist circles. An important intermediary between the Buddhist milieu and the intellectuals at that time was the lay Buddhist scholar and historian Xia Zengyou 夏曾佑 (1863–1924), who introduced Buddhist literature to the reformist official Sun Baoxuan 孫寶瑄 (1874–1924) who was at the time absorbing the Western idea of evolution (*tianyanlun* 天演論). In 1896, Sun and six others met regularly in Shanghai to read Yogācāra literature. Later on, Sun called their group the "seven sages of Shanghai" (*haishang qi zi* 海上七子): Tan Sitong 譚嗣同, Liang Qichao 梁启超 (1873–1929), Wu Jiarui 吳嘉瑞 (unknown dates), Song Shu 宋恕 (1862–1910), Wang Kangnian 汪康年 (1860–1911), Hu Weizhi 胡惟志 (unknown dates) and Sun Baoxuan himself. Xia Zengyou also introduced Zhang Taiyan to Yogācāra in 1897, having him read the *Yogācārabhūmi-śāstra*.

These intellectuals were attracted to Yogācāra because it opened a space for free thought. Ge Zhaoguang mentions their discovery of the notion of emptiness as conditioned arising (*yuanqi* 緣起), which helped free their minds from tradition and ideology. Since all thoughts were only constructions of the mind, they could criticize them freely. This led to the political idea of revolution. But even the overthrowing of tradition should not lead to another ideology, since there should not be any ideology at all. People should embrace change but without creating a new ideology. A political expression of this was anarchism, or as Ge Zhaoguang says: "Intellectuals amid a thought crisis and within the constraints of the tradition were provided with a spiritual basis for breaking off from tradition and for

46. Ge Zhaoguang, "Zijia baozang de shi er fu de 自家寶藏的失而復得" (The Loss and Recovery of Our Own Treasure), *Shixue jikan* (January 2010): 66.

reconstructing their world view."[47] There was therefore a double and simultaneous movement of deconstructing the old and of building something new, which would not be the repetition of the past.

As we have seen in the previous chapters of this volume, Tan Sitong and Zhang Taiyan initiated a new philosophical tradition in reading Yogācāra texts. They used Yogācāra as a tool to respond to intellectual challenges from the West, and simultaneously as a tool to address the perceived debilitated state of their own tradition. They were, in fact, more familiar with Western ideas than they were with Yogācāra and, when they started to study Yogācāra they were thinking within the parameters of Western philosophy, attempting to find in Yogācāra a substitute for Western thinking. In doing so, they came to undertake an exegesis of Yogācāra heavily influenced by Western philosophy, and as such quite different from the traditional exegesis that had previously existed in Chinese Buddhist literature, as shown above.

When Liang started to read Yogācāra texts he was influenced by this trend to employ philosophical exegesis based on Western ideas that had already existed for fifteen years. Liang was sympathetic to a method free of the doctrinal teachings of Buddhism, and so he attempted to return to true philosophical questions, expressing them in the new language of his time, that is, modern Western philosophy. Liang pointed out the limitations of the traditional method of teaching Yogācāra as being replete with statements presenting themselves as definitive truths. This had developed into a "common and absurd practice of opinions" (*yijian de gongtong miuxi* 意見的共同謬習).[48] For Liang, this kind of dogmatic exegesis, which destroys opinions without creating new ones, was contrary to the essence of Buddhism. Therefore, it was useless to read texts such as Vasubandhu's **Mahāyāna-śatadharmā-prakāśamukha-śāstra* (*Baifa mingmen lun* 百法明門論; Lucid Introduction to the One Hundred Dharmas) and *Triṃśikā* (*Weishi sanshi lun song* 唯識三十論頌; Thirty Verses), or even Xuanzang's *Bashi guijusong* 八識規矩頌 (Verses on the Structure of the Eight Consciousnesses), since these texts were intended to assist with memorizing the tenets of the school. Liang wanted to think critically: Why is there consciousness? Why are there eight consciousnesses? Why can we talk about nothing but consciousness?

Liang attempted to go beyond scholasticism and return to the philosophical issue addressed by the Yogācāra texts: the question of the "double attachment to the self and to the world" (*wofa erzhi* 我法二執). Liang claimed that this was the key issue between primitive Buddhism and other Indian schools (*waidao* 外道) at that time, and still remained the key issue. In this regard, texts such as Dignāga's

47. Ibid., p. 68.

48. Liang, *Weishi shuyi*, p. 281.

Ālambana-parīkṣā and Asaṅga's *Mahāyāna-saṃgraha-śāstra* are not helpful because they do not start from the question of double attachment, instead setting up a complex apparatus without the reader being clear about the issues being addressed. Liang saw here the superiority of the *Cheng weishi lun* (probably meaning here its commentary by Kuiji as shown above), since it directly addresses this key issue, right at its beginning.[49]

2.2 Verifying Yogācāra with Western epistemology

Liang believed that the modern concepts of Western philosophy and the most recent discoveries in Western science and psychology could make explicit the basic ideas of Yogācāra. In *Weishi shuyi*, we thus find some Western ideas that had shaped Liang's understanding of Yogācāra and that he used to confirm it.

Liang described Western thought at length as divided into two branches, a rationalist science (*weili de kexue* 唯理的科學) and an empirical science (*jingyan de kexue* 經驗的科學). Liang first described the rationalist branch as the main current in the West, which started from the deductive rationality of the Greeks and established a priori, universal, and formal truths. This current, represented by Descartes, Spinoza, and Leibniz, developed dogmatic affirmations, especially in the realm of metaphysics, and finally claimed to know it all.[50] In reaction to dogmatism, a second branch, represented by Francis Bacon and David Hume, developed an inductive reason based on experience.

So far, this sounds like a familiar account of the history of Western thought, reproduced from one of the manuals available at that time in China.[51] Liang added his own evaluation, since, in fact, there was much at stake for him in this debate between rationalism and empiricism. At one level, Liang very much welcomed the demise of the old metaphysics and the return to experience because this was compatible with Buddhism. Liang, however, felt that empiricism went only half way, and fell into another extreme, skepticism, which is also a form of dogmatism. Empiricism made limited use of reason—its calculative aspect, or, in the vocabulary of Yogācāra, *biliang* 比量 (*anumāna*)—and therefore did not

49. Ibid., p. 282.

50. Ibid., pp. 271–272.

51. Liang drew his description from Chen Daqi 陳大齊 (1886–1983), also called Chen Bainian 陳百年, who studied philosophy and psychology for ten years in Japan. After his return to China in 1912, he taught psychology at Peking University from 1914. Interestingly his book published by Peking University Press in 1918 was entitled *Zhexue gailun* 哲學概論 (Outline of Philosophy), but Liang had it incorrectly as *Xiyang zhexue gailun* 西洋哲學概論 (Outline of Western Philosophy), probably because all the philosophy in that book was Western.

succeed in building a sound metaphysics. This was Liang's main point of contention with Western empiricism and the Chinese rationalists of the New Culture Movement. He opposed the rationalism of his time for confining reason within narrow boundaries.[52] Already in "Jiuyuan jueyi lun" Liang regarded the Dharma Characteristics School to be similar to Kant's philosophy in that both distinguish between the knowable (*kezhi* 可知) and the unknowable (*bukezhi* 不可知). Liang probably took this comparison from Liang Qichao or Zhang Taiyan. What mattered for Liang was the affirmation of the limits of human knowledge and rationality. But unlike Kant, Liang held the possibility of an access to ontological reality through direct cognition, called *xianliang* 現量 (*pratyakṣa*) by Yogācāra. Liang believed that human beings could still have some access to the mystery of life, of the cosmos, and of humanity. And so, he spent many years of his life attempting to build a metaphysics that would be nondogmatic.

Unsatisfied with empiricism and Kantian epistemology, Liang turned to Bergson. Like the empiricists and Kant, Bergson started from human experience, but unlike them, he did not deny the possibility of reaching metaphysical realities. For Liang, Bergson could do this because he did not limit human reason to its deductive or inductive dimensions drawn from experience, but he was able to accommodate extrarational perception, or intuition (*zhijue* 直覺). Liang stated:

> The whole universe is an absolute. As we have said, sensation is made of something perceived and of someone perceiving. Of course, it is impossible to sense the whole universe. When Bergson discusses his concept of perception, he is clearly saying that the subject as perceiver has to get inside the object that is perceived, instead of remaining outside.[53]

There is thus the possibility of an inner knowledge, transcending the barrier between subject and the world. Liang therefore upheld the important Bergsonian idea of "integral experience" (*quanzheng de jingyan* 全整的經驗) and saw it as similar to *xianliang* (direct cognition) in Yogācāra.[54]

Yet, Liang regarded Bergson's method as unable to establish true metaphysics because it was not purely based on direct cognition. First, Bergson introduced some irrational elements, such as an anti-intellectual reason. Second, from the standpoint of Buddhist atomism and of Bertrand Russell's "logical atomism,"

52. See *Yindu zhexue gailun*, p. 166.

53. Liang, *Weishi shuyi*, p. 276.

54. Liang came to know the ideas of Bergson because of a series of articles in the Chinese magazines at that time.

Liang criticized Bergson for believing that life and duration constituted an entity. Liang therefore rejected the idea of identifying Bergson's intuition with Yogācāra's direct cognition as a wild guess.[55] He concluded that the West had failed to harmonize experience with metaphysics, the concrete experience of our world with its hidden and metaphysical reality. Nevertheless, Liang's Bergsonian moment was crucial for the development of his own thought, since it helped Liang to understand how a sound epistemology could lead to metaphysics.

Besides Bergson's concept of intuition, Liang was deeply influenced by the shift to consciousness in modern science and in philosophy at that time, departing from a crude materialism. In this regard, Liang mentioned the name of Karl Pearson (1857–1936), the British philosopher of science, even though he admitted not having read his works.[56] Liang mentioned that Pearson saw the world not as an entity (*shiti* 實體), but as the sum of (*zongji* 總計) sensations.[57]

Also, in *Yindu zhexue gailun*, Liang seems to have been the first in China to draw a parallel between the British empiricist George Berkeley (1685–1753) and Yogācāra.[58] In *Weishi shuyi*, Liang went further, stating that the epistemological question addressed by Yogācāra was solved by Berkeley. Berkeley had criticized the distinction established by John Locke between primary qualities of the object, those intrinsic to it, and the secondary qualities of the object, those added by the subject. Against Locke, Liang sided with Berkeley and Yogācāra, considering that all objects are but mental conceptions.[59]

As another support for the theory of consciousness in Yogācāra, Liang quoted Russell: "The apparent oneness of the world is merely the oneness of what is seen by a single spectator or apprehended by a single mind."[60] As with Russell, Liang welcomed the end of the illusion of the world's oneness. This idea of multiple universes in Russell was also an important point of contact with Yogācāra.

---

55. Liang recognized that the logical formalism of Russell was free from irrationality, but still unable to establish a true metaphysics. *Weishi shuyi*, p. 279.

56. Later, in *Dongxi wenhua ji qi zhexue*, Liang also mentioned the names of two other philosophers of science, the Austrian Ernst Mach (1838–1916) and the French Henri Poincaré (1854–1912).

57. Liang, *Weishi shuyi*, p. 278.

58. In his *Yindu zhexue gailun*, Liang said that he "also attempted" a comparison between the two, but he did not dare to elaborate further (p. 100).

59. Liang quoted Berkeley from Chen Daqi's *Zhexue gailun*. See note 51 on Chen Daqi.

60. Bertrand Russell's "On Scientific Method in Philosophy" was delivered as the Herbert Spencer Lecture at Oxford in 1914, and published the same year by Clarendon Press, London. Liang Shuming read this article in the collection of essays entitled *Mysticism and Logic and Other Essays* (London: Longman, 1918).

2.3 Zhang Taiyan and his abuse of philosophical exegesis

As we have seen, Liang analyzed and explained Yogācāra using Western concepts prominent on the intellectual scene at that time. He did, however, also see the limits of this kind of philosophical exegesis and expressed his concern to preserve the original Yogācāra teachings, rejecting attempts at introducing heterodox teachings. This can be clearly seen in Liang's criticisms of Zhang Taiyan.

Early on, in his first essay, Liang had borrowed the Western notion of evolution from Zhang's "Jufen jinhua lun 俱分進化論" (Theory of *Evolution* in Two Ways).[61] Liang also inherited from Zhang the idea that Yogācāra epistemology could compete with Western epistemology and could be discussed using Western concepts. He also read Zhang's "Jianli zongjiao lun 建立宗教論" (On Founding a Religion), which encouraged Liang to hold the category of religion as something important and even positive.[62]

Yet, in the preface to *Weishi shuyi*, Liang criticized Zhang Taiyan's *Qi wu lun shi* 齊物論釋 (Interpretation of the "Discourse on Making All Things Equal"; 1910) for making Yogācāra a tool for interpreting Chinese philosophy.[63] In the chapter of this volume dedicated to Zhang Taiyan, Viren Murthy shows that Zhang had his own political project in mind while reading Yogācāra texts. Liang considered Zhang's exegesis simply wrong. He discussed the matter with Zhang's associate, Huang Jigang 黃季剛 (1886–1935), who told Liang that he also had some reservations about Zhang's method.

Liang also criticized Zhang's understanding of the notion of self-authentication. In *Zhuo Han weiyan* 菿漢微言 (Subtle Words of Zhang Taiyan; post-face 1917), Zhang had defended Kantian epistemology as a valid formalism, holding that "the determination of validity between correct and wrong concepts needs the intermediary of another concept in order to realize a direct self-authentication."[64]

61. Liang, "Jiuyuan jueyi lun," p. 16. Zhang Taiyan adopted the historical frame of evolution, but he modified it in a significant way, with the idea of a double increase of joy and pain.

62. See "Ru-Fo yitong lun 儒佛異同論" (The Differences and Similarities between Confucianism and Buddhism; 1966), in *Liang Shuming quanji*, vol. 7, p. 159.

63. Liang, *Weishi shuyi*, p. 253. Liang's also criticized Ma Yichu's 馬夷初 (1885–1970) *Zhuangzi zhaji* 莊子劄記 (Reading Notes on *Zhuangzi*; 1919) for the same reason.

64. Quoted by Liang in *Weishi shuyi*, p. 289. "Zhuo Han" is one of Zhang's styles and literally means "making the Han great." 菿 is a loan graph for *zhuo* 倬. The content of *Zhuo Han wei yan* (postface 1917) was dictated in 1915–1916 by Zhang Taiyan to Wu Chengshi 吳承仕 (1884–1939) and first published by Zhejiang Library. Most probably, Liang Shuming received the book directly from Wu Chengshi, his colleague at Peking University.

Zhang had also stated that the Kantian theory for determining the validity of all human knowledge is the same as Yogācāra's "self-authenticating aspect."[65] For Liang, the need of an intermediary invalidates the notion of self-authentication, because *xianliang* (direct cognition) is without a reflexive judgment about something being correct or wrong. In other words, through *xianliang*, one may be wrong, and not even know it. To support his view, Liang referred to Dignāga's *Nyāyamukha*, according to which the self-authenticating of craving and other defilements (*tandeng* 貪等) is also *xianliang*. Therefore, in *xianliang*, there is no judgment of right and wrong; there is no Kantian determination of the validity of knowledge.[66]

As we can see, for Liang, Yogācāra introduces a wisdom that goes beyond the epistemological categories of right and wrong, beyond the moral categories of good and evil. In the authenticating process, there is no self-reflexivity of the subject, but rather the dissolution of any dichotomy between subject and object, between good and evil. In other words, the notion of self-authentication in Yogācāra cannot be used in the realms of psychology or morality. When Zhang Taiyan attempted his dialectical negation of the concepts of good and bad, Liang saw that Zhang ended up only in strengthening these categories.[67]

In short, Liang Shuming's and Zhang Taiyan's methods were opposed in many ways. Whereas Zhang used Yogācāra as an intellectual resource for developing his own philosophy, Liang was more respectful of the texts, history, and project of Yogācāra. When later Liang elaborated his own version of Yogācāra, he was careful to differentiate it from his academic research on historical Yogācāra. In the end, Liang dismissed Zhang as an outsider (*waihang* 外行) to Buddhism, with a very superficial understanding of it.[68]

In the early years of the Republican era, there was indeed a spirit of innovation. Having just started to know about Western thought and having hardly digested it, Chinese intellectuals endeavored to adopt another tradition, which was even more foreign but looked similar, and they attempted to "explain" one by the

65. For Zhang, the first level of authentication is still based on what one perceives and "it immediately provides the knowledge of not being mistaken (猝然念得而當時即知其不誤)." At the second stage, the authentication of the self-authenticating aspect is purely internal, not depending on perceptions.

66. Liang also contested Zhang's association of the self-authenticating aspect with subliminal consciousness (*yuxia yishi* 閾下意識). See Liang, *Weishi shuyi*, p. 289.

67. Liang Shuming further criticized the comparative method of Zhang, who identified self-authentication with Wang Yangming's intuitive knowledge (*liangzhi* 良知), and the authentication of self-authentication with the perfection of intuitive knowledge (*zhiliangzhi* 致良知). See Liang, *Weishi shuyi*, p. 289.

68. See Liang, "Wo de zixue xiaoshi," p. 695.

other. Clearly, many lacked a real understanding of either Western philosophy or Yogācāra. Liang, however, was at the crossroad of Buddhist and philosophical exegeses. In 1920, after nine years of immersion in Buddhism, including four years in Yogācāra texts, he had already attained a respectable understanding of that school. He also studied philosophy intensively and had a truly philosophical mind. Because of his dual skills in Buddhism and philosophy Liang was able to set up a sound method to analyze Yogācāra philosophically, using many ideas and concepts drawn from modern philosophy. In this sense, Liang's explanation of Yogācāra is both well documented and refreshing when compared to traditional Buddhist commentaries.

3. Liang's manual of Yogācāra: Weishi shuyi

I have described above how Liang inserted himself into this double genealogy of Buddhist and philosophical exegeses. In neither case did he passively receive influences from others, but rather developed his own stance. Let us look briefly at his own exposition of the core teaching of Yogācāra. For Liang, the basic problem faced by people is epistemological. They entertain two levels of misperception about reality. At the first level, the crudest, people wrongly believe that perceptions of an object provide true knowledge of it. At a second and deeper level, people believe that the individual operation of a sense gives conceptual knowledge of an external characteristic.[69]

3.1 The epistemological problem of the self

Following the lead of Xuanzang, Liang started to show how Yogācāra cuts attachment to the self and rejected those interpretations that reinforce attachment to the self. Yogācāra epistemology thoroughly deconstructs cognition at its different levels. As Liang said: "The bottle, the whiteness, the sense of white, all three levels can be gradually discarded and made bare."[70] Since Yogācāra theory mostly provides a descriptive analysis of how mind constructs cognition, it may give the impression of affirming the reality of the cognitive process. Yogācāra does not, however, aim at describing the workings of cognition; rather, it deconstructs them, showing that they rest on illusions:

---

69. Liang quoted and explained some verses drawn from Dignāga's *Nyāyamukha*, deconstructing perception into a composite of sensorial elements and deconstructing conceptual knowledge as being the composite of mental operations. *Weishi shuyi*, pp. 283–286.

70. Liang, *Weishi shuyi*, p. 286.

> One cannot say that there is a bottle, or whiteness. Neither one can say the meaning of whiteness. In the end, the only thing that cannot be discarded is sensation. What does this sensation tell? The sensation itself does not authenticate if it exists or not. What are called self-authentication and the authentication of self-authentication are direct cognitions (*xianliang*) without cognitive judgment.[71]

Liang then explained the difference between the three aspects of cognition according to Dignāga: objective aspect (*xiangfen* 相分), subjective aspect (*jianfen* 見分) and self-authenticating aspect (*zizhengfen* 自證分). He stressed that the three aspects designate only three functions (*yong* 用), without constituting three different entities. Liang then introduced the fourth aspect of cognition, which authenticates "self-authentication" (*zhengzizhengfen* 證自證分). Liang's point of emphasis is that the third and fourth aspects do not include any self-awareness or moral judgment, because any self-awareness would presuppose the existence of a subject, and there is no subject at the level of the third and fourth aspects.

Liang added a strong warning to the reader, differentiating what Yogācāra calls nothing but consciousness from the everyday experience of what we call consciousness, or awareness:

> I see a bottle and I think it is a bottle; I see the white and I think it is white. But I am determined that there should be in my mind sensations without thinking; I see the bottle and I do not know it is a bottle; I see the white and I do not know it is white.[72]

In other words, in the third and fourth aspects of cognition, there is a suspension of judgment. Liang criticized Zhang Taiyan for introducing a moral judgment at the level of the third aspect of cognition, as Kant would have also granted. As we can deduce, Liang considered that, through self-awareness and judgment, people were showing their inability to cut attachment to the self. For Liang, Yogācāra introduces one into the wisdom of being in the world, without any self-awareness of being there and without any moral judgment about it.

3.2 The epistemological problem of the world

In *Weishi shuyi*, Liang shows first how Yogācāra can cut attachment to the self through suspension of thinking and moral judgment. He then shows how

71. Ibid., p. 286.

72. Ibid., p. 288.

Yogācāra can cut the attachment to the world. Liang explains how Yogācāra was established as a refutation of a crude epistemology based on the theory of atoms, which would place the truth of perception in external objects. He cites long passages from Kuiji's *Cheng weishi lun shuji* that reject the materialism (*youselun* 有色論) of Indian schools like the Sarvāstivāda and Sautrāntika.

According to Liang, for consciousness (or cognition) to occur, two conditions are necessary: first, there must be a cognitive object; second, cognition must obtain something that is apprehended as a cognitive object (seen by the eyes or touched by the hands and so forth).[73] The mistake of some Indian schools and of Hinayāna was to consider external form as the "condition for the causal support of consciousness," or *suoyuan yuan* 所緣緣 (*ālambana-pratyaya*). On the contrary, Liang maintained that only consciousness itself can serve as a "condition for the causal support of consciousness," since ultimately only consciousness can sense itself.[74]

In support of the Yogācāra theory that the objective aspect is something that appears in consciousness, Liang mentioned some physical explanations:

> We always say that white is the white of the bottle, but, in fact, the bottle in itself has no color. What is called white is only a reflection of our optic nerves when there is an excitation provoked by vibrations. In fact, the bottle has no characteristics, but it acquires them through our sensation.[75]

Liang cited another example: ginger is not spicy as such, but it is perceived such by our gustatory sense. Therefore, the white of a bottle and the spice of the ginger are only transformations that occur in our consciousness. We are mistaken because we imagine that there is a distance and a separation between ourselves and the object. In *xianliang*, however, there is no distinction between near and far, between the self and the object.

For Yogācāra, sensation is completely encapsulated in an individual consciousness. This theory raises many objections, and Liang deals with one: how

---

73. Ibid., p. 297.

74. Liang listed three incorrect theories: consciousness working on the basis of individual atoms; on the basis of an aggregation or clustering of atoms; or on the basis of an association of atoms in close proximity. Liang relates that the rejection of the notion of external objects was a feature of Dignāga's *Ālambana-parīkṣā*, but Liang himself quoted the three-fold refutation he attributes to *Cheng weishi lun* (although it is actually probably based on Kuiji's *Weishi ershi lun shuji* 唯識二十論述記 [Notes on Twenty Verses]). Most probably, Liang knew about Ouyang Jingwu's article, mentioned above, *Explanation of the Ālambana-parīkṣā*, but he did not mention it.

75. Liang, *Weishi shuyi*, p. 302.

to account for the fact of shared, or common, sensations. Liang stated here the Yogācāra theory of a multiplicity of mental universes, one for each person, something similar to Russell's idea of multiple universes, as mentioned above. Although the mental universes are independent from each other, they appear similar, giving rise to the wrong belief that there is an object common to all, as the cause of our sensation. Liang quoted here the classical metaphor of the many lamps illuminating a room and giving the wrong impression that the light is coming from only one source.

At the end of the third chapter, Liang explains the Yogācāra theory from the standpoint of the concept of mind. Here it is made clear that Liang applies Chinese Buddhism in his understanding of Indian Yogācāra, making explicit reference to notion of the mind itself (*xinti* 心體), a central concept in *Dasheng qixin lun*.[76] According to Liang, our ordinary mind is partial because it relies only on partial cognition, based only on the subjective and objective aspects of cognition. This leads to a dualism between the mind and the world. On the contrary, the mind in Yogācāra is complete because it relies on *xianliang*, including the four aspects of cognition. The four aspects represent four different functions of the "mind itself."[77] Liang reasons within the traditional categories of Chinese thought (but influenced strongly by their usage in Sinitic Buddhist thought): ontological reality (*ti* 體 [**svabhāva*; **tattva*]) and function (*yong* 用). He postulates that mind itself really exists, even though it is beyond the grasp of the senses: "The mistake is to see the bottle as real (有體); in fact, that which is real is the reality of the unseen mind."[78] Clearly, Liang here follows the idealist interpretation of Yogācāra, an interpretation quite standard in Chinese Buddhism, but we shall discuss this in more detail below.

3.3 Different levels of consciousnesses and mental factors

When Xuanzang or Kuiji discussed the eight consciousnesses, they started with the eighth or base consciousness. For Liang, however, in our modern age we cannot postulate the base consciousness and then deduce the other seven consciousnesses because this would amount to dogmatism.[79] Liang therefore decided to start with the five consciousnesses. At this level, there is no thought,

76. While it is a key term in *Dasheng qixin lun*, there are only two occurrences of it in the whole text of *Cheng weishi lun*.

77. Liang, *Weishi shuyi*, p. 307.

78. Ibid., pp. 307–308.

79. Ibid., p. 308.

only pure sensation. In the case of the visual consciousness, there is only consciousness of whiteness.

Liang then describes five particularities of the five consciousnesses.[80] First, all rely on the physical aspects of the five sense organs (*segen* 色根). Second, the five consciousnesses only take real "forms" (material entities) as their cognitive objects (*shisejing* 實色境). The third characteristic is that the five consciousnesses are momentary. The fourth characteristic is to allow *xianliang* (direct cognition), without discrimination, without judgment, without understanding, without awareness. Therefore, this kind of sensation cannot be wrong, in the sense that you cannot evaluate it with any external criteria of right or wrong. He states that it is not the senses that are mistaken, but rather our mental perception (*zhijue* 知覺). Finally, the fifth characteristic of the five consciousnesses is to be intermittent. In relation to the five consciousnesses, Liang finally mentions the theory of the nine levels of existence (*jiudi* 九地), as expressed originally in Vasubandhu's *Abhidharma-kośa* (*Apidamo jushe lun* 阿毘達磨俱舍論; Storehouse of Higher Doctrine), and according to which, at the last three levels, the five consciousnesses are deactivated.

In the last part, Liang discusses the fifty-one mental factors (*xinsuo* 心所), quoting Kuiji extensively. Liang also compares Yogācāra with Western psychology. First, he maintains that Western psychology with its three mental activities—reasoning, emotion, and will—lacks in subtlety when compared to the fifty-one mental factors of Yogācāra. Second, for Yogācāra, will and emotion do not constitute independent categories because any cognition includes both emotion and will. Whereas modern psychology tends to objectify the mind, Liang understands the mind to be nothing but a transformation of the different consciousnesses, involving at the same time reasoning, emotion, and will.

Therefore, in the four chapters of his manual on Yogācāra, Liang devoted the first two chapters to deal with questions of methods, and in chapters three and four he explained the doctrines of Yogācāra. The book abruptly stops with chapter four, after the description of the first five consciousnesses and the mental factors. Logically, the next sections would have been the sixth, the seventh, and finally the eighth consciousnesses, in the reverse order to how they are presented in *Cheng weishi lun*. Liang did not finish his book because he interrupted his

80. Liang felt also the need to defend the traditional belief, both in Buddhism and in the West, that there are only five senses, against the theory of modern psychology, which had added three more senses: temperature, strength, and wholeness. Liang read about this theory in Chen Daqi's *Xinlixue dagang* 心理學大綱 (An Outline of Psychology). The theory seems to come from the German professor and founder of psychology Wilhelm Wundt (1832–1920). Liang dismissed this modern theory as ridiculous, because sensations can only be caused by the five consciousnesses, without any further justification.

class for health problems; when he returned to teaching a few months after, he had then shifted his attention to the comparison of the three cultures. Also in 1920, Mei Guangxi 梅光羲 (1880–1947), a disciple of Yang Wenhui, published *Xiangzong gangyao* 相宗綱要 (The Essential Points of the Dharma Characteristics School). This work is more like a dictionary, consisting of 150 entries, and did not bring the philosophical method that Liang had aspired to. Liang probably considered that this own scholarly work was enough for the public and there was no need for him to continue writing on Yogācāra.

As I have argued, Liang's reading of Yogācāra was at the crossroads between two exegeses, one philosophical and one historico-philological. Philosophers like Xiong Shili 熊十力 (1885–1968) or Mou Zongsan 牟宗三 (1909–1995) did not continue this blending of the two methods because Yogācāra would become for them an intellectual tool for reviving Confucianism, quite disconnected from the original intent of Buddhism.[81] Liang's most lasting influence was probably in those Buddhist circles that absorbed his new method of philosophical enquiry. For example, Liang's influence over Taixu is manifest. Taixu read the *Weishi shuyi* and praised Liang's efforts to explain Yogācāra in the language of Western philosophy. Therefore, it is not surprising that, in his *Faxiang weishixue gailun* 法相唯識學概論 (Outline of the Dharma Characteristics School and Nothing but Consciousness School, 1932), Taixu followed a similar philosophical explanation of Yogācāra texts and theory to the one first proposed by Liang.[82]

4. Liang's creative Yogācāra

Liang was worried about Yogācāra's success because misunderstandings were strengthening the illusory notion of a psychological, epistemological, or moral self, creating more attachments to the world and to the self, instead of cutting them off. Liang had written his manual on Yogācāra precisely to prevent those misunderstandings. Nevertheless, in 1921, he came to the realization that Buddhist enlightenment was out of reach for most people and that the time was not ripe for propagating Buddhism. In the present age, it was better to show people

81. For the view that Xiong used his critique of Yogācāra thought to develop dialectically a unique Confucio-Buddhist syncretism, see John Makeham's chapter in this volume.

82. Later, in 1921, Taixu read *Dongxi wenhua ji qi zhexue*, and the same year, criticized Liang's elitist conception of Buddhism and his claim that Buddhism was not adapted to the modern times. See Taixu, "Lun Liang Shuming *Dongxi wenhua ji qi zhexue* 論梁漱溟東西文化及其哲學" (On Liang Shuming's *Eastern and Western Cultures and Their Philosophies*) in *Haichaoyin* 1/11 (1921). Reproduced in *Taixu dashi quanshu* 太虛大師全書 (Complete Works of the Great Master Taixu) (Taipei: Shandaosi, 1946), vol. 25, pp. 302–304.

how to live ethically in the world, and so Liang started advocating Confucianism instead. The shift from Buddhism to Confucianism may not appear as radical if we pay attention to the fact that Liang inserted Confucianism within the general frame of Buddhism. But in order to do so, he had to make some important modifications in Yogācāra theory. In this final section we shall examine how Liang created his own version of Yogācāra in *Dongxi wenhua ji qi zhexue*. First, at the epistemological level, in addition to the two orthodox modes of knowledge, *biliang* and *xianliang*, Liang introduced a third mode of knowledge, moral intuition (*zhijue*). From this revised epistemology, Liang could link the three modes of knowledge to three moral options presented to individuals and to cultures. The three cultures of the West, China, and India, respectively, represented three moral options: the development of the self and of the nation (in the West and based on *biliang*); the deepening of harmonious relations with others (in Confucianism and based on *zhijue*); and the radical quest for transcendence (in Buddhism and based on *xianliang*).

4.1 Liang's transformation of Yogācāra epistemology (*please refer to the chart at the end*)

Both in *Yindu zhexue gailun* and *Weishi shuyi*, Liang faithfully expounded the standard doctrine of Dignāga, that is, Yogācāra epistemology holds only two modes of cognition: *biliang* (inferential cognition) and *xianliang* (direct cognition). In his *Dongxi wenhua ji qi zhexue*, however, Liang claimed he was not satisfied with Yogācāra epistemology on two grounds. First, he considered that since *xianliang* is encapsulated only in unique and discrete moments of consciousness, it has no duration and therefore cannot be used by *biliang* for constructing concepts through comparison over a period of time: "If the first experience of darkness has obtained nothing, the other successive experiences obtain also nothing. How can *biliang* play its analytic and synthetic function in the process?"[83]

Secondly, Liang understood *xianliang* to function in a passive mode; nothing is added to reality by a mind that is purely reduced to a mechanical process. Therefore, Liang saw the need to have another mode of cognition, intuition (*zhijue* 直覺), to which are attached two mental factors:

> Between *xianliang* and *biliang* we should introduce the two mental factors (*xinsuo* 心所) of feeling (*shou* 受; *vedanā*) and discerning (*xiang* 想; *samjñā*), attached to perception and ruling over consciousness. The two

83. Liang, *Dongxi wenhua ji qi zhexue, Liang Shuming quanji*, vol. 1, p. 399.

> mental factors of feeling and discerning are able to obtain a "meaning" (*yiwei*), which is not entirely clear and is difficult to articulate. For example, the two functions obtain the meaning of black at the first occurrence. When the meaning of black is accumulated afterward and through many occurrences, it is linked together through the synthetic function of *biliang*. At the same time, the meaning of black is clearly distinguished from the other meanings of white, yellow, red, green, etc. Therefore, *biliang* exercises analytic and synthetic functions. Only then does the abstract meaning appear. In relation to meaning, the two mental factors of feeling and discerning are *xianliang*. Therefore, between the sensation in *xianliang* and the abstract concept in *biliang*, there must be the stage of "intuition" (*zhijue*). It is not enough to rely on *xianliang* and *biliang*. This statement is my own modification of Yogācāra.[84]

In the Yogācāra theory, the two mental factors of feeling and discerning belong to a group of five "omnipresent" mental factors because they are always active in the mind, like the eight consciousnesses.[85] Liang assigns two mental factors to intuition, or *zhijue*: "feeling" entails an intuition at the sensitive level, and "discerning" entails an intuition at the intellectual level. Because intuition is an active mode of knowledge that involves a judgment made by a subject, a meaning is recorded by that subject. Experience is not encapsulated in discrete moments like in *xianliang*, but forms a meaningful continuum. For Liang, the knowledge apprehended by intuition is an impression, a tendency, an orientation, which in orthodox Yogācāra are regarded as psychological functions that do not qualify as legitimate knowledge. Liang illustrates this by taking the example of something typically Chinese, calligraphy:

> When we contemplate the calligraphy and paintings of some famous artists, we do not rely only on sensation in order to know the several strokes of black and colors—we also rely on intuition to get the meaning of beauty and grandeur of these artworks. This meaning is something alive, different from passive sensation, and also different from fixed concepts.[86]

---

84. Ibid., p. 399.

85. These two mental factors should not be confused with the two aggregates, which are part of the five aggregates (*wuyun* 五蘊): form, feeling, perception, mental constituents, and consciousness. The other three mental factors in this group of five are attention, contact, and volition. See Mizuno, *Essentials of Buddhism*, pp. 100–101.

86. Liang, *Dongxi wenhua ji qi zhexue*, p. 400.

Liang continues, making the content of intuition more explicit:

> What intuition apprehends is called the "object conveying the basic stuff" (*daizhi jing* 帶質境),[87] in which there are both reflection and basic stuff, but the reflection does not resemble the basic stuff.[88] For example, when I hear a sound, I can immediately know its sublimeness thanks to intuition. At this moment, the basic stuff is the sound that the ear is unable to apprehend, and the reflection is the sound's sublimeness. In this case, however, the relation between reflection and basic stuff is different from both *xianliang* and *biliang*. What *xianliang* apprehends is the object as it is in itself (*xingjing* 性境), in which the reflected image and the subjective aspect are not generated from the same seed and this is why reflections necessarily resemble their basic stuff, and are not purely subjective, but rather are still objective. What *biliang* cognizes is the "reflection-only object" (*duying jing* 獨影境) in which the reflection and the subjective aspect are generated from the same seed, but without being accompanied by a basic stuff, and so *biliang* is purely subjective.
>
> Regarding the "object conveying the basic stuff" apprehended by intuition, its reflection is half objective and half subjective. Since there is a sound as its basic stuff, it can be said to be objective, yet the beautiful meaning of it is not in fact in the object itself, but it is a subjective addition. Therefore the reflection cannot be said to be completely objective; cannot be said to be the "object as it is in itself." It can be said only to "convey the basic stuff." (Yogācāra does not recognize the objective, and this statement is only for convenience and as a temporary measure.)
>
> For example, we hear and appreciate the sublimeness of a sound; we see a painting and appreciate its great beauty; we eat something sweet and find it delicious. In fact, there is nothing sublime in the sound as such, nothing beautiful in the painting as such, nothing delicious in the sweet as such. Sublimeness, beauty, sweetness, and other meanings are mistakenly added by human intuition. This is why intuition is called a misconstrued perception. . . . However, the reason I do not use the term

87. Liang provides a novel interpretation of this concept.

88. Charles Muller relates that *benzhi* 本質 is "The raw sensate aspect of something that impinges on our consciousness (Skt. *bimba*; Tib. *gzugs nyid*); the original form of something as contrasted to its reflection, projection 影像 (*pratibimba*), or perceived manifestation. A substance as it is before it undergoes the transformations of consciousness. Thus, the raw substance of things that can't ever be directly received, but can only be 'represented.' " *Digital Dictionary of Buddhism*, s.v. "*benzhi* 本質," by C. Muller, www.buddhism-dict.net (accessed September 3, 2012).

> misconstrued perception, and instead use the term "intuition," is because Yogācāra understands misconstrued perception as belonging to the category which includes pseudo-*xianliang* and pseudo-*biliang*, and therefore the term is completely negative, with bad connotations. In order to express an extraordinary mental activity that is distinct from *xianliang* and from *biliang*, I myself prefer using the term "intuition."[89]

Liang was very much aware that he was changing Yogācāra teachings, and indeed, was harshly criticized by Buddhists for departing from "orthodoxy."[90] As I see it, Liang's theoretical reason is quite weak. He argues that *xianliang* and *biliang* in the standard theory cannot explain the continuum of experience. Yet, in Yogācāra theory it is precisely the eighth consciousness, the base consciousness registering the seeds of the perception occurring in the other seven consciousnesses, which explains the stream of consciousness and its continuum. Also, Liang wrongly understood *xianliang* as being passive, whereas orthodox Yogācāra stresses the dynamic interaction between the object and the mind. Liang's understanding of *xianliang* as a passive mode of cognition comes most probably from the Chan tradition. His misunderstanding about a supposed passivity of *xianliang* leads him to posit *zhijue*, or intuition, as an active and creative mode of cognition. But if *xianliang* is correctly understood in the first place, it is not necessary to posit *zhijue* as an independent mode of cognition.

Yet, the crux of Liang's intent in introducing intuition as a third mode of cognition lies elsewhere. Yogācāra epistemology explains the functioning of the mind, yet ultimately sees the mind as an obstacle to overcome: by deconstructing the mental operations we may succeed in neutralizing them, not letting them operate, and be liberated from them. Although Liang continued to uphold this overall project of liberation, he wanted to accommodate, within the mental operations, some room for judgments that could bear positive meanings. This was precisely what Liang had reproached Zhang Taiyan for, when Zhang understood the self-authenticating aspect as carrying a moral judgment about good and evil. A couple of years after his harsh condemnation of Zhang Taiyan, it seems that Liang identified the same nexus of difficulties in the Yogācāra theory, that is, the connection between mental states and engagement in the world.

---

89. Ibid., p. 400.

90. In 1929, Taixu wrote that "identifying the two mental factors of feeling and discerning was a complete mistake." Taixu, "Renshengguan de kexue 人生觀的科學" (The Science of the Philosophy of Life), in *Taixu dashi quanshu* 太虛大師全書 (The Complete Works of the Great Master Taixu) (Taipei: Taixu dashi quanshu chuban weiyuanhui, 1959), vol. 46, p. 57.

In more general terms, this touches on the traditional tension in China between Buddhism and Confucianism, with Buddhism regularly suspected of not giving value to the present life, of depreciating human life as an illusion. Although Liang remained fundamentally a Buddhist, he believed that the traditional Buddhist teaching did not make enough room for a positive appreciation of human life, and he therefore attempted to establish a Confucian morality that could hold value for the present and prepare the Buddhist liberation for tomorrow.

4.2 Yogācāra being centered on ethics

For Yogācāra, epistemological problems are both the obstacles to and the solutions for enlightenment. For Liang, however, ethical problems come to the forefront, and so he understood the three modes of cognition (discussed above) as three moral options, founded on different value judgments. In traditional Buddhist teachings, ethics plays an important role, but it is essentially a negative morality, avoiding attachment to the self and to others in order to reduce suffering. It is a freedom from something. For Liang, however, even if the aim of life is finally to experience ultimate liberation, it would be wrong to live as if we were only to get rid of our mistaken cognitions, as if we were to avoid only the attachments created by our cognitions. Life itself should be invested with a positive meaning. There should be in this life a legitimate "attachment" to some moral values, to some good people, or to life itself.

Liang saw intuition as belonging to the realm of true morality, giving meaning (*yiwei* 意味) to the world. Starting from around 1937 onward, Liang continued to develop this concept of intuition as a special mode of cognition that he decided to call *lixing* 理性, a term best translated as "moral reason."[91] This change of terminology, from intuition to moral reason, manifests Liang's shift from epistemological problems to ethical issues, applying Buddhist epistemology to Confucian ethics. Distinct from intuition, *biliang* is antimoral, being the cognitive mode of the calculating self, and therefore stained with selfishness, and *xianliang* is amoral, beyond the moral standards of good and wrong.

Liang applied the three modes of cognition to three cultures, *biliang* to the West, intuition to China (Confucianism), and *xianliang* to India (Buddhism). According to Yogācāra, wrong cognitions generate four types of attachment:

91. An Yanming, "Liang Shuming and Henri Bergson on Intuition: Cultural Context and the Evolution of Terms," *Philosophy East and West* 47 (1997): 337–362; see also John Hanafin, "The Last Buddhist," in *New Confucianism: A Critical Examination*, ed. John Makeham (New York: Palgrave, 2003), p. 202.

attachment to the self due to discrimination (*fenbie wozhi* 分別我執); attachment to the world due to discrimination (*fenbie fazhi* 分別法執); innate attachment to the self (*jusheng wozhi* 俱生我執); and innate attachment to the world (*jusheng fazhi* 俱生法執). Liang reorganized the way to deal with these attachments. According to him, while a culture based on *biliang* creates the four types of attachment, a culture based on intuition, like Confucianism, can dissolve the first three attachments, but only a culture based on *xianliang*, like Buddhism, can dissolve the fourth attachment, that is, the mistaken belief in the existence of an external world.

In other words, Confucian intuition could overcome the cognitive hindrances created by the discriminating mind, realizing the first step of perceiving reality without the constraints of the self. What is perceived is not the reality of this or that object, of something perceived by someone; rather it is a whole encompassing all that exists. Moral and aesthetic meanings are added to reality but without creating an attachment to the self. In a second step, realized only in Buddhism, reality is perceived as it is, without any support. Even the perception that there is a world goes away, or as Liang said: "The mountains, the rivers and the earth in front of the eyes have all disappeared. Nothing is seen and then ontological reality (*benti* 本體) appears. As Yogācāra says, fundamental wisdom (*genbenzhi* 根本智; [*mūla-jñāna*]) witnesses Suchness (*zhenru* 真如)."[92]

From the standpoint of orthodox Buddhism, one could point out that the moral function Liang assigns to Confucianism can perfectly be assumed by the Buddhist notion of subsequently obtained cognition (*houde zhi* 後得智; *pṛṣṭha-labdha-jñāna*).[93] Through this mode of cognition, the bodhisattvas are able to use conventional knowledge in helping other sentient beings, but they themselves do not become attached to this knowledge since they know it is only intermediary, unlike fundamental wisdom. Liang, however, did not view this type of wisdom as taking human affairs seriously enough. Indeed, from the perspective of fundamental wisdom, our conventional knowledge and the world itself lack substance and are illusory. Although bodhisattvas may indeed help sentient beings in attaining final liberation, they do not really care about making this world a better place. Subsequently obtained wisdom fails to provide a positive meaning for this present world right now. Therefore, Liang assigns to Buddhism the specific role

92. Liang, *Dongxi wenhua ji qi zhexue*, p. 411.

93. This wisdom is discriminating but without creating wrong ideas about a self and about external reality. In *Yindu zhexue gailun* (pp. 163–164), the subsequently obtained wisdom is associated with the notion of worldly direct cognition (*shijian xianliang* 世間現量). Indeed, Liang's concept of intuition is identical to worldly direct cognition, with the difference that intuition provides a positive meaning to the present world as it is.

of religious transcendence and to Confucianism the role of providing meaning to life and the world. From the point of view of Buddhism, Liang replaces subsequently attained wisdom with Confucian intuition, which he believes is better suited for active engagement with the world. Unlike subsequently obtained wisdom, which is reserved for the bodhisattvas, Confucian intuition is accessible to all, without any precondition of enlightenment.

For Liang, Buddhism and Confucianism complement each other. Through Buddhism, the ultimate and ontological reality can be known, but only Confucianism can provide a positive value for the present world. Liang's vision is deeply rooted in his own personal experiences. He personally aimed at an otherworldly reality. At the same time, he attempted to alleviate the suffering he saw in his own times, actively engaging in social and cultural reform, not only because of Buddhist compassion, but also because he believed that this world could gain a positive meaning. In his fundamentally Buddhist vision, Liang introduced the link of Confucian morality. Although he had opposed any use of Yogācāra that would engage the realms of morality and politics, as shown above, he regarded as acceptable a Yogācāra theory that would integrate moral intuition as a second mode of knowledge, operating within the world, but without creating any attachment to it.

4.3 Yogācāra in human history

The idea of evolution is an important link between Yogācāra and modern discourse from the West. As a theory, evolution describes ongoing transformation in the natural world (natural sciences like biology and physics) and in society (sociology, economics, politics), as well as in human ideas (history of thought) and in the individual mind (psychology). Since Yogācāra theory is about flux, it provided intellectuals with resources to embrace the rapid social and cultural changes happening at Liang's time in China.

The specific contribution of Liang Shuming was to insert Yogācāra theory itself within an evolutionary scheme. Accordingly, the three cultures of the West, China, and India developed on three different epistemological and moral grounds, yet in the modern age, the three cultures have come into contact, enabling humanity to run these three stages of culture successively. The West can no longer continue its focus on *biliang* and needs to learn from China about intuition. China also needs a combination of *biliang* and intuition to preserve China's own identity and at the same time embrace progress. By entering deeper into the ethical age, humanity will advance one step further toward *xianliang* and the final enlightenment of Buddhism.

Within this broad historical frame, Liang attempted to understand how Yogācāra teachings could have appeared so early in human history, describing the intellectual precocity (*zaoshu* 早熟) of Yogācāra as being the sublime product of genius such as that of Asaṅga and Vasubandhu.[94] Because of its complexity, their teaching was not understood at that time. Only today, in the modern age, have people begun to understand Yogācāra because modern Western science is showing people the validity of Yogācāra. Modern science from the West is indeed important, but people should not praise it as if it were absolutely true and perfect. Liang believed in the intrinsic superiority of Yogācāra over all theories of knowledge, including Western and Confucian theories, since only Yogācāra did not introduce dogmatic belief. In this respect, Yogācāra is without rival.[95]

Although I have not found textual evidence to support the hypothesis, I believe Liang's theory about the precocity of Yogācāra can be linked to the theory of the seeds in the base consciousness. As we know, Liang construed culture as a continuum similar to the base consciousness. Therefore, we could say that the seed of Yogācāra was planted by Asaṅga and Vasubandhu in Indian culture but did not immediately manifest its karmic fruit.[96] At that time humanity had not yet developed a strong material basis for society and so Asaṅga's and Vasubandhu's ideas were unable to be implemented. The seed matured much later, in the modern age in China, under the impact of Western thought acting as an external factor.

Liang was probably correct when he stated that Yogācāra would have remained a hidden and obscure theory in China if it were not for its encounter with Western ideas. Indeed, it was only because of the new ideas from the West that Yogācāra was rediscovered in modern times. Liang believed that, in the age of science, Yogācāra would become the basis for modern philosophy. He did not, however, advocate returning purely and simply to the formulations of Asaṅga and Vasubandhu. Yogācāra had to be expressed in the language that people could best understand, and at that time that was the language of Western philosophy. Although language from the West did not add anything to Yogācāra teachings, it was instrumental in showing to all a truth that a few enlightened people had experience and expressed long ago.

Liang did not understand Yogācāra as an abstract theory but as a set of profound insights deeply rooted in the history of humanity. He also warned against

94. Liang, *Dongxi wenhua ji qi zhexue*, p. 526.

95. Liang, *Weishi shuyi*, p. 313.

96. The origin of good seeds in the base consciousness is a difficult point in the theory of Yogācāra. In his cultural philosophy, Liang solved the question by postulating the genius of a few people derived from their meditative practices.

making Yogācāra another political or social ideology.[97] Yogācāra, like Buddhism in general, ultimately aims at leaving the world and history. As we will see in the final section of this chapter, Liang's understanding of Yogācāra is ultimately founded on metaphysics.

4.4 Buddhist metaphysical method in Yogācāra

Liang's interpretation of Buddhism, including the Yogācāra School, was mostly based on Chinese Buddhism. One of the main differences between Indian and Chinese Buddhism relates to the question of ontology. In the 1920s this question became very controversial, as it is today. From 1922 onward, Ouyang Jingwu offered classes on Yogācāra texts at the China Institute of Inner Learning. His textual research on the recently rediscovered Yogācāra classics highlighted the original teachings of Indian Yogācāra. At the same time, this shed new light on important texts in the Chinese Buddhist canon (*Da zang jing* 大藏經), such as *Dasheng qixin lun* (Awakening of Mahāyāna Faith). As Eyal Aviv shows in his chapter in this volume, Ouyang Jingwu rejected *Dasheng qixin lun* because its doctrinal content departed from orthodox Buddhism by establishing some concepts not found in earlier texts. From the perspective of the original doctrines of Yogācāra, Ouyang and his disciples considered *Dasheng qixin lun* to be unorthodox and even non-Buddhist. In the same year, in 1922, Taixu responded to Ouyang with a short answer, "Fofa zongjueze tan 佛法總抉擇談" (A General Choice for Buddhist Teachings).[98] As with Ouyang Jingwu and Liang Shuming, Taixu also held that only Yogācāra could save Buddhism, yet for Taixu, Yogācāra was not the whole of Buddhism, and it was improper to judge *Dasheng qixin lun* only from the point of view of Yogācāra. From his perspective, *Cheng weishi lun* and *Dasheng qixin lun* belonged to two different yet complementary schools within Buddhism.

Liang could not ignore the debate between Ouyang Jingwu and Taixu. He immediately accepted the conclusion of Ouyang about the authorship of *Dasheng qixin lun*, as mentioned above. Concerning the debate about the doctrinal orthodoxy of *Dasheng qixin lun*, Liang remained silent. He probably sided with the traditional Chinese interpretation, defended so vehemently by Taixu, because Liang had previously considered the Yogācāra theory of knowledge to be the necessary

---

97. Liang strongly opposed Taixu's "Buddhism for the human world" (*rensheng fojiao*).

98. The short answer of Taixu was published in 1936: *Faxiang Weishixue* 法相唯識學 (Studies on the Dharma Characteristics School and Nothing but Consciousness School) (Shanghai: Shangwu yinshuguan, 1936; reprint, Beijing: Shangwu yinshuguan, 2004), pp. 385–392.

philosophical basis upon which metaphysics could be built.[99] Unlike Ouyang and some Japanese scholars, Liang was not ready to alter his metaphysical understanding of Buddhism. All his philosophical thought was built on metaphysics, and it would have been difficult for him to abandon it. Another factor may explain why Liang continued holding on to Chinese Buddhism. The controversy between Chinese Buddhism and Indian Buddhism, between metaphysics and antimetaphysics, developed mostly in the 1920s and 1930s. At that time, Liang had already formed his understanding of Buddhism. He was not interested so much in academic debate about the history of Buddhism and he clearly recognized his lack of expertise in this field. Also, when the controversy broke between Ouyang Jingwu and Taixu, Liang had already shifted his interest to rural reconstruction and therefore he chose not to participate in the intellectual and academic debates on Buddhism. Yet, we may suppose that if the thesis on the incompatibility between Yogācāra epistemology and metaphysics had been argued ten years before, this may have seriously undermined Liang's project of establishing an ontological metaphysics on the basis of Yogācāra epistemology.

Following the path opened by *Dasheng qixin lun*, Chinese Buddhism, especially the Huayan and Tiantai Schools, developed in a direction quite different from that of Indian Yogācāra. These schools claimed the existence of a positive ultimate essence, named and described as the "matrix of buddhas (*rulaizang* 如來藏)," buddhahood, or the "mind of the cosmos" (*yuzhou zhi xin* 宇宙之心). This ultimate reality tended therefore to be interpreted as objective, present under two modes, actual and potential. As actual, it was absolutely transcendent, independent from the world; as potential, it was present everywhere in the phenomenal world.

When Westerners started the academic study of Yogācāra in the first half of the twentieth century, many relied on Chinese and Japanese commentaries, and therefore their understanding was heavily influenced by the ontological reading that prevailed in East Asia for over one thousand years. Also, Western scholars of Yogācāra were influenced by their own Western ontological tradition.[100] In modern China, most intellectuals, including Liang Shuming, also followed the

99. Liang, *Weishi shuyi*, p. 271.

100. Louis de la Vallée Poussin (1869–1938) translated *Cheng weishi lun* from the Chinese into French, offering an idealist reading of Yogācāra by which consciousness alone creates the world. See Louis de la Vallée Poussin, *Vijñaptimātratāsiddhi: La Siddhi de Hiuan-Tsang*, (Paris: Librairie Orientaliste Paul Geuthner, 1928–1929). Subsequently, other Western scholars such as the Russian scholar Fyodor Ippolitovich Stcherbatsky (1866–1942) also followed the idealistic reading of La Vallée Poussin. This idealistic reading of the Yogācāra was also prevalent in India with scholars such as A. K. Chatterjee, C. D. Sharma, P. T. Raju, and S. N. Dasgupta.

idealist reading. Contemporary New Confucians, like Xiong Shili and Mou Zongsan, integrated Yogācāra into their own metaphysical system. Despite the efforts of Ouyang and his disciples, the position of Taixu prevailed, and Yogācāra was not revived as an independent Buddhist school but remained integrated into the metaphysical system of East Asian Buddhism. Therefore, both East Asia and the West have mostly approached Yogācāra within a common philosophical framework structured by a fundamental ontology. Only during the relatively short time where Yogācāra was an independent school in India was it able to preserve its epistemology free from ontology.[101]

In *Dongxi wenhua ji qi zhexue*, Liang's ontological interpretation of *Cheng weishi lun* is quite explicit: "*Xianliang* witnesses Suchness (*zhenru*), that is, fundamental reality (*benti* 本體). This is what Yogācāra means by 'wisdom and Suchness are perfectly equal' or 'non-conceptualizing wisdom does not change.'"[102] When Xuanzang talked about equality between wisdom and Suchness, he did not necessarily imply identity. He meant that wisdom and Suchness are at the same level. Liang, however, understood fundamental wisdom and Suchness to be identical. For him, Suchness is the ontological Mind, foundation of human consciousness and of cosmic reality, which "witnesses itself" (*xin zi wei zheng* 心自為證).[103] Here Liang displaced the aim of Yogācāra's epistemology, from an analysis of concrete perceptions to an experience of an ultimate reality that exists prior to and somehow independent of perception.

Interestingly, for Liang, fundamental reality (*benti*) is not to be conquered but to be revealed. Liang uses the metaphor of a "layered curtains" (*zhongmu* 重幕) to express the manifestation of the fundamental reality:

> Inner and outer both come from the base consciousness and are eventually split by us in two sections. In between we add various barriers. This means that in our life—amidst the demands that confront us—we split the world and the self. The seventh consciousness is attached to the self

101. In the last twenty-five years, nonmetaphysical readings have been proposed. The first author to go against the idealistic reading of Yogācāra is the Indian scholar Kochumutton. See Thomas A. Kochumutton, *A Buddhist Doctrine of Experience: A New Translation of the Works of Vasubandhu the Yogacarin* (Delhi: Motilal Banarsidass, 1982). After Kochumutton's "new" interpretation, which attempts to unearth the original meaning of the classical Yogācāra texts, other scholars have followed. More recently, Dan Lusthaus understands Yogācāra as similar to the Western school of phenomenology, especially to Husserl's thought. See Dan Lusthaus, *Buddhist Phenomenology*. Alex Wayman adopts also a similar nonontological reading. Alex Wayman, "A Defense of Yogācāra Buddhism," *Philosophy East and West* 46, no. 4 (1996): 447–476.

102. Liang, *Dongxi wenhua ji qi zhexue*, p. 413; *Cheng weishi lun*, CBETA 31n1585_p0049c21.

103. Liang, *Weishi shuyi*, p. 287.

> and manifests images by itself, so creating a layer of partition within. The first six consciousnesses perceive objects and manifest images by themselves, so [creating] a layer of partition to the outside. Accordingly, the whole universe, the so-called absolute, cannot be apprehended by our own sensation and thought. As long as these tools are active, there is already a separation into two contrasting formations [viz. self and other], with layer upon layer of partitioning. If you want to open up the layers of curtain and truly recognize unique and absolute fundamental reality, you need to get rid of the two attachments. Then, rash desires will stop by themselves; and the layers of curtains will fall automatically. Only then will it be possible to witness the meaning of the one reality. This is the contribution of Yogācāra to the metaphysical method.[104]

Here Liang underlines the fact that the epistemological apparatus put in place by Yogācāra cannot by itself realize fundamental reality. On the contrary, it is only by pacifying the mind that fundamental reality can be manifest. Since fundamental reality is itself tranquil, therefore only a pacified mind can be united with it.

Liang's primary interest in Yogācāra was not epistemological but metaphysical and ontological. The epistemology of Yogācāra, in which the process of negation is pushed to its extreme, opens to the ultimate stage of *nirvāna*, not defined purely in negative terms, but as a positive reality. Liang's thought is unusual in the sense that he combines a radical transcendence of leaving the world, typical of Hīnayāna Buddhism, with an ontological frame, typical of Chinese Buddhism.

I will evaluate Liang's ontological bent from four different points of view. First, from the perspective of Yogācāra, Liang clearly understood the epistemological project of Yogācāra as avoiding any undue metaphysical construction. Liang appreciated Yogācāra for its scientific method and yet he always considered that Buddhist metaphysics could be deduced from Yogācāra epistemology. Although Liang's method emphasized starting from epistemology, he had already presupposed a metaphysical framework.

Second, from the perspective of intellectual history, on the one hand, we have a purely epistemological Yogācāra that existed for a short time, in a limited geographical area; on the other hand, we have a metaphysical Yogācāra that has lasted for more than one thousand years and continues influencing East Asian thought. Therefore, this ontologized version of Yogācāra that has nourished the life and thought of so many people should not be lightly discarded.

Third, from the perspective of philosophy, we could investigate the claim that Yogācāra is free of any ontology. In fact, it is doubtful if it possible to have

---

104. Liang, *Dongxi wenhua ji qi zhexue*, p. 412.

an epistemology completely free from ontology. Furthermore, any comprehensive body of philosophical thought cannot fail to deal with ontological questions. Probably Liang's insistence on the necessity of metaphysics was partly a response to the challenges brought by Western philosophy, but there were also deep philosophical considerations that made Liang believe that an epistemological discourse cut from ontology was insufficient.

Fourth, from the point of view of the individual, it seems that religious practice does not need the supposition of an ontology that may hinder one's liberation. Yet, in Yogācāra epistemology, the self and volition have no ontological foundation and therefore lack intellectual and practical strength. The subsequent development of ontology addresses precisely this need, giving the Buddhist practitioner a firm basis on which he can rely for his practice.

Liang had an ontological faith in the sense that he believed there was a foundational reality of human experience and of the world. As a Buddhist himself, he started with the existential questions of human suffering and impermanence. He adopted the Yogācāra method in order to deconstruct all the elements of experience. In the end, Liang believed that beyond the illusory elements of experience he would find an ontological reality, or Suchness. We can say that Liang had a real faith in Suchness, something that was beyond his words and beyond his intelligence but which could be experienced.

Conclusion

This volume investigates the intellectual reception of Yogācāra thought in modern China. Liang Shuming is a good case of an intellectual embracing the new discourse on rationality, science, and philosophy. As we have seen, Yogācāra is fully rational in deconstructing cognition through reason. Liang even applies the critical tools of reason in order to deconstruct the history of the school (what I have called "historico-critical exegesis"). Liang's ultimate interest, however, is not in the history and dogma of the school, which he uses in order to raise philosophical questions. With Yogācāra, Liang completely embraces the discourse of reason of his age, and yet, with Yogācāra, he is able also to subvert reason from within, showing that the discourse of reason is altogether limited. In this sense, Yogācāra has truly enabled a modern discourse of reason, in which reason is able to criticize itself.

Liang has also shown that, besides being critical, reason should also be ethical. He considered that the highest mode of cognition in Yogācāra goes beyond any judgment of good or evil. In order to make room for an authentic morality, Liang established within Yogācāra an ethical reason (Confucian intuition), which allows a profound communion with others and with the cosmos. Here again,

Table 7.1 The epistemological and moral functions of the mind according to Liang Shuming (see section IV of this chapter: Liang's creative Yogācāra)

Cognitive functions for Liang Shuming	Objects *jing* 境	Presence of raw substance	Presence of image	Correspondence of basic stuff and reflection	Quality of reflection	Content of reflection	Psychological state
Second step of direct cognition *chushi xianliang* 出世間現量	Ontological reality *benti* 本體 *zhenru* 真如	Yes	No				Supreme Passivity
First step of direct cognition *shijian xianliang* (世間) 現量	Object as it is in itself *xingjing* 性境	yes	yes	Absolute correspondence without addition by the mind	Purely objective	Particular characteristics *zixiang* 自相	Passivity
Intuition *zhijue* 直覺 & 2 mental factors –Feeling 受 –Discerning 想	Object conveying the basic stuff *daizhijing* 帶質境	yes	yes	Addition, creativity of mind	Half objective Half subjective	Meaning *yiwei* 意味	Activity without Selfishness –Aesthetic *Miaomei* 妙味 –Moral *Lixing* 理性
Inferential cognition *biliang* 比量	Reflection-only objects *duyingjing* 獨影境	no	yes	Independence of reflection from basic stuff	Purely subjective	Common characteristics *gongxiang* 共相	Activity stained by selfishness

Liang's focus on morality is truly modern. Because he considered morality important as such, he made it an independent mode of reason, distinct from the transcendental reason of religion and distinct from the instrumental reason of worldly affairs.

Finally it is probably Liang's insistence on transcendental reason and metaphysics that may be the most difficult to appreciate. Liang reminds us of the existence of a metaphysical and ontological reality that can only be reached through the type of radical deconstruction as displayed by Yogācāra. For Liang, critical reason did not lead to the rejection of metaphysics, but opened itself to a transcendental ontology that discloses mind's true freedom. We come here to Liang's personal belief in and commitment to Buddhism, and at this point, we may let the reader himself judge if this kind of religious metaphysics is modern or not.

The thought of most of the authors under consideration in his volume displays a strong syncretism, which is indeed characteristic of this historical period. Liang's thought can be said to be syncretic in the sense that he mixes Confucian morality with a Buddhist epistemology expressed in terms of Western categories. However, Liang's view on ultimate reality is clearly expressed in terms of Buddhist metaphysics, and therefore it can be rightly claimed that his thought is ultimately not syncretic but Buddhist.

8

Xiong Shili's Critique of Yogācāra Thought in the Context of His Constructive Philosophy

John Makeham

XIONG SHILI 熊十力 (1885–1968) is conventionally regarded as a founding figure of the modern New Confucian school of philosophy[1] and widely recognized as one of the most original and creative Chinese philosophers of the twentieth century. He began his Yogācāra studies in Nanjing at the China Institute of Inner Learning (Zhina Neixue Yuan 支那內學院) in 1920 under the tutelage of the institute's founder, Ouyang Jingwu 歐陽竟無 (1871–1943).[2] Two years later, Xiong was appointed to teach Yogācāra philosophy in the Philosophy department of Peking University, where he taught for two years. He subsequently led a peripatetic and frequently interrupted academic career. Over the thirty-year period from the early 1920s to the early 1950s, he moved from an uncritical belief in Yogācāra philosophy to a position where it served as a foil for his own constructive philosophy. His criticisms of Yogācāra grew progressively more trenchant over this period.

The incremental nature of this transition is reflected in the different versions of his major philosophical writing, *Xin weishi lun* 新唯識論 (New Treatise on the Uniqueness of Consciousness; hereafter *New Treatise*).[3] In 1923 he published *Weishi xue gailun* 唯識學概論 (A General Account of Yogācāra Learning; 1923),

1. On the distinction between "New Confucian" and "Neo-Confucian," see the Introduction to this volume, fn. 3.

2. The institute was not formally launched until 1922 but it had already been running since 1918, based on the grounds of the Jinling Sutra Press (Jinling kejing chu 金陵刻經處) in Nanking.

3. This English rendering of the title is based on Xiong's own idiosyncratic gloss of *weishi* 唯識, discussed below.

based on his lectures at Peking University. In 1926 this book was revised, but the original title was retained. The title of the next revised version, *Weishi lun* 唯識論 (Treatise on Yogācāra), was published in 1930. The literary redaction (*wenyanwen ben* 文言文本) of *Xin weishi lun* was published 1932 and represents Xiong's mature rejection of Yogācāra philosophy, although he still retained many elements of Yogācāra, deploying them for his own purposes. (As indicated by the title, *Xin weishi lun* is presented as a commentary on, or critical response to, Xuanzang's 玄奘 [602–664][4] *Cheng weishi lun* 成唯識論 [Demonstration of Nothing but Consciousness], a core text in East Asian Buddhism.)[5] As contemporary scholar of Chinese philosophy Guo Qiyong 郭齊勇, has noted, the literary redaction of the *New Treatise* represents Xiong's most foundational and important writing.[6] It was with the publication of the literary redaction that Xiong was catapulted to national prominence (and controversy). A vernacular redaction (語體文本) of the *New Treatise* was published in 1944, and an abridged edition of the vernacular redaction was published in 1953.

Critically appropriating important terms, concepts, and problems from Yogācāra philosophy (strongly mediated through its Chinese interpretation), Xiong Shili went on to develop these elements into his own ontology: a metaphysics in which the primary ontological realm of "Fundamental Reality" (*benti* 本體)[7] transforms and permeates all things such that Fundamental Reality and phenomena are seen to cohere as a single whole. Xiong's ontology was influenced by both Confucian and Buddhist teachings. He was particularly inspired by the view found in *Yijing* 易經 (Book of Change) that the cosmos is perpetually and

---

4. Famous pilgrim to India and translator and editor of key Mahāyāna texts.

5. The title *Xin weishi lun* may well have been intended to echo a second level of meaning. Given that *Xin weishi lun* is presented as a commentary on, or critical response to, Xuanzang's *Cheng weishi lun*, an argument could be made that the title of Xiong's work has the additional implicit sense of *New Demonstration of Nothing but Consciousness*.

6. Guo Qiyong, *Tiandi jian yige dushuren: Xiong Shili zhuan* 天地間一個讀書人: 熊十力傳 (A Scholar Poised between Heaven and Earth: A Biography of Xiong Shili) (Taipei: Yeqiang chubanshe, 1994), pp. 50–54, 61. Unless otherwise noted, subsequent references to *New Treatise* are to the literary redaction. I have used the recension in *Xiong Shili quanji* 熊十力全集 (The Complete Writings of Xiong Shili), vol. 2 (Wuhan: Hubei jiaoyu chubanshe, 2001), collated against a photographic reproduction of the original recension first published by Zhejiang Provincial Library in October 1932, and republished in Taipei by Wenjing chubanshe in 1973. The photographic reproduction was made from a copy of the original recension provided by Tang Junyi 唐君毅 to Zhou Shaoxian 周邵賢, a former student of Xiong.

7. It should also be borne in mind that in addition to the rich history this term has in the context of Sinitic Buddhism (directly influencing its subsequent appropriation by Neo-Confucian philosophy), at the time Xiong was writing, this was also a rendering of Kant's "noumenon."

vigorously changing. He also subscribed to the notion of the mind as inherently enlightened, but obscured by defilements, a view common to several Sinitic systems of Buddhist thought—Tiantai, Huayan, and Chan—influenced by the *Dasheng qixin lun* 大乘起信論 (The Awakening of Mahāyāna Faith). It was also a view that shaped Neo-Confucian philosophy.

The following study—focusing on the *New Treatise*—consists of two parts. The first part introduces Xiong's radical ontological monism and his related critique of Yogācāra philosophy as ontological dualism and pluralism. At the heart of his critique is the charge that key Yogācāra thinkers (Vasubandhu, Dharmapāla, Xuanzang, and Kuiji) had effectively substantialized the concept of seeds (*bīja; zhongzi* 種子)—originally just a heuristic metaphor—by presenting seeds as the ontological basis of all things. Xiong's critique of Yogācāra pluralism extends to the division of consciousness into eight groups, and to Dharmapāla's/Xuanzang's appropriation of Indian logician and philosopher Dignāga's 陳那 (*ca.* 480–540) tripartite theory of consciousness. Xiong's critiques are grounded in the Mahāyāna doctrine of conditioned arising (*pratītya-samutpāda; yuanqi* 緣起)—everything arises from causes and conditions and has no inherent self-nature—and the doctrine that the phenomenal world is not ontologically distinct from undifferentiated absolute reality (*dharmakāya*), a thesis he develops using the *ti-yong* 體用 conceptual polarity.

In the second part I adduce a range of evidence drawn from the *New Treatise* to show that the Huayan Buddhist doctrine of nature origination (*xingqi* 性起) played a central role in Xiong's constructive philosophy, in which he integrated concepts, problems, and themes from traditional Chinese philosophy with elements emblematic of Sinitic Buddhist philosophy to articulate an ambitious philosophical syncretism. The theory of nature origination provides an ontological basis for all phenomena by presenting phenomena as manifestations of the nature (*xing* 性) (which, in turn, is the functional equivalent of Suchness, the Absolute, Fundamental Reality, *dharma* realm [*dharmadhātu*], and so on). The influence of this doctrine is particularly evident in Xiong's conception of the *ti-yong* conceptual model. I begin with Xiong's revisionist account of "transformation" (轉變; [**pariṇāma*]),[8] in

8. Occasionally I have suggested what I believe would have been the particular matching Sanskrit terms in square brackets, based on typical Sinitic Buddhist usage. Inter alia, this serves the purpose of reminding readers that Xiong is drawing upon a long-established technical vocabulary, even though he often chooses to invest certain terms with new meaning. In the context of Yogācāra thought, *zhuanbian* 轉變 refers to the transformation of consciousness—the continual renewal of consciousness from instant to instant. Kuiji 窺基, *Cheng weishi lun shuji* 成唯識論述記 (Commentary on *Cheng weishi lun*), CBETA, T43n1830_p0240c07-08: ". . . relying on the transformations of the inner consciousness [= base consciousness] means that seed consciousness [= base consciousness] transforms into manifest activity and manifestly activated consciousness transforms into seeds." (All references to the *Taishō Tripiṭaka* are to the Chinese Buddhist Electronic Text Association [CBETA] edition.)

which he presents Reality (實體; 本體 [*tattva]) as nothing other than an uninterrupted holistic process of constant transformation (*heng zhuan* 恆轉) that cannot be reduced to subject-object characteristics. In this context he introduces and elaborates two concepts derived from the *Book of Change*: "contraction" (*xi* 翕) and "expansion" (*pi* 闢), adapting them to characterize the inherent processual qualities of transformation, when viewed from the perspective of conventional truth.

Xiong posits Fundamental Reality/Suchness/inherent nature/the Absolute as an underlying "locus" in which phenomenal/conventional reality is ontologically grounded. Being committed to the view that the mind is characterized simultaneously by transformation (change, activity, movement) and constancy (quiescence, being undisturbed) enables Xiong to present the ceaseless flow of phenomenal appearances as nothing other than Reality/inherent nature. Having argued that "Reality cannot be sought independent of phenomena" and that "the True Ruler (*zhen zai* 真宰) is to be discerned amongst the flow [of phenomena]"[9] provides Xiong with a basis on which to present his account of the relationship between productive power and habituated tendencies; the nature (*xing* 性) and form-and-vital stuff (*xingqi* 形氣); and *li* 理 and *qi* 氣. I show that this is a further elaboration of his understanding of the *ti-yong* polarity, and consistent with the nature origination thesis. For Xiong, Fundamental Reality is flow. This constant emphasis on the dynamic nature of Fundamental Reality stands in marked contrast to the Indian emphasis on causality.

The penultimate section in part 2 addresses the topic of theodicy and deals specifically with the relationship between defiled mental associates (*ranshu* 染數)[10] and the inherently enlightened mind/the nature. I conclude that the thrust of Xiong's comments is consistent with the teaching developed in the *Dasheng qixin lun* that nonawakening depends on inherent awakening. The final topic addressed in part two is the thesis that the nature—representing ultimate truth, Suchness, and so forth—and practice (or cultivation) are not two and that this is a further expression of Xiong's understanding of the *ti-yong* paradigm.

1. Xiong's radical monism and critique of ontological dualism and pluralism

Although there is some disagreement among specialists about the basic epistemological stance of Yogācāra thinkers, Xiong was neither an epistemological

9. Xiong Shili, *New Treatise*, p. 70.

10. "Mental associates" is also alternatively translated as "mental factors" because they are aspects of minds, and not merely associated with them. Xiong, however, seems to treat mental factors less as aspects of than qualities that accompany the mind. Thus he describes mental associates as "'helpers and companions' because they are a family relative of the mind." See *New Treatise*, p. 91.

idealist nor a transcendental idealist. He did not hold that all we can know are mental representations or mental constructions; nor did he accept any notions akin to a distinction between the a priori and a posteriori in which things-in-themselves cannot be known by us. Further, he was neither an epistemological realist nor an ontological agnostic. He did not accept that the objects of our knowledge exist independent of the mind; nor did he suspend judgment about the ontological status of external objects. For example, in responding to the claim that there are external objects because we stop seeing white when white-colored objects are removed from before us and we stop feeling hardness when we stop touching hard objects, Xiong replied as follows:

> For consciousness[11] to manifest solidity, whiteness, and other characteristics there must be a cognitive object as cause. I am prepared to accept this meaning. However, the cognitive object that functions as cause certainly does not have an independent existence separate from consciousness. How so? This is because cognitive object and consciousness are a whole (*yiti* 體; [literally "one body"]). Because they are a whole, they resonate with one another (*jiaogan* 交感). Because they resonate with one another, we can say, nominally, that the cognitive object has the power to function as cause, conveying an image of itself [to the mind] (*dai ji xiang* 帶己相). (*Dai* 帶 has the sense of "to appear as" [*si* 似].[12] See *Cheng weishi lun shuji*.[13] The term *ji* 己 is posited as the cognitive object's [*jing* 境] reference to itself. This is saying that it is only because cognitive objects have the power to act as causes that they are able to cause consciousness to manifest images that resemble

11. Here "consciousness" is synonymous with "mind."

12. For a cognitive object or dharma to cause a cognition of itself to appear (*pratibhāsa, nirbhāsa, ābhāsa, avabhāsa*, etc., 現, 顯現, 照, 光影, 似, 似塵, 似顯現, etc.) in the mind of a perceiver, an *ālambana* 所緣 (a cognitive object from which mental impressions are derived) must act as the cause of the cognition, and it must convey an image of the cognitive object (*jing* 境; *viṣaya*). That image, which arises in the mind, is believed to be a resemblance (*si* 似; *sādṛśya*) of some "thing" out there. This is the fundamental point that influential philosopher and logician Dignāga seeks to establish in *Ālambana-parīkṣā* (Treatise on Discerning the Conditions for the Causal Support of Consciousness; *Guan suoyuan yuan lun* 觀所緣緣論), a work that attracted much attention in the first decades of the twentieth century in China and discussed in Dan Lusthaus chapter in this volume. In China Dignāga was considered to be part of the Yogācāra tradition. For a note on Chinese translations of the title *Ālambana-parīkṣā*, see the introduction to this volume.

13. Kuiji, *Cheng weishi lun shuji*, CBETA, T43n1830_p0271c22-28.

> cognitive objects.[14]) If [cognitive objects] are talked about as causes in this sense, then their existence should be accepted. Now, for you to state that there are external causes would be illogical. What is the reason for this? Because you presume [the existence of] external causes, you assert that [cognitive objects] are separate from inner consciousness and exist independently. [According to your reckoning,] inner and outer are separated, neither connecting with the other nor close to the other. Since there is no way for them to affect one another, how can there be a sense in which [cognitive objects] serve as causes? Thus your presumption that there is an external realm that causes the characteristics of solidity and whiteness to appear in inner consciousness is nothing more than your own erroneous presumption and rightfully cannot be accepted.[15]

Underpinning Xiong's position is the view that consciousness or mind and cognitive objects are inseparable because they constitute a single body, an indivisible whole. Even to speak of "them" in these terms is—from Xiong's perspective—to do so only nominally, provisionally (*jia* 假; [**prajñapti*]): "In terms of appearance only, subject and object are mutually entailing; it cannot be said that either issues from the other. As such, subject and object accompany one another with no identifiable boundary between them. (No demarcation between consciousness and cognitive object can be found.) Thus even if one wanted to separate them, there is certainly no place even to begin. This is due to the so-called flow of the whole."[16] Xiong insists that consciousness and the appearance of cognitive objects constitute a single, indivisible whole that cannot neatly be separated into two components:

> The term *weishi* 唯識 [serves] to refute only [the presumption of the independent existence of] external objects and does not mean that objects do not exist. Because cognitive objects and consciousness are the same whole and are not separated, hence it is said to be "*weishi*." *Wei* 唯 means "unique" (殊特);[17] it does not mean "only/solely." Consciousness is able

14. Passages in round brackets are Xiong's inline auto-commentary. In the original text they are marked by use of a smaller font. Xiong discusses *dai ji xiang* 帶己相 in his *Fojia mingxiang tongshi* 佛家名相通釋 (Complete Explanation of Buddhist Terms) (Taipei: Mingwen shuju, 1994/1937), pp. 337 ff.

15. Xiong, *New Treatise*, pp. 15–16.

16. Xiong, *New Treatise*, p. 22.

17. Following the 1932 redaction of the literary edition of *New Treatise* in reading *shute* 殊特 rather than the 2001 redaction, which reads *teshu* 特殊.

> to discern cognitive objects; its potent function is unique. In referring to consciousness and terming it "unique," [this is because] the referent (義; [*artha]) also includes cognitive objects.[18] How could one talk of *weishi* and then say that cognitive objects do not exist?

This is a radical reinterpretation of the term *wei* 唯 (*mātra*) as it occurs in such Sanskrit terms as *vijñapti-mātra* (*weishi* 唯識: consciousness only; nothing but consciousness) or *citta-mātra* (*wei xin* 唯心: mind only; nothing but mind). There is no question that in Sanskrit it means "only," "nothing but" and not "unique."

Occasionally, Xiong did distinguish internal and external cognitive objects, thus giving the impression that he accepted the existence of cognitive objects independent of consciousness. This is not the case.

> Both the sensory consciousnesses and the sixth consciousness[19] get the name consciousness from discerning the characteristics of cognitive objects. Whereas the sensory consciousnesses discern only external cognitive objects, the sixth consciousness discerns internal and external cognitive objects. Internal cognitive objects are the product of cognitive construction. . . . However, because the sixth consciousness is also always responding to cognitive objects it does not preserve a self-nature. This is because when the sixth consciousness arises it conveys the characteristics of the cognitive object (*jingxiang* 境相). For example, when it takes external forms and so forth as its cognitive objects, in consciousness there necessarily appear reflections (*yingxiang* 影像; [*pratibimba*][20]) which resemble external forms and so forth. And even though an *ālambana* (*suoyuan* 所緣) [cognitive object from which mental impressions are derived] is fundamentally not an external cognitive object, in consciousness there still appears a reflection which resembles the *ālambana*. This kind

18. In his *Fojia mingxiang tongshi*, p. 189, Xiong explains this as follows: "Because no dharmas are separate from consciousness it is called '*weishi* 唯識.' Because this does not mean that there is nothing but consciousness, the term '*wei* 唯' is used."

19. The Yogācāra School distinguished eight types of consciousness: The five sensory consciousnesses are the visual, auditory, olfactory, gustatory, and tactile. The sixth consciousness or *manovijñāna* (mental consciousness) is the thinking consciousness. It also brings together and differentiates the sensory impressions derived from the five sensory consciousnesses. That is, it can think about what the other five consciousnesses perceive; the five consciousnesses do not have this reflective capacity. The seventh or self-centered consciousness (*manas*) is the source of self-attachment; and the eighth, or base consciousness (*ālayavijñāna*), retains the impressions of past experiences and "perfumes" new experiences on the basis of that previous conditioning.

20. This reflection contrasts with the original form of something.

> of reflection also resembles an external cognitive object and so functions just the same as an "*ālambana* condition" (*suoyuan yuan* 所緣緣) [condition for the causal support of consciousness].[21]

An *ālambana* is merely a conceptual stop-gap—it represents what is nominally or hypothetically posited to be something that exists "externally" to the mind, to consciousness. As Xiong states, it is not actually an external cognitive object but is merely spoken of as if it were. This, in turn, is entirely consistent with conventional truth and mundane reality:

> As for what is termed "knowledge," it has always been developed on the basis of looking outwards at things. In the universe that constitutes our everyday lives, because we regard that which our senses detect to be real cognitive objects (*shizai jing* 實在境) external to our mind, so we distinguish and deal with them accordingly. This is how knowledge has been developed. Hence knowledge is merely a tool by which to seek principles externally. If this tool is used only in the universe that constitutes our everyday lives—that is, within the world of physical principles—of course it cannot be deemed inappropriate. If this tool is used carelessly, however, when one wants to solve metaphysical problems, and one posits Reality (*shiti* 實體) as a cognitive object of the external realm in order to trace its principles, one will be greatly mistaken.[22]

1.1 Reality

"Reality" is the ontological holistic "locus" of everything. It is the single most important concept in the *New Treatise* and is invoked frequently, albeit under a variety of names: "Reality (*shiti* 實體; [**tattva*]) is not a cognitive realm (*jingjie* 境界) separate from one's own mind, nor is it a cognitive object of knowledge. . . . Moreover, the word 'self-nature' (*zixing* 自性; [**svabhāva*]) is but a different term for Reality."[23] In the vernacular redaction of the *New Treatise*, *shiti* 實體 is largely replaced by *benti* 本體. As Xiong points out, however, the meaning is the same: "Fundamental Reality (*benti* 本體) is but a different term for True Nature (*zhen xing* 真性). As the True Principle (*shili* 實理) by which we and the ten thousand things live, it is called True Nature. As for this True Nature being the True Aspect (*shixiang*

21. Xiong, *New Treatise*, p. 99.

22. Ibid., p. 12.

23. Ibid., p. 10.

實相 [*tattvasya-lakṣaṇam]) of myself and the myriad things as they inherently are (*benran* 本然), it is also called Fundamental Reality. Here, True Aspect is just the same as saying Reality (*shiti* 實體)."[24]

Elsewhere he explains that in Buddhist writings the term *xing* 性 is often used synonymously with the term *ti* 體 to express the meaning of "absolute truth" (*juedui de zhenli* 絕對的真理), which in "Oriental philosophy" is expressed using the terms *benti* 本體, *shiti* 實體, or the *ti* 體 of *ti-yong* 體用.[25] In the *New Treatise*, both mind (*xin* 心)[26] and the nature (*xing* 性) are also synonymous with Reality: "The nature refers to the principle by virtue of which we are living; if we use it to refer collectively to all existents, then provisionally it is called 'transformation.' "[27] One of Xiong's main characterizations of Reality is as an uninterrupted holistic process of constant transformation.

Xiong explains that Reality can be apprehended or realized only by seeking within, returning to one's inherent mind (*benxin* 本心), where Reality, True Principle, can be personally verified or witnessed. Direct awareness of self-nature, being awoken to Reality, is wisdom (*zhi* 智; [**jñāna*]). It is worth pointing out that according to Yogācāra soteriology, it is by transforming the consciousnesses into "direct cognitions" that the eight consciousnesses cease and one attains nonconceptual wisdom (*jñāna*). When all the seeds in the eighth consciousness reach maturity, come to fruition, then the eighth consciousness is transformed and one attains "perfect mirror wisdom" (*dayuanjing zhi* 大圓鏡智; *mahādarśa-jñāna*) enabling direct, unmediated cognition of things just as they are. Xiong similarly describes wisdom as direct, unmediated cognition.

Xiong adamantly opposed any form of ontological dualism or pluralism. He was an ontological monist but in a particular sense—his monism is not reducible to a single quality or characterization. "Although it has always been absolutely nothing yet it is not nothing; although it gives rise to the myriad existents, it does not exist. Hence, dispel both existence and no-existence; sever names and images at the ford of constant stillness. Roll-up or release at will; cease verbal distinction-making [upon the realization of that which lies] beyond snares and traps."[28] "Snares and traps," of course, is an allusion to the fish-trap and

24. Xiong, *New Treatise*, vernacular redaction, p. 20.

25. Xiong, *Fojia mingxiang tongshi*, pp. 45–46,

26. Xiong also uses "mind" to mean consciousness; indeed on occasions he uses the binome "mind-consciousness." When employed in this sense, it does not have the sense of "Reality."

27. Xiong, *New Treatise*, p. 142.

28. Xiong, *New Treatise*, p. 92.

rabbit-snare allegory in *Zhuangzi*. Just as snares and traps are used to catch game, once the game has been caught one no longer needs the snares and traps, so too with words and their referents. In order to be able to understand this Reality—which Xiong also variously refers to as First Thing, and absolute principle, the nature, one mind, and so forth—it must be personally witnessed, personally experienced.

1.2 Criticism of seeds as causes

Xiong identified Paramārtha (499–569)[29] as a representative figure in the "old" tradition of Yogācāra as transmitted in China in contrast to the "new" tradition, which he associates with Xuanzang and Kuiji 窺基 (632–682),[30] but which has its roots in the Weishi teachings of Dharmapāla[31] (fl. sixth century) and Vasubandhu (fourth century).[32]

According to Xiong, the key difference between the old and new traditions in China is that the latter group posited seeds as the ontological basis of all things and so was guilty of promoting an ontological pluralism.[33] Xiong's critique of the account of seeds in *Cheng weishi lun* is a central theme in the *New Treatise*.

The second chapter of the *New Treatise* devotes considerable attention to refuting attachment to consciousness (which in this context refers to the eight consciousnesses, as distinct from consciousness as the True Mind/Reality/*tathatā* and so forth). Xiong freely acknowledges that former Mahāyāna teachers (= Dharmapāla/Xuanzang) had clearly maintained that attachment to the belief that consciousness is real is just as mistaken as attachment to cognitive objects, and had "therefore nominally talked about [consciousness'] being generated by

---

29. Influential Indian translator into Chinese of key Yogācāra texts. As John Jorgensen points out, "Paramārtha was an early translator of Yogācāra texts into Chinese, but because his version of Yogācāra allowed for the existence of the *tathāgatagarbha*, his works became controversial, some even alleging that he introduced an alien doctrine into Yogācāra, although his translations may have reflected a version of Yogācāra found in India."

30. Student of Xuanzang who wrote an important subcommentary on *Cheng weishi lun*.

31. Student of Dignāga, this major sixth-century Indian Yogācāra scholar wrote an influential commentary on Vasubandhu's *Triṃśikā* (*Weishi sanshi song* 唯識三十頌; Thirty Verses on Nothing but Consciousness), translated by Xuanzang, T.1586.31, the text on which Xuanzang's *Cheng weishi lun* comments. Xuanzang's *Cheng weishi lun* is said to draw heavily on Dharmapāla's commentary and privileges many of its interpretations. See, however, the discussion of Dharmapāla under 1.1.3 in the Introduction to this volume.

32. Younger brother of Asaṅga and major figure in the early development of Yogācāra learning and author of key texts, including *Triṃśikā*, the text on which Xuanzang's *Cheng weishi lun* comments.

33. Xiong, *Fojia mingxing tongshi*, B.256.

conditioned arising (*yuansheng* 緣生) so as to show that the characteristics of consciousness are illusory and unreal."[34] Despite this, Xiong maintains that Yogācāra philosophy (as principally represented by *Cheng weishi lun* rather than the Paramārtha tradition) had hypostasized the doctrine of conditioned arising into a doctrine of seeds, which, as Liu Shu-hsien points out, suggests a structural realism.[35] It also entails various forms of ontological dualisms (seeds and consciousness [or so-called manifest activity (*xianxing* 現行)]; seeds and mind/*tathatā* [Suchness]; pure and impure seeds) and even ontological pluralism, with seeds posited as the ontological basis of all things. He found all of these perspectives to be antithetical to his own ontological monism.

For Xiong, consciousness has no self-nature (*zixing* 自性; [**svabhāva*]); it is generated by conditioned arising:

> Nominally saying that [mind-consciousness] is generated by conditioned arising causes [one] to understand that mind-consciousness is only an illusory manifestation and does not truly exist. If consciousness did truly exist, it would have self-nature (*ziti* 自體). . . . Now, in analyzing this consciousness, it is said to be the manifestation of an illusory image [generated by] the interdependence of many conditions. It is thus very evident that consciousness has no self-nature. Hence, with respect to conditioned arising, [my purpose] is not to directly express [the view] that consciousness arises due to the aggregation of many conditions, but rather is to refute effectively those who are attached [to the view] that consciousness really exists.[36]

---

34. Xiong, *New Treatise*, p. 27.

35. Liu Shu-hsien, "Hsiung Shih-li's Theory of Causation," *Philosophy East and West* 19, no. 4(1969): 403.

36. Xiong, *New Treatise*, p. 37. It is important to note who Xiong's target is here. In a corresponding passage in the vernacular text, p. 73, he writes:

> If it leaves its various conditions then there is no such thing as consciousness (*xin* 心). In early times the ways the Indian Buddhists talked about the meaning of conditioned arising was no more than this, and this is as it should be. Later, however, the founders of the Mahāyāna Yogācāra School, the two great masters, Vasubandhu and Asaṅga, gradually changed the meaning of what previous Buddhists had referred to as conditioned arising. It seems that they looked upon each of the many conditions as single parts and thereupon began to construct [their notion of consciousness (心)] by regarding it as the aggregation of many conditions. In this way, they changed the doctrine of conditioned arising into a kind of structuralism. It closely resembles [the belief that] material objects are composed through the aggregation of many parts. This sense is still not fully evident in Asaṅga's writings but in his way of speaking about things, there is already this tendency. As for Vasubandhu and later masters, compared with Asaṅga, it is evident that they changed the doctrine of conditioned arising into a structuralism.

Establishing the claim that consciousness is generated by conditioned arising is a crucial step for Xiong in critiquing the Yogācāra doctrine of seeds. He develops his critique of this doctrine in a number of contexts, one of the most important being in his revisionist account of the Four Conditions (*si yuan* 四緣): (1) causes as condition (*yin yuan* 因緣); (2) continuous sequence of sameness condition (*deng wujian yuan* 等無間緣); (3) condition for the causal support of consciousness (*ālambana* condition) (*suoyuan yuan* 所緣緣); and (4) contributory factors as condition (*zengshang yuan* 增上緣). The Four Conditions are central to Yogācāra accounts of causality, particularly for explaining the causal relationship between seeds, consciousness, and cognitive objects.[37]

According to Xiong, a key defining characteristic of the standard Yogācāra view of causes as conditions is that causes themselves bring to completion their own effects. Thus the seeds of visual consciousness, functioning as cause, bring to completion their own visual consciousness effects. Much of Xiong's analysis and discussion is devoted to critiquing the Yogācāra view—which he associates with Vasubandhu and Dharmapala/Xuanzang[38]—that seeds are causes (*yinti* 因體), in particular the idea that seeds are the cause of consciousness:

> The various Mahāyāna masters before Vasubandhu consistently maintained that consciousness and the various dharmas have no self-nature; that is, they regarded them all to be empty. When Vasubandhu established [the doctrine of] the uniqueness of consciousness (*weishi* 唯識), he started having consciousness subsume the various dharmas and so came to look upon the dharma of consciousness as something relatively real. Furthermore, if we infer on the basis of his account of seeds, consciousness is generated from seeds and so consciousness is a real dharma (*shi fa* 實法) with self-nature.[39]

> [Former teachers] presumed that the appearance of mind-consciousness (*xinshi* 心識) had an origin. Hence seeds were established as causes and mind-consciousness was posited as the effect that seeds themselves had brought to completion.[40]

---

37. See, for example, Xuanzang (trans. and compiler), *Cheng weishi lun*, CBETA, T31n1585_p0040c20– p0041b06; translated in Francis H. Cook, *Three Texts on Consciousness-only* (Berkeley, CA: Numata Center for Buddhist Translation and Research, 1999), pp. 242–250.

38. Dharmapāla was a major sixth-century Indian Yogācāra scholar who wrote an influential commentary on Vasubandhu's *Thirty Verses*. Because Xuanzang's *Cheng weishi lun* purportedly draws heavily on this commentary and privileges many of its interpretations, in Xiong's hands, "Dharmapāla" effectively functions as metonym for views expressed in *Cheng weishi lun*.

39. Xiong, *New Treatise*, p. 95.

40. Ibid., p. 28.

> Using "consciousness" as a name for the manifest activity (*xianxing* 現行)[41] [of seeds], consciousness' existence was affirmed, and seeds were thus the cause from where "manifestly activated consciousness" (*xianxing shi* 現行識) was generated, and so were also the reality (*ti* 體; [**dravya*][42]) of manifestly activated consciousness.[43]

> Manifest activity is not generated without a cause, and so additionally seeds were established as its cause. Each manifestly active mental dharma (*xin fa* 心法) [= mind] has as its cause its own seeds. Each manifestly active mental associate (*xinsuo fa* 心所法)[44] also has as its cause its own seeds. Since there are differentiations in manifest activity . . . seeds [alone] suffice to account for the myriad differences [in manifest activity].[45]

For Xuanzang, seeds are a "potentiality that immediately engenders an actual dharma." Real seeds, as distinct from nominal seeds, can function as causal conditions. This view contrasts with the view upheld in the Abhidharma literature (ancient scholastic Buddhism) that seeds are not real existents (*dravya*), but simply metaphors.[46] Thus Xiong remarks: "Conventionally it is presumed that rice and other things all issue from seeds. Now this is also presumed about mental dharmas (*xin fa* 心法). Is this not a great mistake?"[47] His point is that rather than treating seeds as a nominal (*prajñapti*) device, an expedient means to refer to something that lacks inherent existence, these Yogācāra teachers had effectively substantialized seeds by attributing causal power to them. For Xiong, consciousness or mind-consciousness is not a product of seeds. Indeed it is not a product of anything: it constantly arises as an incessant flow of ever-renewing thoughts.

Xiong was similarly critical of the way Dharmapāla/Xuanzang had appropriated the Indian logician and philosopher Dignāga's tripartite theory of consciousness—that consciousness consists of an object/image part (*xiangfen* 相分;

---

41. The appearance of things in their manifest aspect in the seven consciousnesses as they emerge from seeds in the eighth consciousness; the activity of consciousness.

42. *Dravya*: that which is real and has causal function.

43. Xiong, *New Treatise*, p. 39.

44. Mental activities that accompany and assist the functioning of the mind. They are analyzed in great detail in the last chapter of the *New Treatise*.

45. Xiong, *New Treatise*, p. 52.

46. Tao Jiang, *Contexts and Dialogue: Yogācāra Buddhism And Modern Psychology on the Subliminal Mind* (Honolulu: University of Hawaii Press, 2006), p. 60.

47. Xiong, *New Treatise*, p. 29.

nimitta [**bhāga*]); a perceiving/seeing part (*jianfen* 見分; *darśana* [**bhāga*]); and a self-verifying part or that part which confirms the perceiving part (*zizhengfen* 自證分; *svasaṃvṛtti*).[48] The significance of the tripartite theory is that it relates to Xuanzang's opening comments in *Cheng weishi lun* (apparently following the lead of Dharmapāla) to the effect that self and the external world are to be explained by the transformation of consciousness. According to *Cheng weishi lun*, the transformation of consciousness is the result of being bifurcated into an image part and a perceiving part: "Transformation [of consciousness] refers to consciousness itself coming to be replicated in two parts. This is because both parts, the image part and the perceiving part, arise due to the self-verifying part of consciousness.[49] Self and dharmas are established on the basis of these two parts."[50] Drawing on the scholarship of Katsumata Shunkyō 勝又俊教, Tao Jiang points out that this was a departure from the original verse seventeen of Vasubandhu's *Thirty Verses*, and by adopting Dharmāpala's explanation Xuanzang was able to interpret the verse as stating that "the transformation of consciousness is the result of its being bifurcated into the discriminating and the discriminated. Because neither of the two exists outside consciousness, there can be nothing but consciousness."[51]

Xiong notes that when Dharmapāla (presumably channeled by Xuanzang) discussed transformation, he divided it into two types: seeds functioning as causes capable of bringing about transformation (*yin nengbian* 因能變) in consciousness; and manifestly activated consciousness itself (*xianti* 現體)—the self-verifying aspect unique to each mind and mental associate—functioning as effects that are simultaneously capable of bringing about transformation (*guo nengbian* 果能變) in consciousness. Because each and every self-verifying part is, in turn, able to transform and be manifest as a perceiving part and an image part, they are referred to as "effects capable of bringing about transformation."[52]

48. *Cheng weishi lun shuji*, CBETA T43n1830_p0319a22.

49. This self-verifying or self-corroborating part is seen to be theoretically required because every moment of consciousness needs to be self-aware if memory is to be possible; otherwise there would be just an array of unconnected moments.

50. *Cheng weishi lun*, CBETA, T31n1585_p0001b01-02. In the *New Treatise*, p. 52, Xiong provides the following illustration: "Take for example the auditory consciousness. Sound is the image part. Cognition of the discernment of sound is the perceiving part. The image [part] and the perceiving [part] must have constitutive entity as their basis and that is the self-verifying part. Each mind consists of the combination of these three parts. Each mental associate also consists of the combination of these three parts. . . . In general terms, manifest activity is presented in the appearance of the image [part], hence the name."

51. Tao, *Contexts and Dialogue*, p. 52.

52. Xiong, *New Treatise*, p. 52.

The perceiving part and the image part represent what consciousness becomes, what it transforms into (*suobian* 所變). The reason the perceiving part and the image part together represent what consciousness transforms into is that both are needed in order for perception to occur. Consciousness-as-transformer (*nengbian* 能變)—the capacity of consciousness to transform into a perceiving part and image part—provides the raw material that one re-presents to oneself as what consciousness transforms into (*suobian* 所變). Central to Xiong's objections is this bifurcation of consciousness:

> In regard to causes' being able to bring about transformation, [Dharmapāla] held that seeds are able to transform and to be manifest as that which is transformed. In regard to effects' being able to bring about transformation, he held that manifestly activated consciousness itself (*xianti* 現體) is able to bring about transformation and that the perceiving part and the image part are that into which it is transformed (*suobian* 所變). In sum, subject (*neng* 能) and object (*suo* 所) are each made separate. This is just like taking something that is already whole and then breaking it apart into fragments. How could this possibly explain what transformation is?

He further faults "former teachers" for breaking down mind-consciousness (*xinshi* 心識) into eight groups, comparing this to the analysis of material objects into molecules, and thus mistakenly comparing mind to matter.[53] He also criticizes Dharmapāla for adopting seeds as a metaphor of productive power—which Xiong treats as the dynamic aspect of Fundamental Reality—as this reinforced the impression that seeds were real entities; and for adopting a view of seeds that aligned Dharmapāla with the views of the proponents both of atoms and of the *ātman*,[54] as well as proponents of a mechanistic theory of the universe.

> According to Dharmapāla's doctrine, each sentient being has its own productive power as cause and this productive power is also called seeds. The differences in the self-nature (*tixing* 體性) of sentient beings are as numerous as grains of rice. . . . He did not realize that in taking "seeds" as a metaphor he was both making the mistake of treating the eighth consciousness (*ālaya*) as analogous to things . . . and, moreover, subtly complying with [the views of] proponents of atoms.[55]

53. Ibid., p. 28

54. In Brahmanistic thought, the self that grounds living beings.

55. *New Treatise*, pp. 56, 57.

He also objected more generally to the techniques of "breaking down" (*fenxi* 分析): "When they broke-down mind-consciousness, the contents were extremely fragmented, in order to accommodate multiple seeds. It is just as if a material object was analyzed into atoms, molecules, right down to electrons."[56] The idea here is that consciousness was broken down into eight clusters and these clusters were in turn attributed to seeds. He extended his criticism of the techniques of "breaking down" to the analytic methods used in science and philosophy.

In the vernacular version of *New Treatise*, Xiong further developed these criticisms to portray the above views about seeds as inconsistent with the doctrine of conditioned arising and effectively being a theory of structural realism:

> If it leaves its various conditions, then there is no such thing as consciousness (*xin* 心). In early times the ways the Indian Buddhists talked about the meaning of conditioned arising was no more than this, and this is as it should be. Later, however, the founders of the Mahāyāna Yogācāra School, the two great masters, Vasubandhu and Asaṅga, gradually changed the meaning of what previous Buddhists had referred to as conditioned arising. It seems that they looked upon each of the many conditions as single parts and thereupon began to construct [their notion of consciousness (心)] by regarding it as the clustering of many conditions. In this way, they changed the doctrine of conditioned arising into a kind of structuralism (*gouzaolun* 構造論). It closely resembles [the belief that] material objects are composed by the clustering of many parts. This sense is still not fully evident in Asaṅga's writings but in his way of speaking about things there is already this trend. As for Vasubandhu and later masters, compared with Asaṅga, it is evident that they changed the doctrine of conditioned arising into a structuralism.[57]

1.3 *Ti* and *yong*

Xiong also employed the *ti-yong* (體用) conceptual polarity to criticize dualism and pluralism, as well as to articulate his monism (nor non-dualism) via his views on the mind. Although generally still regarded as an endogenous Chinese philosophical construct, the philosophical development of the *ti-yong* polarity owes more to late Six Dynasties and Sui-Tang traditions of Sinitic Buddhist thought

56. Ibid., p. 92.

57. Xiong, *New Treatise*, vernacular version, p. 73.

than to Wei-Jin Profound Learning (*xuanxue* 玄學).[58] Xiong's understanding of *ti* as Fundamental Reality (*benti* 本體) or just Reality (*shiti* 實體) underscores this Sinitic Buddhist heritage, even if the *ti-yong* polarity was further developed in Neo-Confucian thought during the Song and Ming periods. For Xiong, *ti* and *yong* constitute a single whole and cannot be separated. It is on this basis that he proceeded to criticize various Yogācāra teachers, after first indicating his positive view of the Madhyamakan apophatic (*zhequan* 遮詮)[59] method:

> Since ancient times there have been many who have propounded mysterious words. The most sublime exponents of the apophatic mode of explanation are certainly the Buddhists, with the Emptiness School (Kong zong 空宗) [Madhyamaka or Sanlun in China] being especially skilled. Only they commanded a fully penetrating insight into the absolute (*li* 理) and so their theses encountered no obstacles. Only with the arrival of the Existence School (You zong 有宗)[60] did [Buddhists] begin to turn their back on the apophatic mode of explanation, instead advocating the manifestation of [Fundamental] Reality through function (*ji yong xian ti* 即用顯體). . . .
>
> Those who talk about "the manifestation of [Fundamental] Reality (*ti* 體)[61] through function" would certainly say that although function is also a real dharma (*shifa* 實法) it is not independent of Reality; that is, Reality is manifest through function. This, however, is to fail to understand that since there is certainly nothing in Fundamental Reality that can be established, then how can it be established in function? Suppose we presume that function can be established because it is a real dharma, then function already stands in contrast to Reality, so how can one talk about function's being able to manifest Fundamental Reality? . . .[62]

58. For relevant studies, see for example, Funayama Toru 船山徹, "Taiyō shōkō 體用小考" (On *Ti-yong*), in *Rikuchō Zui Tō seishinshi no kenkyū* 六朝隋唐精神史の研究 (Studies on the Psycho-Spiritual History in the Six Dynasties, Sui and Tang Periods), ed. Usami Bunri 宇佐美文理 (ed.), *A Report of Grant-in-Aid for Scientific Research, Japan Society for the Promotion of Science* (Kyoto, 2005), pp.125–135; Mou Zongsan, *Xinti yu xingti* 心體與性體 (Mind Itself and Nature Itself) (Taipei: Zhengzhong shuju, 1990), pp. 571–657; Huang Lianzhong 黃連忠, *Chanzong gong'an ti, xiang, yong sixiang zhi yanjiu* 禪宗公案體相用思想之研究 (Studies on Thought Concerning *Ti*, *Xiang*, and *Yong* on Chan Case Studies [*Gongan/Kōan*]) (Taipei: Xuesheng shuju, 2002), pp. 125–175.

59. Argument developed on the basis of what may not be said of something; *via negativa*.

60. Xiong, *New Treatise*, vernacular version, p. 79 says that this refers to the Yogācāra School established by Vasubandhu and Asaṅga.

61. Xiong, *New Treatise*, vernacular version, p. 79 explains that the term *ti* 體 here is a contraction of *benti* 本體.

62. Xiong, *New Treatise*, pp. 38–39.

Coming to Vasubandhu, he initiated the establishment of [the doctrine] that consciousness is the transformer (*nengbian* 能變)[63] and thereby controls dharmas. Later, Dharmapāla and Kuiji elaborated the main components of his teachings and expanded them, adding detail to [the function of] cause in [consciousness'] transformation (*nengbian yinti* 能變因體). ("Cause in [consciousness'] transformation" refers to seeds.) Crucially, everything that was established was done in regard to function. (On the basis that all dharmas are grounded within consciousness, Vasubandhu privileged consciousness as the transformer [*nengbian* 能變]. What he referred to as "dharmas [generated by consciousness] the transformer" [*nengbian fa* 能變法] was termed "function" when contrasted to unchanging "Suchness" [*zhenru* 眞如; (**tathatā*)].[64] Since Vasubandhu had established consciousness so as to ground dharmas, he thus established it as really existing in function. Vasubandhu and Kuiji developed this interpretation using the concept of "seeds." Using "consciousness" to name the manifest activity [of seeds], consciousness' existence was affirmed, and seeds were thus the cause from where "manifestly activated consciousness" [*xianxing shi* 現行識] was generated, and so were also the reality [體; (**dravya*)[65]] of manifestly activated consciousness. It is patently evident that they deemed function to have self-nature [*ziti* 自體]. Again, this was to establish [Fundamental Reality] in function and was in fact an elaboration of Vasubandhu's thought.) Yet they did not realize that they had made the mistake of severing Fundamental Reality and function in two. (What Vasubandhu and the others referred to as manifestly activated consciousness are dharmas that arise and cease; "dharmas [that are generated by consciousness'] capacity to transform"; and are function. Suchness, however, is a dharma that does not arise and cease; a dharma that does not transform. It is Reality. It is patently evident that they regarded Reality and function as two parts.) How can one talk about "manifesting Reality through function"?[66]

Consistent with his monism (or non-dualism), for Xiong there is nothing in ontological Reality that can be established, so the proposition that it can be established through function is meaningless. "As a word, 'function' refers to the flow of Reality

63. This refers to the capacity of consciousness to be transformed into a perceiving part and image part.

64. Xiong's implication here is that Dharmapāla had severed *ti* and *yong*, treating consciousness as *yong* relative to the *ti* of Suchness.

65. *Dravya*: that which is real and has causal function.

66. Xiong, *New Treatise*, p. 39.

and describes the appearance of Reality. There is no thing which appears, nor is there any rest in flow. Accordingly, [Reality] cannot be established in function."[67]

Xiong's position can be seen to be implicitly consistent with the views expressed in the *Dasheng qixin lun*, in that the latter does not present the phenomenal world as ontologically distinct from all-pervading, undifferentiated absolute reality (*dharmakāya*). Rather, it posits ignorance as hindering us from realizing that the phenomenal world lacks independent existence, self-nature, reality. This is a view that is also evident throughout much of the *New Treatise*.

2. *Nature Origination*

2.1 Transformation

From the perspective of conventional truth, however, the phenomenal world does exist. How, then, should the appearance of the phenomenal world (including mental phenomena) be explained? Xiong appeals to the concept of transformation (*zhuanbian* 轉變; [**pariṇāma*]) to explain phenomenal appearance. The transformation of consciousness is a key concept in Yogācāra philosophy of mind and cognitive epistemology. As we have seen, in order to establish his positive thesis, Xiong takes critical aim at the account of transformation presented in *Cheng weishi lun*, according to which consciousness—the mind—is bifurcated into a "transforming" (*nengbian* 能變) mode and a "transformed" (*suobian* 所變) mode. *Cheng weishi lun* presents all experience as contained within the transformations of consciousness. Consciousness' transformations into a perceiving part (subject) and image part (object) characterize a range of cognitive activities, including those of each of the eight consciousnesses. Karmic "seeds" (*bija*) or potentials emerge from the eighth or base consciousness (*ālayavijñāna*), giving rise to the "manifest activity" of the seven consciousnesses and causing or "perfuming" future seeds. As described by Tagawa Shun'ei:

> The seeds stored in the ālaya-vijñāna function to generate manifest activities. From this perspective, the causes are the seeds. Then, the manifest activities that were generated by the seeds immediately perfume impression-momentum seeds in the ālaya-vijñāna and in this way those manifest activities are the direct causes of those seeds. Thus there are two kinds of direct causes: seeds as direct cause and manifest activity as direct cause.[68]

Xiong's own account of transformation is presented as a direct challenge to, and radical departure from, the seeds-based causal theory found in *Cheng weishi*

---

67. Ibid., p. 39.

68. Tagawa Shun'ei, *Living Yogācāra: An Introduction to Consciousness-only Buddhism* (Boston, MA: Wisdom Publications, 2009), p. 50.

lun. Xiong sought to develop and defend an ontological account of transformation in which Reality (*shiti* 實體; *benti* 本體; [**tattva*]) is presented as nothing other than an uninterrupted holistic process of constant transformation (*heng zhuan* 恆轉) that cannot be reduced to subject-object characteristics. Doctrinally, it is consistent with such basic Mahāyāna teachings as emptiness (*kong* 空; *śūnyatā*) and conditioned arising (*yuanqi* 緣起; *pratītya-samutpāda*), and its critical edge is closely and explicitly informed by standard Madhyamaka deconstructive ploys. As we will see again later in this chapter, however, Xiong moves beyond a purely Madhyamaka perspective, to adopt a view that remains firmly entrenched in the conceptual genealogy of so-called nature origination (*xingqi* 性起): a doctrine developed in Huayan Buddhism to indicate "that all phenomenal appearances are nothing but manifestations of the nature.[69] Nature origination . . . goes beyond conditioned arising in locating an ultimate ontological basis for the phenomenal world."[70] Equally significant, "nature origination . . . [affirms] that all phenomenal appearances (*hsiang* 相) are nothing but a manifestation (*yung* 用) of the nature (*hsing* 性) that is their very essence (*t'i* 體)."[71]

"Transformation" is one of the concepts Xiong developed to present the absolute unity, and indeed nonduality, of the ontological and phenomenal. To this he wedded concepts taken from the *Book of Change*, adapting them to characterize transformation.

What is transformation? Xiong explains it is as follows:

> One contraction (*xi* 翕) and one expansion (*pi* 闢) is called transformation. (These two "one" words simply highlight different tendencies in dynamism.[72] This is not saying that contraction and expansion each have self-nature [*ziti* 自體]. Nor can one say that contraction precedes and expansion follows.) It

---

69. In the context of Sinitic Buddhism, "the nature" refers to Buddha-nature; for Xiong, it refers to Fundamental Reality.

70. Peter N. Gregory, *Inquiry into the Origin of Humanity: An Annotated Translation of Tsung-mi's Yüan jen lun with a Modern Commentary* (Honolulu: University of Hawai'i Press, 1950), p.18.

71. Ibid., p. 153.

72. Cf. Robyn Wang and Ding Weixiang's observation about Zhang Zai's 張載 (1020–1077) concept of *taixu* 太虛 (Ultimate Void):

> *Taixu* contains *qi*, yet it is not equal to or identical with *qi*. This is a central assumption of his ontology and moral teaching, and it enables Zhang to provide a metaphysical and ontological account of the myriad things. When *qi* coalesces the myriad things begin to exist; when *qi* disperses the myriad things disappear. This is analogous to the way water freezes when cold but evaporates when heated. These physical changes express a metaphysical necessity: "Ultimate Void cannot exist without *qi*; *qi* must coalesce to form the myriad things; the myriad things must disperse to return to the Ultimate Void."

> has always been [the case] that movement's constant transformation is continuous and without end. (Here "movement" is another name for "transformation." Just as the first movement ceases the next movement arises. It is like the uninterrupted flash upon flash of lightening—this is what is called "continuous." It is not a previous movement's continuing into a later moment of time that is called "continuous.")[73] . . . As contraction consolidates it comes close to being matter. It is the basis for nominally talking about material dharmas. The vigor of expansion is such that it is utterly unimpeded. It is the basis for nominally talking about mental dharmas. Because the material and the mental lack reality (*shishi* 實事; [**dravya*]) there is transformation only. ("Real" means real constitutive entity. This is because neither material nor mental dharmas have real self-nature).[74]

For Xiong, contraction is the basis for nominally talking about material dharmas—physical phenomena—and expansion is the basis for nominally talking about mental dharmas—mental phenomena.[75] (As such, contraction and expansion are conventional perspectives, not ultimate perspectives. It is important to bear this in mind.) Material dharmas are associated with the contracting tendency of constant transformation; mental dharmas are associated with the expanding tendency of constant transformation:

> It has always been the case that material and mental dharmas are devoid of self-nature. If one were to talk of their Reality (*shixing* 實性) then it would be constant transformation. Material dharmas are when the movement of constant transformation is contracting; mental dharmas are when the movement of the constant transformation is expanding. Fundamentally,

---

The key point is that *taixu* is in both the dispersion and the coalescence of *qi*. The main difference from Xiong's account of *xi* and *pi*, of course, is that Xiong is proposing an uncompromising monism. Robin Wang and Ding Weixiang, "Zhang Zai's Theory of Vital Energy," in *Dao Companion to Neo-Confucian Philosophy*, ed. John Makeham (New York: Springer, 2010), p 47. The locus classicus of *xi* 翕 and *pi* 闢 is *Book of Change*, "Xici Commentary A."

73. The connection with the Yogācāra concept of "continuous sequence of sameness condition" (*deng wu jian yuan* 等無間緣; one of the Four Conditions)—in which the preceding instant of consciousness extinguishes just as the following instant of consciousness is generated—is evident, and in part explains why Xiong is only minimally critical of this particular concept.

74. Xiong, *New Treatise*, p. 41.

75. In *abhidharma* teachings, dharmas are real and do not pass away; the composite things they constitute change from moment to moment, but dharmas remain. Madhyamaka theory construes dharmas as impermanent and dependently arisen. Xiong is clearly following this latter understanding.

contraction and expansion are separate and contrary trends in movement—this is transformation's unpredictability. Thus it appears to be like arising and ceasing. Yet although it seems to be an illusion it is real and not empty.[76]

For Xiong, the claim that there are real material objects and real minds is a misguided conceptual elaboration. Material and mental dharmas are devoid of self-nature. The various dharmas extinguish at the very moment of their generation. There is only the ceaseless flow of instant upon instant of generation and extinction. Rather, the Reality of material and mental dharmas is "constant transformation":

> I regard the self-nature (*zixing* 自性) of the phenomenal world to be inherently empty. ("*Zixing* 自性" here refers to "*ziti* 自體.") It exists only because of the attachments of false discrimination (妄情). ("Phenomenal world" is the collective name for the various material and mental dharmas that are conventionally attached to. If all of the material and mental dharmas appropriated by views based on false discrimination [*qingjian* 情見] and conceptions of the sixth consciousness [*yixiang* 意想] are cut away, then what thing can be named as the phenomenal world?") If one discerns that the phenomenal world in fact does not exist then one knows that there is no means for causes as condition (*yin yuan* 因緣) to be established. It is only because the phenomenal world to which false discriminations are attached is empty that inherent Reality (*shixing* 實性) which is not empty is able to be profoundly realized by means of proper attentiveness. ("Inherent" means "inherently so of itself" because it is not established by the conceptions constructed by the sixth consciousness. "Reality" is an alternative name for Fundamental Reality. "Attentiveness" [*zuoyi* 作意] means "reflection through accurate cognition" [*guanzhao* 觀照]. Correct wisdom reflected through accurate cognition tallies with the truth, and is far removed from deluded misguided conceptual elaboration, hence it is said: "proper attentiveness.") There has only ever been this Reality. Apart from it there is no phenomenal world to which it stands in contrast. (Grasping neither material nor mental images, and also grasping neither non-material nor non-mental images; being far removed from all conceptual realms [constructed by] the sixth consciousness, in profound mystery that which is encountered is True, and in profound stillness Fundamental Reality is revealed. Could there additionally be a phenomenal realm to which this stands in contrast and which can be talked of?) It is for this reason that

76. Xiong, *New Treatise*, p. 48.

> in talking about productive power I define it on the basis of Reality and do not explain it in terms of causes as condition. (Once the phenomenal world has been dispatched, what causes as condition is there to talk of?)[77]

In other words, just as with the analogy of the ocean and waves employed in *Dasheng qixin lun*, phenomena are not different from Fundamental Reality. In themselves, however, they have no self-nature, no independent existence.[78]

Elsewhere Xiong explains that he used the concept of productive power—which he presents as the dynamic aspect of Fundamental Reality—as a skillful means, an expedient:

> In the chapters "Transformation" and "Productive Power," I nominally established [the concept] of constantly transforming productive power in order to highlight the flow of Fundamental Reality. I nominally established this term so as to show that mental and material dharmas both took flow or transformation as their basis. As with the *Prajñāpāramitā* literature [teaching of] the inherent emptiness of conditioned phenomena and their characteristics, this leads people to begin to grasp the import of Reality. Although the establishment of this concept [on the basis of] skillful means (*fangbian* 方便) seems to differ [in approach] from that of the Mahāyāna Madhyamaka School, the end goal is certainly the same—this is beyond question.[79]

In addressing the topic of material dharmas—physical phenomena— in Chapter 5 of *New Treatise*, "Demonstration of Material [Dharmas], A (成色上), Xiong aims to provide an explanation for conventional accounts of the material world. At the heart of conventional accounts, we are told, is the view that physical phenomena offer physical resistance. Xiong explains that in reality there is no resistance; what we deludedly take to be resistance is actually the process of "constant operation" in which the movement or transformation of phenomena—dharmas—seems to tend toward contraction. Contrary to the conventional

77. Ibid., p. 54.

78. This perspective has obvious connections with the notion of *li shi wu ai* 理事無礙 (the unobstructed interpretation of the absolute and the phenomenal) as interpreted by the Huayan thinker Fazang in relation to the *Dasheng qixin lun*. See Peter N. Gregory, *Tsung-mi and the Sinification of Buddhism* (Honolulu: University of Hawai'i Press, 2002), pp. 157ff.

79. See Xiong Shili, "Jiangci 講詞" (Speech), *Shili lunxueyu jilüe* 十力論學語輯略 (Edited Collection of Xiong's Shili's Discussions on Scholarship), in *Xiong Shili quanji*, vol. 2, p. 253. The speech was given in 1935.

view, because of the nature of constant operation, phenomena—having no self-nature—offer no resistance. As the process of transformation coheres (*sheju* 攝聚), there is apparent contraction: "the illusory construction of countless moving points."[80] As stated in Chapter 2 of *New Treatise*: "Constantly coalescing, and so without any prearranged agreement, countless points of movement are illusorily constituted, the tendency of which seems to be towards solidifying—this is called 'contraction.'"[81] These moving points—analogous to atoms— appear to have material form but do not.

Xiong also employs the concepts of contraction (*xi* 翕) and expansion (*pi* 闢) to elucidate mind and its relation to Reality. Mind, just like phenomena, does not have real existence—it is devoid of a discrete self-nature. There is, however, a self-nature or Reality that makes mind possible. This self-nature or Reality is called constant transformation or constant operation. As the expression of the power of constant operation's self-nature, mind is not different from constant transformation and so is not different from Reality.[82] "It is not the case that the mind is identical to Fundamental Reality (心非即本體也).[83] Nevertheless, because the mind definitely is not transformed by things therefore it may be said that the mind is not different from Fundamental Reality (心即本體耳)."[84] The implicit premise here is that Reality and mind stand in a relationship of *ti* and *yong*.

Thus, on the one hand, "mind does not have a real self-nature within itself." Yet, on the other hand, mind as Reality is transcendent: "This mind has no 'you' and 'me,' and is not constrained by time or space; it is an undifferentiated [whole] without duality and distinctions, and is inexhaustible and without end. . . . The mind of a single person or a single thing is the mind of heaven and earth and the myriad things. This is not something that physical substance can separate and so they are thoroughly interconnected."[85] In providing this description Xiong

---

80. Xiong, *New Treatise*, pp. 72–73.

81. Ibid., p. 41.

82. This is reminiscent of the two aspects of the one mind (*yixin kai ermen* 一心開二門) in the *Dasheng qixin lun*. In its true aspect it is the mind as Suchness, the all-pervading, undifferentiated absolute reality (*dharmakāya*). It its other aspect (its conventional aspect), it is the mind that is subject to birth-and-death; and identified with the *ālayavijñāna*, but grounded in *tathāgatagarbha*. The *ālayavijñāna* also has two modes: an enlightened mode equivalent to the undifferentiated absolute body (*dharmakāya*) of the Buddha, and an unenlightened mode.

83. This is analogous to mind as subject to birth-and-death or the unenlightened mode of *ālayavijñāna*.

84. Xiong, *New Treatise*, p. 83. This is analogous to mind as Suchness or the enlightened mode of *ālayavijñāna*.

85. Ibid., p. 81.

explicitly references the Huayan 華嚴 doctrines of "one and many are united" and "layer upon endless layer." Here mind can be seen to be consistent with the Huayan doctrine of the unobstructed interpenetration of the absolute and the phenomenal (*li shi wu ai* 理事無礙), as propounded by the Huayan and Chan patriarch Guifeng Zongmi 圭峰宗密 (780–841).[86]

2.2 Mind: movement and quiescence

The question of whether the mind is quiescent or moving occupied Xiong for much of his life, and became a key issue of contention in the series of exchanges he had with Lü Cheng 呂澂 (1896–1989) in 1943.[87] Throughout most of the 1920s Xiong upheld the view that the ontological character of the mind was transformation alone. Under the influence of Ma Yifu 馬一浮 (1883–1967), however, beginning in 1929, Xiong adopted the view that the mind was characterized simultaneously by transformation (change, activity, movement) and constancy (quiescence; being undisturbed). He continued to uphold this view until the mid-1950s when he finally reverted to the view he had originally maintained in the 1920s.[88] In the *New Treatise*, Xiong expresses this view of constancy in change as follows:

> Whether moving or at rest it is as one; dissolving the divisions of time and space. (This mind does indeed flow incessantly yet it is also profoundly tranquil and undisturbed. In regard to its incessant flow it is nominally termed "moving." In regard to its undisturbed, profound tranquility it is nominally termed "at rest." Being both in motion and at rest it is devoid of the characteristic of continuously arising, and so time cannot be securely established. Being both in motion and at rest yet lacking a domain, space cannot be securely established either.) Extremely subtle yet manifest; extremely close at hand yet god-like. Empty and devoid of characteristics yet replete with a myriad phenomena.[89] (Hence it says "Extremely subtle yet manifest.") Without arising from its seat yet extending all over the

86. See Gregory, *Tsung-mi and the Sinification of Buddhism*, pp. 158–165.

87. On this debate, see Lin Chen-kuo's chapter in this volume.

88. See Li Qingliang 李清良, "Lun Ma Yifu dui Xiong Shili *Xin weishi lun* zhi yingxiang 論馬一浮對熊十力《新唯識論》之影響" (The Influence of Ma Yifu on Xiong Shili's *Xin weishi lun*), *Taiwan Dong-Ya wenming yanjiu xuekan* 臺灣東亞文明研究學刊 7, no. 1 (2010): 201–232.

89. This phrase is attributed to Cheng Yi in Cheng Yi and Cheng Hao 程顥 (1032–1085), *Henan Cheng shi yishu* 河南程氏遺書 (Surviving Works of the Cheng Brothers), in *Er Cheng ji* 二程集 (Collected Works of the Cheng Brothers) (Beijing: Zhonghua shuju, 1981), p. 153.

> dharma-realm (*fajie* 法界).[90] (A verse [*gāthā*] from the *Flower Ornament Sutra* [*Avataṃsaka-sūtra*; *Huayan jing* 華嚴經] says: "According to conditions, one follows one's feelings and nothing is out of place, yet all the while one constantly occupies the seat of enlightenment.")[91]

Although the phenomenal appearances of arising and ceasing, change and movement, never cease for a moment, they are not real and do not abide even momentarily. They are what they are because of what we mistakenly impute to them through deluded attachment. Xiong is at pains to draw our attention to the ceaseless flow of these phenomenal appearances because it is in this ceaseless flow that inherent nature/Reality is revealed. "One's inherent nature has always been just as it is. Since it has not transformed into something different, it is said neither to change nor to move."[92]

This, in turn, provides the key to interpreting a series of paradoxes and seeming contradictions:

> Arising is non-arising (*sheng ji wu sheng* 生即無生) because arising does not exist (*bu you* 不有). ("Does not exist" means that there is nothing serving as an obstruction.) Ceasing is non-ceasing (*mie ji fei mie* 滅即非滅) because ceasing does not rest (*bu xi* 不息). ("Does not rest" and so is not empty nothingness.) Change is unchanging (*bian ji bu bian* 變即不變) because change is always constant (*zhen* 貞). ("Constant" is to be firm and immovable. Because something is always just like its nature it is referred to as "ever constant" [*heng zhen* 恒貞]. This is because with things and with people, with ordinary people and with sages, their natures never change. It is just like water—even though it is able to become ice, it does not lose its water-nature.) Movement is non-moving (*dong ji fei dong* 動即非動) because movement does not shift. (Master Zhao's 肇公 "Wu bu qian lun 物不遷論" [Things Do Not Shift Treatise] develops this thesis.[93] The Well (*jing* 井) Hexagram in *Change* says: "The well stays in its place [but its

---

90. Dharma-realm is the universe as the Buddha sees it and so co-extensive with everything. This is the universe that features in the key scripture of Huayan Buddhism: *Huayan jing*.

91. Xiong, *New Treatise*, p. 11.

92. Ibid., p. 69.

93. This is a reference to the Buddhist monk Sengzhao 僧肇 (384–414?). Besides being a translator he also wrote a series of philosophical essays on topics such as change, *prajñā*, emptiness, and *nirvāṇa*, collected in the book *Zhao lun* 肇論 (Essays by Shi Sengzhao). In English, see for example, Walter Liebenthal, *The Chao Lun: The Treatises of Seng-Chao*, 2nd rev. ed. (Hong Kong: Hong Kong University Press, 1968). In the original text of Sengzhao's

water always] shifts."[94] "Shifts" is "to flow." This says it flows inexhaustibly yet it always stays in its place, and so it still means does not shift.) When this is understood, "Suchness" will be manifest in each of the ten-thousand things. (Reality cannot be sought independent of phenomena.) The True Ruler (*zhen zai* 真宰) is to be discerned amongst the flow [of phenomena] (The True Ruler does not refer to a spirit or a god. The True Ruler is said to be that which has regularity and cannot be thrown into disarray within this flowing. It is like when we are confronted by a bewildering array of feelings and yet in the midst of these feelings there is always a profound calm, all of one's responses are perfectly appropriate, and one is able to have the restraint not to seek for things. This is the meaning of True Ruler.) and in activity it does not stop being still. (*Zhuangzi* says: "To abide in silence and yet be as manifest as a dragon." "To abide in silence" means to be still, and "to be as manifest as a dragon" means to be active. To issue forth and to stop—movement and stillness are one.)[95]

"Nonarising," "nonceasing," "nonchanging," and "nonmoving" are all references to inherent nature, to Fundamental Reality. Arising, ceasing, change, and movement are references to phenomenal appearances. That which ontologically underpins nonexistent phenomenal arising is this nonindividuated inherent nature which itself is nonarising. That which ontologically underpins phenomenal ceasing is this nonindividuated inherent nature which itself is nonceasing. That which ontologically underpins phenomenal change is this nonindividuated inherent nature which itself is unchanging. And that which ontologically underpins phenomenal movement is this nonindividuated inherent nature which itself is nonmoving. Failure to see this is due either to attachment to things or to being mired in the notion of emptiness, the belief that absolutely nothing exists:

---

essay "Things No Not Shift" (Wu bu qian lun 物不遷論), the unstated premise here is that no event can depart from its moment of occurrence and move to another moment of occurrence (CBETA, T45n1858_p0151a08-51c29). This enabled Sengzhao to argue that past things are stationary and do not move. Past things do not reach the present because they do not move from the past to the present. If they move they would not be past things. Here Xiong is not interested in this original argument.

94. "Xici, shang 繫辭上" (Appended Statements, A), *Zhou Yi* 周易 (Book of Change), 7.15a, *Shisan jing zhushu* 十三經注疏 (The Thirteen Classics with annotations and subcommentaries) edition, comp. Ruan Yuan 阮元 (1764–1849) (Taipei: Yiwen yinshuguan, 1985), 8.18a. Xiong's interpretation differs from the standard one given by Kong Yingda 孔穎達 (574–648) in *Zhou yi zhushu* according to which it is the village or hamlet that changes over time but the well stays in its place.

95. Xiong, *New Treatise*, pp. 69–70.

> From talking about arising without yet understanding that arising is nonarising, right through to talking about moving without yet understanding that moving is nonmoving—this is to be attached to things. From talking about nonarising without yet understanding the arising of nonarising, right through to talking about moving without yet understanding the moving of nonmoving—this is to be mired in emptiness.[96]

Being mired in emptiness blinds one to the Absolute (*shiji li di* 實際理地), to Reality, to the nature, which can be affirmed only by introspection, by self-realization. Being attached to things is caused by a failure to understand that phenomenal appearances have no self-nature; by looking no further than conventional truth. "It is due to following conventional truth that the mundane world is accepted as proven. Earth is nothing but earth, water is nothing but water, right through to the myriad existents. . . . Because absolute truth is experienced, however, there is a categorical refutation of conventional knowing. Hence, earth is not thought of as earth, because earth's nature is empty. What is manifest before one is Reality (真體), perfectly clear." Xiong asserts that phenomenal appearance—the world established by conventional truth—is, in fact, nothing other than Suchness. "Reality cannot be sought independent of phenomena" and "the True Ruler (*zhen zai* 真宰) is to be discerned amongst the flow [of phenomena]."[97]

Here Xiong might seem to affirm the Madhyamakan thesis that absolute and conventional truths are ultimately identical. However, whereas a thoroughgoing Madhyamakan perspective would insist that emptiness is itself empty, that emptiness is also conditioned because it depends on a network of conditions and has no self-nature, Xiong effectively posits Fundamental Reality/Suchness/Original Nature/the Absolute as an underlying "locus" on which phenomenal/conventional reality is ontologically grounded.

2.3 Inseparability of *xing* and *qi*

Arguing that "Reality cannot be sought independent of phenomena" and that "the True Ruler is to be discerned amongst the flow [of phenomena]" provides Xiong with a basis on which to present his account of the relationship between productive power and habituated tendencies; the nature (*xing* 性) and form-and-vital stuff (*xingqi* 形氣); and *li* 理 and *qi* 氣. This is a further elaboration of his understanding of the *ti-yong* polarity, and is consistent with the nature origination thesis.

---

96. Ibid., p. 70.

97. Idem.

One of Xiong's (many) criticisms of Dharmapāla concerns the concept of "productive power" (*gongneng* 功能). As we have seen, Xiong described Reality as nothing other than an uninterrupted holistic process of constant transformation that cannot be reduced to subject-object characteristics, which he characterized as "constantly operating." "With regard to incessantly transforming Fundamental Reality, when the power of its movement is broken down (*fenxi* 分析), it is said to be an alternation of one contraction and one expansion. In directly treating incessantly transforming Fundamental Reality as a category it is called constant operation."[98] He also refers to constant operation as "productive power." Productive power can be understood to be the dynamic aspect of Fundamental Reality.

Xiong identifies three main differences between his understanding of productive power and that of Dharmapāla. First, whereas for Dharmapāla productive power is synonymous with seeds, for Xiong productive power is a further characterization of Reality (albeit like all verbal characterizations it is employed nominally, as a skillful/expedient means.) The second main difference is that for Xiong, productive power is the totality of all things, whereas for Dharmapāla it is individuated: "Taking productive power to be the causal condition for the phenomenal world Dharmapāla divided the phenomenal world into numerous discrete constitutive entities."[99] The third main difference, according to Xiong, is Dharmapāla's conflation of habituated tendencies with productive power by treating habituated tendencies as seeds. Habituated tendencies are the karmic residue of past actions: "It is like when burnt incense has extinguished and there still remains a lingering smell."[100] As Xiong explains, there are said to be two types of seeds: those that have always existed and are already stored in the *ālaya* consciousness when a sentient being is born and which give rise to the "manifest activity" of the seven consciousnesses; and seeds that begin to arise: "This refers to the first seven consciousnesses' perpetual perfuming of habituated tendencies (*xiqi* 習氣),"[101] thus causing future seeds. Dharmapāla's "fundamental error" lay in "his conflation of habituated tendencies with productive power, thus leading him to say that in addition to productive power which had existed without a beginning there were productive powers which began to arise."[102]

Xiong instead proposes using the concepts of heaven (*tian* 天) and humans (*ren* 人) to elucidate the relationship between productive power and form-and-vital-stuff:

98. Ibid., p. 53.

99. Ibid., p. 56.

100. Ibid., p. 56.

101. Ibid., p. 56.

102. Ibid., p. 59.

> Productive power is a heavenly matter; habituated tendencies are a human capacity. . . . "Heaven" does not refer to an independently existing god in some external sphere but rather refers to the principles by which humans are able to live. "Humans" are all those who, ever since the beginningless existence of sentient beings, have brought to completion their productive power, retaining it with self-made [karma], so bringing to completion their own individual life. . . . Habituated tendencies begin together with the body. For example, in human life the existence of this body and also the physical world this body encounters are collectively called "form-and-vital-stuff." We have form-and-vital-stuff to enable us to live, and habituated tendencies commence together with them. As for productive power, it is that by which form-and-vital-stuff is constituted and is the controller of form-and-vital-stuff.[103]

Xiong further endorses the view that this distinction between productive power and form-and-vital-stuff is like the Neo-Confucian distinction between the moral nature (*yili zhi xing* 義理之性) and the psychophysical nature (*qizhi zhi xing* 氣質之性) but emphasizes that because of the vital role the nature plays in coalescing the psychophysical, "one cannot talk of the nature independent of the psycho-physical":

> [Cheng] Yichuan 程伊川 [1033–1107][104] said that the moral nature is simply the name given to the original goodness in the psycho-physical [nature]. In other words, it is simply to talk of the principle by which the psycho-physical [nature] coalesces. Thus the moral nature and the psycho-physical nature do not exist as two. Many Ming *ru* ridiculed Yichuan for saying that there were two roots [to human nature]. They had not grasped Yichuan's meaning. The [idea of a] psycho-physical nature had originally been developed by [Zhang] Hengqu 張橫渠 (1020–1077),[105] and the two Cheng brothers[106] both adopted his teaching. [Cheng] Mingdao 程明道 [1032–1085][107] also said: "To talk of the nature without talking of vital stuff (氣) is incomplete; to talk of vital stuff without talking of the nature is unclear. To treat them as two is wrong." It is thus evident that the nature includes vital stuff within it such that it is all pervasive; it cannot be separated

103. Ibid,, p. 60.

104. Major Neo-Confucian philosopher.

105. Zhang Zai 張載, another major Neo-Confucian philosopher.

106. Cheng Yi 程頤 (Yichuan 程伊川) and Cheng Hao 程顥 (Mingdao 明道).

107. Neo-Confucian philosopher.

> into two. In commenting on the passage in the *Analects* "[Humans] by nature are close to one another" [17.2], in his *Collected Annotations on the Analects* Zhu Xi 朱熹 [1130–1200] said: "Here 'human nature' collectively refers to the psycho-physical."[108] He used the word "collectively" precisely because the inherent nature exists within the psycho-physical.[109]

Xiong's "concept matching" does not stop there—he further suggests that the relation between productive power and habituated tendencies can be understood in terms of principles (*li*) and vital stuff (*qi*): "As for productive power, it is that by which form-and-vital-stuff are able to be constituted and is the controller of form-and-vital-stuff. Thus its wondrousness (*lingmiao* 靈妙) can be described as god-like, and the models it provides as it issues forth are also called principles."[110] The vexed issue of the relationship between *li* and *qi* was central to Neo-Confucian metaphysics, due in large part to an obfuscation between the goal of giving *li* a logical priority over *qi* (so that there would be a "pattern/norm" for a given thing to conform to and hence exist), and the actual ontological and temporal privileging of *li* over *qi*. With Zhu Xi, for example, *li* (*ti*) reveals its function through *qi* (*yong*). He did not, however, always preserve the immanence of *li* within *qi* and thus opened the way for centuries of philosophical debate not only in China but in Korea and Japan as well. Even though Zhu seems to have wanted merely to give *li* a logical priority over *qi* (so that there would be a "pattern/norm" for a given thing to conform to and hence exist), he is widely held to have regarded *li* as ontologically and temporally prior to *qi*. This ambiguity or ambivalence is in consequence of his decision to use terms that convey a temporal sequence such that *li* seems to precede the existence of *qi*. Curiously, this particular controversy continued well into the twentieth century and was discussed as part of Feng Youlan's 馮友蘭 (1895–1990) New Principle-centered Learning (*Xin lixue* 新理學). A good case can also be made that it is prefigured in *Dasheng qixin lun*.

Xiong avoided the trap of granting Suchness/Reality/the nature/productive power a temporal precedence over the phenomenal world by insisting that "one cannot talk of the nature independently of the psycho-physical. . . . The moral nature (*yili zhi xing* 義理之性) and the psycho-physical nature *xing* (*qizhi zhi xing* 氣質之性) do not exist as two. . . . The nature includes vital stuff within it such that it is all pervasive; they cannot be separated into two."[111]

---

108. See my discussion of this passage in *Transmitters and Creators: Chinese Commentators and Commentaries on the Analects* (Cambridge, MA: Harvard University Asia Center, 2003), pp. 213–214.

109. Xiong, *New Treatise*, p. 64.

110. Ibid., p. 60.

111. Ibid., p. 64.

2.4 Theodicy

The topic of theodicy—How does evil arise if God is omniscient and omnipotent?—is another example of the connection between the *New Treatise* and *Dasheng qixin lun*. If, following the idea of inherent enlightenment (*benjue* 本覺)—that all sentient beings are already enlightened[112]—then how is ignorance of our intrinsic enlightenment to be explained? The notion of "one mind two aspects" (*yixin kai ermen* 一心開二門) in *Dasheng qixin lun* is relevant here. Starting from the premise that one mind is the ultimate source of all phenomena, the scripture proposes that this one mind has two aspects. The first aspect is characterized by an original, pristine, pure Buddha-nature intrinsic in all things (*tathāgatagarbha*); the all-pervading, undifferentiated absolute reality (*dharmakāya*). The second aspect is characterized as being subject to birth-and-death. Although this aspect of mind is identified with the base consciousness (*ālayavijñāna*), and hence contains both pure and impure seeds, it is ultimately grounded in *tathāgatagarbha*. Only ignorance prevents us from realizing the fundamental unity of the two aspects of the one mind.

Having noted that the identification of the *ālayavijñāna* with the *tathāgatagarbha* served to ground "the process of conditioned arising on an intrinsically pure ontological foundation," Peter Gregory points out that

> this means that the defilements that appear to obscure the intrinsically enlightened mind of Suchness are merely the manifestation of that mind as it accords with conditions and have no independent basis of their own. The relationship between the tathāgatagarbha and the ālayavijñāna is thus the basis on which the Hua-yen tradition establishes its theory of nature origination and is the central issue in terms of which it distinguishes its type of Yogācāra from that of the Fa-hsiang [法相; dharma characteristics[113]].[114]

As Gregory argues, however, whereas "conditioned arising posits no ultimate ontological basis" enabling it to be claimed that ignorance is beginningless, *tathāgatagarbha* theory was unable to escape the problem of the origin of ignorance.[115] Moreover, in introducing the concept of *ālayavijñāna*, the author of

---

112. This, in turn, is a Chinese elaboration of the *tathāgatagarbha* doctrine: the potentiality for Buddhahood exists embryonically in us of all.

113. This refers to Yogācāra thought associated with Xuanzang and Kuiji. It was a term used by those associated with the Huayan School to distinguish their own self-identification as Faxing 法性 or dharma nature.

114. Gregory, *Inquiry into the Origin of Humanity*, p. 191.

115. Ibid., p. 18.

Dasheng qixin lun did not avoid the ontological problem of theodicy, but only raised it in an altered guise.[116]

While also emphasizing the centrality of the theodicy question in the *Dasheng qixin lun*, Dan Lusthaus is more sanguine that the text did succeed in formulating a solution: "Far from ignoring or giving short shrift to the theodicy question, as has usually been assumed, the main thrust of the text is to provide an answer—in fact, numerous, interweaved answers—to that question." Lusthaus focuses on a key passage that "attempts to explain, step by step, analogy by analogy, model by model, how exactly the relations between inherent awakening, non-awakening, initial awakening and final awakening work. Without understanding how non-awakening depends on inherent awakening, AF [*Awakening of Mahāyāna Faith*] seems to say, neither initial nor final awakening can be possible."[117]

Xiong is vague as to how the afflicted mind—defiled mental associates—first arose, seeming to assume the conditioned arising premise:

> Ever since beginningless time, because afflictions occur together with life, they are intimately connected to the physical form, and have never been severed. Their appearance is like following a familiar path, and so they arise automatically without one even being aware of it.[118]

---

116. Peter N. Gregory, "The Problem of Theodicy in the Awakening of Faith," *Religious Studies* 22, no. 1(1986): 73–74.

117. Dan Lusthaus, "Why, If We Are Originally Enlightened, Is There Non-Enlightenment? The Awakening of Faith's Neglected Answers," unpublished draft paper presented at the Annual Meeting of the American Academy of Religion, Philadelphia, Nov. 18–22, 2005, p. 3. Lusthaus further argues (p. 5) that the *Awakening of Mahāyāna Faith* "plays on several meanings of the term 'awakening' 覺 *jue*, which also can mean 'to be aware of.' Mind is, by nature, awareness. Only when it is aware of its own aware nature, from the moment a thought arises—and thus not distracted by that thought—does it coincide with its original nature." Xiong's following comments (*New Treatise*, p. 145) are consistent with these comments about thought:

> An old saying says: "As soon as we cease our thoughts, then it will be just as it has always been."* This is to be awoken to the pure function (*jingyong* 淨用) of one's mind;** that there has never been anything separating us from [our inherent nature]; that the various afflictions are false; and that upon illumination they are seen to be empty.

*Daoyuan 道原 (comp.), *Jingde chuan deng lu* 景德傳燈錄, CBETA, T51n2076_p0219c16.
** That is, to overcome defiled habituated tendencies, ignorance; to realize one's original nature. The term "pure function" comes from the *Dasheng qixin lun*, CBETA, T32n1667_p0586c01. Even ignorance is ultimately "perfumed" by Suchness. Pure habituated tendencies allow us to realize this.

118. Xiong, *New Treatise*, p. 129.

For no particular reason, human life is endowed with a mass of innate confusion. (Note the phrase "For no particular reason." This benightedness was never an intrinsic part of original nature; it is just that when we are born there is this confusion that occurs together with our life. "Occurs together": because they merely exist with one another, one does not precede the other.)[119]

Human life is constrained by the physical body, and then there are the demons of affliction[120] which arrive without being caused, resulting in [humans'] misleading themselves about their origin.[121]

According to Xiong, mental associates are the manifest activity (*xianxing* 現行) of habituated tendencies. Afflictions are impure mental associates, clusters of "delusional forces that consolidate and do not disperse," arising "only after the human form and spirit issue forth." The accumulation of habituated tendencies means that when cognitive objects are cognized, this leads to attachment to particular characteristics such as "pleasant" and "unpleasant" and so forth, prompting Xiong to contrast mind and mental associates: "Mind is not different from the nature, whereas mental associates are but habituated tendencies. Their fundamental difference is as starkly clear as this." So long as mental associates obey the mind, assist the mind, and remain subservient to the mind, then all will be well. Mental associates will also be the nature because the mind is not different from the nature. If, however, defiled mental associates (*ranshu* 染數) are given free rein, they will attack the nature. "When habituated tendencies attack the nature, the mind cannot be seen, and so the mental associates alone are taken to be the mind. This is what is referred to as deluded mind. Deluded mind is also called deluded consciousness."[122] He further relates that humans have so severed themselves from the inherent principle—the nature—that has always been within us, many of us are not even aware of its existence.

How then is this "mass of innate confusion"[123] able to influence and even control the physical body?

Previously, had I not stated "productive power is a matter for heaven; habituated tendencies are a human capacity"? As the human comes to take

119. Ibid., p. 119–120.

120. This refers to defiled mental associates, a topic taken up in detail below.

121. Xiong, *New Treatise*, p. 86.

122. Ibid., p. 104.

123. Ibid., p. 119.

> control the nature becomes hidden. Thus, with [habituated tendencies'] accumulation on the physical body it becomes difficult to follow one's [nature] as it originally is. (Habituated tendencies start together with the physical body and so habituated tendencies are accumulations on the physical body. If they are defiled habituated tendencies then they are always in close proximity to the physical body and are contrary to one's inherent life principles. Although undefiled habituated tendencies accord with the heavenly-bestowed nature it is extremely difficult to foster and nurture them.)[124]

> Because the mind is not different from the nature (心者即性), it has always been there (*benlai* 本來). Mental associates are habituated tendencies and arise subsequently.[125] That which has always been there is free. (It operates freely.[126]) That which arises subsequently is conditioned (*youwei* 有為). That which has always been there is pure and without defilement; that which arises subsequently brings together both wholesome and defiled mental associates. That which has always been there is "host." (It is this inherent nature alone that is the life of humans. Accordingly, in relation to subsequently arising habituated tendencies it is said to be the host.) The subsequently arising habituated defiled mental associates obstruct the inherent [nature] and so, on the contrary, the host becomes the "guest." (To be without a basis is to be a guest. Being obstructed, the inherent mind is not revealed; and although it exists, it is as if it does not; hence it is said to be the "guest.") That which arises subsequently is the guest; defilements, however, overcome and obstruct that which has always been there, and so the guest becomes the host.[127]

And even though defiled mental associates overcome and obstruct the mind/the nature, Xiong maintains that this is necessary: "If there were no afflictions, then there would be no *prajñā* either. Thus all defilements are the seeds of *rulai* 如來 [*tathāgata*].[128] Confucius said: 'As long as the way prevails in the world [I] will not join them in changing the world.' "[129] This is because when one realizes the

---

124. Ibid., p. 63.

125. They are not inherent in the nature.

126. It is unconditioned and nondeliberative.

127. Xiong, *New Treatise*, p. 141.

128. A reference to the buddhas who have shown the way.

129. Xiong, *New Treatise*, p. 125. This is Confucius's response in *Analects* 18.6 to the suggestion that he, too, might join some recluses and flee the conventional world. The inference is that Confucius realized that the conventional world provides the ground for awakening.

emptiness of afflictions, the role of conditioned arising in their generation, and their fundamental lack of self-nature, then one's perspective is able to move from conventional truth to ultimate truth. The thrust of Xiong's comments would thus seem to be consistent with the thesis proposed in the *Dasheng qixin lun* that non-awakening depends on inherent awakening.

2.5 The nonduality of nature and practice

In the *New Treatise,* Xiong describes how "good mental associates" counteract the afflictions of defiled mental associates, driving them into submission and eventually eliminating them. Further, in order to be able to recover our inherent human nature we must rely upon pure dharmas (*jingfa* 淨法) (pure habituated tendencies, good mental associates):

> Although the nature inherently exists, if it is concealed and not revealed, then it does not constitute the [fully realized] nature. Hence the fact that people themselves are able to create the power of pure [habituated tendencies] so as to recover the nature (*fu xing* 復性) means that this inherently existing nature is no different from one constituted through people creating it anew.[130]

And "even though we are situated within impurities, because of the power of this self-nature, pure dharmas continuously arise."[131] Xiong describes this reliance on pure dharmas as "learning (*xue* 學)" and (paranomastically) glosses learning as "awakening (*jue* 覺)":

> "Learning" means "awakening." In learning, the thorough realization of principle (*qiongli* 窮理) is fundamental; and fully revealing the nature (*jinxing* 盡性) is its final goal. Thoroughly tracing dharmas to their source is what is meant by "thorough realization"; being neither deficient nor in excess is what is meant by "fully revealing." The nature is not different from inherent pure mind; and principle is not different from the principle by which the mind is self-sufficient. They are not fused from outside, nor are they to be sought from others. It is up to you students to experience them personally and to discern them clearly.[132]

---

130. Xiong, *New Treatise,* p. 145. It should be borne in mind, however, that without the inherent nature, this capacity to create the nature, a new would not be possible.

131. Ibid., p. 141.

132. Ibid., p. 142.

The importance of learning is said to be twofold. First, it enables one to realize that psychophysical form is not only not harmful to the nature, it *is* the nature (or perhaps more precisely, it is not different from the nature—again implying a *ti-yong* relationship): "If there were no physical form, then the nature would also be unable to be seen. Psycho-physical form is the coalescence of the nature—that is, psycho-physical form is nothing other than the nature."[133] The villain in the piece is habituated tendencies, which occur together with psychophysical form and gradually obscure the nature. When, however, the nature controls psychophysical form, the power of wholesome habituated tendencies increases and becomes associated with the nature:

> The Buddhists say that when the five aggregates (*wu yin* 五陰) are replete this is [the cause of] suffering[134] because they conceal the mind of the matrix of the buddhas (*rulaizang xin* 如來藏心). If one transforms one's understanding of the five aggregates from that of the perspective of sentient beings to that of the perspective of the true nature of things (*faxing* 法性), then the gate-keepers of the six sense faculties[135] will all become pure qualities.[136]

Second, learning is important because it enables us to realize that the nature and practice are not two. The contrast between the nature—representing ultimate truth, Suchness, and so forth—and practice is a tension with a long history in traditional Chinese philosophy.[137] In the following passage, Xiong presents the

---

133. Ibid., p. 143.

134. Xiong is deviating from standard Buddhist accounts of *wu yin sheng ku* 五陰盛苦, which refers to suffering caused by human existence's consisting of nothing other than the five aggregates. This is one of the "four and eight kinds of suffering" (四苦八苦).

135. The six sense faculties pursue the five sensory fields and the thought-field and only then are the six consciousnesses produced. "Gate-keepers" is simply another name for the six sense faculties.

136. Xiong, *New Treatise*, p. 144.

137. In this connection, Lin Zhenguo's (Lin Chen-kuo) 林鎮國 discussion of early Chinese controversies surrounding such concepts as *lixing* 理性 and *xingxing* 行性 is particularly instructive. See his "Zhenli yu yishi: cong Foxing lunzheng dao Zhu-Lu yitong de er zhong zhexue leixing 真理與意識---從佛性論爭到朱陸異同的二種哲學類型 (Truth and Consciousness: From Buddha-nature Debates to the Two Kinds of Philosophical Types [Represented in] the Differences between Zhu Xi and Lu Xiangshan), *Guoli Zhengzhi Daxue zhexue xuebao* 28(2012): 1–46. For another very useful survey, see Liao Minghuo 廖明活, *Zhongguo Foxing sixiang de xingcheng he fazhan* 中國佛性思想的形成和發展 (The Development of Chinese Buddha-nature Thought) (Taipei: Wenjin chubanshe, 2008), pp. 280–304.

nature and practice as complementary. Cultivation is the continuation and application of the positive qualities associated with the nature:

> *Change* says: "that which continues this is goodness; that which completes it is the nature."[138] The whole that is the nature gives rise to practice and this is called "continuing." (The nature is the incessant flow of the whole; it is the full endowment of the myriad good qualities. Hence, by relying on it to give rise to cultivation then all of the myriad good qualities will be accomplished. This is what is meant by "the whole that is the nature gives rise to practice and this is called 'continuing.'") Full cultivation's dependence on the nature is called "completion." (The full efficacy of cultivation depends on the nature in order to arise. This is because it consists solely in expanding and fully developing (*kuochong* 擴充) the nature rather than adding what is not in the nature. Thus it is said "Full cultivation's dependence on the nature is [called] completion.") The purity of the innate nature is due to heaven;[139] the subsequent arising of pure habituated tendencies is due to humans. Hence it is said: "If it were not for heaven then there would be no cause. (The nature is heaven. If humans did not have their innately (*tianran* 天然) fully endowed nature then by what cause could they do good?) If the heaven-[given] is not [acted upon] by humans then there would be no completion."[140]

The thesis that the nature and practice are not two is yet another expression of Xiong's understanding of the *ti-yong* paradigm: that Fundamental Reality is actively creative and that it is morally inflected. The doctrinal claims that "the whole that is the nature gives rise to practice" and "full cultivation depends on the nature" are both derived from Tiantai writings. Xiong's purpose in glossing the passage from the *Book of Change* with Tiantai Buddhist teachings is to verify "cross-culturally" the thesis that the nature and practice are not two.

In one final example—a variation of the "unity of heaven and humans" (*tian ren he yi* 天人合一) paradigm, which in turn is but a variation of the *ti-yong* paradigm—Xiong employs the images of *qian* and *kun* to reinforce his understanding of the unity of the nature and practice:

---

138. "Xici, shang" (Appended Statements, A), *Book of Change*, 7.11a-12a. "The alternating procession of *yin* and *yang* is the way; that which continues this process is goodness; and that which completes this process is the nature."

139. In other words, it is inherently so; it is due to the nature.

140. Xiong, *New Treatise*, p. 144.

> In the *Book of Change*, Qian 乾 is the way of heaven and Kun 坤 is the way of humans. Kun succeeds heaven by according with it, and so by doing good it continues the virtue of Qian's vigor. (The Kun hexagram represents things, which arise subsequently [to the nature]. When we humans, by ourselves, create pure habituated tendencies, and so give expression to our heavenly-endowed nature, this is Kun emulating the images of heaven.) Therefore, when you students continue [the virtue of Qian's vigor by doing] good things and complete that which is [heavenly-endowed], it is the nature that is involved therein. The *Analects* says: "People are able to make the way great; it is not the case that the way is able to make people great."[141] . . . In succinct terms, for Confucians the goal of making the way great lies in being in accord with the five virtues,[142] whereas for Buddhists it lies in diligently practicing the six perfections.[143] . . . Thus it is said: "There is nothing which does not flow forth from the dharma realm (法界 [*dharmadhātu*]),[144] and nothing which does not return to it."[145]) This is what is referred to as "the united virtue of heaven and man; the non-duality of nature and cultivation."[146]

Conclusion

Over the past three decades there has been a widespread tendency to portray Xiong narrowly as a Confucian philosopher who also happened to criticize Buddhist philosophy, but whose philosophical achievements lie in his accounts of the relationship between *ti* 體 and *yong* 用; the principle of Change; and the two concepts "contraction" (*xi* 翕) and "expansion" (*pi* 闢) derived from the *Book of*

141. *Analects* 15.29.

142. Although there are various lists of "five virtues," the most likely is humanness, rightness, ritual propriety, wisdom, and living up to one's word.

143. The six perfections (*pāramitā*; 波羅蜜): charity, discipline, forbearance, vigor, contemplation, and wisdom.

144. *Digital Dictionary of Buddhism*, s.v. "*fajie* 法界," www.buddhism-dict.net (accessed June 16, 2011): "In Sinitic forms of Mahāyāna teaching, 法界 refers to a religious basis or principle—the origin of all things. In this kind of teaching, where the whole universe is taken as phenomena, it is understood as the manifestation of true thusness."

145. This saying appears in a wide range of Chinese Buddhist texts.

146. Xiong, *New Treatise*, p. 144. This saying appears in a wide range of Chinese Buddhist texts.

Change.[147] Rather than being understood as an essential framework within which to tease out the complexity of Xiong's thought, his engagement with Buddhist philosophy has tended to be dismissed as a passing phase[148] or inconvenient distraction. Too often, Xiong's uncompromising critiques of Yogācāra philosophy—in particular, the Vasubandhu, Dharmapāla, Xuanzang, and Kuiji tradition—seem to have provided a convenient pretext for ignoring other key elements of Buddhist philosophy in his constructive philosophy.

The weight of evidence presented in the chapter shows that Xiong's Confucio-Buddhist syncretism was developed dialectically on the basis of a critique of Yogācāra thought, and as an elaboration of the Mahāyāna doctrines of conditioned arising and the inherent emptiness of conditioned phenomena.[149] Madhyamakan (and Perfection of Wisdom [Prajñāpāramitā]) methodological insights are central to the *New Treatise*, in particular those premised on the view that emptiness and the phenomenal world are not two different things but rather are two characterizations of the same thing. Rather than using conventional Madhyamakan terminology, however, Xiong articulates this perspective using the

147. The following comments by Jiyuan Yu, "Xiong Shili's Metaphysics of Virtue," in *Contemporary Chinese Philosophy*, ed. Chung-Ying Cheng and Nicholas Bunnin (Oxford: Blackwell Publishers, 2002), p. 129, are typical: "His major philosophical contribution has been, through appropriating some aspects of Buddhism and combining them with his sophisticated understanding of the *Yijing*, to provide Confucianism—which has traditionally been regarded as being only an ethics – with a more solid metaphysical basis and a more dynamic character."

148. Lin Anwu 林安梧 even departs from the conventional consensus that Xiong gradually changed his philosophical allegiance from Buddhism to Confucianism, instead insisting that Xiong had always adopted a Confucian stance. See his "Dangdai Ru-Fo lunzheng de yixie wenti: Li Xiangping xiansheng 'Xiong Shili zhexue de queshi yu Ru-Fo huitong' du hou 當代儒佛論爭的一些問題—李向平先生「熊十力哲學的缺失與儒佛會通」讀後" (Some Issues in Contemporary Confucian-Buddhist Debates: On Reading Mr Li Xiangping's "Shortcomings in the Philosophy of Xiong Shili, and Confucian-Buddhist Interconnections"), *Ershiyi shiji* 48 (1998): 126.

149. In this chapter I have drawn attention to the Buddhist elements in Xiong's thought, as they are the most pertinent to his critique of Yogācāra thought. I have also sought to challenge the uncritical view that Xiong was simply a Confucian thinker—a view that seems to have become entrenched, especially in the wake of the retrospective creation of New Confucianism as a philosophical school. In a sense, this essay is a continuation of a polemical project first started when I published the edited volume *New Confucianism: A Critical Examination* (New York: Palgrave Macmillan, 2003). More recently, I have argued that Xiong's strong rejection of nihilism (associated with Madhyamaka) provided the space for a morally-inflected universe and this is where the Confucian side of his syncretism gains added traction. One only needs to take note of the number and variety of Neo-Confucian thinkers Xiong cites, engages with, or alludes to appreciate the place of Neo-Confucian philosophy in his overarching syncretism. See my "Xiong Shili's Understanding of the Relationship between the Ontological and the Phenomenal," forthcoming.

ti-yong polarity. Thus, when we read Xiong's *New Treatise*, we need to remind ourselves—just as Xiong regularly reminds us—that his sustained critique of Yogācāra is matched by a profound respect for Madhyamaka philosophy and that his appropriation of the *ti-yong* polarity and the concepts "contraction" (*xi*) and "expansion" (*pi*) are grounded in Madhyamakan philosophical premises.

It was not, however, exclusively Madhyamakan or Confucian philosophical insights[150] that served as key impetuses in the development of Xiong's creative philosophy. Madhyamaka provided a deconstructive method, a radical apophasis, central to which is the concept of emptiness.[151] Beyond this, however, Xiong also drew substantial (albeit largely unacknowledged) philosophical inspiration from *Dasheng qixin lun* and the doctrine of nature origination, as resources to affirm the phenomenal world, the life-world, and not simply to repudiate it. (Even this "stance" was dictated by the dialectical relationship between ultimate truth and conventional truth—whereby one cannot be realized without the other—as is made explicit in the *ti-yong* paradigm as developed by Xiong.) Surprisingly, the central place occupied by the doctrine of nature origination in Xiong's philosophical system seems to have been ignored in secondary scholarship on Xiong, thus rendering problematic the degree to which his philosophical system has been faithfully represented.

150. In this chapter, the Confucian dimension is represented in his accounts of the nature (*xing* 性) and form-and-vital stuff (*xingqi* 形氣); and *li* 理 and *qi* 氣; nature and practice; that Fundamental Reality is actively creative and morally inflected; and in his use of the *Book of Change*.

151. It should be noted that in the *New Treatise*, Xiong is not prepared to endorse any notion of nihilism, such as might be ascribed to Madhyamaka philosophy. In the 1944 vernacular redaction of *Xin weishi lun*, Xiong is more explicitly critical of Madhyamakan conceptions of emptiness.

PART 5

The Return to "Genuine Buddhism"

9

Ouyang Jingwu: From Yogācāra Scholasticism to Soteriology[1]

Eyal Aviv

THE RECEPTION OF Yogācāra in modern China involved many prominent intellectuals, but few were as central as Ouyang Jingwu 歐陽竟無 (1871–1943). Ouyang was a major force in the modern case of what Hu Shi 胡適 (1891–1962) anxiously called the "Indianization of China." He was a hub around which many other figures, events, and institutions related to the revival of Indian Buddhism were connected.[2] Ouyang was also a charismatic leader who attracted prominent intellectuals to engage in the demanding study of Buddhist thought and logic. Finally, he is also crucial to our subject matter as he was the one who institutionalized the fascination with Indian Buddhist philosophy in the early twentieth century through the foundation of the China Institute of Inner Learning (Zhina Neixue Yuan 支那內學院).

Ouyang was a paradigmatic intellectual of his period. His story and career are idiosyncratic in his decision to turn to Indian scholastic Buddhism, but in many other ways his is the story of the last generation that was born and grew up into the old, imperial, world order only to discover that their reality did not match the old

---

1. I would like to thank Lin Chen-kuo and John Powers for their criticisms and suggestions.

2. He was, for example, a friend of Zhang Taiyan 章太炎 (1868–1936) (for more on Zhang see John Jorgensen's and Viren Murthy's chapters in this volume). Zhang's financial support and his network of connections were crucial to furthering Ouyang's career. He was an interlocutor of Taixu 太虛 (1890–1947) and his interpretation of Yogācāra (see the chapters by Erik J. Hammerstrom and Scott Pacey in this volume for more details on Taixu). He was the teacher and protégé of Lü Cheng 呂澂 (1896–1989) (see Dan Lusthaus's and Lin Chen-kuo's chapters), Xiong Shili 熊十力 (1885–1968) (see Lin Chen-kuo's and John Makeham's chapters), and Liang Shuming 梁漱溟 (1893–1988) (see Thierry Meynard's chapter).

3. The Cheng-Zhu School was the orthodox school of Confucian thought in late-Imperial China. The school was rooted in the philosophical teachings of the Cheng brothers, Cheng Yi 程頤 (1033–1107) and Cheng Hao 程顥 (1032–1085), especially of Cheng Yi, which were systematized by Zhu Xi 朱熹 (1130–1200). For over a millennium the commentaries produced by scholars of this school were the main source of interpretation used in the Imperial examinations.

ideals and worldview anymore. Like many others of his age, Ouyang was trained as a Confucian, only to renounce the orthodox Cheng-Zhu 程朱School[3] and embrace the more idealistic Lu-Wang 陸王 branch of Confucianism.[4] Unlike some of his contemporaries, who gradually gravitated toward so-called Western Studies, Ouyang became known for his conviction that it is within scholastic Buddhism that Chinese people can find the intellectual and spiritual resources a nation needed in dire times.

The primary goal of this chapter is to introduce Ouyang and his role in the Indian scholastic revival of Republican China, a role that has largely been ignored in Western scholarship. I highlight Ouyang as a key figure in the reintroduction of Yogācāra thought into China. I also introduce Ouyang's contribution to Yogācāra studies in China, the texts he studied and published, his career as a teacher, and the kind of scholarship he produced. In order to demonstrate his creative and idiosyncratic approach, I elaborate on his distinction between two aspects of the Buddhist doctrine he called *weishi* 唯識 and *faxiang* 法相. In the second part of the chapter I argue against a common understanding of Ouyang as merely "Mr. Yogācāra." While he certainly deserves his reputation as a leading exponent of Yogācāra in twentieth-century China, he was a complex thinker whose ideas evolved over time, and he changed his philosophical and methodological preferences to adapt to the changing circumstances of his life and the broader historical context of twentieth-century China. I show that after his Yogācāra phase he explored other approaches and shifted from a critical and analytical style of scholarship to a more syncretic style. To analyze the later Ouyang I will focus on his *tathāgatagarbha* (matrix of the buddhas) thought, his initial critique of the *tathāgatagarbha* teaching as it appears in *Dasheng qixin lun* 大乘起信論 (Awakening of Mahāyāna Faith), and his later embrace of this doctrine.

Different phases in Ouyang's career

The division of Ouyang's life into different phases draws in part on the analysis of Cheng Gongrang.[5] There are four main phases: pre-Buddhist early phase; the Yogācāra phase; the Yogācāra-Madhyamaka syncretic phase; and his later thought. In the following pages I will describe briefly his pre-Buddhist phase and then move on to his Buddhist thought and to his later years, where he seems to have returned to embracing Confucianism enthusiastically and gave new direction to his Buddhist thought.

---

4. The main rival of the Cheng-zhu School, the Lu-Wang School was rooted in the teachings of Lu Xiangshan 陸象山 (1139–1192) and later, more famously, in the teachings of Wang Yangming 王陽明 (1472–1529).

5. See Cheng Gongrang 程恭讓, *Ouyang Jingwu Foxue sixiang yanjiu* 歐陽竟無佛學思想研究 (Studies in Ouyang Jingwu's Buddhist Thought) (Taibei: Xinwenfeng Press, 2000).

Early phase: Confucian education (1877–1901)

Ouyang was born to an educated family in Yihuang 宜黃 county, Jiangxi province. His father, Ouyang Hui 歐陽暉 (1822–1876), died when Ouyang Jingwu was five years old, thus leaving the young Jingwu in the hands of his uncle Ouyang Yu 歐陽昱 (1837–1904), an educator, writer, and well-known intellectual in Yihuang who passed the imperial exam as second rank. Between 1877 and 1890, his uncle tutored Ouyang in a broad range of traditional Confucian scholarship, aiming to equip the young Jingwu with the necessary knowledge to advance within the Chinese bureaucracy. He taught him first and foremost the orthodox Cheng-Zhu school, but also tutored him in the methods of evidential learning (*kaozhengxue* 考證學).[6] Wang Enyang 王恩洋 (1897–1964)—one of Ouyang's leading disciples and a well-known Buddhist scholar in his own right—commented on Ouyang's education: "At a young age the master studied language. He then mastered Han Studies and progressed to master Song-Ming Neo-Confucianism, especially admiring the Lu-Wang [School]. He thoroughly mastered poetry and prose, evidential learning, and [Song-Ming] metaphysics."[7] The critical methods of philology and historiography, to which he was exposed at a young age, played a crucial role in his mature Buddhist scholarship. He was the first Buddhist scholar to apply the critical method of evidential learning to the study of Buddhist texts. In 1890 Ouyang Jingwu was admitted into the Jingxun Academy (Jingxun shuyuan 經訓書院) in the provincial capital of Jiangxi, Nanchang. The Jingxun Academy was one of the finest institutions for higher learning in Jiangxi of the late-Qing Dynasty, and it placed a strong emphasis on classical knowledge and scholarship.

Deeply disturbed by the Chinese defeat in the war against Japan, in 1895 Ouyang turned his back on the Cheng-Zhu School and developed a keen interest in the Lu-Wang school of Neo-Confucianism.[8] Lü Cheng 呂澂 (1896–1989), his closest disciple, recounts: "The war in the East has already started and the affairs

---

6. On the Evidential Research movement see Liang Ch'i-ch'ao, *Intellectual Trends in the Ch'ing Period* (Cambridge, MA: Harvard University Press, 1970); Benjamin A. Elman, *From Philosophy to Philology: Intellectual and Social Aspects of Change in Late Imperial China* (Los Angeles: University of California Press, 2001).

7. Xu Qingxiang 徐清祥 and Wang Guoyan 王國炎, *Ouyang Jingwu pingzhuan* 歐陽竟無評傳 (A Critical Biography of Ouyang Jingwu) (Nanchang Shi: Baihuazhou wenyi chubanshe, 1995), p. 20.

8. Here Ouyang seems to have been part of a trend among young Chinese intellectuals who followed the example of Japanese intellectuals in the Meiji who favored the Lu-Wang teaching as a critique of what they saw as the Cheng-Zhu School's inability to face the challenges of the late-Tokugawa period (1600–1868), or in the Chinese case, the late-Qing period (1644–1911). For more, see Oleg Benesch, "Wang Yangming and *Bushidō*: Japanese Nativization and Its Influence in Modern China," *Journal of Chinese Religion* 36, no. 3 (2009): 439–454.

of the state deteriorated day by day. The master indignantly saw miscellaneous studies[9] as unhelpful, and focused on the Lu-Wang School's teachings as a possible remedy for the social problems of the day."[10] This phase, in which Ouyang devoted himself to the teaching of Wang Yangming's more "subjective turn," would eventually lead him to embrace Buddhism.

Early encounter with Buddhism

While studying at the Jingxun Academy, Ouyang was also exposed to new ideas from the West. He befriended an older student named Gui Bohua 桂伯華 (1861–1915), who introduced him to many of the latest intellectual trends. More pertinent to our concerns, however, is that Gui introduced Ouyang to Buddhism. A fellow Jiangxi native, Gui spent most of his early years in the capital, Nanchang. Like Ouyang, he had received a traditional Confucian education. The defeat of China by Japan in 1895 transformed him, and he decided to join the reform movement led by Kang Youwei 康有为 (1858–1927) and Liang Qichao 梁启超 (1873–1929).

The failure of the reform movement had a devastating effect on Gui Bohua. Finding solace in Buddhism after he became sick and depressed, he went on to study Buddhism more seriously with Yang Wenhui 楊文會 (1837–1911), the so-called father of the Buddhist revival in modern China.[11] In one of his letters from the period, Yang Wenhui updated a friend with a letter saying: "This year I have a few students in my residence; Gui Bohua from Jiujiang is the most serious—he has been studying with me for two years already."[12] In fact, many of Yang's early students, including Ouyang, were introduced to him through Gui Bohua.

---

9. "Miscellaneous teachings" probably refers to those traditional teachings he received in his childhood, especially those of the orthodox Cheng-Zhu School.

10. Lü Cheng, "Qin jiaoshi Ouyang xiansheng shilüe 親教師歐陽先生事略" (A Brief Biography of My Teacher Mr. Ouyang), in *Zhongguo Fojiao sixiang ziliao xuanbian* 中國佛教思想資料選編 (An Anthology of Materials on Chinese Buddhist Thought), ed. Shi Jun 石峻 et al. (Beijing: Zhonghua shuju, 1983), p. 354.

11. Ouyang Jingwu, "Jingwu shiwen: Gui Bohua xingshu 竟無詩文: 桂伯華行述" (Gui Bohua's Biography in Jingwu's Poetry and Prose Collection), in *Ouyang dashi yiji* 歐陽大師遺集 (Bequeathed Collected Writings of Master Ouyang) (Taibei: Xinwenfeng, 1976), p. 1855. According to Cheng Gongrang, it is likely that Gui Bohua was exposed to Buddhism even before he returned to his village to hide in the aftermath of the collapse of the reform movement in 1898. This is because most of the prominent reformers in the Hundred Days' Reform, such as Tan Sitong 譚嗣同 (1865–1898), Kang Youwei, or Liang Qichao, had a deep interest in Buddhist practice and thought.

12. Yu Lingbo 于凌波, *Zhongguo jindai Fojiao renwuzhi* 中國近代佛教人物志 (Biographical Records of Modern Chinese Buddhists) (Beijing: Zongjiao wenhua chubanshe, 1995), p. 323.

Gui's initial attempts to introduce Ouyang to Buddhism were unsuccessful as Ouyang was at the time attracted to the Confucian teachings of Wang Yangming. Finally, Gui made a tactical retreat, but not before giving Ouyang two Buddhist texts. Ouyang recounts: "He gave me copies of *Awakening of Mahāyāna Faith* and the **Śūraṃgama-sūtra* (*Lengyan jing* 楞嚴經; Sutra of the Samādhi of Heroic Progress) and said, 'How about that for the time being you take these and put them next to your bed? Make them your bedtime reading.' I did not feel like taking them."[13] Influenced by Gui's enthusiasm and piety, Ouyang eventually did read the two texts and found them interesting but problematic.

Ouyang thought at that point that the teachings of the Lu-Wang School were very similar to what he read in *Awakening of Mahāyāna Faith* and to a certain extent also those in the **Śūraṃgama-sūtra*. According to Cheng Gongrang, for Ouyang, *Awakening of Mahāyāna Faith* provided a better explanation of the origins of life and death than did the teachings of the Lu-Wang School. Despite this, although Buddhism and Lu-Wang Confucianism are so close in many respects, Confucianism has a clear advantage in practical matters and in social engagement. From this perspective it may well have seemed that Confucianism is an improved version of Buddhism. Taking into account the fact that Ouyang turned to the Lu-Wang teachings for solutions to contemporary political and social crises, one can easily see how the Buddhism of texts such as *Awakening of Mahāyāna Faith* was simply not enough to convert him.[14]

There was one more pressing and practical issue that kept Ouyang from pursuing Buddhism more seriously. In 1897, his brother, Ouyang Huang 歐陽滉, passed away. Ouyang Huang was the supporter of the family, and Ouyang was forced to take his place. The Imperial examination seemed like a natural path, in line with his ancestors' heritage, and the safest path for a scholarly and bureaucratic career. In 1903, he took the Excellence Tribute (*yougong* 優貢) examination, which was an examination at the village or town level that allowed him to participate in the Imperial exams. Ouyang passed the examination and in 1904, he took the Imperial examination in Beijing, but only managed to achieve the second rank. This failure was a blow to Ouyang's prospects on the path of public service. He could get a minor position in his county or hold a local teaching position, but it was not enough to support his family. Trying again was never an option, as the examination system was canceled a year later.

---

13. Ouyang Jingwu, "Jingwu shiwen: Gui Bohua xingshu," p. 1855.

14. Cheng Gongrang 程恭讓, "Ouyang xianshang de shengping, shiye ji qi Fojiao sixiang de tezhi 歐陽竟無先生的生平, 事業及其佛教思想的特質" (The Characteristics of Ouyang Jingwu's Biography, Career, and Buddhist Thought), *Yuan Kuang Buddhist Journal* 12, no. 4 (1999): 157.

This failure was a turning point for Ouyang. On his way back from Beijing to Jiangxi, Ouyang had a chance to visit Yang Wenhui. At that point Ouyang had already begun to read Buddhist texts and form a more positive impression of the tradition. After his meeting with Yang, Ouyang's faith "was increased and solidified."[15] At this time, Yang Wenhui was focusing on returning to ancient Buddhism, including Yogācāra. Why Yogācāra? An important reason was Yang's relationship with the Japanese Buddhist scholar Nanjō Bunyū 南條文雄 (1849–1927) whom he met when he served in the Chinese Embassy in London. Nanjō, who befriended Yang, proposed to send him texts that were lost in China but preserved in Japan. Most important among them were Yogācāra texts such as Kuiji's *Cheng wei shi lun shuji* 成唯識論述記 (Commentary on *Demonstration of Nothing but Consciousness*), which is considered to be the most authoritative commentary on Xuanzang's 玄奘 (602–664) *Cheng weishi lun* (*Demonstration of Nothing but Consciousness*).[16] Other texts included Daolun's 道倫 (alt. Dyunlun 遁倫; d.u.)[17] commentary on *Yogācārabhūmi-śāstra* (*Yuqie shidi lun* 瑜伽師地論; Discourse on the Stages of Concentration Practice) called *Yuqie lunji* 瑜伽論記 (Commentaries on the *Yogācārabhūmi*); and *Dasheng fayuan yilin zhang* 大乘法苑義林章 (Essay on the Garden of Dharma and Forest of Meaning), a Kuiji treatise in which he discusses major principles of Yogācāra philosophy.

Perhaps as an attempt to convince Ouyang that Buddhism offers more than *Awakening of Mahāyāna Faith*, and to pacify some of Ouyang's objections, Yang encouraged Ouyang to study the Yogācāra tradition, without which, Yang told Ouyang, there is no way to understand Buddhism.[18] This was where Ouyang finally felt that his doubts regarding Buddhism were beginning to dissipate. In the following years many dramatic events shaped Ouyang's life. His mother's death was a moment of personal crisis that provided another reminder of suffering and

15. Lü Cheng, "Qin jiaoshi Ouyang xiansheng shelüe," p. 354.

16. Kuiji's *Cheng weishi lun shuji* is important for providing the context to understand the *Cheng weishi lun*, the foundational text of the East Asian Yogācāra tradition. Whereas *Cheng weishi lun* presents us with different views about doctrinal issues without clearly indicating who held these views, the commentary by Kuiji provides us with the names and explains that what Xuanzang did was to collect ten different commentaries on the *Triṃśikā* (Thirty Verses) and establish Dharmapāla's (Hufa 護法; *ca.* sixth century) commentary as the orthodoxy. In recent year scholars have challenged Kuiji's motives and conclusions. See, for example, Dan Lusthaus, *Buddhist Phenomenology: A Philosophical Investigation of Yogācāra Buddhism and the Ch'eng Wei-shih Lun*, Curzon Critical Studies in Buddhism Series (London: Routledge, 2002), pp. 382–414; and Sakuma Hidenori, "On Doctrinal Similarities between Sthiramati and Xuanzang," *JIABS* 29, no. 2 (2008): 357–382. Nonetheless Kuiji's *Cheng weishi lun shuji* remained a crucial text, and for Ouyang's generation it was the only way to unlock the meaning of *Cheng weishi lun*.

17. Or Doryun, a Korean monk of the Tang dynasty.

18. Cheng Gongrang, "Ouyang xianshang de shengping, shiye ji qi Fojiao sixiang de tezhi," p. 162.

impermanence. In response he decided to "refrain from meat and sex, stop his career, put his trust in the Buddhadharma and strive for unsurpassed awakening."[19] In 1907, Ouyang met Yang again and then left to study in Japan, where he spent time with other followers of Buddhism such as Zhang Binglin 章炳麟 (Taiyan 太炎) (1869–1936), Gui Bohua, and others. We have no information about Ouyang's whereabouts in Japan. We know he returned to China a year later and embarked on a short-lived experiment of living a reclusive life in the Jiufeng Mountains. The harsh conditions in the mountains took a severe toll on his health, forcing him to return to the city. Giving up the peaceful life of a reclusive scholar in the mountains, Ouyang decided that the second-best option available to him was to travel to Nanjing and join Yang Wenhui.

This he did in 1910. It was in the same year that Yang established a Buddhist research association with other like-minded intellectuals. These intellectuals lamented the antischolarly tendencies Chinese Buddhism had appropriated from the Chan tradition and strove to make Buddhism more compatible with the modern age. Ouyang shared these criticisms of Chan Buddhism; later, he also harshly criticized other indigenous Chinese Buddhist traditions. Ouyang then joined Yang's research institution and continued his studies in Buddhism.

Unfortunately for Ouyang, the decision to move to Yang's vicinity came a little too late. A year later, in August 17, 1911, Yang passed away. This was two months before the 1911 Revolution broke out in Wuhan. Surprisingly, in his will Yang left an important part of the Jinling Sutra Press[20] business under the command of Ouyang. Yang divided the operation of the Sutra Press between three of his disciples, but one of them resigned after a short time and the other one died. Thus, Ouyang remained the head of the Jinling Sutra Press.

At the age of forty, Ouyang found himself beginning his career as a Buddhist leader, heading the most prestigious Buddhist publishing house, and a de facto heir of the "father of the Buddhist revival"[21] in modern China. Ouyang now had the means and influence to promote his vision of Buddhism and his studies of Yogācāra thought. He continued to promote the goals of the Jinling Sutra Press according to Yang's vision. In his will, Yang asked Ouyang to publish two of Yang's own writings, the *Shi Moheyan lun jizhu* 釋摩訶衍論集注 (Collected Commentaries on the *Explanation of the Treatise on Mahāyāna*)[22] and *Deng bu deng*

19. Lü Cheng, "Qin jiaoshi Ouyang xiansheng shilüe," p. 354.

20. Established in 1866 by Yang Wenhui, the Jinling Sutra Press (金陵刻經處), was the first modern publishing house dedicated to the printing and distribution of Buddhist literature across China. The Jinling Sutra Press is still active today and is located in Nanjing.

21. Holmes Welch, *The Buddhist Revival in China* (Cambridge, MA: Harvard University Press, 1968), p. 2.

22. *Explanation of the Treatise on Mahāyāna* is a commentary on *Dasheng qixing lun*.

guan zalu 等不等觀雜錄 (Miscellaneous Records of *Contemplations on the Equality and Non-Equality of Things*). In addition, Yang asked him to publish an outline of the Buddhist canon that would make the variety of Buddhist literature available to a wider readership. Finally, Ouyang was asked to finish and publish the remaining fifty fascicles of the *Yogācārabhūmi-śāstra*, a task that was important to Yang but which he did not complete. This last request is a clear indication of the importance that Yang attached to the study of Yogācāra in his late life and one of the reasons for Ouyang's thorough study of this tradition at that point in his career.

Ouyang's Yogācāra Phase

This phase, which lasted from 1904 until 1923, was the defining phase of Ouyang's career and the phase for which he is best known. From 1904 until the mid-1910s Ouyang was busy with an in-depth study of the scholastic Buddhist tradition, especially Yogācāra but also the *abhidharma* tradition.[23] The latter served as a necessary foundation to the study of the former. Soon after, he began publishing his own writings, which eventually evolved into a large corpus of texts. Ouyang's research into Yogācāra intensified and gained a therapeutic value in 1915 following another tragic event. When he was on a fundraising trip to Gansu, his daughter, Ouyang Lan 歐陽蘭 (1899–1915), fell ill and died in Nanjing. Deeply anguished and stricken by guilt, Ouyang found comfort and strength in his studies of *abhidharma* and Yogācāra.

Ouyang studied the major Abhidharmapāda texts of the Sarvāstivāda School.[24] He read major *abhidharma* commentaries such as the *Mahāvibhāṣā-śāstra*

23. *Abhidharma* (the Higher Teaching or sometimes also About the Teaching) constitutes the third "basket" of the Buddhist canon (*Tripiṭaka*). The Abhidharmikas attempted to systematize the broad range of Buddhist teachings that appeared in the discourses (*sūtra*) and in the monastic discipline (*vinaya*). In the earlier stages of the movement the *abhidharma* texts consisted of a list of doctrinal classifications (*mātṛkā*). Over time, the tradition evolved to include extensive works dedicated to scholastic attempt to present a coherent vision of the Buddhist teaching. It also documents many debates among the different schools of Buddhism about contested doctrinal issues. For more detailed information, see Noa Ronkin's entry on Abhidharma in the *Stanford Encyclopedia of Philosophy*, http://plato.stanford.edu/entries/abhidharma (accessed June 21, 2012); Noa Ronkin, *Early Buddhist Metaphysics: The Making of a Philosophical Tradition* (London and New York: Routledge, 2005); and Collett Cox, *Disputed Dharmas: Early Buddhist Theories on Existence—An Annotated Translation of the Section on Factors Dissociated from Thought from Saṅghabhadra's Nyāyānusāra* (Tokyo: Studia Philologica Buddhica XI, The International Institute for Buddhist Studies, 1995).

24. The Sarvāstivāda School was an important early school of Buddhism. This school is known for several controversial doctrinal positions it held, one of which had given the school its name. Literally, Sarvāstivāda means the teaching that everything exists, namely that each particular (i.e., dharma) exists at all times (past, present, and future). The textual foundation of the Sarvāstivāda *abhidharma* is seven books that constituted the *abhidharma* basket within the Sarvāstivāda canon. Later, many commentaries and summaries were added to the seven canonical books.

(*Apidamo dapiposha lun* 阿毘達磨大毘婆沙論; Treatise on the Great Commentary of Abhidharma); the *Abhidharma-kośa* (*Apidamo jushe lun* 阿毘達磨俱舍論; Storehouse of Higher Doctrine); and also Yogācāra works such as the *Mahāyāna-saṃgraha* (*She dasheng lun* 攝大乘論; Compendium of the Great Vehicle) and *Cheng weishi lun*. He paid special attention to the study of *Yogācārabhūmi-śāstra*, which he deemed a foundational text for the entire Buddhist system. He also lectured on these texts and studied them daily in the research section of the Jinling Sutra Press.

The fruits of these studies began to appear a year later. In 1916, Ouyang published two prefaces. This was the literary medium through which Ouyang wrote most of his scholarly works. As Ouyang headed the Jinling Sutra Press, which published critical edition of canonical texts, much of Ouyang's writing at that time consisted of prefaces to the texts the Jinling staff edited and published. In his prefaces he outlined the major themes of the texts and their philosophical content. He then gave his own analysis, both historical and doctrinal. It was in his analyses that we find the more constructive aspect of Ouyang's teaching.

Which texts did he comment on during his early stage as a writer? To begin with, he published prefaces to two works of Vasubandhu, **Pañcaskandhaka-prakaraṇa* (*Dasheng wuyun lun* 大乘五蘊論 Treatise on the Five Skandhas) and **Mahāyāna-śatadharma-prakāśamukha-śāstra* (*Baifa mingmen lun* 百法明門論; Lucid Introduction to the One Hundred Dharmas). He wrote another commentary for Vasubandhu's *Mahāyāna-saṃgraha* (Compendium of the Great Vehicle). He later published a preface to *Cheng weishi lun*, in which he compared and contrasted *Cheng weishi lun* with *Abhidharma-kośa*. These two different approaches to Buddhism served as the beginning of a theory he began to develop a year later about the two approaches to Buddhism, which he called *faxiang* 法相 and *weishi* 唯識 (discussed below).

In 1917, Ouyang wrote a preface to the **Buddhabhūmisūtra-śāstra* (*Fodi jing lun* 佛地經論; Treatise on the Sutra of the Buddha-stage), and later that year the Jinling Sutra Press celebrated the publication of the one hundred volumes of the *Yogācārabhūmi-śāstra*. As this occasion marked the fulfillment of an important part of Yang Wenhui's will, Ouyang wrote a preface to the *Yogācārabhūmi-śāstra*. In addition to outlining the text, his analysis contained important aspects of his concerns at that point in his career, such as his criticism of the Ming Buddhists' study of Yogācāra, the history of the school, and his first formulation of his idiosyncratic *faxiang* and *weishi* approaches, mentioned above.

But what did Ouyang find in *abhidharma* scholasticism, and especially in the Yogācāra tradition? What did he see in these teachings that deserved so much attention? According to Ouyang himself:

> If one wishes to dispel the five obstacles [of Chinese Buddhism], one must enter the gates of the Yogācāra teaching.[25] The Yogācāra teaching is a skillful means; it is the understanding of the correct principles. A scholar who investigates it will be able to clearly understand the true principle. He will be able to cure the obstacle of vague and unsystematic thinking.[26]

First, it is important to note that unlike others attracted to Yogācāra at that time, Ouyang did not turn to Yogācāra to create a unique synthesis with some larger idiosyncratic philosophical project.[27] He did not necessarily see Yogācāra as a way to save China politically. Although he remained a Chinese patriot throughout his life, his interest in Yogācāra was due more to his genuine concern with the predicament of Buddhism in China rather than to a concern about China itself.[28] For Ouyang, Yogācāra was an antidote to the following problems Buddhism faced during his lifetime: (1) Chan Buddhist anti-intellectual sentiments; (2) the doctrinal errors of the Tiantai and Huayan schools; and (3) the lack of a systematic approach among Chinese intellectuals.

In the following years, Ouyang published and lectured more on Yogācāra teachings. He also founded the institution that would become the center of Indian Buddhist studies in Republican China, the China Institute of Inner Learning.[29]

Ouyang's thought during his Yogācāra phase

It is problematic to summarize Ouyang's understanding of Yogācāra thought in these twenty years as one set of conclusions. It is therefore useful to sample important works that can elucidate his major ideas and innovations. As for his style of scholarship, Dongchu, a monk and historian of modern Buddhism commented:

---

25. Literally, *weishi* and *faxiang*.

26. Ouyang Jingwu, "Weishi jueze tan 唯識抉擇談" (Critical Essays on the Doctrine of Nothing but Consciousness), in *Ouyang dashi yiji*, p. 1360.

27. Some of the intellectuals discussed in this volume such as Xiong Shili, Liang Shuming, and Zhang Taiyan belong to this category.

28. Ouyang's concern for the fate of China was always on his mind. Although this concern is not evident in his Buddhist scholarship, his early engagement with Lu-Wang thought and, to a greater extent, his late-life Confucian writings in the post-Mukden Incident had reinforced his view on the importance of saving the nation. For more see Eyal Aviv, "Differentiating the Pearl from the Fish Eye: Ouyang Jingwu and the Revival of Scholastic Buddhism," PhD diss., Harvard University, 2008, pp. 80–83.

29. The China Institute of Inner Learning is a crucial part of Ouyang's career. In order to focus on Ouyang's intellectual development, however, I will omit, for the most part, the details relating to the founding of the institute that are not relevant for understanding Ouyang's thought.

> When Ouyang studied the Yogācāra texts, he did not pursue the origin of each and every character, but [instead] tried to grasp the general message of the text (*dayi* 大意). This is why he began with the Yogācāra corpus, then [studied] the *Prajñāparamitā* (Perfection of Wisdom) literature, and toward the end studied the *Mahāparinirvāṇa-sūtra* (*Niepan jing* 涅槃經; Sutra of the Great Final Nirvāṇa) while always connecting it to the core of his teaching.[30]

Ouyang considered the *Yogācārabhūmi-śāstra* to be of prime importance, and many regard his preface to the publication of the *Yogācārabhūmi* as the highest achievement of his early writing career. Why was it so important for Ouyang to introduce the *Yogācārabhūmi*? Ouyang explains:

> The Ming revivalists tried to [re]build the wall of the [Faxiang] teaching. They worked hard but had no achievements. Then, over the course of several centuries, those who wished to command this teaching did not carefully study any [Yogācāra] text other than the *Xiangzong ba yao* 相宗八要 (Eight Essential Texts of the Faxiang School)[31] and *Weishi xin yao* 唯識心要 (The Core Teaching of *Vijñaptimātra*).[32] Their discourse was a shambles, and [they achieved only] a narrow sectarian view, whereas [the scope of Faxiang] is as broad as heaven and earth, but they did not know it. It has the excellence of being well structured, but they did not make good use of it. They only cast their eyes over the surface, and then left it at that. Who [among them] bothered with [the challenges of] the *Yogācārabhūmi*?[33]

Ouyang's major reason for choosing the *Yogācārabhūmi* was triggered by the fact that the Ming revivalists failed to include this foundational text in their list of root texts of the Yogācāra tradition. Such a grave error can only yield "no achievements," and a "shambles."

---

30. Shi Dongchu 釋東初, *Zhongguo Fojiao jindai shi* 中國佛教近代史 (History of Modern Chinese Buddhism) (Taipei: Zhonghua Fojiao wenhuaguan, 1974), p. 671.

31. A one-fascicle work by the late-Ming monk Xuelang Hong'en 雪浪洪恩 (1545–1608). Xuelang prescribed eight essential texts of the Faxiang School and summarized their contents.

32. A ten-fascicle work by Ouyi Zhixu 蕅益智旭 (1599–1655) on *Cheng weishi lun*, also known as *Cheng weishi lun guanxin fayao* 成唯識論觀心法要 (The Essentails of the Cultivation of Mind [According to] *Demonstration of Nothing but Consciousness*).

33. Ouyang Jingwu, "*Yuqie shidi lun* xu 瑜伽師地論敘" (Preface to the *Discourse on the Stages of Concentration Practice*), in *Ouyang dashi yiji*, p. 352.

In his "*Yuqie shidi lun* xu 瑜伽師地論敘" (Preface to the *Discourse on the Stages of Concentration Practice*), Ouyang outlined, analyzed, and contextualized the text. Unlike later critical Buddhists such as Lü Cheng, Hakamaya Noriaki 袴谷憲昭, or Matsumoto Shirō 松本史郎, he had only traditional scholarly methods at his disposal and knew no other Buddhist languages. Yet his work was a substantial advance in applying critical methods to the study of Buddhist texts, drawing on evidential research methods developed in the Qing Dynasty.

Ouyang opens "*Yuqie shidi lun* xu" with the claim that one must study the Yogācāra tradition, because Yoga is synonymous with unity, which in turn is synonymous with Suchness, skillful means, and awakening. Yogācāra consists of training oneself in Yoga and of liberating oneself and others. The word "stages" (*bhūmi*; *di* 地) means that which exhausts both principle (*li* 理) and phenomena (*shi* 事). It is similar to ground, which serves as a foundation that supports.[34] He then outlined what he intended to discuss in "*Yuqie shidi lun* xu" and divided it into four sections:

> An outline of the five main parts (*wu fen* 五分) of the *Yogācārabhūmi*, including the seventeen stages and what each of them means;[35] a description of the ten essential principles (*shi yao* 十要) discussed in the *śāstra*;[36] a discussion of the 10 "branches" (*shi zhi* 十支) or concomitant texts of the Yogācāra tradition and how they relate to the *Yogācārabhūmi*; and a discussion of the ten lineages of the traditions (*shi xi* 十系).[37]

34. Ouyang Jingwu, "*Yuqie shidi lun* xu," p. 307.

35. The five sections are: (1) the section on the major stages (*ben di fen* 本地分); (2) the section explaining the stages, called the section on analysis (*viniścaya*; *jue ze fen* 決擇分); (3) the section explaining the meaning of the *sūtra* and *śāstra*, called the explanation division (*shi fen* 釋分); (4) the section explaining the meaning and giving synonyms (*paryāya-saṃgrahinī*; *yi men fen* 異門分); and (5) the section explaining the important points in the *tripiṭaka*, called the division of the doctrinal points (*shi fen* 事分).

36. The ten essentials themes of the text are: (1) the principle of *weishi* (*weishi yi* 唯識義); (2) the principle of *faxiang* (*faxing yi* 法相義); (3) the sublime principle of equality and difference (*pingdeng shu sheng yi* 平等殊勝義) or the *śravaka* and the *bodhisattva* teachings; (4) the principle of being associated (*samprayukta*; *xiangying yi* 相應義), which here means the excellent action associated with *prajñā*; (5) the principle of basis (*yi yi* 依義), which states that everything that arise have "other" cause and condition as its basis; (6) the principle of function (*yong yi* 用義) where he listed major categories other than suchness, such as correct knowledge, atoms, antidotes etc.; (7) the principle of gradualism (*jian yi* 漸義), where he lists practices related to gradual practice, such as the number of eons it takes a Bodhisattva to become a Buddha etc.; (8) the principle of *agotra* (*wu zhong xing yi* 無種性義); (9) the principle of synonyms (*yi men yi* 異門義); and (10) the scriptural base [of the tradition] (*yi jing yi* 依經義).

37. This is the section where Ouyang critiques the Ming revivalists.

The first part is mostly expository, and describes what is written in the five sections of the *Yogācārabhūmi*. In the second part he selectively expands on themes he found important in the text, drawing his readers' attention to those aspects of the texts that support the key concepts he wished to emphasize. One key example of this strategy is his extensive treatment of the first two (of ten) principles of *faxiang* 法相 and *weishi* 唯識. Ouyang treated these two technical terms in a very idiosyncratic and controversial fashion. For him, *faxiang* and *weishi* represent two different approaches to Buddhism. Since this example has far-reaching implications for Ouyang's thought, I will treat it in some detail here.

Historically, both terms were used as translations for the term "Yogācāra," or more specifically for the Yogācāra School in China. Whereas *weishi* is the translation of the term "nothing but cognition/consciousness" (*vijñāptimātra*), the term *faxiang* is often translated as "dharma characteristics" (*dharma-lakṣaṇa*). Interestingly, in texts such as *Abhidharma-kośa*, where we can compare the Chinese with the Sanskrit, the term *dharma-lakṣaṇa* rarely appears. Most often, Xuanzang simply added the word "characteristics" (*xiang* 相) to what is only "*dharma*" (*fa* 法) in the original Sanskrit.[38] After the Tang Dynasty, the term was used for the first time to denote Xuanzang's Yogācāra School but soon became a mildly derogatory expression used by opponents of the school. Huayan thinkers such as Fazang 法藏 (643–712) and Chengguan 澄觀 (738–783) mocked the Yogācāras for pursuing the "characteristics of dharmas" rather than the real nature of dharmas (*faxing* 法性).[39] Later, however, Yogācāras themselves adopted the term, and today it is used by East Asian Yogācāras, especially in Japan, where it is the official name (Hossō in Japanese).

In his analysis, Ouyang extracted these terms from their historical context and introduced them as two approaches to Buddhism (*zong* 宗). These two approaches, he argued, underlie all Buddhist thought, but they are especially pronounced within Yogācāra contexts. As we will see below, the textual evidence for the existence of what he defined as *faxiang* and *weishi* mostly derive from definitive Yogācāra texts.

What are the characteristics of these two approaches? For Ouyang, the *faxiang* approach is the comprehensive and systematic framework that underlines all Buddhist teachings. It transcends sectarian approaches and is universal. The *weishi* approach is soteriologically oriented and rooted in the idiosyncratic

38. See for example the *Abhidharma-kośa* T1558.1b24 and T1558.10c15-16.

39. See, for example, Chengguan's 澄觀 (738–839) commentary on the the *Avataṃsaka-sūtra* (*Huayan jing* 華嚴經; Flower Ornament Sutra) called *Dafangguang Fo huayan jing shou* (大方廣佛華嚴經疏) (T1735.511a08 ff.) for the differences between *faxiang* and *faxing*.

approach and framework of the Yogācāra School. In "*Yuqie shidi lun* xu," Ouyang described some of the main differences between the two. Here I will summarize his detailed—and somewhat unclear—description, and also outline major characteristics of each. According to Ouyang, whereas *weishi* is rooted in Buddhist practice, *faxiang* is rooted in reason and theoretical study. Alternatively, *weishi* discerns objects (*liaobie* 了別), whereas *faxiang* is Suchness (*ruru* 如如). This statement is rather enigmatic and difficult to reconcile with a different distinction Ouyang made between the two approaches, in which *weishi* is equated with principle (*li* 理) whereas *faxiang* is equated with the phenomenal world (*shi* 事). The way that I understand Ouyang's intention is that for him *weishi* is akin to the conventional truth—a particular, limited, perspective that describes reality conventionally for the sake of clarity—whereas *faxiang* embodies the ultimate truth. *Faxiang* denotes the characteristics of *dharmas*, but *dharmas* in their true nature are Suchness.

Furthermore, Ouyang saw *faxiang* as the universal aspect of Buddhism that serves as a vehicle for all Buddhists, whereas *weishi* is narrower in scope and is only designed for bodhisattvas and practitioners of Mahāyāna. Consequently, different Buddhist texts may approach Buddhism through either *faxiang* or *weishi* perspectives. For example, texts with abhidharmic tendencies would approach Buddhism through a *faxiang* prism. *Abhidharma-samuccaya* (*Dasheng apidamo jilun* 大乘阿毘達磨集論; Compendium of Higher Doctrine), for example, is a *faxiang* text, and Ouyang called it "the gate of *faxiang*."[40] Other *faxiang* texts, according to Ouyang, are *Madhyānta-vibhāga (Zhong bian fenbie lun* 中邊分別論; Differentiation of the Middle and Extremes), and Sthiramati's *Abhidharma-samuccaya-vyākhyā* (*Dasheng apidamo zaji lun* 大乘阿毘達磨雜集論; Commentary on the *Compendium of Abhidharma*). The *weishi* paradigm is associated with texts such as *Mahāyāna-saṃgraha*, *Viṃśatikā* (Twenty Verses), and *Triṃśikā* (Thirty Verses).

Although Ouyang adopted this distinction in some of his other texts as well, "*Yuqie shidi lun* xu" is the only text in which it receives a systematic exposition. The reason becomes clear when one reads Ouyang's explanation of the unique role of *Yogācārabhūmi* in the relation between the two approaches or paradigms. Whereas all the other Buddhist texts fall under either the *faxiang* or the *weishi* approach, it is only the *Yogācārabhūmi* that unites *faxiang* and *weishi* into one holistic approach to Buddhism. As such, it is a text that can serve as the textual foundation for what he saw as "authentic" Buddhism, free from the erroneous views of the Chinese Buddhist tradition.

---

40. Ouyang Jingwu, "*Zaji lun shuji* xu 雜集論述記敘" (Preface for Sthiramati's *Commentary on Abhidharma-samuccaya*), in *Jingwu neiwai xue* 竟無内外學 (The Inner and Outer Teachings of Ouyang Jingwu) (Jiangjin: Zhina neixue yuan, 1942), p. 2.

What was Ouyang's goal in introducing new meanings into these terms? After all, it is highly unlikely that Ouyang was unaware of how these terms were traditionally employed in Buddhist texts. It is more likely that he deliberately shifted the traditional meaning of the terms in order for his readers to reappraise traditional views on the topics he highlighted, such as the importance of Buddhist scholasticism, especially of *abhidharma* in the study of Buddhism; the need for more systematic and holistic approaches; and the rejection of traditional taxonomies among Chinese Buddhist schools (*panjiao* 判教).

Opposition to the faxiang *and* weishi *innovation*

The impact of Ouyang's reinterpretation of *faxiang* and *weishi* is best understood by reviewing the strong reaction it provoked. One notable objection came from the reformer monk Taixu, whose agenda and views of Buddhism often opposed those of Ouyang. Taixu wrote many articles repudiating Ouyang's views, four of which are of particular importance.[41]

Taixu states his main argument very clearly at the beginning of his essay "Lun faxiang bi zong weixue 論法相必宗唯識" (Discussing [the Idea] that *Faxiang* Must Follow *Weishi*):

> Nothing but consciousness takes as dharmas the characteristics of dharmas (*faxiang*). Therefore, what is called *faxiang* is subsumed within *weishi* (i.e., nothing but consciousness) within itself. When discussing *weishi*, *faxiang* is contained within it. There were no other opinions about this matter since the time of Xuanzang. In modern times, [however], there are those who distinguish *faxiang* and *weishi* [as if] they were two doctrinal approaches and conclude that there is a huge gap between them. This is an unfounded and trivial side issue that does not correspond to the holy teaching. Therefore, in establishing our own teaching we will deliberate [on this view].[42]

---

41. The first response was a short article in his journal *Haichaoyin* 海潮音, which he published in 1922, entitled "Jingwu jushi xueshuo zhiyi 竟無居士學說質疑" (Questioning the Teachings of Layman [Ouyang] Jingwu). In this article, Taixu responded to Ouyang's "*Yuqie shidi lun* xu" and rejected Ouyang's differentiation of *faxiang* and *weishi*. The second, a more systematic critique, is based on a talk Taixu gave in 1925 at a conference in Lushan. The talk was later also published in *Haichaoyin* entitled "Discussing [the Idea] that *Faxiang* Must Follow *Weishi*." In 1927, Taixu published a "sequel" article, "Zai lun faxiang bi zong weixue 再論法相必宗唯識" (Discussing Again [the Idea] that *Faxiang* Must Follow *Weishi*), in which he addressed the same topic. In 1946, a year prior to his death, Taixu wrote an article about Ouyang's 1938 essay entitled "Yue 'bian faxiang weishi'" 閱 "辨法相唯識" (Reading "Arguments [about] *Faxiang* and *Weishi*").

42. Taixu, "Lun faxiang bi zong weixue," *Haichao yin* 6, no. 8 (1925), MFQ (*Minguo Fojiao qikan wenxian jicheng* 民國佛教期刊文獻集成; Compendium of Republican-Era Buddhist Journals) 163:10.

Both Ouyang and Taixu seem to have been aware of two different approaches within Buddhism that are different to a certain extent. They nevertheless disagree on the nature of the difference. Whereas Ouyang held that *faxiang* is entirely separate from *weishi*, Taixu argued that they could not be separated into two independent aspects; rather, *faxiang* must be subsumed within *weishi*.[43]

Taixu was also critical of Ouyang's classification of the scriptures. He used *Mahāyāna-saṃgraha* as an example. For Ouyang, *Mahāyāna-saṃgraha* was classified as a *weishi* text. Taixu, on the other hand, held that *Mahāyāna-saṃgraha* includes both *faxiang* and *weishi*, arguing that whereas the first chapter in the treatise focused on the *ālayavijñāna* (*weishi* according to Ouyang), the second chapter focused on characteristics and explained the three natures (*faxiang* according to Ouyang).

In his 1922 essay "Jingwu jushi xueshuo zhiyi" (Questioning the Teachings of Layman [Ouyang] Jingwu), Taixu criticized Ouyang's interpretation of the key term *zong* 宗 as a unique approach.[44] Indeed, Ouyang's usage of *zong* was idiosyncratic and deviated from the common understanding of the term as a lineage or a religious or philosophical "school." Taixu's argument was that Ouyang was oblivious to the semantic range that the term carries.[45] Taixu then argued that a correct definition of *zong* was established by Kuiji as "the most revered and major principle" (*chongzun zhuyao zhi yi* 崇尊主要之義). For Taixu, the "the most revered and major principle" means that dharmas do not go anywhere (*wu wang* 無往) and that they are not dharma characteristics (*fei faxiang* 非法相). Consequently, *faxiang* by itself cannot be a *zong*. The only *zong* that Taixu recognizes as "the most revered and major principle" is *faxing*.[46] The term *faxing* has a long history in East Asian Buddhism and is often used as a synonym with *tathatā* (Suchness).[47] *Faxiang* is only an explanation (*shuoming* 說明), a convenient name for all dharmas. In this sense, for Taixu, *weishi* is equal to *faxing*.

---

43. For more, see Aviv, "Differentiating the Pearl from the Fish Eye," pp. 204–213.

44. The word is often used in the tradition to refer to a lineage, a certain teaching, or a school.

45. It is highly unlikely that Ouyang was not aware of the meaning of the terms and the way they were employed in Buddhist texts. It is more likely that he deliberately shifted the traditional meaning of the terms in order to encourage his audience to rethink its traditional views on the topic.

46. Taixu, "Jingwu jushi xueshuo zhiyi 竟無居士學說質疑," in *Haichao yin* 3, no. 6 (1922), MFQ 153:437–439.

47. For more on *faxiang* and *faxing*, see Robert Gimello, "Chih-Yen, 602–668 and the Foundations of Hua-Yen Buddhism," Ph.D. diss., Columbia University, 1976, especially chapter 4; Yoshizu Yoshihide 吉津宜英, "'Hossō-shū' to iu shūmei no saikentō 「法相宗」という宗名の再検討 (Reexamination of name 'Hossō-shū,'" in *Bukkyō shisō bunkashi ronsō* 佛教思想文化史論叢 (Collected Essays on the History of Buddhist Intellectual Culture), ed. Takao kyōju kanreki kinen: Bukkyō shisō bunka shi ronsō 渡邊隆生教授還暦記念仏教思想文化史論叢 (Committee for the Commemoration of Professor Watanabe Takao's Sixtieth Birthday) (Kyoto: Kyoto Nagata bunshōdō, 1997); and Dan Lusthaus, *Buddhist Phenomenology*, pp. 372 and 386–387.

There was another important concern for Taixu in regard to Ouyang's dual-approach theory. For Taixu, this theory blurred the clear boundaries between Mahāyāna and Hīnayāna. Among Chinese Buddhists it is almost axiomatic that Mahāyāna is superior. Ouyang Jingwu was no exception in holding this view. As a monk who had traveled to Europe, Taixu was aware of the growing skepticism in the West about the authenticity of Mahāyāna teaching and the gravitation by some Buddhism enthusiasts and Western scholars toward the perceived pristine Buddhism of the Theravāda school. Generally speaking, skepticism about the authenticity of Mahāyāna did not take root in East Asia, but during the Republican period, many Buddhist intellectuals rediscovered the *āgama*[48] and *abhidharma* literature, traditionally denigrated as Hīnayāna literature by many mainstream East Asian Mahāyāna texts. As a result, East Asia saw a revival of interest not only in Yogācāra but also in Buddhist logic, *Abhidharma-kośa* other *abhidharma* works, and, of course, the *āgamas*. Both Ouyang and Taixu were a part of this trend, but whereas for Ouyang it yielded a critique and a reassessment of the Buddhist tradition in China, for Taixu it reaffirmed the superiority of Mahāyāna Buddhism, particularly of the East Asian tradition.

For example, Taixu noted that in Ouyang's view the *faxiang* approach includes *Abhidharma-kośa*. For Taixu, the fact that Ouyang included a Hīnayāna text as part of *faxiang*, regarding it as a legitimate approach to Buddhism, and equating it with the more quintessentially Mahāyāna *weishi* approach, amounted to legitimizing Hīnayāna and undermining the primacy of Mahāyāna in Chinese Buddhism. In his critique, Taixu insisted on clear boundaries between the two vehicles, arguing that both the five dharmas[49] and the three natures[50] are established only after the Bodhisattva's realization of emptiness:

---

48. The four *āgamas* are the collection of the sutras in the Buddhist canon that are attributed to the Buddha. In the premodern era they were often perceived in East Asia as a rudimentary teachings that preceded the more definitive Mahāyāna teachings. A growing interest in these "Hīnayāna" texts demonstrates the tendency toward a more ecumenical and nonsectarian approach among some Buddhists in modern China.

49. The five dharmas scheme is outlined in texts such as the *Laṅkāvatāra-sūtra*. The five dharmas are: (1) signs or appearances (*nimitta; xiang* 相); (2) names (*nāma; ming* 名); (3) discriminatory conceptions or ideas (*samkalpa; fenbie* 分别); (4) correct knowledge (*samyag-jñāna; zhengzhi* 正智); and (5) Suchness (*tathatā; zhenru* 真如).

50. The three natures (*tri-svabhāva; san xing* 三性) is the teaching that we know the world through three different possible modes of perceptions. (1) The illusory or imagined, which is constructed through false conceptualization (*parikalpita-svabhāva; bianji suozhi xing* 遍計所執性); (2) The dependent nature, which is the mode in which we understand our view of world as a result of causes and conditions (*paratantra-svabhāva; yita qi xing* 依他起性); and (3) a mode of cognition of reality as it is, without false conceptualizations (*parinịspanna-svabhāva; yuancheng shi xing* 圓成實性).

> The five dharmas and the characteristics of the three [natures] are established only in the stage after the attainment of the bodhisattva's emptiness. As such, is the *abhidharma* of the two vehicles[51] sufficient to verify what has been established means after the attainment of emptiness? Having scanned through the **Mahāvibhāṣā* and *Abhidharma-kośa*, [I realized] that neither includes this principle.[52]

Despite Taixu's concern and critique, the revival of *abhidharma* studies is one of the more interesting outcomes of Ouyang's creative distinction between the two approaches to Buddhism. More scholars who were interested in scholastic Buddhism undertook the study of *abhidharma* in order to understand better the teachings of Yogācāra in particular and Mahāyāna in general. Historically, the study of *abhidharma* was marginalized in post–Tang Dynasty China. Its analytical approach was rejected and replaced by a traditional "doctrinal classification" (*panjiao* 判教). In all major *panjiao* taxonomies *abhidharma* and other "Hīnayānic" views ranked very low.[53] Consequently, throughout Chinese Buddhist history *abhidharma* has largely been ignored as a source for genuine philosophical and spiritual meaning.

For Ouyang this was further proof that Chinese Buddhists were ignorant of the roots of their own tradition. A part of his research included, partially as a corrective measure, a thorough study of *abhidharma*, especially the foundational *Abhidharma-kośa*. Toward the end of the Yogācāra phase of his career, Ouyang published and wrote an introduction to *Abhidharma-kośa*, which he opened by saying: "Anyone who studies Yogācāra must study *Abhidharma-kośa*. A tree has its roots, a house has its foundations, and a family member has his ancestral temple."[54] Anticipating Taixu's critique, Ouyang contextualized the study of *abhidharma* from a Mahāyāna perspective. For Ouyang, like many other Yogācāras, studying *abhidharma* without Mahāyāna thought is deficient and unhelpful. He paraphrased the *Mahāprajñāpāramitā-śāstra* (*Da zhidu lun* 大智度論; Great Treatise on the Perfection of Wisdom) by saying: "One who studies *abhidharma* without first grasping the *Mahāprajñāpāramitā-sūtra* (Sutra of the Great Perfection of

---

51. The two vehicles is a term used by Mahāyāna followers to refer to the lesser two vehicles of the śrāvakas (hearers, direct disciples) and pratyekabuddhas (solitary buddhas).

52. Taixu, "Lun faxiang bi zong weixue," p. 14.

53. Fazang, for example, assigned the Hīnayāna teaching to the lowest position, whereas Zongmi ranked it second, above the teachings for the laity. See Peter Gregory, *Tsung-mi and the Sinification of Buddhism* (Princeton, NJ: Princeton University Press, 1991), pp. 134–135.

54. Ouyang Jingwu, "*Apidamo jushe lun* xu 阿毘達磨俱舍論敘" (Preface to the *Storehouse of Higher Doctrine*), in *Ouyang dashi yiji*, p. 821.

Wisdom) will veer off the right path."[55] But at the same time, Ouyang, in sharp contrast to many Buddhists such as Taixu, thought that it was problematic to study Mahāyāna without *abhidharma*. *Abhidharma* is more than Buddhism for those with poor faculties: it is the foundation without which a true understanding of Mahāyāna is impossible. He said: "[The understanding of] one who studies Yogācāra while being deficient in *abhidharma*, will be completely empty and rootless."[56]

Ouyang and his critique of the Dasheng qixin lun (Awakening of Mahāyāna Faith)

Ouyang and the scholastic movement are known for their critique of the theory of Buddha-nature in East Asia. Ouyang never rejected either one of the two approaches to Buddhism and kept developing his theories throughout his career. However, from 1924 onward, Ouyang began to publish works that were different from his early prefaces. He was more syncretic and began to explore texts that were not part of the classical Yogācāra or Abhidharma corpus, and he even began to reconnect with his Confucian heritage.

The term "Buddha-nature" is often used interchangeably with the term *tathāgatagarbha* (womb of the tathāgata; 如來藏). Generally speaking, *tathāgatagarbha* refers to the assumption that sentient beings possess inherent gnosis (*jñāna*) and that this inherent gnosis can lead them to enlightenment. In this chapter I use *tathāgatagarbha* since this is the term Ouyang used most of the time. In the following section I focus on Ouyang's contribution to the debate surrounding the doctrine of *tathāgatagarbha* and his later embrace of the doctrine toward the end of his life.

Although the East Asian interpretation was controversial within scholastic circles, the *tathāgatagarbha* doctrine itself is by no means foreign to Yogācāra, and both traditions intermingled at a very early stage. The term was not used often in the classical Yogācāra texts of Asaṅga's and Vasubandhu's writings (although one interesting exception is Vasubandhu's commentary on Asaṅga's *Compendium of Mahāyāna*, the **Mahāyāna-saṃgraha-bhāṣya* [*She dasheng lun shi* 攝大乘論釋]).[57]

55. Ouyang Jingwu, "*Apidamo jushe lun* xu," p. 824.

56. Ouyang Jingwu, "*Apidamo jushe lun* xu," p. 831. Cf. John Jorgensen's observation in his chapter that in Tokugawa Japan *abhidharma* was used as preparation for the study of Yogācāra.

57. For more on Vasubandhu's usage of the term *tathāgatagarbha*, see Keng Ching, "Yogācāra Buddhism Transmitted or Transformed? Paramārtha (499–569) and His Chinese Interpreters," Ph.D. diss., Harvard University, 2009, pp. 401–404.

But references to similar concepts and to the term itself can be found in the six sutras and eleven treatises cited by Kuiji[58] as the Yogācāra orthodoxy. Among these texts, we can find the *Avataṃsaka-sūtra*; *Laṅkāvatāra-sūtra* (*Lengqie jing* 楞伽經; Discourse on [the Buddha's] Entering [the Country of] Lanka); and treatises such as the *Mahāyāna-sūtrālaṃkāra* (*Dasheng zhuangyan jing lun* 大乘莊嚴經論; Ornament for the Great Vehicle Discourses), all of which are often considered examples of Yogācāra-*tathāgatagarbha* hybrid texts. Kuiji himself is no stranger to the *tathāgatagarbha* discourse. In his commentary on the *Vimalakīrti-sūtra*, Kuiji says: "The *ālayavijñāna* is what contains and conceals; the seeds are what is contained and concealed. Two kinds of what is contained and the two kinds of what is concealed are all called the womb of the Buddha."[59] Although Ouyang's views are different from those of Kuiji, he (and other Buddhists)—critical as they were of East Asian Buddhism—did not reject the *tathāgatagarbha* tradition as a whole.

This is an important point to remember when we look into the changes Ouyang went through in his later career. Ouyang and his disciples are often portrayed as rejecting this central view in East Asian Buddhism, but this chapter will demonstrate that this is not the case. There are two major reasons that led to this misunderstanding. First, there is no doubt that the Yogācāra movement was a controversial phenomenon in Chinese intellectual history, especially the group associated with Ouyang Jingwu and his China Institute of Inner Learning. Consequently, much of our view of them was informed by polemical literature created by their opponents who doubted the patriotism of Ouyang and his followers and the "Chinese-ness" of their Yogācāra teaching. They also saw them as criticizing everything that Chinese Buddhism stood for, and one important aspect was the *tathāgatagarbha* teachings.[60] The opponents' view is not entirely off the mark, but we should not be satisfied with their characterization of Ouyang and his disciples precisely because their opponents won a "narrative contest."

Secondly, one of the prisms through which scholars who study the "Neo-Yogācāras" of the Republican period is a comparison with the Critical Buddhist movement in Japan (*hihan bukkyō* 批判佛教). The leaders of the Critical Buddhist movement in Japan, Hakamaya Noriaki and Matsumoto Shirō, rejected

58. See also the related discussion in Thierry Meynard's chapter.

59. Keng Ching, "Yogācāra Buddhism Transmitted or Transformed?" p. 289.

60. Of the opponents, the so called New Confucians are worth noting, especially Xiong Shili and Mou Zongsan (for more on this, see the essays in this volume by John Makeham, Lin Chen-kuo, and Jason Clower), but there were others, such as the historian Chen Yinke 陳寅恪 (1890–1969) and the intellectual historian Wing-tsit Chan (1901–1994) (for more see Aviv, "Differentiating the Pearl From the Fish Eye," pp. 88–89).

tathāgatagarbha as non-Buddhist.[61] While parallels do exist between the two intellectual phenomena, Ouyang and his circle differed in their approach to the doctrine.

Ouyang's particular view of *tathāgatagarbha* is important for our understanding of the scholastic Buddhist movement for two reasons. First, it contributes to our understanding of Ouyang's teaching as a whole. He is known as a staunch critic of East Asian Buddhist schools, such as Tiantai and Huayan, and of foundational texts in East Asian Buddhism, such as the *Awakening of Mahāyāna Faith* and the **Śūraṅgama-sūtra* and their misinterpretation of Buddhism (and he was especially critical of their *tathāgatagarbha* theories). Thus it may come as a surprise (it certainly did for me) that later in life he studied texts such as the *Avataṃsaka-sūtra* and the *Nirvāṇa-sūtra* that preached a version of *tathāgatagarbha* theory. Either Ouyang's thought had shifted with time or he had developed a more nuanced view of the *tathāgatagarbha* teaching.

Second, Ouyang's peculiar view of *tathāgatagarbha* is important for understanding the different voices amongst scholastic Buddhists. For many, the Critical Buddhist movement demarcated a clear rejection of the East Asian Buddhist tradition. It is important to take into account the diversity of voices and the differences between the first and second generations of scholastic Buddhists in terms of their critical evaluation of Buddhist doctrine and the scholarly methodology and tools they used.

Ouyang's study of Yogācāra earlier in his career brought to his attention the discrepancies between what he understood to be the "authentic" Indian teaching and foundational East Asian Buddhist texts such as the *Awakening of Mahāyāna Faith* and the way the East Asian Buddhist tradition interpreted central doctrines such as *tathāgatagarbha* or Buddha-nature. It is interesting to see the kind of critique that Ouyang leveled against the *Awakening of Mahāyāna Faith* and its doctrine of *tathāgatagarbha*, as it ignited one of the most heated debates in modern Chinese intellectual history.[62] His critique is also interesting because of the importance Ouyang attached to this doctrine later in his life. We will return to this supposed tension in his thought later on.

---

61. See, for example, Matsumoto when he argued: "I do not consider *tathāgatagarbha* thought to be Buddhist." In Matsumoto Shirō, "The Doctrine of Tathagata-garbha Is Not Buddhist," in *Pruning the Bodhi Tree: The Storm over Critical Buddhism*, ed. Jamie Hubbard and Paul L. Swanson (Honolulu: University of Hawaii Press, 1997), p. 165.

62. The debate surrounding the *Awakening of Mahāyāna Faith* is complex and beyond the scope of this chapter. Here I will refer only to Ouyang's treatment of the *Awakening of Mahāyāna Faith*'s interpretation of the *tathāgatagarbha* doctrine. See also John Jorgensen's article in this volume and Aviv, "Differentiating the Pearl from the Fish Eye," pp. 119–165.

The *Awakening of Mahāyāna Faith* became the target of growing criticism as early as the late nineteenth century in Japan and later in China. The debate continued throughout the twentieth century and is still taking place today in scholarly and monastic contexts. For critics of the text, it became the embodiment of what is wrong with East Asian Buddhism. The first Chinese intellectual who wrote about the debate in China was Zhang Taiyan, who concluded that the text was authentic but contained major flaws.[63] Interestingly, in Ouyang's early treatment of the text he accepted the same position. Although I am not aware of a later treatment of the text, it seems plausible that he may have changed his mind later. Most of his students— among them, Lü Cheng, Liang Qichao,[64] and Wang Enyang 王恩洋 (1897–1964)—who contributed to the debate, thought the text was apocryphal. It seems unlikely that their position would directly oppose that of their teacher.

The two kinds of tathāgatagarbha *theory*

According to the *tathāgatagarbha* texts, our inherent gnosis is pure. It is due to adventitious defilements (*āgantuka-kleśa*), that this inherent gnosis is not manifested in most sentient beings. These defilements distort the way ordinary unenlightened people see the world, and consequently they mistake their projection as reality. Once this misconception is rectified, the hindrances to correct knowledge of reality as it truly is are also removed.

This relatively simple view is problematized by: (1) discrepancies in classical Yogācāra texts in the way they understood the relationship between *tathāgatagarbha* and *ālayavijñāna*; (2) different interpretations of *tathāgatagarbha*; and (3) the conceptual and doctrinal problems it created. As for the first problem, there were fundamental inconsistencies between the two views, especially with the Yogācāra tradition of Asaṅga and Vasubandhu. In his *Mahāyāna-saṃgraha*, Asaṅga argued that the *ālayavijñāna*, or the base consciousness where all the karmic seeds are stored (*sarvabījakam*), has three characteristics:

63. Zhang Taiyan, "*Dasheng qixin lun* bian 大乘起信論辯" (Disputing the *Awakening of Mahāyāna Faith*), *Minbao* 民報 19 (1908), reprinted in *Xiandai Fojiao xueshu congkan* 現代佛教學術叢刊 (Collectanea of Modern Buddhist Scholarship) (Taipei: Dasheng wenhua chubanshe, 1978), vol. 35.

64. Liang Qichao was a student of Ouyang for a short time. He was not a disciple in the same sense that Lü Cheng was, but Ouyang left a deep impression on Liang. His commitment to learn from Ouyang is apparent in a letter he wrote to his daughter about his days in Nanjing, "Every week, on Mondays, Wednesdays, and Fridays from 7:30 am-9:30 am (The hardest thing is to wake up at 6 am) I go the Inner Studies Institute to listen to Mr. Ouyang Jingwu lecture on Buddhism." See Xu and Wang, *Ouyang Jingwu pingzhuan*, p. 78.

self-characteristics (*zixiang* 自相), characteristics as a cause (*yinxiang* 因相), and characteristics as a result (*guoxiang* 果相). The second characteristic, as a cause, means that the *ālayavijñāna* serves as "the cause of manifestation of all defiled *dharmas*."[65] The third, the characteristic of *ālayavijñāna* as a result, is defined as the fact that "the *ālayavijñāna* continues and recreates based on the beginningless permeation of those defiled dharmas."[66] As the text suggests, for Asaṅga—who does not mention inherent pure gnosis—the deepest realm of the mind is defiled and needs correction. But where would this correction come from? Naturally if it is not from within the mind, it must come from without.

According to Yogācāras such as Asaṅga, the way to stop the recreation of seeds is to extinguish their "container," namely the *ālayavijñāna*, in a process called "transformation of the basis" (*āśraya-parāvṛtti; zhuanyi* 轉依). But how can the process of the purification of a defiled mind begin? In the *Mahāyāna-saṃgraha*, Asaṅga suggested that the process must begin with an external source, most often one that is associated with the teachings of the Buddha.[67] The Buddhist teaching, or correct Dharma (*saddharma*), which originated in the *dharmadhatū*,[68] is "perfuming" the defiled mind with pure seeds.[69]

By contrast, for many East Asian Buddhists, even among critics of East Asian traditions such as Lü Cheng, the mind contains both pure and impure seeds.[70] The view that dominated most of East Asian Buddhist tradition conceived of the mind as the source of pure seeds. Consequently, the source of defilements was believed to be adventitious.

The *Awakening of Mahāyāna Faith* uses a well-known simile to describe the external source of the defiled states. This resembles the relationship that exists between the water of the ocean and its waves, stirred by the wind. Water and wind are inseparable; but water is not mobile by its nature, and if the wind stops,

65. Asaṅga, *Mahāyāna-saṃgraha*, T.1594.134b27-28. This version was translated by Xuanzang under the title *She dasheng lun ben* 攝大乘論本.

66. *Mahāyāna-saṃgraha*, T.1594.134c01.

67. Since this is a perfuming process that results from listening to the correct teaching, it is technically called "perfuming by hearing" or **śrutavāsanā*.

68. *Dharmadhatū* 法界 is a complex notion and often depends on the context. In the *abhidharma* tradition *dharmadhatū* is the realm (*dhatū*) of thinking, or the realm of human experience. Later, in the East Asian Mahāyāna tradition, *dharmadhatū* became associated with ultimate reality: the principle of reality that underlies human experience of reality.

69. *Mahāyāna-saṃgraha*, T.1594.136b29-c11.

70. Lü Cheng and Xiong Shili, "Bian Foxue genben wenti: Lü Cheng, Xiong Shili wangfu hangao 辯佛學根本問題 – 呂澂，熊十力往復函稿" (Debating the Fundamental Questions of Buddhism: The Correspondence between Lü Cheng and Xiong Shili), *Zhongguo zhexue* 11 (1984): 179.

the movement ceases. But the wet nature remains undestroyed. Likewise, man's mind, pure in its own nature, is stirred by the wind of ignorance. Both mind and ignorance have no particular forms of their own and they are inseparable. Yet mind is not mobile by nature, and if ignorance ceases, then the continuity [of deluded activities] ceases. But the essential nature of wisdom remains undestroyed.[71] The mind is inherently quiet; it is the adventitious winds of ignorance that stir the naturally quiescent sea of mind. As stated above, the *tathāgatagarbha* thesis was assimilated rather early into the Yogācāra tradition, but the two doctrines—early Yogācāra and *tathāgatagarbha*—contained irreconcilable tensions.[72] These tensions resurfaced in the twentieth century in the thought of Ouyang Jingwu.

Keng Ching distinguishes between what he calls the weak and strong *tathāgatagarbha* theses. The strong thesis, popularized in East Asia, sees the *tathāgatagarbha* as an unconditioned ontological foundation of all *dharmas*, the *ālayavijñāna* included. That means that the pure mind is inherently awakened (*benjue* 本覺), as it is the source of everything, and defiled states must be located elsewhere.[73] According to Keng Ching, this view does not appear in Indian texts mainly because the view that "Thusness [Suchness] as an unconditioned *dharma* can serve as the basis for conditioned dharmas goes against the basic distinction between 'unconditioned dharmas' vs. 'conditioned dharmas' established from very early on in the Abhidharma Buddhist philosophy." As we will see, this was also the problem Ouyang grappled with.

The second, weaker, *tathāgatagarbha* theory does appear in Indian texts such as the **Śrīmālādevī-siṃha-nāda-sūtra* (*Shengman shizi hou yisheng da fangbian fangguang jing* 勝鬘師子吼一乘大方便方廣經; Sutra of the Lion Roar of Queen Śrīmālā) and the *Ratnagotravibhāga* (*Baosheng jing* 寶性論; Treatise on the Jewel Nature). It also appears in what are considered Yogācāra texts (according to the East Asian tradition), such as the *Laṅkāvatāra-sūtra*. The weaker *tathāgatagarbha* theory argues for a clear divide between Suchness and the phenomenal realm of conditioned dharmas. *Tathāgatagarbha* is not to be confused with *tathatā* or Suchness. This is the mistake made by the strong *tathāgatagarbha* proponents.

Ouyang's view on *tathāgatagarbha* is rooted in the distinction between the two versions of *tathāgatagarbha* thought. Ouyang agreed with the "weaker" sense of *tathāgatagarbha* and rejected the "stronger" sense. Nonetheless, it is important to note that Ouyang's *tathāgatagarbha* view changed over the years. What began as a critique of the so-called strong *tathāgatagarbha* view and silence with regard to

---

71. Yoshito Hakeda (trans.), *The Awakening of Faith* (New York: Columbia University Press, 1967), p. 41.

72. Richard King, "Is 'Buddha-Nature' Buddhist?" *Numen* 42, no. 1 (1995): 1–20.

73. Keng Ching, "Yogācāra Buddhism Transmitted or Transformed?" pp. 422–424.

the weak *tathāgatagarbha* view evolved into a much milder critique of the strong *tathāgatagarbha* view and an embrace of his own version of the weak *tathāgatagarbha* view. I will now turn to Ouyang's view of the Buddha-nature doctrine.

Ouyang's critique of the strong tathāgatagarbha *theory*

Ouyang discussed his criticism of the strong *tathāgatagarbha* theory as part of his view of correct knowledge (*samyagjñāna; zheng zhi* 正智). For Ouyang, correct knowledge includes both mundane and supramundane knowledge and experiential wisdom (*ru liang zhi* 如量智), as well as wisdom of principle (如理智). Correct knowledge is a separate dharma from Suchness (*tathatā; zhenru* 真如), which is the state in which the principle of no-self is revealed, the holy teaching is actualized, and differs from all the things on which discourses and theories are based.[74]

Ouyang then analyzed how the notion of correct knowledge was distorted in the *Awakening of Mahāyāna Faith*. Correct knowledge should be understood as having two aspects: (1) it is knowledge that perceives the object (*neng yuan* 能緣); and (2) it is that which can function as a cause (*neng sheng* 能生). *Tathatā* or Suchness, on the other hand, "cannot be seeds, perfumer, or perfumed; it has nothing to do with such matters."[75] Here, Ouyang draws a clear line between the strong *tathāgatagarbha* doctrine and what he saw as the genuine Buddhist teaching.

The strong *tathāgatagarbha* doctrine expressed in the *Awakening of Mahāyāna Faith* presented "mind as Suchness" (*xin zhenru* 心真如) and the "mind that arises and ceases" (*xin shengmie* 心生滅) as two manifestations of one and the same mind, such that they are in fact identical, two sides of the same coin.[76] For Ouyang, the two realms were irrevocably isolated from one another. Suchness is beyond language and discursive thought, and it is called Suchness merely because of "forced terminological expedience" (*qiang ming* 強名).

The second problem, according to Ouyang, is that those who followed the wrong interpretation of the *Awakening of Mahāyāna Faith* saw Suchness as giving rise to the myriad dharmas.[77] For Ouyang, relying on a famous passage in *Cheng*

74. See Ouyang Jingwu, "Weishi jueze tan," p. 1378. The explanation is a paraphrase of Maitreya, *Yogācārabhūmi-śāstra*, T.1579.696a01-07. Ouyang gave a general account here of the five *dharmas* and did not include the *Yogācārabhūmi*'s more detailed analysis of correct knowledge. He added that the notion of correct knowledge is also identifiable with two kinds of wisdom: wisdom as experienced (literally as *pramāṇa*) and wisdom according to principle (*ru liang ru li zhi zhi* 如量如理之智).

75. Ouyang, "Weishi jueze tan," p. 1378.

76. *Dasheng qixin lun*, T.1666.576a05-09.

77. Ouyang, "Weishi jueze tan," p. 1379.

weishi lun, this position is similar to that of the Vibhajyavādins.[78] According to Ouyang:

> The Vibhajyavādins (分別論者) did not establish the notion of inherent seeds (*fa'er zhong* 法爾種). [They claim that] the mind is originally pure. When the mind is separated from defilements, its noumenon aspect (*ti* 體) is pure and serves as the cause of the undefiled (*wulou* 無漏), just as milk can become ghee because there is [already] the nature of ghee in milk. Thus, they [i.e., the Vibhajyavādins] take the noumenon aspect [of the mind] as the function [of the mind]. [If] the noumenon aspect is mixed [with the nature of its function], then the function is lost."[79]

Ouyang's later thought and his tathāgatagarbha *phase*

Ouyang's critical tone toward the strong *tathāgatagarbha* doctrine gradually changed. In 1923, after the death of his son and two of his students, Ouyang became more syncretic in his thought. This tendency increased with the years, especially during the last decade of his life when he sought to harmonize the different Buddhist teachings and Buddhist thought with the Confucian tradition.

During the later period of his life, Ouyang intended to work on what he called his definitive teaching.[80] He never explicitly wrote such a piece, but in the summer of 1937 he lectured to his disciples about his definitive teaching.[81] A year earlier, Ouyang also published a commentary on the *Ghana-vyūha-sūtra* (*Dasheng miyan jing* 大乘密嚴經; Sutra of the Secret Adornment), which he considered to be the articulation of his definitive teaching.[82] Ouyang started his commentary by saying:

> There are numerous gates to the Dharma, which can be divided into the three aspects of teaching, practice, and fruit. The fruit aspect is delineated in the *Mahāparinirvāṇa-sūtra*; the practice aspect is delineated in

---

78. *Cheng weishi lun*, T.1585.8c20: "The Vibhajyavādins held the theory that because the nature of the mind is pure and the mind is defiled by adventitious afflictions (*āgantuka kleśāḥ*), it is called defiled. When the mind is separated from [those afflictions] it becomes uncontaminated (*anāsrava*) again, and therefore the uncontaminated dharmas are produced by causes."

79. Ouyang Jingwu, "Weishi jueze tan," p. 1382.

80. Ouyang Jingwu, "Fu Wei Siyi shu 覆魏斯逸書" (Reply to Wei Siyi), in *Ouyang dashi yiji*, pp. 1552–1556.

81. Lü Cheng, "Qin jiaoshi Ouyang xiansheng shelüe," p. 356.

82. Ouyang Jingwu, "Fu Wei Siyi shu," p. 1553.

> the *Mahāparinirvāṇa-sūtra* and the *Avataṃsaka-sūtra*; and the teaching aspect is delineated in the *Ghana-vyūha-sūtra*. This is why it is said that it is one of the summaries of the entire Buddhist teaching.[83]

Ouyang cited and wrote about texts associated with the *tathāgatagarbha* corpus such as the *Mahāparinirvāṇa-sūtra*, the *Laṅkāvatāra-sūtra*, the *Avataṃsaka-sūtra*, and the *Ghana-vyūha-sūtra*, among others.[84] He had largely ignored these texts in his earlier career. The fact that he wrote an extensive preface to the *Mahāparinirvāṇa-sūtra*—a sutra that he often read in his old age—is another indication of a shift in his *tathāgatagarbha* views.

This shift should be seen as a part of his growing interest in the existential questions of the ultimate state and goal of Buddhism (and life), rather than in the study of conditioned phenomena. Themes he explored in his late writings include Buddhist practice (rather than the Buddhist teaching, on which he focused his earlier writings); Confucianism and its relation to Buddhism; and the notion of *nirvāṇa* without remainder (*nirupadhiśeṣa nirvāṇa*).

Ouyang's theory of *tathāgatagarbha* appears in several of his later writings. A detailed account can be found in a series of letters exchanged between Ouyang and his friend and supporter Mei Guangxi 梅光羲 (1880–1947). The correspondence began with a series of questions Mei posed to Ouyang on the difference between *prajñā* and *bodhi* and includes seven letters Ouyang sent to Mei. In the fourth letter, Mei Guangxi asked about the meaning of the quotation from the *Avataṃsaka-sūtra*: "The bodies of all the buddhas are only the one body of *dharma* (*dharmakāya*)."[85] Ouyang replied: "When Dharma dwells among humans it is called the *dharmakāya* (Dharma-body), and when the Dharma dwells in the dharmas it is called the *dharmadhātu* (realm of dharmas). It is therefore called Dharma-body and also can be called *dharmadhātu*."[86]

Ouyang elaborated on this special realm that all Buddhas possess in a later letter to Mei Guangxi. As he had already established that *dharmakāya* is synonymous with *dharmadhātu*, Ouyang explained his notion of *dharmadhātu*, which in a Mahāyāna context often refers to the noumenon, reality as it is, and emptiness:

---

83. Ouyang Jingwu, "*Dasheng miyan jing* 大乘密嚴經," in *Ouyang dashi yiji*, pp. 1011–1012.

84. The *Ghana-vyūha-sūtra* is another Yogācāra-*tathāgatagarbha* hybrid text that resembles the themes discussed in the *Laṅkāvatāra-sūtra*.

85. *Avataṃsaka-sūtra*, T278.429b20.

86. Ouyang Jingwu, "Fu Mei Xieyun shu 覆梅擷芸書" (Reply to Mei Xieyun), http://www.guoxuebook.com/new/0002/bfehyx/041.htm, fourth letter; accessed January 29, 2012.

> [In the notion of] the *dharmadhātu*, *dharma* means the sacred dharmas of all the conditioned and unconditioned. All sacred dharmas arise because of a cause named *dhātu*; therefore the meaning of *dhātu* is a base. The true nature of all dharmas, the true essence of all the buddhas, is called *dhātu*; therefore *dhātu* means the essential nature. Pure and impure, arising and ceasing, like space or void (虛空), it is endowed with merit, it is the same as *nirvāṇa*, it is the same as *tathatā*. "[Whether] the *tathāgata* appears or does not appear in the world, his essence (or nature) is permanently abiding."[87] All the buddhas and sentient beings equally possess it, therefore it is the dharma abode; it is the dharma nature (or *dharmatā*).[88]

In the seventh letter to Mei Guangxi, Ouyang clarified that, based on the *Śrīmālā-sūtra*, the storehouse of *dharmadhātu* (*fajiezang* 法界藏) is in fact synonymous with *tathāgatagarbha*. Returning to a focus on metaphysics of the essence that can be found in any sentient being and is equal to the noumenon (which probably resembled ideas he was concerned with during his neo-Confucian phase) brought Ouyang closer to mainstream East Asian thought.

But what did he mean by *tathāgatagarbha*? Ouyang seems to rely on several examples of textual evidence that aren't always in agreement with one another. In the sixth letter he offered his own solutions:

> *Tathāgatagarbha* is the basis that establishes the pure and impure in the sacred teaching, and it is the basis that gives rise to the sacred practice. The *Śrīmālā-sūtra* says: "The *tathāgatagarbha*, the self-nature of which is pure, is defiled by adventitious afflictions, [and] it is the basis that establishes these defilements." "The seven consciousnesses do not stop even for a moment, do not plant the myriad sufferings; they do not get weary of suffering; and do not aspire to *nirvāṇa*. [But for the *tathāgatagarbha*] there is no past, no arising, and no ceasing; it plants the myriad sufferings [i.e., it can serve as the base for suffering]; and it can be weary of suffering and aspire to *nirvāṇa*."[89] It is also the basis that establishes purity. Being bounded, it is called *tathāgatagarbha*; being free from bondage, it

---

87. This is a quotation from *Dasheng miyan jing*, T682.749a19-21.

88. Ouyang, "Fu Mei Xieyun shu," sixth letter.

89. In his commentary on this passage, Yinshun 印順 (1906–2005), a disciple of Taixu, argued that it is the permanence of the *tathāgatagarbha* that allows it to be the basis for both suffering and liberation. It is this permanence that distinguishes *tathāgatagarbha* texts from other Mahāyāna texts belonging to the Madhyamaka and Yogācāra traditions (see Yinshun, 勝鬘經講記 [Notes on Sutra of the Lion Roar of Queen Śrīmālā], http://www.yinshun.org.tw/books/06/yinshun06-13.html accessed July 16, 2011). It is another indication of the change in Ouyang's approach to Buddhism in his later life.

is called the *dharmakāya*. For the one who has no doubt with respect to *tathāgatagarbha* that is bounded within numerous afflictions, or has no doubt with respect to the *dharmakāya* that is liberated from the numerous afflictions in the afflictions store, for him there is the manifestation of the basis of the sacred practice.[90]

Here Ouyang followed texts such as the *Śrīmālā-sūtra*, arguing that the *tathāgatagarbha* is the permanent essence in the stage where this essence is bounded with afflictions. The question is: What is the difference between the base consciousness (*ālayavijñāna*) and *tathāgatagarbha*? Ouyang followed the *Laṅkāvatāra-sūtra* (and/or very likely the *Ghana-vyūha-sūtra*, which he regarded highly toward the end of his life), arguing that "the *ālayavijñāna* is indeed the *tathāgatagarbha*."[91]

By taking this stance, Ouyang had distanced himself from the classic model of *ālayavijñāna*, as outlined by Vasubandhu and Asaṅga. He did not address these discrepancies, which he had so meticulously denounced earlier. In one essay about the main teachings of the China Institute of Inner Learning, Ouyang stated: "The *Śrīmālā-sūtra* explains that the *tathāgatagarbha* is the same as the intrinsically pure mind of Yogācāra."[92] How is *tathāgatagarbha* different from the classical Yogācāra doctrine? First, the permanence of *tathāgatagarbha* is, of course, radically different from the transient nature of the *ālayavijñāna*. Second, as far as I am aware, neither Asaṅga nor Vasubandhu thought about the *ālayavijñāna* in terms of "innate purity," a characteristic that Ouyang (following the *Śrīmālā-sūtra* tradition) attributed to the *tathāgatagarbha*. Furthermore, as the repository of all the seeds that bring about further rebirth, *ālayavijñāna* cannot be innately pure. It is not of the same nature as *nirvāṇa*. *Nirvāṇa*, or liberation, is attained only when the *ālayavijñāna* is transformed (*āśrayaparāvṛtti*). The idea that the mind is innately pure is simply a different school of early Mahāyāna Buddhist thought.

In his article on Ouyang's *tathāgatagarbha* thought,[93] Zhou Guihua determined that Ouyang offered a compromise between the Indian view of *tathāgatagarbha*

90. Ouyang, "Fu Mei Xieyun shu," sixth letter.

91. Ouyang, "Fu Mei Xieyun shu," fourth letter.

92. Ouyang Jingwu, "Zhina Neixue Yuan yuanxun shi 支那內學院院訓釋" (Explanation of the Regulations of the China Inner Studies Institute), in *Ouyang Jingwu ji* 歐陽竟無集 (Ouyang Jingwu's Collected Writings), ed. Huang Xianian 黃夏年 (Beijing: Zhongguo shehui kexue chubanshe, 1995), p. 79.

93. Zhou Guihua 周貴華, "Ouyang Jingwu dashi de rulaizang sixiang 歐陽竟無大師的如來藏思想" (The Tathāgatagarbha Thought of Master Ouyang Jingwu), in *Rongtong Kong Fo: yidai foxue dashi Ouyang Jingwu* 融通孔佛：一代佛學大師歐陽竟無 (Harmonizing Confucianism and Buddhism: The Life and Time of the Buddhist Master Ouyang Jingwu), ed. Zheng Xiaojiang 鄭曉江 (Beijing: Zongjiao wenhua chubanshe, 2004), pp. 28–49.

theory and the Chinese Buddhist thought expressed in the *Awakening of Mahāyāna Faith*. According to Zhou, the Indian tradition understood *tathāgatagarbha* to be a way of speaking kataphatically about emptiness, while in fact *tathāgatagarbha* and emptiness are synonymous. Later, in texts such as the *Nirvāṇa-sūtra*, we see an evolution of the term to mean a basis and cause of buddhahood. The term *tathāgatagarbha* probably appeared around that time and developed in texts such as the *Tathāgatagarbha-sūtra*. Texts such as the *Śrīmālā-sūtra* (which, according to Paul Williams, can be dated to the third century CE),[94] argued for the similarity between the innately pure mind and the *tathāgatagarbha*. This is the kind of *tathāgatagarbha* theory to which Ouyang subscribed.[95] There are several interpretations of just what *tathāgatagarbha* is. The *Śrīmālā-sūtra* offers a different understanding from that of the *Laṅkāvatāra-sūtra*. Without delving into the different models, suffice it to say that Ouyang, who rejected the notion that *tathāgatagarbha* is equated with Suchness, seemed to be closer in his interpretations to texts such as the *Śrīmālā-sūtra*, the *Laṅkāvatāra-sūtra*, and the *Ghana-vyūha-sūtra*. Early on, Ouyang vehemently rejected the conflation of Suchness, *tathāgatagarbha*, and conditioned phenomena found in the *Awakening of Mahāyāna Faith*. Zhou argued that Ouyang's later teaching served as a kind of compromise. He admitted that *tathāgatagarbha* should be the noumenonal aspect (*ti* 體) of all conditioned phenomena, but he rejected the causal power of *tathāgatagarbha* to give rise to phenomena, as in the inherent enlightenment (*benjue* 本覺) theory of the *Awakening of Mahāyāna Faith*. Following the *Śrīmāla-sūtra*, Ouyang saw *tathātagarbha* as Suchness or *dharmakāya* when it is entangled within conditioned dharmas. But even as Suchness it cannot serve as a direct cause, only as a secondary or auxiliary cause (*adhipati pratyaya*). Only conditioned cause can serve as a direct cause.

Chinese commentators explained this dynamic by utilizing the formula of noumenal reality (*ti* 體) and function (*yong* 用), in which *tathāgatagarbha* is seen as *ti* and conditioned phenomena as *yong*. But they also present us with a problem, because they interpret them as the same thing. From Ouyang's standpoint, this is a mistake that can be found among the indigenous Chinese schools of Tiantai and Huayan: "If one established the unity of 'principle' and 'phenomena' (*li shi* 理事) as his tenet, then truth will surrender to the [false doctrines of]

---

94. See Paul Williams, *Mahayana Buddhism: The Doctrinal Foundations* (London and New York: Routledge, 1989), p. 100.

95. Even Lü Cheng, who was more critical than Ouyang of the East Asian tradition, did not reject the validity of the *tathāgatagarbha* tradition; see Lü Cheng 呂澂, "*Lengqie* rulaizang zhang jiangyi 楞伽如來藏章講義" (Notes of the Tathāgatagarbha Chapter of the *Sutra on the Decent into Lanka*), in *Lü Cheng Foxue lunzhu xuanji* 呂澂佛學論著選集 (Selected Collection of Lü Cheng's Buddhist Writings) 5 vols. (Shandong, Jinan: Qilu shushe, 1991), vol. 1, pp. 258–259.

Tiantai and Huayan. Why is it? The Tiantai saying 'three thousand worlds in one thought' (*yi nian san qian* 一念三千) and the Huayan theory of 'the *dharmadhātu* of no obstruction between principle and phenomena' means [just] that."[96]

Ouyang's solution is to argue that *tathāgatagarbha* is not equal to Suchness (such as it is presented in the *Awakening of Mahāyāna Faith*), but rather that the *tathāgatagarbha* is the aspect of the *ālayavijñāna* that contains the innate untainted (*anāsrava*) seeds. In the words of Ouyang, "The aspect that stores the pure seeds is the *tathāgatagarbha*; the aspect that stores the defiled seeds is called the *ālaya*[*vijñāna*]. It is absurd to further establish a ninth consciousness."[97] As such, Ouyang acknowledged the role played by the *tathāgatagarbha* while avoiding the problem of mixing Suchness (= noumenon aspect) and conditioned phenomena (= function).

What Ouyang seems to have accomplished here is interesting, as he relied on the notion of innate pure seeds that can be found in texts such as *Cheng weishi lun* and harnessed the more orthodox teaching of Yogācāra in order to solve a problem in the *tathāgatagarbha* doctrine, namely how to maintain the integrity of the *tathāgatagarbha* doctrine without falling into the *Awakening of Mahāyāna Faith* trap of mixing Suchness and conditioned phenomena.

Conclusions

In this chapter I have attempted to argue that Ouyang Jingwu well deserves to be considered one of the important intellectuals in the Yogācāra scholastic movement in early twentieth-century China. Ouyang was the first Chinese Buddhist intellectual who recognized Yogācāra as one of the highest achievements of the Buddhist tradition and turned the propagation of Yogācāra into the focal point of his career. More than anyone, Ouyang was responsible for printing and introducing Yogācāra texts and circulating them among Buddhists and non-Buddhist intellectuals. His institution, the China Institute of Inner Learning, was where he conducted his research, taught most of the other figures discussed in this book, and wrote about many *abhidharma* and Yogācāra texts.

We saw Ouyang as a patriotic thinker whose main goal was to rectify flawed doctrines and practices in order to bring about intellectual and spiritual revolution in China. He was a staunch critic of his native Buddhist tradition and used traditional and more modern scholarly methods in order to highlight problems in the history and doctrines of the Buddhist tradition in China. Ouyang was also a creative scholar with a unique interpretation of doctrinal issues. We noted this both

96. Ouyang, "Fu Mei Xieyun shu," fifth letter.

97. Ouyang, "Zhina neixueyuan yuanxun shi," p. 53.

with respect to his unique approach later in life to the doctrine of *tathāgatagarbha* and with his idiosyncratic differentiation of the *weishi* and *faxiang* approaches. We also saw how radical his new interpretation was and how much Ouyang challenged Buddhist orthodoxy with his scholasticism as evidenced by the emotional reaction of Taixu and the debate that ensued between them.

With so many achievements in regard to the revival of scholastic Buddhism, it is not surprising that Ouyang is remembered mainly as a paragon of Yogācāra scholarship in China. In this chapter, however, I have also argued for a more nuanced view of Ouyang's thought as a whole and of the way he dealt with the East Asian Buddhist tradition. Specifically, I have tried to avoid associating him too readily with other critical movements, such as the Japanese Critical Buddhist movement with its complete rejection of basic East Asian Buddhist traditions such as *tathāgatagarbha*. Scholars tend to ascribe to Ouyang and his disciples similar radical views, partially, I argue, because of the polemical context from which this intellectual movement emerged in Republican China.

Although Ouyang himself might not have admitted that his writings about *tathāgatagarbha* were a departure from his earlier teachings, this late phase presented a new tendency in Ouyang's thought that was not present in the earlier stages of the evolution of his philosophy. Ouyang's intellectual trajectory is the story of the complex relationship and dialogue between the different foreign and Chinese forms of thought. To understand the place of Yogācāra in Ouyang's thought, we must locate it in the context of this dialogue. Using this approach will help us see Ouyang as he was, a multifaceted thinker who was transformed by different teachings throughout his life, and not merely as a polemical and sectarian thinker as he has often been portrayed.

10

Lü Cheng, Epistemology, and Genuine Buddhism

Dan Lusthaus

AS THE IMPERIAL age came to an end and the Republican era began, Buddhism, like China, struggled to find a way to respond to the challenges of modernity. Western ideas—especially in philosophy, science, and technology—could not be ignored after a humiliating century of foreign domination. Even Japan, which in the past had been an avid consumer of Chinese culture, now had risen to cultural prominence in East Asia, primarily due to a deliberate and dramatic pursuit of modernity, incorporating Western trends and ideas into its fabric. The cultural vanguard of East Asia—in the arts, science, humanities, fashions, the full gamut of cultural touchstones—had become Japan, not China. China looked within for native tools with which to regain its former preeminence, and looked beyond its borders for new ideas or inspiration in order to remake itself. Buddhism, since it had always been pan-Asian and never exclusively Chinese, provided several conduits for the influx of new ideas. Moreover, of all the traditional Chinese philosophical systems, the one that most nearly matched the epistemological complexity and rigor of the Western systems, such as the Kantian and neo-Kantian systems that had become popular in Europe and Japan in the early twentieth century, was Yogācāra.[1] How to interpret Yogācāra correctly, and the proper way to view its relation to other East Asian forms of Buddhism—historically and

1. A number of scholars, especially in Japan, have drawn attention to similarities between the Yogācāra notion of *vijñapti-mātra* (nothing but mental construction) and Kant's *Vorstellung* ("representation"). One can find additional affinities. For instance, "According to Kant, sensibility can only intuit, understanding can only think; the two cannot exchange their functions." (J. N. Mohanty, *Edmund Husserl's Freiberg Years: 1916–1938* [New Haven, CT: Yale University Press, 2011], p. 195.) This bears a striking parallel to the distinction between perception (*pratyakṣa*) and inference (*anumāna*) in Yogācāra *hetuvidyā* epistemology in that the former only cognizes particulars while the latter only cognizes conceptual universals.

conceptually—became major debate topics among the Buddhist intelligentsia, as well as among some of their rivals.

The foreign conduits were of two basic types: (1) Buddhist traditions and literatures from India, Tibet, Japan, and so on, that had not previously received attention in China; and (2) new methodologies for recontextualizing and reaching new understandings of traditional Chinese Buddhist literature, such as historical and philological criticism.

Buddhism had flowed into China from India and Central Asia from the first through seventh centuries. Within a generation or so from the time of the great pilgrim and translator Xuanzang 玄奘 (600–664), China—and thus East Asia—ceased to receive new ideas and developments, even though translators remained sporadically active until the eleventh century.[2] In the early eighth century it was as if a great spigot was turned and Buddhism ceased to flow into China, instead flowing into Tibet. Absolutely foundational Indian figures for later Indian and Tibetan Buddhism, such as Dharmakīrti (seventh century), Candrakīrti (600–*ca.* 650), Śāntarakṣita (725–788), and so on, were unknown to East Asian Buddhists until the twentieth century. As knowledge of Sanskrit and Indic languages disappeared from China by the end of the Song Dynasty, deciphering difficult texts and obscure translations could go no further than what the traditional commentaries had provided, or what the ingenuity and inventiveness of novel—but frequently uninformed—readings could concoct. As Chinese Buddhists in the early twentieth century earnestly began to study Tibetan and Sanskrit, they suddenly had access to a vast quantity of Buddhist literature previously unknown, and also could now consult alternate translations and commentaries of texts well known within the Chinese tradition, sometimes with startling results. Additionally, many important texts, such as key commentaries by Xuanzang's successor, Kuiji 窺基 (632–682), had long been lost and forgotten in China, but preserved in Japanese or Korean collections. Reintroducing these forgotten texts to Chinese readers spawned excitement, new studies, and new insights.

In addition to gaining a variety of new materials with which to work, new methodological strategies for working on them also emerged. Western philological and textual methods came directly from Western scholars in China—such

2. The major exception were the forms of early tantra that entered China during the eighth and ninth centuries, which, while leaving some tacit traces in China and Korea, passed to Japan where they survived and were further developed as the Shingon 真言 School. See also Tansen Sen, "The Revival and Failure of Buddhist Translations during the Song Dynasty" *T'oung Pao* 88 (2002): 27–80. The last prolific translator was Dānapāla 施護 (tenth century), to whom 115 translations found in the Taishō—either done by himself or in collaboration with others—are attributed. He worked until 1017 or so. Of all the texts he translated only one reflects a significant post-Xuanzang Indian development: Kamalaśīla's *Bhāvanākrama* (*Guang shi puti xin lun* 廣釋菩提心論; Extensive Explanation of the Treatise on Bodhi-mind) T.32.1664.

as Baron Alexander von Stäel-Holstein (1877–1937)[3] and Ferdinand Lessing (1882–1961)[4]—who became influential teachers for a generation of Chinese scholars, or indirectly through the appropriation and deployment of European methods by Japanese scholars, which in turn influenced Chinese exegesis and hermeneutics. A variety of text-critical methods had also been developed during the Qing Dynasty primarily within Neo-Confucian circles in China, helping to set the groundwork for an appreciation of the usefulness of such approaches.

Lü Cheng and "Genuine Buddhism"

Lü Cheng 呂澂 (1896–1989) was both a beneficiary and contributor to these cross-currents. Arguably the key initiator and founder of the modernizing approach to reforming Buddhism was Yang Wenhui 楊文會 (1837–1911) whose lectures Lü attended in Nanjing while still very young, under the influence of his older brother, Lü Fengzi 呂鳳子 (1886–1959). This was also how Lü Cheng first met Ouyang Jingwu 歐陽竟無 (1871–1943) who was working with Yang at that time. Ouyang would influence the course of Lü's life and career. When Ouyang established the Buddhist Research Institute (Fojiao yanjiubu 佛學研究部) at Jinling Sutra Press (Jinling kejingchu 金陵刻經處) in 1914, Lü Cheng became one of its earliest members.

Ouyang was a fierce defender of the Yogācāra promulgated by Xuanzang and of Xuanzang's translations, and he especially valued the *Yogācārabhūmi-śāstra* (*Yuqie shidi lun* 瑜伽師地論; Treatise on Grounds for Disciplined Practice), a huge compendium of Buddhist doctrine and practices.[5] Xuanzang's ostensive motive for undertaking the perilous journey to India across the deserts and mountains

3. On Baron Stäel-Holstein, see the overview of his life and work by Wang Qilong 王啟龍, *Ganghetai xueshu nianpu jianbian* 鋼和泰學術年譜簡編 (A Brief Chronological Biography of Alexander von Stäel-Holstein) (Beijing: Zhonghua shuju, 2008), and a shorter English version, Wang Qilong, "A Brief Review of Alexander von Stael-Holstein: A Great Scholar in Asian Studies," *Chinese Tibetology* 1 (March 2008): 80–93. For examples of the Baron's scholarship, cf. Baron A. von Stael-Holstein, *Kāśyapaparivarta* (China: 1923) [correlated Sanskrit, Chinese and Tibetan editions of the text, with an English introduction]; "The Emperor Ch'ien-lung and The Larger *Śūraṃgamasūtra*," *Harvard Journal of Asiatic Studies* 1, no. 1 (April 1936): 136–146; "Avalokita and Apalokita," *Harvard Journal of Asiatic Studies* 1, no. 3 (November 1936): 350–362; and "On a Peking Edition of the Tibetan Kanjur which Seems to be Unknown in the West," edited and introduced by Jonathan Silk, *Journal of the International Association of Buddhist Studies* 22, no. 1 (1999): 215–249.

4. Lessing, perhaps best known for his works on Tibet, "Lamaism," and Tantra, came to China in 1907 and spent seventeen years there teaching languages and philology at various institutions.

5. For a fuller account of Ouyang, see the essay by Eyal Aviv in this volume.

of Central Asia was to retrieve a complete copy of the *Yogācārabhūmi*; he translated it in one hundred fascicles soon after returning to China.[6] Unlike Ouyang, who apparently never learned Sanskrit or Tibetan, and so could work only with Chinese sources and Chinese translations, Lü studied Sanskrit and Tibetan and came to realize that correlating Chinese texts with their Sanskrit and/or Tibetan versions provided insights otherwise unobtainable from the Chinese texts alone. In the case of difficult texts or passages—and there were many—consulting the Sanskrit or Tibetan could offer invaluable clues to otherwise unsolvable interpretive conundrums. Indian and Tibetan texts not only offered alternative interpretations of important Buddhist concepts, but they also shed light on how to critically read the Chinese translations more accurately, since they could reveal what lay behind a translator's method and choices and clarify the intended denotations of terms that were sometimes obscured by their Chinese literary equivalents.[7] The ability to read the texts more accurately facilitated a clearer understanding of their original purport and meaning. In the sometimes-heated debates over the correct interpretation of Buddhist concepts and models, and over which texts might justifiably serve as reliable proof texts, these textual methods, Lü believed, could help distinguish "genuine" Buddhism (*zhenshi Foxue* 真實佛學) from the

6. Xuanzang left China in 627, arrived in India (Kashmir) in 629, studied at Nālandā and elsewhere, and traveled through most of India. His travelog, *Xiyu ji* 西域記 (Record of Western Lands; T.51.2087) compiled from his notes by the young monk Bianji 辯機 (who suffered an ignoble and painful death shortly after completing that project due to a scandalous intimacy with the Emperor's married sister) remains one of our most important historical documents about seventh-century India and Central Asia. Xuanzang began his return to China in 643 and arrived back in Chang'an in 645. He translated the *Yogācārabhūmi* with a team of over twenty assistants from July 3, 646 to June 11, 648, while simultaneously translating nearly a dozen other texts.

7. To give one example: The Chinese word *xiang* 相 was used by translators for a variety of Sanskrit terms, such as *lakṣaṇa* (characteristic or definition of something), *ākāra* (mental image), *nimitta* (signature feature 標記, or a cause 因), *liṅga* (mark, indicatory feature, sign, cause), and so on. While such terms are clearly distinguishable in a Sanskrit text, the proper intended sense may not be as evident in a Chinese translation using *xiang*. A discussion of the second of the Five Dharmas in the *Laṅkāvatāra-sūtra* [Discourse on [the Buddha's] Entering [the Country of] Lanka] in an essay titled "*Lengqie* guan wangyi 楞伽觀妄義" (An Examination of Erroneous Ideas in the *Laṅkāvatāra Sūtra*) is included in *Lü Cheng Foxue lunzhu xuanji* 呂澂佛學論著選集 (Selected Collection of Lü Cheng's Writings on Buddhism) 5 vols. (Jinan: Qilu shushe, 1991), vol. 1. pp. 266–277, an essay first published on May 28, 1930. In this example, where the Chinese gives *xiang*, Lü Cheng points out that the underlying Sanskrit term is *nimitta* (*ni-mi-ta* 尼彌他), which has two main meanings, "cause" and "signature feature" (有二種釋，一為因義一為標記義); he compares its usage in the *Laṅkāvatāra* with the usage of *nimitta* in a foundational Yogācāra text, *Madhyānta-vibhāga* (*Zhong bian fenbie lun* 中邊分別論; Differentiating the Middle from the Extremes), and concludes that the *Laṅkāvatāra*'s primary sense for *nimitta* is "sign" while retaining aspects of "cause" (p. 269). This determination would have been difficult to reach on the basis of the Chinese texts alone.

"fake" imitations (*xiangsi Foxue* 相似佛學) that had displaced the genuine article in East Asia.

Although Lü Cheng provides no manifesto or tenet-list defining Genuine Buddhism, his writings and those of his contemporaries offer some guidance. It must accord with and not distort the authentic teachings of the Buddha as recorded and transmitted in legitimate Buddhist sutras and treatises. Buddhist texts, especially the treatises, were often very argumentative, and Indian Buddhists contested and disputed the whole gamut of Buddhist doctrines, so Genuine Buddhism was less about adhering to a fundamentalistic or catechismic dogma than thinking with and working from the parameters advised by the legitimate materials. Although ultimately the originating sources were from India, their Chinese transmissions and exemplifications were also "Genuine." In the view of Ouyang and his disciples, like Lü, the Yogācāra tradition developed by Asaṅga, Vasubandhu, and others, and promulgated in China by Xuanzang, Kuiji, etc., provided the necessary basis—doctrinally and methodologically—for developing Buddhism in the twentieth century, embodied in their institutional dream to revive the traditions of Nālandā University—the premier Indian Buddhist institution for many centuries, including when Xuanzang studied there—with its focus on the five "sciences."[8] Lü devoted a good portion of his early career to figuring out and lucidly presenting two of those sciences, *hetuvidyā* (logic and epistemology) and *śabdavidyā* (grammar and linguistics),[9] an immensely significant contribution, since for the last thousand years few in China have correctly understood them.

Ouyang's promotion of Yogācāra in particular struck many of his younger contemporaries as more relevant and authentic than the alternative forms of Buddhism competing at that time. Liang Qichao 梁啓超 (1873–1929), who studied with Ouyang, wrote in the early 1920s: "It is only after having heard the teachings by Master Ouyang Jingwu on the thought of the Nothing-but-Consciousness (Weishi) school that I knew there exists a Genuine Buddhism

---

8. The five sciences (*pañcavidyā*; *wu ming* 五明) are: (1) grammar, linguistics, and literary arts (*śabdavidyā*; *shengming* 聲明); (2) fine arts and mathematics (*śilpakarmasthānavidyā*; *gongqiaoming* 工巧明); (3) medicine (*cikitsāvidyā*; *yifangming* 醫方明); (4) logic and epistemology (*hetuvidyā*; *yinming* 因明); and (5) ethical, psychological, and intellectual cultivation (*adhyātmavidyā*; *neiming* 內明).

9. His main *hetuvidyā* writings are discussed below. His *Shengming lüe* 聲明略 (Précis on [Sanskrit] Grammar), which has been reprinted a number of times—for instance, combined with Ouyang's *Weishi jueze tan* 唯識抉擇談 (Critical Essays on the Doctrine of Nothing but Consciousness) (Nanjing: Zhina Neixue yuan, 1922)—not only presents an overview of Sanskrit grammar (case endings, conjugations, etc.), but discusses how a variety of challenging passages found in Chinese translation should be understood in the light of the underlying Sanskrit.

(聽歐陽竟無講唯識，方知有真佛學。)."[10] Lü held a similar conviction. The ideological nemesis of Genuine Buddhism was the *tathāgatagarbha*-laden metaphysics anchored in *Dasheng qixin lun* 大乘起信論 (Awakening of Mahāyāna Faith) and related texts, almost all of which Lü came to demonstrate were Chinese pseudepigraphic creations pretending to be original Indian texts. Genuine Buddhism eschewed such forgeries and the distorted Buddhism they promoted, an uphill battle in many quarters given that this pseudepigraphic ideology had dominated the East Asian Buddhist scene since the Song Dynasty.

A project based on recovering Genuine Buddhism while discrediting Mistaken Buddhism not surprisingly contains both strong radical and conservative impulses. The radical impulse is to shake up and overthrow the status quo by exposing its fallacies, replacing it with the newly discovered ideas. The conservative urge is to anchor the new discoveries in a notion of a lost "original" meaning, then work to retain the genuine article once recovered while preventing any further deviations and distortions. The genuine is to be uncovered, deciphered, unpacked, propagated, applied, extended, but not "altered" or distorted, since recovering it means to save it from centuries of distortions.

The doctrinal disputes engaging the Chinese intellectuals in the early decades of the twentieth century often turned on the prior ideological commitments and biases that the various disputants brought to the table, each rehearsing ingrained arguments to which they might add new polemical and rhetorical twists, but having no clear criteria with which to adjudicate differences of interpretation. Under such circumstances there was little to prevent each side from talking at or past the other, rather than providing clear and decisive evidence for deciding in favor of one idea or interpretation over another. For Lü, the philological tools he acquired, along with access to the witness of Indian and Tibetan traditions in their original languages, would serve precisely as means to reach definitive understandings of what the Buddhist texts say and mean, and thus what Genuine Buddhism truly is.

---

10. In Liang Qichao, *Liang Qichao quanji* 梁啟超全集 (Complete Collected Works of Liang Qichao), vol. 8, *juan* 20, (Beijing: Beijing chubanshe, 1999), p. 6041; cited in Ni Ping, "Mise en oeuvre de la pensée bouddhique Vijñānavāda (Rien-que-Conscience) dans les écrits littéraires et philosophiques de Yuan Hongdao (1568–1610)," PhD diss., l'Institut national des langues et civilisation orientales [INALCO], Paris, 2012), p. 11; Ni translates Liang's line as: "C'est seulement après avoir entendu l'enseignement de Maître Ouyang Jingwu sur la pensée de l'école Rien-que-Conscience que j'ai su qu'il existe une véritable bouddhologie."

Dignāga, Ālambana-parīkṣā, *and the Yogācāra epistemological tradition*

In December 1928 Lü published his study of the sixth-century Indian logician Dignāga's *Ālambana-parīkṣā* (Investigation of What Lies behind Perceptual Objects)[11] in *Neixue* 內學 (Inner Teachings).[12] He was assisted by the cleric Shi Yincang 釋印滄[13] (1906–1943), who also worked with him on another of his major Dignāga projects, a detailed study of the *Nyāyamukha* (Introduction to Logic) called "*Yinming zhengli men lun ben* zhengwen 因明正理門論本證文" (Evidential Study of *Introduction to Logic*).[14] This is the same period in which Lü published

---

11. A number of the texts to be discussed are well known in Buddhist studies circles by their Sanskrit or Chinese titles, but they lack standard English equivalents.

12. Lü Cheng and Shi Yincang, *Guan suoyuan shi lun hui shi* 觀所緣釋論會譯 (Correlation and Explanation of the Texts of the *Ālambana-parīkṣā*), *Neixue* 4 (1928): 123–164. A French translation of the *Ālambana-parīkṣā* by Susumu Yamaguchi with Henriette Meyer that included a partial rendering of Vinītadeva's (*ca.* 690–750) commentary appeared the following year: *Examen de l'objet connaissance* (Paris: Imprimerie Nationale, 1929). Erich Frauwallner's German translation of Dignāga's text, which includes a Tibetan edition, appeared the year after that: "Dignāga: Ālambanaparīkṣā, Text und Übersetzung," *Wiener Zeitschrift für die Kunde des Morgenlandes*, Bd. 37, Heft 1 und 2 (1930): 174–194. Five years later a German translation of the Dharmapāla commentary by Magdalene Schott was published: *Sein als Bewußtsein: Ein Beitrag zur Mahāyāna-Philosophie* (Heidelberg: Carl Winters Universitätbuchhandlung), in *Materialien zur Kunde des Buddhismus* 28 (1935): pp. 25–50. N. Aiyaswami Sastri published *Ālambanaparīkṣā and Vṛtti by Diṅnāga with the Commentary of Dharmapāla, Restored into Sanskrit from the Tibetan and Chinese Versions and edited with English Translation and Notes and with copious extracts from Vinītadeva's Commentary* (Adyar-Madras: The Adyar Library, 1942), but is deeply flawed: his renderings of Dharmapāla's text bear almost no resemblance to the original. See n. 33 for additional editions and translations.

13. Although the term *shi* 釋 indicates his ordained status, Yincang was actually his secular name; his monastic name was Weizong 葦宗. It is unclear why his name appears in the *Neixue* bylines in a hybrid form—a secular name with a monastic title—rather than simply as one or the other, which would be the normal procedure (technically, once a monastic name is bestowed with ordination, one's secular name should be obsolete). In 1929 Weizong (aka *Shi* Yincang), having completed his studies, left the Neixue institute for the Bolin Doctrinal Academy in Bolin Monastery 柏林寺 in Beijing. From that point on he pursued a monastic rather than an academic career, and died in 1943 of tuberculosis.

14. *Neixue* 4 (1928): 237–264. The *Nyāyamukha* (Introduction to Logic) study does not appear in *Lü Cheng Foxue lunzhu xuanji*, but it was reprinted in *Xiandai Fojiao xueshu cong kan* 現代佛教學術叢刊, v. 42 (1978): pp. 335–361). Shi Yincang received co-author credits with Lü for their work on the *Ālambana-parīkṣā* and *Nyāyamukha* when they were originally published in volume 4 of *Neixue*, but Shi Yincang's name is omitted from the reprinted version of the portion of the *Ālambana-parīkṣā* study reprinted in *Lü Cheng Foxue lunzhu xuanji*. The *Nyāyamukha* study was not included in *Lü Cheng Foxue lunzhu xuanji*, but a study of the related *Nyāyapraveśa* (*Yinming ru zhengli lun* 因明入正理論; Entryway into Logic), the other introductory *hetuvidyā* text translated by Xuanzang, written by Śaṅkarasvāmin) is included in volume 3, pp. 1500–1620 (title: *Yinming ru zhengli lun jiangjie* 因明入正理論講解 [Detailed Explanation of the *Nyāyapraveśa*]).

his detailed overview of Dignāga's *Pramāṇasamuccaya* (*Jiliang lun* 集量論; Compendium on Epistemology) called "*Jiliang lun* shi lüe chao 集量論釋略抄" (An Abridged Exposition of *Compendium on Epistemology*.)[15] His work on these three crucial Dignāga texts— *Pramāṇasamuccaya*, *Nyāyamukha*, and *Ālambana-parīkṣā*—was a stunning achievement, although it undeservedly remains largely unknown among Buddhist scholars until now. It is also a good illustration of what could be accomplished with Lü's textual tools.

Lü's study of the *Ālambana-parīkṣā* provides a good example of his method and approach, showing that despite having three Chinese translations of the same text by three of the most famous and illustrious medieval translators, the Chinese materials themselves prove to be frequently insufficient for solving major problems. Solving such problems would require consulting the original Sanskrit versions, or, in the absence of available Sanskrit, Tibetan versions. Lü's interest lay not in creating an Ur-text (doing philology for its own sake) but rather in recovering Genuine Buddhism. Additionally, such careful textual analysis provides useful insights into how each of the translators worked, thereby resolving uncertainties while helping one to acquire more sophisticated and solidly grounded historical and hermeneutic sensibilities that could carry over to reading other texts by these translators with more confidence. Although eventually *Ālambana-parīkṣā* was superseded in India (and later Tibet) by more sophisticated

---

15. The *Pramāṇasamuccaya* study is in *Lü Cheng Foxue lunzhu xuanji*, vol. 1, pp. 176–243 (it originally appeared in *Neixue* 4 [Dec. 1928]: 165–235). *Neixue* 4 contained, in addition to the *Ālambana-parīkṣā*, *Nyāyamukha* and *Pramāṇasamuccaya* studies (the first two in collaboration with Shi Yincang), another study by Lü Cheng of a Dignāga text, **Hetu-cakra-hamaru* (Wheel of [Inferential] Reasons), in which Dignāga provides rubrics for discerning whether an inference is valid, contradictory, or inconclusive. Lü's study in based on the Tibetan, which alone preserves this text. His essay is titled "Yin che lun tu jie 因車論圖解" (Charts Explaining the *Wheel of Reasons*), *Neixue* 4 (1928): 265–270. This was reprinted in *Lü Cheng Foxue lunzhu xuanji*, v.1, pp. 170–175.

It is notable that Lü focused so much attention on Dignāga and these three (or four) texts. The *Nyāyamukha* survives only in Chinese. *Pramāṇasamuccaya* (Compendium on Epistemology), considered to be Dignāga's magnum opus, survives in complete form only in two poor Tibetan translations; aside from a couple of verses translated into Chinese by Xuanzang, there is no extant Chinese version. Yijing 義淨 (635–713) is reported to have translated it as *Jilianglun* 集量論 in four fascicles, but that has not survived; see *Kaiyuan shijiao lu* 開元釋教錄 (Record of Śākyamuni's Teachings Compiled during the Kaiyuan Reign Period), compiled by Zhisheng 智昇 (730 CE), T.55.2154.568b3-5 and 637c3; and *Zhenyuan xin ding shijiao lu* 貞元新定釋教目錄 (Record of Śākyamuni's Teachings Revised during the Zhenyuan Reign Period) compiled by Yuanzhao 圓照, T.55.2157.972b15-16. I am indebted to Michael Radich for this information. There was no Sanskrit version available to Lü Cheng. The Sanskrit of Jinendrabuddhi's (fl. 725–750) commentary, which contains much of Dignāga's root text has only recently been discovered and is gradually being published. *Ālambana-parīkṣā* is preserved in Chinese and Tibetan translations (see below), and only a few of its Sanskrit passages have been identified as preserved in other Indian texts, although these too were unavailable to Lü.

and complex critiques of atomism, none of those later works reached China and East Asia until the twentieth century. Thus, *Ālambana-parīkṣā* represents the high water mark in the East Asian appropriation of Indian Buddhist critiques of atomism, and as such received much attention among twentieth-century Chinese intellectuals for its seeming relevance to modern scientific atomic theories as well as to contemporary trends in the psychology and philosophy of perception. For Lü, as the essay accompanying his textual correlations and annotations illustrates,[16] this sort of study afforded an opportunity to understand Xuanzang and his influences more insightfully.

Dignāga's *Ālambana-parīkṣā* (Investigation of *Ālambana*) is a short, terse text, consisting of only eight verses with Dignāga's auto-commentary (*vṛtti*). The Sanskrit is not extant, but there are three Chinese versions:

1. Paramārtha translated the entire text in the mid-sixth century: *Wu xiang si chen lun* 無相思塵論 (T.31.1619).
2. Xuanzang translated it—quite differently— in 657: *Guan suoyuan yuan lun* 觀所緣緣論 (T.31.1624).
3. Yijing 義淨, in 710, translated Dharmapāla's 護法 (sixth century) commentary on *Ālambana-parīkṣā* (T.31.1625) which includes nothing related to the last two verses—conceptually the most challenging and innovative section of Dignāga's text. It is unclear whether the omission is because this section was never translated by Yijing, or whether it failed to be preserved in transmission, though there is no mention anywhere of a portion being lost. Unfortunately incomplete translations were not uncommon at that time, but that often went unnoticed since only someone with access to a full text would be aware of the missing parts.

There is also a Tibetan translation of the verses alone, another of the verses with the *vṛtti*, and a Tibetan translation of an illuminating commentary by the eighth-century Yogācāra commentator Vinītadeva.[17]

16. This essay was titled *Fu lun Zangyi ben tezheng* 附論奘譯本特徵 (Addendum: Discussion of the Distinctive Features of Xuanzang's Translation). See below for further discussion.

17. The verse text: *dmigs pa brtag pa*, [Peking No.] 5703; [Derge No.] 4205; [Narthang] ce 180a2-180b1; [Kinsha] 3702, ce 235b6 (p.119-3-6). The text with *vṛtti*: *dmigs pa brtag pa'i 'grel pa*, [P. No.] 5704; [D. No.] 4206; [N] ce 180b1-182a2; [Kinsha] 3703, ce 236b1 (p.119-4-1). The Vinītadeva (dul ba'i lha) commentary: *dmigs pa brtag pa'i 'grel bshad*, [P. No.] 5739; [D. No.] 4241; [N] ze 186b1-200b6; [Kinsha] 3739, ze 243b1 (p.123-2-1), the Vinītadeva text translated into Tibetan by Śākyasiṃha and dpal brtsegs. For a translation and study based on the Tibetan, see F. Tola and C. Dragonetti, *Being as Consciousness* (Delhi: Motilal Banarsidass, 2004), Part I, although I find their interpretation, and at times their translation problematic and unconvincing. For additional translations into Western languages, see n. 12.

The argument of Ālambana-parīkṣā

Often mischaracterized in the secondary literature as an idealist argument that rejects the reality of external objects, Dignāga's goal is more modest and interesting. An *ālambana* is that from which a cognitive image is produced. In Indian Realist schools, such as the Buddhist Sarvāstivādins, an *ālambana* is not only based on a material object conducive to being perceived by the senses (i.e., a *viṣaya*), but it is also composed of atoms, irreducible material entities too tiny to see. The *Ālambana-parīkṣā* has two goals. The first is to refute the claim that either atoms or groupings of atoms can serve as an *ālambana*. The second is to suggest that the mental images (*ākāra*) we see are mentally constructed based on mental habits. Whether these mental constructions do or do not correspond in some way to some sort of materiality *other than atoms* Dignāga explicitly declares indeterminate.[18]

The refutation of atoms works as follows. Dignāga stipulates that an *ālambana* must satisfy two criteria: It must *convey an image of itself* to the cognition, and it must be a *causal factor* in the cognition. Since when one sees an object one does not see the image of an atom, single atoms fail the first criteria. No atom is conveying an image of itself to a cognition. A "group" of atoms would only be many atoms *conceptually* lumped together as a "group," none of which individually conveys its image. Such a grouping would be a mental abstraction superimposed or abstracted from individual, actual atoms (if such existed). For most Buddhists, such a conceptual collocation, or "group," has no 'reality' aside from the actual components comprising it. It is merely a conceptual-linguistic label that lumps actual things together; such heuristic labeling is called *prajñapti* (heuristic label; a merely nominal existent) by Buddhists. A paradigmatic example in Buddhist texts is a chariot, which is simply a heuristic label for the collocation of the various parts—axle, wheels, bucket, reins, etc.—of which it is constituted. There is no whole that exists

18. This explicit declaration is the penultimate sentence of Dignāga's essay, and hence the conclusion he wishes us to draw from his exercise. Perception involves (1) *indriya*, sense-faculties, or, as Dignāga prefers to describe them, "capacities" (*śakti*), i.e., the physical eyes, ears, etc, which are occasions for the capacities to see, hear, etc.; and (2) *viṣaya*, physical sense-objects, like colors, shapes, sounds, etc. Standard Buddhist doctrine classifies the physical *indriya* and *viṣaya* as *rūpa*, sensorial-physicality, or materiality. Having just discussed *indriya* and *viṣaya*, Dignāga concludes in his penultimate sentence the following. Paramārtha's version: 識者或異二或不異二或不可說。 "Some [claim that] consciousness is different from those two [i.e., the *rūpa* or matter of which the sense-faculties and the sense-objects are composed]; some [claim] it is not different from the two; some are unable to say (one way or another)." Xuanzang's version: 根境二色與識一異或非一異。隨樂應說。 "As to whether the two *rūpas*—viz. *indriya* and *viṣaya*—and consciousness are the same or different, or whether they are neither the same nor different: One can say according to one's wishes (*sui le* 隨樂; *yathā-āśaya*)." The Tibetan reads: *rnam par shes pa las de gnyis gzhan nyid dang gzhan ma yin pa nyid du cid gar brjod par bya'o*, "Whether those two are the same as or something other than consciousness, say however you wish."

or acts independent of its parts. The "whole" *qua* group of atoms is a constructed fiction. Being fictional, a "group" is therefore incapable of causing anything. Fictional entities have purely fictional status and are no more capable of producing real effects than Sherlock Holmes is capable of solving a real crime. Again, in Buddhist jargon, such groupings are *prajñapti* (nominal existents), not *dravya* (causally efficacious entities). Thus the group of atoms fails the second criteria.

In short, Dignāga concedes for the sake of argument that an atom *might* cause a cognition, but it does not convey an image of itself. And, even if it is a certain configuration or grouping of atoms that conveys the image of a certain shape, etc., such a grouping being merely a *prajñapti*, with no power of agency beyond the actual individuals that constitute it, it cannot cause the cognition. As Vasubandhu had already argued in his *Viṃśatikā* (or *Viṃśika*) (Twenty Verses), the notion of groupings of partless entities that lack extension is prima facie incoherent. The atom, even if one grants it could be a cause, fails to convey its own image; the grouping, even if arrayed in certain configurations and shapes, fails to be a cause (and thus, by default, cannot be conveying "its" or "their" image). Hence, neither the atom nor the grouping satisfies the criteria for being an *ālambana*.

Having refuted in the first six verses that atoms or atom groupings could serve as an *ālambana*, Dignāga devotes the final two verses with their commentary to explaining that consciousness itself produces mental images based on prior experiences. The "images" it conveys are its own fabrications, and consciousness itself is the cause of the cognizance of such images, thus satisfying both criteria. This is not unlike Kant's *Vorstellung*, which are mental projections that we experience in such a way that the actual noumena that might lie beyond the sensory intuition are obscured and only appear in our consciousness in the form we construct of them, our own mental "representations" that are not the things in-themselves. Or to take a less abstract account, physiological analysis of visual perception shows that "colors" are not properties of objects—as we think we perceive them to be—but are mental constructions fabricated in our visual apparatus and brains.[19] There are no exact objective correlates to such colors. Not only do different species see different ranges of colors (not to mention the variations in different types of "color blindness" in humans), but there is no one-to-one constant between specific light waves and corresponding colors. The same color can be produced by entirely different wave frequencies, so there is no one-to-one correspondence between light frequencies and perceived colors.[20] Dignāga

19. There is a vast scientific literature on this subject based on decades of experiments and tests. See, for instance, http://www.sciencedaily.com/releases/2005/10/051026082313.htm

20. Similarly, see http://www.echalk.co.uk/amusements/OpticalIllusions/colourPerception/colourPerception.html

is arguing that when we perceive objects as "solid," or of this or that "shape" and so on, we are projecting our fictional images and concepts onto these things in the same way modern physiology has demonstrated we see colors, contrasts,[21] or the way we group discrete items into meaningful units,[22] and so on. As with color perception, we take these projected fictions to be intrinsic to the images and meaning-units we experience *as if* they were external to us, while we ourselves are producing them. To what extent something outside the cognitive sphere is participating or contributing is, Dignāga concedes with great honesty, impossible to determine epistemologically.

Problems and Discrepancies between the Chinese Translations

The three Chinese versions of *Ālambana-parīkṣā* differ from each other in numerous small details and in some major ways as well. Starting with their basic formats, Paramārtha's text begins with just the verses, not divided into a first verse, second verse, etc., but simply sequenced together as one continuous string of verse. This is followed by the entire *vṛtti* (auto-commentary) devoid of verses. Paramārtha provides no indication where the verses should be inserted into the commentary. The reader has to determine this on his own.

Xuanzang's text, on the other hand, inserts complete verses into the commentary. However, as he did in his translations of other texts consisting of verse and commentary such as the *Abhidharmakośa-bhāṣya* (Vasubandhu's Autocommentary on *Storehouse of Higher Doctrine*), Xuanzang does not separate out the parts of the verse that go with specific portions of commentary, but places the entire verse as a single unit. Actually, as the Tibetan versions illustrate, the commentary frequently only addresses a phrase or so of a verse at a time, so the relation between verse and comment is much clearer when the verses are broken up and the specific segment is inserted exactly where the comment addresses it. None of the Chinese translations does that.

Yijing's translation of Dharmapāla's commentary, in fact, does *not* demarcate the verses from the comments at all, nor does it mark off where Dignāga ends and Dharmapāla begins. Without an independent version of the text it would be nearly impossible to tell which is which. Yijing's translation is also very obscure in many places, and, as Lü says, "difficult to understand" (*ao nan jie* 拗難解).

21. http://www.echalk.co.uk/amusements/OpticalIllusions/colourPerception/colourPerception2.html

22. "Gestalt grouping" is a well-established phenomenon, with a large literature.

Since in the course of making his argument Dignāga attempts to carefully define a number of terms critical to Indian epistemology—such as *ālambana, viṣaya, ākāra*, etc., all of which denote distinct aspects of the process of producing a mental image in perception—as well as explaining how they relate to each other, determining with some precision the exact underlying terms being rendered by their Chinese equivalents would be a desideratum for getting a handle on his presumed epistemology. With three translations by three of the most prominent translators one might imagine that triangulating between them would be a fairly straightforward task. That turns out not to be the case. There is little consistency when comparing them. In order to find consistency, one expects that when term A is being used by Paramārtha and term B is being used by Xuanzang in the same location, the next time A appears in Paramārtha's text Xuanzang will have B in the comparable position. But that does not happen. And when one factors in the Tibetan, rather than it deciding in favor of one or the other, it frequently introduces a third possibility. To crown off the discrepancies, a few passages of the original Sanskrit have been preserved in other Sanskrit texts, and these sometimes offer a different term from what one might expect in either the Tibetan or Chinese options. There are also entire lengthy passages that lack a corresponding passage in the other texts, so even simply trying to line them all up is a challenge.

The terminological confusion starts from the very beginning. Xuanzang translates the title as 觀所緣緣論 *Guan suoyuan yuan lun*. The word *lun*, although often mistakenly treated as an actual part of a text title and then mechanically treated as an equivalent for *śāstra*, is actually included in many Chinese titles as a classifier, to show that the text is not a *sūtra* (discourse of the Buddha; in Chinese, *jing* 經), but something written by a later Buddhist. It is a classifier, and like a particle, it often should not be translated.[23] *Guan* is a standard equivalent for *parīkṣā*, meaning "investigation" or "examination." *Suoyuan* is the standard Chinese term for *ālambana*. But, as Lü notes, Xuanzang has added an extra *yuan*, "condition"; *suoyuan yuan* is the standard equivalent for

23. Similarly, placing 大乘 *dasheng* (Mahāyāna), 小乘 *xiaosheng* (Hīnayāna), or 佛說 *Foshuo* (Buddha Says) at the front of a Chinese title served to classify the type of text it was, and not to render into Chinese some part of the text's original title. I suspect that is why Paramārtha and Xuanzang translate the title of the *Mahāyāna-saṃgraha* into Chinese as *She dasheng lun* 攝大乘論 (Compendium of the Great Vehicle), placing the "Mahāyāna" (*dasheng*) *inside* the title, to signal that the term "Mahāyāna" is indeed part of the original title and not a mere classifier. While sometimes an Indic title will include *śāstra* and this would be properly rendered into Chinese as *lun*, the *lun* classifier is more commonly added to many texts whose Sanskrit titles did not include the word *śāstra*; either no classifier at all was included in the original title (e.g., *Viṃśatikā* or *Viṃśikā*), or one of a much broader range of Sanskrit text-type classifiers was used (*bhāṣya, vyākhyā, vivaraṇa, pariccheda, saṃgrāha, prakaraṇa, ṭīkā*, etc.).

ālambana-pratyaya, "the type of condition that is an *ālambana*." It is an acceptable gloss since that is what the term *ālambana* means here, but it does introduce something not in the original, and hence is not a strictly literal rendering. Yijing renders the title *Guan suoyuan lun* 觀所緣論釋, dropping the added "condition," while adding *shi* 釋, indicating his text is an explanatory commentary (by Dharmapāla).

Paramārtha's title is initially odd, and actually hard to translate. In his rendering *Wuxiang si chen lun* 無相思塵論, there is no obvious equivalent for *ālambana*. *Chen*, which literally means "dust," is commonly used by Paramārtha and some other translators for "sense-object," and is more typically deployed as an equivalent for *viṣaya*.[24] *Si* means "thought," "idea," or, if taken as a verb, "thinking, considering." So *si chen* could be seen as an imprecise rendering of *ālambana-parīkṣā* (investigation of *ālambana*) as "thinking about or considering the 'dusts' (sense-objects)," imprecise precisely because it fails to distinguish *ālambana* from the other object-words used by Dignāga and other Indian writers to identify the distinct components of the epistemological process active in creating a mental image. *Wuxiang* could be understood a number of ways, depending on how one reads *xiang* here. In some Buddhist literature *wuxiang* might denote something "formless," or something "with no marks or characteristics," or it could mean "without images." On first blush *wuxiang* bears little relevance to the original Sanskrit title, nor does Dignāga discuss being "imageless" or "formless," etc. There are some indications that Paramārtha sought to offer a series of works connected by a theme of *wuxiang* (in whichever sense would have been involved[25]),

24. While the reason translators into Chinese chose *chen* 塵 to render sense-objects (*viṣaya*, etc.) is unclear, two hypotheses suggest themselves. Some may have presupposed a perceptual theory, similar to Jain theory, in which an unhindered consciousness can perceive everywhere and anywhere, until blocked or hindered by some physical obstruction, viz. an object. The bright, luminous consciousness is blocked by "dust," which impedes the full potential range of the sense faculty. The other theory is that "dust" did not necessarily carry negative implications in Chinese thought, but was a euphemism for the things and affairs of the everyday world, the dust kicked up in the marketplace and during one's travels, etc. Cf. *Daodejing* 4 and 56: 挫其銳，解其紛，和其光，同其塵. "Blunt the sharpness, untangle the knots, merge with the light, unify with the dust," with the expression "unify with the dust" usually understood as returning to ordinary affairs after experiencing the merging with light. This interpretation is reiterated in the final two ox-herding pictures that follow the round emptiness of the eighth picture.

25. I suspect the sense of *wuxiang* in that thematic would have stood for the term *nirākāra*, i.e., the idea that enlightened cognition is devoid of (*nir-*) images (*ākāra*), an idea embraced at that time by the Saṃmitīyas, whom, I also suspect, exerted a strong but so far unacknowledged influence of Paramārtha, whose base in India, Ujjain, was famous then as a Saṃmitīya center. Xuanzang debates Saṃmitīyas while in India on the issue of *nirākāra*, with Xuanzang promoting a *sākāra* (enlightened cognitions do include images) position.

but exactly which texts were included remains unclear.[26] If that is the case, then the *wuxiang* in this title would only denote its belonging to that series, and should not to be considered an integral component of the text's title. If, nonetheless, one were to attempt a possible reading of the full title as is, it could be interpreted as: "Treatise on Considerations about Sense-objects as Lacking Materiality," taking *wuxiang* as representing "devoid of materiality," a usage which, I believe, would be unusual for Paramārtha. Another possibility is to take *si* 思 and *chen* 塵 as indicating mental functions and sense-objects, respectively.

Putting this trivia aside, if we look at the first sentence of the Paramārtha and Xuanzang translations, important discrepancies emerge.

> **Paramārtha**: 若有人執眼等六識。緣外境起。
> "There are some people who hold that what the six consciousnesses, such as eye-consciousness, etc., take as an *ālambana* is produced by an external object (境 **viṣaya*)."
>
> **Xuanzang**: 諸有欲令眼等五識。以外色作所緣緣者。
> "There are some wishing to claim that what causes the five sensory consciousnesses, such as eye-consciousness, etc., is an *ālambana-pratyaya* made by external *rūpa* (色)."

Already in this first sentence, differences begin to mount. Paramārtha tells us there are *six* sensory consciousnesses; Xuanzang says *five*. Xuanzang again

26. See Diana Paul, "The Structure of Consciousness in Paramārtha's Purported Trilogy," *Philosophy East and West* 31, no. 3 (July 1981): esp. 298 and 313 n.8, though Paul fails to mention Paramārtha's *Ālambana-parīkṣā* translation as a candidate for a *Wuxianglun*, instead suggesting three other texts as a possible *Wuxianglun* "trilogy" based on the fact that in the Taishō edition the phrase 從無相論出 "extracted from the *Wuxianglun*" appears after the title of two of them, and the comparable phrase 出無相論 appears after the title of the third. A *Wuxianglun* is cited several times by Huizhao 慧沼 (648–714), Kuiji's successor, in his *Cheng weishi lun liaoyi deng* 成唯識論了義燈 (Illuminating the Definitive Meaning of *Demonstration of Nothing but Consciousness*), T.43.1832.729b22-c29, but he seems to be paraphrasing texts, not quoting them verbatim, since not only are the statements he attributes to the *Wuxianglun* not found in any Taishō texts, but the statements he attributes to other texts in the same passage, such as the *Madhyānta-vibhāga* (Differentiation the Middle from the Extremes) and *Laṅkāvatāra-sūtra* (Discourse on [the Buddha's] Entering [the Country of] Lanka) are also not found in the received versions. Fazang 法藏 (643–712), the putative Huayan patriarch, also provides an otherwise unattested quotation from a *Wuxiang lun* in his commentary, *Dasheng qixin lun yiji* 大乘起信論義記 (Notes on the Meaning of *The Awakening of Mahāyāna Faith*; T. 44.1846.262c5-7). Similarly Wŏnhyo 元曉 (617–686), in his **Vajrasamādhi-sūtra* commentary, *Jingang sanmei jing lun* 金剛三昧經論 (Commentary on the *Sutra on the Adamantine Meditation*), T.34.1730.969a14-17, cites another passage from a *Wuxiang lun* that is not found in any extant text.

uses the full term *suoyuan yuan* (*ālambana-pratyaya*) while Paramārtha uses only the single word *yuan* (rather than *suoyuan*), which ambiguates between *pratyaya* ("condition"), for which *yuan* is the common equivalent, and *ālambana*, since, used verbally at the beginning of a phrase, *yuan* can mean "to take as an *ālambana*," i.e., to take up as an object for perception. Notably he does not use *chen*, "dust," that appeared in his title. Both Paramārtha and Xuanzang tell us that the claim these people wish to make is that the *ālambana* is produced by something "external" (*wai* 外); Paramārtha says it is an external *jing* (外境), Xuanzang that it is an external *rūpa* (外色).[27]

As Lü Cheng demonstrates, when Xuanzang stipulates "five consciousnesses," he is following Dharmapāla, who in Yijing's translation explicitly argues that one should understand "five consciousnesses" here because, Dharmapāla claims, all Buddhists are already in agreement about the way the sixth consciousness works, so it is only the first five that need to be debated by Dignāga. Specifically, when the sixth, the *manovijñāna*, takes any or all of the five sensory consciousnesses as its cognitive object(s), it perceives their perception. Thus other Buddhists accept that the sixth consciousness can have for its object the perceptions of another consciousness such that an object appears to the sixth as a material object when it is, in fact, only the perceptual object of a sense-consciousness. For instance, the shape sensed by visual consciousness is perceived by the sixth consciousness also as a physical visual shape. All Buddhists accept the sixth consciousness as a type of "common sense," one that appropriates what each sense discretely senses, combining them into an "object" characterized by color, shape, texture, smell, etc., although each of the senses alone only obtains and provides the data restricted to its specific domain. Eye-consciousness sees shapes, colors, etc.; auditory consciousness hears sounds; and so on. It is the sixth consciousness that takes their percepts and combines them as that rotund, garlic-reeking opera singer intrusively inviting a donation. Hence all Buddhists accept that in such cases so-called perception of a physical object actually involves mental processes that are internal, since one does not take cognizance of a visual, auditory, etc. percept unless it is noticed, processed, and cognized by the sixth consciousness. Perception, therefore, involves one internal mental function apprehending the activity of another mental function. Thus, according to Dharmapāla, what remains in contention is whether this

27. I leave *jing* untranslated here and provide no Sanskrit equivalent since *jing* could be used for many different terms including *viṣaya, gocara, rāṣṭra, deśa; adhiṣṭhāna, arthâkāra, arthya, ārambaṇa, gati, jñeya, jñeya-vastu*, and a host of other attested equivalents. Since deciding which equivalent is at play in this passage is the task, it would beg the question to supply a Sanskrit term. Xuanzang's 色 *se*, on the other hand, is unambiguously an equivalent for *rūpa*.

process, accepted as a legitimate account of how the sixth consciousness functions, can be applied to how the five sensory consciousnesses work as well. Put more simply, Buddhists do *not* argue that the sixth consciousness directly accesses external things, but rather that it gathers data from the five sensory consciousnesses and processes that for its cognitive grist. If, as indicated above, a percept as seemingly primitive as color is actually a mental construction—which is the implicit claim of Dignāga and Dharmapāla—then in an important way the five sense consciousnesses are also operating in a manner similar to the sixth consciousness, constructing a perceptual experience based on internal mental processes. Since Dharmapāla apparently seized an opportunity to make this argument by supplying explicit numbers of consciousnesses involved, one may infer that the original text had no number at all here, leaving him this opening. Thus, one may also conclude that Paramārtha's gloss of "six consciousnesses" is as much an interpretive addition as Xuanzang's "five consciousnesses." Xuanzang specifies "five consciousnesses" because he is following Dharmapāla's interpretation here. We are now on alert that neither Paramārtha nor Xuanzang is translating in a strictly literal word-for-word fashion, but that both are willing to add interpretive glosses to "guide" the reader. Visualizing an imagined Sanskrit original behind either or both translations has now become a shade more difficult and tenuous.

What of the difference between what each identifies as the external producer of the *ālambana*? Is it *viṣaya* or *rūpa*? Can the Tibetan mediate? Where Xuanzang uses *wai se* 外色, "external *rūpa*," the Tibetan has *phyi rol gyi don*, which represents the Sanskrit *bāhyārtha* (*bāhya* = external + *artha* = referent). So the Tibetan has neither *viṣaya* nor *rūpa*, but a third candidate: *artha*. Was the underlying term *artha*, *rūpa*, or *viṣaya*? These are not synonyms, and to conflate them would cloud rather than clarify the epistemological distinctions Dignāga and his contemporaries found important, even necessary, to distinguish.

An *artha* is a "referent," "that toward which an intention intends," and thus *artha* also signifies "meaning," "a target," and "wealth." It is something reached for, grabbed, acquired, and appropriated. Its significance lies in the attitude with which it is approached and considered, not in some quality independent of such an attitude. A *viṣaya* is a sense-object, something amenable to being taken up by one of the senses, such as a certain type of color, shape, sound, smell, etc. When a *viṣaya* is being taken up by a cognition, the *viṣaya* as contributing cause and the cognitive aspect doing the taking up are together called *ālambana*. A *viṣaya*'s ontological status was a matter of dispute between different Buddhist schools. *Rūpa* is physical materiality. Of the three terms, *rūpa* carries the strongest materialist connotations; *artha*, the most abstract metaphysical implications; and *viṣaya*, the most concretely sensorial.

The term suggested by the Tibetan, *bāhyārtha* ("external referent"), is commonly found in Buddhist discourses of this type,[28] so that would be the expected term in this context. But, following the principle of *lectio difficilior*, Xuanzang's rendition is the most appealing, since it would be the least expected of the three. The Tibetan translator may have glossed the original term into *bahyārtha* as reflexively as Paramārtha added "six" to the types of perceptual consciousnesses. That Xuanzang's unexpected choice, *rūpa*, deserves consideration is possibly buttressed by one of the few passages of the *Ālambana-parīkṣā* for which we have a surviving Sanskrit passage, the beginning of the sixth verse, which is attested in two texts (Kamalaśīla's [eighth century] *Tattvasaṃgraha-pañjikā* [Commentary on the *Compendium on the Components of Reality*] and Śaṅkara's [eighth century] *Brahma-sūtra-bhāṣya* [Commentary on the *Brahma Sutra*]). It states: *yad-antarjñeya-rūpaṃ tu bahirvad avabhāsate*, "that *rūpa* is known within [consciousness] but appears as if external." This is, however, not conclusive, since the context is somewhat different (*rūpa* here is probably an abbreviation for *svarūpa*, the basic nature of a thing in-itself), and the Tibetan for verse six is consistent with *rūpa* (though Paramārtha's rendering is not; he again uses *jing* 境!).

In any event, many of the Chinese terms used by both translators have well-known Sanskrit equivalents, but even when we compare all the various translations, the exact underlying Sanskrit term often remains uncertain.

Lü Cheng's edition of the Ālambana-parīkṣā

Having looked only at the title and first sentence, we already see the types of problems that quickly leap out. The discrepancies and problems do not diminish as one continues, but grow increasingly thorny as the disparities accumulate. If one looks only at the Paramārtha and Xuanzang translations, their alternatives are incommensurate and irresolvable. If one then turns to Yijing's text for resolutions, one finds a text that occasionally may shed some light, as it did with the question of why Xuanzang stated "five consciousnesses" rather than the "six" glossed by Paramārtha. The impression that the original text did not specify a number here, so that both "five" and "six" are translators' glosses, is confirmed by the Tibetan, which indeed gives no number here. Although it is helpful in this instance, Yijing's translation frequently becomes inscrutable, eventually posing many more problems than it solves. If one could read only the Chinese versions, attempting to work through these three texts would result in a frustrating interpretive impasse, which may be one reason the East Asian tradition did not

28. When the Yogācāra position is described in Sanskrit literature as the rejection of "external objects," the term typically used for external object is *bahyārtha*.

devote much attention to this text prior to the twentieth century with the efforts by Ouyang Jingwu, Lü Cheng, and others.[29]

Since enlightenment involves purifying the mind of misconceptions and ignorance, logic and epistemology are indispensable. A mind that sees things as they are (*yathābhūtam*) is one that functions with clarity and logically. Muddleheadedness is the antithesis of enlightenment. Hence Lü, from his earliest explorations of Buddhist thought, developed an interest in clarifying Buddhist logic and epistemology, topics that until that point had received more veneration than understanding among East Asian Buddhists. That the *Ālambana-parīkṣā* contained a critique of atomism, seemingly a very modern, scientific concern, gave it pertinence to the effort to address modernity critically with traditional Buddhist tools.

Since it was evident that the Chinese texts alone would not lead to a resolution of the interpretative impasses, and the original Sanskrit was not available, Lü turned to the Tibetan to mediate. He translated the entire Tibetan text into Chinese and then correlated the results between it and the three Chinese versions. He worked over the Yijing text, annotating it, re-punctuating it, trying to make sense of it where it seemed most inscrutable. Consulting the Tibetan and Xuanzang texts, he judiciously determined where in Paramārtha's text to insert Dignāga's verses into the commentary.[30] It is worth emphasizing that his translation of the Tibetan is superb.[31]

---

29. Clearly at a certain stage in the development of Yogācāra epistemology *Ālambana-parīkṣā* was considered a major text, which explains why across three centuries three leading translators produced Chinese versions. As Lü Cheng recognized, *Ālambana-parīkṣā* was a further refinement of the critique of atomism found in several verses of Vasubandhu's *Viṃśatikā* (Twenty Verses). Some centuries later, it was still considered important enough to be translated into Tibetan, along with Vinītadeva's commentary. That it subsequently fell into relative disuse in India and Tibet is easily explained by the exponentially more sophisticated debates on epistemology and atomism that one finds beginning with Śāntarakṣita's *Tattvasaṃgraha* (Compendium on the Components of Reality; eighth century). Dignāga's little text is quaint and simplistic in comparison. However, since these later discussions of atomism were never introduced into East Asian Buddhism, the centuries of relative neglect of Dignāga's text requires a different explanation. There was a revival of interest in the Xuanzang and Dharmapāla-Yijing *Ālambana-parīkṣā* texts during the Ming Dynasty, but then little more until the twentieth century. Ouyang's *Guan suoyuan yuan lun shijie* 觀所緣緣論釋解 (Interpretative Exposition on the *Ālambana-parīkṣā*) appeared in 1914 in *Foxue congbao* 佛學叢報 11.

30. Yamaguchi included editions of the Paramārtha and Xuanzang Chinese texts as appendices to his French translation of *Ālambana-parīkṣā*, which he collated (there are so many substantial divergences, including extended passages with no corollary in the other text, that simply lining them up against each other is a daunting undertaking), and he too inserted the verses where he thought they should go. His correlations and insertion points frequently differ from Lü's. In my opinion Lü's choices for verse insertion and passage correlation are superior.

31. As part of this project, John Powers, Leslie Kawamura, John Makeham and I scrupulously went over Lü's translation, line by line, word by word, comparing it with the Tibetan. We grew to admire his ability to solve—with possibly one or two exceptions perhaps due to his using a different edition of the Tibetan—the text's intricate challenges, while rendering it into a clear, classical Chinese. In my opinion, his translation is superior to and more insightful than any of the published modern translations I have seen.

He titled the study that appeared in *Neixue*, *Guan suoyuan shi lun huiyi* 觀所緣釋論會譯, which we might render as "A Comparative Exposition [of the Chinese and Tibetan] Translations of the *Ālambana-parīkṣā*." It consisted of three parts.

1. A very short introduction (six lines) briefly explaining which texts are involved.
2. The Texts. This section, which is the major portion of the study, presents the versions in the following order. For each passage, first Lü's translation of the Tibetan is given, followed by Paramārtha's text, followed by Xuanzang's, followed by his annotated version of the Yijing text. In other words, the Tibetan is the first version one encounters, followed by the three Chinese versions given in chronological order. A page and a half of endnotes follows the presentation of the passages.
3. An analytic essay that highlights differences and similarities between the texts, and draws some conclusions about the nature of the different versions, their relation to each other, and what can be gleaned about Dignāga's original text on that basis. As the title of the analytic essay explains, "Fu lun Zangyi ben tezheng 附論奘譯本特徵" (Addendum: Discussion of the Distinctive Features of Xuanzang's Translation[32]), its primary focus is Xuanzang's version, viewing the others in terms of how they shed light on it.

In the essay Lü notes from the outset that Xuanzang's translation is unique, different from the others. He concludes that Paramārtha and the Tibetan are closest, and that while Xuanzang was influenced by Dharmapāla's interpretation, there are noticeable differences between his interpretation and the one found in the Yijing translation. One senses that just as Lü is carefully documenting that Xuanzang is, on the one hand, clearly influenced by Dharmapāla, while, on the other hand, remaining sufficiently independent, and thus not a blind follower, of Dharmapāla—being, as Lü puts it, more faithful to the intent and literal wording of Dignāga's text than to doctrinal affiliation—Lü is likewise implicitly declaring his own independence from Xuanzang while acknowledging Xuanzang's deep influence on him. He seems to see Xuanzang more as a kindred spirit than as an infallible beacon.

32. This addendum essay is the only part included in *Lü Cheng Foxue lunzhu xuanji*, where the title is slightly modified as "Lun Zangyi Guan suoyuan shi lun zhi tezheng 論奘譯觀所緣釋論之特徵" (Discussion of the Distinctive Features of Xuanzang's translation of *Ālambana-parīkṣā*). The name of Lü's collaborator, Shi Yincong, is not mentioned (was Yincong only involved in preparing the texts, not this essay?) and there is some minor reworking and rewording of the text primarily for the sake of added clarity, for instance, more clearly demarcating quotations.

It bears noting that of the editions he used and worked on, Xuanzang's text required the least amount of work. The Tibetan had to be translated; Paramārtha's text required parsing and decisions on where to insert the verses meaningfully into the commentary; Yijing's text required much wrestling with obscure passages, decoding difficult terms and phrases, and adding many useful, if sometimes tentative annotations and punctuations. Xuanzang's text, by way of contrast, is left intact. Rather, Lü saw his task as understanding its philosophical meaning, along with an understanding of the motives and techniques used by the translator. Xuanzang's text required analysis and study, but not alteration.

Some implications of Lü's study of Ālambana-parīkṣā

Without recourse to the Tibetan version, solving the countless puzzles and problems posed by even the most scrupulous comparisons of the Chinese texts alone would have been impossible. Lü is warning his contemporaries that they cannot rely on Chinese materials alone if they want to understand "Genuine" Buddhism correctly instead of the imaginary construction of Buddhism that had been forged over the centuries by other uninformed but imaginative readers of the Chinese texts. With an ability to read Sanskrit and Tibetan, a proper and profitable way to read the long venerated Chinese texts was now at hand. In the case of *Ālambana-parīkṣā*, without a careful consideration of the Tibetan, the Chinese versions would be difficult to understand, appreciate and reconcile with each other. Although the Tibetan does not solve everything, at least it makes a more informed reading possible.

Philology and textual-critical method are deployed by Lü Cheng not to produce a scholarly artifact, such as an Ur-text, but to recover the original meaning and import of the text(s) and the ideas it bears. Lü was attempting to understand:

1. What each translator was doing to and with the text;
2. Why they were treating it as they did;
3. What different, considered interpretations were like, in order to have a hermeneutic space within which to make genuine and informed interpretive choices of one's own.

That activity itself—a hermeneutics grounded in careful philology and text-criticism—in a certain sense, is what Genuine Buddhism is about for Lü Cheng. His modus operandi consisted of careful readings designed to pare off questionable or untenable options through strict attention to the basic texts and their history, thereby determining the viability of different interpretations and even of certain texts.

Lü's sustained interest in *hetuvidyā* (Buddhist epistemology and logic), of which his *Ālambana-parīkṣā* study is an important part, paved the way for subsequent East Asian studies, such as those by Yamaguchi Susumu 山口益 and Ui Hakuju 宇井伯壽.[33] Western studies of Yogācāra have tended to focus exclusively on texts dealing with the supposed signature Yogācāra doctrines, such as the three natures (*trisvabhāva*), the eighth consciousness (*ālayavijñāna*), and cognitive closure (*vijñapti-mātra*), while those working on the *hetuvidyā* and *pramāṇa-vāda* (epistemic validation) literature have tended to show little interest in how Buddhist *pramāṇa-vāda* was a natural outgrowth of Yogācāra and remained informed by Yogācāra concerns and concepts (aside from repeatedly trying to find "idealist" elements or "tacit idealist assumptions" in early *pramāṇa-vāda* thinkers such as Dharmakīrti). But *pramāṇa-vāda* in a form recognizable as foundational for the later developments first appears in Asaṅga's Yogācāra works, gets refined in several texts by Vasubandhu (only fragments of which are extant[34]), becomes further refined and sharpened by Dignāga, and reaches a systematic sophistication in Dharmakīrti. Each of them was a Yogācāra thinker. That Yogācāra and *hetuvidyā* are the same tradition has always been understood in East Asia.

Lü Cheng's methods for dealing with other texts

To gain a fuller sense of Lü's project and how he approached controversies, mention can be made of some of his other essays, which take on popular but apocryphal texts. The first has the provocative title "*Lengyan* bai wei 楞嚴百偽," which we might render as "One hundred things wrong with the *Śūraṅgama* [*sūtra*]."[35] In fact, he even provides a bonus example, so the full count is actually 101 things wrong with this text. Even today the *Śūraṅgama* remains very popular among

33. On Yamaguchi's French translation of *Ālambana-parīkṣā* see supra n. 12. Yamaguchi also produced a Japanese translation with Vinītadeva's commentary: Yamaguchi Susumu and Nozawa Jōshō 野澤靜證, *Seshin yuishiki no genten kaimei* 世親唯識の原典解明 (Study of Source Texts of Vasubandhu and *Vijñapti-mātra*) (Kyoto: Hōzōkan, 1953). Ui's *Bukkyō ronrigaku* 佛教論理學 (Buddhist Logic) (Tokyo: Daitō shuppansha, 1933) includes his Japanese translation and study of Dignāga's *Nyāyamukha* (Introduction to Logic) on pp. 363–392. His study of Dignāga, *Jinna chosaku no kenkyū* 陳那著作の研 (Studies of Dignāga's Writings) (Tokyo: Iwanami shoten, 1958), includes his study of *Ālambana-parīkṣā* (pp. 24–130, with his Japanese translation of the Paramārtha, Xuanzang, and Yijing versions), and studies of three other Dignāga texts. Ui's indebtedness to Lü Cheng is clearly evident.

34. E. Frauwallner, "Vasubandhu's *Vādavidhi*," *Wiener Zeitschrift für die Kunde Süd- und Ostasiens* 1 (1957): 2–44.

35. *Lü Cheng Foxue lunzhu xuanji*, pp. 370–395.

East Asian and Vietnamese Buddhists, and is used ritually as well as an object for conceptual study.[36]

After pointing out that there are other popular but "spurious" (*wei* 偽) texts, namely *Renwang jing* 仁王經 (The Benevolent Kings Sutra); the Chinese **Brahmajāla-sūtra* (*Fanwang jing* 梵網經; Sutra of Brahmā's Net);[37] *Dasheng qixin lun* 大乘起信論 (Awakening of Mahāyāna Faith), *Yuanjue jing* 圓覺經 (The Perfect Enlightenment Sutra), and the *Zhancha [shan e yebao] jing* 占察[善惡業報]經 (Sutra on Divination of the Effects of Good and Evil Actions), he proceeds to compare details given in the **Śūraṅgama-sūtra* (Sutra on the Hero's Progress) with comparable information provided by other, authentic sutras. Some of the details he discusses are doctrinal, some are seemingly trivial (such as at what age the Buddha and a certain king meet), and he shows that it is precisely with these other spurious texts that this *Śūraṅgama* shows most consistency, highlighting trains of "spurious" Buddhist themes embedded in spurious texts. Although many of the details on their own might seem slight, almost insignificant, the evidence mounts, as more and more spurious things accumulate, until their sheer number makes the case compelling and decisive.

In another work, "Lengqie rulaizang zhang jiangyi 楞伽如來藏章講義" (Lecture Notes on the Tathāgatagarbha chapter of the *Laṅkāvatāra-sūtra*),[38] Lü's aim is not to challenge the authenticity of the text itself, but to strip away erroneous interpretations that have attached to it, in this case concerning the notion of *tathāgatagarbha*, in Chinese *rulaizang* 如來藏, the *zang* of the *tathāgata* (i.e., buddha). *Tathāgatagarbha* has become a seemingly indelible part of East Asian Buddhism, although, as Lü sets out to demonstrate, how it is understood has

---

36. The full Chinese title is *Dafo ding rulai mi yin xiu zhengliao yi zhu pusa wanxing shoulengyan jing* 大佛頂如來密因修證了義諸菩薩萬行首楞嚴經 (T.19.945), but it is best known by the abbreviated *Lengyan jing* 楞嚴經. This has long been recognized as an apocryphal text written in China, though the "translation" is ascribed to a Pāramiti (Bancimidi 般刺蜜帝), supposedly in 705 CE. This is *not* to be confused with another text titled *Śūraṅgama-samādhi-sūtra* (*Shoulengyen sanmei jing* 首楞嚴三昧經; abbrev.: 首楞嚴經 *Shoulengyan jing*; the Chinese titles being transcriptions of the sounds for *Śūraṅgama* which in Sanskrit means something like "heroic or courageous progress"). This latter *Śūraṅgama-samādhi-sūtra* is an authentic Indian text that was often studied together with the *Vimalakīrti-nirdeśa-sūtra* (The Teachings of Vimalakīrti). The authentic *Śūraṅgama-sūtra*, extant in Kumārajīva's Chinese translation (T.15.642) was translated into French by Étienne Lamotte, *La Concentration de la march héroïque*, in *Mélanges chinois et bouddhiques* v. XIII (Brussels: Institut Belge des Hautes Études Chinoises, 1965), which in turn was translated into English by Sara Boin-Webb, *Śūraṃgamasamādhisūtra: The Concentration of Heroic Progress* (London: Buddhist Text Society, 1998).

37. Not to be confused with the Pāli *Brahmajāla sutta* that begins the *Dīgha-Nikāya*, with which it has nothing in common aside from the title.

38. *Lü Cheng Foxue lunzhu xuanji*, pp. 257–265.

become infected with a variety of spurious concepts derived from spurious texts. How, for instance, should one understand the *zang* of *rulaizang*? The Chinese term suggests a storehouse, someplace where something precious might be hidden. Lü explains: "The '*zang*' should be taken in the sense of 'womb (*zang*) of an embryo,' that from which a buddha is born" (藏謂胎藏，佛由是而生也).[39] He further informs us that *tathāgatagarbha* is a Mahāyānic exposition of the theme that "mind-nature is originally pure," understood by some to mean that this is some sort of special, unique mind. "This mind is *tathāgatagarbha*; when consciousness obtains this mind, it can become buddha . . . [S]tudents of Buddhism already know this. *Tathāgatagarbha* is mind. But what sort of mind is this mind? It is the everyday/ordinary mind of sentient beings, not some special mind out there apart from that."[40] Having presented his thesis, he proceeds to support it, while attacking *Dasheng qixin lun* for having infected the concept of *tathāgatagarbha* with spurious interpretations.

Dasheng qixin lun—one of his favorite foils, since its ideas have become foundational for much of what Lü and some others saw as misguided Buddhism—often gets criticized in the course of analyzing other texts, and he devotes several essays to specifically exposing it as spurious. In one, "*Qixin* yu *Lengqie* 起信與楞伽" (The *Awakening of Mahāyāna Faith* and the *Laṅkāvatāra-sūtra*), he writes:

> Long before *Dasheng qixin lun* became widely circulated, there were translations of the *Laṅkāvatāra* by Guṇabhadra[41] in the Song[42] dynasty and [another] translation[43] by Bodhiruci during the Wei dynasty.[44] (There is a tradition that in ancient times there was also a translation from the Liang, but no details from that text are available.[45]) The ideas in this text are quite unique, but if one examines them in comparison with the Sanskrit text and the Tibetan translation, thereby determining the original wording of

---

39. Ibid., p. 257.

40. Ibid.

41. *Lengqie abaduoluo baojing* 楞伽阿跋多羅寶經, (partial) trans. by Guṇabhadra 求那跋陀羅 in 443 (4 fasc.), T.16.670.

42. I.e., the Liu Song Dynasty 劉宋 (420–479), not to be confused with the later Song Dynasty (*ca.* 960–1279); Guṇabhadra's dates are 394–468; he arrived in China *ca.* 435.

43. *Rulengqiejing* 入楞伽經, trans. by Bodhiruci 菩提流支 in 513 (10 fasc.), T.16.671.

44. Bodhiruci arrived in Chang'an in 502 and died in 527. The Wei Dynasty ran from 386 until 534 or 535. *Dasheng qixin lun* did not appear until the second half of the sixth century.

45. This is the *Lengqiejing sijuan* 楞伽經四卷 trans. by Dharmakṣema 曇無讖 between 412 and 433 (not extant), but listed in *Kaiyuan shijia lu* at T.55.2154.629b11.

the text, the Song translation matches up closely, while the Wei translation is filled with errors and hundreds of deviations [from the original wording].

Now, if we examine *Dasheng qixin lun* in comparison with the *Laṅkāvatāra*, it definitely is not an authentic original [Indian] text. It is based on erroneous translations it stole from the Wei [version of the *Laṅkāvatāra*]. Moreover it barely muddles through their meanings. It could only have been written by a Chinese person, no one else. How could Aśvaghoṣa[46] have been the original author of something that we know could only have been composed by a Chinese scholar who derived erroneous expressions from the Wei translation of the *Laṅkāvatāra*? By applying this criterion one recognizes that the *Awakening of Mahāyāna Faith* is a spurious text – reaching this conclusion is simple, nothing complicated. Now I will prove it with seven demonstrations.[47]

We do not need to explore the seven demonstrations here to appreciate his point. His claim that the *Awakening of Mahāyāna Faith* relies heavily on the vocabulary of the Bodhiruci *Laṅkāvatāra* is spot on, as has been confirmed by more recent studies aided by the power of computer searches.[48] One obvious implication of the fact that it is not an authentic translation, but a forgery composed by someone drawing on Bodhiruci's vocabulary, is that Paramārtha—who developed his own technical vocabulary, which differed from Bodhiruci's—was not involved in the production of *Dasheng qixin lun*. Hence attributing the translation to Paramārtha is as spurious as attributing authorship to Aśvaghoṣa.

Lü mentions three Chinese versions of the *Laṅkāvatāra*: the earliest version by Dharmakṣema, which is no longer extant; the Guṇabhadra translation, which

46. The reputed author of *Dasheng qixin lun*, an attribution universally discredited by scholars today.

47. "*Qixin* yu *Lengqie*," *Lü Cheng Foxue lunzhu xuanji*, vol. 1, p. 293.

48. Cf. Frédéric Girard's French translation of *Dasheng qixin lun*: *Traité sur l'acte de foi dans le Grand Véhicule* (Tokyo: Keio University Press, 2004)—which draws heavily on Japanese scholarship—states: "La version de Paramārtha offer des similitudes et des affinités terminologiques ainsi que stylistiques tout d'abord avec des ouvrages traduits du Sanskrit par Bodhiruci et Ratnamati. . . . C'est ce que suggère le comparaison d'un certain nombre de termes techniques du *Traité* avec ces ouvrages." [The version (of *Dasheng qixin lun* attributed to) Paramārtha shows some similarities and some terminological affinities first of all with works translated from Sanskrit by Bodhiruci and Ratnamati (and *not* Paramārtha). . . . That is what suggests comparing a number of technical terms in the *Treatise* with their works.], pp. xxxi-xxxii. This "thesis" is attributed to Takemura Makio 竹村牧男 in his 1986 article, "Kishiron to Jūjikyōron 起信論と十地経論" (*Dasheng qixin lun* and *Daśabhūmi-sūtra-bhāṣya*), *Tōhōgaku* 72 (July 1986): 1–15. Not surprisingly, Lü Cheng is not mentioned, much less given credit for having already demonstrated this many decades earlier.

he correctly pronounces as closest to the received Sanskrit version; and the Bodhiruci translation, which he also rightly criticizes for a host of deviations from the Sanskrit, deviations he then documents that *Dasheng qixin lun* has appropriated and refashioned in a muddled manner. Since his interest is to show how *Dasheng qixin lun* exposes its own apocryphal status by revealing that it "stole" terms and concepts from an error-riddled predecessor, which it incorporated, reproducing those errors, the fourth Chinese version of the *Laṅkāvatāra*, *Dasheng rulengqie jing* 大乘入楞伽經, translated by the Khotanese monk Śikṣānanda 實叉難陀 in 700 (T.16.672), is irrelevant, since that translation post dates *Dasheng qixin lun* by more than a century.

It is important to keep in mind that without being able to compare the various Chinese *Laṅkāvatāra*-s against the Sanskrit original, Lü's analysis and its conclusions would be impossible, since identifying conclusively which translation is faithful to the Sanskrit and which deviates from it would be impossible.

For Lü Cheng, Genuine Buddhism cultivates logic and clear thinking in order to purify the everyday mind. Distinguishing the true from the false, the authentic from the imaginary, the clear from the distorted, insight from ignorance has always been Buddhism's goal and raison d'être. Shedding centuries, or even *kalpas* of mistaken views—including about Buddhism itself—and thereby "purifying the mental stream of karmic pollution" has always been Yogācāra's project. Few in China did it better than Lü.

11

The Uncompromising Quest for Genuine Buddhism: Lü Cheng's Critique of Original Enlightenment

Chen-Kuo Lin

IT WOULD NOT be an exaggeration to claim that Lü Cheng 呂澂 (1896–1989) and Yinshun 印順 (1906–2005) are two of the most prominent scholars of Chinese Buddhism in the twentieth century.[1] Unlike Yinshun, whose popularity has grown in recent decades due to the strong revival of Buddhism, Lü Cheng has remained relatively understudied.[2] As I will show in this chapter, the failure to recognize Lü's scholarly contribution inevitably leads to a one-sided picture of modern Chinese Buddhist thought and the role of Yogācāra in modern Chinese Buddhist scholarship.

I will further contend that, as far as methodology is concerned, it is also necessary to place Lü Cheng within the broader context of intellectual history in modern China. On the one hand, we need to trace the lineage of Lü's scholarship to European Buddhology through its Japanese assimilation, a development that unfolded from the late-nineteenth century to the early twentieth century. As is quite well known nowadays, Japanese scholarship played a seminal role in the

1. I wish to express my thanks to Ernest Brewster for assistance in proofreading.

2. Cf. Wing-tsit Chan, *Religious Trends in Modern China* (New York: Columbia University Press, 1953; Octagon Books Reprint, 1978). In Chan's work, Lü Cheng is completely overshadowed by Lü's master, Ouyang Jingwu 歐陽竟無 (1871–1943). Also see Eyal Aviv's chapter on Ouyang. For research on Yinshun, see Tien Po-yao, *A Modern Buddhist Monk-Reformer in China: The Life and Thought of Yinshun*, PhD diss., California Institute of Integral Studies, 1995; and Marcus Bingenheimer, *Der Mönchsgelehrte Yinshun (*1906) und seine Bedeutung fur den Chinesisch-Taiwanischen Buddhismus im 20. Jahrhundert* (The Scholar Monk Yinshun and his Position in Twentieth-Century Chinese Buddhism) (Heidelberg: Edition Forum [Wurzburger Sinologische Schriften], 2004).

formation of modern Chinese Buddhist studies.[3] On the other hand, we should not ignore the domestic context of Chinese intellectual history in which Lü's textual-philological and philosophical approaches were rooted. As for the latter, the turn from Neo-Confucian philosophy to philology in the eighteenth century paved the way for Lü Cheng to pursue modern Buddhist scholarship.[4] In this respect, his intellectual career should be investigated within the dual contexts of philosophy versus philology, on the one hand, and idealism versus positivism, on the other hand.[5] In its historical development, especially after Dignāga (sixth century), logic and epistemology (*hetuvidyā*; *pramāṇa-vāda*) became the core of Yogācāra philosophy. In modern China, it was Lü Cheng who brought Buddhist logic and epistemology to the fore once again.

Clearly, Lü favored philology and textual-historical criticism over philosophical speculation. It would, however, be improper to characterize Lü as a philological scholar without considering the philosophical significance of his works. As we will see in the following discussion, Lü articulated a strong philosophical critique of mainstream Chinese Buddhist thought and practice, especially as represented by *Dasheng qixin lun* 大乘起信論 (Awakening of Mahāyāna Faith) and Chan/Zen Buddhism.

This chapter is divided into four parts. First, I sketch Lü Cheng's academic profile over three stages. In the second part I focus on Lü's contribution to the study of Buddhist logic and epistemology.[6] In the third part I argue that Lü's critique of Chan ideology cannot be viewed as separate from his devotion to the study of Buddhist logic and epistemology. In the fourth part, I summarize the debate between Lü Cheng and Xiong Shili 熊十力 (1885–1968). Finally, I sum-up Lü's lifelong intellectual career in the conclusion.

---

3. Chen Jidong 陳継東, *Shinmatsu Bukkyō no kenkyū: Yō Bun'e o chūshin toshite* 清末仏教の研究：楊文会を中心として (Late-Qing Buddhist Research: Centered on Yang Wenhui) (Tokyo: Sankibō Busshorin, 2003).

4. Benjamin E. Elman, *From Philosophy to Philology: Intellectual and Social Aspects in Late Imperial China* (Cambridge, MA.: Council on East Asian Studies, Harvard University, 1984).

5. In the plan to edit the *Zangyao* 藏要 (Essentials of Buddhist Canon), Ouyang clearly expressed his dissatisfaction with the *Taishō Shinshū Daizōkyō* 大正新脩大藏經 (*Taishō Revised Tripitaka*; 1922) claiming that the editorial quality of the Chinese Buddhist canon can be assured only by those scholars who are well trained in Chinese philological and historical-textual criticism and Song-Ming philosophy. See Ouyang Jingwu et al., "Benyuan shiji 本院事記" (Administrative Report), *Neixue* 3(1926): 167–187.

6. In this chapter I pay more attention to Lü's textual-philological contribution to Buddhist logic and epistemology than his exegesis of traditional Yogācāra doctrines. Whereas I undertake a historical-textual survey on this aspect of Lü's work, a more detailed study on Lü's epistemology is presented in Dan Lusthaus's chapter.

1. Life and works

The early stage (1896–1922)

The fourth of seven children, Lü Cheng was born in Danyang County, Jiangsu, in 1896.[7] According to Lü, it was under the influence of his eldest brother, Lü Fengzi 呂鳳子 (1886–1959), who had studied Buddhism under Yang Wenhui 楊文會 (1837–1911) and who later became a nationally famous artist, that Lü became interested in both art and Buddhist learning. As a high-school student, young Lü often purchased Buddhist scriptures at the Jinling Sutra Press (Jinling kejing chu 金陵刻經處) where he came to know Ouyang Jingwu. In 1914 Lü joined the Buddhist Seminary newly established by Ouyang as an affiliated institute of Jinling Sutra Press.

In 1917 Lü traveled to Japan to study language and art, but due to the anti-Japanese sentiment in China, he returned to China in 1918. As we will see, the Japanese connection played an important role in Lü's intellectual career. In 1919, Lü officially worked with Ouyang in setting up the China Institute of Inner Learning (Zhina Neixue Yuan 支那內學院). During the same period, Lü was also appointed as Dean of Academic Affairs at the Shanghai School of Art, teaching Aesthetics and History of Western Art. It is worthy of note that during this period Lü never gave up his interests in art history and aesthetics that led to the publication of four books in the early 1920s.[8] Lü served as dean of the China Institute of Inner Learning in 1922 when the institute was officially established. He did not give up his interest in art until he completely devoted himself to Buddhist studies from 1924.

---

7. Lü Cheng, "Wo de jingli yu Neixue Yuan fazhan licheng 我的經歷與內學院發展歷程" (My Experiences and the History of the China Institute of Inner Learning), *Shijie zhexue* 3 (2007): 77–86. This was documented in 1959 when Lü worked at the Chinese Academy of Social Science.

8. (1) Lü Cheng, *Meixue qianshuo* 美學淺說 (Aesthetics for the Beginner) (Shanghai: Shangwu yinshuguan, 1923); (2) Lü Cheng (ed.), *Meixue gailun* 美學概論 (Introduction to Aesthetics) (Shanghai: Shangwu yinshuguan, 1923); (3) Lü Cheng, *Wanjin meixueshuo he mei de yuanli* 晚近美學說和美的原理 (Modern Theories of Aesthetics and the Principles of Beauty) (Shanghai: Shangwu yinshuguan, 1925); (4) E. Meumann, *Wanjin meixue sichao* 晚近美學思潮 (Einführung in de ästhetik der gegenwart), trans. Lü Cheng (Shanghai: Shangwu yinshuguan, 1924); and (5) Earnst Meumann, *Xiandai meixue sichao* 現代美學思潮 (Einführung in de ästhetik der gegenwart), trans. Lü Cheng (Shanghai: Shangwu yinshuguan, 1931). See *Minguo shiqi zongshumu* (1911–1949): *zhexue-xinlixue* 民國時期總書目 (1911–1949)：哲學•新理學 (Comprehensive Bibliography in the Republican Era 1911–1949: Philosophy & Modern Neo-Confucianism), ed. Beijing tushuguan 北京圖書館 (Beijing: Shumu wenxian chubanshe, 1991): pp. 211, 213. It should be noted that the last translation is the reprinted edition.

The middle stage (1922–1949)

The halcyon era in Lü's lifelong scholarly career was witnessed in the thirty-year history (1922–1952) of the China Institute of Inner Learning. According to Lü's work statement in 1950, the mission of the Institute was to restore Genuine Buddhism (*zhenshi Foxue* 真實佛學) through refuting the False Buddhism (*xiangsi Foxue* 相似佛學).[9] According to his recollection, the institute pursued three steps to accomplish its mission. The first step was to edit critically Buddhist texts available in their Sanskrit, Tibetan, and Chinese versions. The second step was to establish accurate knowledge of Indian Buddhist doctrines as the criterion to evaluate critically the historical development of Chinese Buddhism, especially Chan and Huayan. For Lü, this quest for Genuine Buddhism finally precipitated his critique of the Chan doctrine of inherent enlightenment (*benjue* 本覺), which was said to have been rooted in *Dasheng qixin lun*, a Chinese Buddhist apocryphal. Another famous episode in the same period was Lü's debate with Xiong Shili, a former colleague who was later converted to Neo-Confucianism. The last step was to establish the Five Subjects of Buddhist Teachings as a comprehensive curriculum of Buddhist scholasticism.

Before summarizing the works completed during this period, we should be aware that Lü studied Sanskrit and Tibetan with Huang Shuyin 黃樹因 (1898–1925),[10] a young colleague who had learned Tibetan with Tibetan monks at Yonghe Temple in Beijing and had studied Sanskrit with Ferdinand Lessing (1882–1961), a German linguist living in Shandong,[11] as well as Baron Alexander von Stäel-Holstein (1877–1937), a Russian Sanskrit scholar who taught at Peking University between 1918 and 1929.[12] According to Lü's recollection, Huang brought him several Sanskrit and Tibetan dictionaries for the purpose of self-learning. It took

9. Lü Cheng, "Zhina Neixue Yuan yanjiu gongzuo de zongjie he jihua 支那內學院研究工作的總結和計畫" (Report and Plan of the Research Work in the China Institute of Inner Learning), *Xiandai Foxue* 1, no. 1(1950). On Genuine Buddhism, see also Dan Lusthaus's chapter in this volume.

10. For Huang's biography, see Ouyang Jingwu, "Huang Jian shilüe 黃建事略" (Biography of Huang Jian), *Neixue* 1(1924): 179–180. See also Ouyang's and Lü's talks on the occasion of the opening of Shuyin Seminar Room: "Shuyin yanjiushi chengliji 樹因研究室成立記" (On the Opening of Shuyin Research Center), *Neixue* 3(1926): 172–178.

11. University of California (System) Academic Senate, "Ferdinand Diedrich Lessing, Oriental Languages: Berkeley" University of California: In Memoriam, April 1963, http://www.oac.cdlib.org/view?docId=hb0580022s&chunk.id=div00016&brand=oac4&doc.view=entire_text.

12. For Baron Alexander Von Stäel-Holstein, see Wang Qilong 王啟龍 (ed.), *Ganghetai xueshu nianpu jianpian* 鋼和泰學術年譜簡編 (A Brief Chronological Biography of Alexander von Stäel-Holstein). Wang Qilong, "A Brief Review of Alexander von Stäel-Holstein —A Great Scholar in Asian Studies," *China Tibetology* 1(March 2008): 80–93.

Lü about five years of self-training to read Sanskrit and Tibetan texts, which was crucial to completing the critical edition of the *Zangyao* (Essentials of the Buddhist Canon).[13]

The Tibetan texts Huang brought back to Nanjing in the early 1920s include Sthiramati's (sixth century) *Trimśikā-vijñaptimātra-bhāṣya* (Commentary on the *Thirty Verses on Nothing but Consciousness*) and **Sūtrālaṃkāravṛttibhāṣya* (Commentary on the *Adornment of the Great Vehicle Scripture*); Asvabhāva's (fifth to sixth centuries) **Mahāyāna-sūtrālaṃkāraṭīka* (Commentary on the *Adornment of the Great Vehicle Scripture*); Guṇamati's (sixth to seventh centuries) *Vyākhyāyuktiṭīkā* (Commentary on the *Explanation of Reasoning*); Dignāga's (*ca.* 480–540) *Pramāṇasamuccaya* (A Compendium of Epistemology) and its auto-commentary; and Asaṅga's (fourth century) *Mahāyāna-saṃgraha* (Compendium of the Great Vehicle) and auto-commentaries.[14] This shows that the seeds of Sanskrit and Tibetan studies, planted in Chinese soil by Alexander von Stael-Holstein, successfully germinated in the China Institute of Inner Learning.

Lü's philological enthusiasm should be also placed within the broader context of the emergence of comparative philology and religious studies in the nineteenth century. That is, Lü came to be acquainted with this new trend of treating religious studies as a science through his acquaintance with Japanese scholarship. In this connection the lifelong friendship and cooperation between Yang Wenhui and Nanjō Bun'yū 南條文雄 (1849–1927) should be noted. Nanjō studied with Max Müller at Oxford during 1880–1884 and later took the first post of Sanskrit lecturer at Tokyo University.[15] It was quite natural for young Lü to come to know Japanese and European Buddhist scholarship through the seminar held at Yang's Jinling Sutra Press.

Regarding textual-philological approaches to the study of Yogācāra texts, it is first necessary to mention Sylvain Lévi's discovery and preparation of critical editions of the Sanskrit manuscripts of Asaṅga's *Mahāyānasūtrālaṃkāra* (Treatise on the *Adornment of the Great Vehicle Scripture*) and Vasubandhu's *Triṃśikā* (Thirty Verses) and *Viṃśatikā* (Twenty Verses) in 1907 and 1925. Lévi's works

---

13. Gao Zhennong 高振農,"Huainian enshi Lü Cheng xiansheng 懷念恩師呂瀓先生" (In Memory of My Teacher Mr. Lü Cheng), *Wutaishan yanjiu* 1 (1998): 32–34.

14. Recently a list of Buddhist texts, including Sanskrit and Tibetan texts collected in the Shuyin Research Center, were found and published. See Gao Shanbin 高山彬, "Zhina Neixue Yuan Fojiao shiliao sanzhong 支那內學院佛教史料三種" (Three Documents of the China Institute of Inner Learning), in *Shijie zhexue* 3 (2010): 151–160.

15. Judith Snodgrass, *Presenting Japanese Buddhism to the West: Orientalism, Occidentalism, and the Columbian Exposition* (Chapel Hill: The University of North Carolina Press, 2003), pp. 118–121. For Nanjō's role in Meiji New Buddhism and his relation to Chinese intellectuals, also see John Jorgensen's chapter.

immediately attracted the attention of Japanese scholars, especially Ui Hakuju 宇井伯壽 (1882–1963) and Yamaguchi Susumu 山口益 (1895–1976), who became devoted to this new field of research. As far as the scholarly genealogy of Buddhist studies is concerned here, we should not overlook the fact that in 1916, Ui studied under Louis de la Vallée Poussin (1969–1938) in Cambridge, while Yamaguchi worked with Lévi in the1930s.[16] In was through working in such intellectual milieux that Ouyang, Huang, and Lü came to realize that there is no way to ignore the textual-philological studies of Sanskrit, Pāli, and Tibetan texts if they sought to revitalize Buddhist studies in China.

Lü's interest in the textual-philological studies resulted in his early works. These works are as follows: (1) *Shengming lüe* 聲明略 (A Brief Introduction to Śabdavidyā), published by the China Institute of Inner Learning in 1923; (2) *Yindu Fojiao shilüe* 印度佛教史略 (A Brief History of Indian Buddhism), published in 1925; (3) *Yinming gangyao* 因明綱要 (A Primer of Buddhist Logic), published in 1926; (4) *Fojiao yanjiufa* 佛教研究法 (Research Guide for Buddhist Studies), published in 1926; and (5) *Fodian fanlun* 佛典汎論 (A Survey of Buddhist Literature), published in 1929. As evidenced in those early works, Lü demonstrated his zeal for learning European Buddhology through Japanese scholarship. Among others, Ogiwara Unrai 荻原雲來 (1869–1937) and Fukaura Seibun 深浦正文 (1889–1968) are two scholars to whom Lü remained deeply indebted. Lü's *Yindu Fojiao shilüe* was (largely) adapted from Ogiwara's *Indo no Bukkyō* 印度の佛教 (Indian Buddhism), whereas both *Fojiao yanjiufa* and *Fodian fanlun* were adapted from Fukaura's works.[17] It is also interesting to note that the above five books were not included in his collected works, *Lü Cheng Foxue lunzhu xuanji* 呂澂佛學論著選集 (Selected Collection of Lü Cheng's Writings on Buddhism), edited by Li An 李安 in 1986 and published in 1991.[18] Although Lü might have not been fully satisfied with his early works, they nevertheless provide invaluable clues to the sources of Lü's early scholarship.

---

16. Takasaki Jikidō 高崎直道, "Yugagyōha no keisei 瑜伽行派の形成" (The Formation of the Yogācāra School), in *Kōza Daijō Bukkyō: Yuishiki shisō* 講座大乘佛教•唯識思想 (Series of Mahāyāna Buddhism: Yogācāra Thought, volume 8), ed. Hirakawa Akira et al. (Tokyo: Shunjūsha, 1982); Lin Chuanfang 林傳芳, "Jindai Riben Foxue yanjiu de kaizhan 近代日本佛學研究的發展" (The Development of the Buddhist Studies in Modern Japan), in *Xiandai shijie de fojiaoxue* 現代世界的佛教學 (Buddhist Studies in Modern World), ed. Zhang Mantao 張曼濤 (Taipei: Dacheng wenhua, 1979): pp. 41–98.

17. Ogiwara Unrai 荻原雲來, *Indo no Bukkyō* 印度の佛教 (Indian Buddhism) (Tokyo: Hinoeuma shuppansha, 1917); Fukaura Seibun 深浦正文, *Bukkyō seiten gairon* 佛教聖典概論 (A Survey of Buddhist Literature) (Kyoto: Ikuta shoten, 1924); *Bukkyō kenkyū hō* 佛教研究法 (Research Methods in the Buddhist Studies) (Tokyo: Hinoeuma shuppansha, 1923).

18. Lü Cheng, *Lü Cheng Foxue lunzhu xuanji*, 5 vols. (Jinan: Qilu shushe, 1991). See also Li An, "Editorial Note," in vol. 1.

From the outset, Lü was interested in the study of Buddhist canonical texts, biographies of the Buddha, doctrinal history, logic, and epistemology. He quickly picked up Western scholarship through Japanese writings. Without doubt, young Lü greatly admired Western scholars such as E. Burnouf, K. Kern, H. Oldenburg, and Rhys Davids. By contrast, he looked down upon the traditional Chinese commentaries as "outmoded and strange."[19] In this regard, Lü also closely followed in the ideological footsteps of Japanese scholarship. For example, he keenly noticed the controversy aroused by Mochizuki Shinkō's 望月信亨 (1869–1948) article of 1919 on the authorship of *Dasheng qixin lun* that threatened the doctrinal ground of East Asian Buddhism.[20] As we will see below, Lü's interest in textual-philological study undergirds his uncompromising quest for "Genuine Buddhism." On the contrary, "False Buddhism," which was said to have been embedded in the East Asian Buddhist apocrypha, especially *Dasheng qixin lun*, should be rejected without reservation. Lü's lifelong critique of *Dasheng qixin lun* finally concluded in two articles published during the 1950s and 1960s.[21]

Lü's interest in canonical literature was realized with the completion of the *Xinbian Hanwen dazangjing mulu* 新編漢文大藏經目錄 (New Catalogue of the Chinese Buddhist Canon) in 1963.[22] The catalogue is divided into five parts: (1) Sutra, (2) Vinaya, (3) Abhidharma, (4) Tantra, and (5) Chinese Commentaries. Regarding the classification of scriptures, Lü avoided adopting the traditional East Asian hermeneutic framework, for instance, the Tiantai classification of teachings. In contrast, he attempted to restore the Mahāyāna system from the Indic sources, especially Asaṅga's *Mahāyāna-saṃgraha* (Compendium of the Great Vehicle).[23]

19. Lü Cheng, *Fojiao yanjiufa* 佛教研究法 (Research Guide for Buddhist Studies) (Taipei: Xin wenfeng chuban gongsi, 1977), p. 84: "In the main trend of Buddhist studies in recent decades, Western scholars are more advanced in studying Buddhism with the methods of historiography. They search for truth in every subject with the aid of philology, archaeology, aesthetics, and historical chronology. . . . In comparison, the hermeneutic speculation as seen in Chinese works looks like something outmoded and strange."

20. Ibid., p. 93.

21. Lü Cheng, "*Dasheng qixinlun* kaozheng 大乘起信論考證" (Textual Criticism of the *Awakening of Mahāyāna Faith*), in *Lü Cheng Foxue lunzhu xuanji*, vol. 1, pp. 303–369; "*Qixin* yu Chan: duiyu *Dasheng qixin lun* laili de tantao 《起信》與禪——對於《大乘起信論》來歷的探討 (*Awakening of Mahāyāna Faith* and Chan: Investigation into the Origin of the *Awakening of Mahāyāna Faith*), *Xueshu yuekan* 4 (1962): 32–37. See also Lou Yulie 樓宇烈, "Lü Qiuyi xiansheng xueshu nianbiao 呂秋逸先生學術年表 (Chronology of Lü Cheng's Scholarship), in *Zhongguo xiandai xueshu jingdian: Yang Wenhui, Ouyang Jian, Lü Cheng juan* 中國現代學術經典•楊文會•歐陽漸•呂澂卷 (Academic Classics in Modern China: Yang Wenhui, Ouyang Jian, Lü Cheng) (Hebei: Hebei jiaoyu chubanshe, 1996).

22. *Lü Cheng Foxue lunzhu xuanji*, vol. 3, pp. 1621–1896. The catalogue was originally edited in 1963 and published in 1981.

23. *Lü Cheng Foxue lunzhu xuanji*, vol. 3, 1622–1626.

The most significant contribution of *New Catalogue* can be seen in the critical examination of the translators in Chinese Buddhist canon. Compared with Nanjō Bun'yū's *Catalogue*, in which, for instance, fifty-four works in fifty-nine fascicles are ascribed to An Shigao 安世高 (second century CE), Lü Cheng identified only twenty-two works in twenty-six fascicles as An Shigao's works.[24] It is also worth of note that Lü never made a secret of his admiration of Nanjō and his magnum opus.[25]

Furthermore, Lü's interest in Buddhist history, which developed from his adoption of Ogiwara's work, is evidenced in his *Yindu Foxue yuanliu lüejiang* 印度佛學源流略講 (Lectures on the History of Indian Buddhism) and *Zhongguo Foxue yuanliu lüejiang* 中國佛學源流略講 (Lectures on the History of Chinese Buddhism), two of the most widely circulating works. Both works were records of lectures delivered in 1961 (prior to the Cultural Revolution, 1966–1976) and published in 1979.

The greatest achievement in the period 1928–1937 was the completion of the *Zangyao* (Essentials of the Buddhist Canon), which consists of seventy texts in more than 400 fascicles. Before *Zangyao* was edited, it had taken seven years for the China Institute of Inner Learning to prepare a critical edition of the complete works of Xuanzang's translation in nearly 1000 fascicles. All were published in woodblock print. Lü summarized the main findings of the project as follows: (1) The entire *mātṛkā* (matrix) of *Saṃyutāgama* (Miscellaneous Collection) was discovered for the first time in the last section of the *Yogācārabhūmi-śāstra* (Discourse on the Stages of Concentration Practice). The findings help to clarify the historical origin of the Yogācāra School and restore the textual order of the Chinese translation of *Saṃyutāgama.* (2) The textual relationship between the *Yogācārabhūmi* and *Ratnakūṭa-sūtra* (The Scripture of Forehead Jewelry) was also identified. (3) The project concluded by drawing a distinction between the Old Yogācāra School—represented by Bandhusri, Citrabhanu, Nanda, and Paramārtha—and the New Yogācāra School—represented by Dharmapāla and Xuanzang—with the teachings of Sthiramati lying between the two schools.[26] (4) For Lü Cheng this framework was instrumental in reconstructing the entire system of *abhidharma* literature.[27]

---

24. Ibid., bol. 3, 1629.

25. Lü Cheng, *Fojiao yanjiufa*, pp. 19–20.

26. Lü Cheng, "Lun *Zhuangyan jinglun* yu weishi guxue 論莊嚴經論與唯識古學" (On the *Mahāyāna-sūtrālaṃkāra* and the Old Yogācāra School), *Lü Cheng Foxue lunzhu xuanji*, vol. 1, p. 73. The article was published in 1924. For Lü's later interpretation, see *Yindu Foxue yuanliu lüejiang* 印度佛學源流略講 (Lectures on the Development of Indian Buddhism), *Lü Cheng Foxue lunzhu xuanji*, vol. 4, pp. 2220–2234.

27. Lü Cheng, "Neixue Yuan yanjiu gongzuo de zongjie he jihua."

The *Zangyao* demonstrates a high standard of textual-philological criticism, yet unfortunately it has not been properly recognized by contemporary scholars. As one example to highlight why it should be better appreciated, take Lü's edition of Xuanzang's *Cheng weishi lun* 成唯識論 (Demonstration of Nothing but Consciousness). *Cheng weishi lun* was edited on the basis of the Sixi 思溪 edition of the Song Dynasty, while other editions, such as the Korean copy and the Ming copy, were compared. For the critical edition, the following textual sources were also consulted: (1) Vasubandhu's *Triṃśikāvijñaptikārikā* (Thirty Verses) and Sthiramati's *Triṃśikāvijñaptibhāṣya* (Commentary on the *Thirty Verses*), which are collected in Sylvain Lévi's *Vijñaptimātratāsiddhi* (Paris, 1925); (3) Jinamitra's Tibetan translations of *Triṃśikā* and (4) Sthiramati's *Triṃśikābhāṣya*; (5) Tibetan translation of Vinitadeva's *Triṃśikātīkā*; (6) Paramārtha's Chinese annotated translation of *Triṃśikā, Zhuanshilun* 轉識論 (Treatise on Evolution of Consciousness); and (7) Kuiji's *Cheng weishi lun shuji* 成唯識論述記 (Commentary on *Demonstration of Nothing but Consciousness*).[28] Lü also edited the main text of *Cheng weishi lun* into three layers: (1) the root verses, (2) the main commentaries, including Sthiramati's commentary, and (3) the other subcommentaries. With the distinction of three layers, Lü's new edition of *Cheng weishi lun* is not only user-friendly, but also convenient for checking the difference between Dharmapāla's and Sthiramati's commentaries. Lü also translated Sthiramati's *Trimśikā-vijñaptimātra-bhāṣya* from Sanskrit into Chinese in 1926, only one year after Lévi's publication of Sanskrit text and two years before the new edition of *Cheng weishi lun* was published.[29]

Lü spent ten years (1928–1937) compiling *Zangyao*, which in total comprises seventy Indian Buddhist texts. However, he never considered his textual-philological work to be purely scientific research. On the contrary, the ambitious project was motivated by his quest for the Indian origins of Genuine Buddhism. Lü believed that as far as the true form of Buddhism has been fully disclosed, there should not be any difficulty in refuting the corrupted form of Buddhism in its later development.

In 1937, Lü moved along with the China Institute of Inner Learning to Sichuan when the Second Sino-Japanese War broke out. This event precipitated a most difficult and chaotic time for the Chinese people. In 1943, Ouyang passed away in Sichuan and Lü was elected as dean of the institute. After Ouyang's death, Lü devoted his energies to designing the Buddhist curriculum, "Five

28. Lü Cheng, "*Cheng weishi lun* jiaokan shuoming 成唯識論校勘說明" (Editorial Note on *Cheng weishi lun*), *Zangyao* 藏要, series I, (Nanjijng: Zhina Neixue Yuan, 1929), volume 8.

29. Lü Cheng, *Anhui sanshi weishishi lüechao* 安慧三十唯識釋略抄 (An Abridged Translation of Sthiramati's *Triṃśikāvijñaptibhāṣya*), *Neixue* 3 (1926): 115–142. It is worthy of note that the publication of Lü's translation was even earlier than Takakusu Junjirō's 高楠順次郎 (1866–1945) and Ogiwara Unrai's Japanese respective translations of 1927.

Buddhist Subjects Seminar," in which thirty Buddhist texts were designated as the core curriculum.[30] Lü lectured on fifteen canonical texts over three years (1943–1946).[31]

The final stage (1950–1989)

After the war ended, Lü moved back to Nanjing in 1947 when China was yet again drawn into the civil war. In 1949, the People's Republic of China was established. According to Lü's recollection:

> When Danyang was liberated in April, 1949, I read Chairman Mao's writings and learnt New Philosophy by myself. Thus, I came to have deeper understanding of revolution. In September, I was invited to be a representative of religious groups in the Chinese People's Political Consultative Conference. I did not attend the meeting due to the fact that I do not harbor religious beliefs.[32]

The editorial note of Lü's résumé also mentions his self-examination, claiming that what he had accomplished was nothing but the academic work of Buddhist studies.[33] Although it is not easy to tell whether Lü's statements were politically distorted, I am rather inclined to believe that Lü was politically transformed through the revolution. This can be testified by his thought as it developed in the last stage of his career.

Most of Lü's later works were published in *Xiandai Foxue* 現代佛學 (Modern Buddhist Studies) in the 1950s. In Communist China, as he recollected, he participated in various political movements, including the "Three Protests,"[34]

---

30. The five subjects are (1) *abhidharma*, (2) vinaya, (3) Yogācāra, (4) Prajñāpāramitā, and (5) Nirvāṇa.

31. Lü Cheng, "Wo de jingli yu Neixue Yuan fazhan licheng," pp. 78–79.

32. Ibid., p. 79.

33. "The China Institute of Inner Learning, where I have worked for many years, is a religious institute. Mr. Ouyang, the founder of the institute, espoused strong religious faith. However, his case is different from so-called religious belief, because he believed what he believed, which stemmed from his authentic quest and profound understanding of human ascendance. . . . All my research and editing work undertaken in the China Institute of Inner Learning were done for academic purposes. After liberation, I did my best to transform the Institute into an academic institute." Lü, "Wo de jingli yu Neixue Yuan fazhan licheng," p. 79.

34. In 1951–1952, the political movement of the "Three Protests" was directed toward corruption, waste, and bureaucracy.

political learning, especially learning Marxism and logic, and participating in agricultural labor.[35] The China Institute of Inner Learning was forced to close its door in 1952 for the reason that "the state is in charge of academic plans and projects, and hence there is no need for the existence of private institutions."[36]

Lü's academic career completely ceased at the outset of the Cultural Revolution in 1966. Unfortunately, most of Lü's manuscripts were lost in the political turmoil.[37] Fortunately, however, Lü had enough time to systemize his life-long study of Buddhist teachings before the Cultural Revolution. A series of Lü's articles on the fundamental topics in Buddhism was published in *Xiandai Foxue*. At the same time, probably owing to state ideology, Lü also returned to the critical study of Chinese Buddhism. From 1961 to 1966, he taught at the Seminar of Buddhist Studies in Nanjing, where his *Zhongguo Foxue yuanliu lüejiang* (Lectures on the Development of Chinese Buddhism) and *Yindu Foxue yuanliu lüejiang* (Lectures on the Development of Indian Buddhism) were recorded in 1961. Both can be considered as milestones of Lü's scholarly career. In the same year, he also lectured on the *Nyāyapraveśaka* (Commentary to *Entryway into Logic*), which was published in 1983.

2. *Buddhist logic and epistemology*

Before exploring Lü Cheng's contribution to the study of Buddhist logic and epistemology, we need to bear in mind the fact that the booming interest in Chinese logic at the turn of the twentieth century reflects the anxiety of modernity among Chinese intellectuals. As culturally imagined, Chinese intellectuals assumed that European modernity had been grounded in the rationality of logic

---

35. Lü, "Wo de jingli yu Neixue Yuan fazhan licheng," p. 79.

36. Ibid., p. 79.

37. In recent years some of Lü Cheng's unpublished works have been discovered and published. Here are some of the most important findings: (1) Chinese draft translation of Dignāga's *Ālambana-parīkṣā* (Treatise on Discerning the Conditions for the Causal Support of Consciousness) from the Tibetan version, which was completed before the finalized version in *Neixue* 4 (1928). See Gao Shanbin, "Zhina Neixue Yuan Fojiao shiliao sanzhong," pp. 151–160. (2) Chinese translation of Bhāvaviveka's (sixth century) *Madhyamakahṛdaya* (The Heart of the Middle Way), Chapter V, "Yogācāratattvaviniścaya" (Discerning the Reality in Yogācāra), which was completed in the 1950s. See Lü Cheng, "*Zhongguan xin lun* 'Ru jueze yuqieshi zhenshi pin' " 中觀心論•入決擇瑜伽師真實品 (Chinese translation of Bhāvaviveka's *Madhyamakahṛdaya*, Chapter V, "Yogācāratattvaviniścaya"), in *Shijie zhexue* 6 (2011): 72–91. (3) Modern Chinese translation of Vasubandhu's *Viṃśatika*. The date is not specified. See Lü Cheng, "*Ershi weishi* baihua yiben 二十唯識白話譯本" (Modern Chinese translation of *Viṃśatika*), in *Shijie zhexue* 1 (2009): 120–133. (4) Lecture on the *Diamond Sutra*. The date is not specified. See Lü Cheng, "*Jingang bore jing* jiangyi 金剛般若經講義" (Lecture on the *Diamond Sutra*), in *Zhongguo zhexue shi* 4 (2008): 5–15, 24.

and epistemology, while in contrast the same rationality is considered absent in non-Western civilizations. For Chinese intellectuals, science rooted in logic and epistemology was part of the project of searching for "wealth and power."[38] The best example in China is Yan Fu's 嚴復 (1854–1921) translation of John Stuart Mill's *A System of Logic* in 1905. Another example is Hu Shi's (1891–1962) *The Development of the Logical Method in Ancient China* (Shanghai, 1922). It was in this intellectual milieu that there was a revival of scholarship on ancient Chinese and Buddhist logic.[39] The new era of the latter started from the reprint of Kuiji's *Yinming ru zhengli lun shuji* 因明入正理論述記 (Commentary on *Nyāyapraveśa*) in 1896, the most influential text of Chinese Buddhist logic which had been lost for a thousand years in China before being retrieved from Japan by Yang Wenhui and Nanjō Bun'yū. This text was immediately used by Yang as one of the main textbooks in the Buddhist Seminary in 1907.[40] After that, more than thirty monographs on Buddhist logic were published in the Republican period.[41] Among those works Lü Cheng's *Yinming gangyao* 因明綱要 (A Primer of Buddhist Logic) was viewed as one of the finest.

As seen in the annual record of China Institute of Inner Learning, most of the graduate seminars and undergraduate courses Lü Cheng had conducted during 1923–1926 were on Yogācāra and Buddhist logic. Lü used Kuiji's *Yinming ru zhengli lun shuji* as the main text for the 1923–1924 Buddhist logic seminar. Śaṅkarasvāmin's (sixth century) *Nyāyapraveśa* (Entryway into Logic),[42] Dharmakīrti's (eighth century)[43] *Nyāyabindu* (A Drop of Logic), and Dignāga's *Nyāyamukha* (Introduction to Logic) and *Pramāṇasamuccaya*

38. Cf., Benjamin I. Schwartz, *In Search of Wealth and Power: Yen Fu and the West.* (Cambridge, MA: Belknap Press of Harvard University Press, 1964); Song Wenjian 宋文監, *Luojixue de chuanru yu yanjiu* 邏輯學的傳入與研究 (Importing and Studying the Logic from the West) (Fuzhou: Fujian renmin chubanshe, 2005), pp. 7–16.

39. Jochim Kurtz, *The Discovery of Chinese Logic* (Leiden: Brill, 2011); John Makeham, "The Role of Masters Studies in the Early Formation of Chinese Philosophy as an Academic Discipline," in *Learning to Emulate the Wise: The Genesis of Chinese Philosophy as an Academic Discipline in Twentieth-Century China*, ed. John Makeham (Hong Kong: Chinese University Press, 2012), pp. 73–101.

40. Shen Jianyin 沈劍英, Yao Nanqiang 姚南強, Xu Donglai 徐東來, Shen Haibo 沈海波, *Zhongguo Fojiao luojishi* 中國佛教邏輯史 (History of Chinese Buddhist Logic) (Shanghai: Huadong shifandaxue chubanshe, 2001), p. 323; Lou Yulie, *Zhongguo xiandai xueshu jingdian*, pp. 24, 264–265.

41. Li Kuangwu 李匡武, Zhou Yunzhi 周云之, and Zhou Wenying 周文英 (eds.), *Zhongguo luojishi xiandai juan* 中國邏輯史•現代卷 (History of Chinese Logic: Modern Period) (Gansu Renmin Chubanshe, 1989), pp. 135–138.

42. A primer on Dignāga's logic.

43. Another Yogācāra scholar in the tradition of Dignāga.

(Compendium on Epistemology) were also studied. In 1927, Lü Cheng read Dignāga's *Pramāṇasamuccayavṛtti* (Exposition on the Compendium on Epistemology) with those scholars interested in Tibetan Buddhism.[44] The research output of this meeting of minds was published in the journal *Neixue* 內學.[45]

Although extending research to Dharmakīrti in the later stage, Lü Cheng began his study of Buddhist logic with Kuiji's *Yinming ru zhengli lun shuji*, a commentary on Śaṅkarasvāmin's *Nyāyapraveśa*. The result was the publication of "*Rulun* shisi yinguo jie 入論十四因過解 (On the Fallacies of Reasoning in the *Nyāyapraveśa*) and *Yinming gangyao* (A Primer of Buddhist Logic) in 1926. Instead of confining the study to the Chinese commentarial tradition, Lü Cheng read the *Nyāyapraveśa* in comparison with (1) two Tibetan translations, one of which was rendered from the Sanskrit original, while the other was Xuanzang's translation from the Tibetan into Chinese; (2) a Tibetan translation of Dignāga's *Pramāṇasamuccayavṛtti*; (3) a Tibetan translation of Dharmōttara's *Nyāyabinduṭīkā*; and (4) *Lo-pan mav-pos mdsad-pahi bye-brg-tu rtogs-par byed-pa chen-po* (The Great Volume of Precise Understanding).[46] It should be noted that the Sanskrit text of *Nyāyapraveśa* had not been available to Lü until it was published in 1930 and 1931. In Lü's 1935 critical edition of Xuanzang's Chinese translation of *Nyāyapraveśa*, the Sanskrit text and Tibetan translations were included as basic materials for cross-reference.[47] Lü lectured on the *Nyāyapraveśa* again in 1961.

Lü Cheng's textual-philological study of Buddhist logic reached its climax with his research on Dignāga's texts. In 1926, he published *Jilianglunshi lüechao* 集量論釋略抄 (An Abridged Translation of *Pramāṇasamuccayavṛtti*) on the basis of two Tibetan translations by (1) Kanakavarman and Dad-pa śes-rab; and (2) Vasudhararakṣita and Seṅ-rgyal. Another unique contribution of Lü's work can be seen in his "*Yinming zhengli menlun ben* zhengwen 因明正理門論本證文" (Cross Reference to the *Nyāyamukha*), a cross reference of *Pramāṇasamuccayavṛtti* and *Nyāyamukha*. The methodology adopted in this work is briefly explained in the preface:

> Recently I read the Tibetan texts of *Pramāṇasamuccayavṛtti* and found that [Dignāga's] thesis [in that work] was adopted from *Nyāyamukha*. Two thirds of the quoted passages are the same as those in *Nyāyamukha*.

---

44. See the annual reports in *Neixue*, vols. 1–4, 1924–1928.

45. See also Dan Lusthaus's chapter for further discussion of some these works.

46. Lü Cheng, "*Rulun* shisi yinguojie 入論十四因過解" (On the Fallacies of Reasoning in the *Nyāyapraveśa*), *Neixue*, 3(1926): pp. 145–146.

47. *Zangyao*, series II (1935), vol. 6.

> Although the Sanskrit origin of *Nyāyamukha* is no longer extant, it is sufficient to interpret this text with the aid of *Pramāṇasamuccayavṛtti*. Hence I follow the method of cross reference to produce a critical edition in which the original meaning is gradually disclosed and the accumulated uncertainty suddenly melts away. It is the most delightful work I have ever undertaken in my study of Buddhist logic.[48]

In the same year, 1928, Lü Cheng also published a Chinese translation of Dignāga's *Hetu-cakra-ḍamaru* (*Yinlun juezelun* 因輪決擇論; The Drum Wheel of Reason). He noted that this text seeks to illuminate the theory of *trairūpya* (three conditions of logical reason), which according to Lü, was not properly understood in Satis Chandra Vidyabhusana's *A History of Indian Logic*.[49]

One of the purposes of Lü Cheng's enthusiastic study of Sanskrit and Tibetan texts was to develop a critical understanding of Buddhist logic texts preserved in the Chinese canon. Unlike his predecessors, Lü believed that it was impossible to approach a correct understanding of Buddhist thought merely through the Chinese commentaries. In this regard he was so critical-minded that he would not readily accept even the authority of Xuanzang and Kuiji without due evidence. A good example of Lü's textual-philological criticism is seen in his comparative study of four translations of Dignāga's *Ālambana-parīkṣā* (Treatise on Discerning the Conditions for the Causal Support of Consciousness).[50] For the purpose of understanding Dignāga's thesis correctly, Lü Cheng translated the Tibetan version of *Ālambana-parīkṣā* into Chinese and compared it with other translations.[51] As a result, Lü concluded his findings as follows: (1) Xuanzang's translation is different from both Paramārtha's and Tibetan translations. Paramārtha's and the Tibetan translations are almost identical in both the verse and prose sections,

---

48. Lü Cheng, "Yinming zhengli men lun zheng wen 因明正理門論本證文" (On the Text of the Nyāyamukha) *Neixue* 4 (1928): pp. 237–264.

49. Lü Cheng, "*Yinlunlun* tujie 因輪論圖解" (Diagrammatic Explanation on the *Treatise on the Wheel of Reason*), *Neixue* 4(1928): pp. 1–6.

50. See also Dan Lusthaus's chapter in this volume. Among the three Chinese translations, the first, by Paramārtha, is dated between 557 and 569. The second, by Xuanzang, in dated 657. The third one, completed in 710, was included in Yijing's 義淨 (635–713) translation of Dharmapāla's commentary (*Guan suoyuan lunshi* 觀所緣論釋), CBETA, Vol. T31, No. 1625.

51. Yamaguchi Susumu 山口益 also acknowledged his indebtedness to Lü's exegetical reading of Dharmapāla's text. See Yamaguchi and Nozawa Jōshō 野澤靜證, *Seshin yuishiki no genten kaimei* 世親唯識の原典解明 (Study of Source Texts of Vasubandhu and *Vijñapti-mātra*) (Kyoto: Hōzōkan, 1953), pp. 413–414, 432, 446. According to Ui Hakuju 宇井伯壽, Lü Cheng's works on Dignāga held up favorably when compared with European and Japanese scholarship. See Ui Hakuju, *Jinna chosaku no kenkyū* 陳那著作の研究 (Studies on the Works of Dignāga) (Tokyo: Iwanami, 1979), pp. 8, 13–14.

whereas Xuanzang's translation stands for his own lineage of learning. (2) Xuanzang's translation is not as faithful as is usually assumed. He often changed the wording of the text in order to match the commentarial interpretation he had received from his own Indian lineage of exegesis. (3) According to his comparative study on Dharmapāla's commentary on *Ālambana-parīkṣā*, Lü Cheng found that Xuanzang's translation of the *Ālambana-parīkṣā* might be based on the commentarial interpretations that appeared after that of Dharmapāla. For Lü Cheng, the myth of Xuanzang as a faithful translator was no longer sustainable in light of textual-philological criticism.[52]

3. Critique of Dasheng qixin lun, *Chan, and Neo-Confucianism*

Lü Cheng's life-long devotion to the study of Buddhist logic cannot be taken as scholarly interest only. It should rather be explained by his strong motivation to uphold an uncompromising distinction between Genuine Buddhism and False Buddhism. For Lü Cheng, the criteria of Buddhist truth can be found only in logic and epistemological analysis, such as was privileged in Yogācāra. According to this view, Sinitic Buddhist teachings, such as Huayan and Chan, completely deviated from the true path of the Buddha's teaching. As a result, in addition to promoting Buddhist logic and epistemology, it is quite natural for Lü Cheng to regard "False Buddhism" as the target of criticism.

What is "False Buddhism"? For Lü Cheng it referred to those Sinitic forms of Buddhist teachings stemming from the doctrine of inherent enlightenment (*benjue* 本覺) that appeared in *Dasheng qixin lun* for the first time. For Lü Cheng and Ouyang Jingwu, one of the reasons for the incompatibility of the doctrine of inherent enlightenment with authentic Buddhist teachings can be traced back to the apocryphal misconception in *Dasheng qixin lun*. Inspired by Mochizuki Shinko's findings in 1919 and Ouyang's critique in 1922 on the doctrinal authenticity of *Dasheng qixin lun*,[53] Lü Cheng sharply expressed his critical stance

52. Lü Cheng, "Fu lun Zang yi ben tezheng 附論奘譯本特徵" (Addendum: Discussion of the Distinctive Features of Xuanzang's Translation), *Neixue* 4 (1928): pp. 34–42.

53. See Ouyang Jingwu 歐陽竟無, *Weishi jueze tan* 唯識抉擇談 (Critical Essays on the Doctrine of Nothing but Consciousness), especially the section of "Jueze wufa tan zhengzhi 抉擇五法談正智" (On the Meaning of "Correct Cognition" in the Theory of Five Dharmas) (Nanjing: Zhina Neixue yuan, 1922). Ouyang argued that *tathatā* as the object of cognition is separate from *jñāna* as the subject of cognition. In the *Dasheng qixin lun*, however, *tathatā* and *jñāna* are confused and mingled as Mind-Suchness (*xinzhenru* 心真如) which is further taken as the transcendental ground of existence. For a brief critique of *Dasheng*

in the epochal debate with Xiong Shili right at the occasion of Ouyang's death in 1943, claiming that the doctrine of "the enlightened nature [of mind]" (*xingjue* 性覺) was completely incompatible with the doctrine of "the quiescent nature [of mind]" (*xingji* 性寂)."[54] The latter was regarded as being faithful to the Buddha's teaching that mind (*citta*) is "naturally pure" (*prakṛti-viśuddhi*) or "brightly shining" (*prabhāsvara*).[55] With the "naturally pure/quiescent mind" sentient beings are capable of realizing the truth (*tathatā*) as the object of cognition. By contrast, as claimed in *Dasheng qixin lun*, with the "naturally enlightened mind" sentient beings are by nature always already enlightened. As a consequence, it is unnecessary to go through the course of epistemic transformation to achieve enlightenment. Precisely in this respect, we see that Lū Cheng must have been influenced by Dignāga's epistemological approach than by the pre-Dignāga Yogācāra teachings. For Lü Cheng, Genuine Buddhism must take the epistemological stance to pursue valid knowledge first. On the contrary, if any one takes a metaphysical stance as exemplified in *Dasheng qixin lun*, one will be led to an impure form of "enlightenment". To be genuine means to be faithful to the Buddha's teaching. The fundamental ground of Genuine Buddhism is valid cognition that can serve as the basis for spiritual and social liberation.

In short, the "quiescent nature of mind" is a reflective mind, whereas the "enlightened nature of mind" is a self-reflexive mind that guarantees sentient beings will be enlightened as soon as they return to the origin of mind. Lü

qixin lun, Tiantai, and Huayan, see Ouyang Jingwu, "Yang Renshan jushi zhuan 楊仁山傳" (Biography of Yang Renshan), in Ouyang Jingwu, *Ouyang Jingwu wenxuan* 歐陽竟無文選 (Selected Writings of Ouyang Jingwu) (Wuhan: Wuhan daxue chubanshe, 2009), pp. 378–381. See also Cheng Gongrang 程恭讓, *Jueze yu zhenwei zhijian: Ouyang Jingwu Foxue sixiang tanwei* 抉擇於真偽之間—歐陽竟無佛學思想探微 (Determining Truth and Falsity: An Investigation of Ouyang Jingwu's Buddhist Thought) (Shanghai: Huadong shifan daxue, 2000), pp. 112–135. For Ouyang's changing views, see Eyal Aviv's chapter in this volume. For textual and doctrinal criticism by Ouyang's student and successor, see Lü Cheng, "*Dasheng qixin lun* kaozheng." The date of this lengthy article is not known.

54. Lü Cheng and Xiong Shili 熊十力, "Bian Foxue genben wenti: Lü Cheng, Xiong Shili wangfu hangao 辯佛學根本問題一呂澂, 熊十力往復函稿" (Debating the Fundamental Questions of Buddhism: The Correspondence between Lü Cheng and Xiong Shili), *Zhongguo zhexue* 11 (1984): 171.

55. Cf. Peter Harvey, *The Selfless Mind: Personality, Consciousness and Nirvana in Early Buddhism* (London: RoutledgeCurzon, 1995/2004), pp. 166–167. To cite Harvey's exposition (see p. 167), the naturally pure mind "exists whether or not it is 'corrupt' and 'defiled' or 'translucent' and 'freed from defilement'. Even the corrupt person destined for hell thus has a 'brightly shining' *citta* 'covered', so to speak, by the defilements which obscure it. This expresses a very positive view of human nature and, indeed, of the nature of all beings." For more details of this notion, see Takasaki Jikidō 高崎直道, *Nyorai zō shisō no keisei* 如來藏思想の形成 (The Formation of Tathāgatagarbha Thought) (Tokyo: Shunjūsha, 1976), pp.754–758.

Cheng labeled this mode of praxis as "returning to the origin" (*fanben huanyuan* 返本還源), a dictum that is archetypical in Huayan, Chan, Daoism, and Neo-Confucian schools. Lü Cheng argued further that the practice of "returning to the origin" inevitably leads to ethical and religious corruption, for if one assumes that one's mind is inherently enlightened, why bother to go through the painstaking process of religious and philosophical practice? Lü contended that it is precisely due to the influence of the concept of inherent enlightenment that Chinese Buddhism, especially the Chan Schools, became corrupted and retrograde. On the contrary, if the doctrine of "the quiescent nature of mind" can be firmly upheld, then one will be encouraged to practice ceaselessly self-transformation in order to attain a spiritual goal.[56] In this regard, Lü Cheng clearly discerned the practical relationship between metaphysics and ethico-religious practice. That is, it is absolutely critical to fight for the correct understanding of Buddhist teachings, because the wrong view leads to unwarranted consequences.

The critique of Chan and *Dasheng qixin lun* is a motif that is evident over the entirety of Lü's intellectual career. In the early period, he already held that *Dasheng qixin lun* was distortedly adapted from Bodhiruci's translation of the *Laṇkāvatāra-sūtra*. This led to absolute idealism through the invention of the "naturally enlightened mind," which resulted from the confusing conglomeration of objective truth (*tathatā*) and subjective mind (*ālayavijñāna*).[57]

Later, when he taught at the Seminar of Buddhist Studies in Nanjing in 1961, Lü Cheng explicated his thesis in more detail in three articles on *Dasheng qixin lun* and Chan. He emphasized the idea of the sociality of doctrine, claiming that the theory of "the inherently enlightened mind" is ideologically conservative because its concerns are nothing other than a return to the origin, whereas the theory of "the quiescent nature of mind" is ideologically progressive because it requires the transformation of cognition as the foundation of ethical, religious, and societal change. Of course, Lü's emphasis on the sociality of religious theory might reflect the dominance of Marxist ideology in China, providing Lü with further philosophical resources to construct his version of "Critical Buddhism."[58]

---

56. Lü Cheng, "Bian Foxue genben wenti: Lü Cheng, Xiong Shili wangfu hangao," p. 173.

57. Lü Cheng, "*Qixin* yu *Lengqie* 起信與楞伽" (*Awakening of Mahāyāna Faith* and the *Laṅkāvatāra-sūtra*), *Lü Cheng Foxue lunzhu xuanji*, vol. 1, pp. 292–302. In 1961, Lü Cheng published another important article, "*Qixin* yu Chan 起信與禪" (*Dasheng qixin lun* and Chan), to elaborate the same issue in a more sophisticated way; in *Lü Cheng wenji* 呂澂文集 (Collection of Lü Cheng's Works), ed. Hong Qisong 洪啟嵩 and Huang Qilin 黃啟霖, (Taipei: Wenshu, 1988), pp. 21–40.

58. See Chen-kuo Lin, "Metaphysics, Suffering, and Liberation: The Debate between Two Buddhisms," in *Pruning the Bodhi Tree: The Storm over Critical Buddhism*, ed. Jamie Hubbard and Paul L. Swanson (Honolulu: University of Hawai'i Press, 1997), pp. 298–313.

For Lü Cheng, the theory of "origin-returning"—which he held was rooted in Bodhiruci's distorted translation of *Laṇkāvatāra-sūtra*, in *Dasheng qixin lun*, and in all Chinese Buddhist schools (Tiantai, Huayan, and Chan)—was "made possible through deliberate alteration and paraphrasing. They used dirty tricks to justify the status quo, including the social system. Hence the theory was accepted without suppression for it was not against the interests of ruling class."[59] In this regard, we see the same pathos of anti-traditionalism shared by the Chinese liberals and socialists since the May Fourth Movement down to the Cultural Revolution. The same call for social and political reform was clearly witnessed in Lü Cheng's critique of Chan ideology.

4. The Lü-Xiong Debate in 1943

The following section documents the Lü-Xiong debate in more detail as it is crucial for our understanding a key event in modern Chinese intellectual history. The following account summarizes the Lü-Xiong correspondence as found in Xiong Shili, *Xiong Shili quanji* 熊十力全集 (The Complete Writings of Xiong Shili) (Wuhan: Hubei jiaoyu chubanshe, 2001), vol. 8, 420–467; hereafter XSLQJ.

March 10, 1943, Xiong's letter to Liang Shuming and Lü Cheng

On February 23, 1943, Ouyang Jingwu died in Sichuan. Two weeks later, in a reply to Lü Cheng's call for memorial essays, Xiong Shili also enclosed a letter he had sent to Liang Shuming 梁漱溟 (1893–1988) in which Xiong expressed his strong discontent about Ouyang's life-long career:

> Master Jingwu stands for the system of "dharma characteristics" (*faxiang* 法相) and "nothing but consciousness" (*weishi* 唯識). Later he also occasionally promoted the thought of the *Prajñāpāramitā*[-*sūtra*] (Perfection of Wisdom Scriptures) and the *Mahāparinirvāṇa*[-*sūtra*] (The Nirvāṇa Scripture), which is [unfortunately] nothing but a reflection of a trend. At the bottom of his thought, he did not really go beyond the Yogācāra position. It is just like Kuiji's *Boreboluomiduo xin jing zan* 般若波羅蜜多心經幽贊 (Commentary on the *Heart Sutra*) that is not completely faithful to the definitive Mādhyamaka teaching.

59. Lü Cheng, "Shilun Zhongguo Foxue youguan xinxing de jiben wenti 試論中國佛學有關心性的基本思想" (On the Fundamental Theory of the Nature of the Mind in Chinese Buddhism), *Lü Cheng Foxue lunzhu xuanji*, vol. 3, p. 1417.

> Master Jingwu's strength of vow is great indeed. It is a pity his approach to external learning (*wenxun* 聞熏, literally "perfuming through hearing")[60] is thoroughly committed to Yogācāra. Yogācāra campaigns [that the way to attain Buddhahood] consists of more external learning. Those who adopt external learning, even though having taken a great vow, are not commensurable with those who inwardly return to their own mind, nurturing and expanding the subtle sign of moral sentiment without the aid from external learning. Throughout his entire life Master Jingwu disparaged the Neo-Confucians of the Song and Ming dynasties. Nevertheless, the Song-Ming Neo-Confucians insist that learning should cut into the bone for one's own need. This precisely is what Master Jingwu needed.
>
> Although Master Jingwu also occasionally talked about Chan public cases (*gong'an* 公案 [*kōan*]]) he did not seem to be interested in inwardly discovering his own treasure. What people love is the inspiring rhetoric of Chan discourses. I am afraid that Master Jingwu's Chan talk does not necessarily owe much to Chan. The resoluteness of Master Jingwu's personality is truly great. If he were capable of exhausting his mind, instead of ending up merely as a scholar, he would definitely become a hero such as is rarely found in history.
>
> (XSLQJ 8: 421–422)

At the end of the letter, Xiong also used the opportunity to promote his *New Treatise on the Uniqueness of Consciousness* (*Xin weishi lun* 新唯識論), claiming that the *New Treatise* fundamentally synthesizes Buddhism and Confucianism into an independent system, which he considers to be "the crystallization of Oriental philosophy" (XSLQJ 8: 423).

March 16, 1943, Xiong's letter to Lü

After his letter of March 10 to Lü, Xiong sent a follow-up letter to apologize for his offensive comments. Xiong still, however, insisted that he disagreed with the Yogācāra doctrine of external learning, contending that returning to one's own treasure, i.e., the transcendental mind, is the only way to the realization of the ultimate truth.

---

60. *Wenxun* 聞熏 is an abridged term of *zhengwen xunxi* 正聞熏習, meaning "perfuming through hearing the correct teaching."

April 2, 1943, Lü's reply

I do not understand what you mean by being discontent with the idea of "perfuming through hearing." As stated in the *Yogācārabhūmi-śāstra* (*Yuqie shidi lun* 瑜伽師地論; Discourse on the Stages of Concentration Practice),[61] the perfuming for production of pure seeds is a mere auxiliary (*adhipati*) condition, and is not the same as being forced from outside (*wai shuo* 外鑠, literally "externally to fuse metal [onto something] using heat").[62] As to its ultimate intent, [Yogācāra] takes insight (*prajñā*) as Reality (*shixiang* 實相 [*tattvasya-lakṣaṇam*]), implying that the latter is not found externally. Unfortunately, the true meaning has been concealed due to the misunderstandings inherited from Tang-dynasty scholarship. Your opinion is totally rooted in the theory of "the enlightened nature [of mind]" (*xingjue* 性覺), which is in opposition to the theory of "the quiescent nature [of mind]" (*xingji* 性寂). Since your opinion is in line with the Chinese apocryphal scriptures and treatises, how could it be taken as the measure of the Buddha's teaching? If you want to find out [the distinction between] truth and falsity, I think the issue should be examined more carefully.

(XSLQJ 8: 424)

April 7, 1943, Xiong's reply

Xiong's reply is divided into two parts. In response to the first half of Lü's reply, Xiong rejoined that if pure seeds are not inwardly produced by Reality/Suchness (i.e., *shixiang*, *dharmatā*, *tathatā*), which is found in each sentient being, then they are caused by external conditions. If pure seeds are not produced by Reality, then they are not essentially related to Reality. As a result, the realization of Reality becomes contingent because it is possible to realize Reality only when one is inwardly aware of one's own transcendental ground as Reality.

Regarding the second half of Lü's reply, Xiong argues that the question of whether Buddhist scriptures such as **Śūraṃgama-sūtra* (*Lengyan jing* 楞嚴經;

61. Traditionally attributed to Maitreya, *Yogācārabhūmi-Śāstra* was composed in India between 300 and 350 CE and translated into Chinese by Xuanzang between 646 and 648.

62. Cf. *Yogācārabhūmi-śāstra*, CBETA, T30n1579_p0282a15; T30n1579_p0301c02.

Sutra of the Samādhi of Heroic Progress),[63] *Yuanjue jing* 圓覺經 (The Perfect Enlightenment Sutra),[64] and *Dasheng qixin lun* are Chinese apocrypha has not been definitively settled. Further, Xiong disagreed with Lü about the direct opposition between *xingjue* (enlightened nature) and *xingji* (quiescent nature), maintaining that the nature of quiescence and the nature of awakening must be regarded as the two aspects of the same nature. If Reality/Suchness was merely quiescent and not enlightened, it would be no different from the Sāṃkhya's dark force.[65] Hence Xiong contended that *xingjue* (enlightened nature) and *xingji* (quiescent nature) cannot be separated. In his own words:

> I think that in reality enlightened nature and quiescent nature cannot be separated. Whenever there is enlightenment in nature, there is quiescence in it. Whenever there is quiescence in nature, there is enlightenment in it. The nature [of mind] itself (*xingti* 性體) is truly both quiescent and enlightened. That is, whenever it is enlightened it is quiescent; whenever it is quiescent it is enlightened. If either is missing, the nature will be concealed. As for those who hold the theory of *xingjue* while rejecting *xingji*, they will misconceive the delusive mind as the self-nature. As for those who hold the theory of *xingji* while rejecting *xingjue*, they will misconstrue ignorance as the self-nature.
>
> (XSLQJ 8: 426)

It should be noted that although Xiong is more in favor of the theory of *xingjue*, he regards it as an extreme view. For Xiong, the difference between *xingjue* and *xingji* should be dialectically synthesized.

In the final remark, Xiong interpreted the meaning of *jue* 覺 in terms of the Confucian concept of *ren* 仁, claiming that "*jue*" (awareness) means "humanity"

---

63. This scripture was supposedly translated by the Indian monk Pāramiti in 705. Although it has been enthusiastically received and considered as one of the most influential texts in the history of Chinese Chan Buddhism, its textual authenticity has been strongly questioned. Lü Cheng is famous for his critique of **Śūraṃgama-sūtra*. See Lü Cheng, "*Lengyan* baiwei 楞嚴百偽 (Hundred Forgeries of *Śūraṃgama-sūtra*), in *Lü Cheng Foxue lunzhu xuanji*, vol. 1, 370–395. See also Dan Lusthaus's chapter in this volume.

64. For a comprehensive study of this scripture, see A. Charles Muller, *The Sutra of Perfect Enlightenment: Korean Buddhism's Guide to Meditation* (Albany: State University of New York Press, 1999), "Introduction."

65. Xiong criticized Lü for confusing the Buddhist notion of emptiness (*sūnyatā*) with Sāṃkhya's theory of universal nature (*pratkṛti*). The dark force Xiong refers to is one of the three tendencies or qualities (*gunas*) that characterize this universal nature. Ironically, when *Xin weishi lun* was published, Xiong's philosophy was viewed by some as a Chinese version of Sāṃkhya.

(*ren*), and "humanity" (*ren*) in turn means "creative transformation" (*shenghua* 生化), a notion adopted from the *Book of Change*. In this regard, Xiong practiced the hermeneutics of metonymy by deliberately displacing the semantic meaning of key terms for the purpose of justifying his own thesis. In the Buddhist contexts "*jue*" is often used to render the Sanskrit terms *buddhi* or *bodhi*. The term *buddhi* is used in various syntaxes to indicate "intellect, mind, perception, comprehension, understanding, etc." *Buddhi*, however, in the sense of "the awakened state of mind" is an established meaning within Sinitic Buddhism. The clearest example can be seen in *Dasheng qixin lun*, where it is claimed that the nature of mind itself, free from conceptualization, is "inherently enlightened" (*benjue* 本覺). When Xiong attempted to defend the theory of *xingjue*, he semantically altered *jue* to mean "being capable of feeling or acting," while the meaning of *bujue* 不覺 is understood as "being incapable of feeling or acting." This distinction of sensibility and insensibility in the medical sense was used for the first time by Cheng Yi 程頤 (1032–1085) to describe the meaning of *ren* as the existential state of nondifferentiation between self and other. Following Neo-Confucian usage, Xiong went further to interpret *ren* as the onto-theo-logical ground of existence. Accordingly, the affirmation of the Buddhist idea of "inherent enlightenment" is semantically transformed to the affirmation of the Confucian concept of human nature as *ren* in both a moral and a cosmological sense. Here we see the semantic play of metonymy in Xiong's hermeneutics.[66]

April 12, 1943, Lü's reply

Lü Cheng continued to clarify the distinction between *xingji* and *xingjue*:

1. The theory of nature of mind in quiescence is based on the notion of "the nirvāṇic self-nature" (*zixing niepan* 自性涅槃), whereas the theory of nature of mind in enlightenment is based on the notion of "the awakened self-nature" (*zixing puti* 自性菩提). The former emphasizes that cognitive transformation is based on the object of cognition, whereas the latter emphasizes that the cognitive transformation is based on seeds (*bīja*) as the subjective cause and conditions. Since the emphasis is different, the practical consequence is different:

66. See Chen-kuo Lin, "Hsiung Shih-li's Hermeneutics of Self: Making a Confucian Identity in Buddhist Words," *Guoli Zhengzhi Daxue zhexue xuebao* (*NCCU Philosophical Journal*) 8 (2002): 69–89. For the view that Xiong's constructive philosophy took the form of an ambitious Confucio-Buddhist syncretism, in which Xiong integrated concepts, problems, and themes from traditional Chinese philosophy with elements emblematic of Sinitic Buddhist philosophy, see the chapter on Xiong Shili by John Makeham in this volume.

the former searches for reform (*gexin* 革新), while the latter is inclined toward origin-returning (*fanben* 返本).

2. The theory of *xingji* is authentic, whereas the theory of *xingjue* is false. The reason for this judgment is that the theory of *xingji* is based on the correct understanding of *prakṛti-prabhāsvaratāṃ cittasya* (the shining/illuminating nature of mind), while the theory of *xingjue* is based on the false understanding of the same concept. Lü accused Xiong of falling into the trap of *xingjue* because Xiong did not realize that under the insidious influence of a series of Chinese Buddhist apocrypha—*Dasheng qixin lun*; *Zhancha* [*shan e yebao*] *jing* 占察[善惡業報]經 (Sutra on Divination of the Effects of Good and Evil Actions); *Jin'gang sanmei jing lun* 金剛三昧經論 (Commentary on the *Sutra on the Adamantine Meditation*;[67] *Yuanjue jing*; and *Śūraṃgama-sūtra*—the theory of *xingjue* confuses the mind as the subject and the truth (*tathatā*) as the object, therefore it also does not correctly capture the significance of "transformation of the basis" (*āśrayaparivṛtti*).[68] Accordingly, those who adopt the theory of *xingjue* neither correctly know the goal (i.e., *tathatā*) of practice, nor commit to the task of epistemic and religious reform. Because they do not rely upon the correct teaching, their understanding is nothing but sheer speculation. In short, Lü accused Xiong of ascribing to false teaching.
3. Lü claimed that Xiong did not understand the fact that, according to the theory of *xingji*, the illuminating mind (*prakṛti-prabhāsvaratāṃ citta*) and illusive conceptualization (*abhūta-kalpana*) are two aspects of known reality. At this point, Lü seems to refer to the middle way of existence and emptiness as stated in *Madhyānta-vibhāga (Zhong bian fenbie lun* 中邊分別論; Differentiation of the Middle and Extremes), which should not be confused with Xiong's synthesis of *xingjue* and *xingji* (XSLQJ 8: 430)

April 13, 1943, Lü's postscript to the letter of April 12

Lü continued to explain the practical implications of the distinction between *xingji* and *xingjue*. For the theory of *xingji*, one will be lead to cognitive and practical reform in search of the world of truth (*dharmadhātu*). For the theory of

67. For this Chinese Buddhist apocryphon, see Robert E. Buswell, *The Formation of Ch'an Ideology in China and Korea: The Vajrasamadhi-Sutra, a Buddhist Aprocryphon* (Princeton, NJ: Princeton University Press, 1989). For more studies on the same subject, see Robert E. Buswell (ed.), *Chinese Buddhist Apocrypha* (Honolulu: University of Hawaii Press, 1990).

68. "Transformation of the basis" (*zhuanyi* 轉依) is a fundamental concept employed in the Yogācāra system to explain the path of conversion from the deluded state of mind to the enlightened state of mind.

xingjue, on the contrary, one will be attracted to the practice of origin-returning, viz., returning to the inherent mind, which could actually still be within the state of deluded mind. In other words, according to Lü, the followers of *xingjue* theory are unable to apprehend correctly the distinction between pure mind and deluded mind and so easily confuse the inherent mind (pure mind) with the psycho-physical mind (XSLQJ 8: 429). It should be noted that Lü's criticism is quite similar to the approach that Zhu Xi 朱熹 (1130–1200) adopted in critiquing Lu Xiangshan 陸象山 (1139–1193).[69]

April 17, 1943, Xiong's reply

In response to Lü's statement, "Reality can be verbalized only within the context of cultivation (*gongfu* 工夫)," Xiong asked: Whose practice? Which Reality? In Xiong's answer, Reality is none other than the inherent mind (*shixiang ji benxin* 實相即本心). Hence, the subject of practice must be the inherent mind, not the defiled empirical mind. If one practices with the defiled mind, then one will be unable to reveal the inherent mind. Only if one practices with the original mind can reality be disclosed. The key question is: how is it possible to know one's original mind? In our everyday experience all we know are the contents of the defiled mind. How can we reach the inherently pure mind? According to Xiong, the inherent mind can be known only by the self-awareness of the inherent mind

69. Historically and ideologically speaking, the Xiong-Lü debate can be traced back to the polemics between the Chinese Yogācāra and the *tatāgatagarbha* thought in the seventh century, which was later echoed in the debate between Zhu Xi and Lu Xiangshan in the twelfth century. This indicates that the debate cannot be explained by sectarian doctrines alone. It should be rather understood as the contest between two modes of philosophical thinking. That is, two theories are developed in both the Buddhist and the Neo-Confucian traditions to cope with the conflict between two different philosophical modes. (1) The first theory, which I label as the "Cognitive Theory," contends that the condition for the possibility of attaining buddhahood/sagehood is found in the mind that is capable of cognizing the truth. Truth is taken as the object of cognition, whereas mind is the subject of cognition. *Truth is independent of the mind.* Accordingly, buddhahood/sagehood can be attainedonly when one has cognized truth objectively. This theory is held by both Yogācāra and Zhu Xi. (2) The second theory, which I call the "Ontological Theory," holds that the condition for the possibility of buddhahood/sagehood is found in the subjectivity that is transcendentally grounded in truth. *Truth is not independent of the mind.* Truth is rather seen as the transcendental ground of mind. This theory even goes further to claim that the mind itself *is* truth. To claim that mind *is* truth is the same as claiming that truth is found in the self-realization, or self-disclosure of mind, which is in turn grounded in truth. This theory is held by both the *tathāgatagarbha*-influenced schools and Lu Xianshan. See Chen-kuo Lin, "Zhenli yu yishi: cong Foxing lunzheng dao Zhu-Lu yitong de er zhong zhexue leixing 真理與意識---從佛性論爭到朱陸異同的二種哲學類型" (Truth and Mind in Vijñaptimātra-Tathāgatagarbha Polemics: A Comparative Approach), *Guoli Zhengzhi Daxue zhexue xuebao* (*NCCU Philosopical Journal*) 28(2012): 1–46.

itself. It cannot be known by any mind other than the inherent mind. Furthermore, there is no inherent mind other than the mental subject that functions, because function is always already the function of inherent mind. The inherent mind in itself (*ti* 體) is not different from its function (*yong* 用).[70]

On the other hand, Xiong accused Yogācāra of mistaking the defiled mind (*ālayavijñāna*) as the true subject while relying on the hearing of correct teaching as the means for awakening. In this regard, Xiong explicitly expressed his agreement with the Chan dictum, "transmission through the direct witness of inherent mind without the need of scriptural teaching." Looking through the traditional dichotomy between meditative practice (*chan* 禪) and scriptural learning (*jiao* 教), Xiong apparently sided with the former and rejected the latter. He also conceived his disagreement with Ouyang and Lü as an instance of the paradigmatic conflict between *chan* and *jiao* (XSLQJ 8: 436).

Regarding Lü's distinction between *xingjue* and *xingji*, Xiong disagreed with any attempt to distinguish the two concepts in terms of subject and object, maintaining that if the self-nature (the ontological ground of existence) is divided into subject and object, this would be tantamount to saying that the self-nature exists external to itself, a logical contradiction. On the contrary, Xiong argued that the self-nature should be characterized as both quiescent and aware. That is, self-nature as the transcendental ground of existence is quiescent because it is empty of essence. It is aware, because when one's self-nature is manifest, it is based on the self-awareness of its own nature. In this connection, Xiong cited the Chan self-cognition of mind as the theoretical support. He further argued that if there were no self-awareness of mind, then there would be no subjectivity as the starting point to gain access to that enlightenment. Therefore, Xiong disagreed with Lü's conclusion about the practical consequence of two theories. For Xiong Shili, awakening is possible only if subjectivity itself is capable of being self-aware (XSLQJ 8: 438).

April 18, 1943 Xiong's follow-up reply

In this follow-up letter, Xiong continued to clarify two main points. First, responding to Lü's distinction between the theory of *xingjue* as the teaching of origin-returning and the theory of *xingji* as the teaching of progressive reform, Xiong criticized the latter theory for its outward searching for the ideal world (*dharmadhātu*), which was said to be similar to the idea of God as the transcendent being in the Christian faith. Xiong pointed out that

---

70. For further discussion of Xiong's understanding of the *ti yong* conceptual polarity, see John Makeham's chapter on Xiong Shili in this volume.

the teaching of origin-returning is based on nondualist thinking, whereas the theory of *xingji* is mistakenly based on the dichotomy of subject-object. Insofar as the ideal world is viewed as a transcendent object, it will become an object of speculation leading inevitably to illusory discrimination. Hence, Xiong argued that authentic reform should be rooted in the "true origin," viz., the "true mind."

Second, Xiong clarified further the distinction between the theory of *xingji* and the theory of *xingjue* from the perspective of the *ti-yong* (noumenon-function) dyad. The theory of *xingji* is based on the duality of *ti* and *yong*, whereas the latter is based on the nonduality of *ti* and *yong*. According to Xiong's criticism, both Lü and Ouyang differentiate ontological truth (*tathatā*) as the object of cognition, and the mind (*prajñā*) as the subject of cognition. This is the epistemological approach. In contrast, Xiong contended that the cognition of mind qua function cannot be separated from the ontological truth qua noumenon. For Xiong, truth can be disclosed only within the inherent mind (= transcendental subjectivity). If there is any distinction, it lies between the empirical aspect of mind and the transcendental aspect of mind. Ultimately speaking, there is only one mind ("inherent mind"). Xiong concluded that the ontology of inherent mind should be considered as more fundamental than what Lü understood in his epistemological approach. In this respect, the philosophical conflict between Lü and Xiong should be characterized as the conflict between the ontological approach and the epistemological approach. Xiong concluded as follows:

> One who has witnessed ultimate reality cannot merely dwell in quiescence. The foremost task is not to act against authentic subjectivity (*zhenzai* 真宰, i.e., inherent mind; Reality). Instead, one should act progressively and vigorously, as if shooting an arrow that approaches the sky ceaselessly without falling to the earth. Creating ceaselessly amounts to saying that ultimate reality discloses itself ceaselessly and its virtue also manifests endlessly. Hence ceaseless cultivation is nothing but the ceaseless functioning of ultimate reality. In this regard, how can profound function not be in quiescence? In the beginning, the learning of origin-returning requires human beings to practice diligently in accord with heaven (i.e., ultimate reality). As a result of persistent practice, human beings are not differentiated from heaven. [In this final state of practice,] one is dynamic yet also quiescent, quiescent yet also dynamic. One becomes creative through knowing the origin, and vice versa. When one has returned to the origin, one is always both dynamic and quiescent. How could it happen to corrupt the body and lose the nature?
>
> (XSLQJ 8: 442–443)

April 22, 1943, Lü's reply

In this brief reply, Lü refused to refer to Xiong's *New Treatise*, stating that he merely sought to clarify issues of Buddhist teaching. He also pointed out that the theories of *xingji* and *xingjue* are different interpretations of the same notion of "the shining/illuminating nature of mind" (*prakṛti-prabhāsvaratāṃ cittasya*). If the theory of *xingji* is correct, the theory of *xingjue* must be false. Hence no compromise is allowed. The issue also has nothing to do with the notion of "Two Modes of the One Mind" referred to in *Dasheng qixin lin*. In other words, Lü accused Xiong of confusing the distinction between *xingji* and *xingjue* with the ontological model of "Two Modes of the One Mind." As for the latter, Lü regarded this doctrine as the proto-typical example of "inherent enlightenment" theory.

May 21, 1943, Xiong's reply

In this reply, Xiong confessed that he was not a Buddhist and so was not obliged to confine his discussion to Buddhist discourse. Secondly, he strongly defended the priority of ontology, which he argued is evidenced in the Buddhist concept of *dharmatā* being understood as "ultimate reality." Accordingly, how could it be illegitimate to talk about ontology in Buddhism? Thirdly, Xiong accepted Lü's distinction between *xingji* and *xingjue* as two interpretations of the same illuminating nature of mind. He refused, however, to accept the claim that the theory of *xingji* is correct only, while the theory of *xingjue* is false. Regarding Lü's accusation that Xiong had resorted to the doctrinal model of *Dasheng qixin lun*, although Xiong did not continue to elaborate his position, there is no doubt that Xiong's position is highly sympathetic with that of *Dasheng qixin lun*.

May 25, 1943, Lü's reply

> According to your theory, *dharmatā* is the same as ultimate reality (*benti* 本體), which can be testified in the Hināyāna literature. This interpretation is sheer speculation. [As a matter of fact,] *dharmatā* as "universal" (*sāmānya-lakṣāṇa*) cannot be taken to mean "noumenon." (In *Cheng weishi lun*, fascicle 8, *dharma* and *dharmatā* are considered as neither identical nor different. In this context, *dharmatā* refers to "universal" too. This usage had become obvious since the *Abhidharma-sūtra* was highly praised by the Yogācāras.[71]) In Hināyāna, it [*dharmatā*] also refers to "general law,"

71. *Abhidharma-sūtra* (*Apidamo jing* 阿毘達磨經) is quoted in Asaṅga's *Mahāyāna-saṃgraha*. Although it has never been found in any extant Buddhist canon, it is regarded as one of the foundational scriptures in the Yogācāra School.

"general habit," and "natural law," and so forth. (Cf. The Pāli Text Society's *Pāli-English Dictionary*. This dictionary provides accurate knowledge, for it took ten years to edit on the solid basis of philological study in Buddhist canons.) Anyone who realizes the *dharmatā* realizes this [universal] only. How could it be viewed as "ultimate reality"? As to "Reality/Real Characteristic" (*shixiang* 實相) and "real nature" (*shixing* 實性), they refer to "characteristics" (*lakṣaṇa*). In this regard, we cannot play metaphysical speculation simply because there is "real" (*shi* 實) in the Chinese translation. In short, the central concern of Buddhism is to detach oneself from defilement and to transform the basis (*āśrayaparivṛtti*). Hence practice is directed toward the true characteristics of illusion. ("Illusion" refers to what is experienced in the defiled stage.) It is in this context that the fundamental notion of "the illuminating nature of mind" is established. The term "illumination" refers to the reality of illusory appearance, and is not disturbed by any discourse. (In Sanskrit, "*prabhāsvarah*" means "clear" or "shining brightly," but not "purity.") This is what is meant by the theory of *xingji*. (The terms "the self-nature in *nirvāṇa*," "the dwelling of *dharma* (*fazhu* 法住)," and "the seat of dharma (*fawei* 法位)" refer to the existence in itself which does not depend on awareness (*bodhi*; *jue*). Hence the word *jue* cannot be used here.) Unfortunately, since the Six Dynasties onward this forged translation [of the *Laṅkāvatāra-sūtra*] has contributed to widespread misunderstanding. The phrase "inward cognition of the *dharmatā* detached from verbalization" ("inwardly" means "detached from verbalization") was misunderstood as "enlightenment by itself." This misunderstanding even goes further to become "enlightenment in itself." Hence the notion of "the illuminating nature of mind" was corrupted as "the enlightened nature of mind." As a result, the true meaning of Buddhist teaching was completely lost.

In short, the theory of *xingji* is based on the object of cognition (*jñeya*; *suozhi* 所知), which is the cause of defilement, whereas the theory of *xingjue* mistakes the subject of cognition (*jñāna*; *nengzhi* 能知) as the fruit which has been purified. If one follows the theory of *xingji*, one knows defiled falsity as defiled falsity. As a result, one practices both detachment from defilement and abandoning falsity. If one follows the theory of *xingjue*, one will mistake deluded thought as pure thought to the extent that one will fall into defilement and error. The two theories are fundamentally different. Since the theory of *xingjue* appears like a Buddhist teaching, however, it creates great confusion. As such, should we not criticize it as a false teaching? If we recognize this as a false teaching, should we not do everything to destroy it?

(XSLQJ 8: 447–448)

June 3, 1943, Xiong's reply

Xiong suggested that correspondences with Lü Cheng be included in the third volume of Xiong's *Yuyao* 語要 (Record of Essential Sayings), hoping that the debate would be adjudicated in public.[72] For Xiong, the most important issue involved in the debate concerned the distinction between *xingji* and *xingjue*.

June 12, 1943, Lü's reply

In this reply, Lü did not conceal his anger toward Xiong, who had shifted the focus of the debate from Ouyang Jingwu's interpretation of "perfuming through hearing" to Xiong's own *New Treatise*. Lü questioned Xiong's intellectual integrity for glossing over the critical differences between the two parties and refused to continue the discussion.

June 21, 1943, Xiong's reply

Xiong expressed his sadness at Lü's emotional accusation but still continued to clarify a few points of controversy.

July 2, 1943, Lü's reply

In his reply, Lü restated his lifelong concern with rectifying misunderstanding of the Buddha's teaching. He explained that he reacted so strongly to Xiong's criticism because he could not excuse any false Buddhist teaching such as that of *xingjue*. He also continued to clarify some key issues related to the debate. First, as regards the distinction between the [School of] Emptiness (Madhyamaka) and the [School of] Existence (Yogācāra), Chinese scholars were misled by Madhyamaka philosopher Bhāvaviveka (*ca.* 500–570 CE) who overlooked the fact that both Nāgārjuna (*ca.* 150–250 CE) and Asaṅga taught the middle way. Second, the distinction between Mahāyāna and Hināyāna lies in the different ways of teaching. The Mahāyāna takes a synthetic approach, whereas the Hināyāna takes an analytic approach. The former is called *yiqie shuo* 一切說, while the latter is called *fenbie shuo* 分別說. According to Lü, in Chinese Buddhism the distinction between emptiness and existence when framed in terms of

72. Xiong Shili published *Shili Yuyao* 十力語要 in 1941. When Xiong proposed to include the correspondences with Lü in the *Yuyao*, he was obviously referring to the sequel volume, *Shili yuyao chuxu* 十力語要初續, which was published in 1949.

xing 性 (essence/nature; *svabhāva*) and *xiang* 相 (appearance; *lakṣaṇa*) is conceived as the difference between reality and appearance. This is totally misleading because the usages of *svabhāva* and *lakṣaṇa* are interchangeable in the Indian Buddhist context. Third, Lü accused Xiong of uncritically appealing to the authority of Xuanzang's School. According to Lü, "Xuanzang's translation is not precise enough because he altered the Indian texts in accord with later doctrinal developments" (XSLQJ 8: 454).

Lü's criticisms were also directed at Xiong's *Xin weishi lun*, arguing that Xiong's knowledge of Buddhism was totally distorted. For example, Xiong cited the "Maitreya Questions" chapter in the *Mahāprajñāpāramitā-sūtra* (The Large Scripture on Perfect Wisdom) as the textual source in his critique of Asaṅga's doctrine of three natures (*trisvabhāva*). According to Lü this is just bad scholarship, pointing out that the "Maitreya Questions" chapter was an accretion to the corpus of the *Mahāprajñāparamitā-sūtra* added during the later period of the Yogācāra system and its development. It had nothing at all to do with the Prajñāpāramitā (Perfection of Wisdom) thought. Lü checked the Sanskrit and the early Tibetan versions of the *Prajñāpāramitā-sūtra* and the Tibetan version of Asaṇga's *Mahāyāna-saṃgraha*, concluding that the "Maitreya Questions" chapter is a later addition.[73] In short, Lü employed philological and textual criticism to refute Xiong's *Xin weishi lun*. At the end of his letter, Lü rejected Xiong's standpoint of *xingjue*, claiming again that it was based upon spurious translations of Indic texts. Furthermore, there was no way for the doctrine of *xingjue* to be reconciled with the doctrine of *xingji*. If *xingji* is correct, then *xingjue* must be false, and vice versa. More importantly, for Lü, the doctrine of *xingjue* inevitably leads to mysticism, which has never been the true Buddhist position.

July 19, 1943, Xiong's reply

In addition to defending the Chinese Buddhist distinction between the School of Emptiness (Madhyamaka) and the School of Existence (Yogācāra), *dharmatā* and *dharma*, in this reply Xiong also refuted Lü's interpretation of the theory of three natures (*trisvabhāva*) in the "Maitreya Questions" chapter. The central point in the debate, according to Xiong, lies in the differing conception of *tathatā*. Xiong contended that *tathatā* is nondifferentiated reality. He rejected Lü's interpretation of *tathatā* as merely an empty universal. At the end of the letter, Xiong concluded:

73. See also Edward Conze and Iida Shotaro, "'Maitreya Questions' in the Prajñāpāramitā," *Melanges D'Indianisme: A La Memoire de Louis Renou* (Paris: E. De Boccard, 1968), pp. 229–242. Lü's findings with regard to this issue was made well before the publication of Edward Conze's article.

After all, the Buddhist teachings have lots of problems. I would simply like you to clarify the truth [of Buddhist teaching]; there is no need to go out of your way to defend them. As I have seen, even though one can find something profound and truthful in Buddhism, there are also lots of illusory features, which are especially prevalent [in the works of] Asaṅga. Indians are fond of playing with conceptual slogans; some slogans are useful, some are not. Chinese thinkers do not like to play with concepts, which is both their strength and weakness. I do not completely believe in the Buddha. Therefore, I do not mind whether [the Buddha's teachings] are false or true. What I do want is to find the truth in myself.

(XSLQJ 8: 467)

Concluding remarks

As a scholar, Lü Cheng's academic accomplishment in preparing the critical edition of *Zangyao* (Essentials of the Buddhist Canon) and his studies of Buddhist logic and epistemology still stand as a landmark of Buddhist studies in China. As a thinker, Lü's critique of the doctrine of Original Enlightenment, as embedded in *Dasheng qixin lun*, Chan, and Neo-Confucianism, reflects his conception of Genuine Buddhism as that which emphasizes the practice of cognitive transformation underlying social-political reform. For Lü, the quest for the true spirit of Buddhism reverberates with the call of modernity in early twentieth-century China. This is especially resonant in a series of articles published in 1954, in which Lü Cheng repeatedly emphasized the importance of the Yogācāra notion of "transformation of the basis" (*zhuanyi* 轉依) as a fundamental concept that should be employed so that social and political reform can be achieved through the progressive development of cognition.[74] In this regard, Lü's emphasis on the notion of "sociality of cognition" might be indebted to Marxism.[75]

---

74. Lü Cheng, "Guanxing yu zhuanyi 觀行與轉依" (Contemplative Meditation and Transformation of the Basis), *Lü Cheng Foxue lunzhu xuanji*, vol. 3, p. 1378.

75. Lü Cheng, "Yuanqi yu shixiang (II) 緣起與實相（下）" (Dependent Arising and Reality) (II), *Lü Cheng Foxue lunzhu xuanji*, vol. 3, p. 1364. Regarding the continuity or the discontinuity of Lü's thought after the establishment of PRC in 1949, the new policy of religion had a great impact on Buddhism, including on the China Institute of Inner Learning. Did Lü change his understanding of Buddhist philosophy after 1949? As the work statement of 1951 shows, in addition to learning Marxism and Maoism, Lü also gave fifteen lectures on the critique of the *Dasheng qixin lun*. This indicates that the policy of the Chinese Communist government did reinforce Lü's critique of Original Enlightenment, which had been clearly raised before 1949. That is, it may be reasonable to say that Lü articulated more explicitly the critical stance of Buddhism in Marxist and Maoist terms in the early period of New China.

In 1966, Lü Cheng's intellectual career was suddenly interrupted by the Cultural Revolution. We do not know the extent of his anxiety and suffering in the ensuing political turmoil. Neither do we know whether he had become disillusioned about his quest for "radical reform". All we know is the silence that he left for us in his tracks.[76]

76. Why has the study of Lü been relatively neglected? One reason for the failure to recognize the contributions of Lü Cheng and Ouyang might be due to their identity as lay scholars. This can be clearly seen in the ideological tension between Taixu's school and Ouyang's school. Another reason might be attributed to the persistent popularity of the traditional form of Chinese Buddhism. Historically, the critique of inherent enlightenment has always remained a minority voice in Chinese Buddhism. Its modern fate is no exception. The traditional forms of Chinese Buddhism, such as Chan, Pure Land, and Tiantai, continue to flourish. However, the success of philosophy should not be measured by popularity. Philosophically speaking, Lü's thought deserves more appreciation for its persistent critique.

PART 6

Dénouement

12

Chinese Ressentiment and Why New Confucians Stopped Caring about Yogācāra

Jason Clower

"The crisis of the last hundred years has caused Chinese culture to lose its self-confidence entirely . . . The renewal of the Chinese nation is inseparable from the renewal of Chinese culture, which first requires achieving cultural self-consciousness and finding our way back to our lost spiritual home."[1]

BEFORE WORLD WAR II, Yogācāra was a central influence on New Confucians, traditionalists who wanted to save China by reviving Confucianism as a living force in Chinese culture. For Liang Shuming 梁漱溟 (1893–1988) and Xiong Shili 熊十力 (1885–1968), the grandfathers of the movement that thrives today, Yogācāra was both a resource and a foil, a philosophy from which they borrowed ideas and against which they defined themselves by contrast. After the war, however, Mou Zongsan 牟宗三 (1909–1995) and Tang Junyi 唐君毅 (1909–1978) removed Yogācāra from the New Confucian agenda. They no longer found Yogācāra important. And since then, Yogācāra has lingered far from the center of the Chinese intellectual scene. What happened?

It is not that New Confucians somehow forgot about Yogācāra. Mou Zongsan and Tang Junyi still wrote about it, but without great interest. Consider this contrast: as with other disciples of Ouyang Jingwu 歐陽竟無 (1871–1943),[2] Xiong Shili treated Yogācāra as the best representative of Buddhism as a whole and what it had to offer. Then, after learning all that Xiong had to teach, Mou demoted Yogācāra to

1. Jing Haifeng 景海峰, "Ershi shiji ruxue de sanci zhuanzhe 20 世紀儒學的三次轉折" (Three Turning Points in Twentieth-century Confucianism), *Xueshu yanjiu* (2008.3): 51, 52.

2. Ouyang was one of the chief promoters of Yogācāra in China in the early part of the twentieth century, and Mou was implacably opposed to him. See Eyal Aviv's chapter in this volume.

the second-poorest kind of Mahāyāna philosophy, and Tang ranked it dead last. Mou and Tang considered Yogācāra a spent force and passed that belief on to later Confucians. Aside from Confucianism itself, Mou turned most of his creative energy to Immanuel Kant (1724–1804), "the great Chinese of Königsberg," and the rest to Tiantai Buddhism. Tang formed an affinity with Friedrich Hegel (1770–1831) and felt even less need to deal with Yogācāra. And with that, New Confucians moved on, still interested in German philosophy, Tiantai Buddhism, theories of science and democracy, and after that in postcolonialism, American neoconservatism, and almost any other intellectual import from the West—but not in a dead letter from India.

I will try to explain why New Confucians have lost interest in Yogācāra, and I will argue that the reasons are both straightforwardly philosophical—that they believe Yogācāra has already been tapped out and superseded as an inspiration for Chinese philosophy—and also emotional: the New Confucians' cultural nationalist *ressentiment* motivates them to spirited exchange with thought from the West specifically, not with that of a formerly colonized country.

In the first part, I will detail the philosophical critique of Yogācāra by Mou Zongsan, the New Confucians' most prolific scholar of Buddhism and their most influential figure, with supplementary remarks on Tang Junyi. Together, Mou and Tang will serve as a case study for New Confucians' philosophical opinions about Yogācāra and the relative obscurity of Yogācāra in recent decades. In the second part of the essay, I will try to explain the emotional reasons that New Confucians have stopped engaging with Yogācāra. I will argue that the New Confucian project is based partly on national *ressentiment* directed toward the West, and that to the considerable extent that New Confucians are also cultural nationalists, they wish to match Chinese cultural products against those specifically from the West rather than from one of its former colonies.

1. New Confucians take the measure of Yogācāra

New Confucians did not reject Yogācāra hastily. Rather than ignore it or take it lightly, the New Confucians accompanied their verdict against Yogācāra with long, detailed opinions based on a scrupulous, diligent trial.[3] In the main, I will relate the substance of Mou Zongsan's writing about Yogācāra, which is by far the most sophisticated treatment by any New Confucian before or since. Indeed, Mou's disposition of Yogācāra became almost literally the last word on the subject within New Confucianism. After Mou, the most influential voice on Buddhist philosophy was Tang Junyi, and I will supplement my account of Mou's researches with comments about how Tang did and did not concur with Mou.

---

3. For a less technical treatment of this subject see my *The Unlikely Buddhologist: Tiantai Buddhism in Mou Zongsan's New Confucianism* (Leiden and Boston: Brill, 2010), chapters four and six.

Apart from being a leader of the "New Confucian" movement, Mou Zongsan was also an influential interpreter of Buddhist thought for academic Chinese philosophy in Hong Kong and Taiwan. In that latter capacity, his buddhological works[4] became a standard point of reference for academic scholars[5] of Buddhist philosophy in those areas and, more recently, in the PRC. Mou studied at Peking University with Xiong Shili after reading Xiong's landmark *New Treatise on the Uniqueness of Consciousness*,[6] and Xiong confirmed Mou in his cultural nationalist commitment to renew the native Chinese philosophical tradition and also indelibly stamped Mou's judgments about Buddhism.

In 1949 Mou fled Communist rule, which he detested biliously, and lived out the remainder of his life at a series of teaching posts in Hong Kong and Taiwan. Along the way he met Tang Junyi, another Confucian philosopher with a deep interest in Chinese Buddhism who had studied with Xiong in 1932 when Xiong was a visiting professor at Central University in Nanjing. The amiable and mild Tang helped Mou find stable employment in 1960 in Hong Kong after the crotchety and undiplomatic Mou was dismissed from a string of jobs. Both men were charismatic teachers, and it was as teachers rather than as scholars that their New Confucianism first gained

4. Chief among these is *Foxing yu bore* 佛性與般若 (Buddha Nature and *Prajñā*), 2 vols. (Taipei: Xuesheng shuju, 1977; reprint, 2004) (hereafter cited as *FB*), a formidable monograph that is, in effect, a doxographic (*panjiao* 判教) treatment of the whole of Buddhist philosophy as traditionally known in China. There are also significant buddhological portions of Mou's *Zhi de zhijue yu Zhongguo zhexue* 智的直覺與中國哲學 (Intellectual Intuition and Chinese Philosophy) (Taipei: Taiwan shangwu yinshuguan, 1971); *Xianxiang yu wu zishen* 現象與物自身 (Phenomenon and Thing-in-itself) (Taipei: Xuesheng shuju, 1990); and *Yuanshan lun* 圓善論 (Treatise on the *Summum Bonum*) (Taipei: Xuesheng shuju, 1985). Far more commonly read, however, is a series of Mou's transcribed lectures that encapsulates much of his interpretation of Buddhist thought, *Zhongguo zhexue shijiu jiang* 中國哲學十九講 (Nineteen Lectures on Chinese Philosophy) (Taipei: Xuesheng shuju, 1983). The same is true of *Siyin shuo yanjianglu* 四因說演講錄 (Lectures on Four Kinds of Cause) (Taipei: Ehu, 1997), another series of lectures published after Mou's death.

5. That is, for university scholars. Owing to an undeserved reputation for anti-Buddhist prejudice, he is seldom read by Buddhist monastic scholars. Even Yinshun 印順 (1906–2005), a major influence on Mou's buddhology, did not know that he was mentioned in Mou's buddhological writings until years after they first appeared. See Yinshun "Lun sandi sanzhi yu laiye tong zhenwang: du *Foxing yu bore* 論三諦三智與賴耶通真妄：讀《佛性與般若》" (On the Three Truths, Three Kinds of Wisdom, and the Co-extensiveness of the *Ālaya* Consciousness with Truth and Delusion), *Ehu yuekan* 7, no. 4 (1981): 17.

6. See Clower, *The Unlikely Buddhologist*, 32–35. Li Shan 李山 gives a delightful biography of Mou in his *Mou Zongsan zhuan* 牟宗三傳 (Biography of Mou Zongsan) (Beijing: Zhongyang Minzu Daxue, 2002). Also see Umberto Bresciani's chapter on Mou in *Reinventing Confucianism: The New Confucian Movement* (Taipei: Taipei Ricci Institute for Chinese Studies, 2001), and Joël Thoraval, "Idéal du sage, stratégie du philosophe, Introduction à la pensée de Mou Zongsan (1909–1995)" (Ideal of the Sage and Strategy of the Philosopher: Introduction to the Thought of Mou Zongsan), in *Spécificités de la philosophie chinoise* (The Uniqueness of Chinese Philosophy) (Paris: Editions du Cerf, 2003).

a following. In 1958, the two men collaborated with a handful of others in writing a "Declaration to the World on Behalf of Chinese Culture."[7] A communiqué as grandiose as its title suggests, they intended it to serve as the founding document of not just an intellectual movement but of a renaissance in Chinese civilization, a sort of Declaration of Independence from an exclusively Western scholarly orientation.

They were disappointed in the short term. Their "Declaration" attracted no great attention and they remained marginal in the academy and elsewhere. But from their base at New Asia College, then still a marginal institution only recently accredited and located in Hong Kong's unglamorous Kowloon side, Mou and Tang slowly built a movement from the bottom up, winning large followings among students. The very popular Tang died young by the standards of modern Confucian luminaries, who seem to enjoy a Daoist longevity, but Mou continued to teach and write through his eighty-fifth year and achieved break-out academic celebrity after his retirement through guest lectures in Taiwan.[8] Philosopher and buddhologist Lin Chen-kuo [Lin Zhenguo] is a critic of Mou in virtually every way possible, but he often recounts walking across Taipei in the 1970s with throngs of classmates to hear those lectures, which were moved to the other side of the city after the audiences swelled the original venue to bursting point, and he explains Mou's impact on his generation by saying, "We grew up drinking the milk of Mou Zongsan."[9] Long before his death in 1995, Mou became a landmark figure

7. Mou Zongsan, Xu Fuguan 徐復觀, Zhang Junmai 張君勱 and Tang Junyi 唐君毅, "Wei Zhongguo wenhua jinggao shijie renshi xuanyan: women dui Zhongguo xueshu yanjiu ji Zhongguo wenhua yu shijie wenhua qiantu zhi gongtong renshi 為中國文化敬告世界人士宣言—我們對中國學術研究及中國文化與世界文化前途之共同認識" (A Declaration to the World on Behalf of Chinese Culture: Our Common Opinion about Chinese Scholarship and Culture and the Future of World Culture), *in Dangdai xin rujia* 當代新儒家 (New Confucianism) edited by Feng Zusheng 封祖盛 (Beijing: Sanlian, 1989), pp. 1–52. Xie Youwei 謝幼偉 (1903–1976) also had an often unacknowledged role in drafting the "Declaration." See John Makeham, "The Retrospective Creation of New Confucianism," in *New Confucianism: A Critical Examination*, ed. John Makeham (New York: Palgrave Macmillan, 2003), p. 46. n. 11.

8. Wang Xingguo 王興國 argues that the road to fame in Taiwan was opened to Mou only after the 1962 death of Hu Shi 胡適 (1891–1962), who thwarted Mou's chances at any important job since the thirties, and after Mou's 1972 reconciliation with Fang Dongmei, once the vengeful colleague who pushed the prideful and often tactless Mou from his job in Nanjing in 1946. "Luomo er bu luomo: Mou Zongsan yu san suo zhuming daxue—Beijing Daxue, Xinan Lianhe Daxue, Taiwan Daxue 落寞而不落寞—牟宗三與三所著名大學: 北京大學、西南聯合大學、台灣大學" (Aloof but Not Aloof: Mou Zongsan at Three Famous universities—Peking University, Southwest Associated University, and Taiwan University), *Huanan Shifan Daxue xuebao (shehui kexue ban)* (2011.1): 19–27. See also Carine Defoort, "Fu Sinian's Views on Philosophy, Ancient Chinese Masters, and Chinese Philosophy," in *Learning to Emulate the Wise: The Genesis of Chinese Philosophy as an Academic Discipline in Twentieth-Century China*, ed. John Makeham (Hong Kong: Chinese University Press, 2012), pp. 275–276.

9. Personal communication, August 1, 2010.

in philosophy in Taiwan and Hong Kong, whom everyone in Chinese philosophy must now address one way or another, and something like the Thomas Aquinas of the New Confucian movement just as it began spreading to the Chinese mainland in the 1980s. One exceptionally loyal group of former students, called the "Goose Lake" (*ehu* 鵝湖) circle after the journal they publish, remains so committed to Mou's teachings that their detractors liken them to a cult.[10]

Mou described his system of philosophy as "moral metaphysics" (*daode de xingshangxue* 道德的形上學), meaning an epistemology and soteriologically oriented ontology that teaches that the human mind's experiencing moral valences in the universe is the underlying *ti* 體 of the mind or mind-in-itself, of reason itself, and of the universe itself.[11] When writing in a more historical mode, Mou supported this enterprise through detailed exegeses and analyses of classic works in Chinese Confucianism, Buddhism, and Daoism.[12] These are in effect works of philosophical doctrinal critique (*panjiao* 判教): at once both descriptive and also evaluative and doxographical.

2. *Mou's study of Yogācāra*

Within Mou's extensive writings on Buddhism, his work on Yogācāra is the most philologically nuanced. He is forced to make it so partly by the clear tensions in the broader Yogācāra-derived tradition over the idea of the "matrix of the buddhas" (*tathāgatagarbha*).[13] He is aware of a tension in the *Mahāyāna-saṃgraha* (Compendium of the Great Vehicle) between the verses by "Maitreya" and

---

10. The usual quip is to call them the "*Mou men jiao* 牟門教," a play on the Mandarin word for "Mormonism." Ivan Kamenarovic describes his first meeting with Mou this way: "He was in the process of talking with some students, or rather, some disciples. In fact, Prof. Mou is there every afternoon, and whoever wishes goes to the Institute, where a group of the faithful attend as often as possible to listen and discuss." "Une visite au Professeur Mou Zongsan" (A Visit to Prof. Mou Zongsan), *Perspectives chinoises* 4 (1992): 57.

11. Useful outlines of Mou's moral metaphysics are available in English in Bresciani, *Reinventing Confucianism* and John Makeham, *Lost Soul: "Confucianism" in Contemporary Chinese Academic Discourse* (Cambridge, MA: Harvard University Asia Center, 2008). More advanced studies are Sébastien Billioud, *Thinking Through Confucian Modernity: A Study of Mou Zongsan's Moral Metaphysics* (Leiden: Brill, 2011) and N. Serina Chan, *The Thought of Mou Zongsan* (Leiden: Brill, 2011).

12. These include *FB* as well as *Caixing yu xuanli* 才性與玄理 (Talent and Profound Principle) (Taipei: Xuesheng shuju, 1993); *Xinti yu xingti* 心體與性體 (Mind Itself and Nature Itself) (Taipei: Zhengzhong shuju, 1968–69); and *Cong Lu Xiangshan dao Liu Jishan* 從陸象山到劉蕺山 (From Lu Xiangshan to Liu Jishan) (Taipei: Xuesheng shuju, 1979).

13. For background on the technical terms, key texts, and major figures of the Yogācāra tradition mentioned in this section, see John Powers, "Yogācāra: Indian Buddhist Origins" in this volume.

the commentary by Asaṅga and Vasubandhu (*fl.* fourth century CE) over the issue of *tathāgatagarbha* and aware of the interpolations and apparent skewing in Paramārtha's (d. 569) translations. He also argues philologically about the *Laṅkāvatāra-sūtra* (Discourse on the Buddha's Entering the Country of Lanka) in order to defend the orthodoxy of the *Dasheng qixin lun* doctrine of the matrix of the buddhas (*tathāgatagarbha*) against the criticisms of Ouyang Jingwu and Lü Cheng 呂澂 (1896–1989).[14]

Where Yogācāra proper is concerned, Mou cites the *Mahāyāna-saṃgraha* and, to a lesser degree, *Yogācārabhūmi-śāstra* (Discourse on the Stages of Concentration Practice),[15] *Cheng weishi lun* 成唯識論 (Demonstration of Nothing but Consciousness),[16] and *Mahāyāna-sūtrālaṃkāra* (Ornament for Great Vehicle Sutras).[17] He also makes a significant excursus on the *Foxing lun* 佛性論 (Treatise on

14. *Dasheng qixin lun* 大乘起信論 (Awakening of Mahāyāna Faith) was arguably the most influential treatise in East Asian Buddhism in the last thousand years and supported the wish of many Chinese Buddhists to believe that there is something deeply *right* about the base consciousness, despite its problems, and that consciousness can liberate itself. Many of the indigenous East Asian schools of Buddhism embraced that doctrine warmly, and Mou thinks it was one of the greatest contributions to world philosophy. However, some of Mou's contemporaries attacked the *Dasheng qixin lun* and its teachings. Beginning in the 1920s, first in Japan and then in China, philologists compiled evidence that the text was a forgery, written in China in the sixth century and fraudulently attributed to a more ancient Indian authority. Mou and others defend the text by arguing that although the *Dasheng qixin lun* probably was indeed written in China, it simply codified *tathāgatagarbha* doctrines that could already be found in unsystematic form in unimpeachably Indian scriptures. One of those scriptures is *Laṅkāvatāra-sūtra*, a text first written in Sanskrit in perhaps the third century and extremely popular in China, whose doctrinal similarity to *Dasheng qixin lun* was noticed immediately by medieval Chinese commentators.

Critics of *Dasheng qixin lun* had to account for that similarity. Ouyang Jingwu argued that even though the *Laṅkāvatāra-sūtra* did use the word "*tathāgatagarbha*," it only used it as a figure of speech, a personification of emptiness of own-nature (*svabhāva-śūnyatā*). (For a nuanced discussion of Ouyang's views on *tathāgatagarbha*, see Eyal Aviv's chapter.) Going farther, Ouyang's student Lü Cheng identified what he thought were flaws in one of the Chinese translations of the *Laṅkāvatāra-sūtra* (viz. the 513 translation by Bodhiruci, T. 671) and theorized that *Dasheng qixin lun* had been written by someone in China who had been misled by that translation and then memorialized his misconceptions in the *Dasheng qixin lun*. (Dan Lusthaus comments in detail on Lü's opinion about the Bodhiruci connection in his chapter in this volume.) For Mou's response to both Ouyang's and Lü's arguments, see *FB* 435–453.

15. One of the texts supposed in East Asian tradition to have been spoken by Maitreya and recorded by Asaṅga.

16. A selection of Indian commentaries to Vasubandhu's *Triṃśika* (Thirty Verses) compiled and translated by Xuanzang 玄奘 (602–664), the great Buddhist translator who tried to mold Yogācāra in China into closer conformity with that in India. This became the guiding text of Xuanzang's lineage in East Asia.

17. Long treatise variously attributed to Asaṅga or Vasubandhu, and one of the sources drawn on in the *Demonstration of Nothing but Consciousness*.

Buddha-nature)[18] and refers at times to the *Madhyānta-vibhāga* (Discriminating the Middle and the Extremes).[19] He treats the mature Vasubandhu (i.e., the Vasubandhu of the *Mahāyāna-saṃgraha-bhāṣya* [Commentary on the Compendium of the Great Vehicle] and *Foxing lun*)[20] and Xuanzang as the main spokesmen for Yogācāra proper (i.e., Yogācāra uninflected by Paramārtha's emphasis on the womb of the buddhas).[21] Where Yogācāra is concerned, Mou naturally cites treatises more often than sutras,[22] but he frequently refers to the *Saṃdhinirmocana-sūtra* (Discourse Explaining the Thought)[23] and *Śrīmālādevī-sūtra* (Queen Srimala Sutra).[24] As for Paramārtha's version of Yogācāra, Mou gives the most attention to the *Dasheng qixin lun*, which he takes as its paradigmatic statement. He also devotes a great deal of commentarial attention to Paramārtha's *Jueding zang lun* 決定藏論 (*Viniścaya* Section on the Eighth Consciousness),[25] *Zhuanshi lun* 轉識論 (Operations of the Consciousnesses),[26] *San wuxing lun* 三無性論 (Treatise on the Three Non-Natures),[27] and *Shiba kong lun* 十八空論 (Treatise on the Eighteen Emptinesses).[28] Among the sutras, he refers to the *Śrīmālādevī-sūtra, Avataṃsaka-sūtra* (Flower Adornment Sutra),[29] and *Laṅkāvatāra-sūtra* as

18. Work dubiously attributed to Vasubandhu that explains Buddha-nature as equivalent to emptiness of self-nature.

19. Another of the Yogācāra texts attributed to Maitreya, with a commentary by Vasubandhu.

20. Work dubiously attributed to Vasubandhu that explains Buddha-nature as equivalent to emptiness of self-nature. Regarding Mou's treatment of the text, see, e.g., *FB*, 277, 290.

21. Like many scholars, Mou believes that when the mid-sixth-century translator Paramārtha rendered Asaṅga and Vasubandhu into Chinese, he interpolated doctrines of innate, latent buddhahood that were foreign to the originals and had to be weeded out by Xuanzang.

22. That is, he refers to essays attributed to great Buddhist *thinkers* more than to scriptures supposed to be have been spoken by the Buddha himself.

23. Early Yogācāra text from about the second century CE. For Mou, it is interesting mostly for its description of the base consciousness, how it functions, and how it is related to enlightenment.

24. Short sutra that is one of the main scriptural sources for "matrix of buddhas" doctrines. Full title: **Śrīmālādevī-siṃha-nāda-sūtra* (*Shengman shizi hou yisheng da fangbian fangguang jing* 勝鬘師子吼一乘大方便方廣經; Sutra of the Lion Roar of Queen Śrīmālā).

25. Translation by Paramārtha of one of the chapters of the *Yogācāra-bhūmi*.

26. Short treatise attributed to Vasubandhu and translated by Paramārtha.

27. Treatise variously attributed to Asaṅga or Vasubandhu, translated by Paramārtha.

28. Short commentary on Vasubandhu's *Madhyānta-vibhāga* translated by Paramārtha.

29. Long scripture that influenced the early Chinese reception of Yogācāra and also the Huayan tradition, which can be seen as one of the indigenous Chinese variations on Yogācāra.

scriptural authorities for this line of thinking (i.e., for identifying the base consciousness as the womb of the buddhas). He also refers to the *Saṃdhinirmocana-sūtra*, but less commonly.

Mou accepts a fairly standard Chinese view of the history of Yogācāra.[30] And caring about Buddhism only to the extent that it advances Chinese philosophy, he expresses no interest in the history of Yogācāra in India except as a necessary historical precursor to the tradition's reception in China, and he displays no curiosity about Yogācāra in Tibet, Korea, or Japan. Hence he follows the story of Yogācāra proper only as far as its evolution from the Dilun and Shelun schools into the high Yogācāra tradition as taught by Xuanzang and his successor Kuiji 窺基 (632–682).[31] The more historiographically minded Tang Junyi continues the story further, mentioning the frustrated efforts of Mingyu 明昱 (1527–1616)[32] in the late Ming to reconstruct the school's teachings without the benefit of most of Kuiji's commentaries, and thence to the recovery of

30. Whereas Xiong Shili supposed that Asaṅga and Vasubandhu composed the Maitreya verses themselves, Mou differentiates without hesitation between the brothers and the author of the verses. (However, it is not clear whether Mou takes Maitreya-nātha as a mere human commentator or the bodhisattva in the Tuṣita Heaven.) Mou recognizes the verses as implicitly enunciating a *tathāgatagarbha*-type position and says that Asaṅga and Vasubandhu stripped away the *tathāgatagarbha* implications, interpreting them instead according to their own lights, in a way which Mou thinks brilliant but ontologically dualistic. (For details, see Clower, *Unlikely Buddhologist*, chapter 4.) One and the same Vasubandhu wrote both the *Abhidharmakośa-bhāṣya* (Storehouse of Higher Doctrine) (in his earlier period) and the *Mahāyāna-saṃgraha-bhāṣya* (Commentary on the Compendium of the Great Vehicle). Paramārtha later doctored that text to make it appear as a *tathāgatagarbha*-type document, and Mou believes that this was in fact faithful to the spirit of the Maitreya verses. Later on, Xuanzang, speaking for Dharmapāla, re-interpreted the seminal Yogācāra documents according to the intent of Asaṅga and Vasubandhu. Thereupon the larger Yogācāra tradition developed in two opposite directions, a "psychological" one represented by Xuanzang and a "transcendental" one, emphasizing the *tathāgatagarbha*, represented for Mou by Fazang. (On the slippage in Mou's use of 'transcendent' and 'transcendental', see Clower, *Unlikely Buddhologist*, p. 63, n.14.)

Mou drops Xiong's distinction between an "old" Yogācāra (represented by Paramārtha), and the "new" Yogācāra of Vasubandhu, Dharmapāla, Xuanzang, and Kuiji (concerning which, see John Makeham's essay in this volume, including his note on the problem with including Dharmapāla in this list).

31. The Dilun 地論 and Shelun schools 攝論 were loosely organized traditions in sixth-century China that represented early Chinese efforts to understand Yogācāra thought as it drifted into China. The latter concentrated on the translations of Paramārtha. Tang goes on to write about Xuanzang's attempt to recast the Chinese understanding of Yogācāra in more faithfully Indian terms, followed by the consolidation of his legacy by his student Kuiji into an independent Yogācāra School (*weishi zong* 唯識宗).

32. Ming-Dynasty commentator who tried to pick up the threads of Yogācāra epistemology that were dropped after Kuiji's time. See Introduction.

those commentaries by Yang Wenhui 楊文會 (1837–1911)[33] in the late Qing and their study and propagation by Ouyang Jingwu and his followers.[34] Also unlike Mou, Tang briefly mentions the life of the larger Yogācāra tradition in Japan and Tibet.

Although Mou claims little influence on his buddhology from Xiong explicitly,[35] he models much of his interpretation of Yogācāra after that of Xiong Shili. In his treatment of *saṃskāras*[36] he also quotes extensively from Xiong's *Fojia mingxiang tongshi* 佛家名相通釋; (Complete Explanation of Buddhist Terms; 1937). And when it comes to criticizing the Yogācāras' construal of Buddhism, as well as finding shortcomings in the entirety of Buddhist thought itself, Mou essentially recapitulates points already made by Xiong, such as the Yogācāra "seed" model of mind, and the Yogācāra commitment to a three-vehicle model of liberation.[37] His analysis of Buddhism differs from Xiong's most simply in that he focuses on Tiantai rather than Yogācāra as the strongest and best construal of

33. Publisher of Buddhist texts whose home in Nanjing served as a meeting place and starting point for many of the most interesting trends in modern Chinese Buddhism and Confucianism. Most relevant here is that Yang was instrumental in reviving interest in Yogācāra thought in modern China. He reintroduced key Yogācāra texts that had been lost in China from Japan with the assistance of Nanjō Bun'yū 南條文雄 (1849–1927), a Japanese student of the Oxford orientalist Max Müller (1823–1900), and taught Yogācāra thought to both Ouyang Jingwu and Taixu 太虛 (1890–1947). Regarding these latter two figures, see the chapters by Eyal Aviv and Scott Pacey.

34. Tang Junyi, *Zhongguo zhexue yuanlun: yuandao pian* 中國哲學原論:原道篇 (Origins of Chinese Philosophy: The Way) (Taipei: Xuesheng shuju, 1980), p. 1179. On the history involved, see John Jorgenson's chapter in this volume.

35. In fact, Mou sometimes flaunts his independence from Xiong. For example, in a 1991 keynote address to a large conference, he recalls: "Xiong Shili was my teacher and I was with him every day while he criticized Yogācāra for this and that, and so I finally took Xuanzang's *Demonstration of Nothing but Consciousness* (*Cheng weishi lun*) together with Kuiji's commentary and other people's commentaries and gave it a good reading, sentence by sentence. It was hard to understand and tough work. And after I had read it, I said to Xiong, "Sir, your understanding is not that right." Xiong scolded me, because Xiong had some biases. . . . It is a shame that nobody could persuade Xiong. He was an undetached, stubbornly arrogant reader." Mou Zongsan, "Keguan de liaojie yu Zhongguo wenhua zhi zaizao 客觀的瞭解與中國文化之再造" (Objective Understanding and the Re-making of Chinese Culture), Vol. 27, *Mou Zongsan xiansheng quanji* 牟宗三先生全集 (Complete Works of Mou Zongsan) (Taipei: Lianjing, 2003), p. 433.

36. The fourth of the five *skandhas* or "aggregates" that make up a person in classical Buddhism.

37. Buddhists who subscribe to a three-vehicle model of liberation teach that, aside from enlightenment as a full-fledged buddha, there are also two lesser paths or "vehicles" to liberation that terminate in a somewhat lower grade of enlightenment. As East Asians developed indigenous forms of Buddhism, they overwhelmingly preferred a "one-vehicle" model of liberation, which denies any lesser form of enlightenment than full buddhahood.

the Buddhist message, and in his criticism of Yogācāra he deviates from Xiong by adopting only a few of Xiong's many criticisms as his own, leaving the rest unmentioned.[38]

2.1 Special features of Mou's view of Yogācāra

Notwithstanding his broadly unremarkable views of the history of Yogācāra, Mou does adopt some interpretations of the tradition's place in the larger history of Buddhism.

1. Continuity between "deluded mind" and "True Mind" systems: Consistent with Chinese tradition, Mou does differentiate between the "deluded mind system" (*wangxin xitong* 妄心系統) of Yogācāra in the narrow sense and the "True Mind system" (*zhenxin xitong* 真心系統) of the *tathāgatagarbha* tradition. He does, however, veer from what Keng Ching calls the "traditional view" that Yogācāra and *tathāgatagarbha* are antagonistic to one another.[39] Instead, Mou thinks of *tathāgatagarbha* thought as simply a more advanced and more faithfully Buddhist unpacking of the essential Yogācāra premise, namely, that there is an *ālaya* consciousness that is related to enlightened mind in some way other than perfect, commutative identity.
2. Continuity between Yogācāra and Tiantai traditions: If indeed other scholars overlook the Yogācāra influence on Tiantai, as Dan Lusthaus suggests,[40] curiously, the New Confucians have not. Although both Mou and Tang recognize a particular affinity between Yogācāra and Huayan,[41] Mou shows awareness that Zhiyi 智顗 (538–597) was carrying on a conversation with the Shelun and Dilun traditions, which represented the fledgling efforts of Chinese Buddhists to make sense of fragmentary Indic Yogācāra writings, and that when Zhiyi described his famous "here-and-now momentary mind" (*xianqian yinian xin* 現前一念心), he was drawing from the idea of the *ālaya* consciousness almost as much as the *Dasheng qixin lun* did.[42] Putting it more simply,

38. On Xiong's critique of Yogācāra philosophy, see John Makeham's essay in this volume.

39. Keng Ching, "Yogācāra Buddhism Transmitted and Transformed? Paramartha (499–569) and His Chinese Interpreters," Ph.D. diss., Harvard University, 2009, pp. 36ff.

40. Lusthaus writes: "The popular formula . . . [that] T'ien-t'ai comes from Mādhyamika and Hua-yen comes from Yogācāra is too simplistic, to the point of being wrong and misleading . . . Chih-I was as influenced by Yogācāra as he was by Mādhyamika . . ." *Buddhist Phenomenology: A Philosophical Investigation of Yogācāra Buddhism and the Ch'eng Wei-shih Lun*, Curzon Critical Studies in Buddhism Series (London: Routledge, 2002), p. 369.

41. *FB*, p. 483; Tang Junyi, *Yuandao pian*, p. 1172.

42. *FB*, p. 281.

Mou sees Tiantai as the dialectical fulfillment not just of Madhyamaka but also of Yogācāra.

3. Unconcern with dichotomy between epistemology and ontology: William Chu writes that Chinese scholars of Buddhism view Yogācāra, like their Japanese and Anglophone colleagues, in a "bipartite" way, as fundamentally a statement about either epistemology or ontology (usually the former).[43] He points out, for example, that Yinshun distinguishes between an "epistemological Yogācāra" (*fenbie shibian zhi weishi* 分別識變之唯識), in which "transformation of objects occurs through discriminating conceptualization," and an "ontological (*bentilun shang de* 本體論上的) Yogācāra," in which "mind is the substrate (*benti* 本體) of everything" and the "creation of objective reality . . . [is] effected through 'seeds' in the *ālaya* consciousness."[44]

Mou was aware of both interpretations, of course, and of the fact that the ontological view has generally prevailed in China.[45] Unlike Yinshun, however, Mou does not believe in such a dichotomy nor does he try to endorse one side or another, for in Yogācāra Mou finds both a conceptual constructivism and also a seed-based account of the contingent existence of conditioned dharmas that contributed to what he calls "Buddhistic ontology" (*Fojiao shi de cunyoulun* 佛教式的存有論).[46] And although it does not entirely succeed, in Mou's opinion, it does provide advances that were subsumed into the Tiantai tradition's "complete" or "perfect" (*yuan* 圓) theory.

3. Mou's approach to and critique of Yogācāra

3.1 Truth à la chinoise

In his history of Buddhist philosophy, Mou tells the story of how China got it right, so to speak, how it saved Buddhism from the Indian commentators. And

43. William Chu, "A Buddha-Shaped Hole," Ph.D. diss., University of California Los Angeles, 2006, p. 293. Also see Lusthaus, *Buddhist Phenomenology*.

44. Yinshun, *Weishixue tanyuan* 唯識學探源 (Exploring the origins of Yogācāra) (Taipei: Zhengwen, 1992), pp. 200–207. See Chu, "Buddha-Shaped Hole," p. 287.

45. For example, he comments that Chinese people had a hard time understanding Xuanzang's teaching that "object is not separate from consciousness but rather is nothing but transformed consciousness" (*jing bu li shi, weishi suo bian* 境不離識，唯識所變) in an epistemological way but did find it natural to take it as a statement of "pan-mind-ism" (*fan xinli zhuyi* 泛心理主義). Mou Zongsan, *Siyin shuo*, pp. 176–177.

46. The English translation is Mou's own, and it often misleads people into thinking that Mou has in mind something Parmenidean, or Confucian, namely an account of svabhāvic Being. Mou refers to the Parmenidean sort of theory as "*bentilun* 本體論" which is the usual Chinese rendering of the English "ontology." For the "Buddhistic" sort, Mou reserves the more unusual word "*cunyoulun*." On the meanings attached to the two, see Clower, *Unlikely Buddhologist*, p. 84.

in the case of Yogācāra, Mou's is the story of how Paramārtha rescued the legendary Maitreya's verses from Asaṅga and Vasubandhu's misinterpretation and developed the basic Yogācāra model (of an *ālaya* consciousness that is somehow distinct, if not completely separate, from enlightened mind) just about as far as it could go (with a little help from Fazang)[47] producing an explicit, systematic theory of "*tathāgatagarbha*-arising" (*rulaizang yuanqi* 如來藏緣起). This higher, True Mind version of Yogācāra represented the penultimate form of Buddhist philosophy, surpassed only by Tiantai thought, which maintains that "*ālaya* consciousness" and "enlightened mind" are co-referential terms.

3.2 The value of Yogācāra thought

We have already seen that, like Tang, Mou analyzes Yogācāra thought as a dialectical stage in a certain process of philosophical development, which for Mou culminates in the Tiantai "perfect teaching." What exactly does he think is its dialectical value?

3.3 "Empirical" or "psychological analysis"

Yogācāra gives a good model of the cognitive mind and empirical knowledge and supplies (so Mou believes) an ontology of concrete particulars as mind-involved. Although the Yogācāra model of the mind lacks the "transcendental analysis" (*chaoyue fenjie* 超越分解) that emerges in the True Mind tradition, Mou is not only satisfied but also impressed with its analysis of mind's mundane, "psychological" (*xinli* 心理) or "empirical" (*jingyan* 經驗) aspect,[48] including an account of the ontological basis of conditioned things, and thinks it second only to Kant's treatment of the same problem.[49] In particular, Mou approves of Yogācāra's account of the "factors not associated with a specific mental function" (*citta-viprayukta-saṃskāra; bu xiangying xingfa* 不相應行法). Although Yogācāra philosophy fails

47. At least in some of his moods, Mou takes Fazang's "separate one-vehicle perfect teaching" (*biejiao yisheng yuanjiao* 別教一乘圓教) as the most complete possible expression of this *tathāgatagarbha* system.

48. In Mou's nomenclature, a "transcendental" analysis would be a metaphysics that recognizes an ontological basis to things that transcends what is empirically knowable (for which the paradigm case is the *Dasheng qixin lun*), whereas an "empirical" or "psychological" one limits itself to giving an account of phenomenal particulars.

49. See, for example, his endorsement of Yinshun's view that the Yogācāra "deluded mind school" is quite satisfactory in its account of the arising of defiled dharmas (*FB*, pp. 309–310). Note that Mou accepts Yogācāra learning as roughly on a par with modern psychology or what Erik Hammerstrom calls "mind science" in his chapter; Mou simply finds both limited and unsatisfactory.

to account for the existence of pure dharmas such as liberation in a coherent way, it excels at theorizing the arising or existence of impure dharmas, which is to say, of samsaric minds and things. Put another way, although Yogācāra yields no "ontology without attachment" (*wuzhi de cunyoulun* 無執的存有論), it does produce an "ontology with attachment" (*zhi de cunyoulun* 執的存有論).[50]

3.4 Epistemological advance

A further reason Mou prizes the Yogācāra development of this "ontology with attachment" is that he values it as a sort of Buddhist (and thus, Chinese) counterpart to the Kantian critical turn, for Mou is concerned to show that premodern Chinese philosophy did incorporate a theory of empirical knowledge, even if it did not originate in China and even if it did not give birth to modern science.[51] Unlike Xiong Shili, who chose to purge the entire Yogācāra model of eight consciousnesses and seeds from his philosophy,[52] Mou's solution is much gentler, inasmuch as it "opens up" (*kaijue* 開決) the Yogācāra model of mind, after Zhiyi's fashion, installing it in a larger and considerably different context from any Yogācāra ever intended but leaving it largely intact.

As with Tang, Mou thinks of Yogācāra as Huayan philosophy's less perfect antecedent. Hence in Mou's eyes, Yogacara is an evolutionary relative of the Tiantai "perfect teaching." It teaches that conditioned dharmas are deeply mind-involved, after which the Tiantai School tinkers with the theory and improves it by presenting the totality of *dharmas* as one big thing, as it were, which is coextensive with mind. This is interesting to Mou because, as he sees it, the Confucian "perfect teaching" is a still further improvement of the theory since it identifies the real essence of mind, its moral nature.

3.5 Critique of Yogācāra

For all that, Mou pillories Yogācāra. He inherits the essential problematic of Xiong Shili's debate with Lü Cheng over whether our nature is one of simple, neutral quiescence (as Lü preferred) or of intrinsic enlightenment,[53] and he shares Xiong's

50. That is, although Yogācāra teaches no ontology of a transempirical substance, it does give a good account of empirical things. For Mou, this is equivalent to saying that Yogācāra gives an "empirical analysis" but no "transcendental analysis." See *FB*, pp. 429–431.

51. Clower, *Unlikely Buddhologist*, pp. 246–247.

52. Edward F. Connelly, "Xiong Shili and his Critique of Yogācāra Buddhism," Ph.D. diss., Australian National University, 1978, pp. 106–110.

53. On the Lü-Xiong debate, see Lin Chen-kuo's contribution to this volume.

assumption that a cause of enlightenment that is exogenous to mind cannot be reliable. Thus, also like Xiong, Mou criticizes Yogācāra seed theory, but he does so in a much simpler way than that developed by Xiong. Xiong argued that, in several ways, Asaṅga's and Vasubandhu's theories of seeds (which he distinguished as significantly different from one another) did not give a satisfactory account of the causes for the workings of mind, with or without defilements.[54] But Mou does not complain that, say, seed theory yields an unacceptably atomistic account of the *ālaya* consciousness or that there cannot be eight consciousnesses. In fact, he more or less retains the Yogācāra account of the consciousnesses in his final construal of Buddhist philosophy. The only problem he raises is soteriological. He argues first, relying heavily on Yinshun's work, that the seed theory alone still cannot explain how enlightenment happens, and second, that any seed-based model is incompatible with a "one-vehicle" (*ekayāna*) universalist soteriology in which everyone becomes a buddha eventually, which he thinks that any good system of Buddhist must teach in order to remain faithful to shared Mahāyāna principles.[55]

3.6 No "transcendent," or unconditioned, cause of liberation

Mou will not accept that a theory of necessary, universal liberation is possible unless it posits a robust cause of liberation in each sentient being that is so intrinsic and inalienable that it can be called "transcendent" (*chaoyue* 超越).[56] By this, Mou means that it must be unconditioned (*wuwei* 無為; *asaṃskṛta*). He denies the coherence of any theory that supposes such a cause could lie in unconditioned seeds (*bīja*) of liberation.

Mou tries to explain this conviction partly through his own analysis of the *Mahāyāna-saṃgraha*[57] and partly by quoting Yinshun: "The opinion of the treatise is that [the doctrine of] original undefiled seeds (*benyou wulou zhong* 本有無漏種) cannot obtain. The treatise's definition is this: 'Internal seeds can exist only by way of perfuming (*vāsanā*)' (*neizhong bi you xunxi er you* 內種必由熏習而有). Without *vāsanā* there are no seeds. When could [innate] defiled seeds be perfumed into being?"[58] Although Mou quibbles with other

54. See section 1.2 ("Criticism of seeds as causes") in John Makeham's essay in this volume.

55. See Clower, *The Unlikely Buddhologist*, pp. 107–112.

56. *FB*, p. 311.

57. *FB*, pp. 300–302, concerning Asaṅga's *Mahāyāna-saṃgraha*, CBETA, T1594.31.136b29-c4. More broadly, see *FB*, pp. 296–329.

58. *FB*, pp. 311ff., quoting and discussing Yinshun's *She dasheng lun jiangji* 攝大乘論講記 (Explanation of the *Compendium of the Great Vehicle*) (Taipei: Zhengwen chubanshe, 1992), pp. 147–150. I have not been able to locate the statement "Internal seeds can exist

parts of Yinshun's treatment of the topic of defiled seeds, he agrees with Yinshun that the very idea of an unconditioned seed is incoherent.

Hence Mou concludes that, because perfuming by hearing (*wenxun* 聞熏; *śrutavāsanā*) is a conditioned circumstance, it is therefore contingent:

> As for the turning of the basis (*zhuanyi* 轉依; *āśraya-parāvṛtti*)[59] from delusion to purity, if we could be content with a gradual teaching, this turning of the basis would itself present no problem. The problem is this: going down that road, is it even possible to obtain final turning of the basis? That is, is it [apodictically] necessary? Or is it ultimately an endless process that is never complete? Is *āśraya-parāvṛtti* ultimately an accident, not an [apodictic] necessity?[60]

What it lacks, of course, is a concept of a *tathāgatagarbha* that can be more than a "supporting cause" (*pingyi yin* 憑依因), an entity that is "transcendent" in Mou's sense of the word.[61]

Mou passionately endorses a radical soteriological optimism, whereby full spiritual perfection must be inalienable and ever-available to everyone. Indeed, this issue is the plank in Mou's own philosophy that he cares most about, and he devotes his last monograph, *Yuanshan lun*, to this subject. He also considers it a flaw that Yogācāra teaches a three-vehicle model of enlightenment.[62] He spends little time on this point, however, neither showing that it is required by the seminal texts of the tradition nor arguing that it is entailed by nonnegotiable first principles of the tradition. I surmise that in reading Xiong and Yinshun, Mou was persuaded that there was simply no dispute on the matter.

4. The targets behind the target

From what Mou does not criticize, we can infer that he is focusing his critique of Yogācāra in general on the issues that are relevant to his attack on the China

---

only by way of perfuming" (*neizhong bi you xunxi er you* 内種必由熏習而有) in *Mahāyāna-saṃgraha*. Yinshun may have been thinking of a nearly identical statement in *Cheng weishi lun*: "*neizhong bi you xunxi shengzhang* 内種必由熏習生長" ("Internal seeds can grow only by way of perfuming." T 1585.31.9c2-3).

59. In Yogācāra terminology, the piecemeal transformation of the base consciousness that brings about liberation.

60. *FB*, p. 310.

61. At this point Mou writes a large section arguing what I think is not in much doubt, that the 'buddha nature' referred to in (pseudo-)Vasubandhu's *Foxing lun* does not answer this description, since it refers to nothing more than the bare fact of emptiness of own-nature or, as Mou calls it, the "principle of empty Suchness" (*kongru li* 空如理).

62. *FB*, p. 430.

Inner Studies Institute (Zhina Neixue Yuan 支那內學院)[63] and, more importantly, his response to Kant and Western philosophy in general. He never targets the question of beings who are thought to be incapable of liberation (*icchantika*). In fact, he seldom even mentions the word "*icchantika*." Yet the doctrine of the *icchantika* is a central feature of the historical Yogācāra tradition, and it would be an easy target for Mou's criticism. The omission is even more peculiar because of Mou's passionate zeal for universalism, his special commitment to theorizing human perfection as a possibility inherent in human nature, where "nature" refers to something sufficiently transcendent that it is fully present in any human being and does not depend on arbitrary endowment.[64] So if Mou's main purpose was merely to show the failings of Yogācāra philosophy as it existed in history, why not at least gesture to the repugnance of a belief in the *icchantika* doctrine to Chinese people's Mencian sensibilities?

But it is not Mou's main aim to show the failings of Yogācāra as it existed historically. His main aim is to advance his cultural nationalist project of improving Chinese philosophy and its standing in the world. It is not worth Mou's time to refute the *icchantika* doctrine because nothing like it is defended, in China or the West, by anyone over whom Mou would like to score a victory. That is, even the most smashing criticism of the *icchantika* question would not gain esteem for Mou's philosophy in the eyes of anyone he cares about.

When Mou criticizes Yogācāra in his histories of philosophy, he is also using it as a stand-in for more contemporary rivals, namely the modern-day Yogācāra revivalists Ouyang Jingwu and Lü Cheng of the Inner Studies Institute, whom he loathes as traitors to Chinese culture,[65] and also for Immanuel Kant, whom Mou regards, with "admiration and competitiveness,"[66] as both the epitome of the Western philosophical tradition and also a Western analog to Yogācāra's emphasis on the empirical mind at the expense of the transcendental mind.[67]

63. Ouyang Jingwu's Yogācāra academy, founded in 1922 in Nanjing.

64. This is the point of the first of Mou's books that he still endorsed at the end of his life, *Caixing yu xuanli*.

65. In Mou's opinion, Ouyang and Lü denigrate native Chinese thought as such and hence swoon over Yogācāra precisely because it is foreign. Even as a young man, Mou felt disgusted by Ouyang for denigrating China's own tradition, dismissing Song-Ming Neo-Confucianism entirely, and ranking Confucius himself as only a bodhisattva of the tenth level. "If this was not undermining the cultural basis of the Chinese people," writes Mou's biographer Li Shan, characterizing Mou's feelings about Ouyang, "what was it? If one could not look to the life of wisdom (*huiming* 慧命) of the Chinese people for great sagacity . . . how could China but die away?" Li Shan, *Mou Zongsan zhuan*, p. 46.

66. N. Serina Chan, *The Thought of Mou Zongsan* (Leiden: Brill, 2011), p. 217.

67. This is the formal type that Mou calls the "Beginning Theory of Separation." See Clower, *The Unlikely Buddhologist*, pp. 106, 181–184.

4.1 New Confucian cultural nationalism

The other, not strictly philosophical, reason that Mou Zongsan and later New Confucians dropped Yogācāra from the Confucian agenda is that a philosophy from India ceased to be a helpful foil for their cultural nationalism.

Like other intellectuals of his generation, Mou is a nationalist, his foremost worldly concern being to "save" China. Mou's nationalism, like other New Confucians', takes the form of cultural nationalism, a celebration of the Chinese nation specifically for its unique culture and an advocacy for the revitalization of that unique culture "so as to restore the nation to its former status in the vanguard of human progress."[68] For Mou, as for other New Confucians, that means renovating Chinese philosophy in such a way as to win the respect of modernist Chinese and dismissive Westerners.

4.2 Kinds of New Confucians

In the present day, the New Confucian movement has grown enough that we need to distinguish among New Confucians in a couple of different ways:

1. Narrow and broad senses: It is now common to distinguish between New Confucians in a narrow sense and a broad sense.[69] New Confucians in the narrow sense identify closely with Mou Zongsan, Tang Junyi, and the other authors

---

68. John Hutchinson, "Re-Interpreting Cultural Nationalism," *Australian Journal of Politics and History* 45, no. 3 (September 1999): 402. On the concept of cultural nationalism in general, see Liah Greenfeld, *Nationalism: Five Roads to Modernity* (Cambridge, MA: Harvard University Press, 1993) and Hutchinson, "Re-Interpreting Cultural Nationalism." As applied to China, see Yingjie Guo, *Cultural Nationalism in Contemporary China: The Search for National Identity Under Reform* (New York: RoutledgeCurzon, 2004), and on its application to New Confucianism, see Makeham, *Lost Soul*, pp. 14–16. For a sustained study of Mou Zongsan as cultural nationalist, see Chan, *The Thought of Mou Zongsan*, especially chapters two and eight.

It would not be out of place to call Mou a cultural conservative either, and indeed in *A Cloud Across the Pacific* (Hong Kong: Chinese University Press, 2005), Thomas Metzger likens Mou and other New Confucians very astutely to a species of Western conservative typified by Leo Strauss. However, for my own part I now lean toward a characterization of the New Confucians as cultural *nationalists* as I find more and more evidence, detailed later in this paper, of an emotional need in New Confucians to affirm the classical Chinese inheritance less for its antiquity than for its Chinese-ness, its non-Western-ness.

69. Cai Degui 蔡德貴, "Dangdai xin rujia xiang duoyuan ronghe xing zhuanhua de biranxing 當代新儒家向多元融和型轉化的必然性" (The Necessity for New Confucianism to Shift toward Pluralist Inclusion) *Wen shi zhe* 2 (2003): 17. Lin Anwu 林安梧, "Dangdai xin rujia yu Taiwan xiandaihua de fazhan jincheng 當代新儒家與台灣現代化的發展進程" (New Confucianism and the Development of Taiwanese Modernization), August 30, 2006, http://www.mcu.edu.tw/department/genedu/2echelon/92report/a03/0807_13.htm, accessed July 11, 2011.

of the "Declaration," and also their forebears Liang and Xiong, and they are often associated with New Asia College, Taiwan's Academia Sinica, and the Goose Lake (*Ehu* 鵝湖) journal. In the broad sense, however, a New Confucian is any active Confucian revivalist. For them, Mou and Tang remain required reading, and their prominent contemporary disciples such as Tu Wei-ming and Lee Ming-huei remain something like the elder brothers of the whole movement. Nowadays, however, they are only first among equals, and they are joined by other influential figures who have grown away from the lineage of Mou and Tang, such as "political Confucian" Jiang Qing 蔣慶, one of the mainland Confucian theorists who reject the narrow-sense New Confucians' enamorment with democracy.[70]

2. Cultural nationalists and pluralists: One type of New Confucian, relatively active and visible in the West, praises Confucianism as simply one interesting "cultural resource" among the world's many and tries consciously to renounce the more exclusivist cultural nationalism of the earlier generation of New Confucians. Exemplified by cosmopolitans such as Tu Wei-ming, Liu Shuxian 劉述先, Jing Haifeng, Cai Degui, and Guo Qiyong 郭齊勇, this is the group that I will call the "pluralists." They may not succeed at transcending nationalism and remaining consistent in their pluralist inclusivism in all their moods—probably no Chinese New Confucian has lived who was not motivated to take up the cause in part by nationalism—and it could even be less a sincere conviction than a public posture. But these figures have declared themselves for pluralism repeatedly and have maintained a considerable self-consistency.

The New Confucians who remain are the ones I will call the "cultural nationalist" wing of the movement, those, like Xiong Shili and Mou Zongsan, who declare unreservedly that Confucianism holds a special, unique claim on people, whether Chinese people specifically (as is common on the mainland now) or on all human beings.[71] In this chapter, I am concerned instead with that bulk of the movement that is consciously nationalist.

---

70. Bai Tongdong 白彤東, "Xinxing ruxue haishi zhengzhi ruxue? Xin bang jiu ming haishi jiu bang xin ming? Guanyu ruxue fuxing de jidian sikao 心性儒學還是政治儒學? 新邦舊命還是舊邦新命?—關於儒學復興的幾點思考" (*Xinxing* Confucianism or Political Confucianism? New Country with an Old Destiny or Vice Versa? Thoughts about the Confucian Revival), *Kaifang shidai* 11 (2010): 5–25.

71. To highlight the differences between this orientation and the pluralist one, I am using the phrase "cultural nationalist" here in a more restricted sense than that used by John Makeham, who describes New Confucianism *as such* as culturally nationalist in that it celebrates the Chinese nation specifically for its unique culture and aims to revitalize that unique culture (*Lost Soul*, pp. 14–16). Also see N. Serina Chan, *The Thought of Mou Zongsan*.

4.3 Made in China: New Confucian *ressentiment* and *amour propre*

Often I feel dissatisfied with attempts to explain a social phenomenon as an effort by persons or groups to distinguish themselves in a favorable light from others, as though the desires for identity and recognition were surely the *nec plus ultra* of human motivation. However, even such a giant as Mou Zongsan, whom I count as creditably close to a philosopher of the first rank, does not hide his cultural nationalism—indeed he positively trumpets it in interviews and lectures—and plainly states that his career and his very life are devoted to the revitalization of Chinese culture as a force in Chinese people's hearts and as a cultural player on the world stage. According to Mou's beliefs, there is no conflict among the commands of reason, duty to the Chinese nation, and the yearning for renewed Chinese prestige, because these are all aspects of one principle (*li* 理). However, since I do not accept this belief of Mou's as a fundamental postulate, I do not assume that modern Confucians' purely intellectual reasons and choices are simply identical to their more emotional ones and therefore not worth noticing. Simply put, I allow myself the liberty of differentiating between modern Confucians' reasoning in general and the many instances that are colored by cultural nationalist feelings.

In demonstrably large measure, New Confucian nationalism is a cultural product of *ressentiment*, a feeling that Nietzsche made a theme of his writing and that we can describe as a chronically thwarted amour propre that can motivate limitlessly vast, intellectually and politically powerful philosophizing and culture building. The key causal element of *ressentiment* is forced deprivation relative to expectations, "being denied access to that which you constantly are told is and believe to be rightfully yours."[72] Psychologically, "*ressentiment* denotes an attitude which arises from a cumulative repression of feelings of hatred, revenge, envy," and impotence engendered by that relative deprivation.[73] On a national scale, *ressentiment* finds "double nourishment" when "colossal national pride" is thwarted by a sense of having been slighted by other nations, and then the modern expectation of enjoying equality with all others a priori is again thwarted by the perception that one's nation is being discriminated against in practice.[74] Denied the opportunity to defeat the oppressors on their own terms, people suffering ressentiment seek revenge or vindication in a domain where that is possible, in symbols they create themselves.

---

72. John Sugden and Alan Tomlinson, "Football, *Ressentiment*, and Resistance in the Break-Up of the Former Soviet Union," *Culture, Sport, Society* 3, no. 2 (Summer 2000): 91.

73. Lewis A. Coser, "Introduction," in Max Scheler, *Ressentiment* (New York: The Free Press, 1961), pp. 23–24, 28–29.

74. See Scheler, *Ressentiment*, p. 51.

At its most ineffectual, this is the "method of spiritual victory" (*jingshen shengli fa* 精神勝利法) of the bitter wretch in Lu Xun's 鲁迅 "True Story of Ah Q" (*AQ zhengzhuan* 阿Q正傳) (1921–1922), the symbolic and mostly imaginary defiance of the man in the joke who, told by a robber to stand inside a circle on the floor on pain of death while the robber fleeces him and bullies his family, later exults, "Ha! Did you see how many times I stepped outside the circle when he wasn't looking?"

However, the defiance born of *ressentiment* and the pained symbolic victories are not always as hollow as that. Sometimes *ressentiment* gives birth to ways of thinking that succeed in changing the world. People or groups chafing against intolerable subordination may end up producing what becomes a great cultural system to alleviate their frustration and assert themselves. Nietzsche famously analyzed Christian love as "the most delicate 'flower of *ressentiment*.'"[75] The hallmark of such creativity fueled by *ressentiment* is that it is "by definition a reaction to the values of others and not to one's own condition regardless of others."[76] That is, the cultural products of ressentiment take the form of a self-justification against a dominating other. A movement animated by *ressentiment* is recognizable for beginning, not from the affirmation of something thought be valuable, but from nay-saying against the Other, and "this No is its creative deed."[77]

In popular, official, and academic discourse, a dominant narrative of the modern Chinese nation is the story of China's "hundred years of national humiliation" (*bainian guochi* 百年國恥) that began with the Opium Wars (1839–1842 and 1856–1860),[78] which is a classic story of *ressentiment*: "The profound sense of humiliation, including all the setbacks and frustrations that the Chinese have experienced, has planted in the Chinese people a certain complex that is accumulated and settled in the deepest recesses of the Chinese mentality. This complex can be called 'the dream of becoming a strong nation'."[79] "In short," writes Xu Wu, "Chinese people, for the last 150 years, have been trapped in a bottle, half filled with burning fire and half with freezing ice.[80]

---

75. The phrase itself is Scheler's. See ibid., p. 43.

76. Liah Greenfeld, *Nationalism: Five Roads to Modernity*, p. 16. Emphasis added.

77. Friedrich Nietzsche, *On the Genealogy of Morals and Ecce Homo*, ed. Walter Kaufmann, (New York: Vintage, 1989), § 1.10.

78. A particularly thorough study of popular and elite feelings about national humiliation in contemporary China and their roots in the Republican era is William Callahan's *China: The Pessoptimist Nation* (Oxford and New York: Oxford University Press, 2010).

79. Xiao Gongqin, "Nationalism and the Ideology in China's Transitional Period," *Chinese Economic Studies* 28, no. 2 (March–April 1995): 28.

80. Xu Wu, *Chinese Cyber-Nationalism: Evolution, Characteristics, and Implications* (Lanham, MD: Lexington Books, 2007), p. 93. One can at least *imagine* other species of nationalism motivated less by a resentful feeling of woundedness and more by some other

Indeed, since Lu Xun and Lao She 老舍 (1899–1966), Chinese writers have been outstanding conveyers of what it is to feel the acidic, heart-biting discontent of being consumed by *ressentiment*, and with the renewed interest in Nietzche in China since the late 1990s, Chinese scholars in China have built up a large literature about the Nietzschean and Schelerian concepts of *ressentiment*.[81]

Chinese intellectuals brought this nationalist *ressentiment* and thirst for national vindication to their thinking. Indeed "no school of modern Chinese thought emerged without a nationalist colour except perhaps anarchism," Wu Guoguang says bluntly. "[A]ll joined China's search for countervailing power and wealth."[82] Chinese intellectuals have been expected to act as forces of national vindication, and their work reflects this sense of mission. In her writing about the phenomenon of the Chinese intelligentsia's "patriotic worrying," Gloria Davies notes the "instrumentalist" eye with which Chinese intellectuals try to select ideas for China, which they believe will raise the country higher:

> [H]abits of writing that evolved out of worrying about China have resulted in a discourse dominated by formulations that are aimed at evaluating the pros and cons of particular sets of ideas in the common higher interest of improving Chinese society and culture. Because Chinese critical inquiry is predominantly undertaken in the general interest of advancing the national culture, it tends characteristically to include a moral evaluation as

---

complex of feelings that are more "healthy-minded," to use Nietzsche's word, from pride in the nation's strength to rejoicing in its implementation of a treasured value such as individual liberty or multicultural comity. And my own sense is that we can find actual specimens of diverse non-*ressentiment* based nationalisms. However, Jing Tsu goes so far as to suggest that all nationalism is based on a feeling of victimization or the threat of it: "At the core of nationalism lies a perpetually incitable sense of injury. Nationalism does not rely on just any kind of emotion. Rather than pride, feelings of injury provide the most versatile and undying desire for ambition. The reconstitution of national identity is always pursued with the utmost conviction and energy after suffering successful attacks . . ." See *Failure, Nationalism, and Literature: The Making of Modern Chinese Identity, 1895–1937* (Stanford, CA: Stanford University Press, 2005), p. 24. I am grateful to Peter Zarrow for his suggestions on this point.

81. Fang Weigui 方維規, "Minzuzhuyi yuanze sunshang zhi hou: Zhongguo 150 nian xianzeng qingjie 民族主義原則損傷之後—中國 150 年羨憎情結" (After the Harm to the Principle of Nationalism: One Hundred and Fifty years of Chinese *Ressentiment*), *Shehui kexue* 5 (2005): 18–31. The earliest notable example of this body of Chinese scholarship is Liu Xiaofeng's 劉小楓 essay "Yuanhen yu xiandaixing 怨恨與現代性" (*Ressentiment* and Modernity), in his book *Xiandai shehui lilun xulun: xiandaixing yu xiandai Zhongguo* 現代社會理論續論—現代性與現代中國 (Continued Discussion of Modern Social Theory: Modernity and Modern China), (Shanghai: Shanghai sanlian shuju, 1998).

82. Wu Guoguang, "From Post-Imperial to Late Communist Nationalism: Historical Change in Chinese Nationalism from May Fourth to the 1990s," *Third World Quarterly* 29, no. 3 (2008): 469.

well as an inspection of utility or functionality, with a view to determining whether an idea or a theory will benefit China.[83]

Drawing for a moment on more recent examples than Mou's, let us observe that New Confucians too tell their story routinely in the language of *ressentiment*. Tu Wei-ming tells of the "sense of impotence, frustration, and humiliation" that "framed the context for [Chinese intellectuals'] quest for identity . . . in an increasingly alienating and dehumanizing world."[84] In describing Chinese culture's relationship to the West, New Confucians write about Western "challenge," "impact," "attack," "assault," "intrusion," "invasion," "conquest," "domination," and "occupation." This is true not only of New Confucian cultural nationalists but also of the pluralists, whether in China, in Taiwan and Hong Kong, or abroad. Even the irenic pluralist Tu Wei-ming follows the invasion narrative, writing that post-Imperial Chinese intellectuals felt about the influx of Western learning "as if the Buddhist conquest and the Mongol invasion had been combined."[85]

Beijing University's Zhang Xianglong provides a particularly piquant example of these metaphors:

[A]s with American Indians, Confucian culture . . . was destroyed or severely devastated by murderous, vicious Western invaders. . . . The only difference between the fates of the Confucians and the Indians is that in the case of the final extinction or severe devastation of Confucianism in mainstream society, it was not the Westerners wielding the knife directly but those Westernized Chinese intellectuals. . . . One can imagine that if the Westerners had been able, they would have done in China exactly as they did in the Americas, slaying the men, raping the women, snatching

83. Gloria Davies, *Worrying About China: The Language of Chinese Critical Inquiry* (Cambridge, MA.: Harvard University Press, 2007), pp. 11–12.

84. Tu Wei-ming, "Cultural China: The Periphery as the Center," *Daedelus* 134, no. 4 (Fall 2005): 146.

85. Tu Wei-ming, "Cultural China," pp. 148, 146. Also see Guo Qiyong 郭齊勇, "Zonglun xian-dangdai xin ruxue sichao, renwu ji qi wenti yishi yu xueshu gongxian, jiantan wo de kaifang de ruxue guan (shang) 綜論現當代新儒學思潮、人物及其問題意識與學術貢獻—兼談我的開放的儒學觀(上)" (Comprehensive Discussion of Trends and Figures in Modern and Contemporary New Confucianism and Their Problematics and Scholarly Contributions, As Well As My Own Thoughts on Open Confucianism [part one]), *Tansuo* 3 (2010): 47–56 *passim*; and Guo Qiyong, "Zonglun xian-dangdai xin ruxue sichao, renwu ji qi wenti yishi yu xueshu gongxian, jiantan wo de kaifang de ruxue guan (xia) 綜論現當代新儒學思潮、人物及其問題意識與學術貢獻—兼談我的開放的儒學觀(下)" (Comprehensive Discussion of Trends and Figures in Modern and Contemporary New Confucianism and Their Problematics and Scholarly Contributions, As Well As My Own Thoughts on Open Confucianism [part two]), *Tansuo* (2010.4): 50–59 *passim*.

> the land, and also snuffing out local culture. . . . The disappearance of the Confucian entity from modern China is the result of the West's military and cultural invasion.[86]

Few other Confucians may wish to walk quite this far with Zhang, in effect calling even Mao Zedong and the Red Guards mere cat's paws of Western imperialists, but the point is made. The New Confucian memory of their tradition's past is one of *ressentiment*: indignation over past victimization by the West, in which Confucian culture itself—not places like the Summer Palace or structures of Qing power, but Confucianism itself—suffered military conquest and plunder.

As for the future, *ressentiment* entails a fantasy of vindication and role reversal, and Zhang Xianglong writes accordingly that "restoring Confucianism and Confucian culture to life is the unshirkable duty of the Chinese government, the Chinese nation, and Chinese intellectuals," as doing so "will confirm the guilt of racially other (*yizu* 異族) invaders as perpetrators and the right of Confucian culture to demand they acknowledge their guilt and make reparations."[87] It is important to note that Zhang's argument in favor of reviving Confucianism is an instrumental one: he supports the resurrection (*fuhuo* 復活) of Confucianism because it will underscore China's victimhood, not because Confucianism is right or good or because of intrinsic merits of its own. We can make use of Scheler's observation here: "The formal structure of *ressentiment* expression is always the same: A is affirmed, valued, and praised not for its own intrinsic quality, but with the unverbalized intention of denying, devaluating, and denigrating B. A is played off against B."[88] In this argument, Confucianism is a cultural-political football for ressentiment, a happenstantial symbol for Chinese indignation and defiance to "the West."[89]

86. Zhang Xianglong 張祥龍, "Rujia yuan wenhua zhudao diwei zhi hanyi: rujia fuhuo de yishi qianti yiji yu Yindi'an wenhua de duibi 儒家原文化主導地位之含義--儒家復活的意識前提以及與印地安文化的對比" (The Implications of the Leading Role of Confucianism as Indigenous Culture: The Ideological Preconditions for the Resurrection of Confucianism and the Example of Native American Culture), *Xiandai zhexue* 108 (January 2010): 106, 109–110.

87. Zhang Xianglong, "Rujia yuan wenhua zhudao diwei," p. 106.

88. Scheler, *Ressentiment*, p. 68.

89. In another contemporary example, Wu Xuan 無炫 and Jin Jianren 金建人 write in their introduction to Gong Pengcheng's article about Chinese cultural resources for challenging the hegemony of the modern West: "All over the world, [scholars] are asking: What are the things that Western theory cannot do? How, on the basis of our reception of traditional Eastern culture, can we strengthen creative research into Eastern theories and concepts of modern culture? Delving into these questions can have great significance for ameliorating Chinese theory's loss of its voice in front of Western theory and erecting a modern spirit and cultural self-confidence among Easterners." The thing to note is Wu

Is Zhang just an unrepresentative case from some lunatic fringe? No. He does express *ressentiment* more plainly than other New Confucians, for his style is more polemical and his vocabulary is bloodier than usual. Thus, where others use a relatively abstract word ("invade, attack, impact"), Zhang sometimes chooses a more concrete one ("murderous, vicious, kill, rape, snatch, snuff out, wield the knife"), helping the reader to see vivid violence. Also, Zhang is less sophisticated than the leading New Confucians and does not discipline and temper his *ressentiment* with the truth-seeking appetite of a Mou Zongsan. However, Zhang's *ressentiment* itself is entirely standard for a cultural nationalist New Confucian, and others in that wing of the movement express this *ressentiment* and appeal to it in others routinely.

Beijing University's Wang Yuechuan 王岳川 calls on China to create a space-age Confucianism that will preserve and renew Chinese culture and liberate itself from a Western paradigm of linear time forced on it by the West. Why did China never give birth to an ocean-going civilization like the West's, he asks, with which it could have expanded, colonized, and opened up new markets? Dwelling on the lost opportunities of the Tang and the Ming, Wang concludes that Chinese culture did not sufficiently value the sea and hence "China and the West crossed swords three times, and the last time the West, backed up by its powerful seafaring civilization, won victory. . . . The struggle between China and the West at the beginning of the twentieth century is fresh in our memory."[90]

New Confucian Xu Hongli frets anxiously about the possibility that the West will still conquer China culturally and warns his countrymen thinking of deserting their ancestral culture for the West's that they can never escape:

> Cultural DNA is an established gene. Being born a Chinese is a lifetime fact: you can dye your hair blond but you cannot change your eyes to blue, and it is harder still to change your spiritual nature. Easterners who westernize do so from self-loathing . . . but in their bones they still are not Westerners . . . If [a people's] independent character becomes rootless and floating, it will eventually evaporate and they will choose to accept slavery. Much of the fault for problems in China belongs to invaders, but even more of the fault lies with traitors to the Chinese nation (*hanjian* 漢奸).

and Jin's other-referentiality and instrumentalism. They are looking for resources not by reference to what they *are*, for an intrinsic interest they hold, but for what they are *not*, namely Western. See Gong Pengcheng 龔鵬程, "Xiandai wenming de fanxing yu lunli chongjian 現代文明的反省與倫理重建" (Reflection on and Renewal of Modern Civilization), *Zhejiang Daxue xuebao (renwen shehui kexue ban)* 40, no. 3 (May 2010): 51.

90. Wang Yuechuan, "Taikong wenming shidai yu wenhua shouzheng chuangxin 太空文明時代與文化守正創新" (The Age of Space-faring Civilizations and Cultural Preservation and Innovation), *Dongyue luncong* 31, no. 10 (October 2010): 173–174.

> Among the various levels of people in Chinese tradition, there has always been a special class of scum, perfidious scoundrels willing to be slaves, first to emperors and later to foreigners, whose basic livelihood is doing tyrants' dirty work for them.[91]

To defeat the Western cultural invasion, Xu envisions Chinese universities that refuse any Western model:

> If our universities adopt international norms unselectively, they will lose their independent character and produce culturally marginal people, or even rebellious, Westernized elites, progressives who believe that China must be colonized in order to be modernized, a deformed kind of Eastern intellectual, a fifth column for cultural invasion.[92]

Above I have given several examples from the present day, but these are not simply a phenomenon of post-1989 nationalism. Indeed, the postwar New Confucians' founding "Declaration" is a document conceived in *ressentiment*, addressed not to the Chinese people who did or did not bother to read it but to the West. As with much New Confucian writing, close to the beginning it offers a narrative of *ressentiment*. It describes the early Jesuit encounters at the Qing court as a "battle front" (*zhanxian* 戰線) and goes on to recall the Opium War and the Eight-Nation Alliance.[93] And in complaining about the reduction of the study of the Chinese cultural inheritance by Western scholars and their characteristic agendas, depriving indigenously Chinese kinds of scholarship of much voice, the signatories of the "Declaration" anticipate Said's Orientalism by twenty years. If there is a difference, though, it is that they did not so much write a declaration of independence from Western scholarship as call on China to win the West's admiration and to the West to yield to China the respect they feel has been unfairly withheld.

Mou continued to nurture this *ressentiment* throughout his career and made it his mission to improve the quality and standing of Chinese philosophy relative to the West and role reversal with respect to the West, and to restore China's Confucian culture to a place of leadership in the world. Asserting the value of Chinese philosophy relative to the West, he writes:

---

91. Xu Hongli 徐宏力, "Dongfang xiandai ren yu rujia wenhua 東方現代人與儒家文化" (Modern Oriental People and Confucian Culture), *Dongfang luntan* (2006.1): 18. The rendering of *dongfang* as "Oriental" is Xu's own (p. 25), possibly as a deliberate way of reclaiming the term.

92. Xu Hongli, "Dongfang xiandai ren," p. 24.

93. Mou, Xu, Zhang, and Tang, "Wei Zhongguo wenhua jinggao shijie renshi xuanyan," pp. 4–5.

> Turning our eyes to the West, there is not even a handful who can be mentioned in the same breath with such great philosophers as [Zhiyi and Fazang]. There is truly no reason for Chinese people to underestimate ourselves. . . . I would say that in the history of Western philosophy, only Kant came close to purifying the six sense-bases [as Zhiyi did].[94]
>
> In its simple essentials, [our] responsibility is to revive the ancient meaning of Greek philosophy. . . . This ancient meaning of philosophy has already been lost in the West. Nowadays all that is left is linguistic analysis under the conditions of advanced civilization, with logic having been reduced to applied computing. This does not actually count as philosophy, only the degeneration of philosophy into a technology. To enter into the depths of philosophy, it has to be that "love of wisdom," the "yearning after the highest good." Although the West has forgotten it, this sense of philosophy has been preserved in the Chinese tradition.[95]

On his conviction that China has a mission for world leadership, he writes:

> Along with its progress as a highly scientific civilization, the West has ended up destroying philosophy, which now only handles technological questions and is reduced to a satellite of science. We have nothing against technology; we respect experts. In keeping with the Confucian broad-mindedness of the "one mind with two gates," we affirm all these things as fitting contents for human reason, and all such fitting contents for human reason should make their appearance in history. Why should Chinese people alone not be able to bring them forth?[96]

And expressing his wish for China to reverse roles with the West, he writes:

> Therefore Westerners should also look to China for instruction and not just expect Chinese people to seek instruction from them. But Westerners are able not to respect Chinese because Chinese do not read their own books and hence have no instruction to offer. For example, a few years

94. Mou Zongsan, "Keguan de liaojie," p. 430.

95. Mou Zongsan, "Keguan de liaojie," pp. 431–432. Cf. Mou Zongsan, *Siyin shuo yanjiang lu*. Incidentally, in this speech Mou expresses not only his *ressentiment* toward the West, but toward the reputations of many of his Chinese contemporaries: Liang Shuming 梁瀨溟 (1893–1988), Feng Youlan 馮友蘭 (1895–1990), Hu Shi 胡適 (1891–1962), and even Tang Junyi.

96. Mou Zongsan, "Keguan de liaojie," p. 436.

> ago there was a foreign student who wanted to study Mencius. . . . He said the concept of outer kingship is lacking in the West, which shows that he learned a few things. And so I say that Chinese and Westerners should each first stabilize their own basis and then go on to learn from one another. China lacks science and already knows that it needs to learn from the West. And Westerners, for their part, aside from the civilization of science and technology, should be able to get some ideas about how to solve the problems of cultural post-modernity from diligent study of China's three traditions of Confucianism, Buddhism, and Daoism.[97]

Mou also expresses *ressentiment* about what he takes to be China's thwarted destiny. Most of this indignation is focused on the Manchus, but for whom China would not have fallen behind the West:

> If there had been no three hundred years of Manchu rule, the natural course of the Chinese nation's development would have been little different from the West's. It was exactly during the seventeenth, eighteenth, and nineteenth centuries of the Qing that the West progressed quickly toward modernization . . . Of itself, the cultural life of the Chinese nation was poised to open outward. It was only that it was repressed by the Manchus.[98]

None of this is to say Mou and later champions of Confucian revival do not also find intrinsic value in Confucianism, that they are propelled only by *ressentiment*, or that their philosophy is all a fluffy ideological superstructure for their nationalist feelings. Mou for one strives to support his emotional conviction with philosophical rigor, and so do all the better New Confucian theorists who come after him. It is no insult to Mou that we acknowledge he was a human being, as all scholars are human beings with human foibles, and to acknowledge that he had an agenda, in the legitimate and neutral sense that he had a to-do list, a mission to carry out. But the fact remains that, as we have just seen, Mou and other Confucian cultural nationalists respond to the West with a measure of anger, resentment, and wounded national pride, and they tell us so plainly. But it is a tense thing to be a rigorous scholar and also a New Confucian and a committed cultural nationalist as well. It is a challenge simply to balance the truth-seeking, self-reflexiveness, and intellectual probity that constitute academic integrity

---

97. Mou Zongsan, "Keguan de liaojie," p. 437.

98. Mou Zongsan, "Ehu zhi hui: Zhongguo wenhua fazhan zhong de da zonghe yu Zhong-Xi chuantong de ronghui 鵝湖之會：中國文化發展中的大綜和與中西傳統的融會" (The Great Synthesis in the Development of Chinese Culture and the Merging of Chinese and Western Tradition), in vol. 27 of *Mou Zongsan xiansheng quanji*, p. 447.

with Confucian advocacy, and this balancing act is written all over the work of the movement's pluralist wing, which struggles to make a case for the special and unique value of Confucian thought with resorting to emotional appeals to nationalist sentiment. However, to the extent that a scholar's advocacy for Confucianism also partakes of *ressentiment*—that is, to the extent that one inhabits the cultural-nationalist wing—there is now much greater tension in one's goals. For a cultural nationalist's Confucianism must serve three disparate aims: to advance the Confucian cause and also to gratify national pain, but all in a way that does not rely on nationalist feelings of pride and enmity to camouflage vagaries and weaknesses in one's evidence and arguments.

One usual consequence of the cultural-nationalist aim is ambivalence about the Confucianism of Korea, Japan, and Vietnam. Contemporary Confucians are fully aware of a Confucian heritage in those countries, of course, for the topic of a "Confucian capitalism" in emerging Asian economies is now decades old, and they point to the success of the "Asian Tigers" as evidence of the economic powers of Confucian culture. And since Tu Wei-ming took note of the thought of Korean Neo-Confucian Yi T'oegye 李退溪 (1501–1570),[99] some New Confucians have looked more closely at Korean, Japanese, and Vietnamese Confucianism and produced a small body of Chinese literature that examines the Confucianism of those countries in some detail. Some of these efforts show a belief that modern Chinese Confucianism might gain something by trading notes with Korea, Japan, and Vietnam, where Confucianism did not suffer anything close to the same level of tumult and disgrace as it did in China, and which have already experienced their own Confucian cultural-nationalist movements. A majority of these efforts appear in area studies journals or obscure provincial publications,[100] but

99. For example, Tu Wei-ming, "Yi T'oegye's Perception of Human Nature: A Preliminary Inquiry into the Four-Seven Debate in Korean Neo-Confucianism," in *The Rise of Neo-Confucianism in Korea,* Wm. Theodore de Bary (New York, Columbia University Press: 1985), pp. 223–242.

100. Liu Qiubing 劉邱兵, "Cong zhanhou Xiaodao Youma de sixiang kan Riben de xiandai xin ruxue 從戰後小島祐馬的思想看日本的現代新儒學" (Looking at Japanese New Confucianism through the Post-war Thought of Ojima Sukema), *Ribenxue luntan* (2003.1): 23–28; Lin Qiuwen 林秋雯, "Zhongguo xin rujia he Riben jinshi ruxue 中國新儒家和日本近世儒學" (Chinese New Confucians and Modern Japanese Confucians), *Guangxi Youjiang minzu shizhuan xuebao* 18, no. 2 (April 2005): 54–56; Zhang Bo 張波, "Riben ruxue bentuhua licheng ji tese 日本儒學本土化歷程及特色" (The Process and Characteristics of the Nativization of Japanese Confucianism), *Dongjiang xuekan* 25, no. 2 (April 2008): 16–23; Ding Yuanming 丁原明, "Cong *Dongfang lunli daode* kan dangdai Hanguo ruxue de zoushi 從《東方倫理道德》看當代韓國儒學的走勢" (A Look at the Trend of Contemporary South Korean Confucianism from the Perspective of *Eastern Ethics*), *Shangqiu Shifan Xueyuan xuebao* 24, no. 8 (August 2008): 1–6; Wu Guanghui 吳光輝, "Xitian zhexue yu ruxue sixiang de duihua 西田哲學與儒學思想的對話" (Dialogue between Nishida Kitarō's Philosophy and Confucian Thought), *Riben yanjiu* 2 (2009): 4–9.

some are written by prominent scholars, sometimes in high-profile journals.[101] Such interest, however, is far from the mainstream of modern Confucianism.[102] Furthermore, in cultural-nationalist Confucian circles, the connection to other East Asian countries' Confucianism is considered to run in one direction, from China to its younger brothers. When cultural-nationalist Confucians mention "East Asian culture," there is often an explicit assumption, common in contemporary Chinese nationalism in general,[103] that China is to lead and those smaller countries will follow. Hence the Confucian philosopher Chen Lai of Qinghua University writes, "We must understand that in the revival of modern East Asia culture, unlike Japan and Korea, Chinese culture will take up the responsibility for spiritual creativity (rather than spiritual imitation), and in fact the East Asian cultural sphere hopes for this from China."[104]

A related consequence of their nationalism is directly relevant to our question of why New Confucians stopped being interested in Yogācāra: Yogācāra is Indian and hence it is irrelevant to their nationalist purposes.

---

101. Guo Qiyong 郭齊勇, "Dongya ruxue hexin jiazhiguan ji qi xiandai yiyi 東亞儒學核心價值觀及其現代意義" (The Core values of East Asian Confucianism and Their Modern Significance), *Kongzi yanjiu* (2000.4): 17–25; Cai Degui 蔡德貴, "Dangdai xin rujia xiang duoyuan ronghe xing zhuanhua de biranxing," pp. 15–18; Zhang Liwen 張立文, "Jiegou yu quanshi—Fan Ruanyou *Lunyu yu'an* de lixue tezhi 結構與詮釋—范阮攸《論語愚按》的理學特質" (Structure and interpretation—the Neo-Confucian character of Phạm Nguyên Du's *Luận Ngữ Ngu Án [The Analects in My Humble Opinion]*), *Xueshu yuekan* (2008.8): 22–26; Xiang Shiling 向世陵, "Yili de chengjie yu chuangxin: Li Yu lixue Yixue de juese yu chuangxin 易理的承接與創新: 黎敨理學易學的角色與論域" (Inheriting and Innovating on the Principles of the *Book of Change*: The Role and Context of Lê Văn Ngữ's Neo-Confucian Philosophy of the *Book of Change*), *Xueshu yuekan* (2008.8): 26–32.

102. An instructive case is that of Taiwanese historian Huang Junjie 黃俊傑, who tries to persuade other scholars to think in terms of an "East Asian Confucianism" (*dongya ruxue* 東亞儒學). One can gain a fairly accurate measure of his success, however, in persuading other scholars writing in Chinese to follow him from the title of one of his articles, "How Is 'East Asian' Confucianism Possible?" ("'Dongya ruxue' ruhe keneng? 「東亞儒學」如何可能?," *Qinghua xuebao* (Taiwan) 33, no. 2 [2003]: 455–468) and from the fact that he routinely feels it necessary to put the term inside quotation marks. On efforts to expand the focus of Chinese Confucian studies to encompass all of East Asia, and Huang's efforts in particular, see Makeham, *Lost Soul*, pp. 85, 88–94.

103. See Peter Hays Gries, *China's New Nationalism: Pride, Politics, and Diplomacy* (Berkeley: University of California Press, 2003), pp. 35–39. Note also that uninterest about the traditional culture of the rest of Asia is not peculiar to Confucian cultural nationalists but Buddhist ones as well. Taixu felt much more rivalry with Japanese Buddhism than kinship, and his one effort at building a bridge through importation of Japanese tantra ended in what he considered disaster. Ouyang Jingwu did not care to look to Japan for guidance concerning Yogācāra Buddhism, neither to the traditional Hossō school nor to indologically sophisticated modern Japanese buddhology. For both men, Japan's utility was as a sort of fireproof storage locker for Chinese texts which were lost or burned by the Taiping.

5. *Sunset of Yogācāra studies among New Confucians*

Like the other New Confucians, Mou and Tang proclaimed a deep unity between subject and object, and although it is not surprising that later they gravitated to German idealists, they both began down that path studying Yogācāra with Xiong Shili. Both Mou and Tang were interested in mind-only thought and the relationship of subjects and objects and they made this the main concern for their philosophical *panjiao* schemes. From there Mou became fascinated with Kant, indeed "almost obsessive" as Joël Thoraval puts it,[105] and Tang gravitated to Hegel, but both of them first cultivated their interest in the unity of subject and object in their study of Yogācāra with Xiong Shili. Despite this, none of Xiong's students followed him into a primary dialog with Yogācāra.[106] In fact, Yogācāra ceased to arouse much interest or respect from New Confucians. To take Mou as our main example again, he was a diligent all-around buddhologist and did respond to Yogācāra, but he did not engage with Yogācāra creatively.

Mou certainly did his homework on Yogācāra. He devoted a substantial part of the first volume of *Foxing yu bore* to sorting through not just the primary texts but also the Yogācāra scholarship of Ouyang, Lü Cheng, and Yinshun. Indeed, Mou's treatment of Yogācāra is his most historically and philologically sophisticated buddhological writing. However, Mou saw Yogācāra as only *historically* important, a dialectical stepping-stone in Buddhist philosophy's evolution from its primitive form toward its perfection in Tiantai. To Mou's mind, Yogācāra

---

104. Chen Lai 陳來, "Fazhan Zhongguo wenhua benwei de zhexue yanjiu, canyu jiazhi tixi he minzu jingshen de chongjian 發展中國文化本位的哲學研究, 參與價值體系和民族精神的重建" (Develop Philosophical Research Which Takes Chinese Culture as the Measure of Things and Participate in the Reconstruction of the Value System and the National Spirit), *Beijing Daxue xuebao (zhexue shehui kexue ban)* (1994.4): 56–57. Chen has since become more receptive to Korean Confucianism, for example, as is reflected in writings such as his *Dongya ruxue jiu lun* 東亞儒學九論 (Nine Essays on East Asian Confucianism) (Beijing: Sanlian shudian, 2008) which are directed to a more international audience. I am grateful to John Makeham for pointing this out.

105. Joël Thoraval, "La question de l'intuition intellectuelle et la philosophie confucéenne contemporaine" (The Question of Intellectual Intuition and Contemporary Confucian Philosophy), *Revue internationale de philosophie* 232, no. 2 (2005): 35.

106. Shuxian Liu, "Contemporary Neo-Confucianism: Its Background, Varieties, Emergence, and Significance," *Dao* 2, no. 2 (June 2003): 220. Lin Chen-kuo has pointed out that whereas in the 1950s Mou ranked *Cheng weishi lun* as one of only five bodies of work that formed "the backbone of human learning," together with Kant's *Critiques*, Russell and Whitehead's *Principia Mathematica*, Aquinas's *Summa Theologica*, and the Neo-Confucian writings on mind and nature (*xinxing* 心性), in his mature years he no longer had any such interest in Yogācāra, Russell and Whitehead, or Aquinas, the bulk of his attention going to Kant and the Neo-Confucians. Personal communication, July 31, 2010, referring to Mou Zongsan 牟宗三, *Wushi zishu* 五十自述 (My Life at Fifty) (Taipei: Ehu chubanshe, 1993).

had already been completely "digested" into Chinese philosophy by the seventh century. Like Tang Junyi, who rated Yogācāra even lower than Mou did,[107] Mou thought it was tapped out and long since superseded by Huayan and Tiantai. Yogācāra writings were only important for the sake of historically understanding the development of Buddhism, much as a serious historian of physics would read Newton's *Principia*, namely, as a formidable contribution that nevertheless ceased to be a going concern long, long ago.

So although Mou still engaged with Yogācāra seriously, he saw no reason to bother grappling with it in a prolonged and creative way. When Mou would enter into a creative engagement with what he considered the really indispensable influences, like Kant and Tiantai, he insisted on doing it on a gargantuan scale, publishing completely new interpretations that spanned thousands of pages. Each of these took an investment of energy and lifeblood that most of us can scarcely contemplate making just once in a career. Even a scholar of such mind-boggling energy as Mou, who over the decades engaged Song-Ming Confucianism, Sui-Tang Buddhism, and Kant in this depth, needed an extremely compelling reason to sacrifice so much in a dialogue with a given tradition. For Mou, there were three reasons to give all that was required for a full-scale creative engagement, and Yogācāra was not qualified under any of them. Mou might tackle a thinker or tradition (1) because he believed it to be simply The Truth (as with Confucianism); (2) in order to appropriate uniquely brilliant features of its philosophical system (such as the "non-systematic system" of the Tiantai "perfect teaching"); and/or (3) because the thinker is an influential player in world philosophy who would make a valuable partner for sparring and dialogue for Chinese philosophy during its rise to world prominence (as in the case of Kant).

5.1 India doesn't matter

When Mou and later Confucian nationalists lost interest in a tradition such as Yogācāra, it was not only for narrowly philosophical reasons but also because their ultimate goal was to vindicate Chinese culture with respect to the West, and they did not think that winning against an Indian has-been would get them a title fight with the West. Put bluntly, India did not matter to them. It did not seem relevant enough to their cultural nationalist concerns to be worth the work.

Tang Junyi and Mou Zongsan found a fitting home in New Asia College because it was an entire institution conceived for the purpose of reestablishing a leading role for traditional Chinese learning in the wider world. As Grace Ai-ling

---

107. For Tang, Yogācāra parallels the structures of Xunzi's thought (*Yuandao pian*, vol. 1, p. 18).

Chou points out, however, the conception of the world that informed the New Asia curriculum's map of "the world" was a strangely bipolar one, and very blurry at the edges, a "lopsided equation" that reduced the world deserving of study to China and the West:

> [I]t was their homeland China that was really at the core of their concern. Thus, not only was there no evident effort to teach about Asia as a whole but very minimal attention given to any area or aspect of Asia other than China. In this framework, China was most significant or most representative of 'Asia' or 'the East' while 'the West' served as the counterpart to which China was relating and could be compared. . . . For this reason, the two entities in the world most deserving of study were China, on the one hand, and the West on the other. . . . The primary global relationship of concern was not between the East and the West but between China and the West.[108]

This is a reference to the curriculum, of course, and we should not suppose from that fact alone that the New Asia faculty thought in such simple terms. On examination, however, the universe of Mou's concern includes China and the West (particularly the modern West, the West of science and democracy), but little else. In one of his discourses on the unique merits of Chinese philosophy, Mou explains, "In the West, ideas are always regarded as objects, and . . . they are not themselves the mind. Therefore only China has thorough-going mind-only philosophy."[109] Not to put too fine a point on it, but Mou's map does not include any Arab, Persian, Orthodox Christian, Southeast Asian, Inner Asian, Tibetan, Korean, or Japanese contenders, nor any Indian thought except as a historical precursor to Chinese Buddhism. Mou's mission, and the mission of all New Confucians, is to reconcile Confucianism with the West in particular.

This is not to say that New Confucians have paid no mind at all to India as a civilization. Liang Shuming went so far as to divide the world's major civilizations into three and included India for consideration, and Tang Junyi borrowed his scheme.[110] Among fourth-generation New Confucians, pluralists do often mention India in a list of respected intellectual traditions: "In matters of thought and learning," writes Guo Qiyong, "all these have their brilliance and their

108. Grace Ai-ling Chou, "Confucian Cultural Education on the Chinese Periphery: Hong Kong's New Asia College, 1949–1976," PhD diss., Univ. of Hawai'i at Manoa, 2003, pp. 74–75.

109. Mou Zongsan, "Ehu zhi hui," p. 455. Emphasis added.

110. Meynard, *Religious Philosophy of Liang Shuming*, p. 35.

advantages: China, the West, Marxism, [China's] non-Confucian masters (*zhuzi* 諸子), Confucians, Buddhists, Daoists, Christians, Muslims, and Hindus."[111] Even though lists such as this are important statements of inclusivism, they are honorific. They do not result in the same engagement and fascination with India as with (certain aspects of) the recent Western tradition. "The authors of the 1958 Declaration paid no attention at all to Indian culture," Serina Chan points out, "and at one point dismissed it for 'lacking a consciousness of history.'"[112] New Confucians do not look to India with the same excitement and energy and engagement as they do to the West. Even such a pluralist as Tu Wei-ming, in one of his most famous essays, mentions India not as a partner for exciting new dialog but simply as a luckier, less traumatized victim of Western impact:

> Although China has never been subjected to the kind of comprehensive colonial rule experienced by India, China's semicolonial status severely damaged her spiritual life and her ability to tap indigenous symbolic resources. Chinese intellectuals have been much more deprived than their Indian counterparts ever were. While Indian intellectuals have continued to draw from the wellsprings of their spiritual lives, despite two centuries of British colonialism, the Western impact fundamentally dislodged the Chinese intellectuals from their Confucian haven.[113]

It is the West, not India, that New Confucians take as their foil, their point of reference and self-comparison and the Other to their *ressentiment*. If Indian ideas could be instrumentally useful for raising China relative to the West, New Confucians would do so, but lacking such a promise they have no imperative to divert their attention and energy.

Mou Zongsan replaced Yogācāra from its role as touchstone and foil for Xiong Shili and his generation with Kant. First, for the internal purposes of Mou's metaphysical system, Kant could offer much of what Yogācāra could, and in some cases more. Mou did appreciate Yogācāra's account of the empirical mind and mind-involved concrete particulars, but he thought Kant could do the same job better since his scheme of forms and categories was more parsimonious and cleaner than Yogācāra's functionally identical list of one hundred dharmas, and Kant provided a good epistemology of scientific understanding in the bargain. And although Kant did not recognize the possibility

111. Guo Qiyong, "Zonglun xian-dangdai xin ruxue sichao (xia)," p. 57.

112. Serina Chan, *Thought of Mou Zongsan* p. 268.

113. Tu Wei-ming, "Cultural China," p. 147.

of "intellectual intuition" in human beings (i.e., something like enlightenment, sagehood, or buddhahood), Mou found that Kant came very close to a correct understanding of morality, which is the criterion of good philosophy in Mou's opinion.[114]

So for internal philosophical reasons, Mou no longer had great need of Yogācāra. But, arguably, neither did Xiong Shili. After all, Xiong knew what he believed and knew that he would not find it in Yogācāra. The difference is that where Xiong argued with Yogācāra as a stand-in for the West, "actually using the occasion of his criticism of Yogācāra Buddhism to criticize Western learning,"[115] Mou could argue with the West much more directly and fluently, because of his excellent Peking University education, good English, prodigious study, and the readier availability of both foreign books and a community of university-trained scholars. Mou was able to construct Kant as a spokesman for Western philosophy, its best and most representative product, and through his relationship with Kant he wished to "digest Western philosophical wisdom" for the purpose of "propping up" or "supporting Chinese doctrine."[116] As Zheng Jiadong observes: "The influence of Western philosophy, including Kant's philosophy, on Mou was mainly in terms of the form of articulation. In other words, Western philosophy did not influence or change Mr. Mou's basic understanding of the cosmos or human life; it merely influenced and changed the way he expressed this understanding."[117]

In plain language, Kant was the champion whom Mou the challenger aimed to unseat;[118] a respected rival worthy of learning from. Since Mou, New Confucian nationalists with even better formal educations and even quicker access to and understanding of Western intellectual currents have been able to spar with

114. Mou writes, "If the original import, the true meaning and the deep and far-reaching significance of [Ruxue] in China can be brought out, then I think the person who can really understand Ruxue is none other than Kant." (*Zhi de zhijue yu Zhongguo zhexue*, pp. iv-v; translation by Serina Chan, "The Thought of Mou Zongsan," p. 151. The same sentiment is already found in the 1958 "Declaration."

115. Guo Qiyong, "Zonglun xian-dangdai xin ruxue sichao (shang)," p. 53.

116. Mou Zongsan, *Zhongguo zhexue shijiu jiang*, p. 437; "Keguan de liaojie," p. 434; "Ehu zhi hui," p. 456.

117. Zheng Jiadong 鄭家棟, *Mou Zongsan* 牟宗三 (Mou Zongsan) (Taipei: Sanmin, 2000), p. 231, as translated by Serina Chan, "Thought of Mou Zongsan," p. 207.

118. Indeed, by the end of his life Mou believes he *had* unseated Kant. "Chinese wisdom can take Kant even further. If Kant experts read only Kant and Westerners read only Western philosophy, they will not necessarily understand Kant's original meaning. . . . My foundation is Chinese philosophy, and therefore I can discern Kant's original meaning and take him a step further." Mou, "Keguan de liaojie," p. 435.

Western ideas even more readily, quickly appropriating recent Western scholarly discourses of *ressentiment* from postcolonialism to American neo-conservatism and putting them to Chinese nationalist ends. Except to the extent that they cite Gayatri Spivak and Homi Bhabha, New Confucian cultural nationalists have no need to expend still more energy trying to gather inspiration from India. A philosophy from India has ceased to be useful opponent for contemporary Confucian cultural nationalists. They have the opponent they want now.

Glossary

Glossary of translations for the more common Sanskrit and Chinese terms used in this volume

abhidharma "higher learning"; scholastic presentations of Buddhist doctrine
ālambana cognitive object from which mental impressions are derived; *suoyuan* 所緣
Ālambana-parīkṣā *Investigation of the Object; Investigation of the Percept*
Ālambana-parīkṣā (*Guan suoyuan yuan lun* 觀所緣緣論; Xuanzang's translation): *Treatise on Discerning the Conditions for the Causal Support of Consciousness; Investigation of What Lies Behind Perceptual Objects*
Ālambana-parīkṣā (*Wu xiang si chen lun* 無相思塵論; Paramārtha's translation): *Treatise on Considerations [of the Fact That] Objects of Thought Have No Characteristics; Treatise on Considerations about Sense-objects as Lacking Materiality*
ālambana-pratyaya conditions for the causal support of consciousness; *suoyuan yuan* 所緣緣
ālayavijñana base consciousness; eighth consciousness
benjue 本覺 inherent enlightenment; inherent awakening
benti 本體 noumena/noumenon; Fundamental Reality; ultimate reality
Dasheng qixin lun 大乘起信論 *Awakening of Mahāyāna Faith*
dharma physical and mental phenomena
Dharma Buddhist teaching
dharmadhātu *dharma* realm; realm of dharmas; the principle of reality that underlies human experience of reality; world of truth
dharmakāya "truth body"; undifferentiated absolute reality; Dharma-body
dharma-lakṣaṇa dharma characteristics; characteristics/marks of the dharmas
dravya that which is real and has causal function
faxiang Dharma characteristics
Faxiang alternative name for the Weishi School; Yogācāra School

Faxiang zong Dharma Characteristics School; Yogācāra School
faxing 法性 real nature of dharmas
hetuvidyā epistemology and logic; *yinming* 因明
jianfen 見分 subjective aspect; perceiving/seeing part; *darśana* (*bhāga)
jñāna nonconceptual wisdom
Kong zong 空宗 Emptiness School; Madhyamaka
Madhyamaka Middle Way School; Emptiness School
manas the seventh consciousness
manovijñāna sixth consciousness; the mental consciousness
panjiao 判教 doctrinal classification; doctrinal critique
prajñapti nominal; provisional; heuristic label
pratyakṣa pramāṇa direct cognition; direct perception; *xianliang* 現量
qi 氣 vital stuff
rulaizang 如來藏 matrix of the buddhas (*tathāgatagarbha*); store of the thus come; womb of the thus gone ones
rūpa form
sūtra canonical discourses
suoyuan 所緣 cognitive object from which mental impressions are derived; *ālambana*
suoyuan yuan 所緣緣 *ālambana-pratyaya*; conditions for the causal support of consciousness; the type of condition that is an *ālambana*
tathatā Suchness
tathāgatagarbha matrix of buddhas; womb of the thus gone ones; store of the thus come
ti 體 ontological reality; noumenal reality
vijñāna consciousness
vijñapti-mātra nothing but consciousness; nothing but mental construction
vijñānavāda nothing but consciousness
Vijñānavāda Way of Consciousness; Consciousness School
weishi 唯識 nothing but consciousness
Weishi 唯識 Nothing but Consciousness School; Yogācāra School
weixin 唯心 nothing but mind
xiangfen 相分 object/ image part; objective aspect; *nimitta* (*bhāga)
xianliang 現量 *pratyakṣa pramāṇa* (direct cognition/perception)
xinsuo 心所 mental functions; mental associates; mental activities that accompany and assist the functioning of the mind
xing ji 性寂 innately quiescent
xing jue 性覺 innately enlightened
yinming 因明 lit. "knowledge of reasons"; logic; logic and epistemology
Yogācāra Yogic Practice School
You zong 有宗 Existence School (Yogācāra)
yuanqi 緣起 conditioned arising
zangshi 藏識 store consciousness (eighth consciousness)

Index